"The Kurukshetra Battle" from *The Mahabharata*. © The British Library Board: Or. 13180. Used with kind permission from the British Library.

Tragic Views of the Human Condition

Tragic Views of the Human Condition

Cross-cultural comparisons between views of human nature in Greek and Shakespearean tragedy and the *Mahābhārata* and *Bhagavadgītā*

LOURENS MINNEMA

B L O O M S B U R Y
NEW YORK • LONDON • NEW DELHI • SYDNEY

Bloomsbury Academic

An imprint of Bloomsbury Publishing Plc

175 Fifth Avenue	50 Bedford Square
New York	London
NY 10010	WC1B 3DP
USA	UK

www.bloomsbury.com

First published 2013

Library of Congress Cataloging-in-Publication Data
Minnema, Lourens, 1960–
Tragic views of the human condition: cross-cultural comparisons between views of human nature in Greek and Shakespearean tragedy and the Mahabharata and Bhagavadgita/Lourens Minnema.
pages cm
Includes bibliographical references (pages   ) and index.
ISBN 978-1-4411-9424-4 (hardcover: alk. paper)
1. Tragedy–History and criticism. 2. Tragic, The. I. Title.
PN1892.M56 2013
808.2′512–dc23
2012042522

ISBN HB: 978-1-4411-9424-4
ePub: 978-1-4411-0069-6
ePDF: 978-1-4411-5104-9

Typeset by Deanta Global Publishing Services, Chennai, India
Printed and bound in the United States of America

For Thierno Ibrahima Bah

Chaque homme porte en lui un monde composé
de tout ce qu'il a vu et aimé
et où il rentre sans cesse alors même qu'il parcourt et semble habiter
un monde étranger.

Chateaubriand, Voyage en Italie, *Lettre troisième à M. Joubert*
Tivoli, 11 décembre 1803

Contents

Acknowledgements

This book is the unintended fruit of a comprehensive research project on religious and humanist views of human nature initiated by the then Head of Department of Philosophy of Religion and Comparative Study of Religions at VU University, Amsterdam, Prof Dr Hendrik M. Vroom. I am grateful for his energetic efforts to have facilitated the research. I also thank my colleague, Dr Victor A. van Bijlert, for his comments on the Hindu sections. I am greatly indebted to my colleague in the Faculty of Philosophy, Dr Louise D. Derksen, who has been of tremendous support at the time I most needed it. She suggested many ways of abridging the earlier draft of the manuscript, as well as stylistic improvements and grammatical corrections. I also wish to extend my thanks to Prof Dr Jan C. Heesterman (University of Leiden) for his continuous readiness to share his insights with me, and to Prof Dr Michael McGhee (University of Liverpool) for his moral support and for bringing me into contact with Continuum.

Regarding substantial sections in Part II, paragraphs 3 and 4, of Chapter III Artistic–Communicative Aspects, I thank Peeters Publishers and Booksellers (Louvain) for granting permission to reproduce identical sections of my article 'One Dialogue—Four Relationships: The Different Layers of Meaning in the Dialogue between Krishna and Arjuna in the Bhagavadgītā', which was published in *Studies in Interreligious Dialogue* 21/1 (2011), 96–111.

Lourens Minnema
Amsterdam, in the autumn of 2012

1

Introduction

1 Scope and key questions

Gliding silently over the fields, flying across one cultural landscape to the other and back again, this book aspires to compare cross-culturally Western and Indian tragic views of the human condition. The wider scope of interest of the cross-cultural comparisons is marked off by a *broad key question*: Can tragic views of the human condition, as known to Westerners through Greek and Shakespearean tragedy, be identified outside European culture, in the Indian culture of Hindu epic drama?

This broad key question has to be narrowed down for practical reasons. For one thing, of the core texts that can be considered prototypical of Greek and Shakespearean tragedy, I will mainly concentrate on Sophocles' *Oedipus Tyrannus* and *Antigone* and on Shakespeare's *Hamlet*. These three texts are widely held to be among the best examples of what tragedy is about, as a literary genre. Hindu epic drama appears to be quite different as a literary genre, but the *Mahābhārata* epic, which includes the *Bhagavadgītā*, can be used to make a good comparison when it comes to issues regarding views of human nature. The anthropological *issues* seem much more similar cross-culturally than the literary *genres* which contain them might suggest. My main interest is in the anthropological issues.

Whether this first impression will hold remains to be seen, but it can serve to narrow down the broad key question of the wider scope of interest. The *major key question* limiting the actual frame of reference and guiding the cross-cultural comparisons can then be formulated as follows: in what respects can the *Mahābhārata* epic's and the *Bhagavadgītā*'s views of the human condition be called 'tragic' in the Greek and Shakespearean senses of the word? There are no universal criteria to measure the extent to which views of the human condition in various cultures differ. However, this observation does not make the question altogether impossible to answer. It makes the question answerable in many different ways depending on the framing of the comparisons. Properly *framing the comparisons* is one methodological problem to be faced.

Taking seriously the generic variety of cultural sources is another problem at hand. Views of human nature are expounded in theories, condensed in concepts, imagined in symbols and embedded in stories. Tragic views of the human condition are primarily embedded in stories, the plots of tragedies. Only afterwards are these tragic views of the human condition expounded in theories of tragedy and in philosophical anthropologies. In order to trace tragic views of the human condition, the methodological starting point has to be the stories in which these tragic views of human nature are embedded. In the West, these stories and their dramatic performance constitute a specific narrative genre – 'tragedy'.

2 Aspects of tragedy and embedded anthropological issues

In ancient Greece and in early modern England, the tragic genre represents an art form whose 'tragic' character is related to a wide range of *aspects*. In this book, I shall heuristically identify seven (clusters of) aspects of tragedy – narrative aspects (Chapter II), artistic–communicative aspects (Chapter III), socio-political aspects (Chapter IV), literary–cultural aspects (Chapter V), martial aspects (Chapter VI), psycho-ethical aspects (Chapter VII) and religious aspects (Chapter VIII). Why these aspects instead of other ones? How has the drawing of demarcation lines between these aspects come about? It was not inspired by a particular scholarly tradition or theory. In fact, the aspects and issues presented here could have been defined differently, and most likely would have been if the material at hand had been processed by a different mind. Those salient aspects related to Greek and Shakespearean tragedy that struck me as characteristic of the tragic genre had to be arranged and presented in a form that would both cover the most important anthropological issues raised and make for good cross-cultural comparison, enabling the reader to perceive more clearly some fundamental similarities and differences between Western and Indian views of (wo)man.

Each set of aspects of tragedy will have its own chapter. By devoting separate chapters to these seven aspects of tragedy, I try to cope with several methodological problems simultaneously.

First of all, by describing each cluster of aspects of tragedy in detail, I stay *as close as possible* to the Greek and Shakespearean cultural sources from which the *embedded* tragic views of human nature have to be extracted in order to be compared to their Indian counterparts. Embedded views of human nature are identified in terms of the anthropological *issues* raised in the stories (issues such as coping with evil, suffering, loss, death, power, gender, injustice, fate and freedom) and they are understood in terms of their particular settings before being compared cross-culturally. In my partly phenomenological approach to tragedy and to embedded views of human nature, I try to stay as close as possible to the *phenomena* at hand, that is to say, to the images of human nature as they are presented in the stories. Taking as their starting point 'that which lights up and appears to us', phenomenological approaches expect understanding to emerge out of the description of patterns, that is to say, they take their point of departure in the appearances instead of imposing thought on 'objects', attempting, as Douglas Allen puts it, 'to uncover various structural differentiations within their data'.[1] But, I hasten to add that I highly welcome the light that *theories* can shed on these images. Different theories enable different views of the same phenomena, which then appear differently under different angles. Different theories all cast some light, one way or another, and are presented in this study to do just that. Pure description does not exist, let alone pure understanding. More on that will be said in the following sections. At this stage, let me underscore that the focus is on the appearance of the phenomena themselves under the conditions of a variation in lightning. Basically, I am inclined rather to observe and show than to judge and argue for or against phenomenal patterns and theoretical views, to observe and show the particular ways in which anthropological issues are raised and understood culturally.

Secondly, doing justice to the richness and complexity of each set of aspects of tragedy also allows for a wide range of specific cross-cultural comparisons. Thus, generalizations are avoided. Each set of aspects of tragedy provides for a *particular context* within which specific anthropological issues will be treated and compared. In other words, each particular context (and thus every single chapter) constitutes its own frame for cross-cultural comparisons. The *framing* operates in two ways. On the one hand, a particular context raises particular anthropological issues. This *enables comparisons* with corresponding issues elsewhere. In India, for example, similar questions will be dealt with differently, depending on the cultural differences. On the other hand, the framing does not only enable comparisons, it also *limits and specifies their scope*. Western and Indian views of the human being will turn out to be strikingly similar when it comes to certain issues, yet very different when it comes to other issues.

Tragedy deals with issues it does not expound philosophically, politically or historically, but which it raises artistically. The main purpose of discussing several aspects of tragedy in some detail is to develop a sense of what the related issues (concerning human affairs) and the various ways they are dealt with are about. Methodologically speaking, I shall not be comparing texts, but the main issues the texts and contexts are dealing with. Of concern are the *anthropological issues* which the texts and contexts have in common cross-culturally and the respects in which they differ. The same species of dolphin jumping out of the water seems to generate fairly similar patterns of jumping and of waves on the surface in different oceans worldwide, but the same species of *homo sapiens* appears to generate fairly different patterns of expression and association when raising the 'same' anthropological issues in different cultures worldwide. The 'same' human suffering, for example, is not experienced and expressed identically everywhere. Similar issues are addressed differently to such an extent that the difference may strike one as more impressive than the similarity. In this study, common anthropological issues are described as embedded within their original cultural contexts before being compared cross-culturally.

A summary of the most important anthropological issues that will be raised in the following chapters is meant to convey a first impression of what one should expect in terms of points of cross-cultural comparison. Each set of aspects of tragedy raises certain issues dealing with human affairs. In the chapter on *narrative* aspects, attention is drawn to the extreme ways in which life stories develop into tragic life stories; disorder has to be rectified at terrible cost; suffering and loss determine the mood; a sense of unavoidable necessity takes over; evil and destruction have a long-lasting disturbing effect; and despair, obscurity and irony colour the world views of communities and individuals alike. The chapter on *artistic–communicative* aspects highlights the ways in which dialogues on the tragic stage seem doomed to fail. Audiences are not only influenced by the tragic effects of the representation of events, but also themselves influence the extent to which life stories, characters and events are perceived as tragic or comic. The chapter on *socio-political* aspects brings to the fore how the state, the family, religion and the theatre have been prominent institutional sources of legitimation and conflict, and how 'serious' tragedy was often, despite its democratic origins, expected to exclusively feature aristocratic characters and treat majestic affairs. In the chapter on literary–cultural aspects, it is shown that there are historical shifts in dealing with traditional norms and values, introducing critically reflective views of (wo)man in the transition from epic stories and heroes to tragic stories and heroes that are symptomatic of increased individualization and internalization. The chapter on *martial* aspects demonstrates some striking ways in which the martial values of warrior heroism have cross-cultural parallels in cultures that are separate in space and time, especially when it comes to status, honour and manliness. Also, the use of violence can be seen from a victim's perspective instead of a victor's perspective. The chapter on *psycho-ethical* aspects raises the issues of personal moral responsibility, individual freedom and social constraint, of the weight of human intention and action, of the power and powerlessness of passion, will and reason, of the available vocabulary for attitudes of mind and heart, and of the acquisition of human self-knowledge. The chapter on *religious* aspects touches upon the tensions and interactions between human freedom and supernatural necessity, fate and fortune, and upon the issue of divine intentions and interventions.

3 Definition and cross-cultural applicability of the notion of the 'tragic'

To define what is 'tragic' about tragic views of the human being is not an easy task. It goes without saying that there is no one concept of the 'tragic'. In fact, a wide range of aspects of the tragic genre has to be accounted for because each cluster of aspects generates its own definitions. Definitions of 'tragedy' and the 'tragic' will, therefore, be addressed in all chapters. Readers familiar with, say, philosophical definitions and approaches may appreciate and benefit from reading more on narrative or socio-political approaches, and vice versa.

In order to define the 'tragicness' of tragedy and consider the applicability of the notion cross-culturally, I shall, in the first instance, apply Benson Saler's *prototype approach* of conceptualizing religion. Prototype theory exploits the practical competence of users of a category to distinguish between obvious examples and dubious examples of the category involved.[2] All examples are more or less debatable. This 'more or less', however, is not considered to be the problem, but the solution. It allows for the broadening and application of categories beyond the initial prototypes from which they derive.[3] In establishing resemblances, 'unbounded' analytical categories guide us from the better known to the less known or unknown.[4]

Sophocles' *Oedipus Tyrannus* and *Antigone* and Shakespeare's *Hamlet* are nowadays considered to be among the most outstanding examples of what tragedy is all about. It seems that these examples are already being recognized as such before scholars can prove whether this so-called 'recognition' is justified, but their recognition as prototypes depends on the cultural fashion of the age.[5] Saler's prototype approach suggests that we should take these plays particularly seriously as actual prototypes. What the three plays have in common is that they are about killing one's own relatives and oneself. To turn against and kill one's own relatives and oneself is widely considered a drama and a crime, but it is not necessarily considered a tragedy; if the killing is done inevitably and/or unwillingly, however, the event has turned into a tragedy. This intuitive insight into a good example of what tragedy is about can guide us in recognizing tragic constellations in the first instance, even if it does not exhaust the notion of the 'tragic'.

The examples of Sophocles' *Oedipus Tyrannus* and *Antigone* and of Shakespeare's *Hamlet* are not on a par with each other if one takes the *historical development* of the Western notion of 'tragedy' into account. Saler suggests that history should be taken seriously as a matter of fact, as the actual starting point from which the specific meanings of categories have developed into broader ones. The history of a category does not just refer to its origin, but includes the very development of that category away from its origin, provided the later development has been recognized as such by dramatic practice or by a considerable number of scholars. Such a development is, in fact, illustrated by the plays of Shakespeare being called 'tragedies'. The occurrence of the category 'tragedy' in early modern England marks a historical move of the genre from classical Greek culture (via Roman culture) to modern English culture, but the historical move is based more on literary links to Roman culture than on historical continuity with Greek culture, as we shall see. This invites us to undertake a first cross-cultural comparison within Western culture itself, before pushing the limits even further by comparing issues in two bodies of Western texts and their contexts with the corresponding issues in a body of Indian texts and their contexts. The cross-cultural move from Greece to England has become an integral part of the history of the development of the 'tragic genre'. Hardly any scholar would deny that Shakespeare has written real tragedies. Since Gotthold Ephraim Lessing (1759), the neo-classic recognition of Greek tragedy at the expense of Shakespearean tragedy has been dismissed as false classicism.[6] Whether the category of the 'tragic genre' can be extended beyond the borders of Western culture remains to be seen. Whatever the outcome, the category of the 'tragic', even broader than that of the 'tragic genre', still draws from the history of the genre for its distinctiveness, despite the fact that it is applicable to many more phenomena than to a dramatic or literary genre. Within that history, Greek tragedy continues to be the first point of reference. Greek tragedy remains the historical starting point from which the specific meanings of the notion of 'tragedy' have developed into broader ones.

Greek tragedy remains the first point of reference and Shakespearean tragedy complements and transforms the associations connected with the Greek notion of 'tragic' in 'tragic views of the human being'. This picture should provide enough of a hold as an initial *comparandum* from where the challenge of cross-cultural comparisons beyond the boundaries of Western culture is taken up. Whether a Hindu version of Western tragedy can be identified remains to be seen. Issues related to Western tragedy and tragic views of the human condition function as a productive springboard for entering the cross-cultural stage of comparative research. That is to say, Western issues are 'productive' in the sense that they highlight certain points (of potential comparison) in the Indian material that come to our attention. These would be different from, say, if Chinese issues were being raised. But the cross-cultural comparisons will not be straightforward. The Hindu views of (wo)man under consideration do not emerge from Western tragic literature and drama, but from Indian epic literature and drama, and the socio-political, cultural and religious aspects will turn out to be very different too. The Indian cultural landscape has already constituted its own central points and patterns, thus marking and framing its views of the human condition accordingly. The central points and patterns in the Indian cultural landscape that are now highlighted by a Western interest in certain issues have nonetheless emerged from within the Indian cultural landscape. The reading of the landscape is a predominantly Western one, but the landscape remains a recognizably Indian landscape, a landscape whose patterns are sufficiently characteristic to resist Western reductions of the Indian landscape to a projection screen of Western wishful thinking. Central points and patterns can be recognized as formal structures, even before their meaningfulness is expressed in Western or Indian language games. Hindu views of human nature will be compared as such to certain Western counterparts, not as isolated cases, but as deeply embedded in their own Indian settings. In the second part of each chapter, the Indian tradition will be studied and presented as much as possible in its own terms before being compared to the Western tradition in the third part of each chapter. I realize, however, that this presents a problem in that the Indian tradition is submitted to a predominantly Western reading.

It takes a certain distance, a bird's eye view, to engage in cross-cultural comparisons. It also takes time to fly across one landscape to the other and back again, building up a gradual picture of what the Western and Indian landscapes look like, especially if one wants to include the observations regarding historical developments within each of these regional landscapes. After all, these cultural landscapes are not static structures, but have taken ages to grow into their current state.

There is a tension in my method between moving through time and moving through space. In presenting the historical shift from Sophocles to Shakespeare as a move from one culture to the next, I take my starting point in Greek tragedy, move from there to cross the boundary of Greek culture and enter into English culture, but I then move further on, to a culture which is earlier in time – in fact, turning classical again – but remote, albeit still Indo-European – the Indian culture. On the one hand, my spatial imagery suggests a sideward movement at the expense of chronological considerations. On the other hand, I take my actual starting point in the oldest expression of tragedy, in ancient and classical Greek tragedy because that is where the category originally developed and because I agree with Saler that categories become more transparent if they are not taken as timeless, but are understood as part and parcel of the history of a specific culture where they have proven useful – which includes the extension to *later times*. The category of 'tragedy' is *not a timeless notion*. And yet, the notion of 'tragicness' or the 'tragic' may point to a human experience which is *of all time*, a human experience best exemplified in stories about killing one's kin and oneself unwillingly, which is known beyond Western culture under different names.

4 The scholarly art of comparing cross-culturally

What it means to be a human being varies from one culture to another. Views of the human being differ from one religious or secular world view to another. To be human is something all human beings have in common, but cultures transmit different perceptions of what that commonness consists of. One method of developing a deepened understanding of human nature is to study several perceptions of the human being from different cultures, and to compare them cross-culturally. But this is easier said than done. How is one to find commonness cross-culturally if each culture has its own methods of identifying that very commonness?

The following comparative enterprise was initially triggered by the naive impression that cross-culturally, certain human issues which are presented in 'tragic' literature and drama are strikingly similar worldwide. I decided to submit this impression of cross-cultural similarities to a scholarly testing of its potential for new insights into the similarities and differences between cultures. These similarities and differences are likely to exist, but are hard to spell out.

Comparisons are born from the discovery and *recognition of patterns* in what seem, at first glance, incoherent and unrelated configurations. Basic patterns, such as ice crystals, are recognized without being meaningful in any narrative sense of the word. Ice crystals appear to present us with patterns that we can recognize. Their formal structures are seductively easy to use as projection screens for 'recognizing' (frost) flowers or other images. But they do not represent flowers. Cultural patterns too, can be discovered and 'recognized' as formal structures (full of unknown meaning), but although they tell a story, they do not necessarily tell *your* story. They may tell a different story unrelated to your own meaningful patterns, patterns of cultural expression and association. Cultural patterns are like landscapes. Cultural landscapes are difficult to identify and yet visibly bear the traces of cultural patterns manifest to those who have the academic skills to read them. Such patterns can only be seen from the air, or from a certain distance and angle, in a bird's eye view, at a certain speed. Different angles or contexts enable different perspectives.

One of my main methodological assumptions is that views of the human condition cannot be depicted properly without depicting the *specific cultures* in which they emerge. Views of human nature are deeply embedded in their respective cultures and should be presented as such. Comparing views of (wo)man cross-culturally implies, therefore, comparing the cultural patterns or contexts that mark and frame these views.

I shall not put forward my own textual analysis of each of the texts concerned, but will present the outcome of exegetical and historical analyses done by well-known scholars who are specialists in their fields, and make explicit my personal preferences within the ongoing debate. All these scholarly commentators are extremely helpful in tracing the blinkers and blind spots that form our personal intuitions, preferences and conjectures. My assumption is that scholarly theories tend to shed light on issues more (often) than they cast shadows on them.[7] Also, I assume that one single theory is less likely to shed light on matters than a variety of theories juxtaposed. The juxtaposition of a variety of scholarly theories has the additional advantage that scholars mutually criticize and complement each other's approaches. This again generates the feedback scholarly debate needs in order to constitute a more reliable general impression of the issues being raised. The scholarly debate itself is more important than particular positions within it, in my opinion, because it is the broad debate that conveys a general impression of the issues at stake. Moreover, this general impression of the issues at stake, or rather, my version of that general impression, seeks to avoid getting too abstract and getting lost in details.[8] In the humanities, a sophisticated general impression is as close as one can get to the truth or plausibility of cross-cultural comparisons. But as such, it is worlds apart from a casual first impression. Academic rigour in constantly re-examining the original appearance from different angles makes the difference. It takes time, patience and discipline to withhold from making comparisons until one has carefully charted each issue within its own context.[9]

The main question is a cross-cultural one, and it is a question pertaining to patterns. Such a comparative project presupposes, of course, the possibility and validity of cross-cultural questions. In that respect, much will depend on the reader's affinity with cross-cultural questioning and with the balancing act that every comparative enterprise is. After all, cross-cultural comparisons are closer to impressionistic painting than they are to natural science.[10] I can only offer my personal picture as an informed attempt to grasp some fundamental similarities and differences regarding certain views of human nature in classical Western and Indian literature, and speculate about the value of the picture.

5 Main purpose of the comparative enterprise

Admittedly, tragedies are not everybody's favourite genre. One of my classmates in grammar school would compose her lists of works of modern literature in different languages for the exam by first quickly reading through the last chapter of a book in order to find out whether the plot had a happy ending. If not, she would decide without further consideration that the book would not become part of her reading lists. She did not like tragedies. I later found out that she had gone into business management.

The *main purpose* of my overall comparison is to extend the discussion, not of tragedy as such, but of (tragic) views of the human condition, beyond its Western origins and scope by including (parts of) the Hindu epic tradition of classical India in the discussion. That is one reason why the sections on the *Mahābhārata* epic and on the *Bhagavadgītā* are more elaborate than the sections on Greek and Shakespearean tragedy. The other reason is that the Indian literary and religious traditions are much less well-known outside Indian culture than Western tragedy is.

To identify how close the *Mahābhārata* epic's and the *Bhagavadgītā*'s views of the human condition come to a tragic view (in the Western senses of the word) should serve the *wider purpose* of extending comparative exercises beyond the boundaries of the known and the familiar, and of appreciating to the full, among other things, what it means when a book like *The Go-Between* by Leslie Poles Hartley does not end, but begins, in the present tense, with this opening line: 'The past is a foreign country: they do things differently there'.

But why would one want to extend the discussion of (tragic) views of the human being beyond its Western origins and scope? Shedding some extra light on what it means to be human, trying out different angles, tracing one's own blinkers and blind spots, broadening one's horizon, communicating cross-culturally, empathizing with fellow human beings elsewhere – those are the kinds of things one would wish to be the point of this academic exercise. In the end, the *underlying question* of this study is – are Indian views of human nature very different from Western views of human nature after all?

2

Narrative aspects

PART I: GREEK AND SHAKESPEAREAN ISSUES

1 Introduction

The phenomenon of tragedy is related to a number of narrative aspects. Many scholars have made efforts to define the notions of 'tragedy' and 'the tragic' in terms of these narrative aspects. Scholars have asked themselves what exactly it is about tragedies and tragic stories that qualifies them as tragic. Is it the plot pattern? Is it the tragic end? Is it a perspective or a message? Is it a particular world view or a particular view of man? Is it specific topics? Is it the way the subject matter is being dealt with? Is it the combination of atmosphere, mood and tone? In this chapter, we will be looking at tragic plot patterns, tragic world views, tragic irony, tragic mood and tragic subjects. Three tragic stories will be highlighted in particular – for Greek tragedy, Sophocles' *Antigone* and *Oedipus Tyrannus*; for Shakespearean tragedy, Shakespeare's *Hamlet, Prince of Denmark*. The *main question* of this first part on Greek and Shakespearean issues will be – what is it about these and similar stories that qualifies them as tragic?

In the second part of the chapter, on Indian and Hindu issues, it will be shown which of these narrative aspects are present (or absent) in the *Mahābhārata* epic and the *Bhagavadgītā*.

The third part, on cross-cultural comparisons, will be dedicated to the task of comparing the Greek and Shakespearean material with the Indian or Hindu material. The main question of the third part will be – in what respects do or do not the discussed narrative aspects of Greek and Shakespearean tragedy have parallels in the *Mahābhārata* epic and the *Bhagavadgītā*?

2 Three tragic stories in particular

2.1 Introduction

As mentioned before, three tragic stories will be highlighted. Sophocles (496–406 BCE) wrote his *Antigone* many years before he wrote his *Oedipus Tyrannus*. His *Antigone* was performed in 442 BCE, while his *Oedipus Tyrannus* won the second prize at the Athenian festival in 425 BCE. In terms of the narrative, one might expect them to have been in reverse order since Antigone was Oedipus' daughter returning to her father's city, Thebes. William Shakespeare (1564–1616) wrote his own manuscript version, his 'foul-papers' (the completed draft as opposed to a fair copy submitted to his theatre company) of *Hamlet* most probably around 1600–01, during the final years of the Tudor reign of Queen Elizabeth I (1558–1603). Published text versions appeared in 1603 (an unauthorized, corrupt version), in 1604 (Second Quarto version) and in 1623 (First Folio version), during the first years of the Stuart reign of King James I (1603–25).[1] We start with brief outlines of the plots of these tragedies.

2.2 Summary of the plot of Sophocles' Oedipus Tyrannus

Sophocles' *Oedipus Tyrannus* begins when the city of Thebes has been struck with a plague. Its king Oedipus does not know that he is the cause of this divine punishment. On his way to Thebes, he had unknowingly killed his father Laius, the previous king of Thebes. Moreover, on arrival, he had unknowingly married his mother, queen Iocaste, as a reward for having liberated the city from the Sphinx. Oedipus has sent Creon, Iocaste's brother, to Delphi to ask the oracle what to do. Creon notices that the gods are angry at Thebes because a murderer is polluting the city, and that the murderer is the one who killed Laius. Oedipus vows to find the murderer and starts his investigations. He also questions the blind seer Teiresias who clearly knows more and is reluctant to speak, but gives in under pressure from Oedipus and mentions Oedipus as the pollution. Oedipus does not believe him and suggests instead that there is a conspiracy between Teiresias and Creon. Eventually, Teiresias plainly states that Oedipus has murdered his father and married his mother. The chorus pledges not to condemn Oedipus without evidence. Creon returns to defend himself. Iocaste tells how Laius was told by the oracle that his son would kill him, and how the baby boy had been abandoned, suggesting that the oracle must have been mistaken because Laius was supposed to have been killed by robbers at a crossroads. Uneasy about the crossroads detail, Oedipus questions Iocaste about Laius and starts to link this information to his own killing of an old man at a crossroads, to rumours in his youth that he was not the son of Polybus, king of Corinth, and his wife Merope, and to Apollo's oracle telling him that he would kill his father and marry his mother. A messenger from Corinth announces that Polybus has died of natural causes, but also reveals that Oedipus is the adopted son of Polybus and Merope. The messenger had received Oedipus as a baby from a shepherd of Laius, who then shows up in person at the palace as the only surviving witness of Laius' murder. Having fled the city when Oedipus became king, Oedipus has summoned this former servant of Laius to testify.

In the subsequent discussions, Iocaste is the first one to realize the truth. Oedipus learns the truth more slowly. Both run off-stage. The chorus sings about the transitory nature of human happiness, using Oedipus as an example. Out of the palace comes a messenger, describing how Oedipus, after discovering that Iocaste has hanged herself,[2] gouged out his own eyes. Oedipus wants to face the citizens before retreating into exile, reappears with his eyes mutilated, sings in lamentation with the chorus and blames Apollo. The chorus suggests that Oedipus would be better off dead, but Oedipus counters that blindness is appropriate, since he cannot *see* the results of his actions. He *tells* them instead. Creon is now the new king. Creon refuses to exile him. Oedipus asks Creon to bury Iocaste and to let him touch his two daughters, Antigone and Ismene. They appear, are lamented by their father and commended to Creon's care. While Oedipus goes into exile, the chorus pronounces the Solonian axiom that no one should be judged fortunate until after his life has ended.

2.3 Summary of the plot of Sophocles' Antigone

Sophocles' *Antigone* describes the conflict between Antigone and Creon. Preceding this conflict is the other conflict within the doomed family – the conflict between Eteocles and Polyneices, the subject of Aeschylus' *Seven Against Thebes*. Oedipus had two sons, Eteocles and Polyneices, who agreed to rule Thebes in alternate years. Eteocles refused to step down at the end of his first year of rule, however. Polyneices then raised an army against Thebes. Both brothers are killed by each other's hand. Creon now becomes the ruler of Thebes.

Sophocles' *Antigone* begins when Creon declares that Eteocles' body will be buried properly, that is, ritually, since Eteocles was the protector of the city, but that Polyneices, having attacked the city, will be left unburied on the battlefield. Antigone, in defiance of Creon's edict, resolves to ceremonially bury her brother Polyneices. She is caught in the act by Creon's watchmen and brought before the king. Her sister Ismene had refused to help Antigone for fear of the death penalty. Creon questions Antigone, who does not deny that she has buried Polyneices. She justifies her action, asserting that she was bound to obey the divine laws in spite of any human ordinance. Creon grows even angrier, suspects Ismene to have been involved too, and condemns both women to be locked up in a chamber. Haemon, Creon's son and Antigone's fiancé, seems initially willing to obey his father, but when he tries to persuade his father to spare Antigone by lecturing him on wise leadership, the discussion deteriorates drastically and the two men separate, bitterly insulting each other. Creon decides to spare Ismene, but to imprison Antigone in a cave – to bury her by sealing her underground. Antigone bewails her fate, but remains defensive of her act.

The blind seer Teiresias warns Creon that the gods side with Antigone. Creon will lose his child because of his mistakes, and the sacrificial offerings of Thebes will not be accepted by the gods. The chorus, terrified, asks Creon to take their advice to bury Polyneices and free Antigone. Creon finally relents, but it is too late. Creon decides to free Antigone, only to find that she has committed suicide. Haemon too, kills himself. Upon his return to the palace, Creon, carrying Haemon's body, learns that his wife Eurydice has killed herself, having cursed her husband with her last breath. Creon blames himself for everything that has happened. The chorus closes by saying that the gods punish the proud, but that punishment brings wisdom.

2.4 Summary of the plot of William Shakespeare's Hamlet, Prince of Denmark

The one Shakespearean tragedy that will take centre stage is *Hamlet*. The play begins with some guards talking about a ghost who resembles Hamlet's father, the former King of Denmark. The ghost tells Hamlet that he was poisoned by Claudius, Hamlet's uncle, who quickly assumed the throne and married Hamlet's mother, Gertrude. The ghost instructs Hamlet to revenge his murder. Hamlet, however, delays doing so, and spends most of the play debating his inability to take revenge and acting as if he had gone mad (taking on an 'antic disposition'). By mistake, he kills Polonius, the Lord Chamberlain, and is sent to England, supposedly mad. On his return, he fights a duel with Polonius's son, Laertes, and is killed by a poisoned sword. But before he dies, Hamlet kills Claudius. Gertrude, drinking from a poisoned cup, also dies. Hamlet's close friend, Horatio, is given the task of telling Hamlet's story, while Fortinbras, the new King of Norway, takes over Denmark's throne.

These summaries of the plots are meant to facilitate a closer look at some of the narrative aspects of these and other tragedies, such as the characteristics of tragic plot patterns, the roles of irony and of a tragic mood, the presence of a specific world view and the recurrence of specific subjects.

3 Specific plot patterns

One narrative aspect that has to be dealt with is the cluster of questions related to tragic plot patterns. What role does the plot pattern play in defining the tragic character of tragedies? Does a tragic plot have a specific beginning or end? Does it revolve around a specific conflict? Is 'plot' the soul of tragedy because of its movement to a promised (disastrous) end? Is a 'tragic mechanism' essential to turn a story line into a tragic plot? Different answers will be given for different Greek plays and it seems that even more answers will be given when it comes to Shakespeare's *Hamlet*.

3.1 *Tragic beginning and audience expectation*

Every writer who shapes a tragic plot pattern faces the problem of 'setting in motion and achieving the gradual narrowing-down from an opening situation, in which a wide range of alternative possibilities is available, towards the point where a destiny has taken its full shape', as Michael Ewans puts it.[3] How is a tragic plot set in motion? John Peck and Martin Coyle observe in Shakespeare's case that, whereas in history plays, such as Shakespeare's *Antony and Cleopatra,* the disruptive force is love, in tragedies, it is the overwhelmingly disruptive force of evil.[4] The release of evil sets the tragic plot in motion. According to Ewans, one of the most common ways of shaping a tragic story (both ancient and modern) is:

> to show a pattern of disorder rectified, but at terrible cost; for this reason, several Greek tragedies begin with a *miasma*, a literal and psychic pollution which indicates that the community has in some way violated the normal order of the world and incurred the displeasure of the gods.[5]

Ewans points out that this pattern is first seen in the *Iliad* (I.43.ff.). Sophocles' *Oedipus Tyrannus* explicitly qualifies the opening situation of the plague in

Thebes as pollution (*miasma*) in need of purification (*catharsis*).[6] Shakespeare's *Hamlet* reveals the same pattern:

> of unlawful usurpation and eventual re-establishment of order; but it is grounded upon the concept of *miasma,* brought out in the early exchange between Marcellus and Horatio: 'Something is rotten in the state of Denmark.'\'Heaven will direct it' (I.iv.90–1).[7]

The plot of *Hamlet*, Joan Rees observes, only gradually reveals a *revenge pattern*.[8] Due to his encounter with the Ghost, Hamlet becomes 'a man with a mission' who must henceforward keep his distance from others, such as Ophelia, lest they weaken or contaminate his purpose, Rees notices. But there is not just one single revenge. Hamlet's father, the Ghost, demands revenge for having been poisoned secretly by his brother Claudius. But Hamlet has been offended by his disappointing mother when she married Claudius overhastily and thus committed incest. Besides, Harry Keyishian argues, the revenge agenda of the Ghost and the revenge agenda of Hamlet do not coincide.[9] The Ghost is focused on killing Claudius while leaving his former wife Gertrude out of the affair. 'The Ghost has, in addition, political motives for desiring revenge. He is outraged by the contamination of the state by an unworthy usurper (I.v.36–8)' and the court's licentiousness.[10]

Hamlet wants to take revenge on his mother and Claudius for their marriage. The Ghost's revelations turn him into a new person – a young man with a sacred mission. 'The crucial thing is that Hamlet *remember*, that he honor his father's cause by keeping it alive', Keyishian emphasizes.[11]

3.2 Tragic development

If there is one category that overarches tragic plot patterns, it is *conflict*, the starting-point of all storytelling, Peter Burian contends. In general, tragic plots seem to require certain kinds of conflicts. Burian mentions three aspects of tragic conflicts. First of all, tragic conflict is *extreme*. Compromise or mediation are unlikely options, even though reconciliation between enemies or 'late learning' may occur afterwards or too late, 'In *Antigone*, for example, Creon recognizes his mistake only after he has caused Antigone's death, and Haemon and Eurydice have committed suicide'.[12] Secondly, the conflict involves factors such as past action, ignorance and divine intervention, factors that go beyond choices, clashing between free human agents. Burian mentions the example of the maddening of Heracles in *Heracles*. In addition, one may also think of the religious curse that struck the entire Labdacid dynasty to which Oedipus,

Eteocles, Polyneices, Antigone and Creon belong – a common fate which they re-enact over the generations. The third aspect of tragic conflicts is the community aspect – the whole city, the royal family, the ordering of human life. The downfall of tragic heroes such as Oedipus is never just a personal tragedy.[13]

In the case of *Hamlet* being a revenge tragedy, revenge itself is at the heart of the tragic conflict to the extent that it constitutes an immoral solution to a moral problem and is, therefore, part of the *moral conflict* of choosing between two evils.[14] Thomas McAlindon does not focus on the revenge pattern in *Hamlet,* but on the *psycho-social conflict* in Hamlet, who is basically a loving person trapped in a situation of psychological and social chaos – fratricide, incest, sincere love and the call to violence and hatred.[15] John Lee sees Hamlet's psychic conflict as a *conflict of identity*. The real tragedy, Lee argues, is that Hamlet's repetitive self-exploration does not lead to a consistent story that establishes a unified self. Instead, like Montaigne, Hamlet discovers, in his interior, a landscape of terrifying inner instability. Though the soliloquies, in creating a form of autobiography, give the Prince a story, it is a 'failed story'.[16]

According to Burian, there is no specific plot pattern that could be called a 'true' tragic plot, just a number of *plot patterns* which involve a characteristic *type of conflict* – the retribution pattern, the sacrifice pattern, the supplication pattern, the rescue pattern and the return-recognition pattern.[17] Burian's *recognition pattern* recalls Charles Segal's plot *pattern of riddle and decipherment*, which appeals to our desire for knowledge. Segal calls *Oedipus Tyrannus* the first detective story of Western literature, dramatizing the lonely path of self-discovery.[18] Tragic plots, Burian observes, often combine two or more underlying patterns in unexpected and disturbing ways. In *Antigone*, a pattern of divine punishment involving Creon emerges from the action shaped by Antigone's self-sacrifice.[19]

What strikes me in Burian's list is the absence of the *revenge pattern* as a tragic pattern of its own,[20] one that dominates Aeschylus' entire *Oresteia* trilogy. According to Simon Goldhill, in the *Oresteia*, as in Shakespeare's *Hamlet*, the narrative of revenge is used to explore the nature of human action and obligation, as well as the broadest ideas of justice and transgression (from which revenge draws its force as a principle). As in *Hamlet*, the *Oresteia*'s focus on revenge within a single household leads to the tragedy of intrafamilial violence and conflicting obligations. The structure of the Aeschylean trilogy, however, also links this pattern of revenge to a *pattern of reversal*, where the very act of taking revenge repeatedly turns the revenger into an object of revenge.[21]

Very influential in identifying basic characteristics of tragic plot patterns has been Aristotle's *Poetics*. One of Aristotle's ideas was *peripeteia* (tragic reversal), with Sophocles' *Oedipus Tyrannus* as Aristotle's model play.[22] Bernd Seidensticker points to the feature of 'dialectic reversal', which *intensifies the tragic effect* of the plot and which gives a play its special tragic effect – the unexpected turn of events that develops paradoxically, but inevitably out of the nature of the *dramatis personae* or out of their intentions, plans or actions. He calls this unexpected turn of events, this Aristotelian *peripeteia* ('reversal'), 'dialectic' reversal because 'impending or actual destruction' (Peter Szondi's vocabulary) is not due to an external force operating independently from human action, but to a force arising in interaction (dialectic!) with these actions or intentions, bringing about 'a switch of actions to the contrary'.[23]

Sophocles' *Oedipus Tyrannus* exemplifies a perfect coincidence of this moment of dialectic reversal with the moment of 'recognition' (*anagnōrisis*) by the main character, who himself is not just overturned but turning round. This sudden change in attitude does not come about so suddenly in *Antigone*, or not at all. Ger Groot shows how the structure of *Antigone* deals with a possible reversal of events through a turnabout of its main characters. The crucial third episode shows *a failed reversal*, whereas the first and the fifth episodes show *successful reversals*. Interestingly, the second and the fourth episodes, featuring Creon and Antigone, show *no reversal* at all.[24]

Another element which is considered truly 'tragic' and which is part of the Aristotelian tradition, has been particularly dominant in tragic criticism. It emphasizes *hamartia* (mistake, *tragic error*) and its punishment – the tragic hero, although caught in circumstances beyond his ken and control, is finally to be understood as destroyed by the gods (or fate) because of his own failings. Burian points out that the search for tragic errors in tragic plots is doomed to fail because 'this schema is inadequate and even irrelevant' to many of the plays.[25]

If one is in search of tragic errors in tragedies, the case of Sophocles' *Oedipus Tyrannus* is an interesting one because Oedipus does not make errors. He immediately acts upon and even anticipates the problems he faces, starting to investigate thoroughly the cause of the Theban plague. He is quick to respond and he takes the decisions needed and expected. And yet, his very choice to constantly opt for further investigation, time and again, turns out to be his fatal error. In fact, his conscious urge for knowledge, for truth and insight, could be interpreted as the fatal error defining human nature in general. But that need not be because a search for knowledge is disastrous by definition. Only the extreme pursuit of knowledge which knows of no boundaries seems to be. Defining human nature in terms of an unrelenting search for knowledge is very Greek. One is reminded of the Delphian oracle's adage 'know yourself'. In tragedy, this crucial characteristic of human beings turns out to be their fatal error. But it is also their greatness, not just their weakness. Oedipus is prepared to face the truth at the cost of his own suffering.

If, in the Aristotelian tradition, the plot pattern of a tragedy creates the audience expectation that a nobleman behaves like a nobleman, and that the audience is, therefore, surprised by vice and failure, Shakespeare's *Hamlet* is certain to take us by surprise. As a nobleman, Prince Hamlet is expected to actively take revenge. The more active he becomes, however, the more (self)destructive his actions turn out. Final success coincides with final failure. Like a Greek fate, this outcome only gradually takes shape. It is fuelled by human action, but gets out of human control. The ironic-paradoxical structure of this *reversal* heightens the tragic effect of the plot pattern.

Peter B. Murray's behaviourist approach allows him to draw attention to those aspects of the plot pattern that make Hamlet's character or attitude change under the influence of his own 'habits' or behaviour. As an agent of sincerity and honesty, Hamlet becomes an actor fatally obsessed with his act, Murray argues.[26] Hamlet has a disposition not only to be a noble and honest prince, but also to play roles (the 'antic disposition') and to reflect on his subjectivity. However, under the circumstances, Hamlet gets caught up in a vicious circle of obsession with his own sense of honour, honesty and self-reflection. He is even able to think about how his thinking may be in error. The audience can identify with the way in which Hamlet's disposition gradually turns into a fatal habitus. But the dynamics of the plot pattern can *only in part* be described by tracing the consequences of Hamlet's antic disposition:[27]

> The Gravedigger is less a character than a figure whose primary function is to be a mirror held up to Hamlet's antic disposition as this disposition fades. Thus the statement about the Gravedigger's habituation leads to the question whether Hamlet now finds it easy to jest about death, too. If Hamlet comes to terms with death here, he does so on the basis of a hardening of his sensitivities in which he excludes awareness of matters that might cause him pain.[28]

His only regret seems to be that death ends all distinctions of social class.

One general theory of tragedy that focuses on a specific plot pattern (and specific subjects) as criteria for defining the tragic genre is offered by Clément Rosset.[29] Rosset holds that a 'typically tragic' plot pattern in well-known plays develops in a direction contrary to the expectations or intentions of the agents involved, but not to their advantage. He calls this trap plot the *tragic mechanism*.[30] His general analysis starts with the psychological observation that it is not the situation which is tragic, but the relationship between situations, the transition from one situation to the next. To be more precise, this transition from one state to the next that constitutes the tragic mechanism only becomes tragic when we have grasped it as such afterwards. Tragic is not the dead body that is now carried away, but the idea that this body of flesh and bones is the very same as the one which fell just a moment ago. We have to make the connection. There is nothing tragic about the realization that the body is dead. The tragedy lies in the fact that just a minute ago, the body was someone alive. This realization is horrifying for the intellect because the transition is an absurd identification of two utterly incompatible states in favour of the unfavourable one. At one moment, one is alive; at the next, one is dead. The realization is normally afterwards, but it may be anticipated by imagining its completion in advance. In that case, the tragic is felt at the very moment it takes place.

The imaginative realization of the tragic outcome of the unfolding event turns *time* as actually unfolding into essential timelessness. Tragic time is different from normal time in that it is tragedy in disguise. The tragic movement that unfolds does not, in fact, contain a development of something new. It is fixed, not mobile. It takes time, but it does not allow time to take place since, in essence, the movement is already completed. What we realize – and only after we realize it – is the immobility of the movement. It is the realization that the movement from one state to the next is a solidified mechanism following a rigid scheme, as if time did not exist. Realizing its outcome, we have already drawn up the balance when time starts running. That is why tragic time – our time-consciousness of the non-progressive impact of time proceeding – goes in the opposite direction from normal time, in the sense that it starts from the end, at the culmination point of the tragic movement, and then returns from there to its starting point. Rosset's notions of mechanism, timelessness and immobility, all suggest that a tragic plot pattern is structured to the effect that the realization of incompatibility and necessity becomes a horrifying state of mind of the audience.

Rosset's theory helps to explain why the plot pattern of Shakespeare's *Hamlet* often evokes the question – why did Hamlet *delay*? By the time we realize that the play is a revenge play, we realize its outcome. Realizing its outcome, we have already drawn up the balance when time starts running. But the main character, who himself makes the decision to take revenge, starts running in all directions except towards his goal. He takes plenty of time before actually conforming to time's inevitable, that is, non-progressive outcome.

The Elizabethan concept of revenge, David Margolies points out, has three components – the victim must not only suffer, but also know the reason for it, and the punishment should be appropriate to the original injury. The revenger, then, must be sure that the victim feels his guilt, without which the revenge would seem to be arbitrary. Hamlet has to wait for the appropriate moment, the moment when Claudius actually *feels* his guilt and '*appears* worthy of vengeance—which clearly is not when he is at prayers'. Hamlet's delay is justified.[31]

According to Rees, the reasons for the delay may be many, but basically the delay relates to *dramatic structure*. The dramatic question is – how does Shakespeare fill the interval between instigation to revenge and execution of vengeance?[32] Anthony Brennan too, focuses on dramatic structure. A constant aspect of Shakespeare's dramatic method, he argues, is the development of plots that involve a separation of the major characters. Separation is a primary motif of the romance form, and romance is a major influence on Shakespeare's drama. The action of *Hamlet* is developed around two characters locked in a deadly struggle who hardly ever share the stage together, but constantly spy upon each other through intermediaries and through acting as part of a game of hide-and-seek – Hamlet and Claudius.[33] Claudius' spies 'have a vested interest in promoting their own theories', Brennan suggests. 'Through them Hamlet can encourage all the false speculative theories about his madness'. Claudius 'serves agents like so many tennis balls and Hamlet sends them spinning back determined to keep them in play until it is time to bat them out of court'.[34] Spying is about the acquisition of certain knowledge, Brennan argues, as is the play as a whole, 'From the point of the Ghost's appearance at the outset, all of the action is related to two urgent searches for certain knowledge: Hamlet's need to know if the Ghost is honest, and Claudius's need to know the cause of Hamlet's antic disposition'.[35] Brennan concludes that Shakespeare has imposed a 'severe limitation on the face-to-face relationship with Claudius'. Hamlet only reveals their secret knowledge of the murder publicly in his last words to Claudius. When doing so (V.ii.314–15), Hamlet 'has still spoken less than forty lines to Claudius'.[36]

Bert O. States maintains that it is quite easy to write a long revenge play without arousing suspicions of delay. It is basically a matter of the kinds of things Shakespeare put in Hamlet's path. In fact, this is the dramatic function of the three members of the Polonius family. Instead of attacking Claudius directly, Hamlet follows the trebling device of anticipating the attack by repeating its rehearsal in a 'series of surrogate or mini-revenges' on Ophelia, Polonius and Laertes, the repetitive delays imitating the denouement before it actually takes place, much like the playing out of the murder in *Murder of Gonzago*, constantly 'killing someone *other than* Claudius'![37]

Keyishian concentrates on the *dynamics of revenge* – how revenge is provoked, justified, concluded. He defines revenge primarily as a psychic conflict, as a response to victimization. He focuses more on its psychological than on its moral and ethical dimensions. In fact, he stresses the potentially redemptive functions of revenge.[38] Vengeful violence has its roots in humiliation and finds its solution in symbolically remaking the damaged self. Though 'vengeance composes the plot of the revenge play, grief composes its essential emotional content'. Because victimization is related to the process of mourning, revenge may function as a remedy for grief, even though it is a remedy that risks madness.[39]

Shakespeare, Keyishian argues, distinguishes sharply between authentic revenge and vindictiveness. Authentic revenge is about just retaliations for real injuries. Characters like Titus Andronicus turn 'to revenge because other avenues for achieving vindication, honour, and equity have been closed to them'. Vindictiveness is 'a malicious state of mind that resembles authentic revenge like an evil twin'. Characters like Iago and Shylock 'are moved to chronic resentfulness by a combination of envy, excessive pride, and self-loathing'. Mixed characters like Hamlet and Othello are problematic types 'in whom conflicting, complexly textured impulses struggle for supremacy'.[40]

3.3 Tragic end and tragic mood

Well-known plays like *Oedipus Tyrannus* and *Antigone* give the impression that the difference between comedy and tragedy can be determined by the outcome – *a tragedy always ends in tragedy*. Aristotle's examples of the tragic genre include Homer's epics. The plot of the *Odyssey* is much closer to comedy – which ends in opposite directions for the good people and the bad[41] – than it is to real tragedy, whereas the plot of the *Iliad* is real tragedy – good people ending up badly.[42] According to A. Maria van Erp Taalman Kip, disaster is not the outcome of about one quarter of all the remaining plays. For the Greeks, Aristotle included, the catastrophic end is not a *conditio sine qua non*.[43] She writes:

> In *Poetics* 13 (1453a 27–30), . . . he asserts that when staged at the dramatic contests, tragedies ending in disaster prove to be the most tragic, and that Euripides, in this regard at least, proves to be the most tragic of poets. However, at 14, 1454a 1–9 Euripides' *Iphigenia in Tauris*, a play which does *not* end in disaster, seems to be given preference even over *Oedipus Tyrannus*. I will not discuss here the relation between this passage and the earlier one, but I am fairly convinced that Aristotle would not have denied to *Iphigenia in Tauris* the predicate 'tragic' (*tragikón*).[44]

There is something to be said against this, however. First of all, the predicate 'tragic' could mean 'dramatic' here.[45] Secondly, *Iphigenia in Tauris* may be much closer to 'melodrama' than it is to 'tragedy', but this alternative would not have been a category available to Aristotle. Taken seriously as a 'tragedy,' even if there is no actual destruction in the end, there is an *impending destruction*[46] during the performance, which fully satisfies Aristotle's need for proof of the pedagogic role of tragedy because it stimulates the moral imagination of the audience, which Aristotle considers necessary to avoid possible error.[47] This impending destruction can evoke a *long-lasting worrying effect*, to the extent that the audience remains in a *disturbed mood* afterwards, beyond the initial cathartic relief at the end of the play. A future impending catastrophe is as horrifying as an actual crisis that pollutes the city and is overcome by a pyrrhic victory – both leave a sense of tragicness.[48] In my opinion, the mood of plays is more decisive than the actual end. In the case of tragedy, from the overall mood, a tragic sense of unforgettable and disturbing suffering remains[49] and turns a final victory into a pyrrhic victory. If my argument is solid, the difference between tragedies and comedies depends, at least in part, on the audience's response, in particular, in doubtful cases. If the audience's response is taken into account here, some tragedies can be marked as better examples of tragedy than other ones. The higher the price paid in suffering, the more intense the tragic effect.

A tragic mood is characterized by suffering, grief and mourning. Songs of lamentation, lamenting loss and death, were a formal aspect of Greek tragedies.[50] In *Hamlet*'s case too, if we are to go by Keyishian, though 'vengeance composes the plot of the revenge play, grief composes its essential emotional content'. Because victimization is related to the process of *mourning*, revenge may function as a remedy for grief.[51]

A tragic mood is also characterized by a sense of unavoidable necessity, of inescapable destiny and doom. There is a disturbing sense of no escape, no exit. Johan Taels reminds us of Kierkegaard's distinction between tragedy and comedy. While in both tragedy and comedy, a contradictory relationship is being perceived, the comic approach registers not just the hurtful contradiction, but also its mental (or speculative) escape, whereas the tragic approach registers the same hurtful contradiction but, seeing no way out, becomes desperate.[52]

What about Hamlet's mental 'escape' from the worldly necessities of revenge into providential necessities? Does the shift turn this tragedy into a comedy? Under the guidance of Hamlet's belief in providence, all's well that ends well. Or, is it? Do the providential necessities reduce or double the inevitabilities of fate? Or, does providence take on the form of a series of coincidences – the working of necessity taking on the ironic form of something accidental? And, indeed, does it end well if so many characters die at the end, the morally exonerated main hero included? That Hamlet will die at the end of the play is, Keyishian writes, as much a matter of dramatic convention as of anything in the play's internal dynamics or the psychology of the characters – the killing of Polonius and the death of Ophelia are events that arouse audience expectations of his death. What is in the playwright's hands is how his revenger will meet that fate.[53] The playwright should provide an emotionally satisfying closure, and that is indeed what is being provided. But is Hamlet's final mood also the mood that persists after the play? Or, does the play evoke a long-lasting worrying effect, to the extent that the audience remains in a disturbed mood afterwards? Keyishian, in any case, remains in a disturbed mood.[54]

Hamlet's final mood of calmness in Act V.ii has also drawn the attention of William Kerrigan. His analysis takes the Graveyard scene as its clue.[55] Once obsessed with the facts of life, Hamlet is now fixated on the facts of death. He now meditates on the earthy afterlife of the body, 'How long will a man lie i'th'earth ere he rot?' (V.i.161) He now stares at skulls. What does he *learn* during this *self-education of the prince?*[56] The *first lesson* is that death, playing no favourites, delivers the supreme rebuke to human pride. High and low, man and woman, prince and pauper, jester and king – death undoes all the terms that divide and separate human beings by reducing difference to indistinction. But there is a *second lesson*, which has to do with literal dissolution, death's attack on the integrity of the body, Kerrigan suggests – we do not rest in peace. There is death after death, the dissolution and dispersion in and from the grave, the posthumous death of bodily corruption and putrefaction, to be given to 'Lady Worm' (V.i.87). Hamlet not only refers to imperial Caesar (V.i.209–12), 'but also shifts to verse, clearly proud of his thought' – death is 'one hell of a revenger'. 'The lessons of the Graveyard scene relieve the pressures on Hamlet'. Hamlet 'will avenge his father but need not plan a rivalrous Senecan atrocity', because the task of total revenge in the form of death after death is something he can leave to the plotting God of Christianity. He can do without ambition, passion, hatred and aggression.[57] Hamlet wins for himself the *calm* of V.ii.[58] He 'takes care to assess one final time the fit between his conscience and his task' of eradicating evil (V.ii.67–70). 'Perfect conscience to do it, damnation not to do it. He is not indifferent to damnation. He seems rather to have lost his fear of it'.[59] Kerrigan concludes that Hamlet's last idea of revenge is very different from his first, 'We remember Hamlet for the effects of vengeance on his mind (Acts I–IV) and at last for his mind's effects on vengeance (Act V)'.[60]

Rees is even more positive. During the disastrous end, he argues, it is Hamlet who is cleared of the stigma of cold-hearted butchery and of underhand plotting. Instead, it is Claudius who does the underhand plotting, and it is Laertes who assumes the role of unscrupulous pursuer of blood-vengeance while daring damnation (IV.v.132–8). It is Hamlet who, before the duel, apologizes to Laertes and addresses him as the brother he would have been if Ophelia had become Hamlet's wife. Rees does not stress the disastrous aspects of the end of the plot but its aspects of *reconciliation* and *brotherhood*.[61] He basically argues that if brotherhood has been at the heart of the *tragic conflict*, then the conflict has *not* turned out to be *unresolvable*, despite the fact that they do not survive their reconciliation. Which is not the same, in my opinion, as saying that the conflict is unambiguously solvable.[62] After all, Hamlet and Laertes do not survive their reconciliation.

4 A specific world view

Another narrative aspect to be dealt with is the question whether 'tragedy' can be defined in terms of a specific world view. Several approaches will be presented. Again, occasionally, I shall add my own position, opinion or comment, but my main aim is to enable the reader to have a balanced view of the issues at stake and of ways in which they are being debated.

One way of approaching tragedy as a specific world view amidst other world views starts from cultural differences among world views regarding the origin of and coping with evil in time. These cultural differences have inspired Paul Ricoeur to develop a typology of mythical imagery concerning the origin and end of evil, by distinguishing between four types – the 'drama of creation' type, the 'creation completed' type, the 'tragic' type and the 'myth of the banned soul' type.[63]

Does this typology clarify matters? I am not sure.[64] The 'tragic' type seems to be applicable to Greek tragedy, but not to Shakespearean tragedy. Even the applicability to Greek tragedy is disputable. What if time itself, and death as its embodiment, are considered the origin of evil? Doesn't Dionysus stand for the time-bound character of nature caught up in an inexorable flux of creation and destruction, the instability and perishability of all things, origin of both sorrow and joy? Shouldn't Greek tragedy be defined as the performance of the Dionysian drama of time-bound nature stricken with death and life, that is to say, as expressing a 'dramatic' worldview?

Regarding the applicability of Ricoeur's typology to Christianity during the Middle Ages and the Renaissance, for one thing, the 'eschatological' world view of Christianity is no doubt responsible for the fact that early and medieval Christianity did not produce any tragedies at all – at least not in the artistic sense of the word. George Steiner notices how a medieval distinction between tragedy and comedy in terms of *plot pattern only* (no dramatic performance, just 'a certeyn storie') was intertwined with the *Christian world view*. He points to Chaucer's medieval definition of 'tragedy' as 'a narrative recounting the life of some ancient or eminent personage who suffered a decline of fortune toward a disastrous end'.[65] Steiner puts Chaucer's medieval definition of tragedy in terms of a decline of fortune as the decisive plot pattern in perspective:

> Chaucer's definition derives its force from contemporary awareness of sudden reversals of political and dynastic fortune. . . . But the rise and fall of him that stood in high degree was the incarnation of the tragic sense for a much deeper reason: it made explicit the universal drama of the fall of man. . . . It is in a garden also that the symmetry of divine intent places the act of fortunate reversal. At Gethsemane the arrow changes its course, and the morality play of history alters from tragedy to *commedia*. . . . Of this great parable of God's design, the recital of the tragic destinies of illustrious men are a gloss and a reminder.[66]

According to Steiner, Early Renaissance is still optimistic but the *world view of High Renaissance* introduces a much more tragic world view:

> With the decline of hope which followed on the early renaissance—the darkening of spirit which separates the vision of man in Marlowe from that of Pico della Mirandola—the sense of the tragic broadened. It reached beyond the fall of individual greatness. A tragic rift, an irreducible core of inhumanity, seemed to lie in the mystery of things. The sense of life is itself shadowed by a feeling of tragedy. We see this in Calvin's account of man's condition no less than in Shakespeare's.[67]

Yet, a comparison of contents, of underlying world view or basic tone, has led Steiner to the conclusion that the mature Shakespeare is, on the whole, tragicomic instead of tragic.[68]

Steiner has a different way of approaching tragedy as a specific world view from Ricoeur. Steiner could arrive at his conclusion about Shakespeare only because he had identified the 'tragic' character of tragedy, not on the basis of its form, but on the basis of its contents. In his opinion, the common denominator of tragedy's contents, through the centuries, is the world-view that human life *per se* is an affliction leading to total despair. His criterion of *total despair* implies that a 'tragic' world view is *extreme* by definition. (Burian's qualification of 'tragic conflict' as 'extreme' comes to mind.) Men and women's presence on this earth is fundamentally absurd or unwelcome, a self-punishing anomaly. Tragedy then, in its purest and simplest form, is defined as 'a dramatic representation, enactment, or generation' of the world view that human life is basically a state of homelessness leading to total despair.[69]

Steiner has been sharply criticized on this point by Terry Eagleton:

George Steiner rehearses his familiar case . . . that the mildest whiff of hope is fatal to tragedy. Even the author of the last act of *Lear* fails to be glum enough to qualify for kosher tragic status. . . . It is not only that such a dogmatic stance constrains one to dismiss as nontragic a ridiculously large sector of distinguished tragic art, not least the *Oresteia*. It is also that it is in a certain sense illogical. Pure tragedy, Steiner claims, must be immune to hope; but hope is bound up with human possibility, which is in turn bound up with value. And without some sense of value there can be no tragedy.[70]

Precisely because man can 'conceive of a more humane condition' does he conceive of the human condition as tragic, Eagleton argues. In everyday language, the word 'tragedy' means something like 'very sad', but surely, Eagleton argues, tragedy involves more than this. Tragedy is traumatic as well as sorrowful. In fact, like sorrow, it implies value. We grieve over the 'destruction of what we rate as especially valuable'.[71] The *basic mood* is one of horror, sorrow *and* life-affirmation through sacrifice, not of resignation or wisdom. Tragic protagonists are not exhorted to be reconciled to their suffering. Tragic suffering is not necessarily ennobling either (cf. Sophocles' Heracles and Philoctetes), and 'nobody in Aeschylus' *Oresteia* really learns from their suffering, least of all Agamemnon himself'.[72] However, 'only by accepting the worst for what it is, not as a convenient springboard for leaping beyond it, can one hope to surpass it. Only by accepting this as the last word about the human condition can it cease to be the last word'.[73]

Eagleton does not convince *me* in *one* respect. He blames Steiner for being illogical. But Eagleton's own logic does not strike me as logical. Hope is bound up with a sense of value, but a sense of value is not necessarily bound up with hope. One can stick to a value for value's sake, despite its hopelessness. Besides, the more a tragedy tends to total despair while sticking to a value, the more it is felt to be tragic. It makes all the difference whether Steiner's definition is used essentialistically or prototypically. Steiner's phrasing is essentialistic. That is why Eagleton has a point.

Like Eagleton, Heering leaves open the possibility of recognizing 'the tragic' without assigning it a final and ultimate role in life, without embracing a tragic world view.[74] 'Tragedy' ('the tragic') can imply a tragic world view, but the notion cannot be defined exclusively in terms of a tragic world view. 'Tragedy' can be *a way of being* but also *a way of seeing*. But *if* a world view is tragic, being itself has a tragic structure, not just its appearance or our perception of being. Many ancient religions testify to a tragic structure of being, symbolized by a suffering and dying god, manifesting the conviction that life can only originate from or through death.[75] And since Hegel, a pan-tragic world view has dominated the turn from the nineteenth to the twentieth century. However, whether one embraces a tragic world view or not is a matter of choice, Heering argues.[76] Besides, one need not declare the world tragic as such. The universe may be opaque, obscure, unintelligible, but that does not make it tragic, just inaccessible. The tragic occurs on the *border* between human existence and its environment where engaged human beings face their limits and experience the discrepancy between human existence and the surrounding world – as their responsibility and failure, Christianity adds emphatically.[77]

Kathleen M. Sands objects not only to Steiner's definition of tragedy as a pessimistic world view, but also to Eagleton's less pessimistic version of it. Why? In her approach, it is better to say that *tragedies shatter world views* because they are not world views of any kind. On the contrary, they tell of worlds and times that are broken such that *no coherent view* of them can be had.[78]

What about Shakespeare's *Hamlet* or its hero, Hamlet? Does the play *or* the hero express a non-tragic or a tragic, a Christian or a secular world view, a clash of world views or a crash of world views? What happens after Hamlet's departure for England, Keyishian argues, reflects a sort of Euripidean manipulation.[79] Hamlet turns from a Machiavellian strategist into a Christian fatalist, or rather, the playwright has Hamlet move, in act V, *from a Machiavellian world order to a providential one.*[80] This is the playwright's method of rescuing Hamlet from his dilemma. The trials and constraints, the dilemmas and errors of the hero are the means by which Shakespeare invites his audience to identify with his articulate and attractive protagonist. They also tend to largely exonerate the compromised hero for his excesses, because the hero suffers more from his evil world around him than his world around him suffers from his immorally contaminated violence. In Jacobean tragedy, reflecting the turmoil of political and social instability, the Aristotelian fatal flaw is not ascribed to the character of the hero, but to the criminal and intrusive world around him.[81]

The striking thing in Keyishian's argument is its avoidance of assuming outright a Christian world view as Hamlet's ultimate frame of reference. The issue at stake is, of course, to what extent Shakespeare in general, and *Hamlet* in particular, can be interpreted as expressive of a Christian world view. The only substantial evidence for that in this play might be Hamlet's reference to providence. Keyishian prefers 'Euripidean manipulation' and 'providential world order' to 'Christian fatalism', for two reasons. First of all, there is the shift in world view from a religious focus on interfering inscrutable powers destroying the individual, to a secular focus on interfering social powers destroying the individual. But there is also an artistic reason – the playwright has to provide a satisfying closure *and* a sympathetic hero. That is to say, the main tragic characters have to die, and they have to be sufficiently moral as to make the audience suffer from their deaths and immoralities and 'constitute the audience as a forgiving community' (note the Christian vocabulary!).[82] In addition to these reasons, however, there is one other artistic reason that relates to the provision of a satisfying closure and that has been highlighted by Steiner – Christianity has an anti-tragic vision of the world.[83]

The play as a whole, in *my* understanding, represents *a clash of world views,* tragic and non-tragic ones alike. This clashing of world views, to which we will return in later chapters, was typical of the Renaissance, an era of competing and contested representations, as Stephen Greenblatt puts it.[84] As to the hero of the play, a secular tragic world view, if any, seems to dominate Hamlet's basic mood. Hamlet's response to death in the Graveyard scene, Murray argues, shows no grief or compassion until his personal relationship with Yorick begins to bring death closer to him. His view of life as a base pursuit of worldly goods that death shows to be futile is also found in Christian thinking, but the Christian idea is to renounce worldly values for the sake of the soul. 'Nowhere in this scene does Hamlet express any hope, or any concern for the human soul'. His only regret seems to be that death ends all distinctions of social class. 'Hamlet's perception that death brings human greatness to "base uses" moves him to a deep sense of loss that he counters with irony', not with faith or prayer (V.i.209–12).[85]

5 Irony

A further narrative aspect of tragedy is irony. It is virtually impossible to imagine tragedy without irony. Irony has to do with *a sense of discrepancy*, between words and their real meaning, between good people and their bad performance or ending, between good intentions and bad results, between lavish form and poor content, between divine plans and human initiatives, between certainties and their limits, between present and past events or narratives. But this sense of discrepancy can accompany both tragedy and comedy, Taels points out while explaining Kierkegaard.[86] It is not specific to tragedy. The discrepancy is *hurtful and potentially witty.* Besides, the sense of discrepancy can spring from the situation itself, from the ones who play a part in it, from the intention or world view of the dramatist, from the spectators who include a wider context or their own feeling of it. Who is supposed to *recognize* the irony of a situation, statement, or behaviour? At some level or stage, the discrepancy must be recognized if it is to be a case of irony.

Moreover, the capacity to construct or show recognized discrepancies can be used for different *purposes*. In the Western history of the concept of irony, with the initial exceptions of Plato's Socrates and Aristotle, irony meant no more than straightforward lying for Aristophanes, and a *rhetorical skill*, an artful way of making speeches more effective and persuasive, for Roman, medieval and Renaissance authors on irony.[87] It was in Plato's Socratic dialogues that irony referred not just to an isolated *figure of speech*, but to an entire life style, an *attitude to existence*. But it took until the Romantic nineteenth century before this was recognized and embraced. Since then, it has become possible to think of irony in terms of a capacity to remain distant and different from what is said in general, to practise a self-conscious attitude of *detachment*, to abstain from commitment. And even as a detached attitude, it could be used for different purposes. Taels points out that Socrates used his ironic attitude *for moral purposes* – bringing out the real truth behind apparent certainties – and that his ironic attitude presupposed the existence of a moral order inherent in (human) nature and the cosmos, while the postmodern cultivation of constant reflectivity and multiperspectivism, and the corresponding lack of commitment, belief and ideals, lead to a use of the ironic attitude *for purposes of comic entertainment*, disinterested relativism, socio-political opportunism and an aestheticism that is free of moral obligations because it is no longer founded in a given, moral order – as it still used to be in Shakespeare's time.[88] For example, at the prospect of Hamlet committing a self-damning crime, the Ghost's insistence that Hamlet not 'taint' his mind in the course of taking revenge (I.v.84–5a)[89] encourages a detached attitude for moral purposes – albeit more of a clean conscience than of a stoic state of mind in this context of a doomed and passionately enraged Ghost.

Thomas G. Rosenmeyer has introduced a distinction between *four types of irony* – forensic, blind, structural and Fiktions-irony.[90] *Forensic irony*, 'the irony of attack and defence', either deliberately tells the truth in such a way that nobody will believe it, or understates the case in order to disdainfully deflate the victim. *Fiktionsirony* is connected with the creative intelligence felt to operate through the play. *Blind irony* is defined as 'revealing one's nature without being aware of doing so, or expressing an unintentional *double entendre*, or unknowingly pronouncing a prophetic truth which the addressee does not, and the audience may or may not, accept'.[91] Blind irony in drama shows up the ignorance of the agent/victim.[92] Oedipus's error about himself and about others falls under this heading. *Structural irony* is produced by the text or the plot rather than by a specific speaker. Irony of circumstances comes under this rubric, as in Beckett's *Godot,* 'There is the irony I call "Godot": the irony that triggers the feeling that in spite of the progress of the action, nothing has changed'.[93]

Distinctively 'tragic', according to N. J. Lowe, are *blind irony* and *structural irony* because they 'highlight the gap between individual and cosmic value: things that mean a great deal to individuals become futile or infinitesimal when viewed in the objective proportions of time, multitudes, or divinity'.[94] Lowe then extends his notion of 'tragic irony' to *epic* literature by stating that such an image of the universe goes back to Homer's *Iliad.* Its bipartite cosmos of mortal humans and immortal gods constantly reminds the audience of the discrepancy between the two levels. In Homer's *Oddyssey*, discrepancies such as disguise and intrigue occur on the human level only, just between humans. Tragedy, Lowe concludes, draws from the ironies of the *Iliad*'s bipartite world view and combines them with the ironies of the *Odyssey*'s narrative repertoire of particular effects on the interpersonal level.[95]

Time's eternal order has always been a major source of *structural irony* because the plot takes time to have the heroes reach their fatal destinies. Rosset's observations on the 'tragic mechanism' come to mind, but also McAlindon's observations on Shakespeare's treatment of time. At first, Shakespeare seems to have been focusing on the ironies of reversal. After the first tragedy, *Titus Andronicus*, this focus on reversal and violent change is intertwined with a metaphysical sense of time, 'In essence, tragic action is identified as conflict with time's order. . . . The deeds which generate the tragic action are untimely or mistimed in the sense that they are dilatory or (much more often) either rash or cunningly swift'.[96] Harry Levin argues that *Hamlet*'s revenge pattern includes a reversal that presents a case of 'cosmic irony'. Vengeance is about humans trying to arrange their own lives by taking into their own hands what is almost bound to get out of hand. If it does, Levin suggests, 'if the mistaken purposes fall upon their inventors' heads, then that reversal is an ironic commentary upon the ways of human destiny'.[97] This 'cosmic irony' of 'providence plotting' against the revenger is a clear case of *structural irony*. One of many examples of *blind irony* in *Hamlet* would be the players performing the (first) play-within-the-play, as discussed by Brennan (see Section 3.2). But Brennan's discussion also suggests the *structural irony* of the second play-within-the-play mirroring the first one. Bloom offers his own insight into the role of irony in *Hamlet*:

Unlike Oedipus or Lear, Hamlet never seems victimized by dramatic irony. What perspectives can we turn upon Hamlet other than those he himself has revealed to us? Hamlet's power of mind exceeds ours: we haven't the authority to regard him ironically. For all his brilliance, Oedipus the

King—and not the blind wanderer at Colonus—is contrived by Sophocles to know less than the audience does. Hamlet's unique relation to the audience is just the reverse: he knows that he knows more.[98]

The *blind irony* in this case does not show up the ignorance of the agent/ victim, but that of the audience.

6 Specific subjects

A final narrative aspect of tragedies concerns the question of whether 'tragedy' can be defined in terms of specific subjects. In fact, it cannot. But at least, some recurrent themes are recognized as typically tragic – suffering, loss, death, evil, disorder and transgression. A brief discussion of these topics should suffice to form a picture of the ways in which these subjects are relevant or prominent in tragedies.

6.1 Suffering and loss

Can the tragic genre be defined in terms of a typically tragic subject determining the basic mood? One general approach to tragedy worth recalling here is suggested by Kathleen M. Sands.[99] She begins by observing that tragedy is about *suffering* – not simply about suffering as such, or even profound suffering, but the *telling* about suffering in such a way that the tension between finding meaning in suffering and not finding meaning in it is upheld.[100] The typically tragic subject of suffering is intertwined with the typically tragic subject of loss. The tragic experience of profound loss includes the loss of a meaningful world and a meaningful life. The experience of loss is traumatizing because of the finality of the loss. 'Because it cannot be integrated or expressed, trauma demands reenactment'. Similarly, tragedies 'disrupt and defy the narration of time as meaning'.[101] Yet, Sands argues, telling a story about the meaninglessness of life seems to make sense, seems to imply some sense of meaning. There seems to be a plot pattern in the narrative worth being told. If there were no meaning at all to the telling of the loss of meaning, one would keep silent and stick to the re-enactment of the trauma. In fact, there is a decisive difference between trauma and tragedy:

> Tragedy, as an aesthetic form, consigns trauma to a ritual space where, rather than being silently reenacted, it is solemnly voiced and lamented. Just as marking off the sacred creates the profane, so tragedies mark off trauma and in so doing wrench back from trauma the rest of life, during which time does not stand still and from which swaths of meaning can be made.[102]

In the case of melancholia, the loss that generates mourning is invisible, has itself been lost. In the case of tragedy, tragedy does not recover the loss, but uncovers the loss, recognizes the loss precisely as such, uncovers the grief and the pleasure. Healing, meaning and pleasure are tragedy's recovering by-products, which it generates precisely because it tells the story of a loss clearly lacking them. 'Only by finding the pleasure can we know what the grief was about. . . . But pleasure, resurrected, does not come up in the same condition as it went down, because it has been to the netherworld and back, and grief still clings to it', Sands concludes.[103]

6.2 Death

Rosset identifies three main areas of tragedy, namely death, failing affection and the meanness of man. Rosset then discusses *Oedipus Tyrannus* as an example in the tragic area of the discovery of death.[104] Death is definitely one of the recurrent themes in tragedy and, in that sense, a typically tragic topic. Easterling suggests that even the formal links between Greek tragedy and the typically Dionysiac satyr plays indicate the importance of death as a main subject because of a fundamental 'connection between tragic meditation on violence and suffering, guilt, punishment, mortality, human limitations', and the belief that 'what Dionysus is believed to offer is "salvation"' from the cycle of change, time, mortality and death, 'rather than a manifestation of divine power to help or harm'.[105]

Death never ceased to be a defining feature of tragedy. Fiona Macintosh draws attention to two formal features that Greek tragedy and the modern Irish drama of Yeats, Synge and O'Casey have in common – the 'big speech' of the dying heroes and the lament of their mourners. These two formal features are seen to be parallel to each other and, in their parallelism, to reflect ritual relationships between the mourners and the mourned.[106]

The Graveyard scene in *Hamlet* shows Hamlet meditating on the skull of the court jester Yorick and on the posthume impact of death as the utter loss and complete annihilation of everything life stands for, far beyond any devastation a simple human revenger would ever be able to bring about, according to Kerrigan.[107]

6.3 Evil, disorder and transgression

Apart from loss, death and suffering, evil is omnipresent in tragedies. One might even say that, in terms of content, the release of evil as a disruptive force and the corresponding human suffering (and deaths) as a result of it constitute the subject matter of tragedies. The release of evil sets the tragic plot in motion. 'Several Greek tragedies begin with a *miasma*, a literal and psychic pollution which indicates that the community has in some way violated the normal order of the world and incurred the displeasure of the gods', Ewans points out.[108]

In this matter, Shakespeare's history plays are different from his great tragedies (*Hamlet*, *Othello*, *King Lear* and *Macbeth*), as Peck and Coyle observe. Whereas in the history plays, things go wrong because people are weak, ambitious or resentful, in the major tragedies:

> the passions that disrupt life are far more extreme: there is a focusing on the evil in human beings, an evil that results not just in the death of the tragic hero but also in the deaths of the innocent and good who seem to be singled out for destruction for no other reason than that they are innocent. . . . The moment the façade of order is shattered, we begin to see the cruel, vicious and murderous side of people, to see the self-seeking, hatred and violence.[109]

Evil takes many forms, but the most menacing form of evil in tragedies is the extremely serious threat of *chaos*. Comedies too have their disorder, but the disruptive force of comic disorder is much more innocent. The terrifying occurrence or menace of disorder in *Oedipus Tyrannus* and *Hamlet* includes the disastrous destruction of entire kingdoms and a relapse into chaos. In *Hamlet*, Rees notices, Claudius embodies evil and Hamlet is dedicated to destroying evil. The Ghost's theological insistence on sin and divine judgement, on his stay in purgatory for sins committed in his lifetime that he could not clear himself from before he suddenly died, introduces a religious dimension that links murder to damnation, Claudius to Milton's Satan in *Paradise Lost* (Book IV), confession to conscience and repentance to redemption.[110] Watson argues that Hamlet's revenge is doomed to fail because it lacks the same capacity to balance things as its counterpart, ambition. Revenge aims at the restoration of a balanced order, but it is disproportionate by nature.[111] Social chaos can take many forms – mixed marriage, incest, parricide, fratricide – all of them being forms that cross the natural and normative borders violently, disrespectfully or accidentally, all of them leading to psychological states of confusion and distress. That is why *transgression of borders* is a related 'specifically tragic' subject.

7 Conclusions

What is it about these and similar stories that qualifies them as tragic? Tragedy cannot be defined in terms of specific subjects, but some subjects are prominent in tragedies. Suffering, loss, death, evil, disorder and transgression are examples of such themes.

It is the disruptive force of evil that sets a tragic plot in motion. An initial constellation of escalating disorder has to be rectified. A polluting situation is in need of purification. An extreme conflict is in need of an extreme solution. Tragic conflicts are extreme, and even if they have not turned out to be unresolvable, they are never solved unambiguously. Tragic solutions never solve everything entirely. There may be reconciliation between the main characters, but not between the characters and the audience. There may be reconciliation at the mental level of accepting one's fatal destiny, but this hardly ever implies a simultaneous reconciliation on the practical level of social conflicts. Burian maintains that there is no such thing as a typically tragic plot, but that it is nonetheless helpful to categorize the existing plot patterns according to their types of conflict.

Aristotle's tragic 'reversal' is a switch of actions to the contrary and not for the better. Real tragedy is about good people ending up badly. The Aristotelian unexpected turn of events develops inevitably out of the actions or intentions of the dramatic characters themselves, not just accidentally. This unforeseen active involvement of the characters in the fatal outcome intensifies the tragic effect. It suggests some fatal error on the part of the tragic characters. Fatal errors do not always occur in tragic plots, however.

In tragic plot patterns, time plays an ambiguous and ironic role. On the one hand, time means progress, opportunity, future. On the other hand, when time starts running, it brings about failure, inevitability, gloom. The more time unfolds, the more some disastrous outcome seems unavoidable. In the face of a fatal outcome, time seems to be counterproductive.

After all, tragedies always end in tragedy. The outcome of tragedies is a high goal, which the tragic heroes fail to achieve, or which they lose at the very moment they achieve it. This can be an act of revenge, which is successful, but too destructive to restore the balance. Neither moral justice nor psychological satisfaction can compensate for the injustice done to the victims, for the deaths of the revengers and for the collateral damage. The injustice and destruction cannot be undone. The price to be paid for successful revenge is, by all standards, too high. The outcome of tragedies is not necessarily death, but the bitter taste of death – a tragic mood that has a long-lasting worrying effect on the audience afterwards, beyond the initial cathartic relief at the end of the play. The psychic damage of severe suffering cannot be undone.

The tragic mood in tragedies may or may not be the fruit of a tragic world view. When Steiner defines pure tragedy as 'a dramatic representation, enactment, or generation of the world view that human life is basically a state of homelessness leading to total despair', his phrasing is essentialistic, not prototypical. His definition is based on the essential presence (or absence) of total despair in a play's world view. Eagleton prefers to distinguish between a play's world view and a play's basic subjects, plot and mood. Plays can still be identified as 'real tragedy' (not 'pure tragedy'!) when one recognizes in their contents the omnipresence of tragic suffering and of horror, even if they do not embrace a tragic world view in Steiner's sense of the word. They may, though, embrace a tragic world view in Heering's sense of the word, manifesting the conviction that life can only originate from or through death. Eagleton would call it 'life-affirmation through sacrifice'. In Sands' approach, tragedies shatter world views because they tell of worlds and times that are too broken to allow for any coherent views. For each of these approaches, Greek examples can be found. As for the play *Hamlet*, Greenblatt's interest in competing and contested representations typical of the Renaissance has led me to conclude that *Hamlet* does not represent a crash of world views, but a clash of world views – tragic and non-tragic ones alike. As to its main character, a secular tragic world view, if any, seems to dominate Hamlet's mind. More on that in the chapter on religious aspects.

Tragedy without irony is hardly imaginable. But where and whose is the irony? All kinds of incongruent combinations of things or people can evoke a sense of discrepancy. Lowe has identified two of Rosenmeyer's types of irony – blind irony and structural irony – as distinctively tragic, because these types of irony highlight the gap between individual and cosmic value; things that mean a great deal to individuals become futile on a cosmic scale. Tragedy has Odyssean deception built in into the Iliadic structure of the world, Lowe argues. Levin suggests that, in *Hamlet*'s revenge pattern, if the mistaken purposes of the revengers fall upon their inventors' heads, then that 'providential' reversal is an ironic commentary upon the ways of human destiny (and apparently not a case of *karma*!).

PART II: INDIAN AND HINDU ISSUES

1 Summary of the plot(s) of the Mahābhārata and Bhagavadgītā

1.1 Introduction

In this second part of the chapter, on Indian and Hindu issues, it will be shown how the narrative aspects that have been discussed are present (or absent) in the *Mahābhārata* epic and the *Bhagavadgītā*.

The Indian *Mahābhārata* epic constitutes the primary narrative context of the *Bhagavadgītā*. To some extent, one could argue that both the epic as a whole and the *Gītā* can be taken to have a plot pattern of their own, but the two plot patterns are intertwined. The entire episode of the *Gītā*, the Book of the *Bhagavadgītā*, forms the third episode of the Book of Bhishma, the *sixth* of the eighteen major books of the epic. The basic epic may have been composed between the mid-second century BCE and the year zero, but it includes an unknown number of interpolated texts and is therefore notoriously difficult to date.

1.2 Summary of the plot(s) of the Mahābhārata epic

The *outermost frame* of the *Mahābhārata* epic is constituted by a story about an epic singer paying a visit to gatherings of ascetic *brahmins* in the Naimisha Forest where he tells them the story of the ritual performance of a snake sacrifice at the court of King Janamejaya.

The *outer frame* of the epic is constituted by a story about King Janamejaya who is performing a snake sacrifice during which the epic is being told. Taking many days to perform, Indian rituals used to have breaks, which were filled with recitals. During this snake ritual, the *brahmin* seer Vyāsa has his pupil Vaiśsampāyana recite the epic he had composed.

The *inner frame* of the epic story itself is constituted by many stories and a main plot revolving around a socio-political conflict concerning royal succession. The *Bhagavadgītā* constitutes[112] the very heart of that plot – the moment when the military conflict is about to break out on the battlefield. Within its narrative corpus, the epic has philosophical sections. These are called the 'didactic sections' because, within the context of the narrative, they are put into the mouths of characters who take on the role of teachers. The two most important didactic expositions are in the twelfth book, the 'Book of Peace' (*Śānti-parvan*) by Bhīshma, and within the sixth book, in the 'Song of the Lord' (*Bhagavadgītā*) by Krishna, respectively.

The epic's plot pattern turns around the actual *succession* to the Kuru throne of Hāstinapura by its *legitimate* heirs. The problem consists of the legitimate heirs, the Pāndavas, failing to live up to their duty of organizing a smooth and morally convincing transition of power in favour of the Pāndava clan, and the illegitimate heirs, the Kauravas, their cousins, claiming, seizing and holding to the throne by all means and at any cost.

The second book, the 'Book of the Assembly Hall' (*Sabha-parvan*), recounts how Yudhisthira builds a new assembly hall at Indraprastha and how the jealous Duryodhana, the eldest Kaurava cousin, challenges Yudhisthira, the eldest Pāndava cousin, to a dice game. Yudhisthira, addicted to gambling, loses everything and everybody, including 'his' wife Draupadī who offers strong resistance to her illegitimate treatment by appealing to *dharma* and challenging Yudhisthira's understanding of it during the dice game, and is spared the shame by divine intervention. The Pāndavas are free to leave, but are then challenged to a second dice game, which Yudhisthira loses again. All the Pāndavas and their shared wife Draupadī are sent into temporary exile in the forest. After their return from exile, their cousins still refuse to hand over the kingdom. Krishna, a Yādava chieftain, functions as a neutral mediator between the two rival parties, even though he sympathizes with the Pāndava side, since Krishna and Arjuna have been maternal relatives by marriage and friends for a long time, burning the Khāndava Forest together. He offers the two rivals, Arjuna and Duryodhana, the choice between either his personal service as a charioteer and a counsellor or his armies. While Arjuna prefers Krishna's service in person unarmed, Duryodhana is happy to get Krishna's armies. Peace negotiations fail and the two parties prepare for war. The conflict has thus seriously escalated. The two sets of cousins and their allied armies face each other at Kurukshetra, the Kuru battlefield, on the brink of a fratricidal and suicidal war that will destroy not only the two clans, but also the very prospect of any heir surviving in order to succeed to the throne. In the end, the fatal battle takes place and the two clans are virtually destroyed. In the 'Night Attack', the surviving Pāndava allies are killed off by the few surviving Kaurava partisans. The five Pāndava brothers themselves remain alive, along with Krishna and his compatriot, Satyaki. The one single Pāndava heir to the throne, Parikshit is killed in his mother's womb. But Parikshit is promised revival by Krishna, whose divine intervention saves him and the Kuru lineage for the future. He will be Arjuna's grandson and Janamejaya's father.

1.3 Summary of the episode of the Bhagavadgītā

Within the epic, the *Bhagavadgītā* depicts the Kurukshetra battlefield as its stage. Two mighty armies face each other. The Pāndava side is led by Arjuna, who is accompanied by his charioteer Krishna. Arjuna faces a moral dilemma. On the one hand, he is expected to fight a righteous war in order to regain the kingdom from the Kauravas, who took over the kingdom from the Pāndavas by unlawful means and are unwilling to return it. On the other hand, Arjuna is expected to fight a deadly war involving the killing of some of his own kinsmen, affectionate friends, respected elders and revered teachers. Facing the killing of kin and a deadly war, he suddenly hesitates and refuses to fight. His charioteer Krishna tries to convince him to return to fighting. He does so by preaching to Arjuna, thus behaving as Arjuna's teacher (*guru*). In the end, Krishna reveals himself as the Lord of Time, the Lord of the universe, and Arjuna becomes the devotee of Lord Krishna as his only God. Arjuna surrenders to Krishna's might. He is asked to dedicate all his actions to Lord Krishna and return to the battlefield, actively performing his caste duty without an individual desire for the fruits of his actions.

2 The Mahābhārata's specific plot pattern

2.1 One overall plot pattern

Despite some scholarly doubt whether the *Gītā* originally constituted an integral part of this famous epic, one can certainly state that it has become an integral part of the written Sanskrit version of the *Mahābhārata* as it has been transmitted through the ages. The Sanskrit version became the archetype.[113] The plot of the *Mahābhārata* as a whole has become unthinkable without the *Gītā*'s description of the battlefield of Kurukshetra as its central stage.[114] Some scholars doubt whether the *Mahābhārata* actually constitutes a whole and contains an overall plot that convincingly integrates all the various elements that make up the text. After all, the text is eight times the size of the *Odyssey* and the *Iliad* put together. The sheer size of the text prevents a convincing integration of all the narrative and didactic materials involved. A strong point in favour of this argument are the interruptive repetitions, most notably the *Gītā* itself.[115] But before focusing on the plot of the *Gītā* and its links to other books of the epic, let us turn to the traditionally presumed overall plot of the epic as a whole.

The written Sanskrit version of the *Mahābhārata* epic, as it has been transmitted through the centuries, constitutes a narrative that reveals *an overall plot pattern*. Whether all materials fit into that overall plot pattern is not the point. A. K. Ramanujan admits that a text like the *Mahābhārata* is much more of a living and ongoing tradition than of a fixed and finished text. Its many narratives have provided materials and allusions to every artistic genre – from plays to proverbs, from folk performances to movies and TV. But he goes on to say that most traditional Hindus would never have been able to remember and recall in great detail this enormous epic if the epic had lacked an underlying narrative structure.[116]

2.2 The release of evil

A closer look at the overall plot pattern of the epic teaches us that the epic's plot pattern is centred on the actual succession to the Kuru throne of Hāstinapura by its *legitimate* heirs. This presentation of the epic's plot pattern refers to the *release of evil* as a disruptive force, which sets the plot in motion – the jealousy, greed and ambition of the Kaurava cousins, who start out to claim, seize and hold on to the throne by all means. The Book of the Assembly Hall, as mentioned in the plot summary, recounts the jealousy of the eldest Kaurava, Duryodhana, at the prosperity of the Pāndavas as evidenced by their newly built assembly hall at Indraprastha. Duryodhana responds by challenging the Pāndava cousins to a dice game, held in the Kauravas' assembly hall. Due to the dicing incompetence and lack of self-control of Yudhisthira, the rightful heir to the throne, the Pāndavas lose everything, are reprieved and lose again. They are then sent into temporary exile in the forest. After thirteen years, they legitimately reclaim their share of the kingdom, but the Kauravas refuse to give in. All peace missions by the mediator Krishna fail, and the conflict over succession escalates into a suicidal war among the two branches of a common lineage, the Kuru lineage, which gives its name to the fatal battlefield and war, the Kurukshetra war. As was the case with the two dice games, the use of trickery is not being shrunk from, but this time, it is the Pāndavas who break the predetermined rules of battle on a regular basis.

In fact, the epic's great interest in victory by trickery is a reflection of its obsession with *dharma* (natural, social and moral order). The war represents *dharma*'s decline. The release of evil is a release of *adharma*, contaminating all sides. More than that, the disruptive force of evil assumes apocalyptic proportions. World history becomes the stage of this drama. The entire known world is involved in the battle and is almost entirely destroyed. The Pāndava side finally emerges victorious, but they have no reason to be in a victorious mood. The women mourn and funeral rites are observed. Yudhisthira is persuaded to organize a horse sacrifice in order to legitimate the Pāndava rule. The surviving parents of the Pāndavas and the Kauravas retire to the forest, where they die in a forest fire. The Vrishnis, Krishna's people, kill each other in a fateful club fight. Krishna too, retires from the world. So do the Pāndava brothers and Draupadī. Yudhisthira is left with his dog, a scene of utter misery.

A final turn of events has Yudhisthira being invited to ascend to heaven, provided he leaves his dog behind. He refuses. The dog turns out to be Dharma, his father. Yudhisthira and Dharma ascend to heaven together. Upon his arrival, Yudhisthira finds out, to his dismay, that his brothers have gone to hell, while the evil Kauravas appear to have attained heaven. Then, he is told by Indra that his brothers' sojourn in hell and his vision of them there are only products of illusion, imposed upon the Pāndavas so that they may expiate the evil deeds they perpetrated in the war. Afterward, the epic characters go back to being aspects of the gods, demons, and other supernatural beings from whom they had originally emerged and attain heaven.

2.3 Happy ending and disturbed mood

So far, the epic's plot pattern, on a 'historical' or 'mundane' level, is about two related problems – legitimate succession and the reign of *dharma*, or rather, the failure or lack of them. The *plot's ending* seems to have solved both problems. First of all, a legitimate heir to the Kuru throne is provided for, and a single undisputed one at that, as Ruth Cecile Katz notices.[117] Secondly, all the epic characters end up in heaven – actually a glorified Rajput fortress. The *conflicts* are *solved*. And the disastrous end is not that disastrous after all.

Or is it, after all? A literal reading that focuses on facts cannot account for the *disturbed mood* which is brought about along the road to heaven. The war is nothing less than disastrous, and the mood of the survivors testifies to a deep sense of tragedy, of loss instead of gain, of grief instead of victory. All is not well that ends well. The epic ends in a minor key. Irawati Karve once pointed out that her family always viewed the epic as a tragedy, an expression of the futility of human life.[118] In contemporary Northern India, there is a saying: 'That household is a *Mahābhārata*!', meaning 'That household is full of quarrels and strife!' James L. Fitzgerald speaks in the same vein when he draws his readers' attention to the traditional Hindu reception of the epic as an *inauspicious* text, which was not read or recited in their homes by pious Hindu people.[119]

Alf Hiltebeitel's reading of the plot pattern comes to similar conclusions, even though he identifies the core set of problems differently. First of all, the release of evil as a disruptive force has to do with classification, with loss of distinction, with *blurring distinctions between social groups*, and the need to keep categories distinct. Bhīshma tells Yudhisthira that 'by *dharma* beings are upheld apart'.[120] Separation is crucial to upholding the social order.[121]

One of the chief objects of the *Mahābhārata*, according to Hiltebeitel,[122] is to instruct kings and other warriors in how to curb endless cycles of *violence*, particularly as such cycles effect and implicate *brahmins*. After the war, Yudhisthira is stricken with *grief* because of the *loss* of so many warriors and the *weeping* of the Kaurava women, and has to be consoled.

The one quality that Yudhisthira has to develop is the quality of non-cruelty (*ānrśamsya*).[123] Yudhisthira is being put to the test three times. By the epic's end, Yudhisthira has lost his brothers and his wife. The only creature left is his devoted dog. About to enter heaven, he is told that he can only enter heaven if he leaves his dog behind. (the second test.) He refuses, out of non-cruelty. He has learnt his lesson and is rewarded for it – the devoted dog turns out to be his father Dharma, and they enter heaven together. The third test that Dharma puts Yudhisthira through is the upside-down experience of heaven and hell. At first, Yudhisthira sees his enemy Duryodhana shining in heaven, and is shocked, blaming him for the war and the mistreatment of Draupadī.[124] Nārada 'tells him that in heaven, enmities cease; Yudhisthira should not think of what was done at the dice game, the pain (*parikleśa*) done to Draupadī and the other pains that followed'.[125] Yudhisthira refuses to enter heaven. Nārada then takes him to the edge of hell. Overwhelmed by sorrow and grief, Yudhisthira gives way to anger and '"censures" Dharma for what is in effect his cruelty'.[126] It is the moment where Yudhisthira, hearing the piteous cries of his brothers and Draupadī from hell, wonders whether he is hallucinating or imagining things. (18.2.48) According to Hiltebeitel, Yudhisthira is back to the question that was raised about him in the assembly hall where he played the dice game – was he mindful about what went on or was he going out of his mind? Indra comforts Yudhisthira, 'He has had to see hell because he killed Drona by fraud; for similar reasons the others also experienced hell'. They are 'now freed from sin in their celestial bodies'.[127] What Yudhisthira saw, Dharma continues, was an illusion displayed by Indra; hell must be seen by every king. His brothers (including Karna) did not deserve hell for long. And Draupadī did not deserve hell at all. (18.3.34–7) Yudhisthira then enters the sacred purifying divine river Gangā and is purified from enmity and grief. However, when he sees Draupadī in heaven, 'suddenly King Yudhisthira was wishing to question her'. (18.4.8) But Indra cuts him off by telling him about her divine origins. 'So Yudhisthira wants to ask Draupadī a question, but never gets to ask it'. Hiltebeitel suggests, isn't the 'best clue to what Yudhisthira is thinking about the one thing Nārada has told him not to think about' – Draupadī's pain at the dice game and the other pains that followed?. He continues:

> van Buitenen gives us one of his most memorable insights: 'the epic is a series of precisely stated problems imprecisely and therefore inconclusively resolved, with every resolution raising a new problem, until the very end, when the question remains: whose is heaven and whose is hell?' This design is one of deferral. The question Yudhisthira doesn't get to ask comes even after this, and is the *Mahābhārata*'s very last deferral. . . . Yudhisthira will never answer Draupadī's question and he will never ask her his own.[128]

In terms of the *plot's ending*, the *final mood*, and the *resolving of conflicts*, Hiltebeitel's reading is very interesting. Where exactly does the plot end? In heaven? Is the plot's ending a happy ending, just because friends and enemies end up in heaven together? Why is Draupadī temporarily in hell if she did not deserve hell at all? If Yudhisthira finds peace of mind, a human heart without enmity and grief, why does he wish to question Draupadī when he sees her in heaven? Why is he not allowed to ask his question? Which question? Will Draupadī's question ever find an answer? Conflicts are 'inconclusively resolved'. The final mood is not cut off from the lingering thought that Yudhisthira is not supposed to have – the thought of suffering. That this determines the final mood is strikingly confirmed by Yudhisthira passing his three tests – he has learnt non-cruelty and compassion or pity (*anukrośa*).

3 Mahābhārata's specific world view

There are, however, both ritual and mythical dimensions to the plot's pattern, which I have virtually left out so far, but which are no less related to the release of evil. That is to say, the release of evil as a disruptive force has to do with the ritual consecration of kings, with the ups and downs of fortune, with the destructive and recreative cycle of cosmic time and with the battle between gods and demons. These dimensions constitute the epic's world view.

3.1 Ritual consecration of kings

The dice game is connected to the traditional rite of consecrating the king as a universal monarch (*rājasūya*). The king is to lead an agonistic sacrifice against contenders as a way of ritually establishing order and legitimacy. The fact that this rite follows its own pattern has interesting implications for the epic's plot pattern too. Just as in the ritual texts, the royal ritual is concluded by a dice game, similarly in the epic, Yudhisthira's royal ritual is technically incomplete without the dice game.[129] The epic's *plot pattern* corresponds to, and in fact follows, the *ritual pattern* of the royal consecration ritual, according to Jan C. Heesterman. The dice game, the war and the horse sacrifice are part and parcel of the royal ritual cycle.[130] The dice game determines the course of the epic's plot pattern. But there is an important difference between the epic and the royal consecration ritual. In the ritual, the dice game is to take place at the height of the ritual, right after unction, chariot-cum-cattle raid and enthronement. In the epic, the dice game is the central event, but is not part of the consecration ritual itself. Rather, it is causing the reversal of the consecration. Heesterman welcomes Herman Tieken's recent interpretation of the dice game in terms of a competitive counter-consecration ritual put up by the rivals of the Pandavas as a challenge because this interpretation underlines the originally cyclical alternation among opponents in a (yearly) repeatable agonistic sacrifice. The risk of agonistic sacrifice, Heesterman argues, was the dynamic centre of the archaic potlatch society. Out of the cyclical rhythm, the ritualists then built a linear sequence of yearly sacrifices to be viewed as a single, once-for-all event, as the epic suggests.[131]

3.2 Fortune and royal succession

The five Pāndava brothers and the Kaurava opponent Duryodhana constitute the fourth generation of the Kuru lineage. Down the generations of the epic, each generation is given a period of glory from which there is an inexorable decline. Each generation follows the characteristic rise to a peak, from which there is a characteristic *reversal of fortunes*. After the death of Pāndu (third generation) and after Dhrtarāstra's (also third generation) agreement to partition of the kingdom among the two sets of cousins, Yudhisthira's star is clearly on the ascendant and he endorses Nārada's suggestion that he legitimize his sovereignty by performing the *rājasūya*, the ritual for consecrating the king as a universal monarch. Julian F. Woods, following Madeleine Biardeau, describes how he then loses everything at the height of his power and wealth before recovering the kingdom and witnessing conditions reminiscent of a Golden Age, and concludes, 'The pattern of history has repeated itself for the fourth time in as many generations'.[132] The dice game, thus, symbolizes the evils of passion, of collapse of the natural order, of the ups and downs of fortune, and also of the supreme determination of fate.[133]

The wife of the five Pāndavas, Draupadī, plays a central role in the ups and downs of *fortune*. Draupadī is Yudhisthira's last stake in the dice game. Why? What does it mean if she is lost to another king? She had been won by the Pāndavas in a *svayamvara* ('self-choice'), a public contest of suitors in which a princess chooses her own bridegroom. 'The emphasis' in this mythologem, according to Hiltebeitel, 'is on a feminine figure, goddess rather than heroine, "choosing" her partner(s) amidst a wooing contest'.[134] It is the goddess Śrī who is incarnate in Draupadī. Śrī, the goddess of prosperity, in her choice of bridegrooms, is interested in royal virtues and in kings. In the 'royal horse sacrifice' (*aśvamedha*), the horse confers prosperity (*Śrī*) on the king. The goddess Śrī is a repository of royal virtues, which she does not so much incorporate as confer or transfer. The specific gift which Śrī bestows is royalty or sovereignty. Śrī is the source of the king's sovereignty, provided the monarch is omni-virtuous. She is unfaithful to those she favours. The rhythm of time is her only regulative principle. Her fickleness coincides with a 'pessimistic' view of time. If Prosperity embraces a king, his kingdom will thrive; if she leaves the king for some other king, the decline of the kingdom will be his 'portion' of fortune, Hiltebeitel concludes.[135]

3.3 Cosmic time for Śiva and Vishnu, cosmic battle between gods and demons

Biardeau's observation that Draupadī's marriage to five husbands simultaneously is the result of an intervention by the god Śiva illuminates and complicates the coherence of the plot pattern even further, because it points out the complementary roles of Śiva and Vishnu in destroying and recreating the entire cosmos. 'The *adharmic* side of Draupadī's irregular marriage is initiated by Śiva: "When Śiva intervenes and breaks the rules of the ideal society, it is always with an eye to destruction, but a destruction necessary to the renewal of the world"'.[136] It is the role of Krishna, Krishnā Draupadī, Vyāsa (Krishna Dvaipāyana), and Nārāyana, Hiltebeitel argues, first to sanction Śiva's disruption and then meanwhile, even while *dharma* wanes, to preserve it in essence through its suspension. The mysterious workings ('subtle *dharma*') of the so-called 'three Krishnas' have the potential to bring the Kurukshetra *conflict* to *cessation* – whether through peace, or, as happens, *through war*.[137] Due to their respective complementary roles, Śiva is associated with the dice game whereas Krishna, Vishnu incarnate, is conspicuously absent from it.[138] If, in the hands of Śiva, dicing reflects the increase of *adharma*, the loss of 'prosperity', and an intoxicated aloofness to matters of gain and loss, there is a clear contrast with Krishna who leaves nothing to chance. 'The arbitrary, addictive, and destructive character of dicing runs counter to' Krishna's 'constructive efforts toward the "restoration of *dharma*"'.[139]

Śiva's connection with dicing through the waning course of dharma is literally a fatal throw of the dice that substitutes one better world epoch in the *cosmic* cycle of time for another worse epoch. The four *yugas,* or cosmic world epochs, have the names (or numbers) of the throws of dice – Krta (Golden Age), Tretā (three), Dvāpara (two) and Kali (the worst throw). The fact that the dice game is played and won with deceit is indicative of the waning course of *dharma,* but also of either the onset of the Kali epoch (Katz) or of the apocalyptic dissolution at the end of the Kali epoch (Biardeau). Unlike the 'cleverness' of the gods, the importance of human deceit in the epic's plot is characteristic of the Kali epoch because, as Katz seems to imply, deceit is a dubious compromise between effort (*purushakāra*) and fate (*daiva*).[140] While Śiva and Pārvatī play at dice on a mythic level, symbolizing the course of the world epochs on a cosmic scale, Śakuni and Duryodhana, Dvāpara and Kali incarnate, that is to say, personifications of the respective *yugas* in the form of demons, play dice on an epic level, symbolizing the course of the world epochs in a transitional microcosmic moment 'between the *yugas*', on a 'historical' scale.[141]

The cosmic destruction that takes place at the end of a cosmic time period is called *pralaya*.[142] On a much more down-to-earth level, there are the four subsequent world epochs (*yugas*), which were referred to earlier on. The cosmic saviour incarnate (*avatāra*) intervenes at times of cosmic crisis at the conclusion of a *yuga*. There has been a lot of scholarly debate on the (in)exact way in which the epic makes use of mythical time schemes for its own plot pattern. Several mythical time schemes are likely to have inspired the plot pattern, but no single scheme is applied literally or accurately.[143]

'For the epic', Woods points out, the conflict between Pāndavas and Kauravas

> is simply an episode in the perennial battle of the gods and the demons for the control of heaven, temporarily shifted to the Earth where incarnations [manifestations of aspects, *LM*] ('sons' and 'daughters') of these same gods and demons are continuing this battle for supremacy. . . . The growing ascendancy of the demon hordes is marked here below by the gradual moral entropy of human society. This situation can only be reversed by the Creator Himself who engineers a renewal of society through the complete destruction of the old order.[144]

Biardeau stresses the *apocalyptic* character of the epic.[145] First of all, the epic is constructed as a 'revelation', in the original sense of the term 'apocalypse', which goes until the end of time, or until the promise of a non-end of time. The epic reveals a hidden continuity *beyond* the crisis. The final destiny of all the warriors who die in the battle will be heaven. This Indian style apocalypse does not lead to a triumph at the end of the war or to a description of a Golden Age ever after, but to a simple renewal of the world.[146] Secondly, the epic reveals that this continuity takes place *through* the crisis, in the second sense of the word – the catastrophe grows to universal proportions, time itself reveals itself as the supreme disruptive force of evil that sets in motion the destruction of the current world order. Yet, this fatal force of time also assures some form of continuity by allowing destruction to be transformed into recreation. Again, the *epic's ending* is *ambiguous*. The Kurukshetra War, therefore, represents the eschatological crisis of an age that is in urgent need of the apparition of one of Vishnu's saving incarnations (*avatāras*), Krishna. According to Biardeau, there is an air of doom in the epic. The *apocalyptic mood* dominates.[147] One thing is certain – the plot pattern moves towards our age, and our age is the worst one, the *Kali-yuga*, in a cosmic setting.[148]

3.4 Tragic or dramatic world view

Does this view of time and world history qualify as a tragic world view? Both Biardeau and Hiltebeitel identify Buddhism as the main rival in the background. Hiltebeitel notices that 'the epic's emphasis on the relentlessness of time . . . creating and collapsing worlds . . . is in all likelihood an answer to the time-emptying and deconstructive Buddhist teachings of radical momentariness'.[149] In Hinduism, time is related to the gods Śiva and Vishnu. The destructive role of Śiva and the constructive role of Vishnu in the epic are complementary roles, as Biardeau and Hiltebeitel have shown. Śiva represents the cosmic principle that brings about perpetual movement. If the impact of Śiva becomes too strong, the destabilizing forces of nature, which uphold an oscillating universe, have to be restabilized. Vishnu represents the restabilizing forces of nature without undoing the perpetual movement of this fluctuating universe. The stability of the universe consists of its capacity to redress extremely destructive fluctuations.[150]

The framing of the tragic plot pattern in the restricted sense of earthly affairs within a widening, transcendent perspective, on the one hand, reinforces the impression that the human being and world history are suffering from the ups and downs of a fortune that reveals cosmic timing, and on the other hand, enhances the impression that the down-to-earth level of human suffering is left behind as a lower level of reality that only stages the cosmic drama temporarily on the earth whereas the real battle between gods and demons is decided elsewhere. Human suffering from human action is dominant on the historical level, but cosmic timing and divine victory are decisive on the cosmic level. The epic's world is a *tragic* world, but its wider world view is not. Rather than a tragic world view, I suggest, the epic's world view is a *dramatic* world view. I do not only mean 'dramatic' in the *modern* sense of the word, as John Gibert uses it, 'For a modern sensibility, the word "drama" carries connotations of gripping emotion and momentous action'.[151] I mean 'dramatic' in the *pre-modern* sense of the word, the way it is used by Jan Assmann with regard to the ancient Pharaonic religious world view:

> Underlying the cult was a concept of the world that we might call "dramatic," and this in two respects: because the world consists of acts, the work of a deity in action occurs in everything that happens, and humankind, in the person of the king, participates actively in this dramatic reality; but dramatic also in the sense that because reality is continually at play, the result of a success must always be repeated and can in no way be understood in and of itself. Given the prospect of a "virtual apocalypse" that proceeds from

the ever-present possibility of a standstill, a catastrophe, every sunrise is an event to be greeted with rejoicing: 'The earth becomes bright, Ra shines over his land; he has triumphed over his enemies!'[152]

In terms of contents, basic tone and world view, I would argue that the *Mahābhārata* epic's world is a *tragic world* within the wider perspective of a *dramatic world view*. But this 'within' requires further explanation. The tragic world of human affairs is *juxtaposed* with the dramatic world of cosmic affairs as an entirely different, transcendent perspective on the immanent outlook. Juxtaposition means a lack of tension and conflict between the two. What is tragic on the historical level is simultaneously dramatic on the cosmic level. The point is that one should not equate the historical with the cosmic levels. Instead, one should maintain both of them while keeping them apart. This juxtaposition is comparable to Bhīshma's description of *dharma* as upholding beings apart.[153] The potential or logical conflict between the two worlds or perspectives is 'solved' by keeping them apart. The conflict is not solved, but transcended by shifting from one perspective to the other without creating a short circuit. Such a cosmic transcendence of the conflict is, of course, also one way of solving the conflict, in the sense that one is liberated from its compelling inevitability. In its own right, the potential or logical discrepancy represents a real clash. But taking one perspective at a time reduces its impact to the extent that a conflict can be denied or neglected.

This juxtaposing approach is characteristic of a *differentiated society* that copes with complexity by dividing society up into segments, layers or classes that do not mutually interfere – neither vertically or horizontally. This approach is also characteristic of a *polytheistic world view* that upholds the diversity that the universe manifests, at the cost of its unity. Rather than reducing diversity to unity, polytheistic world views tend to be impressed by the irreducibility of diversity.[154]

In a more specific sense, the juxtaposing approach is very characteristic of *Hinduism*, according to Biardeau and Heesterman. Biardeau argues that the three goals of *kāma*, *artha* and *dharma* constitute one pole; the one goal of *moksha* constitutes the other pole of that fundamental bipolarity which has become the very structure of Hinduism.[155] But, much more on that later.[156] Heesterman argues that the *brahmin* priest who started to incorporate the values of asceticism within society came to represent absolute, transcendent authority cut off from the social world, while the sacral king came to represent the social world.[157] The *brahmin* priest came to represent the transcendent pole as opposed to the immanent pole of the sacral king. This fundamental juxtaposition of radical transcendence and radical immanence has been characteristic of Hinduism ever since. While Biardeau stresses the *complementarity* of the juxtaposition, Heesterman stresses its *inner conflict*. In Heesterman's understanding, the inner conflict is ultimately about the enigma of life and death and how to deal with it; or rather, about the impossibility of dealing with it. The juxtaposition of transcendence and immanence is offered as the solution, but at the same time, the offered 'solution' is one way of expressing the problem of the insolvability of the inner conflict. In this sense, the inner conflict is deeply tragic since it is not solved. Instead, the inner conflict is dissolved and radicalized by splitting up the difference between its poles. By dissolving and radicalizing the inner conflict, the difference between transcendence and immanence becomes a radical gap. The two poles mutually exclude each other, but are held together by their juxtaposition. The tragic character of the inner conflict is neither solved nor recognized. Juxtaposition implies not just the transcendence of tragedy taking place on the immanent level by making it a part of a wider dramatic perspective; it implies the denial of tragedy taking place by shifting grounds from the immanent to the transcendent level. The absolute opposition between life and death on the immanent level, which constitutes a linear conflict in which one of the two poles has to be eliminated, is ultimately denied by adding a cyclical pattern of re-balancing exchange, reversal and eternal return. The juxtaposition consists of adding a cyclical pattern to a linear pattern. *The linear pattern is deeply tragic* because the conflict between the two poles is unsolvable. One of the opposites has to be eliminated, but there is no way in which that can be done without eliminating the other pole as well. *The cyclical pattern is deeply dramatic, but not tragic*, I would add, because it denies the very opposition it reverses.[158]

Heesterman's observations are very helpful in assessing the relative importance of the tragic dimensions of the epic's plot pattern. The *plot's second ending* of all the warriors in heaven is an abrupt and– at least for Yudhisthira – an unexpected *shift* from the opposition between good and evil, justice and injustice, not towards the elimination of the evil and unjust side of the opposition, but towards the elimination of the opposition itself. Shifting grounds from earth to heaven, the plot pattern leaves behind the historical, mundane level and, in transcending it, declares it an illusion while retreating into the cosmic level. The juxtaposition of a historical level and a cosmic level takes shape in the plot pattern by shifting from earth to heaven in such a way that the human tragedy, which is enacted by human agents, is being *framed* by a cosmic drama that enacts a reshuffle of the very agents involved in the human tragedy. Whereas the *historical arrangement* of the Kurukshetra war manifests a *linear pattern* that ends in a disaster for virtually all agents involved, the *cosmic rearrangement* of the war, its outcome and its warriors manifests a *circular pattern* of re-balancing exchange, reversal and eternal return. The ending of the story appears to consist of *one tragic ending on the historical level*, which culminates in the disaster of total war and destruction – of the eighteen armies, only nine souls survive, the five Pāndavas with Krishna on one side, and only three minor warriors on the other – and of *another, dramatic ending on the cosmic level* that makes the main opponents in heaven equal and puts the story in an entirely different framework. The terror of time and history is confirmed in the story's first ending, denied in its second; it is overcome by temporarily recycling it.

The literary device of *framing* a story within another story is used in the epic to *juxtapose* a historical, tragic perspective and a cosmic, dramatic perspective, rather than to oppose the two perspectives or even to superimpose one of them. To a great extent, both perspectives are taken seriously in their own right. It is only from the cosmic perspective that the historical perspective is being disqualified as an illusion – a clear case of superimposition. But even this superimposed disqualification tends to confirm the extent to which the two perspectives do not oppose each other since an illusion can never, within this cosmic perspective, be an ultimate opponent to reality, only a temporary and secondary one. Moreover, the superimposed cosmic perspective is playing a marginal role in the epic's plot. Superimposition is less decisive for the plot pattern as a whole than juxtaposition. Both perspectives are mainly upheld apart by juxtaposition, that is to say, by using the literary device of framing.

That the plot's second ending is a clear case of framing instead of simply taking a different turn is evident from the plot's beginning in the first chapter of the epic. The epic's beginning touches upon the cosmic origins of its main characters while shifting to the historical level. That is to say, the main human characters are presented in the epic as sons and daughters or manifestations of aspects of gods, goddesses and demons. Bhīshma is Dyaus incarnate, Yudhisthira is the son of Dharma, Arjuna is the son of Indra, Draupadī is Śrī incarnate, Duryodhana is Kali incarnate, Krishna is Vishnu incarnate and Vyāsa is Nārāyana incarnate.[159]

Hiltebeitel pays much attention to this mythic background for specific psychological character traits of the epic's main characters, which he interprets as epic continuations of mythic models.[160] In this context, he also points out the aspects of simultaneity and juxtaposition:

But even where there are mythic models, the epic continuations (I avoid here the mechanical tone of terms like 'copy' and 'transposition') can be of the greatest psychological subtlety. Things occur differently on the two different planes, and that is the value—and for the *Mahābhārata* the purpose—of having both. . . . Moreover, some of the *Mahābhārata's* most intriguing characterizations emerge directly from a juxtaposition of mythic and epic themes. One thinks of Arjuna, the son of Indra who is reluctant to fight, and of certain other mythic-epic correlations handled with restrained but unmistakable irony.[161]

Indra is the god of fighting, battle and war whereas his son Arjuna is inclined to pacifism on the battlefield at the very moment he is expected to live up to his duty of main warrior.

3.5 Irony

The conflict between the Pāndavas and Kauravas is simply an episode in the perennial battle of the gods and the demons for the control of heaven, temporarily shifted to the Earth. It illustrates *a bipartite cosmos*. But does it also constitute *a source of irony?* The parallelism between the 'mythic' and the 'epic' levels indicates correspondence. Does it also indicate discrepancy? It does, on the level of individual characters – Arjuna, son of the warrior god Indra, is suddenly inclined to pacifism on the battlefield. But does it evoke 'a sense of discrepancy' (as I would define 'irony') on the level of the plot pattern? Do divine interventions change the direction of the plot? Does fate bring about an unexpected turn of actions to the contrary?

Let us examine the plot's first ending of Yudhisthira's lonesomeness during the aftermath of the war, and the plot's second ending of his entrance into heaven in the company of friends and foes alike. Does this shift from the 'epic' to the 'mythic' level coincide with a shift from the 'illusory' to the 'real', from 'mortal' to 'immortal', in such a way that it evokes an ironic tension? The plot's ending appears to consist of one, tragic ending on the historical level, and another, dramatic ending on the cosmic level, which retakes the story within an entirely different frame. Framing is used in the epic to juxtapose rather than to oppose the two perspectives. The framing of the plot within a widening, transcendent perspective by Indra and Dharma could, with the benefit of hindsight, reveal the *bitter* irony of the previous events. But irony is not used here for purposes of bitterness, neither by Indra and Dharma nor by the story-teller Vyāsa nor by Janamejaya, the king to whom the story is retold. The final focus is on having passed beyond the stage of hostility by crossing the heavenly Ganges, the river of *purification*, not on the illusory nature of waging war; although the evil warriors all end up in heaven as a reward for having died on the battlefield and, to that extent, really benefit from having waged war, the huge difference between heaven and hell is simply undone by calling it an illusion and turning the page. There is not enough of an active ironic tension between the previous situation and the new perspective because the new perspective is much less about the old situation than it is about cutting the last ties with the old situation and about qualifying the new situation as absolutely different from the previous one. The new perspective is presented as having all along interacted and interfered with the previous one by imposition of its hidden agenda from above in a bipartite cosmos in which the individual mortal characters are simultaneously framed in an immortal perspective. Yet, the new perspective is not presented as such explicitly in any way that *confronts* the historical level of human affairs with the mythic level of cosmic affairs. The clash between heaven and hell that was supposed to correspond with the earthly opposition between good and evil no longer applies. The imagined correspondence between the 'mythic' and the 'epic' levels that evoked within Yudhisthira a sense of hurt, indignation and incomprehension is disqualified as invalid. The conflict situation is not between human and cosmic affairs, but remains within the historical level. The two levels are juxtaposed as two entirely different perspectives. The difference between these two perspectives is as radical as the gap between dreaming or fostering an illusion and waking up to ultimate reality. Either one is dreaming or one is awake. There is no directly experienced tension between the two because the dreaming experience is cut off from the awakening experience. These experiences of the cosmos are too far apart to constitute a bipartite cosmos in the Homeric sense of the word.

But more needs to be said about the development of the epic plot than what has been said so far about the epic's plot ending(s). There are two main characters in the epic whose presence highlights the gap between individual and cosmic value: things that mean a great deal to individuals become futile or infinitesimal when viewed in the objective proportions of time, multitudes, or divinity. In the Homeric model of a bipartite cosmos, we are constantly reminded of the different narrative vistas of the same events as perceived by the mortal characters, the gods and the audience. In the *Mahābhārata*, it is the story-teller Vyāsa and the mediator, counsellor and god Krishna who move around freely on all levels of knowledge, past, present and future. They have access to the human and superhuman perspectives and realities alike. King Dhrtarāstra, for example, asks Vyāsa to change developments on the ground by changing the plot he is composing – but Vyāsa answers that he cannot change destiny. Vyāsa is, after all, the all-knowing narratorial voice that Greek tragedy lost on its way from epic 'telling' to tragedic 'showing'.

Krishna is an even more complicated figure because he is Lord of the Universe, actively intervening at the historical level of bringing about the war for the sake of necessary renewal; he is also the peace mediator intervening for the sake of peace; and he is the yogic fighter who teaches 'peace of mind' to a warrior. Krishna is both all-knowing and all-powerful. Krishna has divine foreknowledge and (mis)uses it to pursue his superhuman goals by immoral means. Sometimes, his whispered counselling contains silent treachery; at other times, his outspoken counselling contains all the teachings of Hindu philosophies combined. In my understanding, Krishna's presence in the epic is full of irony in every respect. His irony is not just a figure of speech or a tricky intervention in disguise and recognition (cf. the *Harivaṃśa*[162]), but an attitude to existence.

When it comes to tricky interventions, the role Krishna plays in the epic plot is reminiscent of that of a trickster, not of that of a jester. A divinely connected trickster can do extraordinary things that are not normally possible. A professionally paid court jester makes fun of things by commenting on them, not by connecting to the realm of the inaccessible. But Krishna's tricky interventions are saving, moral interventions, not egotistical, amoral, ludicrous (trickster) or moralistically ridiculing (jester) interventions.

4 The Bhagavadgītā's plot pattern and world view

4.1 The Gītā's specific conflict and specific solution

Since (an earlier literary version of) the *Bhagavadgītā* has often been considered an interpolation into the epic, that is to say, an independent literary work, does the *Gītā* as we know it from the epic, have a *plot pattern* of its own and/or does it fit into the epic's overall plot pattern? The answer to this question will not only define the narrative relationship between the epic and the *Gītā* but also contribute substantially to the identification of a Hindu version of Western tragedy.

In the *Gītā*, the opening scene depicts two mighty armies facing each other on the stage of the Kurukshetra battlefield. But while the *Mahābhārata* epic is about *mourning*, the *Gītā* is only about *grief*.[163] The Pāndava side is led by Arjuna, who is accompanied by his charioteer Krishna. Arjuna faces a moral dilemma. On the one hand, he is expected to fight a righteous war. On the other hand, it is a deadly war involving the killing of some of his own kinsmen. Facing the killing of kin and a deadly war, he suddenly hesitates, breaks down and gives a moving description of his heart-rending grief.

Krishna too, in his response, shows that Arjuna's grief appears as the prominent feature of his mental state. But instead of evoking compassion, with Krishna it evokes indignation and a rebuke. Krishna's answer is everything but compassionate, 'The Lord said: You are grieving over those that deserve no grief, and yet are uttering seemingly wise talk. The truly wise grieve neither over the retention nor the departure of life'.[164] There is no doubt that Arjuna's faintheartedness, this specific emotion of the situation, is considered unmanly, lacking nerve and willpower, confused, and consequently, anything but courageous or holding out against feelings of fear of the consequences of one's actions. Despite Krishna's doubts about the lucidity and firmness of Arjuna's deliberations, Krishna's powers of persuasion make an appeal to reason. Apparently, despite his confusion Arjuna still has a reasoning capacity that can be addressed. His deliberations cannot be dismissed as sheer blindness. Arjuna does have a point. In fact, the problem is that he has several points. His reasoning capacity could generate equally good reasons for both horns of the moral dilemma. What Arjuna's mind or reason does not generate is the kind of knowledge necessary to solve the moral problem itself.

The solution Krishna comes up with is neither a psychic nor a moral nor a rational one, but beyond that. What Krishna has to offer is a spiritual solution. It takes Krishna quite some time to lead Arjuna all the way from his psycho-ethical problem to its spiritual solution. Krishna turns out to be a sophisticated counsellor and a teacher acquainted with the major spiritual traditions of ancient India. In fact, most of the *Gītā* is dedicated to Krishna restating the dilemma in such a way as to encompass and integrate or transcend all previous philosophical debate on action and knowledge in the Indian religious realm at the time.

Rhetorically speaking, Krishna's teaching begins with pointing out the impermanence of existence and the dualism between the mortal body (*deha*) and the 'embodied one' (*dehī*), the immortal soul or self (*Gītā* 2.13–30). Besides, it is the duty and glory of a warrior to fight instead of incurring evil and disgrace (2.31–8). It is the (short-term) destiny of warriors who fight that they gain access to heaven (2.32). But, from then onwards, Krishna begins to focus on the notion of action. It becomes the (long-term?) destiny of anyone who acts according to Krishna's teaching to avoid rebirth and to be one with Krishna. The focus has shifted from Arjuna's war action to the value and nature of action in general. The main thrust of the argument is that if Arjuna's spiritual self does not attach to and identify with (the results of) his action because it knows of its own immortality and transcendence, the spiritual actor remains separated from the actual action of the agent.

But the decisive *turning-point* or catalyst, both in the plot pattern of the *Gītā* and in the Hindu mainstream devotional (*bhakti*) experience, is that God takes the initiative, in an act of favour, grace or kindness, which expresses his divine feelings of protective care (or love) for the devotee, to reveal himself to the devotee as the supreme Self. The devotee acquires his personal knowledge of God because God makes himself known to his devotee. Krishna does so verbally. His verbal revelation awakens in Arjuna the desire to actually see the cosmic appearance of the Lord of the universe. Arjuna is unable to see Krishna with his natural vision; Krishna has to endow him with a divine eye to see the divinity (11.8). Arjuna receives a frightening vision of Krishna as Time devouring the universe. He is shattered and persuaded by it. Calmed down by Krishna – Krishna restores his appearance to 'normal' – Arjuna is invited to act accordingly. He receives additional teachings from Krishna as his Lord. Destroyed is his delusion; his doubts are gone. He has gained wisdom (memory, *smrtis*) through Krishna's favour, grace or kindness (18.73). He is back on the battlefield, ready to act as Krishna commands, ready to fight.

So far the story line. In order to find an answer to the question whether the *Gītā* has a plot of its own and/or whether it fits into the epic's plot, and with the prospect of identifying a Hindu version of Western tragedy, two types of reversals in the plot pattern call for a closer look – ironic reversal connected with the martial issue and cosmic reversal connected with the revelatory issue.

4.2 The martial issue and ironic reversal

Regarding the martial issue of the *Gītā*'s plot, the most impressive of moments, no doubt, is the moment that Arjuna himself, the main warrior hero and commander-in-chief of the Pāndava armies, hesitates and even refuses to fight.

Hiltebeitel has pointed out the unmistakable *irony* of the situation – Arjuna, the son of the war god Indra, is reluctant to fight.[165] This is (implicit) irony on the borderline between the mundane and the cosmic levels.

There is also irony on the *mundane* level, as Ramanujan notices. Ramanujan has a structuralist approach to the problem of literary unity of the Sanskrit version of the *Mahābhārata* and the *Gītā*. He suggests that one central structuring principle of the epic is an ironic kind of repetition, illustrated by the *Gītā* repeating a scene in *Virāta Parvan*. During the thirteenth year of exile, incognito in the Matsya kingdom, Arjuna, disguised as a eunuch dancing master to Prince Uttara, becomes his charioteer in battle after Uttara's failure of nerve and attempt to flee from the battlefield, and after Arjuna has asked Uttara who he thinks he is. The very next book opens with Arjuna in the chariot with Krishna as the charioteer, and the same thing happens.[166] Several *ironic reversals* take place between actor and agent, charioteer and warrior, eunuch and potent male.[167] What seems like a *playful* rehearsal in the Virāta episode becomes *serious* in the *Gītā*'s plot. Both Ramanujan and Doniger seem to confirm my understanding that the anticipating Virāta episode has a *comic* character, as opposed to the subsequent *Gītā* episode, which has a *tragic* character. They also demonstrate a literary embeddedness of the *Gītā's* plot in the epic's broader plot pattern. The *Gītā's* plot fits into the epic's plot as a whole.

4.3 The revelatory issue and cosmic reversal

Regarding the revelatory issue of the *Gītā's* plot, the terrifying appearance of Lord Krishna as Time devouring the universe (11.9–49) can be interpreted as an *esoteric vision* or as an exclusive (and potentially mystical) vision or as a mystical experience, including a vision that transmits esoteric knowledge. Potentially mystical, because Arjuna is not at all depicted as a mystic, but later *bhakti* audiences developed mystical access to this vision. The esoteric knowledge would have remained secret if Krishna were not to have taken the initiative to reveal it to Arjuna. That is to say, the *Gītā* makes the truth emerge as a deliberate act of revelation on the part of Krishna. Krishna's efforts to persuade Arjuna to fight take a decisive turn when Krishna reveals his true identity and the way it is related to Arjuna's true identity. This *revelatory truth* is not a wise advice. It is simply overwhelming. It is persuasive because it is self-evident as a spiritual experience. Krishna's appearance disarms Arjuna's unwillingness to fight, clears his mind and liberates his heart from the burden of potential guilt feelings and depression.

Krishna's battlefield theophany in the *Gītā* is not the only one. Apart from one later epic theophany (14.54.3–7), supposedly redisclosing the *Gītā* form to the desert sage Uttanka, there is another important theophany a short time before the battlefield scene of the *Gītā*, at the moment of the final breakdown of Krishna's peace negotiations at the Kaurava court, when Krishna has failed to persuade Duryodhana and when he addresses Duryodhana personally (5.129.1–15). In this court theophany, Krishna's ostensible purpose is to make peace, whereas in the battlefield theophany, it is to make war, Hiltebeitel explains. In the *court theophany*, Krishna, seemingly alone (in the deluded view of Duryodhana), 'produces or "releases" all classes of beings (except demons) from his own person' – a vision (*darshan*) of Krishna's creative aspects addressing Duryodhana and heading for peace. In the *battlefield theophany*, Krishna puts Arjuna in a position where he can view the assembled hosts, and 'appears at the very center of all beings', dissolving them into himself – a vision of Krishna's destructive aspects addressing Arjuna and heading for war.[168] Biardeau has shown that Arjuna's outsider position within the battlefield theophany itself is the position of the delivered, who are free to witness, firstly, the fate of the delivered (11.21–2); secondly, the fate of the undelivered (11.26–8) and; thirdly, the fate of the three worlds (11.29–30).[169] So, Arjuna receives a vision of fate.

In Doniger's literary approach to narratives, our narrative vision varies between the extreme ends of the entirely personal, 'microscopic' view and the entirely general, 'telescopic' view.[170] As Doniger puts it; 'On this continuum between the personal and the abstract, myth vibrates in the middle' – in the sense of spanning both extremes. Myth, ranging 'from the most highly detailed' to 'the most stripped down', has the ability 'to capture simultaneously the near and far view', thus offering a peculiar kind of *double vision* of things.[171]

In order to explain how and why texts provide us with microscopes and telescopes, Doniger takes a closer look at the *Book of Job*, the *Gītā*, and the *Bhagavata Purana*.[172] These three texts contain a combination of the down-to-earth view of things (the microscopic view) and the cosmic, god's-eye view of things (the telescopic view). In the *Book of Job*, 'God and Satan look down through their telescopes and decide to use Job as a pawn in a test of their own powers'. On earth, Job is ruined by God. With words, Job tries to cope with the disaster, but he has no reply to the overpowering riddle of creation and its creator. The plot takes another turn when God restores Job's life to normal. Doniger points out that 'the trick of undoing it all at the end ("It was all a dream")' has 'two Hindu parallels that use this trick of the illusion-shattering epiphany'.[173] In the (probably) tenth-century-CE *Bhagavata Purana*, Lord Krishna, as a little naughty boy scolded by his mortal mother Yashodha for having eaten dirt, is asked to open his mouth to prove his innocence. When he opens his mouth, his mother sees in it the whole universe. She becomes frightened and confused by this cosmic vision. God restores life to normal. Likewise, Doniger argues, the *Gītā* has Lord Krishna *shift from word to image*, from Krishna's verbal arguments, which must persuade Arjuna to Krishna's even more persuasive display of his cosmic form.

I would like to draw attention here to the fact that a *philosophical reading* of the *Gītā* may register the minimal presence of the doctrine of illusion (*māyā*) from Krishna's teaching – the word *māyā* occurs only in *Gītā* 4.6, 7.14–15, and 18.61 – but that a *literary reading* can register the overwhelming presence of the idea of illusion all the more clearly. Terrified, Arjuna begs Lord Krishna to turn back into his friend Krishna, which the god consents to do, switching back from image to word. Calmed down by Krishna (11.50) Arjuna is comforted by the reassuring, but illusory familiarity of human life.

Doniger's comment goes in a political direction, 'Outside the text, however, the reader has been persuaded that since war is unreal, it is not evil'.[174] This comment underlines her point that myth is able to present two viewpoints simultaneously by switching from the microscopic to the telescopic viewpoint and back again. Moreover, she suggests, 'the myth as a whole offers a way of balancing the two views so that the reader is not in fact forced to accept either one, or to choose between them'. The two viewpoints are valid simultaneously – our lives are both real and unreal.[175] Juxtaposition of viewpoints is its corresponding literary device.

Also, Doniger's comment illustrates that 'the wide-angle lens can be theological and political simultaneously. . . . Using microscopic and telescopic viewpoints to link daily reality with global—indeed, galaxial—politics, myth enables us to . . . think globally and act locally. And this is exactly what the *Gītā*'s message is all about: think globally, act locally', Doniger argues.[176] Arjuna should forget about local politics, concentrate instead on his immortal self, or rather, on Krishna's supreme Self, and then fight nonetheless (*Gītā* 11.32–3).

In my understanding, it is not, despite *Gītā* 11.1, Krishna's teaching, but Krishna's theophany which brings about this shift in attitude and in the development of the Gītā's plot. Switching from a microscopic view to a telescopic view brings about a *first shift in mood*, in my opinion, a move from moral defiance and grief to existential shock and desperation; switching back from a telescopic view to a microscopic view brings about another shift in Arjuna's mood, a move from existential shock and desperation to reassuring comfort and devoted acceptance of his 'acting locally'. This is to be Arjuna's *final mood* in the *Gītā*. It is presumed to consist of the kind of state of mind Krishna has promised to all those who practise yogic action – indifference, equanimity, serenity, tranquillity, peace of mind (2.48; 2.64–71; 6.27), release from evil or impurity (4.16; 6.27, 28; 9.1) and happiness (5.21; 6.21, 27–8). This yogic happiness clearly transcends the straightforward happiness Arjuna was referring to in 1.37, 'How could we be happy having killed our own folk'? It is referred to by Krishna in terms of 'the wise one to whom happiness and unhappiness are the same' (2.15). Within the narrative scope of the *Gītā*'s final chapter, Arjuna's final mood consists of that state of mind which Krishna had called for in 2.37, being resolved to fight.[177]

If the shift from Krishna's teaching to Krishna's theophany and back again is the decisive turning-point in Arjuna's attitude and in the development of the *Gītā*'s plot, it is also the decisive *solution to the conflict*. That is to say, it confirms the strong impression that scholars such as Katz have – 'the paths of knowledge and devotion intertwine. Yet in the *Gītā* and most of the epic, devotion is the dominant solution, which seems to absorb knowledge'.[178] If Krishna's theophany enables Arjuna to (almost) fully grasp Krishna's teaching,

Arjuna's devotional attitude enables him to fully integrate absolute knowledge (purify his mind). This progress implies a move from *juxtaposition* of viewpoints to a *superimposition* of the transcendent viewpoint, from immanent conflict to transcendent solution. To the extent that the transcendent level of the spiritual solution is upheld while returning to the immanent level of the moral conflict, the telescopic view remains the decisive one, *framing* the microscopic view.

From a literary point of view, the *juxtaposition of perspectives* – of Arjuna's dilemma, a tragic scene, and Krishna's revelation, a visionary scene of fate – may not seem strong *as a plot device* because it comes out of the blue, like a Euripidean *deus ex machina*, except that Krishna's teaching awakens in Arjuna the desire to have slightly more of it – not to have more than he can cope with, however. But, it is strong in two respects.

First of all, the juxtaposition has the same function as *anagnorisis* (recognition) in tragedy. Of course, Arjuna has come to understand a lot already during Krishna's teaching, including the recognition that Krishna is the supreme Lord of the Universe. But that was recognition by human standards. On a cosmic scale, however, Krishna's supreme Self is out of proportion, beyond anything Arjuna can cope with. Arjuna recognizes Krishna as Vishnu (11.24, 11.30), but simultaneously begs him to tell him who he is, of so terrible a form (11.31). Krishna then reveals that He is Time devouring the Universe. What Arjuna also recognizes is his inevitable *fate*, which consists of his warrior action having become inevitable and doomed to bring about death. The same word *kāla* means both 'time' and 'death'. It is Arjuna's human destiny to recognize and assume death (killing and being killed) as the fate of his warrior caste.[179] Arjuna's vision of Krishna's appearance is a potentially traumatizing vision of fate. Is this *dramatic* vision a *tragic* vision of time, death and inevitable destruction?

The juxtaposition of perspectives is strong in a second respect. The recognition of his fate leads Arjuna to see his human smallness, but it leads the audience to see his cosmic greatness, in the sense that the smallness of his human action and suffering takes part in a great cosmic plan of which he is fully conscious. Arjuna will not just perform his duty, but he must perform his duty on stage – a cosmic stage in the theatre of Krishna's providential drama of creation and destruction:

> The Lord abides in the hearts
> Of all beings, Arjuna,
> Causing all beings to revolve,
> By the power of illusion, as if fixed on a machine.
> [*Gītā* 18.61][180]

Illusory as it may be, the creative power of appearance and illusion (*māyā*) constitutes a play that must be taken very seriously.[181]

Arjuna's human suffering and evil (the evil of killing one's relatives and of engaging in a total war) participate in a cosmic (periodical) deliverance from suffering and evil. (Cf. 9.1, 9.30–32, 10.3) Thus, the *second function* of the juxtaposition of Arjuna's dilemma, a tragic scene, and Krishna's revelation, a tragic *and* visionary scene of fate *and* predestination, as a plot device is that it represents *a Hindu version of Western tragedy* – tragedy is upheld on the immanent level, and simultaneously, it is recognized and overcome on the transcendent level as part of the same plot. Part of? The revelation does not intervene in the sense that the plot takes a different turn from what was to be expected – Arjuna is, after all, expected to fight – but it does intervene in the sense that it triggers what was to be expected to happen – Arjuna fighting. The two are not on the same level, but the transcendent level is perpendicular to the immanent level. The narrative sequence of the two does not resolve, but expresses the problem of bipolarity; and yet, the transcendent pole is the ultimate one which does resolve the problem on its own terms. The tragic conflict is both maintained and transcended – except that the plot shifts back to the battlefield, to the tragic conflict, albeit with a heightened, purified consciousness. One is reminded of Spinoza's adage that freedom is the recognition of necessity. Does this Hindu human drama imply a dramatic deliverance *from* tragedy or a dramatic deliverance *in* tragedy?[182] It implies both. The double perspective of the juxtaposition maintains both poles of the bipolarity, precisely because the ultimate, non-tragic perspective is not the final perspective in the *Gītā*. The final outcome is that Arjuna has to fight a disastrous war after all. By switching back from the *ultimate* to the *final* perspective, the plot upholds the oscillation. The oscillation consists of a shifting of two levels that are always there.

Does this development of the *Gītā's* plot fit into the epic plot pattern as a whole? The microscopic focus of the *Gītā's* beginning is *widened* half-way down the plot, with Krishna's theophany, into a telescopic focus, and then *narrowed down* again to human affairs, whereas the telescopic focus of the epic's beginning, with the divine origin of the main characters, is immediately *narrowed down* to human affairs, and then finally *widened* again into a telescopic focus on the main characters, gods and demons in heaven. But both plots use the same literary device of framing, which can be read both ways. The *Gītā* and the epic have this *double scope* in common, which enables a smooth match between them, because the literary device of framing allows for a two-way traffic interpretation of things, depending on the viewpoint taken, and allows for a simultaneous appreciation of both perspectives on their own terms.

5 Conclusions

The narrative aspects of tragedy that have been discussed in connection with the Greek and Shakespearean material are also present in the *Mahābhārata* epic and the *Gītā*. Subjects that are prominent in tragedies are also recurrent topics here – suffering, loss, death, evil, disorder and transgression. The release of evil as a disruptive force that sets the plot in motion is the Kauravas' jealousy, greed and ambition to seize the kingdom, but also the Pāndavas' loss of the kingdom due to Yudhisthira's obsession with dicing, which marks a reversal of fortunes. The disorder consists of the escalation of the conflict to a fatal war in which trickery on both sides illustrates a transgression of the moral order of an entire epoch that is declining. The disastrous war seems to settle the conflict of succession, but the grief over the loss of so many warriors and the weeping of the Kaurava women set the tone for a disturbed mood after the end of the war. There is a second end to the plot, however, in heaven, where the warriors from both parties are welcomed in a mood purified from enmity and grief.

A regular reversal of fortunes determines the plot pattern down the generations of the Kuru lineage, each generation witnessing glory and decline. Yudhisthira's dice game and ensuing exile constitute one such turning point. The occurrence of these crucial topics testifies to the influence of the ritual pattern of the royal consecration rites on the narrative pattern. The dice game also symbolizes the evils of passion, the collapse of the natural order and the determining power of fate, of which fortune distributes its short-term portions. The god Śiva is associated with the dice game and with the threat of chaos, whereas Krishna (the god Vishnu), who is conspicuously absent from the dice game scene, leaves nothing to chance and counterbalances the destructive impact of Śiva. A fatal throw of the dice substitutes one better world epoch in the cosmic cycle of time for another worse epoch. The fatal conflict between the Pāndavas and the Kauravas is about the succession to the Kuru throne. In the background of the battle between the Pāndavas and the Kauravas is also the perennial battle between the gods and the demons.

The world view embedded in the plot pattern of the epic is not easy to identify if one is to take into account that the plot pattern has two endings, until one realizes that one story frames the other story instead of being its linear continuation with a twist. The epic's world, I suggested, is a tragic world, but its wider world is 'dramatic' in the pre-modern sense of the word – it is about the workings of the cosmos as actions of the gods who are involved in a permanent battle of establishing order at the expense of chaos. The epic presents a tragic world within the wider perspective of a dramatic world view. In the plot pattern, the two worlds or perspectives are juxtaposed, not opposed to each other. The juxtaposition consists of a cyclical and deeply dramatic pattern being added to a linear and deeply tragic pattern. The terror of time and history is confirmed in the plot's first ending, denied in the plot's second ending, overcome by temporarily recycling it. This juxtaposition holds true for the plot pattern of the *Gītā* as well, but the other way around. The *Gītā*'s plot shifts from the immanent world to the transcendent world and back again, whereas the epic shifts from the divine world to the human world and back again to the heavenly world. The juxtaposition is upheld. Both perspectives remain valid. By juxtaposing instead of opposing them, tragedy is upheld on the immanent level and simultaneously, tragedy is recognized and overcome on the transcendent level. This amounts to a Hindu version of Western tragedy.

PART III: CROSS-CULTURAL COMPARISONS

1 Introduction

The third part of this chapter, on cross-cultural comparisons, will be dedicated to the task of comparing the Greek and Shakespearean material with the Indian or Hindu material. The *main question* of this third part will be: in what respects do or do not the narrative aspects of Greek and Shakespearean tragedy have parallels in the *Mahābhārata* epic and the *Bhagavadgītā*?

2 Specific subjects

At least some recurrent themes in the Greek and Shakespearean tragic genre are recognized as 'typically tragic' – suffering, loss, death, evil and transgression. These subjects are not only prominent in tragic literature, but also in epic literature, including Indian epic literature. The main subject of the *Mahābhārata* is a typically *epic* cluster of subjects – the battle between warrior heroes fighting each other for the sake of victory, a power struggle among legitimate and illegitimate intendants to the throne. Epic literature contains many stories about ruling families trying to cope with infighting because of rival claims to succession to the throne, and so does tragic literature – in Aeschylus' *Seven against Thebes*, Polyneices opposes the rival claim of his brother Eteocles; in *Hamlet*, Claudius opposes his Hamlet.[183] The so-called 'typically tragic' subjects of suffering and loss, death, evil and fatal conflict are omnipresent in the *Mahābhārata* epic too. This is nowhere more explicit than in the figure of King Yudhisthira. He is stricken with *grief* after the war because of the *loss* of so many people and he is in need of consolation. It is also explicit in the weeping of the Kaurava women whose relatives lost the war and who lost their relatives. An entire book, the Book of Women, is dedicated to their *mourning*. The finality of the loss is traumatizing, but it is solemnly voiced and lamented; it is suffering worth being told, as Sands would say. In Greek tragedy, the chorus is not the only 'character' to do so. In *Hamlet*, the lamentation of Hamlet's father and of Ophelia play an important role. In the *Bhagavadgītā*, Arjuna's grief is crucial to his refusal to fight. The main plot of this epic can be said, paradoxically, to be made of the stuff of tragedy. Whether the themes coincide with the message remains to be seen.

Evil takes many forms. One form of evil is the injustice of illegitimate succession to the Danish and Kuru thrones by King Claudius and Crown-Prince Duryodhana, respectively. Vices that these two royal characters have in common are the passions of envy and ambition. Hamlet's revenge is an equally menacing passion doomed to fail as its counterpart 'ambition' because it lacks the same capacity to balance things. Disproportionate by nature, neither ambition nor revenge can restore the order of equilibrium. The by far most menacing form of evil in epics and tragedies alike is, after all, the extremely serious threat of *chaos*. Comedies too have their disorder, but the disruptive force of comic disorder is much more innocent. The terrifying occurrence or menace of disorder in *Oedipus Tyrannus* and *Hamlet* and in the *Mahābhārata* epic includes the disastrous destruction of entire kingdoms and a relapse into chaos. In Greek and Shakespearean tragedies, the violation of the normal order has already brought about a pollution, a tangible form of evil that has to be removed. In the *Mahābhārata* epic, the violation of the normal order is symbolized by the dice game ('the evils of gambling') and by *brahmins* living as warriors and warriors living as *brahmins*. In the *Gītā*, the threatening prospect of blurring distinctions between groups is symbolized by the picture of women marrying outside their caste – the functional equivalent of *Hamlet*'s incest, another form of loss of distinction. In the Gravedigger scene, Hamlet depicts death itself as the ultimate destroyer of all social class distinctions. Social chaos can take many forms – mixed marriage, incest, parricide, fratricide, internecine war. All of them are forms that cross the natural and normative borders violently, disrespectfully or accidentally, all of them leading to psychological states of confusion and distress. That is why *transgression of borders* is a related 'specifically tragic' subject. In the epic, separation is necessary to uphold the social order.

3 Specific plot patterns

3.1 Order at stake

The release of disorder as a disruptive force that has to be fought, contained and undone is crucial to epics, tragedies and comedies alike, but in the case of tragedies, the occurrence or menace of contaminating pollution, catastrophe and *social chaos* is an extremely serious one. Even if the counterforces are mobilized successfully, tragedies show a pattern of disorder rectified, but at terrible cost. In *Oedipus Tyrannus*, the pollution is purified by the virtually suicidal self-removal of the king from power. The sense of a family curse has been reinforced. In *Hamlet*, the pollution is purified by Hamlet committing the crime of murderous revenge. The crown is lost to his Norwegian rival, even though the illegitimate king, Claudius, has been removed from power and his father avenged successfully. Hamlet's successful mission is linked up with murder, death and eternal damnation. In the *Mahābhārata*, the release of evil disorder is constituted by the jealousy, greed and ambition of Duryodhana, who seizes and holds on to the throne illegitimately, although even the epic itself argues that his inner blindness is only to be expected from a son whose father is a blind king – a blind king being a contradiction in terms according to traditional standards. But the disorder is reinforced by the Pāndavas, who fail to be installed as the legitimate heirs, due to Yudhisthira's vow always to accept a challenge, to his dicing incompetence and to his lack of self-control. The power struggle escalates into a fatal war. An entire generation of warriors dies. This total war also has a mythic cause, namely the goddess Earth's complaint to Brahma that she is overburdened. It is the gods who incarnate as Pāndavas in order to remove the Earth's burden of demons (Kauravas). The social drama takes on cosmic proportions right from the beginning. However, it was not only power that was at stake. What has become most apparent is Yudhisthira's failure to protect and uphold the natural and just order (*dharma*) of the world which is, after all, the purpose of kingship. The Kuru war had turned out to be a total war and a relapse into social chaos. After the war, there is a period of the Pāndavas' successful rule, helped by Dhrtarashtra and Vidura. But eventually, Krishna, Yudhisthira's brothers and their wife retire from the world. Yudhisthira is left with his dog. This scene of misery is a close-up that works like a wide shot, which summarizes an entire epoch – left with his dog, a lonesome hero who has successfully removed his rivals from power, but at a terrible cost.

The unfolding of social chaos in tragedies leads to *mental instability*. Mental disorder, confusion and madness are a real risk. Hamlet, on top of that, discovers in his interior, a landscape of terrifying inner instability. Certain knowledge and a clear vision of the order of things are crucial, as is *remembrance*. But Oedipus' search for certain knowledge turns against him. Polonius' spying habits are equally self-destructive, and the storage capacity of his orderly memory is of no avail under extreme circumstances. Hamlet has his own problems in acquiring reliable knowledge about the Ghost, about Claudius and about himself. The Ghost has summoned Hamlet to remember him, but Hamlet also has other things on his mind. In the *Mahābhārata*, Yudhisthira's pyrrhic victory leaves the Kaurava women mourning, and himself in need of consolation, tormented with guilt feelings. He remembers the unjustifiable use of violence. However, he also remembers the teachings of Vyāsa. He is, after all, the son of Dharma, god of order and justice. In the *Gītā*, Arjuna too, initially suffers from grief and confusion when faced with his destiny. But Arjuna is in the blessed company of Krishna. He receives certain knowledge and a clear vision of the cosmic order of things and his role in it. Yet, he will not remember Krishna's teachings very well.

Duty represents order and necessity on the level of expected behaviour. In tragedies, the actual performance of duty does not meet expectations. Oedipus performs his duty as a king if he can liberate Thebes from its murderous polluter. Likewise, Hamlet performs his duty as a son and crown prince if he can liberate the state of Denmark from its murderous and illegitimate usurper Claudius. Yudhisthira performs his duty as a king if he can liberate the throne from its illegitimate usurper Duryodhana, Arjuna likewise as a warrior. But they never only perform their duties. Their performance of duties does not uphold order, as one would expect, but leads to a transgression of borders and taboos, to violation of the natural order and to self-destruction. Revengefully or violently restoring order is a duty that implies violating that very order. The more the plots advance, the sharper the notions of 'order' and 'duty' unfold their ambiguities. Antigone has the duty to bury her brother; does this duty include the self-imposed duty of challenging her uncle? Hamlet has the duty to kill his uncle; does this duty include the self-imposed duty of challenging his mother and the performance of self-imposed role-playing? Yudhisthira has the duty to take up the responsibilities of kingship; does this duty include the duty to violently conquer the throne by force and the self-imposed vow always to accept a challenge, even a deceitful one? The practical necessities of daily life impose their own constraints on the necessary performance of duty. Some necessities, if practised, compromise other ones. The implementation of order may trigger chaos. The necessary performance of duty is not necessarily on the side of order and necessity. As in *Hamlet*, Aeschylus' *Oresteia*'s focus on revenge within a single household leads to the tragedy of interfamilial violence and conflicting obligations. In the epic, the Pāndavas fail to live up to their duty of organizing a smooth and morally convincing transition of power in their favour. It is the Pāndavas who break the rules of battle. Even Krishna is actively involved in the use of trickery on the battlefield. Like Hamlet, the Pāndavas are a morally mixed lot. Both Yudhisthira and Arjuna are faced with the violating consequences of their performance of duty, which is not necessarily on the side of order and justice. They are not on a revenge mission, like Hamlet, but they too fail to accomplish their mission to restore the order of the world.

3.2 Tragic conflict

Tragic conflicts are *extreme*, Burian pointed out. Tragic conflicts do not ordinarily admit compromise or mediation. There is no easy way out when Creon and Antigone, or Claudius and Hamlet, oppose each other. Similarly, the two armies in the *Mahābhārata* oppose each other precisely because all previous mediation efforts have failed. Also, Hamlet's many dilemmas – to be or not to be, to act or not to act, to be passionate or to be rational, to kill or not to kill, to believe or not to believe – illustrate the extreme nature of his cluster of conflicts. Likewise, Arjuna faces the dilemma to kill or not to kill his own relatives and teachers or to violate his duty as a warrior. Besides, Hamlet's specific dilemma to act or not to act, to take up arms or to be stoic, has striking parallels in Yudhisthira's dilemma to choose between kingship and asceticism, and in Arjuna's dilemma to take up arms or to withdraw from active life. Yudhisthira appears as much at home in the world of thought and inaction as Hamlet; in fact, he is – not as much, but much more.

Secondly, Burian argued, conflict in tragedies involves more than human freedom in action. It involves past actions, ignorance or misunderstanding and divine intervention. The Labdacid dynasty is struck by a religious curse. The Kuru dynasty is struck by the ups and downs of fortune, by the destructive and recreative cycle of cosmic time, and by the battle between gods and demons. Neither the Pāndavas nor the Kauravas are free from ignorance or misunderstanding. They make solemn vows, but do not realize that these vows turn against them. They receive divine boons such as supernatural weapons, but then imagine themselves invincible. Karna and his rivals, the Pāndavas, do not know that they share the same mother Kuntī who suffers extremely from being mother to both camps. The Kauravas and the Pāndavas vaguely know that they are fallible mortal incarnations of demons or gods who occasionally show support on their behalf. Only Krishna has superior background information and foreknowledge precisely because he fully incarnates Time destroying the universe and Vishnu recreating the universe.

Thirdly, Burian observed, conflict in tragedy is never limited to the opposition of individuals. In the epic too, the future of the royal house, the welfare of the community, even the ordering of human life itself is at stake.

3.3 The counterproductive nature of time

In general, in the West, when events unfold, time seems to make progress and to open up new possibilities. Time appears to advance towards goals and results ahead. This progress directs one's expectations, or, for that matter, the expectations of characters in stories, and corresponds to their intentions, at least in principle. In tragedies, however, the plot pattern develops in a direction contrary to the expectations or intentions of the agents involved, but not to their advantage. Rosset argued that it is only due to our realization of the discrepancy that the painful contradiction between the expected direction and the actual direction will be felt as tragic. Moreover, as soon as one has realized that the events lead nowhere or that the disastrous outcome is already inescapable, time appears to be timeless – lacking progress – because nothing new can happen in the meantime. Whatever happens only illustrates the counterproductive nature of time. *Oedipus Tyrannus* is its finest exemplification. Hamlet's revenge mission too is leading nowhere, or rather, into the opposite direction. But this is felt by the audience, not necessarily by the characters on stage. In the *Mahābhārata*, time is not on the side of progress either. Śiva's connection with dicing through the waning course of *dharma* is literally a fatal throw of the dice, which substitutes one, better, world epoch in the cosmic cycle of time for another, worse epoch. The fact that the dice game is played and won with deceit is indicative not only of the waning course of *dharma,* but also of the Kali epoch. On the stage of the Kurukshetra battlefield, most participants realize, in one way or another, that the imminent war will be counterproductive. This realization culminates in Arjuna's mental breakdown. His imminent performance of duty will turn out to be counterproductive, and Arjuna realizes this in advance, anticipating its completion imaginatively, as Rosset would put it. The battlefield scene in the *Gītā* constitutes the lull before the storm, not a delay imitating the ending that is eventually to come, as in *Hamlet*. It constitutes timeless suspense, timeless itself, but limited in time, or rather, suspense *of* Time devouring the universe; this is more comparable to 'Pyrrhus' pause' in *Hamlet* II.ii.487–80:

So as a painted tyrant Pyrrhus stood,
And like a neutral to his will and matter
Did nothing.[184]

Does the *Gītā* exemplify Aristotle's moments of 'reversal' (*peripeteia*) and 'recognition' (*anagnōrisis*)? Does the battlefield scene in the *Gītā* intensify the tragic effect by constituting a dramatic turn of events to the contrary? The situation shows no 'switch of actions to the contrary', but an imminent crossing of the line of no return. The intensification of the tragic effect is evident, but it is not caused by a switch of actions. It takes the form of an imaginative realization of the imminent danger and inescapable necessity of crossing the line of no return. The fear of catastrophe is intensified precisely because the danger is expected. It is brought about by the anticipation of the next step. It is not an unexpected turn of events. The probability of disaster is about to be narrowed down to inevitability and necessity. Aristotle's 'reversal' too, follows the rules of probability and necessity, but it gives them an ironic, paradoxical twist by having the reversal 'develop cogently out of the premises of the action', as Seidensticker puts it.[185] There is, however, the warrior duty of Arjuna to fight, a compelling obligation and a social necessity which, in this case, produces actions that are counterproductive and will lead to a change of the actions into their own opposites, that is to say, to an ironic-paradoxical 'reversal'. The 'reversal' is not on the level of events, but on the level of performance of duty. Arjuna's imminent performance of duty will turn out to be counterproductive, and the irony is that Arjuna knows this in advance. This constellation also fits Seidensticker's suggestion that 'reversal' be qualified as 'dialectical' – the destructive force arises in interaction with and appears to rise out of Arjuna's role-performance.

Arjuna's realization of impending disaster through his own action is not presented as a case of sudden 'recognition' but, if anything, as a case of confusion and weakness. Arjuna is not expected to recognize and lament the tragic quality of his doomed destiny, but to learn how to cope with it. He asks to be instructed. His conscious urge for knowledge, for truth and insight is not the fatal error defining human nature in general, as *Oedipus Tyrannus* may suggest. Religious teaching is Krishna's initial coping strategy. But Arjuna's moment of 'recognition' comes when Krishna appears to him as Time devouring the Universe. This vision puts Arjuna where he belongs cosmically speaking – on the battlefield. Arjuna is now reconciled with his warrior role as his ultimate destiny, on the elevated level of the knowledge of the audience, as a passive witness to his own action. The vision brings about a full 'recognition' of Arjuna's doomed destiny, but neither the recognition nor the reconciliation take place on the tragic level. They do not take place on the mundane level of action, but *sub specie aeternitatis*. This cosmic level is too transcendent to be part of the tragic experience of mortal suffering the way in which Groot interpreted *Antigone*. Groot argued that reconciliation takes place on a different level, not between the main characters, but on the level of knowledge and the recognition of one's destiny, between a character and his or her insight into the inevitability of limits, pain, contradictions, and the ambiguities of life itself. Arjuna's 'recognition' would, in Greek tragedies, only intensify his sense of tragedy. In the Hindu epic, however, Time devouring the Universe is not the epitome of the counterproductive nature of time. Instead, it is the necessary transitional stage before the next recreation of the universe.

But there is another scene in the epic which may, in the first instance, seem to come close to Aristotle's moments of 'reversal' and 'recognition'. It is the scene of Yudhisthira's upside-down experience of heaven and hell. Yudhisthira sees his enemy Duryodhana shining in heaven and his brothers and Draupadī in hell. This turns out to be a (third) test, an illusion displayed by the god Indra. Friends and enemies end up in heaven together. This is certainly an unexpected turn of events for Yudhisthira, but it is not the characters' actions or intentions out of which a dramatic turn of events develops. Nor is it the victory of reconciliation and brotherhood over hatred and fratricide, as Rees suggested for *Hamlet*. It is simply turning the page. Yudhisthira does acquire a deepened understanding of his own destiny, however. Recognition takes place. But this 'recognition' does not increase his suffering. Instead, his heart is purified from enmity and grief. Yet, when he sees Draupadī in heaven, he wants to question her. But Indra is not in the mood for further questions and tells him instead the story of her divine origins. What comes to mind here is Hamlet's failure to tell his own story (and charge Horatio with the task). Lee pointed out that though Hamlet's soliloquies, in creating a form of biography, give the prince a story, it is a 'failed story'. Draupadī's story too, in Yudhisthira's mind, remains after all a 'failed story'. Indra's version of Draupadī's story is ultimately a 'completed story'. From a literary point of view, they constitute two 'juxtaposed stories'.

4 A specific world view and the role of irony

4.1 Tragic and dramatic worlds and world views

Steiner states that a tragic world view is extreme by definition, presuming as it does that human life is basically a state of homelessness leading to total despair. If stated in this way, however, tragedies rarely have a tragic world view. Eagleton and Heering did not start from a tragic world view, but from tragedies and tragedic world views. This allows them to leave open the possibility of recognizing 'the tragic' without assigning it a final and ultimate role in life. Heering stressed that, for a tragic world view, it is not sufficient that the universe be obscure and unintelligible. If being itself really has a tragic structure, as tragic world views hold, the tragic occurs on the border where humans face their limits and experience the discrepancy between their existence and the surrounding world. In a tragic world view, this border is ontologically real, not just a perceived or illusory one, and its crossing either way hurts extremely. Sands argued that tragedies shatter world views. Tragic stories tell of worlds and times that are broken such that no coherent view of them can be had. Borders are, in fact, cracks splitting up coherence beyond repair, rifts opening up dazzling gaps beyond orientation, as Sands would put it. I would argue that, prototypically speaking, both a tragic and a tragedic world view strongly tend towards despair, face a hardly bearable number of borders, limits, cracks, gaps and rifts, are much more impressed with the terrible cost of a resolution than with the resolution itself, and much more with the disruptive forces of evil and chaos than with the forces of justice and order.

In the *Mahābhārata*, the war tends towards total destruction, and so does time. But the contrasts between order and disorder, good and evil, gods and demons, are not black and white. The plots of the epic and the *Gītā* present a tragic world (view) within the wider perspective of a dramatic world view – a dramatic perspective that frames the tragic perspective without transforming it. The tragic and the dramatic perspectives are juxtaposed. By switching back from the ultimate to the final perspective, the plots uphold the oscillation. The oscillation consists of a shifting of two levels that are always there. But there is more to it, if the role of irony is taken into account.

4.2 Irony

Tragedy is impossible to imagine without *irony*, even though irony is not exclusively tragic. The sense of discrepancy in tragedy springs from the many occasions where speeches, coincidences or perspectives clash and hurt.

Among human characters, irony is likely to occur in situations of disguise, mistaken identity, intrigue and lying, that is to say, in cases where agents, speakers, listeners or victims are ignorant without realizing their ignorance; in the meantime, their counterpart exploits their ignorance and their audience knows. Rosenmeyer called this type of irony 'blind irony'. *Oedipus Tyrannus* and *Hamlet* illustrate this type. But, so does the *Odyssey*. The *Mahābhārata* epic too, contains a lot of blind irony. Heroes make vows that will later on turn against them. The Pāndavas live in disguise during the thirteenth year of their exile without being recognized by their enemies. Arjuna, by nature a male warrior, takes up the role of a transvestite and dance teacher. Karna is ignorant of his semi-divine origin as a son of the sun god, but strong when the sun rises and weak at night. King Dhrtarāstra is blind – a contradiction in terms. *Brahmins* live like warriors, and warriors behave like *brahmins*. Arjuna, the main warrior, refuses to fight, behaving like an ascetic *brahmin*. Deceit and trickery are abundant during the dice game and the war proper. These are all ironies on the human level and on the level of individual characters.

Apart from blind irony, Rosenmeyer's structural irony is also distinctively tragic, Lowe suggested. It is the plot and, thus, the circumstances that produce structural irony. Things do not develop according to expectations. Aristotelian reversals take place. Solutions create problems. Blindness becomes the source of sight (the seer Teiresias), and sight becomes the source of blindness (Oedipus). In the *Mahābhārata* plot pattern, for example, the scene in the *Gītā* is the reversal of the parallel Uttara scene in the Virāta in several respects – a reversal between the actor and agent, charioteer and warrior, eunuch and potent male. What seems like a playful rehearsal in the Virāta episode becomes serious in the *Gītā*'s plot. This ironic reversal or repetition is strikingly similar as a literary device to Hamlet's playful rehearsals of killing Claudius and his serious killing of Claudius in the end.

The most decisive source of (mainly structural) irony in epic and tragic literature, however, is the tension between the cosmic level of immortal gods, demons and fate, and the earthly level of mortal humans. This tension may also take the form of a discrepancy between the timeless and the temporal or between the real and the illusory. The bipartite cosmos of the *Iliad* has the gods intervene in the plot pattern of the Trojan war among humans on both sides. The bipartite cosmos of *Hamlet* has the world of the Ghost, eternal damnation and providence interfere in the world of the Danish royal court. In the *Mahābhārata*, while Śiva and Pārvatī play at dice on a mythic level, symbolizing the course of the world epochs on a cosmic scale, Śakuni and Duryodhana, Dvāpara and Kali incarnate, that is to say, personifications of the respective *yugas* in the form of demons, play dice on an epic level, symbolizing the course of the world epochs in a transitional microcosmic moment 'between the *yugas*', on a historical scale. The conflict between Pāndavas and Kauravas is simply an episode in the perennial battle of the gods and the demons for the control of heaven, temporarily shifted to the Earth. The dice game and the war illustrate a *bipartite cosmos*. But do they also constitute a source of *irony?* The parallelism between the mythic and the epic levels indicates correspondence. Does it also indicate discrepancy? It does, on the level of individual characters: Arjuna, son of the warrior god Indra, is suddenly inclined to pacifism on the battlefield. But the literary device of *framing* a story within another story is used in the epic to *juxtapose* a historical, tragic perspective, and a cosmic, dramatic perspective, rather than to *oppose* the two perspectives. Irony is not used here for purposes of bitterness. The final focus is on having passed beyond the stage of hostility by crossing the heavenly Ganges, the river of purification. There is not enough of an active ironic tension between the previous situation and the new perspective. The new perspective is not presented in any way that *confronts* the historical level of human affairs with the mythic level of cosmic affairs.

When it comes to *irony as an attitude to existence*, since the Romantic nineteenth century, it has become possible to think of irony in terms of a capacity to remain distant and different from what is said in general, to practise a self-conscious attitude of detachment, to abstain from commitment. And even as a detached attitude, it could be used for moral purposes (Socrates and Shakespeare's time) or for purposes of comic and aesthetic entertainment (modernism and postmodernism). In the *Gītā*, Krishna too, as his reply to Arjuna's prospect of committing a crime, calls for Arjuna's (yogic) stainlessness (in *Gītā* 4.30 and 6.27). Krishna too, teaches Arjuna a self-conscious attitude of detachment for moral purposes, for the sake of renewal of the cosmic order, not for lack of commitment, beliefs and ideals. Arjuna is summoned to take Lord Krishna's combination of yogic detachment and saving interventions in human history as a supreme example of the perfect attitude to existence. Taels reminded us of Kierkegaard's distinction between tragedy and comedy. While both tragedy and comedy recognize a contradictory relationship, the comic approach registers the hurtful contradiction, but also its mental (or speculative) escape, whereas the tragic approach registers the same hurtful contradiction but, seeing no way out, becomes desperate. Note the *Gītā*'s difference with Romantic irony, tragic and comic alike – *yogic* detachment does not register hurt in the same way as comic irony does; yogic detachment does not feel the hurt; it has been purified by meditation – by crossing the heavenly Ganges, the river of purification. Yet, one may ask, does Kierkegaard, in disqualifying Hegelianism as the mental or speculative escape of a typically comic world view, implicitly demonstrate a striking correspondence between Hegelianism and the *Gītā*'s world view? Does the *Gītā*, in Kierkegaard's terms, propagate a *comic* world view? Krishna's message is, after all, one of sticking to one's inner-worldly duty while escaping its consequences mentally and speculatively. Do Hindus respond to the world of suffering the way Hegelians do if held against the obscure light of Kierkegaard's concept of 'the tragic'? Hindu theology suggests some strong tendencies in this direction. It developed full-fledged theologies of 'divine play' connected with Shiva or Vishnu. The 'divine comedy' of Shiva or Vishnu is an inner-worldly affair. The world of creation is a product of the creative power of illusion, but God or Consciousness is beyond that manifestation of divine power. The serious world of illusion is framed within a comic world view, it seems. Total freedom of the Spirit, at last. Maybe,

Hegelians envisioned nothing different from that Hindu vision of the world. But this is highly unlikely, since the Hegelian project was never intended to accomplish a complete withdrawal from – in the sense of 'voluntarily letting go of' – the empirical world. Instead, it was intent on getting a superior grip on it, through violent conflict, active resistance, hard labour and forced self-transformation, based on the awareness of one's own greedy grasping and then realizing that one cannot hold on to it; of the ambition of the Master to be in control and then realizing that he cannot hold on to power, but is forced to recognize his dependence on his Slave's consent. This is not to suggest, however, that yogic aspirations themselves are always free from desire for power. In the epic, in fact, yogic self-discipline is depicted as generating the kind of cosmic power (*tapas*) that deserves to be rewarded with military boons, such as the acquisition of weapons. But this is not the way in which yogic detachment is depicted in the *Gītā*, despite the military context of its use. Its purpose is to be absolutely free from what has to be done.

3

Artistic–communicative aspects

PART I: GREEK AND SHAKESPEAREAN ISSUES

1 Introduction

The artistic–communicative aspects of tragedy are connected with the formal dimensions of tragedy as an art form. The artistic transformation of tragic stories into tragic drama raises the key question of whether the formal dimensions of tragic plays and their performances play a decisive role in bringing about a sense of tragedy. Is there something about their formal structure that is specifically tragic? Is it specific settings, characters and casting? Is it the effect of the art form on the mood of the audience? Or is it the audience response, the way in which the audience relates to the stories and the characters, which determines whether the audience is witnessing a real tragedy? Defining tragedy as a literary genre also distinguishes it from comedy, satyr play, melodrama – distinctions themselves drawn differently through the ages. The following sections will focus on three formal aspects in particular – the literary genre, the dialogues and the audience response.

2 A specific literary genre

The first artistic aspect to be dealt with is the question whether 'tragedy' can be defined in terms of a specific literary genre. Several approaches will be presented. Occasionally, I shall add my own position, opinion or comment, but my main aim is to enable the reader to have a balanced view of the issue at stake and of the ways in which it is being debated.

2.1 A dramatic genre

Historically speaking, the notion of 'the tragic' (*tragikos*) originally referred to the Greek art form of tragedy (*tragikē technē*). The first users of the term, therefore, were Greek spectators attending theatre plays and judging them within the institutional setting of an open competition. The notion was used to point out the formal characteristics of this genre of drama. That is to say, the 'tragic' character of tragedies was first of all a matter of form. It encompassed elements such as a chorus, a few actors, narrative song, including songs of lamentation, dance, dialogue, stage acting, and a certain unity of plot time, action and place, due to the constant presence of the chorus.[1] The primal meaning of the word 'tragic' is 'tragedic' – that which relates to tragedy as a theatrical institution. The genre started as a fifth century BCE art form in Athens. From the fourth century BCE onwards, it spread throughout the Mediterranean. Its decontextualization from Athens lead to substantial transformations in its form, content and function, but within the Greek and Latin speaking world of Hellenism, people continued to identify certain stories and their stage performances as belonging to the genre of 'tragedy'.[2]

A second wave of plays called 'tragedies' by contemporaries is to be found in the sixteenth and seventeenth centuries of West-European Renaissance, and above all, in the Elizabethan England of Shakespeare. The fact that the Elizabethan plays are also called 'tragedies' raises an important theoretical issue – should we limit the category of 'the tragic' to its contemporary fifth century BCE use as referring to those plays which, for whatever reasons, the ancient Greeks happened to call 'tragedies', because that is how they called them? This is A. Maria van Erp Taalman Kip's position.[3] What Van Erp Taalman Kip cannot, in my opinion, convincingly exclude from her effort to concentrate on the sheer facts is the fact that the use of categories such as 'the tragic' proved useful not just to the fifth-century contemporary users, but also to the Hellenistic heirs to this tradition, who not only changed the meaning of the term, but also recognized its inherited meaning. Apparently, 'the tragic' referred to a fifth-century genre of drama which could be recognized as such, put on stage, create certain expectations with the audience, and on the basis of that be varied upon in order to surprise the audience by fulfilling their expectations differently from what conventions would have predicted. Play-going is different from ritual in the sense that play-going presupposes the performance to be excitingly different from one's conventional expectations. The play-goer expects to be surprised. The phenomenon of 'genres' is based on the pre-philosophical capacity to recognize certain patterns to be different from other ones and to adjust one's expectations accordingly, but also, to be pleasantly surprised if the genre is given shape differently. Or, unpleasantly surprised, for that matter, because plays can still be recognized as 'bad plays' or as 'bad examples' of the genre in case. The responses of the audience are the responses of an informed audience, an audience informed about the repertoire of forms and contents. The tragic genre can have its conventional shape and character changed within the limits of what people can still recognize.[4]

In one respect, Greek tragedy is worlds apart from Shakespearean tragedy – Greek tragedy was performed under the sign of Dionysus, the god of the drama that took place during the Great Dionysia festival at Athens. After the performance, the masks were dedicated to the god. The most obviously Dionysiac element, P. E. Easterling points out, was the satyr play, satyrs being part of the god's entourage.[5] The satyr play was performed by the same chorus and actors as the three preceding tragedies. It was connected to the worship of Dionysus, who presided over the dramatic festival. Dionysus was both the chorus leader (leader of the dance) and the divine spectator for whom the shows were put on. The Greek gods in general, and Dionysus in particular, were engaged in musical and theatrical performance, as Steven H. Lonsdale argues.[6] The gods were not just honoured by organizing a festival around a principal rite, be it a choral performance, a procession, a contest or a sacrifice. They were also persuaded to attend the festival, to be pleased by the performance of their worshippers and to take delight in the spectacle as spectators. Greek religious festivals typically display this temporary rapprochement between humans and gods who engage in giving pleasure and taking pleasure in festival dancing. This is very similar to the younger generation dancing and the older generation watching and feeling rejuvenated.[7] Examining the Delian festival for Apollo, Lonsdale underscores the Greek emphasis on the visual component of the spectacle. He suggests that 'the pleasure in viewing presupposes a critical judgment concerning composition and performance', not just on the part of the human audience, but also on the part of the gods. Judging the performance is both a human and a godly affair. 'The divine pleasure is shared by and reflected in the glow of the human spectators', Lonsdale suggests. He then highlights the Greek criterion of ideal human judgement by pointing out that the ideal judge is *talapeiros*, 'one who has much experience of suffering'. 'Ideally, a performance should console and compensate for mortal suffering by providing, through music and dance, a temporary antidote to death and a defense against old age', Lonsdale explains.[8]

2.2 *Tragedy versus comedy*

Different cultures generate different patterns of composition, expectation, and recognition, of course, and the main distinction in dramatic genres that classical Greek culture upheld was the distinction between 'tragedy' and 'comedy'.[9] Right from the beginning, however, this effort to identify what is 'tragic' about tragedy inevitably went beyond a form definition to include references to their respective contents and to the audience's response.

Crucial to Aristotle's distinction between tragedy and comedy are the attitude and response of the spectators. The attitude is evoked by the poet's capacity to create expectations with regard to the (im)moral quality of the action's results. According to James M. Redfield, comedy and tragedy, in Aristotle's approach,

> imply the same ethical standards. But they differ in their expectations of achievement. The poet of comedy established a pervasive expectation that his characters will behave badly, the poet of tragedy that his characters will behave well. Each presumes the descriptive norm of his culture, but in a reduced form. . . . In comedy we are surprised by virtue and success, in tragedy by vice and failure.[10]

Redfield's *emic* (insider's) perspective is very helpful in grasping the gap between Aristotle's approach to comedy and tragedy from within classical Greek culture, and Henri Gouhier's approach to comedy from within modern Western culture. According to Gouhier, in the case of comedy, laughing comes from the idea that *I* am superior to them.[11] Aristotle presumes the 'objective' norm (public, social expectations) of his culture, whereas Gouhier presumes the 'subjective' norm (private, individual convictions) of his culture. A postmodern approach is offered by Northrop Frye, who presumes the 'intersubjective' and 'contingent' norm (comedy as a playful agreement to limit and transgress the field of possibilities, and tragedy as an almost accidental loss of freedom) of his culture.[12] Tragedy is linked to necessity (or loss of freedom) and is therefore serious, while comedy is linked to contingency and is therefore funny. Falling by accident is funny, not tragic, because it is contingent.

Regarding the usual distinction between generic categories such as 'comedy' and 'tragedy', Shakespeare's work poses several problems. First of all, in the case of Shakespeare's plays, besides 'comedy' and 'tragedy', a new category, solely based on the content of the plays, emerges – 'history'. In fact, the very category of 'history' seems to have been introduced because of Shakespeare's success in staging historical topics.[13] Secondly, different editors use different ways of applying these three categories. The Quarto edition of

Hamlet calls it a 'tragedical history' whereas the first Folio edition calls it a 'tragedy'. Nineteenth-century critics will add a fourth category – 'romance', applicable to Shakespeare's last plays, except that in Shakespeare's own time, this popular mixed genre would have been considered 'tragicomedy'. This genre was vehemently rejected by Sir Philip Sidney, an Elizabethan courtier and literary critic, for violating the decorum that separates plays featuring kings (tragedies) from plays featuring clowns (comedies). Twentieth-century critics will add yet another category, that of 'problem play', also applicable to *Hamlet*.[14] Lastly, Shakespeare himself was well aware of the genre distinctions that were in use, but also of their fluidity and arbitrariness. On the one hand, Lawrence Danson suggests, he 'would also have read Donatus' fourth-century treatise on comedy when he was learning Latin in his Stratford grammar school'. In this treatise, comedy represents a didactic form of teaching an audience by example, that is to say, by imitating types like 'the young lover' or 'the bragging soldier', not by focusing on individual characters. Roman and Elizabethan tragedies, by contrast, are expected to be centred around distinct individuals.[15] On the other hand, Shakespeare explicitly ridiculed the genre distinctions when he had Polonius proclaim, 'The best actors in the world, either for tragedy, comedy, history, pastoral, pastoral-comical, historical-pastoral, tragical-historical, tragical-comical-historical-pastoral' (II.ii.395–8).[16] And he did not obey Sir Philip Sidney's classical style rules. By allowing clownish characters to feature prominently in tragedies (the Fool in *King Lear*, the Gravedigger in *Hamlet*), he broke not only the classical genre conventions, but also the social conventions of keeping 'high culture' separate from 'low culture'.[17]

3 Specific dialogues

There is one formal aspect of Greek tragedy as an art form that is supposed to have both a political function and an educational (didactic) function – its dialogical character. Dialogue on stage symbolizes public debate, rational, moral, and political criticism, consensus building and democracy. At least, that is what it has come to represent to a Western mind that perceives classical Greek culture as the cradle of democracy and secular philosophy.

From a cross-cultural, comparative perspective, however, it is not self-evident that these qualities should automatically be attributed to its formal dialogical character. Dialogue is not, by definition, a democratic and rational form of communication – unless it is defined as such by a specific context. Ancient Greek tragic dialogue symbolizes these qualities because tragic dialogue is performed on stage and in a political context. *Dialogue is a contest*.

Dialogue is a power struggle between dominant males who should allow healthy conflict to flourish, according to the democratic chorus in Sophocles' *Oedipus Tyrannus* (880–1), while rejecting the arrogant tyrant's silencing of his opponents (873). Also, dialogue has become part of an art form instead of part of a ritual recitation. It has lost the religious authority of divine inspiration, Redfield points out.[18] Tragic poets are awarded prizes in staged contests. For Homer and Hesiod, the power of the word had been a magic power; for the Sophists, it had become rhetorical power. Like rhetoric, poetry became increasingly technical and associated with competition before a panel of judges. But, Redfield argues, 'poetry never became rhetoric. For one thing, poetry maintained some distance from everyday life—comedy through fantasy, tragedy through the heroic world inherited from Homer'.[19] A secularization of the poet's authority brought about the loss of his standing of prophet and the acquisition of his standing of teacher – except that the narrative poet does not explain and instruct, but shows and affects his audience.[20] I agree, but would like to recall Lonsdale's point that judging the performance was both a human and a godly affair. The context was still that of religious festivals attended by the gods as spectators.

Although Redfield takes care not to throw rhetoric and tragic poetry together, he rightly points out their common roots in the historical context of Athenian democratic procedures. As does Hall, when she emphasizes 'the multivocal form of tragedy, which allows diverse characters to speak (and, more importantly, to disagree with each other)'.[21]

The most expressly *didactic* voice of a play was the authoritative collective voice of the chorus, surrounded with other dissenting voices but, according to Goldhill, itself also one particular voice among other voices.[22] Rhetoric and tragic poetry not only share the same historical roots, tragic dialogue, in fact, critically explores the language of rhetoric used in the socio-political arena of public debate, he argues. The power of persuasion on which democracy depends is highly ambiguous, tragedy suggests.[23]

The dialogical structure of Sophocles' *Antigone* has been analysed by Groot. As we have seen in detail earlier,[24] his analysis shows that the crucial third episode reveals a *failed dialogue*. How does Creon respond to Haimon's efforts to persuade his father? At first, Creon is willing to listen. But Haimon makes a tactical mistake by referring to Antigone's support by the people – a small, but fatal mistake (*hamartia*) because Creon, who was about to be persuaded, slides back into his previous position. And yet, Philippe Van Haute argues, there is one figure in the play who actually changes thanks to a successful dialogue, and he is, the only one – Creon. At the end, Creon takes Teiresias' intervention seriously, recognizes his failure and assumes his responsibility.[25] The dialogue between Teiresias and Creon is tragic because it comes too late, but it is successful because it brings out human greatness, Van Haute concludes. Greek contemporaries would not have agreed; they would have seen human failure recognized.

The dialogical character of *Oedipus Tyrannus* has been discussed by Burian.[26] Greek tragedy is essentially a drama of words, Burian states. Characters enter, talk with each other, exit. Very little 'happens' on stage – no battles and no blindings, as in Shakespeare. Tragic discourse is still responsive to a notion of the ominous quality of language itself:

> The power of such words is not easily controlled, and it should come as no surprise that their effects are often diametrically opposed to what the speaker intended or the hearer understood. A familiar case is Oedipus' curse on the slayer of Laius, who turns out to be himself (*Oedipus Tyrannus* 222–75). Even more arresting is the succession of speech-acts that produce the *peripeteia* of *Oedipus the King*: for Oedipus' downfall is constituted not by deeds, the killing of the father or wedding of the mother (outside the drama, as Aristotle would say), or even the self-blinding (after the fact and off stage), but by a dialogue sequence that puts special emphasis on the code of communication.[27]

Discourse, verbal interaction, is the essential action, not merely reference to or representation of the action. 'The issues of tragedy . . . are enacted through speech-acts', Burian concludes.[28]

Greek dialogues were masked dialogues. In the ritualistic contexts of traditional societies, masks do not hide the inner voice from external speech-acts, but reveal the persons ritually represented by the masks. In the theatrical contexts of modern societies, masks play hide-and-seek with the other characters on stage and with the audience, hiding the persons and their intentions behind the masks. Historically, there has been an institutional shift worldwide from ritual to theatre,[29] from representative enactment to fake role-playing, but this is not to be confused with a shift from serious drama to entertaining play. In the ancient Greek case, tragedy was considered serious drama, and as such, it was closer to the traditional ritualistic contexts, whereas comedy was playful entertainment and was closer to modern theatrical contexts. Both made use of masks. The use of masks did not itself constitute revelation or disguise. Tragic heroes such as Orestes were fully capable of disguising their intentions, hiding them from other characters – not behind masks, but behind words.

Shakespearean tragic dialogue too, is performed on stage, and in a politically sensitive context. The audience may be royal or common. The dialogues may be staged as public or private contests. But their political function seems less prominent than their cultural function of articulating a 'clash of civilizations'. There is a contest between competing cultural and religious ideologies and a 'clash of characters', which is a contest between competing social and psychological identities. Culturally, one is expected to be contradicted, but there are no clear winners.[30]

Does the play *Hamlet* have a dialogical character? For a start, one aspect of the play is certain to be intertwined with it – the importance of theatricality to the play's forms of communication.[31] The court is supposed to display order, the king is presumed to distribute grace, and the courtiers are expected to display rhetorical graciousness, playing their respective roles on the royal stage, as Jorge Arditi will explain elsewhere.[32] David Margolies points out that King Claudius

> conveys order in his rhetoric. His balanced phrases, alliteration, end-stopped lines and contrived oxymorons resolve contradictions into a sense of higher unity, as when he says Denmark is 'contracted in one brow of woe'. . . . It is Hamlet, rather than the Ghost or Claudius, who appears as the disruptive element. . . . His replies to Claudius and Gertrude are strikingly brief, one-liners that constitute a stylistic disruption, a rudeness in the midst of rhetorical graciousness comparable to Cordelia's 'nothing'.[33]

Hamlet invalidates the court rhetoric and destabilizes the spoken text by altering its context. The royal court betrays a constant 'slippage between form and content', and a 'naturalization of corruption' and complacency. This is embodied by the otherwise insignificant courtier Osric. He lacks individualizing traits, but he is Laertes's accomplice in plotting Hamlet's poisoning. Behind his meaningless language, he is murderous, Margolies argues. 'The problem is not that he uses language to *disguise* his meaning . . . but that the slippage of meaning allows him to *escape* personal responsibility'.[34] Hamlet's verbal virtuosity parries Osric's hollow language, but his verbal victory is of no avail. The reality has changed, but the language has not, Margolies concludes. I fully agree, but would add to his last point that, in my opinion, Hamlet rehearses his verbal duelling skills against Osric in anticipation of his physical ones against Laertes, certain of his victory (V.ii.203f.).

The importance of theatrical performance is also felt when a dialogue is spied upon. A dialogue spied upon is a dialogue on stage, according to Anthony Brennan:

> Whenever Hamlet for a moment thinks he can drop his mask and open his heart he discovers that he is on stage with another spy in an undeclared play within the play. . . . The Prince's ideas on acting are not simply a

matter of taste, they are critically related to his situation. To survive the spies Claudius rains on him he has to be acute in detecting a bad performance.[35]

In terms of roles and the conversations that go with them, Prince Hamlet is many things to many people. Many of his dialogues are highly rhetorical. His conversations with Horatio are among the rare exceptions, but these can hardly be called dialogues, since Horatio fulfils the roles of 'listener' and 'recorder'. What *Hamlet* is really famous for is Hamlet's soliloquies, his monologues. Or rather, his *inner dialogues* with himself.

However, these soliloquies do not address his presumed true inner self in a fully dialogical sense of the word. Hamlet never asks the main question 'Who am I'? Instead, they explore the self and, in doing so, constitute self-images that create a story that should establish the continuity of a stable self, but fail to do so, according to John Lee.[36] The tragedy is that these efforts at self-exploration never achieve the stability and certainty of a solid picture of that self. Hamlet's attempts to capture himself show, in their repetitiveness, his frustration at his inability to pin down his self. Each renewed effort demonstrates his failure to establish an inner dialogue with his presumed true self. All he knows is that he is not what people hold him to be.

But even the 'inner dialogues' testify to the dialogical character of the play, according to Anthony Gash. The dialogical character of *Hamlet* is related both to Hamlet's mirroring of other persons' ways of communicating with him and to the presence of an audience during the performance of the play.[37] Hamlet's self-conscious dialogue with third-person conceptions of himself, in questions like 'Am I a coward'? [II.ii.568], gives voice not merely to his own responses, but to the audience's hypothetical responses to him.[38] In many of the mirroring dialogues, Hamlet plays the Socratic role of questioner, even though his interlocutor tries to retain it for himself. The reversal of the roles of questioner and respondent that occurs in almost all of the Hamlet dialogues, including those with Rosencrantz and Guildenstern, Polonius, and Hamlet's mother, depends on Hamlet's refusal to identify with the 'you' whom the requests and concealed threats imply. By answering with an inappropriate logicality, Hamlet thus strikes a blow at a picture of language as primarily logical or referential, Lash argues.[39] The pattern in such dialogues is the disclosure of a verbal ambiguity where none seemed possible, the refusal to be identified as this or that, and finally the reversal by which the questioner becomes the implicit subject of the conversation. Gash points out that Hamlet's feigned madness ('antic disposition') is to be equated with that other kind of feigned madness, the Socratic idiom of philosophical fooling. The Socratic fool has no wisdom prior to his dialogue with another person, and functions only as a mirror to the partner in dialogue.[40] The improvisatory quality of Hamlet's dialogues and the interactive quality of Socrates' philosophical fooling have in common a discourse that is less oriented towards a self that it might express or a reality that it might represent than towards another person as a person to whom we are responsible. But in the shameless world of Elsinore politics, relations have become instrumental and have been reduced to subject–object relations. *Genuine dialogues* are doomed to fail or are simply absent, except for some extraordinary, other-worldly exceptions.[41]

Whereas epic depicts heroes who have battle comrades as friends, tragedy depicts heroes as *lonesome*. Greek tragedies like Sophocles' *Antigone* show tragic heroes engaged in failing dialogues, instead of epic heroes engaged in riddle-solving dialogues. Sophocles' *Oedipus Tyrannus* shows a hero who starts out as a dialogically open person, but whose riddle-solving dialogues turn him into a lonesome figure, who will be lamented by a sympathetic chorus as his collective audience, who will be left behind when his wife and mother commits suicide, and who will voluntarily mutilate himself out of shame, physically and psychologically isolating himself for ever. His riddle-solving dialogues turn out to be failed dialogues. And failed dialogues imply nothing less than failed lives, failed communities and failed states. H. J. Heering observes that tragedy is always a lonesome adventure, even though its components, 'freedom' and 'constraint', are not.[42] Freedom and constraint presume a relationship. Tragic adventure loses touch and does not find its way back to the relationship. Sophocles' Antigone suffers from a lonesomeness, which still knows a secret that breaks open the isolation. 'I was born not to share in hatred [*sun-ekthein*], but in "nearness and dearness" [*sum-philein*]'. (*Antigone* 523) There is alliance, connection in that secret. This is what Hamlet lacks. The secret task of the Ghost's appearance makes him distrust every friendship, makes the love-access to Ophelia impossible, makes every prayer a monologue. Nowhere can he speak his mind, pour out his heart, share his feelings. According to Sartre, therefore, he should be considered the perfectly free man, but his insecurity betrays a different man. The problem of lonesomeness is already there in Oedipus, who could have seized the opportunities of his dialogues with his mother and wife, and with the seer Teiresias, to reach a deeper mutual understanding, but whose blindness turned each conversation into a monologue, each appeal to the gods into self-justification. The tragic adventure lacks dialogical openness, cuts off contacts, blocks entries, refuses gifts. It is tragic, Heering suggests, and symbolic of Hamlet's unanswered lonesomeness as a human being and decision-maker, that his last request to his friend Horatio was to tell his story on his behalf.[43]

4 A specific audience response

How does define the 'tragic effect' of tragedy? Does tragedy bring about a specific 'tragic experience'? Does a specific audience response exist, which goes with watching or witnessing a tragedy?

4.1 Audience response defining the tragic genre

For Richard H. Palmer, the audience response is the best methodological access to achieve a sustainable definition of tragedy. Reviewing all the major theories of tragedy, especially those from the nineteenth and twentieth centuries, Palmer then presents his own, embracing definition, 'Tragedy is a dramatic form that stimulates a response of intense, interdependent, and inseparably balanced attraction and repulsion'.[44] This definition does not define Greek tragedy, but Western tragedy in general. It does not do so by referring to contents and specific plot patterns, to a tragic world view, or to the status of human action and responsibility, but by referring to more formal aspects, such as the ability to arouse intense emotions and to keep a constant balance between attraction and repulsion.[45] As to the comparison of the tragic and the epic genres, a difference in scope tends to separate the two genres. The emotional needs of an audience demand the restricted scope of tragedy. The more expansive epic form dissipates the constant connection between stimuli for attraction and stimuli for repulsion.[46]

Palmer's approach is very valuable but, from my perspective, fairly monocausal as well if the audience response is the only factor providing the criterion for a definition of tragedy. I agree that the tragic effect brings about an ambivalent response, characterized by a balance between attraction and repulsion. It is not possible, however, to reverse the argument the way Palmer does, and argue that the very balance between attraction and repulsion among the audience provides sufficient ground to infer that the play in question is a tragedy. In that case, horror stories and horror films would be tragedies by definition.[47] Also, some comedies would equally qualify as tragedies, except that, in those cases, the audience would feel repelled by less awesome things, like the pretentiousness or incompetence of the main characters, and would feel attracted either by their surprising success or by its own sense of superiority, while being in a constant balance between attraction and repulsion. Apart from that, is the constant balance between attraction and repulsion itself an expression of imbalanced excitement or of emotional equilibrium?

4.2 *Catharsis*

What specific audience response is a tragic drama supposed to arouse? (1) Is a tragic play expected to morally and didactically instruct the audience by example or counter-example to curb their own emotions? (2) Is it expected to intellectually clarify their confusing dilemmas and states of mind? (3) Is it supposed to therapeutically relieve their excessive emotional stress or to ritually purify their emotional life from unbalancing passions, thus restoring emotional equilibrium? (4) Is it to socio-psychologically sympathize with fellow human beings? (5) Or is it supposed to homeopathically fortify and immunize their souls against misfortune by having them exposed to the greater sufferings of others? All these five options, and variations on them, have been ways of interpreting Aristotle's notion of *catharsis*, according to Stephen Halliwell.[48] What is at stake when involving Aristotle's notion of *catharsis*?

There has been a lot of controversy on the exact stance Plato and Aristotle have taken in the philosophical debate on the moral and epistemic role of the emotions in tragedy. Is tragedy to be avoided for relying too much on creating illusions and appealing too much to irrational emotions, as Plato has it, or does an audience learn from watching tragedies, as Aristotle suggests? How powerful are the rhetorical and moral roles of language and the senses? Is the tragic audience response caused by affective effects or by cognitive effects, or by both? If so, how do emotions and reason relate?[49]

Broadly speaking, Aristotle argues that tragedy has a didactic function. By showing what human beings are like, in general, tragedy teaches the audience what humans can be like if they (fail to) become fully human, that is to say, virtuous, but also socially and politically active, not just isolated individuals. Tragedies such as *Oedipus Tyrannus* show that isolated individuals are doomed to lack happiness. Tragedies are persuasive because they appeal to emotions in ways much more powerful than pedagogical lessons. The best tragedies bring about a change of attitude in the audience, a change of hearts and minds that culminates in *catharsis*, the last stage in the learning process. On the intellectual level, the audience comes to understand what they are like; on the emotional level, their pity and fear are cleansed.

In Martha Nussbaum's opinion, the role tragedy assigns to emotions is one crucial reason for Aristotle's ethical appreciation of tragedy. The two tragic emotions of pity and fear are a direct source of genuine learning. As feelings, pity and fear are themselves forms of growing understanding, reliable sources of 'clarification' (*katharsis*).[50]

Segal admits that for Aristotle, 'the emotions also have a cognitive basis and so presumably can be "identified" by intellectual processes' of recognition and learning, but in the case of *catharsis*, 'the intellectual function does not seem to be uppermost'.[51] What Aristotle seems to refer to is the audience's emotional response of cleansing release, as manifested in the 'shudder' of fear, in the 'weeping' of protagonists and choruses alike, and in the 'common grief' among 'all the citizens' (*Hippolytus* 1462). 'Aristotle's *catharsis*, which his *Poetics* seems to envisage as a primarily individual response', should therefore, Segal suggests, be extended 'to this public participation in the release of emotion in the theatre',[52] characterized by 'the sharing of tears and suffering', which 'creates a bond of common humanity between mortals. This is the bond that the two bitter enemies Priam and Achilles discover at the end of the *Iliad* (24.507–17)'.[53] Such emotional participation enlarges our sympathies and thus our humanity.[54]

Margolies points out that the audience of tragedies is cued right from the beginning by one of the essential principles of tragedy – the principle of necessity. The conclusion of a tragic process of events is felt to result necessarily from the conditions that preceded it. Margolies, then, defines *catharsis* as the resolving of 'the tension between aversion and recognition of necessity', and as the result of the acceptance of inevitable disaster (necessity).[55] Palmer's way of defining tragedy comes to mind; however, Margolies does not just focus on the sustained ambiguity of the tension – he focuses on its cathartic resolution.

Margolies gives the example of *Hamlet* to illustrate his point. The audience knows that the corrupt court at Elsinore and the refusal of Hamlet to join its dirty games puts both parties on an inevitable collision course. Faced with the inevitability of a disastrous outcome, the audience must accept it and recognize necessity. The ambiguity of the tension is sustained until the disaster actually occurs. The disaster itself resolves the tension because it constitutes the completion of the process leading up to it. 'In that sense the completion of the process is *formally* pleasurable, even though its content is unpleasant', Margolies observes.[56]

Bert O. States would agree wholeheartedly, but not for the same reason. Since States is more concerned with the continuity of 'character', he offers a slightly different perspective. The lives of real characters differ from the lives of the characters on stage. In the artistic setting of a constructed plot pattern, dramatic lives unfold in a closed field; dramatic characters are therefore more likely to come to a conclusion, to culminate in some form of completion, to arrive at something, to actually become what they are, to coincide with their character, to lead lives in accordance with their personal nature. Watching them coincide brings about a *catharsis* in the audience, who lack this perfect completion. The character 'is offered an opportunity by fate to become himself in essence'.[57]

Michael Ewans' suggestion that a tragic story often shows a pattern of disorder rectified, but at terrible cost, brings to mind Robert N. Watson's understanding of the function of Aristotle's *catharsis* – to restore equilibrium.[58]

If ambition is a doomed effort to rise above a position of equality, and if revenge is a doomed effort to restore equality, a Shakespearean revenge tragedy does not only rectify, through revenge, the disorder brought about by the release of evil; it also rectifies, through the coincidence of revenge succeeding and failing simultaneously, the disorder brought about by the release of revenge.

Segal places *catharsis* in the context of the ritual closure of tragedy within the plays themselves. Ritual-like actions in scenes of formal lament and burial that often end Greek tragedies (including the *Iliad*) are emotionally powerful means of bringing about a sense of (Aristotelian) 'purification' from strong and dangerous theatrical emotions, of order restored and of communal solidarity.[59] In *Oedipus Tyrannus*, Oedipus 'not only completes the movement towards ritual purification but also attends to the detail of burying Jocasta's body (1446–8)'.[60] The end seems all the more disturbing if the expected closing ritual is withheld or postponed, as in *Antigone* (1257), when Creon enters with the polluting dead body of his son Haimon at the end of a play that started out with Creon's very refusal to allow funeral rites.[61]

Segal's suggestion of a link between *catharsis* and ritual closure (speeches, weeping and ritual burial of bodies) is also very much applicable to *Hamlet*'s final scene. Fortinbras allows the body of Hamlet to be buried as a soldier with military honour:

> Let four captains
> Bear Hamlet like a soldier to the stage.
> For he was likely, had he been put on,
> To have proved most royal. And for his passage
> The soldiers' music and the rites of war
> Speak loudly for him.
> Take up the bodies. Such a sight as this
> Becomes the field, but here shows much amiss.
> Go, bid the soldiers shoot.
> [V.ii.390–7][62]

Easterling appreciates Segal's definition of *catharsis* in terms of 'cleansing release', and also his suggestion that it should be associated with tragedy's use of ritual action.[63] She suggests an alternative model to that of the ritual sharing of tears – the idea of the witnessing role of the audience, of the community taking cognizance of what the characters do and suffer. She too, gives an example from *Oedipus Tyrannus*:

> It comes immediately after the climactic moment when Oedipus discovers his identity, and the chorus respond with 'Alas, generations of men, I

count your life as equal to nothing' (1186–8). Having witnessed what has happened to their king ('With your fate as my example, *yours*, unhappy Oedipus, I call nothing that is mortal blessed', 1193–6), the men of Thebes reach a new understanding of human nothingness as well as of human achievement: if these disasters could happen to Oedipus, of all people, they can happen to anyone.[64]

Such directions and appeals cue the audience response, and 'it is worth noting that this guidance is given in intellectual as well as emotional terms', Easterling underlines.[65]

For the witnessing role of the audience in *Hamlet*, one may turn to Horatio, who has been listening to Hamlet's comments all along and is finally asked by Hamlet to tell his story to the audience. As the prime and privileged listener to Hamlet's story, he is qualified to represent the audience in much the same way the chorus plays this role in Greek tragedies. Horatio is all the more credible since he is, as Easterling would put it, 'the prime witness of the tragic events', and in principle, confronted with the Ghost, a sceptical witness at that. The very last scene of the play, where Fortinbras finds Horatio amidst the dead bodies of the protagonists, is indeed telling. Harry Levin's brief remark should suffice, 'Pity and fear are the usual tragic components; but here, while Fortinbras surveys the damage, Horatio bespeaks the emotions of "woe or wonder" (V.ii.374 [357]). The play has kept us guessing; it leaves us wondering'.[66] This appeal to wonder cues the audience response.

It may sound odd that tragedy and Aristotle's notion of *catharsis* should ever have been interpreted in terms of the first option mentioned by Halliwell – to morally and didactically instruct the audience by example or counter-example to curb their own emotions. But this was the neo-classical view of tragedy and *catharsis*, and therefore, a leading view in *Shakespeare*'s time, together with the 'loosely stoical' view, in the Renaissance, of tragedy fortifying the soul against the fickleness of fortune (fourth option), Halliwell explains.[67] Elizabethan contemporaries would have been inclined to reduce the mirroring function of art to that of moral mirroring, and this is probably how plays were perceived by the audience at the time.

Shakespeare, however, *plays* with the moral mirroring function of plays, in the case of *Hamlet* by turning it into a play-within-the-play while having Hamlet say:

I have heard
That guilty creatures sitting at a play
Have by the very cunning of the scene

Been struck so to the soul that presently
They have proclaimed their malefactions.
[II.ii.586–90][68]

Within *Hamlet*, the Player's Speech (II.ii.450–516) functions as a moral mirror, but it is also itself an anticipatory mirror to the crucial play-within-the-play 'Murder of Gonzago', which Hamlet calls 'The Mousetrap' (III.ii.247) and which exposes Claudius as the murderer of Hamlet's father.[69] Levin writes, 'The art of painting, almost as frequently as the art of drama, is Hamlet's analogy for the hypocrisies of the court, the discrepancies between appearance and reality'.[70]

We are only one step removed from the initial philosophical debate on the moral and epistemological role of the emotions in tragedy, on the affective and cognitive effects cueing the audience response. The issue at stake in the classical Greek debate is now itself being staged by Shakespeare. On the emotional level, the simulating power of playing may or may not stimulate the corresponding passionate action and moral conversion. On the intellectual level, the simulating power of playing may or may not lead to existential recognition, learning and basic human understanding. Also, the two levels interfere with each other. In the 'Mousetrap' mirror, guilty creatures sitting at a play suffer existential recognition, being cued to instantly display a self-betraying form of behaviour. But does witnessing a play automatically lead to a recognition that incites action? A full understanding of the tragic implications may, instead of clearing the way for action, dramatically turn against it, as Gash notices in his comments on 'Pyrrhus' pause':

For lo! his sword,
Which was declining on the milky head
Of reverend Priam, seemed i'th'air to stick.
So as a painted tyrant Pyrrhus stood,
And like a neutral to his will and matter
Did nothing.
[II.ii.475–80][71]

The player not only re-enacts the killing of Priam, but intervenes in it, Gash argues, by breaking the chain of cause and effect which binds 'will' (motive) to 'matter' (physical action). Here, acting demonstrates the value of inaction, or, at any rate, of the contemplative distancing from action. The player thereby sheds a different light on Hamlet's own hesitation to act. Hamlet does not hesitate out of psychological or moral weakness. He makes one realize that 'understanding kills action, for in order to act we require the veil of illusion', and 'the player lifts the veil of illusion', Gash suggests.[72]

5 Conclusions

Tragedy, as an art form, has formal dimensions that highlight the artistic–communicative aspects of tragedy. The key question is whether these formal dimensions of tragic plays and their performances play a decisive role in bringing about a sense of tragedy.

The 'tragic' character of tragedies has to be recognized as such by an informed audience. The audience has certain expectations about the conventions of the genre, about the formal ways in which a specific repertoire will be put on stage. Greek tragedy encompassed elements such as a chorus, a few actors, narrative songs (including songs of lamentation), dance, dialogue, stage acting and a certain unity of plot time, action and place, due to the constant presence of the chorus. Greek and Shakespearean tragic language, Silk pointed out, tend to emphasize a specific vocabulary, that of 'must', 'too' and 'name', that is to say, of compulsion, excess and identity.

A literary or dramatic genre is expected to surprise the audience within the limits of what the audience can recognize at a particular moment in time. This implies that generic conventions have the potential to change over time. The Greeks and Romans recognized tragedy as a specific genre and distinguished it from comedy and the satyr play. According to Aristotle, in comedy, the audience is surprised by the virtues and successes of bad characters, in tragedy by the vices and failures of good characters. The English too, recognized tragedy as a specific genre and distinguished it from comedy. They did not distinguish it from the 'satyr play' but from 'history', a new genre, probably introduced as a category due to the popularity of Shakespeare's 'histories'. Shakespeare makes fun of current generic distinctions when he has Polonius enumerate a ridiculous list of supposedly different genres. (*Hamlet* II.ii.395–8) Shakespeare uses the generic distinctions of his time freely and playfully. He does not respect the neo-classical rule that tragedy should stick to 'majestical matters' and comedy to 'clownish matters', but he seems to follow Donatus' rule that tragedies are centred around distinctive individuals whereas comedies contain character types, as Danson argued.

In order to evoke a sense of tragedy, the audience should not just be enabled to cognitively recognize the formal generic conventions, it should be moved by them. In fact, according to Palmer, the audience should be moved in a specifically 'tragic' way by stimulating an emotionally intense response of constantly balanced attraction and repulsion. I argued that this typically 'tragic' audience response is not exclusively 'tragic' since it is also aroused by horror movies. Margolies defined *catharsis* as the resolving of the tension between aversion and recognition of necessity, and as the result of the acceptance of inevitable disaster (necessity).

Is the tragic audience response caused by cognitive effects or by affective effects or by both? Aristotle's notion of *catharsis* has been at the centre of the many debates on this issue. At stake are the educational function of art and the classical discussion of the relationship between rational and emotional ways of acquiring valid knowledge. The weeping of the chorus or the lament of a major player on stage may cue the intended audience response of emotional sympathy with fellow human beings and of a deepened cognitive understanding of human nature. The ritual closure may bring about *catharsis* in the sense of restoration of equilibrium as a collective experience, both within the plays and among the audience, but such a satisfying closure can be withheld or suspended, Segal observed. The witnessing role of the audience is both an emotional and a cognitive affair, Easterling argued.

Elizabethans were convinced of the educational function of tragedies. A theatre play was considered a moral mirror held up to the audience. Shakespeare's *Hamlet* displays the hypocrisies of the court and the moral corruptibility of human nature and action. But Shakespeare plays with this mirroring function of playing on stage by having his characters both enact their acts as forms of acting and simultaneously question the effects of acting. There is a Shakespearean sense of tragedy about the discrepancy between acting and actions which is, after all, symbolic of the discrepancy between art and reality, Levin suggested.

The dialogues constitute an artistic–communicative aspect that is connected with the educational and political functions of Greek tragedy. Greek tragic dialogue is performed on stage, as a public contest, and in a political context. Dialogue is a power contest between dominant males, and staged in a democratically competitive and rhetorical context. Its poetry is associated with competition before a panel of judges or fellow voters. The poet has no religious authority. His secularized authority is that of an artist and a teacher who articulates the issues that preoccupy Athenian society. Competitive dialogues may be seen as typically 'tragic', but they are not exclusively 'tragic' because the epic genre too, contains many competitive dialogues, except that these epic dialogues are not staged in a democratic context.

Shakespearean dialogues are performed on stage, often as public or private contests, but unlike Greek tragic dialogues, their staging does not formally take place in a political context. Instead, one might say that they are staged in the cultural context of highly politicized clashes of contested ideologies and of competing social identities.

The forms of communication displayed in *Hamlet* show a high degree of theatricality. Rhetorical graciousness defines social status, but it is unmasked as corrupt. Hamlet, despite the verbal virtuosity in his contests with several opponents, invalidates the court rhetoric. His dialogues are spied upon, overheard and reported, as if they were performed on stage. The presence of an audience is felt. Hamlet mirrors other persons' ways of communicating with him and reverses the roles of questioner and respondent. Dialogue itself becomes an issue. The presence of an audience is felt even stronger during Hamlet's inner dialogues with himself. Lee considered them failed dialogues with his presumed true self.

Failed dialogues may be seen as typically 'tragic'. Whereas epic heroes engage in riddle-solving dialogues, tragic heroes, such as Oedipus and Antigone, engage in failed dialogues doomed to turn dialogical partners into lonesome drifters. The tragic adventure lacks dialogical openness.

PART II: INDIAN AND HINDU ISSUES

1 Introduction

In ancient and classical Indian and Hindu culture, literary and dramatic genres have developed that differ from their Western counterparts. In what respects do these genres differ? Have literary genres and dramatic genres developed as separate categories in India? What are poetry's specific mood effects and audience responses, according to classical Indian aesthetics? And should the *Mahābhārata* epic be classified as an 'epic' genre? One aesthetician will turn out to be crucial to answering these questions – Anandavardhana.

Also, dialogues play an important role in the *Mahābhārata* epic as a whole – a role that will be discussed later on. In this chapter, we shall focus on one dialogue in particular – the dialogue between Arjuna and Krishna in the *Bhagavadgītā*. What does this specific dialogue mean to whom, and what is its corresponding audience response?

2 The Mahābhārata's specific literary genre

2.1 Hindu religious classification

The outer frame of the epic presents Vyāsa as its composer. Vyāsa is a *brahmin* seer and an incarnation of the deity Vishnu-Nārāyana, and as such, endowed with the priestly authority of a religious teacher. Despite that, the epic is not as sacred a scripture as the *Vedas* and *Upanishads*, which are considered as *śruti*, the 'hearing' of the inviolable word, of the sacred revelation, of the eternal knowledge, of the original vision seen by the first seers.[73] The *Mahābhārata* epic is part of that oral tradition whose religious authority is categorized as *smrti*, the 'remembrance' of the collective wisdom and shared memory of the past, 'the collective experience that has been recorded and ratified for posterity by the elders of the community', as Julius Lipner puts it.[74] On occasion, the epic refers to itself as on par with the *Vedas* (*Mahābhārata* 1.56.15) precisely because the *Vedas* remained *the* symbol of scriptural authority. But the epic's authority is not beyond all criticism. Also, one may add, there is a subcategory within *smrti* called *itihāsa*, 'sacred narrative' or 'sacred (hi)story', represented in an exemplary way by the *Mahābhārata* because it portrays itself as Vyāsa's account of the victory of the Pāndavas over their cousins, a (hi)story retold on two subsequent occasions by the *Mahābhārata* itself. But, is this the only way to categorize this 'epic'?

2.2 Indian literary classification

Apart from the classification in terms of religious authority, a literary classification developed in circles of the royal courts of the classical and medieval periods. To which literary genre does the *Mahābhārata* belong according to this tradition? Indian tradition has expressed its understanding of the nature and significance of the *Mahābhārata* in many ways – in terms of 'story' (*ākhyāna*), 'legendary history' (*itihāsa*), 'instructive treatise' (*śāstra*) and 'poem' (*kāvya*) alike, since it contains all these styles.[75] D. P. Chattopadhyaya agrees that the *Mahābhārata* contains many styles, ranging from 'history' and 'story' to 'poem', but in the end, he confirms Ramanujan's position that one should regard the *Mahābhārata* as a 'great poem' (*mahākāvya*).[76]

This conclusion would not have been drawn originally. Initially, the epic was classified as a 'story' (a category including 'legendary history'), Gary A. Tubb points out.[77] Previously, there had been a distinction between the older Sanskrit epics, the *Rāmāyana* and the *Mahābhārata*, and the younger 'court epic' genre (of the 'great poem'), which was also called 'literary epic' or 'classical epic' and which had its own classical form, style and themes, according to Indira V. Peterson.[78] So, what had happened? The *Mahābhārata* which, so far, had been considered a legendary history and a story, was now considered a poem that could be evaluated according to the aesthetic standards of Sanskrit classical or court poetry.

The theoretician of aesthetics responsible for putting the *Mahābhārata* on the map of Indian aesthetics was among the most outstanding and influential Sanskrit aestheticians of all – Anandavardhana. I would like to present his position, bearing in mind that our exploration should give us an answer to two questions: 1. whether Hindu aestheticians themselves considered the plot to have some 'tragic' effect; and 2. whether the audience response was considered to play a decisive role in bringing about the plot effect.

2.3 Mood effects and audience responses in classical Indian aesthetics

Indian aesthetics has always been transmitted mainly by example and oral instruction, by practising the arts, hardly by writing and discussing theoretical treatises, Susan L. Schwartz emphasizes.[79] But, according to Shyamala Gupta, sometime between the first and the fifth century CE, Bharata Muni wrote a 'treatise on dramaturgy', his *Nātyaśāstra*, which became very influential.[80]

In its sixth chapter, he unfolds a 'theory of taste/mood (*rasa*)'. The most important condition for the spectator who intends to derive delight (*rasa*) from a dramatic performance is his capacity to identify (to a great extent) with the emotional state of the character presented on stage. To a great extent, but not entirely, the *mood* of the spectator is not a copy of the *emotion* of the character, but a generalized version of it, less particular to one person, more universal, less contaminated by other emotions, more purified, less unstable, more sustained, as Daniel H. H. Ingalls points out.[81] The mood contains an ingredient of detachment that allows the audience to elevate itself to a pure (*sāttvika*) state and to share the emotions of other persons without getting personally involved in them.[82] If a drama is to be successful, it should bring about a correspondence between the dominant 'stable emotion' (*sthāyībhāva*) of the main characters on the one hand, and the subsequent mood (*rasa*) of the audience that tastes its performance, on the other.

According to Bharata Muni, there are eight 'stable emotions' and eight corresponding 'tastes' ('flavours' or 'moods' or 'delights') – love or sexual excitement (*rati*) evokes the erotic taste (*śrngārarasa*); laughter or amusement (*hāsa*) evokes the comic taste (*hāsyarasa*); pathos or grief (*śoka*) is the source of the pathetic or compassionate taste (*karunarasa*); anger (*krodha*) evokes the cruel taste, 'distorted with anger' (*raudrarasa*); energetic exertion (*utsāha*) is the source of valour, the heroic flavour (*vīrarasa*); fear (*bhaya*) evokes the terrifying taste (*bhayānakarasa*); disgust (*jugupsā*) evokes the nauseating or horrid taste (*bībhatsarasa*); and astonishment or wonder (*vismaya*) is the source of dismay or marvel (*adbhutarasa*).

It is no coincidence, Schwartz argues, that 'food' and 'cooking' are the dominant metaphors from which *rasa* derives its meanings of 'juice', 'liquid abstract', 'essence', 'flavour' and 'delight'. Taste (mood) is generated by the spices (emotions) and by the cooking process (performance) in which the ingredients must be cooked through and thus transformed fully, but also by the digestive process (audience) of burning the food and of thus 'cooking' and refining it even further, for the sake of nourishing the body (cosmic life). The aesthetic experience is brought about by a combination of the characters' dominant emotion, the dramatic performance, and the appreciation by a sophisticated audience, a combination creatively processed into a 'transformed whole', Schwartz emphasizes. The emotion is intensified, experienced, connected with, digested, refined. This refinement process leads to *rasa* as its final result, and it is the 'refined product', the result that counts, she seems to suggest.[83]

2.4 The Mahābhārata's mood effect and audience response in Anandavardhana's aesthetics

In Anandavardhana's famous *Dhvanyāloka*, written in Kashmir in the second half of the ninth century, the *Mahābhārata* 'served as his chief example of a work that fulfills in its entirety the demanding requirements of poetic unity', Tubb writes.[84] It is precisely the way in which Anandavardhana reflected on the relationship between plot effect and audience response that is crucial to its perceived unity. Anandavardhana brought out the significance of *rasa* in poetry by emphasizing the notion of *rasa-dhvani*. But while Abhinavagupta wanted to retain the position of *rasa* as the soul of poetry, Anandavardhana intended to treat *dhvani* as the soul of poetry.[85] What did he mean by that?

Anandavardhana expounded his theory of *dhvani* in his work *Dhvanyāloka*. The word *dhvani* literally means 'sound' or 'overtone' and even suggests the sense of echo, Gupta notices.[86] Chantal Maillard points out that 'the ear and the heart register the sounds of the poetic word like a succession of waves', like registering the resonance of the initial sound of a drum, not the initial bang itself. The metaphor of resonance implies that 'the spectator, as the word *sahrdaya* indicates, is not just any observer but "someone with heart", meaning someone capable of resonating with what he sees and hears'.[87] The crucial importance of having a sensitive spectator on the receiving end reminds me of Lonsdale's point that the ideal judge of Greek tragedy is *talapeiros*, 'one who has much experience of suffering'. According to Anand Amaladass, *dhvani* is usually translated as 'suggestion', but should be rendered 'evocation' because it is not an indirect idea or meaning, but is what is evoked through a meaning, and because of the emotional factor involved in the *dhvani*-process.[88]

The savouring of the 'flavour' of a work of art, according to Anandavardhana, does not come about by logical implication or by direct imitation. Words mean what they stand for or what they indicate, but through their denoted (conventional) or indicated (implied) meaning, 'a further meaning comes into being when the functions of denotation and indication are exhausted', as Gupta puts it, a suggested sense that is not expressed, but evoked, and thus revealed to our consciousness, awakened in our imaginative minds. The unexpressed or evoked sense of words is called *dhvani*. It is declared the soul of poetry because the best poetry is that poetry in which the evoked sense predominates and supersedes the expressed sense.[89]

The mood effect of the work of art is cueing the response of a sensitive audience.[90] But the highly developed understanding of the sensitive reader is also a capacity of the poet who is able to transform his personal experience into a generalized, universalized consciousness. 'That is why *rasa* is said to be neither the personal emotions of the artist, nor of the experiencer, though based on the experience of the artist, now divested of its "limiting" factors', Amaladass explains.[91] If applied to our issue of plot effect and audience response, the 'aesthetic experience' or 'taste' or 'mood' (*rasa*) presupposes both.[92]

Anandavardhana takes the *Rāmāyana* and the *Mahabharata* as paradigms of literary unity. His criterion for literary unity is the employment of a single predominant *rasa,* to which all the other *rasa*s are subordinated. Anandavardhana considers the *Rāmāyana* to be a paradigm of grief and of the compassionate flavour. He writes:

> For in the Rāmāyana the First Poet [Vālmiki] has set forth *karuna* as the *rasa* by making such statements as "Grief was made into verse," and he has carried it through by composing his work so as to extend to the final separation [of Rāma] from Sītā.[93]

However, Ingalls notices, in Sanskrit aesthetics, such a compassionate mood is not allowed to have a long-lasting effect on the audience. Art has its purposes of representing the world as it is and of teaching virtues like 'kindliness', but it cannot have the purpose of disturbing the audience too much. Art is instructive, but above all, its purpose is delight, according to the Sanskrit literates.[94]

In the case of the *Mahābhārata* and its plot, Anandavardhana is struck by the actual destruction of the 'good' parties involved at the very end, and by the mood this disastrous end brings about. How is *dhvani*, poetic evocation, at work in the *Mahābhārata*? It contains all the *rasa*s but, he argues, ultimately the predominant *rasa* is the flavour of peacefulness (*shāntarasa*). Amaladass, paraphrasing and quoting the argument:

> The story of the Pāndavas in all their greatness, success, and glory ends in tragedy. This turn of events in their life is meant to produce a sense of *vairāgya*, detachment. This is surely a means of reaching liberation at the feet of the Lord. This is to inculcate an attitude in the mind of the readers so that they interpret the events of history, the human failures, glory or humiliation in their life according to the model of the *Mahābhārata*. Thus the main purpose of the *Mahābhārata* is to lead others to the realisation of *parabrahman* [Supreme Reality, LM] through the *vibhūtiyoga* [manifestation of a deeper reality, LM] and through the *vairāgyayoga* [discipline of detachment, LM].[95]

But if the predominant flavour is peaceful in the detached sense of the word, it should correspond to the stable emotion of tranquillity in the main character, according to the interpolated verses in Bharata Muni's treatise. The main character, however, Yudhisthira, is all but tranquil when he is left alone with his dog and finds his brothers and wife in hell. Tubb writes that 'what Yudhisthira seeks and finds is not the liberated state of one who has passed beyond attachment, but rather the engaging world of a warrior's paradise'. In fact, the way Yudhisthira and Arjuna are drawn by the poets seems 'intended to evoke the heroic flavor rather than the flavor of peace'.[96]

The epic poem evoking the heroic flavour rather than the flavour of peacefulness? In fact, there are two forms of evocation, Tubb explains.[97] The primary form of evocation of *rasa* is evocation through correspondence between a *rasa* and the stable emotion in the main character. The secondary form of evocation of *rasa* is evocation through aftertone – the reader takes time to think over the implications of what he reads and the evoked sense (*dhvani*) thereby accomplishes its effect. The mind of the audience is the place where the plot effect is realized. The audience response is crucial to the plot effect.

Interestingly, Anandavardhana considers the *Mahābhārata* both a treatise and a poem, but not a story (*ākhyāna*). Being in the form of a treatise or didactic work, its pronouncements have the authority characteristic of a prescriptive work. The educational function of a work is not, however, limited to prescriptive works. As Tubb points out, any Sanskrit work of value, whatever the principal aim of its author, will necessarily provide instruction in at least one of the four major goals of human life.[98] According to Anandavardhana, the *Mahābhārata* teaches all the goals of man, as it contains all the *rasas*, but its major goal, conveyed through evocation, is ultimate liberation (*moksha*). The adventures of the Pāndavas are meant to produce detachment, and detachment leads to liberation.

Ultimately, despite the unsolvable conflict between the Kauravas and the Pāndavas, despite the structural ambiguity of *adharma* and *dharma*, and despite the disastrous end of the Pāndavas, who perish and evoke a long-lasting worrying effect, to the extent that the audience runs the risk of remaining in a disturbed mood afterwards, the plot effect of producing a despondent feeling in response to the miserable end of the Pāndavas is not qualified as 'tragic' by Anandavardhana. On the contrary, the disturbed mood itself is not the final one, but evokes, through aftertone, a deep sense of detachment in the sensitive reader, who then realizes the implication of the statement that Lord Vāsudeva alone is eternal and that everything else is illusory, and who then experiences peacefulness.

Anandavardhana's reading seems a clear case of Hindu hermeneutics. The shift from disturbed to peaceful mood draws from Hindu traditions such as *vibhūtiyoga*, the basic principle that 'the world and all the created things in it are the manifestations of the Lord' and therefore capable of drawing one closer to the Supreme Reality by leading to a spiritual experience of complete detachment (*vairāgyayoga*), Amaladass explains. While interpreting the *Mahābhārata* according to his ideal of predominant flavour, he makes use of the *Gītā*'s notion of *parabrahman* (Supreme Reality) and of 'what is known as *vibhūtiyoga* in the terminology of the *Gītā*', as Amaladass points out.[99]

It is also a clear case, not of specifically Hindu but of general hermeneutics, however, in that it simply takes the message of the texts themselves seriously. After all, the *Gītā*'s message of complete detachment and ultimate liberation is part of the *Mahābhārata*, and the message of the *Mahābhārata* plot itself shifts at the very end from a disturbed mood to a peaceful mood by disqualifying the disturbing scenes at the end as the last illusion the main character should leave behind.

Our exploration gives us an answer to the two questions posed at the outset – whether Hindu aestheticians themselves considered the plot to have some 'tragic' effect, and whether the audience response was considered to play a decisive role in bringing about the plot effect.

Hindu aestheticians such as Anandavardhana did, in fact, consider the plot of the *Mahābhārata* to have some 'tragic' effect, to the extent that the miserable end of the Pāndavas produces a despondent feeling, which I would qualify as a 'disturbed mood'. This despondent feeling, however, is not considered the final or dominating mood of the *Mahābhārata*, but is claimed to evoke, through aftertone, a sense of detachment that releases the spiritual 'flavour of peace', in accordance with Sanskrit literary convention, which does not allow the 'compassionate mood' – let alone some 'ironic mood' – to persist until the very end.

The audience response was considered to play a decisive role in bringing about the plot effect because the sensitive reader was supposed to grasp the emotional significance of the poem by taking time to think over the implications of its key statements. That is to say, the evoked sense of the *Mahābhārata* accomplishes its effect by evocation through aftertone, turning the mind of the audience into the place where the plot effect is realized.

2.5 A dramatic and religious genre

If the audience response was considered to play a decisive role in bringing about the plot effect, it is because the theatrical setting was considered part and parcel of 'poetry' (*kāvya*). In India, 'poetry' (works of *belles lettres*) was, and still is, expected to be performed, put on stage, recited, sung, danced, dramatized if it was and is going to be complete and if it was and is going to be tasted aesthetically, Lyne Bansat-Boudon emphasizes.[100] Song, music and dance accompanied the theatre from the very beginning.

Also, the theatre is related to the temple. 'The design of a theatre was considered a branch of temple architecture', Schwartz writes. Moreover, many Hindu gods and goddesses are dancers themselves, not just the deities who protect the theatre.[101] It is telling that the *Bhagavadgītā* is not known as a didactic treatise within the epic, but literally called the 'Song (*gītā*) of the Lord'. It has to be performed on stage for both aesthetic and religious purposes. Its pious readers are also pious spectators.[102] Being part, even as a spectator, of the occasion of the enactment of one of the epics, and of the *Ramāyāna*, in particular (*Rāmlīlā*), is regarded as a pious act. The performers are, in fact, ritually initiated, and thus transformed into people of the status of their roles within the performance. This does not diminish its entertainment value in the least.[103] It does, however, as Richard Schechner shows, exclude the Greek framing of aesthetic appreciation within a competitive setting, which transforms spectators into judges and critics, and performers into winners and losers. Instead, the aesthetic enjoyment (*rasa*) of the performance is shared between the performers and spectators alike, and the joyful celebration tends towards the Hindu framing within a ritualistic setting, a communal act of piety drawing its performers and spectators into the sacred narrative that is celebrated.[104]

The fact that the *Gītā* represents a song sung by a god, Lord Krishna, brings to mind the first and last chapters of Bharata Muni's (much later) *Nātyaśāstra*, which has another supreme god, Brahmā, teach the rules of dance and theatre to its mythical author, the seer and sage Bharata. The highest gods are engaged in theatre. The gods attend the theatrical spectacle for their own pleasure, and they play their own part in it. Note also that the very term *avatāra*, 'descent' (by the Supreme God for the good of the world), has associations with the theatre, as Freda Matchett notices.[105] The boundaries between the representation and celebration of the empirical world *in* theatre, on the one hand, and the creation of the empirical world *as* theatre, as the staging of a play by a creator god who exercises the power of appearance and illusion (*māyā*), on the other, have become even less clear-cut after the theism of the epics developed into 'theologies of play' (Vaishnavite and Śaivite equivalents of monotheistic 'theologies of creation') in later ages.[106] This theological development only reinforced the continuous categorization of the epics as *smṛti*, sacred narrative to be recited (cf. Greek *diēgēsis*) and/or enacted (cf. Greek *mimēsis*). The song sung by Lord Krishna in the *Bhagavadgītā* is his dialogue with Arjuna.

3 The Gītā's specific dialogue

3.1 Friend–friend relationship

Regarding the dialogical character of the *Gītā*'s plot, the most striking thing about the dialogue between Krishna and Arjuna is that it does not seem to be what one would expect it to be in terms of their previous friend–friend relationship so far in the epic as a whole – a dialogue between friends who have been battle comrades in the Khāndava Forest. As such, they had been identified as incarnations of two ancient sages, Nara and Nārāyana respectively (1.219.12–18, 3.41.1). Ruth Cecile Katz explains that 'as a pair, Nara and Nārāyana are born *yuga* after *yuga*, "for the sake of maintenance of the world" (7.172.81), Arjuna and Krishna incarnating the pair in the present age'.[107] Nara and Nārāyana are, in turn, identified with the human being and Vishnu (God), respectively.[108]

In the *Gītā*, Krishna does not seem to speak as a friend, although he explicitly addresses Arjuna as 'comrade' or 'friend' (*sakhā*) in *Gītā* 4.3. Nor does he seem to speak as a military adviser. Throughout the war, however, Krishna plays a crucial role as friend and military adviser to the Pāndavas. He 'combines cunning and ruthlessness with a preparedness to bend or set aside the *dharmic* rules of warfare to achieve his end', like in the destruction of Drona, Peter Hill writes.[109] In fact, Krishna's role as charioteer combines the roles of friend and military counsellor. In the (later) *Book of Karna* (*Karna Parvan*), which deals with the themes of friendship and fratricide, Krishna will be on speaking terms with Arjuna as a friend and battle companion when fighting Karna and his charioteer Śalya. Hiltebeitel has credited Walter Ruben for pointing out that it is this (later) contrast of the true friendship between Arjuna and Krishna on the chariot, as opposed to the betrayed friendship between Karna and Śalya on their chariot, which sheds a positive light on the (previous) dialogue between Arjuna and Krishna in the *Gītā*.[110] One of Arjuna's reasons for his refusal to fight is his abhorrence of committing the crime of treachery to friends (*mitradrohe*, 1.38).

The social relationship associated with 'friendship' (*sakhyam*) is a *dharmic* relationship, which includes notions like 'companionship in battle', 'warrior pact' and 'mutual trust and loyalty'.[111] The relationships of the combatants with their charioteers are crucial to the outcome of the battle and 'part of a wider network of complicated social relationships centered on the themes of partial or symbolic brotherhood and friendship', as Hiltebeitel puts it elsewhere.[112] There should be a fine attunement and maximum mutual trust between the chariot warrior (*kshatriya*) and his charioteer (*sūta*) because they fully depend on each other in battle. The horse guiding skills of the charioteer are crucial to protect the warrior, and the weapon skills of the warrior are crucial to protect the unarmed charioteer. This allows for friendship between unequals, 'Indeed, the relationship between them is precisely one which relies on friendship because it is based on an inherent inequality. The warrior, of course, has the higher rank'.[113]

The contrast with the blatant lack of friendship between Karna and Śalya is striking. Here, inequality is a source of insults. King Duryodhana had requested Śalya, a chariot warrior, to serve as charioteer for Karna. Śalya considers this an insult. Nobody is aware that Karna, in reality, is a chariot warrior and a half-brother to the Pāndavas. (8.23.19–36) Karna and Śalya, instead of showing mutual respect, start to insult each other. This is even more inappropriate against the background of the charioteer's role of uttering praise when the warrior inflicts defeat and of uttering reproach when the warrior is defeated.[114] This is exactly what Śalya as charioteer is lacking, and what Krishna as charioteer is doing in the *Gītā*. Krishna behaves and speaks as a real friend when he reproaches Arjuna. 'Arjuna and Krishna's success will be related to their true friendship, while Karna and Śalya's failure will be related to their false friendship', Hiltebeitel concludes.[115]

3.2 Master-disciple relationship

Yet, Krishna's role as a counsellor in the *Gītā* is different. He tries to convince Arjuna that he should fulfil his warrior duties and fight. But he does much more than simply trying to persuade him. Krishna turns out to be a sophisticated counsellor and a spiritual teacher acquainted with the major spiritual traditions of ancient India. The solution Krishna comes up with is neither a psychological nor a moral nor a rational one, but beyond that. What Krishna has to offer is a spiritual solution. As a counsellor and a teacher, he offers a spiritual truth. Gradually, Krishna becomes a spiritual *guru* while Arjuna becomes a guided pupil.

The dialogue between Krishna and Arjuna in the *Gītā* is part of the ancient tradition of transmitting knowledge through the master–disciple relationship. Originally and archetypically, the biological father–son relationship is the primary seat of learning. According to the *Laws of Manu* (2.142, 2.149), the *guru* was originally the father himself, who performed the sacraments for his son and taught him a part of the Veda. It is from the *Atharva Veda* (11.5.14–15) onwards 'that the Vedic master-disciple relationship between the teacher (*ācārya*) and the unmarried Veda-student (*brahmacārī*) appears in the literature as an institution of highest authority', Ralph Marc Steinmann maintains.[116] The early *ācārya-brahmacārī* relationship was mainly determined by the transmission of ritual and secular knowledge in order to prepare the student for his duties as a future householder.

Within the development of a bipolarity between the immanent and the transcendent, between the mundane and the cosmic, between the social and the individual, between ritualism and asceticism, from the *Upanishads*[117] onwards, the master–disciple relationship tends to become a lifelong, ascetic relationship, exclusively devoted to the spiritual goal of self-realization by attaining metaphysical knowledge, Steinmann writes.[118] On the part of the disciple (*śishya*), the ascetic master–disciple relationship requires discipline, celibacy, renunciation, asceticism, absolute faith in the *guru*'s knowledge and transforming power, truthfulness, mental alertness and discrimination; on the part of the teacher (*guru*), it requires comprehensive knowledge of the Veda, existential experience of the transcendent reality, self-control, peacefulness, etc. The ascetic *guru* becomes the spiritual father of the disciple and replaces the biological father. This is possible, Axel Michaels explains, through an initiation rite, that is to say, through a ritual father–son identification.[119] The ascetic *guru* is a much more intimate, trustworthy, personal, warm figure than the secular *ācārya*, comparable to the difference in French between *maître* and *professeur*.[120]

3.3 God–devotee relationship

With the development of the henotheistic or monolatric *bhakti* devotion (venerating one favourite god only amidst many gods), from the *Śvetāśvatara-Upanishad* and the *Gītā* onwards, the master–disciple relationship tends to become a devotional relationship that cultivates the adoration of the master *like*[121] a god (*guru-bhakti*), and ultimately *as* a god (*deva-bhakti*).[122] The *upanishadic* love of the truth reached through argument and counter-argument is gradually being transformed into the *bhakti* love of the *guru* reached through his spiritual and physical presence, a relationship of mutual love.[123] Mutual love (*bhakti*) should not yet be interpreted sentimentally, but in the sense of 'loyalty' and 'taking refuge' on the part of the devotee, in the sense of 'favour' and 'affording refuge' on the part of the lord (king or god). One would expect the notion of *bhakti* to have arisen in the circles of warriors. The symbiotic relationship between a lord and his favourite one is illustrated by Krishna and Arjuna in the *Gītā*, Steinmann suggests.[124] In the very same verse Krishna calls Arjuna 'friend' or 'comrade' (*sakhā*), Krishna speaks to him as His devotee, within the context of the transmission of esoteric knowledge from the Vedic seers onwards:

> This ancient yoga is today
> Declared by Me to you,
> Since you are My devotee and friend.
> This secret is supreme indeed." [*Gītā* 4.3][125]

Still under the spell of Krishna's overwhelming visual appearance as Vishnu, Arjuna finally praises Krishna as the father (*pitā*) and *guru* of the world, who should be adored (*pūjyas*):

> You are the father of the world, of all things moving and motionless.
> You are to be adored by this world.
> You are the most venerable Guru.
> [*Gītā* 11.43a][126]

In this passage, the *guru* is not (yet) being venerated as a god or like a god, but the god, Lord Krishna, is being venerated as a *guru*. It is quite clear that the master–disciple relationship is less important than the god–devotee relationship between Krishna and Arjuna. But the two cannot be separated. Krishna's act of loving grace consists of instructing his devotee Arjuna[127] and of initiating him into the spiritual world of immortal truth. From a *bhakti* theological perspective, *the god–devotee relationship assumes the form of a master–disciple relationship*. This relates to one aspect in particular. Krishna presents himself as the paradigm of what he urges Arjuna to become – someone who acts without attachment (*asakta karmin* or *karmayogi*) (3.22, 4.14). In Krishna's case, this happens within the *avatāra* context of His divine interference in worldly affairs for the sake of *dharma* if necessary (4.7–8, 9.7–9).

From a *literary* perspective, in terms of the development of the plot, *the master–disciple relationship assumes the form of a god–devotee relationship.* The transformation is the other way around. Krishna first tries to persuade Arjuna to fight by using arguments and by his teaching. From *Gītā* 10.12 onwards, Krishna seems to have achieved his goal, but Arjuna continues to ask for more explanation (10.18). Krishna continues to point out that He is the origin and essence of all things, including their dialogue, 'I am the logic of those who debate'. (10.32) Krishna also mentions that He is all-destroying Death, and the origin of those things that are yet to be (10.34). Arjuna then asserts that his delusion is gone (11.1). The decisive turning point or catalyst in their dialogue, however, is the shift from Krishna's teaching to his overwhelming appearance (11.9). At this sight, Arjuna confesses that he loses his sense of direction and finds no comfort (11.25). In fact, he is terrified. He speaks in a choked voice to Krishna (11.35) and starts to apologize for having spoken to Him as a friend and comrade:

> Whatever I have said impetuously as if in ordinary friendship,
> 'Oh Krishna, Oh Son of Yadu, Oh Comrade,'
> In ignorance of Your majesty,
> Through negligence or even through affection,
> And if, with humorous purpose,
> You were disrespectfully treated,
> While at play, resting, while seated or while dining,
> When alone, O Krishna, or even before the eyes of others,
> For that I ask forgiveness of You, immeasurable One.
> [*Gītā* 11.41–2][128]

Then follows the verse quoted above, which contains the line, 'You are the most venerable Guru'. (11.43) After Krishna's theophany, Arjuna's questions no longer have dramatic value; he is 'convinced' and is merely asking for clarifications on points of doctrine (12.1, 14.21, 17.21, 18.1).

The dialogue between Arjuna and Krishna is hardly a dialogue at all in the reciprocal sense of the word.[129] In accordance with the *bhakti* tradition, the god, Lord Krishna, has the initiative. Arjuna is being instructed. He is allowed the role of asking questions, but he is not allowed the role of discussing the answers. Arjuna is expected to listen carefully and not to forget. This dialogue is quite different from a Socratic dialogue. Socrates puts the questions and discusses the answers, whereas here Arjuna, not Krishna, puts the questions and Krishna gives the answers.[130] India has its tradition of competitive debate in some places in texts such as the *Brahmanas,* and most visibly in the *Nyāya Sūtra.* But debate in India is not the tool to find truth. Ultimate truth is, in any case, inexpressible and has to be learnt authoritatively from a teacher (who is not to be questioned). This is precisely what is found in the *Gītā*, Victor van Bijlert argues.[131]

Moreover, the dialogue takes a surprising turn when the plot shifts from Krishna's teaching to His appearance. Interestingly, in the previous chapter, Doniger qualified such a shift as a shift from the level of words and arguments to the level of imagery and vision, that is to say, from the level of *logos* to that of *mythos*, and on the level of *mythos,* the arguments do not count and the questions are not answered for they cannot be answered.[132] In the case of the *Bhagavata Purana*, the focus moves from the child Krishna's mouth, the place of *logos*, to its interior, the place of speechless myth. In the case of the *Gītā*, the focus moves from the level of argument to the level of vision – not a subject of discussion, but of surrender.

From a different perspective, however, the sudden *shift from argument and discussion to vision and surrender* should come as no surprise. In his dissertation and two outstanding articles, one comparing Greek and Indian epics, the other comparing Greek and Indian architecture, Gregory D. Alles offers valuable insights into two different concepts of 'power' and 'the power of persuasion' that may be applicable here.[133] In Homer's *Iliad*, Alles argues, persuasive speeches presuppose a different image of what constitutes effective persuasion from those in Valmiki's *Rāmāyana*. Ancient Greek and Indian images of the power of persuasion differ because their concepts of power differ. In the *Iliad*, the power of persuasion is a social power that only depends on and only extends to successful interaction among humans and between humans and the gods; it is systemic or organic in the sense that it gains force as small units, such as arguments and other devices 'combine to form an interconnected web, an organically functioning speech'.[134] The power of persuasion is also relational in the sense of residing in the social relationships that have to be mobilized in order to be obligingly influential, and it is economical in the sense that exact repetition and elaborate additions would spoil the effect of integrating all parts into an efficient whole. In the *Rāmāyana*, Alles explains, power is natural and generative rather than social, like the unrestrained irruption of a hidden source into the visible realm of a variety of manifestations; power is 'dividuated', like seeds, concentrated in separate, isolated and opaque, but dense units of solid mass radiating below the surface and applied in isolated 'spurts', rather than systemic or organic. Power is also like a ritual or magic force, 'concerned with generation and destruction',[135] mobilizing and spending itself in a creative or destructive way, rather than residing in social relationships, and it is cumulative and repetitive in the sense that each addition to the impressive variety of its visible manifestations, honouring it by repetition, enhances its persuasive effectiveness.

Krishna's power of persuasion, viewed at in that light, can be understood as an accumulation of isolated arguments that gain force precisely because they are accumulated and repeated and because they draw from a hidden, esoteric knowledge of divine origin, a massive, transcendent power that mobilizes itself by irrupting into the visible realm as the overwhelming vision of a destructive force, devouring all the manifestations of the manifold universe. Krishna's power of persuasion starts on the level of words and arguments but it is only logical that the eruption of his divine power on the level of *logos* be continued on the level of *mythos*. This is how the power of persuasion operates effectively from an ancient Indian point of view. It is the literal illustration of Krishna's claim, 'I am the logic of those who debate'. (10.32) Krishna addresses a socially sensitive, but mentally isolated individual, Arjuna, on the battlefield, but ignores the social setting, focusing instead on Arjuna's separate Self and preaching an intrapersonal solution to the interpersonal problem of social order, justice and duty, appealing to Arjuna's asocial inner nature and its spiritual potential instead of appealing to the potentially (anti-)social results of his morally intended actions. Removed from all social pressures, everything about Krishna's dialogue with Arjuna seems personal, not social, mobilizing the intrapersonal powers of their respective natures, not the interpersonal powers of their respective social networks.

Let us have one more look at this specific dialogical scene. Krishna as *guru* participates in the oral tradition of transmitting religiously authoritative knowledge to the next generation. His pupil, Arjuna, imagines the cosmic state of affairs that is being preached, and afterwards, he cognitively concludes that his delusion is gone – the picture has come across and he therefore has a clear picture now. But then, Krishna replaces his didactic and imaginative traditional teachings with an actual vision that takes the palpable form of an overwhelming appearance. This appearance is so frightening that it can no longer be called 'didactic' in the traditional sense of the word because the teacher's message is banged into Arjuna's head so shockingly that the vision risks to traumatize Arjuna if it goes on for too long. It works like shock therapy. Afterwards, the patient has been cured of his delusion. Krishna's vision has been instilled into Arjuna's heart and mind when Arjuna was at his most vulnerable – a well-known practice in initiation rituals that aim at structural and long-term effects. What is left for Arjuna to learn is to face the full consequences of this vision. But he does not face them inwardly, in the interior world of an inner dialogue between one part of his soul and another part, as one would expect from a scripture that had already incorporated the Upanishadic teachings. Arjuna's outlook is not turned inward. Instead, he is taught the full consequences by Krishna in the subsequent chapters. The social dialogue is being continued. That is why this *social dialogue* can only become an *inner dialogue* if it is interpreted afterwards as an allegory of the soul or as a symbolic expression of a mystical experience. In the Hindu *Wirkungsgeschichte* of this dialogue, only the visionary scene has been interpreted as symbolic of a mystical experience, but the dialogue as a whole has been interpreted as an allegory of the soul, as will be shown in the next section.

Having surrendered, it is evident that Arjuna has no choice, but to live up to his immortality and act accordingly because Krishna's revelatory truth is simply overwhelming. Or is it?[136] Krishna's revelatory truth is not simply overwhelming if one takes seriously that the revelation is not the end of the story. The terrified Arjuna (11.35) is calmed by Krishna who reveals his own previous form again (11.50), and restores Arjuna's mind to normal (11.51). Krishna then strikes a very different note. He does not impose his commanding view, but leaves Arjuna some real scope for reflection and choice, 'Thus the knowledge that is more secret than all that is secret has been expounded to you by me. Having reflected on (*vimrśya*) this fully, do (*kuru*) as you wish (*icchasi*)'. (18.63) All of a sudden, we are back on the battlefield, the 'field of doing' (*kuru-kshetra*) which coincides with the 'field of Kuru' (*kuru-kshetra*), the royal family to which Drtarāshtra belongs (1.1).[137]

The return to the battlefield is also a return to the friend–friend relationship. But this relationship can no longer be seen without its transformations into a master–disciple relationship and into a god–devotee relationship. The dialogue between Krishna and Arjuna in the *Gītā* testifies to all the three relationships, even though the god–devotee relationship ultimately dominates the dialogical scene in the plot. In this respect too, the *Gītā*'s plot fits well into the epic plot pattern as a whole. The *Gītā* itself establishes the narrative bridge by having Samjaya, minister to King Dhrtarāshtra and the narrator, finish the *Gītā* while addressing the King. The narrator Samjaya retrospectively characterizes the dialogue between Krishna and Arjuna as 'wondrous' (*adbhutam*) and 'pure' or 'sacred' or 'holy' (*punyam*). (18.74, 76)

4 The Gītā's specific audience response

4.1 I-Self relationship

There is, however, one dialogical relationship that has been left out so far – the dialogue of the hero with his own self. The I–Self relationship is of crucial importance to any contemporary Hindu audience around the world. The West has a substantial tradition of reading myths psychologically. So does India. Translating mythology into psychology is not a Western monopoly. The difference between Western culture and Indian culture in this regard is that Western psychology has become part of an exclusively secular discourse and practice whereas Indian psychology has remained part of an inclusively religious discourse and practice called 'spirituality'. From a *Hindu* point of view, 'spirituality' is everything that broadens the mind beyond the realm of this-worldly affairs, everything leading to an expansion of self-consciousness. The plot pattern of the *Gītā* is precisely about that – leading Arjuna to an expansion of self-consciousness. That is why the *Gītā* has become a *spiritual manual* and why it evokes a corresponding audience response. Many famous Hindu authors have contributed to its interpretation as a spiritual manual. In terms of *Western* literary genres, it has become an *allegory*, and it has become categorized as *wisdom literature* and *world literature*.[138]

One of the authors who has interpreted the *Gītā* as a spiritual manual, but one who includes in his interpretation the *Mahābhārata* epic as a whole, is V. S. Sukthankar. He claims that the Ultimate Reality that is immanent in, and also transcends, the diversity of the phenomenal world was synthesized by the *Upanishadic* seers and localized in the 'cave' of man's own heart. 'To galvanize this Internal Ruler into activity again', Sukthankar continues, 'the epic poets made the daring . . . experiment of leading the King out of his Dark Chamber into broad daylight as Lord Krishna in order to expose him to the gaze of his disconsolate devotees'. The picture of Lord Krishna is, in fact, a challenge to man to understand his own true Self, mindful of *Gītā* 10.20 – 'I am the Self, O Gudākeśa, dwelling in the heart of every being'. This equation is the basis of a symbolism that gives an entirely new and universally valuable dimension to the story, he argues.[139]

Sukthankar's symbolic reading of the *Gītā* can draw on a famous passage in the *Katha Upanishad* (1.3.3–13), in particular, where the relationship between chariot warrior and charioteer symbolizes the spiritual relationship between the Self, the body, the intellect, and the mind:

Know the Self (*ātman*) as the lord of the chariot and the body as, verily, the chariot, know the intellect (*buddhi*) as the charioteer and the mind as, verily, the reins. . . . He who has understanding for the driver of the chariot (*vijñānasārathiḥ*) and controls the rein of his mind, he reaches the end of the journey, the supreme abode of the all-pervading.
[*Katha Upanishad* 1.3.3 and 1.3.9][140]

In Plato's *Phaedrus* 246–56, Socrates describes the soul as a winged chariot in which a charioteer drives a team of two horses, the first one noble and modest, the second one ignoble, desire-driven and hard to control.[141]

According to Sukthankar, Arjuna and Krishna are consistently represented in the epic as Nara and Nārāyana. Nara stands for Man, the human being in the abstract (or as the epic says Narottama, Man *par excellence*, the Superman), while Nārāyana stands for the Supreme Being. 'Thus the pair Nara-Nārāyana stands for Man and his God'. Their relationship is hinted at, he suggests, in the episode of king Dambhodbhava, 'a plebeian version of the classic *Upanishadic* parable of the two birds, eternal friends, seated upon the same tree—symbol of the body—of whom one (*jīvātman*, the human soul) eats the sweet fruit, while the other (*Paramātman*, the divine Self) sits, in a pleased mood, silently looking on'. The empirical soul and the transcendental Self are incarnated in one body. The epic poets, Sukthankar argues, view Arjuna and Krishna simultaneously as the human soul and the divine Self.[142]

The implication is that the dialogue of the hero with his own self, as I introduced it, is not a dialogue but a potential friendship and an actual battle. Sukthankar emphasizes the battle and calls it 'the battle royal with one's own self'. He points out the importance of self-conquest in the epic (5.34.53, 55) and quotes several verses from the *Gītā* which distinguish between friend and enemy in the battle for self-conquest (6.6, 3.41, 3.43). Your real friend, as your real enemy, is within you, not outside:

For him who has conquered himself by the Self,
The Self is a friend;
But for him who has not conquered himself,
The Self remains hostile, like an enemy." [*Gītā* 6.6][143]

It is the battle with one's lower self, the empirical ego, along with its adjuncts of desires and passions, hate and greed, envy and malice, combining to form a formidable army of opponents, which is the real battle of Kurukshetra. The internecine war clearly hints at the psychological conflict within man between evil and good propensities, Sukthankar argues.[144] Dhrtarāstra, the blind king of the Kurus, is the empirical ego, the lower and transient personality, blinded by egoism and foolish infatuation. Duryodhana, the chief of the Kaurava brothers, combines lust, anger and greed, which are the ruling passions. Vidura, wise counsellor to Dhrtarāstra, always by his side, but never listened to, symbolizes conscience (*buddhi*), the capacity to discriminate between good and evil. Bhīsma stands for tradition and memory. When he dies, all knowledge will die with him. Arjuna faces his opponents. By practising self-control, he has to purify himself, conquering the baser part of his own nature. Above all, he has to learn that his essential identity is realized by Lord Krishna, the Superself from whom he ultimately does not differ.[145] The battle is a *dialogue with one's deepest self*, a process of growing self-awareness, which the dialogue between Krishna and Arjuna stands for and inspires to.

It is within the narrative context of growing self-awareness and ultimate self-knowledge that Hiltebeitel points out the striking similarities between Arjuna, Draupadī, and Vārshneya Krishna, on the one hand, and Nala (Nala being a homonym for Nara, 'Man'), Damayantī and Nala's charioteer, Vārshneya in the famous love story of Nala and Damayantī, a mirror story within the *Mahābhārata*, on the other hand.[146] The charioteer Vārshneya is the first to recognize Nala in his company as a 'great self' (*mahātman*), 'evoking for readers Krishna and Arjuna on the chariot in the *Gītā*, and also Arjuna's disguise as "the great Nalā" '. When Damayantī sends her maid to test Nala, his reply shows that 'Nala now recognizes the autonomy of his own self: that his self is not Nala who knows himself, but the self that knows Nala (*ātmaiva hi nalam vetti*)'.[147] In short, in terms of self-knowledge, Krishna is to Arjuna as the Self is to the I.

4.2 A pious audience response

If the *Gītā* is considered a spiritual manual by the Hindu audience, one would not expect its language to be very specific about certain rules of behaviour but, within a context of Hindu spirituality, to evoke an attitude of pious awe and meditation. This is precisely what the *Gītā*'s language tempts one to engage in, according to Kees Bolle:

> Like the Upanishads, the *Bhagavadgītā* has always been a text of meditation in India. . . . Redundancies can be pruned a bit in translation, but they cannot be removed. They belong to the meditational function of the book. . . . The redundancy has a purpose, exactly because it is a matter of 'rubbing things in' and therefore repeating them. Wisdom is not something to be *attained* at a certain moment. It is not bestowed on Arjuna like an academic degree. It is a thing practised continually. A verse I have quoted before and which I like most in the *Gītā* is the one in Chapter 10 where Arjuna addresses Krishna, after having been taught concerning the highest:
>
>> 'Tell me more, and in detail
>> of your mystic power and mighty forms,
>> For I cannot listen enough, o Stirrer of Men,
>> to your immortal word.'[148]

Through the identification with Arjuna, the audience is cued to have a similar response. The *Gītā* itself cultivates meditation as the proper audience response. In short, the *Gītā* has a meditational or spiritual function.

Should the *Gītā*, therefore, be considered a mystical poem instead of a practical manual? The Hindu audience is expected to identify with Arjuna as the supreme devotee who has been granted a mystical vision in the midst of a lot of didactic teaching by Krishna. The prominent moral function of the *Gītā* (encouraging caste duty performance) is unmistakable, but in later devotionalist circles, it seems increasingly meant to serve a mystagogical purpose, of leading to a similar mystical experience as Arjuna's, as a spiritual consciousness underlying one's actions. And yet, the very realization of this spiritual awareness is meant to underlie one's actions, that is to say, to serve a practical purpose. This juxtaposition and linking of the two functions is exactly what makes the *Gītā* irresistible for a Hindu audience because it is at the core of what Hinduism is all about. The *Gītā's moral function* of learning how to act socially is upheld, but superimposed by the *Gītā's devotional function* of learning how to act spiritually, and the other way around.

Piety or devotion (*bhakti*) has meant different things in different periods, however. Krishna remained the object of devotion through the ages, but the Krishna cult underwent changes. In the long term, devotionalist movements would not only cherish the Arjuna–Krishna relationship of the *Gītā* but also the *Rādhā-Krishna relationship* of Jayadeva's *Gītāgovinda*. Developments in the Krishna devotion can be traced in subsequent scriptures. Historically speaking, the *Gītā* is older than the *Harivamśa* (first–second century CE), the *Bhāgavata Purāna* (ninth–early tenth century CE) and the *Gītāgovinda* (eleventh century CE). David R. Kinsley has pointed out a historical development from devotion in the first to devotion in later scriptures. Kinsley sketches an opposition between the subservient attitude of the devotee, typified by Arjuna, in the *Gītā*, a trembling servant before the majesty of his lord, and the extraordinarily free attitude of the devotee, typified by the cowherd girls in the *Bhāgavata Purāna*, a spontaneous, ecstatic lover outside the normal confines of society and its duties. In the *Gītā*, devotion

is not an intimate, passionate affair but a disciplined concentrating of mind upon a god who reveals himself to transcend and awe man. In the *Bhāgavata-purāna* (and even before) devotion is intimate, passionate, intense, and topsy-turvy. The context of devotion has moved from the battlefield to the isolated glades of Vrndāvana. The devotional paradigm is no longer a strong-willed, heroic warrior who trembles with fear before the divine, but lowly *gopī* women who do not hesitate to rush off to the forest to revel with their god. And, finally, the god himself has changed from a noble, cunning charioteer and politician to an irresistable, beautiful cowherd youth who plays a flute that intoxicates all of creation.[149]

The shift in focus from 'devotion to duty' towards 'devotion to (the be)love(d)' is likely to have been part of another shift: the *historical shift* from a primarily warrior *(kshatriya)* audience to an audience that included both warriors and merchants *(vaiśya)*. Romila Thapar describes an increasing influence of the merchant classes during the opening up of trade with the Mediterranean world and Central Asia that followed from the rule of foreign kings in India (Indo-Greeks, Śakas and Kushānas) between 200 BCE and 300 CE.[150] As Matchett points out, agricultural and merchant values are embraced by the cowherd Krishna of the *Harivamśa* (59), a scripture chronologically somewhere between the *Bhagavadgītā* and the *Bhāgavata-purāna*.[151]

5 Conclusions

Three formal aspects of the *Mahābhārata* and the *Bhagavadgītā* have been discussed – the literary and dramatic genre, the *Gītā*'s dialogue and the audience response. One conclusion is strikingly clear – both are fully recognized as works of art and appreciated as such but more than that, they are considered spiritual works that should be classified, interpreted and responded to religiously. The epic's religious authority is not beyond all criticism, but it draws from its status as being part of the genre of traditional wisdom, orally transmitted by the community from the venerated past as 'sacred story', 'legendary history' and 'instructive treatise'.

Later on, the epic was also classified as a 'great poem', that is to say, evaluated in terms of court poetry according to aesthetic categories that identify a correspondence between certain emotions of the characters and the taste of certain moods. As a poem on warriors waging a war, one would expect the energetic exertion and valour of the epic's characters to evoke the corresponding mood called the 'heroic flavour'. Or one would expect the misery of the war, the weeping of the women and the disastrous end of the Pāndavas to evoke the 'compassionate flavour', which corresponds to the emotion of grief among the characters; this aesthetic category would characterize the poem as 'tragic' in the sense of leaving a disturbed mood among the audience due to the grief of the characters. But Sanskrit literary convention did not allow the 'compassionate flavour' to dominate a poem and thus create a long-lasting worrying effect. Anandavardhana argued that the epic should be interpreted religiously and therefore be 'tasted' in terms of its evocation through aftertone (instead of evocation through correspondence). He concluded that the flavour that a sensitive audience will taste after the plot effect has done its work in the mind of the audience is the detached 'flavour of peacefulness'.

The *Bhagavadgītā*, literally 'Song of the Lord', represents a song sung by a god, Lord Krishna, and therefore constitutes a religious work of art. It contains a dialogue between Krishna and Arjuna. This dialogue embodies four relationships, most of them religious – the friend–friend relationship, the *guru*–disciple relationship, the God–devotee relationship and the Self–I relationship. The *Gītā* is not just an ethical treatise teaching Hindus to act socially, it is simultaneously a devotional manual guiding Hindus to act spiritually.

PART III: CROSS-CULTURAL COMPARISONS

1 Introduction

Three formal aspects in particular are the focus of this chapter on tragedy's artistic–communicative aspects – the literary genre, the dialogues and the audience response. The cross-cultural comparisons in the third part of this chapter will be dedicated to the task of comparing the Greek and Shakespearean material with the Indian or Hindu material. The main question of this part will be: in what respects do or do not the discussed artistic–communicative aspects of Greek and Shakespearean tragedy have parallels in the *Mahābhārata* epic and the *Bhagavadgītā*?

2 Specific literary genres

2.1 Dramatic genres

Art forms may be categorized according to their artistic genre. The notion of 'genre' implies that a specific art form has certain characteristics by which to recognize its specificity. In the Western tradition, the literary genre has two subgenres – the narrative genre, in which a narrator tells the story of the actions of the characters, and the dramatic genre, in which the actions are acted out on stage.

Tragedy belongs to the dramatic genre. Historically speaking, the Greek notion of 'the tragic' (*tragikos*) originally referred to a fifth-century genre of drama that could be recognized as such, put on stage, create certain expectations with the audience, and on the basis of that, be varied upon in order to surprise the audience by fulfilling their expectations differently from what conventions would have predicted. Genre and audience expectation are intimately related to each other, but neither of them is static or timeless. Seneca's Roman tragedies, in particular, had a long-term impact, also on Shakespearean tragedy. But Shakespearean plays have been distinguished in terms of three genre categories – 'tragedy', 'history' and 'comedy'. The very category of 'history' seems to have been introduced because Shakespeare's success in staging historical topics brought it about. Shakespeare plays with a genre's conventions, with the social realities to which they refer, and with the audience's expectations that go with them.

According to these Western audience's expectations, the *Mahābhārata* 'epic' belongs to the narrative subgenre. But the very distinction between the narrative and the dramatic subgenres is not recognized in the Indian tradition. Indian 'poetry' was expected to be performed as a theatrical spectacle in one way or another, a recital accompanied by song, dance and play. In this regard, there was always a dramatic dimension to the narrative. However, the narrative genre, in the Indian tradition, is referred to as *ākhyāna*, or 'story', for the focus on the meaning of the plot, to be distinguished from a *kāvya*, or 'work of belles lettres', for the focus on the expression of beauty. This Indian distinction has been applied to the *Mahābhārata* too, with different outcomes. At first, it was considered a 'story'. Within the category of 'story', the *Mahābhārata* 'epic' was traditionally the foremost example of a 'work of mythology or legendary history' (*itihāsa*). Under the influence of Anandavardhana, the *Mahābhārata* acquired the status of 'great poem' (*mahākāvya*).

In one respect, there is a close parallel between Greek drama and Indian drama: the gods are engaged in theatre, especially as spectators who take pleasure in the dramatic performance. Compared to the religious context of Greek and Indian drama, Elizabethan drama is strikingly secular.

2.2 Tragedy versus comedy

One Western way of trying to identify what is 'tragic' about tragedy is by comparing tragedy to comedy. Right from the beginning, however, this identification effort inevitably went beyond a form definition to include references to their respective contents and to the audience's response. Comedy and tragedy, in Aristotle's classical approach, imply the same ethical standards, but they differ in their expectations of achievement. The comic characters are expected to behave worse than the norm, the tragic characters are expected to behave better than the norm. In comedy, we are surprised by virtue and success, in tragedy by vice and failure. The tragic hero is a worthy and noble, but unfortunate man whom middle-class citizens can identify with because he is not too close a relative, and not too distant a fellow human being either. We feel pity for unfortunate men who are like ourselves because we imagine ourselves in the place of the other. Murray argued that *Hamlet* emphasizes Hamlet's nobility, especially following the dialogue with Osric. However, if the plot pattern of a tragedy creates the audience expectation that a nobleman behave like a nobleman, and that the audience is, therefore, surprised by vice and failure, Shakespeare's *Hamlet* is certain to take us by surprise. As a nobleman, Prince Hamlet is expected to actively take revenge. The more active he becomes, however, the more (self) destructive his actions turn out to be. In the *Mahābhārata*, the epic heroes are expected to behave similarly to the gods and demons whose incarnations or offspring they are on earth. Like Greek epic heroes, they are immortal, but only after death; and before death, they are larger than life. The good heroes, the Pāndavas, are expected not to fail or cheat, but they do. The audience is surprised by their failures and vices, and expects the semi-divine heroes to behave well, in conformity with the(ir) *dharma*, and to get the corresponding reward (victory, wealth, honour, sons, heaven).

In terms of the generic distinction between tragedy and comedy, the Indian aesthetic tradition with its categories in terms of mood effects acknowledges, as one out of eight stable emotions, 'laughter' or 'amusement' (*hāsa*), evoking the corresponding 'comic' flavour, but it does not acknowledge 'weeping' or 'mourning' as a stable emotion evoking a corresponding 'tragic' flavour. Anandavardhana's reading draws from Indian traditions, such as Bharata Muni's aesthetics, in that it does not consider the 'tragic' flavour (in the Greek sense of the word) a flavour. A 'tragic' flavour is not listed, only a 'comic' flavour. Closest to a 'tragic' flavour is the 'compassionate' flavour (*karunarasa*) because the compassionate flavour corresponds to the stable emotion of grief (*śoka*). One is immediately reminded of tragedy's laments as a formal characteristic of all tragedies, and of Aristotle's notion of pity as part of the audience's response. If tragedy has grief as its 'stable emotion' and if its corresponding 'flavour' or 'mood' is compassion or pity, the analogy is striking.

Anandavardhana considers the *Rāmāyana* to be a paradigm of grief and of the compassionate flavour. Should then, instead of the *Mahābhārata*, the *Rāmāyana* be called 'tragic' in the Greek sense of the word? The conflict between the personal virtue of integrity of both Rāma and Sītā, on the one hand, and the collective virtue of public honour defied by the community's suspicion of Sītā's lack of honour and by Rāma's impotence to protect Sītā, on the other, seems unsolvable. Hegel would call it the unsolvable conflict between private family and public state interests. But, it is also a conflict between (mainly Sītā's) personal feelings and (mainly Rāma's) social duties. Whatever good

Rāma and Sītā are doing, their separation is never finally overcome, despite the fact that Rosset's 'tragic mechanism', in my opinion, is clearly lacking. Final separation is not unavoidable because Sītā's innocence is proven several times and the final separation is never imminent. Palmer would argue that the restricted scope of tragedy is lacking and that the more expansive epic form dissipates the constant connection between stimuli for attraction and stimuli for repulsion, transforming the *Rāmāyana* into a melodrama for most of the time, full of unexpected turning events.[152] Anandavardhana would not agree, and stresses the unity of the epic as a whole held together by a single predominant mood. The audience response of Hindus has been unambivalent throughout the ages – during the marriage ceremony, bride and bridegroom are compared to Rāma and Sītā and honoured as such. The grief-stricken life of a separated married couple, symbolizing the 'flavour of love' (in separation), and the corresponding compassionate flavour or tragic mood have won the hearts of the Hindu population. This Hindu epic seems as close as one can get to a Greek tragedy.

If Palmer's definition of the 'tragic' in terms of constantly being in a constant balance between attraction and repulsion on the bipolar scale of audience response is a criterion to go by, the *Mahābhārata* is much more of a *melodrama* that, in the end, encourages the audience to forget the painful past and to rejoice in seeing peace restored instead, and which thus appeals to the pole of attraction only. Calm in the face of fatal necessity fits the noble dignity of a tragic character, as is the case when Hamlet faces Yorick's skull, contemplates death, seems to lose his fear of damnation and 'defies augury'. But final calm in tragedies does not undo the disturbed mood afterwards on the part of the audience. If it does, the sense of tragedy fades away and melodrama takes over. Anandavardhana's reading of the epic leaves no doubt as to its emotional effect on the sensitive reader, with the reservation that the audience's attraction should not consist of the attached emotional state of melodramatic rapture, but should consist of a detached form of delight.

3 Tragic mood and audience response

3.1 The cueing of an audience response

Traditionally, it is the all-knowing narrator who is in the best position to cue the audience response by evaluating the story in retrospect. In *Hamlet*, this role is taken over by the all-knowing witness Horatio, who has been listening to Hamlet's comments all along and is finally asked by Hamlet to tell his story to the audience. As the prime and privileged listener to Hamlet's story, he is qualified to represent the audience in much the same way the chorus plays this role in Greek tragedies. Horatio is not just the prime witness, but also a sceptic one who, in the end, appeals to 'woe' and 'wonder'. The *Gītā* establishes the narrative bridge by having Samjaya, minister to King Dhrtarāshtra and the narrator, finish the *Gītā* while addressing the King. Samjaya retrospectively qualifies the dialogue between Krishna and Arjuna as 'wondrous' (*adbhutam*) and 'pure' or 'sacred' or 'holy' (*punyam*). (18.74, 76) One is reminded of Bharata Muni's aesthetic theory that the 'stable emotion' of astonishment or wonder (*vismaya*) is the source of the corresponding 'flavour of dismay' or 'marvel' (*adbhutarasa*).

The Book of Women is dedicated to the weeping by the Kaurava women after the war, leading to Segal's sharing of tears and suffering, since the Kaurava women are the women of the enemies who lost the war. The ritual closure of the war takes place when Yudhisthira is persuaded to perform the consecratory horse sacrifice as an expiation for the catastrophic bloodshed. But this ritual closure and the weeping are not the end of the story. One hero after the other dies or disappears into the forest, until only Yudhisthira is left behind with his dog – a scene no doubt evoking Aristotle's pity and fear. Aristotle's pity is not, in my understanding, like Anandavardhana's 'flavour evoked through aftertone', but like his 'flavour evoked through correspondence' (between a *rasa* and the stable emotion in the main character). The Aristotelian 'flavour evoked through aftertone' is a consoling sense of restored balance, and therefore a 'cleansing release' (*catharsis*), strikingly illustrated by the next scene, of Yudhisthira showing compassion with his dog by not leaving him behind, and being rewarded for it.

The language of the *Gītā* evokes an attitude of pious awe and meditation, according to Bolle. Through the identification with Arjuna, the audience is cued to have a similar response, to identify with Arjuna as the supreme devotee who has been taught how to simultaneously act socially and spiritually.

3.2 The educational function

Does an audience learn from watching tragic drama? Aristotle maintained that it does. By showing what mortal human beings are like in general, it teaches the audience what they can be like if they (fail to) become socially and politically active. Aristotle focused on the general experience of *human action*. Anandavardhana too, had an aesthetic and therefore by definition generalized experience in mind. But the difference is equally striking. Anandavardhana focused on the general experience of *human emotion*.

And this is not the only difference. For Aristotle, the aesthetic experience of attending a dramatic performance is a *learning process* that brings about a change of hearts and minds, culminating in recognition (*anagnorisis*) and cleansing release (*katharsis*). His notion of *catharsis* may suggest that the imbalanced emotions inherent in the audience response during the play are overcome at the end, when the emotional equilibrium is restored, or maybe already during the play, by watching the tragic characters from a relatively safe distance instead of identifying with them too much and feeling devastated as well. For Anandavardhana, the aesthetic experience of listening to poetry is a *cooking process* that brings about a refined taste, culminating in the mood of peaceful delight (*shantarasa*). The role he assigns to emotions is a positive one, provided they lead to an aesthetic experience, and a very positive one if they lead to a spiritual experience, as is the case with tranquillity and the peaceful mood that draws one closer to the Supreme Reality. Their initial function may be educational in the artistic context of providing instruction in one of the four major goals of human life, but the ultimate aesthetic function is not educational or pedagogical, but mystagogical and therefore religious or spiritual. Keijo Virtanen writes:

> In comparing the above with Aristotle's concept of *katharsis*, it can be stated that *katharsis* is more strictly associated with medical treatment. Thus Aristotelian *katharsis* emphasizes removal, discharge—which is brought about homoeopathically—while the Indian concept of *rasa* is based on relishing, though the consequents are not ignored. *Katharsis* returns the experiencer back to a normal state, but adds unity and harmony; *rasa* is considered to change the whole awareness into an abnormal state by lifting it to an extraordinary, transcendental (*alaukika, lokottara*), and joyful level.[153]

The scope of Aristotle's focus on human action and purification is a this-worldly return to daily life, whereas the scope of the Indian focus on emotion and purification, Virtanen concludes, is extraordinary, beyond the realm of the observable, including the other-worldly.[154]

Edwin Gerow argues that for Aristotle, in poetry, the learning experience and the affective experience are not identical, whereas for Anandavardhana, they are.[155] Poetry is a learning experience accompanied by, and validated by, the emotional part of that experience. Since learning is about change and thus implies *process*, 'the emotional adjunct of this transformational process is also understood dynamically—not understood so much as the evocation of an emotion, as the alteration of emotions'.[156] Powerful plays are moving – they alter the emotions of the audience. Anandavardhana's *rasa*, on the other hand, is not viewed in terms of process, but of *result*. Gerow writes, 'what the Indian play teaches us, directly and straightforwardly, are truths about our emotional make up. The integration sought is an integration of response rather than an integration of action'.[157] Gerow seems to draw on Schechner when he sees yet another difference – whereas the destiny of the Greek play is directional, the destiny of the Indian play is immanent. Unlike the Greek play, the Indian play 'goes nowhere'[158] but instead, while manifesting movement in all directions (backwards, forwards, circular) on the surface, reveals the constant presence of the transcendent whole that is always immanent in the fragmentary parts and amidst hostile experiences. Gerow concludes, 'Direction is *manifestation only*, as Śamkara might say. The emotional response to the play thus becomes the message of the play, purely and simply'.[159] That is to say, not the parts (characters, events) signifying something (e.g., Creon signifying Pericles), but the delight of the audience in emotionally connecting to the always present and significant underlying greater whole, is what makes the play meaningful. In the light of this all-encompassing result, the process becomes illustrative, but also decorative, illusory and ultimately negligible. Gerow's interpretation of Anandavardhana's view of mood effect and audience response is in line with what I argued about framing and juxtaposing plot patterns in the previous chapter. But, above all, it is very helpful in comparing Anandavardhana (affective experience, integration of response, result, the immanent whole) to Aristotle (learning experience, integration of action, process, the directional parts).

The moral mirroring function of plays instructing the audience by example or counter-example represents the neo-classical view of tragedy and *catharsis*. It is probably how Shakespeare's plays were perceived by the Elizabethan audience. Shakespeare himself plays with the moral mirroring function of playing on stage, in the play-within-the-play 'Murder of Gonzago', for example. It turns the moral question 'How to behave?' into the dramaturgical question 'How to act?' and the other way around, and it turns both the moral question and the dramaturgical question into the all-confusing question 'To act or not to act?' Similarly explicit evidence is not available for Greek tragedies. It is telling that Plato and Aristotle do not seem to agree on the question whether watching tragedies can be a reliable source of moral learning. Aristotle seems to think it can be. But even Aristotle prefers reading plays to attending them.

Traditionally, the *Mahābhārata* has not been perceived as a morally edifying story, but as a story full of quarrels and strife. In the previous chapter, Fitzgerald was quoted as pointing to the traditional Hindu reception of the epic 'proper' as an inauspicious text not to be read or recited in their homes by pious Hindus. This attitude seems to have changed dramatically since the 1989 serialization of the *Mahābhārata* on Indian national television, which brought Indian public life to a standstill during its broadcast each Sunday morning between 10.00 am and 11.00 am – whether on television or on stage, seeing Lord Krishna's image, having a *darshan* (tele-vision!) of the god, can be experienced religiously as having a vision of Krishna himself. After all, like the Greek gods, the Hindu gods are engaged in theatre. Unlike the Greek dramatic practice, however, the Hindu dramatic practice excludes the Greek framing of aesthetic appreciation within a *competitive* setting that transforms spectators into judges and critics, and performers into winners and losers. The Hindu performance takes place within a *ritualistic* setting that evokes piety. In the West, the tragic genre enjoys *cultural* authority as serious drama and literature; in India, the epic genre enjoys *religious* authority as serious drama and (pre)history. It seems that the *Mahābhārata* used to be more popular in the countryside whereas the *Rāmāyana* used to be more popular in the cities. Shubha Pathak suggests that both epics have the same function of moral mirroring because 'both heroes exemplify an ideal of righteousness', but 'adopt different strategies to instruct their audiences in *dharma*', the life story of Rāma offering a 'mastery model' of internalization and imitation for those who can achieve *dharma* easily, the life story of Yudhisthira offering a 'coping model' of internalization and imitation for those who face difficulties in attaining *dharma*.[160]

In the case of the *Gītā*, one might expect this scripture, which has a long history of constituting a spiritual manual that is being read and transmitted at home, to have the function of moral mirroring. Arjuna, then, becomes the exemplary role model for all Hindus who try to abide by their caste duties. But this function of moral mirroring is much more prominent in the case of the *Rāmāyana* than it is the case in the *Gītā* whose function is rather more spiritual. This is illustrated by the allegorical interpretation of the dialogue between Arjuna and Krishna in terms of a spiritual battle between man and God, the I and the Self, a Hindu interpretation that perceives the entire epic war as a spiritual battle. Although both the West and India have a tradition of reading myths psychologically, the difference is that Indian psychology has remained part of an inclusively religious discourse and practice whereas Western psychology has become part of an exclusively secular discourse and practice.

4 Specific dialogues

4.1 The authoritative collective voice of the teacher

In the West, dialogue on stage symbolizes public debate, rational, moral and political criticism, consensus building and democracy. At least, that is what it has come to represent to a Western mind that perceives classical Greek culture as the cradle of democracy and secular philosophy.

From a cross-cultural, comparative perspective, however, it is not self-evident that these qualities should automatically be attributed to the dialogical character of tragedy. Dialogue is a formal aspect of Greek tragedy, but beyond this context, it is not by definition a democratic and rational form of communication – unless it is defined as such by a specific context. Ancient Greek tragic dialogue symbolizes these qualities because tragic dialogue is performed on stage and in a political context. Dialogue has become part of an art form instead of part of a ritual recitation. It has lost the religious authority of divine inspiration. A tragic poet is awarded prizes in staged contests. The poet has lost the religious standing of priest or prophet and acquired the secular standing of teacher, Redfield argued.

But what kind of secular teacher? What, or rather, how does the narrative poet teach? He does not explain anything, but shows something. His teaching is not didactic. Yet, like rhetoric, tragic poetry has its roots in the historical context of democratic debate, of appreciating both arguments and counter-arguments. Even the most expressly didactic voice of a play, the authoritative collective voice of the chorus, is itself also one particular voice among many other, dissenting voices, Goldhill pointed out. Common wisdom (traditional knowledge) is no longer transmitted as shared memory making common sense. To Hamlet's mother, Gertrude, nature as presented by traditional knowledge is universal and therefore makes sense, but to Hamlet, it seems particular, and Gertrude is forced to ask herself and Hamlet why. Apparently, one has to be persuaded, and the power of persuasion on which Athenian democracy depends is highly ambiguous, as Sophocles suggests in *Philoctetes*. In this play, Sophocles critically explores lying and deceit in rhetorical speech-making, that is to say, the potentially moral and immoral authority of any rhetorical speaker, Goldhill suggested.

There is a lot of debate in the didactic sections of the *Mahābhārata* epic on issues concerning moral norms and values, a dimension that will engage us in the next chapters. One aspect may be stated beforehand – these debates do not take place within the historical context of an emerging democracy. The outer frame of the epic presents Vyāsa as its composer. Vyāsa is a *brahmin* seer and an incarnation of the deity Vishnu-Nārāyana, and as such, endowed with the priestly authority of a religious teacher. The epic is less authoritative than the *Vedas* and *Upanishads* which are considered divine revelation. The epic has the religious authority of divine inspiration, albeit not of divine revelation.

A not just religiously, but divinely, authoritative teacher turns up in the *Bhagavadgītā*. Strikingly, the narrative setting of Krishna trying to persuade

Arjuna to rejoin the fighting in a crucial war is similar to Sophocles' Neoptolemus and Heracles trying to persuade Philoctetes to rejoin the fighting in a crucial war. Moreover, in his dialogue with Arjuna, Krishna offers counter-arguments to Arjuna's arguments. Apparently, norms and values are debatable since Krishna's counter-arguments do not immediately convince Arjuna. Krishna's powers of persuasion gradually turn Krishna into a learnt secular instructor and a spiritual teacher. The dialogue between Krishna and Arjuna, then, is part of the ancient tradition of transmitting knowledge through the master–disciple relationship. Krishna's comprehensive knowledge is authoritative. Like Hamlet by Hamlet's real father, Arjuna is summoned by his spiritual father to 'remember', to participate in this shared memory and not to forget the message of this collective voice of tradition, of collective expectations and duties. But Hamlet's 'ghostly father' is outdone by Arjuna's 'spiritual father' (Krishna as *guru*), who first speaks with religious and then even with divine authority.

The emergence of the truth as a deliberate act of revelation on the part of Krishna as the one God makes Arjuna 'cross the hairline from uncertainty to certain knowledge' in a way very different from that of Oedipus. Arjuna does not arrive to his conclusions through a rational and investigative search for the truth. He is taught the truth by his spiritual teacher, and he is shown a vision by his supreme Lord. Unlike Oedipus, Arjuna is not making a final decision to face the truth for himself. Yet, in both these cases, the truth was hidden from its witnesses, who dwell in confused ignorance or blindness. And as the truth breaks through, it overrules the empirical knowledge of mortal human beings. It is beyond their imagination. It changes their entire perception of the world, either positively or negatively.

4.2 Failed dialogues

Whereas epic depicts heroes who have battle comrades as friends, tragedy depicts heroes as lonesome. Greek tragedies such as Sophocles' *Antigone* show tragic heroes engaged in failing dialogues, instead of epic heroes engaged in riddle-solving dialogues, and *Oedipus Tyrannus* has a hero who starts out as a dialogically open person, but whose riddle-solving dialogues turn out to be failed dialogues. And failed dialogues imply nothing less than failed lives, failed communities and failed states. The tragic adventure lacks dialogical openness, cuts off contacts, blocks entries, refuses gifts. It is tragic, Heering suggested, and symbolic of Hamlet's unanswered lonesomeness as a human being and decision-maker, that his last request to his friend Horatio be, to tell his story on his behalf. Despite the display of rhetorical graciousness conveying stately order at Claudius' court, Hamlet invalidates the court rhetoric as hypocritical and deceitful, according to Arditi and Margolies. Hamlet's destabilizing responses to the questions of his partners in dialogue reveal to what extent these courtly dialogues, staged to be spied upon, are failed dialogues right from the beginning for sheer lack of going beyond role-playing. Hamlet realizes this by mirroring the other persons' way of communicating, Gash argued, that is to say, by his reversal of the roles of questioner and respondent, thus refusing to identify with the 'you' whom the requests and concealed threats of his partners in dialogue imply.

The *Bhagavadgītā* does not depict Arjuna as a lonesome hero who lacks dialogical openness. Arjuna has friends on both sides of the battlefield. One of the reasons for his refusal to fight is his abhorrence of committing the crime of treachery to friends. His best friend and battle comrade is his charioteer Krishna, who behaves and speaks as a true friend when he reproaches Arjuna. The secular instruction of the counsellor is not just being complemented by the spiritual teaching of the *guru,* but transformed into the revelatory experience of the one God. This constitutes a successful dialogue. It brings about a positive reversal – Arjuna is persuaded to fight – but more than that, the dialogue is deepened. It leads to a revelatory and devotional exchange between God and the human being as His personal devotee.

Or does it? The decisive turning-point or catalyst in their dialogue is the shift from Krishna's teaching to his overwhelming appearance. The focus moves from the level of argument to the level of vision, from an instructive debate among friends to a speechless display of divine authority provoking an abrupt abortion of the dialogue, Arjuna's apology in a choked voice for having spoken as a friend, and Krishna's terrifying call for surrender. There is no room left for reciprocity in this dialogue. It has become the monologue of the Lord of the Universe who is the origin of everything, including the logic of those who debate. And yet, the previous dialogical setting is restored and suggests that Arjuna is left with some real, but no ultimate scope for reflection and choice, precisely because he is now endowed with secret knowledge and imbued with divine love. Is this a failed dialogue, a successful monologue or a successful dialogue? Clearly, it is not meant to represent a failed dialogue, and there is nothing tragic about it. It is meant to be instructive, 'oral tradition' in the fullest sense of the words *sampradaya* and *sampradana,* both 'teaching' and 'giving', gifts that cannot be refused.

4.3 Inner dialogues

In Greek tragedy, inner dialogues are hardly staged as such. Instead, heroes let out heartfelt cries – thus thinking aloud. In Elizabethan tragedy, Hamlet's soliloquies seem to be monologues, but these soliloquies can also be taken to represent as many failing dialogues with himself. Each renewed effort, Lee argued, demonstrates his failure to establish an inner dialogue with his presumed self. Bloom stressed the astonishing breakthrough of (tormented) modern self-consciousness in Hamlet's staged expression of self-overhearing and self-awareness. This self-awareness of and dialogue on the ever-changing nature of one's strictly personal experience, taking place between one part of one's soul and another part of one's soul, in the interiority of the mind and heart as an entire inside world, which is independent from the social world and its social dialogues, and from the outside world and its cosmic order, is widely considered a new stage in the cultural history of the West. Before that, as Charles Taylor explains eloquently, the inner dialogue was taking place within the Christian framework of the soul's dialogue with God in prayer and in Augustine's reasoning about and love of truth as an inner light enabled by the divine light of God as the ultimate Truth enlightening everything, including one's reasoning, memorizing and desiring capacities. That is to say, it took the form of an inner dialogue within the scope of an upward one.[161] And until Augustine, the classical Greek and Roman traditions understood the world of the soul to be one cosmic level among many – not an inner world as opposed to an external one, but one aspect of the cosmic world and its natural order, an aspect either (rationally) attuned to that eternal order or arbitrarily ruled by the appetites and their chaotic tendencies, lacking harmony and permanence.[162] A play like *Hamlet* is still far removed from the literary genre of the novel, of course, which will allow the author and the reader to express their emotions and thoughts freely in the public space of a recognized art form, but *Hamlet* marks the start of dramatic experiments with inner dialogues on stage.

Outside the West, the specific literary genre of the novel did not arise independently from Western cultural influences. Stories were told, including autobiographical ones, and heartfelt cries like prayers, psalms, hymns and love songs were heard. But did they commit one's soul to paper as a purely inner dialogue? One literary way of turning existing stories into inner dialogues was by treating them as allegories of the soul. The journey of a traveller could be read as the searching of a soul for its inner sources, for example. This is also how the Hindu audience took up the story of the battle of two armies fighting each other in the *Mahābhārata* epic, and the scene of Arjuna and Krishna's dialogue on the battlefield in the *Gītā*. In the *Katha Upanishad* (1.3.3–13), the relationship between the chariot warrior and charioteer symbolizes the spiritual relationship between the Self, the body, the intellect and the mind. In Plato's *Phaedrus* 246–56, the soul is similarly compared to a chariot in which a charioteer (reason or intellect) drives a team of two horses. According to

Sukthankar, the epic poets view Arjuna and Krishna simultaneously as the human soul and the divine Self. The implication is that the dialogue of the hero with his own self is not a dialogue, but a battle with his lower self, and the Kurukshetra war is really the psychological conflict within man between evil and good propensities. The battle is a dialogue with one's deepest self, a process of growing self-awareness, which the dialogue between Krishna and Arjuna stands for and inspires to.

4

Socio-political aspects

PART I: TRAGIC AND DRAMATIC ISSUES

1 Introduction

The phenomenon of tragedy is related to a number of basic aspects, the third set of which can be identified as the historical origins and functions of the texts and what they represent socio-politically. The tragic texts themselves refer to their respective socio-political contexts either explicitly or implicitly. Categories such as 'tragedy' and the 'tragic' cannot be understood properly without paying serious attention to their historical occurrence in specific periods of time, originally in ancient and classical Greek society and later on in early modern English society. In what ways could the 'tragic genre' and the notion of the 'tragic' be considered *historical products of their time*, moulded or nurtured by a heightened sensitivity to certain problems rather than to other ones – problems springing from this specific socio-political context? Historically, what impact did social status have on the definition of the 'tragic genre'? What roles did the 'tragic genre' have in the socio-political context? What *functions* did tragedy have vis-à-vis the socio-political *status quo,* as represented by the main institutions of the state, the family and religion? A variety of views will be presented. The *main question* of this first part of the chapter on socio-political aspects is – what socio-political functions were connected with the historical origins of Greek and Shakespearean tragedy?

In the second part of the chapter, on Indian and Hindu issues, there will be a presentation of the ways in which these socio-political aspects are present or absent in the *Mahābhārata* epic and the *Bhagavadgītā*. The third part will try to draw some cross-cultural comparisons between the Western material and the Indian material. The main question of the third part will be – in what respects do or do not the socio-political aspects of Greek and Shakespearean tragedy have parallels in the *Mahābhārata* epic and the *Bhagavadgītā*?

Several institutions have been historically connected with tragedy, either as socio-political sources of conflict or as socio-political sources of legitimation and education – the theatre, the state, religion and the family. We will start this chapter by presenting Hegel's theory of tragedy because his theory is particularly relevant to the discussion of two of these institutions – family and the state – and of one play in particular, Sophocles' *Antigone*. Hegel's way of defining the nature of tragic conflicts is too particular to be universally applicable, but its substantial contribution to the theoretical debate on tragedy remains a challenge to new research into the tragedies themselves. After the section on Hegel's theory of tragedy, the theatre, the state, religion and the family will then be addressed in separate sections.

2 G. F. W. Hegel's theory of tragedy

Georg Friedrich Wilhelm Hegel's theory of tragedy focuses on ethical conflicts that appear intrinsically unsolvable, but are full of potential progress.[1] The historical necessity of these conflicts can be understood, Hegel argues, in the light of world history, which has to pass through certain stages in order to actually realize progress. Hegel suggests that tragedy does not oppose (human) freedom and (supernatural) necessity, but two heroes who embody two justified values the audience identifies with. This moral conflict is in itself and to the tragic protagonists involved unsolvable, but leads to the necessity of 'solving' the moral conflict by transcending it, by achieving a higher moral consciousness, which includes these two rights within a superior hierarchy of values. Two valid but partial claims come into inevitable conflict, but in the tragic resolution, they are reconciled, even at the cost of the destruction of the characters who stand for them, because of a painful realization that each position is only a partial one and that life is ultimately one and all-embracing, instead of divided and particular. One realizes the necessity to step beyond partial identifications in order to be at-one with life. In Hegel's way of thinking, inspired by the spirit of the age of the French Revolution, the active dynamics of reflection and self-reflection have the dramatic potential to turn an intrinsically unsolvable conflict into a historically progressive conflict, driving moral consciousness to the limits of self-contradiction and beyond those limits into the next stage of unity, of contradiction experienced, of consciousness enriched.

Hegel's sense of tragedy does not just pertain to the fact that the conflict is both necessary and unsolvable (in life, but resolved in death). It also relates to the fact that ideas and ideals have to be put into practice and exposed to the harsh realities of life in order to become substantial. One cannot remain an observer of 'being' and admire ideals such as the Greek *polis* for representing the early Romantic ideal of political freedom. One has to consciously engage in the 'action' of dirty politics and warfare if one is to actualize this ideal. That is a lesson Hegel draws from Napoleon, whose 'necessary tyranny' actualizes the ideals of the French Revolution by imposing his Enlightenment laws in Europe by force.

Creon embodies this inherently tragic position in Hegel's interpretation of *Antigone*. He cannot escape the suffering that results from the conflict of taking a position in real life for the sake of an ideal. Yet, Hegel argues, Antigone's position is even more tragic than Creon's. Antigone too, must take 'action' in order for her brother to return to a state of 'being' (home), but unlike Creon, Antigone is conscious of the guilt her action implies. Her tragic action includes tragic consciousness. It does not, however, include an understanding of her action as her own individual action. She ascribes to the gods – not to herself – her necessity to act. She does not become an autonomous subject in Hegel's sense of recognizing oneself as a male agent of history. She remains a female who is excluded from the public sphere of the male. She represents the domestic sphere of life and death, the natural order of the woman and the gods. Gods do not oppose men, but the divine laws of nature oppose the human laws of culture. The domestic sphere is the sphere from which the alienated man is banished into the cultural exile of history despite his efforts at homecoming. In Romantic idealism, as George Steiner and Renée van Riessen explain, this motif of exile and attempted homecoming is represented by the ideal love between brother and sister.[2]

Both Antigone's and Creon's positions are partial ones, but in Hegel's initial interpretation, Antigone's claim is more 'legitimate' than Creon's tyranny. Antigone reveals the internal division of the *polis* into colliding interests while the state denies and suppresses the internal conflict of interests. In fact, the play enacts the opposition between several spheres and between several values, embodied by Antigone and Creon, respectively.[3] However, these oppositions are neither pure and unambiguous nor static. Creon is not entirely or truly blasphemous, universal, reasonable, representing the public interest, lawful, or legitimate. Antigone is not entirely or truly pious, passive, devoid of reason, or unconscious.[4] Steiner emphasizes that in Hegel's interpretation, it is only on the 'historical' level that the agonistic encounter takes place between 'human' and 'divine' laws. On the whole, in the long run, if there is divinity in the household gods, under feminine guard, so too there is in the gods of the city and in the masculine legislature. Hegel's Antigone, Steiner concludes, possesses an insight into the quality of her own guilt, which is denied to

Creon – The body of Polyneices *had* to be buried if the city of the living was to be at peace with the house of the dead.[5]

Steiner points out that it is only later on, in Hegel's *Vorlesungen über die Philosophie der Religion*, that Creon's position becomes equally moral. From this later approach derives the Hegelian notion of tragedy as a conflict between two equal 'rights' or 'truths'. Creon is no longer presented as just a tyrant who doesn't understand the quality of his own guilt, as opposed to Antigone, but an ethical power on equal terms with Antigone. Undeniably, Hegel's statement that Creon is not a tyrant reflects his turn to a Prussian, authoritarian conception of the nation state. But more than that, Steiner suggests, it reflects 'Napoleon's recession from a metaphysical into a political-contingent force'. History no longer coincides with Spirit. 'It is within the realm of the state that man must pursue his homeward journey'. Creon now represents the insight that it is only within the state and by virtue of tragic conflict with the state that morality can make progress.[6]

Hegel's theory of tragedy is helpful in highlighting the socio-political aspects of tragedy, in particular Greek tragedy. A closer look at the Greek and Shakespearean material itself is also needed, of course, in order to properly examine the issues raised.

3 The state and the theatre as institutional sources of legitimation and conflict

Greek tragedies were commissioned by the city authorities of Athens and, in that sense, were a political affair. The actors were not just citizens, they were 'performing a properly civic function—in sharp contrast to the theatre in Rome, where acting was rather despised as something foreign, effeminate, fake, licentious, in short illegitimate and un-Roman', Paul Cartledge points out.[7] He suggests that tragic theatre was a political learning experience – Athenian citizens attended mass meetings and open debates between peers, and in doing so, learnt 'to be active participants in self-government'.[8] Jan Assmann and Joseph M. Bryant emphasize that, unlike ancient Egyptian and Chinese concepts of citizenship and the state, the Athenian concept of citizenship (*politeia*) and the state (*polis*) since Solon's reforms is defined in terms of a community (*koinonia*) of, and a constitution (*politeia*) by, its active and free citizens (*politai*), not in terms of a state stronger than society.[9]

Greek tragedies were also a political affair in the sense that they could, implicitly and by analogy, hint at contemporary conflicts, such as the Peloponnesian War (431–404 BCE) between Sparta (ally – Thebes) and Pericles'

Athens suffering from the Great Plague (Oedipus in contaminated Thebes), in Sophocles' *Oedipus Tyrannus*, probably performed around 430 BCE.[10]

There is much disagreement or ambivalence regarding the exact socio-politically critical and subversive features and functions of (Dionysiac) tragedy in general. Is Greek tragedy meant to *subvert* or to *sustain* the political status quo of the city state?[11] Scholars such as Nicole Loraux suggest that Greek tragedy is the tragic outcry of lamentations from the Pnyx, a distant sound voicing feelings of mourning and antipolitical protest against the civic ideology of the political establishment at the Acropolis.[12] Like Cartledge, Simon Goldhill points out that in the political context, 'to be in an audience is above all to play the role of democratic citizen'.[13] But he too, seems to highlight tragedy's subversiveness. Focusing on the opposition between individual heroism and civic society, Goldhill's choice of *Ajax* and *Philoctetes*, according to Rainer Friedrich, implies the replacement of pious Sophocles by subversive Sophocles. This is part of the current trend to 'euripidize' Sophocles.[14]

Wolfgang Rösler too stresses that Greek tragedy was an intrinsically socio-political affair.[15] He illustrates his point by discussing Sophocles' *Antigone*. The burial of Antigone's brother, Polyneices was, in the view of Athenians, a sacred duty and a judicial order laid down in Athenian laws. For the Athenian public, there was no doubt that Creon was acting illegitimately. Creon represents brute tyranny over and against communicative democracy, he argues. Portraying Creon as an autocratic ruler demanding total obedience and showing a total incapacity to communicate created among the Athenian audience a good feeling about themselves. Plays such as *Antigone* fulfilled the internal function of self-confirmation and consolidation for the Athenian *polis*. At the same time, they fulfilled the external function of propaganda directed at the representatives of non-democratic allies also present at the theatre.

Rösler's reading of *Antigone* is different from Cartledge's reading. Cartledge describes the conflict in terms of 'two in principle compatible and indeed mutually supportive public norms—the unwritten laws of the gods and the man-made laws of the *polis*'.[16] Rösler draws the conclusion that neither an apolitical interpretation of Greek tragedy in terms of timeless classical literature nor a Hegelian interpretation in terms of two equally legitimate, but opposing socio-political principles (the state and the family) is tenable. From Aristophanes' *Frogs* (405), Rösler infers that the Greek audience in those days considered the playwrights teachers of moral and political virtues addressing the citizens of the *polis* by offering them role models (Aeschylus) or analytical and critical capacities (Euripides).

Heinrich Kuch would agree with Rösler that plays such as Sophocles' *Antigone* fulfilled the internal function of self-confirmation and consolidation for the Athenian *polis*. He remarks that the *Antigone* was performed in 442, during the flourishing period of Pericles' rule when opposing forces were temporarily in equilibrium.[17] Kuch links the religious and the socio-political aspects historically by taking up the political theme of the *aristocracy–democracy polarity*. The sixth century was characterized by several social and political reforms in favour of the common people. Drama was instrumental in stimulating public debate on social and moral issues, and in establishing a political consensus on a democratic basis. But Kuch also draws attention to the fact that the tyrants or democratic leaders were themselves often aristocrats, and to the fact that the Attic Sea Alliance constituted one of many efforts to establish an *undemocratic* hegemony over the region (Athens, Sicily, Sparta, Boeotia, Thessaly and finally, Macedon). Edith Hall points out that it was only in the imagination of the spectators that tragedy affirmed the social world in which they lived. In reality, male Athenians did not interact on an equal basis with outsiders, women and slaves. Yet, in tragedy, all these groups had a voice, and a powerful voice at that, which would have been unthinkable in real life.[18] Nonetheless, amidst the presence of many ethnicities on stage, the Athenian self-confirmation on stage is evident. The Athenian virtues are idealized as opposed to the barbaric vices of 'Theban tyranny, Persian despotism, Thracian lawlessness and eastern effeminacy', she explains.[19]

In the fifth century BCE, the audience response had been intimately related to the socio-political functions of tragedy. The political disintegration of the Athenian city state, however, led to the loss of tragedy's *political function* of public debate and consensus building. Likewise, the increase of socially loosening ties, in the form of privatization and individualism, led to the loss of tragedy's *social function*. Tragedy in the fourth century was more about special effects than it was really effective.[20] Its main function became *popular entertainment*. In the meantime, theatres were now built all over the Hellenistic world. This decontextualization (from Athens) reinforced the tendency to depoliticize tragedy. These new developments influenced the way tragedy and 'the tragic' were defined and appreciated. Tragedy continued to be defined by focusing on its specific form (drama, story pattern) and contents (topics and world-view), but additionally, it was described in terms of its general effect on the audience and in terms of the audience's response.

The socio-political context of *Shakespearean tragedy* is closely related to the emergence of English tragedy in general. Like all early modern European theatre, English tragedy had been preceded by the ritual festivities of the medieval church and the medieval court. Since the collapse of the Roman Empire, depopulation and the cultural influence of Christianity, the formally planned Roman towns with their theatres, amphitheatres, temples, baths and other civic institutions, had fallen prey to deregulation. The defence of public space had become weak or non-existent, Spiro Kostof observes.[21]

Religion and the state continued to appeal to visual drama. Medieval predecessors of what was to become public theatre in its own right, such as the mystery cycles, processions and tournaments, had been part and parcel of church and court affairs. It was not until the early Modern Age that *public theatre* gradually developed into *a separate institution,* more or less independent of what had been the involvement, but now became the interference, of religion and the state.[22]

The *interference of religion and the state* in matters connected to the new phenomenon of a separate public theatre turned out to be an ambiguous one in early modern England. Religion had split up into several branches, which were involved in a theological and political power struggle whose outcome was as yet unforeseeable. Anglicans, Roman Catholics and Puritans contested each other by all means, including the use or repudiation of public theatre. When the first permanent playhouse in London, called 'the Theatre', was built in 1576, it was located in the district of Shoreditch, to the north of the City of London 'and well outside its walls', Dominic Shellard writes, that is to say, away from the jurisdiction of the Puritans who controlled the City of London and 'who objected to theatre on the grounds that the process of mimesis— the act of taking on another role—was heretical because actors were denying their God-given role'.[23] Besides, due to the huge political tensions that religiously divided factions generated, right at the beginning of the Tudor reign of Elizabeth I (1558–1603), the proclamation of May 1559 – the Church Settlement with Elizabeth that re-established Protestantism as the national religion – had ordered that magistrates in charge of plays 'permit none to be played wherein either matters of religion or of the governance of the estate of the common weal shall be handled or treated'.[24]

During the Tudor reign, acting was widely held to be a 'base' profession. The construction of the next permanent playhouses – 'the Curtain' in 1577, 'the Rose' in 1587, 'the Swan' in 1595, 'the Globe' in 1599, 'the Fortune' in 1600 and 'the Hope' in 1614 –was again outside the City walls, most of them at Southwark, the 'base' night life district south of the river Thames, which was also far away from the royal palaces of Whitehall, Hampton Court and Greenwich. Theatre companies would play in their own playhouses or move around, each one of them under the private patronage of a local landlord since the 1572 *Act for the Punishment of Vacabondes.*[25] The Tudor court would command several theatre companies at a time for special occasions, especially during the Christmas–New Year period, and pay them by the performance. The spatial distance from the court was primarily indicative of a *social* distinction between people and court, rather than a *cultural* division between entertainment and politics. The performance of theatre plays was meant to entertain the people. Its main function was *popular entertainment.* But some of the more popular plays would be screened for suitability to be performed at the royal court, and polished accordingly. Whereas the City government disliked the performances and popularity of the theatres, the court took continuing pleasure in their performances which, as a result, 'initiated a trend towards a more court-based drama' (especially after 1597 due to Privy Council restrictions).[26] A main function of public theatre became *royal entertainment*. Royalty and public theatre grew closer. On the one hand, 'courts developed around the persons of the divine-right kings that dictated the tone of the national culture', as Alvin Kernan points out.[27] On the other hand, new monarchs such as James I, intent on weakening the barons and establishing their own absolute authority, started to monopolize public theatre through exclusive patronage and general censorship. 'The Stuart monopolization of theater was a strategic move, putting a powerful propaganda medium in James's hands'.[28]

Public theatre had become a more or less independent institution, but it continued to have a *public function*. What that means becomes much clearer if compared to the private function of public theatre in the nineteenth century. Steiner highlights the sharp diminution in the role of the theatre in the community, the altered socio-political balance between public and private life and the expansion in the means of communication (newspapers and novels) as the crucial causes of a shift from theatre's public to private function.[29]

Since many of the selected plays were about royal courts and the aristocracy, there was a real risk of royals or diplomats feeling offended by what they were confronted with. The Lord Chamberlain's Men, as Shakespeare's company was called at that time, were also exposed to such risks that simultaneously demonstrated the power of public theatre to unsettle those in authority, as the Southhampton incident during the Essex revolt strikingly illustrates.[30]

Shakespeare and his company appear to have shared in the royal gratitude for support in a critical time. Soon after James had arrived in London, the Crown issued a warrant to the Lord Chamberlain's Men, which brought them under the King's patronage and turned their name into 'the King's Men'. The players continued to work in the public theatres downtown and probably still made most of their money there but, 'as the monarch's servants, the King's Men was the star company among several royal companies at the Jacobean court, providing 177 of the 299 plays performed there between 1603 and 1616. And whenever his company played at court, Shakespeare's plays were those most preferred', according to Kernan.[31]

This turn of events only fuels the question to what extent and in what way Shakespearean tragedy meant to *subvert* or to *sustain* the political *status quo* of the English monarchy around 1600. All one can say with certainty is that Shakespeare's plays could not have explicitly offended the king or court.[32] Stuart censorship would take place under the surveillance of the Master of the Revels, who was charged with controlling all aspects of theatre in both the palace and the city. Kernan writes:

> Hamlet performs the major functions of the Master of the Revels when he greets the players and welcomes them to Elsinore, listens to a recital of lines from their Dido and Aeneas play, chooses *The Murder of Gonzago*, modifies the play for court performance with his famous "dozen lines, or sixteen", lectures the actors on dramaturgy and acting style, arranges for the players to be housed, and, during the performance, ironically assures an uneasy king of the propriety of the play for the royal ear:
> King: 'Have you heard the argument? Is there no offense in't?'
> Hamlet: 'No, no, they do but jest, poison in jest—no offense i' th' world.'
> [III.ii.232][33]

Poison in jest, politics in entertainment. By fairly presenting the political arguments of all sides, it remains unclear whether Shakespeare took sides in the debates.

In Shakespeare's studies of the degradation of powerful men and women, Michael Hattaway argues, he inevitably engaged not only with morality, but with the nature of power and authority. Comic scenes in the tragedies do not just provide comic relief, but occasions for popular voices to scoff at their superiors, similar to the 'fine revolution' in the Gravedigger scene (V.i.89).[34]

The actual stage where *Hamlet* and all the other Shakespearean plays about rulers and decision making are performed is, in the end, a theatre stage, of course. Or is it? I agree with Kernan and Diehl that the actual stage is as much the political stage of the English Renaissance kings, who are struggling with the issue of legitimate kingship in general and with the issue of legitimate succession in particular, as it is the theatre stage, which reflects the political stage and the ideological debate accompanying it. The *entertaining function* and the *political function* of Shakespearean tragedy are intertwined. Public theatre and royal theatre have become linked with each other, for both the existence of theatrical entertainment and the existence of the monarchy are politically threatened, and both institutions are in need of all the support they can mobilize. Shakespeare's plays could not have offended the monarchy or the religio-political establishment. But as part of a more or less independent institution, his plays are much more likely to have functioned in a challenging way than in a legitimizing way, by displaying the dangers of excess.

4 Religion as an institutional source of legitimation and conflict

As a Greek art form, tragedy is historically rooted in the *cult* of the god Dionysus. All drama was performed under the sign of Dionysus, the god of *theatre*, associated with illusion, transgression and metamorphosis, Cartledge writes.[35] Richard Seaford also mentions Dionysus' association with initiation and the mysteries, which explains his contradictory nature, his embodiment of anti-structure and his link with periods of crisis and transformation of identity, like Pentheus in Euripides' *Bacchae*.[36]

Euripides' Dionysus in the *Bacchae* can also be interpreted *politically*, according to Hendrik S. Versnel. He argues that the Hellenistic henotheism (the complete and exclusive worshipping of one's personal and only saviour god amidst the acknowledgement of many other gods) characteristic of Euripides' portrayal of Dionysus is not only similar to the totalitarian despotism of the Hellenistic empires, but also emerges around the same period.[37] For Kuch, the cult of Dionysus was political right from the start. He claims that Dionysus, the god of fertility and wine, was, by his very nature, venerated by the farmers. For the tyrants of the sixth century BCE, promoting the cult of Dionysus was a politico-cultural opportunity to fight their aristocratic opponents by relying on the common people for their political support. Seaford notes that the Dionysus of the *Antigone*'s final choral ode is invoked to come and purify the city as 'the civic god who in tragedy after tragedy presides over the self-destruction of the ruling families of the mythical past, to the benefit of the *polis*'.[38] Seaford is, in fact, in line with Cartledge's argument that the religious festivals of the Athenian 'theatre state' 'served further as a device for defining Athenian civic identity'.[39] In Athenian tragedy, religion and politics were intertwined.

The religious conflict between Protestantism and Roman Catholicism is a constant source of outright war in *Shakespeare*'s time. The theatre is a potential stage for taking sides in the religious conflict and legitimize one religion over the other. It is also the object of a religious controversy. The Protestantism of the Puritans in the City of London is anti-theatrical, while that of the Court promotes the theatre. According to Huston Diehl, 'Shakespeare actively seeks to dissociate his own theatre from . . . superficial spectacles' associated with the theatricality of Roman Catholicism, 'and he claims for the theatre an ethical purpose and an emotional power that seem to align it with early Protestantism', like in Hamlet's use of drama to arouse the guilty conscience of the king.[40]

Religion constitutes an institutional conflict in other respects as well. The issue of eternal damnation or redemption, for example, used to be related to the belief in the existence of purgatory and the institutionalized practice of celebrating Mass for the dead. Hamlet's father is doomed to stay in purgatory and the Lutheran prince studying in Wittenberg is no longer expected to believe in his redemption from purgatory by praying for the deceased. Suddenly, the only option left for the mourners to do on behalf of the dead was blood-revenge, Robert N. Watson notes, 'and promptly the Elizabethan stage began depicting characters using worldly revenge (as in *The Spanish Tragedy* as well as *Hamlet*) to redeem tormented ghosts'.[41]

Religion was also in conflict with political theory. Niccolò Machiavelli argued that state authority does not derive from God, but from man. Rulers can come to power in many different ways. The inherited authority of monarchs is different from power seized by force or being elected into an office for only one year. State authority derives from a combination of being wanted by the people and being pragmatic in the exercise of power.[42] 'Pragmatic comparisons between different political systems revealed that authority might be secular rather than divine in origin', Hattaway notes, and based on theatrically creating the image of a ruler that would make a powerful impression on his subjects and command their respect – quite the opposite of Prince Hamlet's 'antic disposition' (I.v.172), but also quite the opposite of the Tudor and Stuart kings' claim to the throne as a divine right. Hamlet's reference to Calvin's 'special providence' when he decides to accept Laertes' challenge to a duel is illustrative, Hattaway explains, of this claim – a duel was a species of trial whose outcome was divinely ordained. But, Hallaway concludes, 'Shakespeare indicates that the actions have their origins not in divine providence but in a decision of the king'.[43]

In addition to the issue whether state authority actually derives from God, religions such as Christianity claim that state authority *must* derive from God as the moral lawmaker and guarantee of good governance. Machiavelli's idea of strategically calculated killing for the sake of power represents rather a secular virtue, the immoral virtue of pragmatic reasoning, of 'great men' like Claudius and Fortinbras, who are competent statesmen, as opposed to 'good men' like Hamlet, who is clearly incompetent when it comes to effective governance. Do men have to be 'good' in order to be 'great'? Again, Hattaway argues, religion as a source of legitimation is challenged.[44]

5 The family as an institutional source of legitimation and conflict

Greek *epic* heroes are socially rooted in their families. Their participation in society is embedded in their participation in the family. Homer's hero,

Odysseus, is destined to come home, to be in charge of the family affairs and to rule the society of Ithaca accordingly. Steven Shankman and Stephen Durrant point out that Odysseus displays strikingly more individual independence, intentional testing (of his father) and emotional distance with regard to his own family members than ancient Chinese models for social participation in the family demonstrate. Greek epic heroes are socially embedded in the family, but there is more room for individuality and adventure than in the ancient Chinese ideal of staying at home and participate fully in the corporate body of the family.[45] Greek *tragic* heroes, however, witness their homes uprooted. Homecoming is no longer the solution to their social problems. The family has become a source of social conflicts.

An important socio-political issue in tragic plays is the *polis–oikos* polarity. The *polis–oikos* polarity, that is, the state–family polarity, has been cited, since Hegel's interpretation of Sophocles' *Antigone*, as a perfect example of the conflict between two equal rights, the collision between the right of the state on one side, and familial love and the law of the household gods on the other. Both sides are considered to give rise to injustice because they are one-sided, but both are considered to have validity. The fall of both characters, Creon and Antigone, who succumb because they cannot yield, is seen as an illustration of the antagonism between the new *polis* and the earlier kinship systems in ancient Greece. Hegel's interpretation has been extremely thought-provoking because several, from a Western point of view 'universal', oppositions are mobilized at a time (divine–human, feminine–masculine, family–state, individual–community, particular–general, nature–culture, unconscious–conscious) and because these oppositions are presented as dynamic instead of static, and much less pure than a clean antagonism between two mutually exclusive positions would have presented. Their contamination generates the dynamics and tensions Hegel is looking for.

Many scholars have dealt with Hegel's reading of *Antigone* and the *Oresteia* and suggested alternative readings. In John D. B. Hamilton's view, Antigone appears as the very embodiment of '*justice*' *(dikē)* in the *polis*, arguing that her act of disobedience, in fact, reconciles the values of lineage (kinship) and city (state). The point is not her private conscience, but the public consciousness of the age-old customs (*ta nomina*) preceding the new laws (*nomoi*). It is Antigone who has the established customs on her side and therefore represents the *polis*. Creon, on the other hand, is simply wrong and tyrannical – the unjust ruler who destroys the very foundation of the body politic, the family.[46]

Judith Butler writes that the figure of Antigone cannot be reduced to a purely un-political embodiment of kinship and that Creon cannot be reduced to a purely political embodiment of the state. Antigone is very political in her public voicing of rebellion and Creon is very much involved in family affairs and blood lines enabling his succession. Both idealized kinship and political sovereignty, she suggests, emerge as socially deformed. Antigone has already departed from kinship, herself the daughter of an incestuous bond, herself devoted to an impossible incestuous love of her brother, while Creon has assumed his sovereignty only by virtue of his kinship line, Butler points out.[47]

In Ger Groot's view too, Antigone is not the family-minded person usually presented.[48] There is much more ambiguity in the stance she takes. Polyneices is not her only close relative. Ismene and Creon are close family members too, and Haimon is her husband-to-be. Her vocation to obey (which she calls 'love') the laws of the gods is stronger than any sense of human love. She cruelly laughs at her sister's wish to die with her (551), and she never shows any affection whatsoever towards Haimon. The love for her dead brother is denied her living sister and her husband-to-be. Moreover, if performing a valid ritual burial is her true and only concern, she has fulfilled her task by performing it once and for all, without being recognized by the guard. Instead, she insists on doing it a second time and in such a provocative way that she is arrested and brought to her uncle, Creon. She is, in fact, as extremist and stubborn as Creon, and in no way a character to identify with. Ismene and Haimon constitute the wiser mirror image of these two tragic characters. Creon may be extremely stubborn when it comes to state affairs, but he is more flexible than Antigone when it comes to family members and matters. She ignores the expected marriage with her full cousin, is entirely obsessed with her one and only dead brother, and never has any doubts about the gap between right and wrong, between her and her opponents.

The *polis–oikos* issue is also crucial to the socio-political focus of Aeschylus' *Oresteia*. Goldhill shows how the story of Orestes is always told in Homer's *Odyssey* to be exemplary in a positive sense, whereas in Aeschylus' *Oresteia*, this key example becomes problematic due to a shift of focus – a focus on gender. The conflicts of the *Odyssey* are among men, for male authority within the household. The proper men should have proper control of the household. Women do not play a significant role. 'Both the transgressions . . . and the resolutions of these transgressions are to be located in the paternal order of the *oikos*'. Aeschylus shifts the focus by allowing women a position of power in family and city affairs. Orestes becomes famous for matricide – instead of being famous for restoring order in his paternal house. 'Whereas for Homer the answers to the conflicts of his narrative were to be located in the order of the *oikos*, for Aeschylus the answer is to be found in the *polis*. . . . In Aeschylus' trilogy, the household itself needs to be relocated within the frame of the city' and its institutions, where the transgressions, violence and revenge within the household are more or less dealt with. To a great extent, the *Oresteia* becomes a charter for the *polis*.[49]

It is telling, Hall suggests, that the *polis–oikos* issue should be raised 'in the marginal space immediately outside the door of the private home'. This location marks the opposition between the public and the private domain, but also their problematic interrelatedness, from a man's perspective. After all, a man's private ruling of the household was considered an indication of his public performance. 'Creon in Sophocles' *Antigone* fails both as a father and as a civic leader, and the two failures are interdependent'.[50] Like children and slaves, women are considered dependent by nature. The woman should stay at home but the man should 'come home' (*nostos*, homecoming) to restore male order. Hall writes, 'Women only become disruptive (that is, break one of the "unwritten laws," act on an inappropriate erotic urge, or flout male authority) in the physical absence of a legitimate husband or lord (*kurios*)'.[51] Women like Penelope, Clytemnestra and Antigone, who are unsupervised by men, are supposed to lack the guardian or command they need to take proper decisions,[52] a view of intrinsic female dependence that has its Indian parallel in the famous story of Nala and Damayanti (a fairy tale that is also part of the epic), as Wendy Doniger has demonstrated.[53] Hall comes to the conclusion that, taken as a whole, tragedy both recognizes the *legitimacy* of Athenian institutions, such as the patriarchic family and slavery, and *challenges* them, by giving women and slaves a voice.[54]

If religion and the state were two main sources of instability to draw from for *Hamlet*, family was another disruptive force. Not just the royal family, but family ties, in general. A characteristic of royal family ties is, of course, that family matters are, by definition, mixed up with state affairs. John Peck and Martin Coyle suggest that the second and the third scene of Act I in *Hamlet* should be taken together because both the desire for power in the state and sexual desire in the family reveal a far more general sense of disruptive forces lying beneath the surface of society and life in general.[55] Family and the state seem to represent two battlefields for the same emotions when it comes to violent power and love.

If this interpretation is correct, the focus is on the legitimacy of strong emotions and desires, not on the legitimacy of institutions such as the family and the state. Thomas McAlindon, in line with this interpretation, stresses the psycho-social conflict in Hamlet between the initial feelings of affection for his parents, Ophelia and his friends, and the subsequent pressure to use violence for the sake of revenge, the feelings of hatred regarding the murderer of his father, the feelings of disgust regarding his mother's readiness to marry his uncle.[56]

But it is not just psychological chaos that reigns. Hamlet's royal family has lost all legitimacy. McAlindon points to social chaos too, 'Fratricide is a primal symbol of the shattering of human bonds'. The marriage of Claudius to his sister-in-law is presented as incestuous, 'as a reflection of primal chaos where human bonds and the order of society may be said to begin'.[57] The contamination effect, of an immoral royal family upon the moral order of a legitimate state authority, is a source of outrage for the Ghost, who embodies the family and the state as a source of legitimation, not of conflict.

Even in real life, in the family history of the Tudor royal family, the reputation of King James' mother Mary, Queen of Scots, was tainted by the suspicion that she had, like Gertrude, 'over hastily' married Bothwell, after the two of them had murdered Mary's previous husband, Darnley, Henry King of Scots, the proclaimed father of James, whose duty it thus became to take revenge on Bothwell and on his mother, if one goes by the version of Darnley's relatives, the Lennox family, who commissioned a painting commemorating the events and having James pray for revenge, as Kernan explains in detail.[58]

6 Social status defining the tragic genre

One way of defining tragedy that focuses on its socio-political context revolves around the formally artistic question – who are, socio-politically speaking, allowed to be represented and what do they represent on stage in classical tragedy?

Aristotle is well-known for his conviction that aristocracy is superior to democracy. He therefore holds that, compared to epic, tragedy is vulgar and inferior because epic appeals to a cultivated audience that had no need of an actor's poses, while tragedy appeals to a lower class.[59] Aristotle recommends reading tragedies instead of watching actors. He holds that, compared to tragedy, comedy is vulgar and inferior because comedy wants to imitate people who are worse than the people we know, whereas tragedy wants to imitate people who are better.[60] Tragic actors imitate excellent men (*spoudaioi*),[61] men more virtuous, nobler, more honourable, more reputable and successful than we are on average, Aristotle says. Tragedy is an imitation of a serious and complete action that has magnitude. Does this imply that only noblemen and their aristocratic affairs are worthy of being staged? Is 'excellence' the same as 'nobility' and 'dignity'?

We saw in the previous chapter that the Elizabethan neo-classic critics who were opposed to Marlowe, Kyd and Shakespeare were very outspoken in their view that only noblemen and their majestic matters were worthy of being staged in tragedy. Sir Philip Sidney's *Defense of Poesy* became the most eloquent expression in England for this neo-Aristotelian view. Raymond Williams explains:

> The neo-classical rules for tragedy, while assuming that tragic themes must be historical because they must concern great matters of state, tended to argue from the necessary dignity of tragedy rather than from its general and representative quality. And if dignity was the real criterion, the discussion of method was then governed mainly by considerations of decorum. Socially, this is an aristocratic rather than a feudal conception. Rank in tragedy became important because of its accompanying style rather than because the fate of the ruling family was the fate of a city, or because the eminence of kings was the very type of worldliness.[62]

Williams' compact formulation is, in fact, a summary of the entire development so far. In Greek tragedy, royal aristocrats feature prominently because their actions have a visible impact on the lives of others and on the destinies of entire city states; their actions demonstrate the public and metaphysical importance of action in general; theirs are the real actions, the actions that make a difference, ruling the people and mediating between gods and men, Williams argues.[63] Senecan tragedy displays a shift of focus. Williams observes an emphasis 'on the nobility of suffering and enduring misfortune, which provided a basis for the later transfer of interest to the suffering individual, away from the general action'. In medieval Christian ideas about tragedy, the 'fall of princes' stands for the divine warning against the sin of seeking worldly success instead of seeking God. Tragic action is now limited to the worldly action of princes only, 'under the pressures of . . . the alienation of feudal society'. In Renaissance tragedy, the medieval stress on the fall of princes is combined with an aesthetic interest in methods of writing tragedy and in its effects on the audience, governed by considerations of noble dignity and decorum. Rank in tragedy becomes important because of its accompanying aristocratic style. Dignity becomes both a matter of aristocratic rank (content) and a matter of aristocratic style (form).[64]

This way of defining tragedy raises interest in the question whether tragedy is basically an *exclusively aristocratic affair*, or potentially a *democratic affair*, or even the best proof of early (Athenian) democracy, and whether classical tragedy is different from modern tragedy in this respect.

Steiner describes tragedy as in essence an aristocratic and therefore public affair of grave importance, and the rise of the middle classes as coincident with the decline of true tragedy ('serious tragedy').[65] With the rise to power of the middle class, the centre of gravity in human affairs shifted from the public to the private. In the eighteenth century, there emerges for the first time the notion of a private tragedy and private tragedy became the chosen ground not of drama, but of the new, unfolding art of the novel, a literary form appropriate to a fragmented modern audience, Steiner argues. What Steiner seems to hold against the middle classes is their down-to-earth empiricism, their materialist and physical needs, and their sense of language. The idea of 'prose tragedy' is singularly modern, whereas verse stands for 'high tragedy'. 'Kings, prophets, and heroes speak in verse' because 'their style of utterance must reflect' their elevated and exemplary status.[66] Traditionally, the distinction between verse and prose corresponds not just to a separation between the higher and lower classes, but also between tragedy and comedy.[67] Steiner's point is that tragedy is, by definition, an elitist affair.[68] The protagonist must be an outstanding, towering, exceptional personage in order to face and be able to cope with the exposure to supernatural forces like gods and evil, to a threatening 'otherness' in the physical world. The perception of the metaphysical ('of the agonistic to being') is not given to everyman, and this does not please the mediocrity of the middle and lower classes who claim egalitarianism. Rightly or wrongly, social status, a representative role in the community, was an unexamined correlative to excellence until the rise to power of the middle classes.[69]

Steiner has been criticized from different angles. From a self-proclaimed Marxist and Irish Catholic angle, Terry Eagleton is particularly outspoken in his criticism and dismisses Steiner's world as 'an austerely patrician world constructed so as to exclude common feeling', excluding also the Judeo-Christian wisdom that transcendence lies 'in the outstretched palm of a starving child'. Eagleton concludes that 'Steiner insists on the littleness of humankind, but not on its preciousness'.[70] Eagleton sees the late-capitalist system as 'Promethean', in the sense that it is tragically self-undoing, exactly in so far as it has, materially speaking, produced the means of emancipation while, politically speaking, thwarting that end at every turn. Late modernity has recreated in its own way some of the conditions that gave birth to tragedy, and has therefore, in fact, witnessed the renewal of tragedy, not the death of it.[71]

So, who is allowed to be represented and representative on stage in *Greek* drama? Tragedy is different from comedy in this respect. But in what sense? Hall explains that *group* identity was crucial and that it depended on citizen status. The citizen was a male belonging to several groups simultaneously, such as his household, his city district, his tribe, the assembly and specific bodies. She also writes:

Comedy is interested in the competing identities to which this internal civic organisation gave rise, but tragedy's examination of identity is more generalised. Human/divine, male/female, adult/child, free/slave, citizen/non-citizen, Athenian Greek/non-Athenian Greek, and Greek/barbarian are the most significant social boundaries negotiated by tragedy. The answer to the sphinx's riddle, solved by Oedipus, is 'man'. A crucial frontier defined by tragedy is that between man and god.[72]

As Lawrence Danson pointed out in the previous chapter, the very titles of *Shakespearean* tragedies (*Hamlet, Othello, King Lear, Macbeth*) seem to reflect Donatus' view that tragedies should be centred around *distinct individuals* while comedies represent *character types*. In Shakespearean tragedy, the focus is not exclusively on rulers, aristocrats and superiors either. Commoners too play a role on stage. That is precisely why neo-classic critics such as Sir Philip Sidney objected to such tragedies – the prominence of commoners turned these tragedies into tragicomedies or outright comedies. Shakespeare, in turn, exploited class distinctions, for example by having clowns and menials 'speak prose in the very same scenes in which their masters speak in iambic verse', as Steiner notes.[73] If clownish characters belong to comedy because 'clowns' are both funny and of low social status, Shakespeare breaks classical genre conventions, but also the social conventions of keeping 'high culture' separate from 'low culture', Danson argued.[74]

7 Conclusions

Several institutions have been historically connected with tragedy, either as socio-political sources of conflict or as socio-political sources of legitimation and education – the theatre, the state, religion and the family. In the case of Greek tragedy, the theatre is not a separate institution independent from religion and the state. In sharp contrast to Roman theatre, its functions are properly civic – to show fellow citizens the implications of what it means to be or not to be democratic citizens. In Greek tragedy, these implications tend to be disturbing, but this can be for many reasons, not just for socio-political reasons. Moreover, if it is for socio-political reasons, it need not be because tragedy is intent on subverting the *status quo*. Tragedy has the potential to be subversive, but its criticism of the *status quo* is itself part of the socio-political *status quo* organizing it and is often interpreted as having an educational function – people learn to appreciate public debate and community. To the extent that tragedy is part of the main Athenian city festivals, one may argue that it fulfils the legitimizing function of celebrating the city's identity. Since tragedy takes place under the sign of Dionysus, it also fulfils the religious function of honouring the gods. Simultaneously, tragedy has an entertaining function. It is only after the fifth century BCE that it loses its socio-political functions in favour of its function of popular entertainment.

In the case of Shakespearean tragedy, the theatre becomes a separate institution relatively independent from religion and the state. The state and religion may interfere and try to exercise censorship. By law and practice, the theatre is not allowed to put on stage religious or state matters. Shakespearean tragedy is expected to limit itself to fulfilling the function of popular and royal entertainment. Within these limits, its 'majestic' contents raise all kinds of cross-border issues that seem to be permissible as long as they are meant to be purely entertaining. There is always the potential of public theatre to unsettle those in authority, and this is a risk for actors and authorities alike. The theatre's relative independence as an institution specializing in the field of pure entertainment is much more likely to have functioned in a challenging way than in a legitimizing way. This is illustrated by the fact that Shakespeare dares to withhold kings in his plays (and in his audience!) their divine right to rule and that he has his characters draw arguments from both sides of the violent religious controversy between Protestantism and Roman Catholicism.

The family is another institutional source of conflicts that tragedy raises as a disruptive socio-political issue. The Greek interrelatedness of the household and the city and the Shakespearean interrelatedness of the royal family and the state are presented as highly problematic. Their conflicts are connected with the tensions between the private and the public domain, between women and men, between loyalty and ambition, between the powerless and the powerful, between legitimate rule and illegitimate rule, and between order and chaos. To raise the family issue fulfils the socio-political function of reflecting not only on its rootedness in society, but also on the rootedness of society in the family.

Who are, socio-politically speaking, allowed to be represented and what do they represent on stage in classical tragedy? Is tragedy basically an aristocratic affair or a democratic affair? In Greek tragedy, the aristocratic cast symbolizes the public and metaphysical importance of the action and it enacts the clash between aristocratic and democratic values while favouring the democratic ones. In Senecan tragedy, the aristocracy is the bearer of violent actions and noble emotions and states of mind. In neo-classical Elizabethan tragedy, the aristocracy represents the seriousness of 'majestic' affairs, the superior rank and honour of the fighting and ruling classes, and the aesthetics of a gracious and rationally disciplined lifestyle. Only these upper ranks of society are considered worthy of constituting tragedy's representative cast. In Shakespearean tragedy, aristocrats tend to be distinct individuals who interact not just with other aristocrats, but also with commoners. They represent human beings in general and socially embedded, but distinct individuals in particular.

PART II: INDIAN AND HINDU ISSUES

1 Introduction

The third set of aspects of Western tragedy discussed in the first part of this chapter was identified as the historical origins and functions of the texts and what they represent socio-politically. This second part is dedicated to the original socio-political context of the *Mahābhārata* epic and the *Bhagavadgītā*. Did issues similar to those in Western tragedy play a role, issues regarding the state, the family, religion? Did similar sensitivities to problems occur in connection with the classical Indian epic tradition as it presents itself to us in the *Mahābhārata* epic as a whole and in the *Bhagavadgītā*, as a part of it? Did similar functions play a role in the case of the epic genre?

What makes a discussion of the historical origins and functions of the *Bhagavadgītā* and of the *Mahābhārata* epic as a whole complicated is the difficulty of dating the events to which the epic seems to refer and of dating the text layers within the epic that reinterpret the events and reshape the contextual framework. The *Mahābhārata* seems to have been written over a period of several centuries while telling and retelling stories about a period several centuries earlier. Should one focus on events or on idea(l)s in order to date the main themes in the *Mahābhārata* epic? D. P. Chattopadhyaya points out that whereas events are causally traceable, at least in principle, of ideas one can only meaningfully speak of rise, development, decline and fall. The epic must be presumed to construct and reconstruct the socio-political reality it is referring to. Historians, in turn, take up the challenging task of reconstructing this process and of getting as close to the original socio-political reality as possible. But it remains extremely difficult to pin down the dividing line between imagination and rootedness in socio-political realities.[75]

Despite these difficulties concerning the historical reconstruction of a dividing line between imagination and rootedness in socio-political realities in the epic and concerning the tensions between diachronic and synchronic interpretations of the epic, some scholars have been able to shed substantial light on the socio-political functions of the Indian counterparts for three out of four institutions connected with the historical origins of Western tragedy – the state, the family and religion. In India, the theatre remained part and parcel of religion and the state, their rituals and their festivals. It was not institutionalized separately for many centuries. What follows in this second part of the chapter is a presentation of the Indian epic's material on the state, the family and religion as institutional sources of conflict, legitimation and education.

2 The state and the family as institutional sources of conflict and legitimation

2.1 Clan-based societies and monarchical states

Romila Thapar offers a historical approach to the *Mahābhārata* epic and its subject matter.[76] Historians such as Thapar have abandoned the concept of an 'epic age', but the social assumptions implicit in the narratives are of value to them even if the events are fictional.[77] Her knowledge of early Indian history allows Thapar to recognize a difference in the depiction of society in the earlier, narrative sections reciting a series of stories based on bardic material, and the didactic sections relating to the duties of the king, to ultimate liberation and to practices drawing on the law books, respectively:

> The narrative sections seem to depict societies of tribal chiefships moving towards the change to a state system with monarchy as the norm. There is a strong emphasis on lineage rights and functions and a fairly flexible inclusion of a variety of kinship forms. The economy tends to be pastoral-cum-agrarian in which cattle raids and gift-exchange are important components. Heroism is wrapped up in the defence of territory and the honour of the kinsfolk. The didactic sections in contrast assume a highly stratified society with frequent reference to caste functions rather than lineage functions. The political system assumes well-established monarchies and an increasing concentration of authority in the hands of the king. The economy is essentially agrarian with a familiarity with urban centres as commercial units. Gift-giving involves the granting of land in addition to other forms of wealth.[78]

According to Thapar, therefore, political forms in the epic are not sharply differentiated, but they tend to mark a transition from *tribal chiefships* or oligarchies to *kingdoms*.[79]

One characteristic of lineage society noticeable in the *Mahābhārata* is 'the resort to migration to ease tension and conflict, particularly in relation to political power. Thus the Pāndavas build a new capital at Indraprastha'. The conflict between the non-state and state system is more clearly noticeable in the *Rāmāyana*, the other main epic of Hinduism, which favours the monarchical state. 'Whereas in the *Rāmāyana* the difference is projected in the depiction of two entirely different societies, in the *Mahābhārata* the change is interpolated into the same society but is evident in the difference between the narrative and didactic sections'.[80] In the later didactic texts of the *Mahābhārata*, 'the king has rights which place him above his kinsmen but he also has to perform an elabo-rate number of duties'. Also new is the development of elaborate rules regarding the functioning of the various classes (*varnas*).[81] In *Gītā* 1.40–44, a class struc-ture defines every group's place in terms of a necessary hierarchical order.

So, the basic *socio-political source of conflict* underlying Indian society, as it is expressed in the epic, is a conflict *between tribal chiefship and monarchy*, the monarchy and the caste system introducing hierarchy in the process of political and social differentiation at the expense of clan-based societies.[82] Thapar's perspective sheds an interesting light on the meaning of the Kurukshetra war, which dominates the main story of the epic – the epic betrays a socio-political change of historical proportions, a transition from one type of society to the next.[83]

2.2 The rise of empires

In Alf Hiltebeitel's understanding, it would seem that the epics' main narratives refer to former kingdoms that no longer existed by the time of Magadha's metropolitan states, but were presented as glorious empires of the past by *brahmin* poets.[84] On the basis of the link between empire and epic, on the basis of the numerous references to Greeks and on the basis of negative allusions to Buddhism, he agrees with E. W. Hopkins that the epic was composed or compiled after the Greek invasion of Alexander the Great and after the overthrow of the (heterodox, Buddhist) imperial Mauryas by Pushyamitra Śuṅga, between the mid-second century BCE and the year zero.[85] The core motif of the epic as a whole is, according to Hiltebeitel, the education of king Yudhisthira, who has to learn throughout the epic what it means to be(come) a righteous king.[86] The basic *socio-political source of conflict* underlying Indian society at the time that the epic genre becomes prominent is *the rise of empires and moral resistance to them*. The tribal warrior order to which the epic refers is long gone by then.[87] By the time of the epic's composition, the old warrior order has been replaced by empires that are morally reflected upon the epic by reference to an imagined historical warrior order as charter for a better future.[88]

2.3 The family as an institutional source of legitimation and conflict

Simon Pearse Brodbeck situates Arjuna's concerns on the battlefield within the same historical context, but Brodbeck stresses the link between the transition from a tribal, kinship group (*kula*) setting to a more differentiated society, on the one hand, and higher population densities due to the economic transition from pastoralism to agriculture, on the other hand.[89] When the population rises above a certain level, it is necessary to have a hierarchical structure, with certain groups having a monopoly on the use of force, in order to resolve conflicts between strangers. Descriptions of the warrior (*kshatriya*) in ancient Indian texts seem to fit in with this picture. When, as an inevitable correlate of increasing population density, chiefdoms conglomerate to form states, the social and ethnic mix becomes larger, and the *insider–outsider ideology* must give way to a *more inclusive ideology* if the state is to be viable. In the Indian context, he argues, it is the ideology of reincarnation (*samsara*) and binding action (*karmabandha*) that functions as such. It helps to *legitimate* the existing *status quo* – one's fate is due to one's previous actions.[90]

On the Kurukshetra battlefield, Brodbeck points out, Arjuna is primarily concerned with two things – his own future mental state traumatized by the war experience, and the loss of the integrity of his kinship group.[91] He asks Krishna, 'How could we be happy having killed our own folk?' (1.37) If women become promiscuous, sons will not know who their male ancestors are and those ancestors will starve from lack of ritual riceball offerings by descendants:

> Because of the ascendancy of lawlessness, Krishna,
> The family women are corrupted;
> When women are corrupted, O Krishna,
> The intermixture of caste is born.
>
> Intermixture brings to hell
> The family destroyers and the family, too;
> The ancestors of these indeed fall,
> Deprived of offerings of rice and water.
>
> By these wrongs of the family destroyers,
> Producing intermixture of caste,
> Caste duties are abolished,
> And eternal family laws also.
> [*Gītā* 1.41–3][92]

Strikingly, Brodbeck notes, Krishna's answer to Arjuna deals with all kinds of concerns, including Arjuna's appeal to happiness, but it does not deal at all with his concern for the continuity of the family. *Krishna simply ignores the family issue* because it does not fit the new context of dense population, a context which no longer allows for a tribal concern with lineage maintenance.[93] The old insider–outsider ideology no longer holds. The new morality and soteriology must be universalizable; tribal morality and soteriology are not. Arjuna is being taught to purify his mind, and in doing so, to let go of his family concerns.

3 Religion as an institutional source of legitimation and conflict

3.1 Priesthood (brahmins) and aristocracy (kshatriyas)

Right from the beginning, in the very framing of the story, the epic is about the complex and symbiotic relationship between the aristocratic warrior and ruling class of the *kshatriyas* and the priestly class of the *brahmins*, Biardeau argues. The *brahmins* control the spiritual power in Indian society while the *kshatriyas* control the material power. The *kshatriyas* benefit from the spiritual power needed to uphold the world order and generated by their common sacrificial activities, while the *brahmins* benefit from the material wealth of gifts bestowed upon the priest by the patron. In the *Law Books* (*dharmaśāstras*), 'this ritual symbiosis finds its complement at the administrative level. Though, in actual fact, the kings had to issue decrees and rules of all kinds, they were not considered as legislators' because only *brahmins* were 'qualified to know what *dharma* is and how it should be maintained', Biardeau explains.[94] I have to point out explicitly here that this brahminical ideology that keeps *brahmins* and *kshatriyas* rigorously separated presented a normative ideal, not a practised reality.

The relationship between *brahmins* and *kshatriyas* is, from a brahminical perspective, a potential source of conflict and a perpetual source of tension. In the epic, there is a progressive breakdown of the traditional functional relationship between the *kshatriyas* and the *brahmins*. The (honorary) grandfather of the entire family, Bhīshma, though a *kshatriya*, opts for a higher status reserved for the *brahmin* – he renounces both the throne (his royal duties) and his marriage duties (to provide a legitimate heir). But a *kshatriya* is not supposed to act like a *brahmin* even for the sake of ultimate liberation since his specific duties differ from those of a *brahmin*. 'Everywhere in the epic the benevolence and peacefulness of the *brahmin* is opposed to the warlike nature of the *kshatriya*. Each time Yudhisthira wants to give up war and his kingship, and take to forest life, he is suspected to be more like a *brahmin* than a *kshatriya'*. Expressing such a suspicion is an insult.[95] Despite their complementarity, the epic seems to especially emphasize the contrast between kings and *brahmins* and their division of labour. Their mixing up marks a general decline in *dharma* (cosmic, social and moral order), which culminates in the *Gītā*'s presentation of Arjuna's war acts as both the fulfilment of his warrior duties and the performance of his participation in the sacrificial ritual of battle. The war becomes a sort of Vedic 'sacrifice' of the decadent moral and social order (*adharma*) for the rejuvenation of society and for the establishment of a new path to salvation for the warrior caste (in particular, the king).

The basic *socio-religious* source of *conflict* between material power and spiritual power as it is expressed in the epic and as it reflected the brahminical view of Indian society is a conflict *between aristocracy and priesthood*. This basic conflict does not take the form of a historical transition from, say, aristocracy to priesthood, but remains the structural backbone of society as seen through the eyes of the dominant, that is, *brahminic*, culture of the Indian society.

3.2 Religion as an institutional source of conflict

According to Biardeau, the apocalyptic mood of the epic is a reflection of the threat Buddhism poses to the brahminic culture and influence, especially since its Buddhist imperial king Ashoka conquered Northern India.[96]

According to Peter Hill, Arjuna's problem is society's problem.[97] Arjuna's individual crisis in the *Bhagavadgītā* reflects *the crisis facing brahminic orthodoxy* at the time. Arjuna questions that most sacred of all orthodox concerns – the *dharma* (cosmic, social and moral order). This challenge is set for the author(s) of the *Gītā* by the contemporary socio-political climate. Shaken to its foundations, *brahminic* orthodoxy needed to promote a new, simple and uplifting religious vision that was readily accessible to all members of society if it was to survive the challenge of the ascetic movements, in particular Buddhism and Jainism.[98]

In the opening scene of the *Gītā* proper, Arjuna faces a moral dilemma and responds to it with a psychic breakdown. According to Brodbeck, this crucial scene is symptomatic of the period of socio-cultural and religious change that the Indian culture was going through when the epic was written. It could not have happened any time and anywhere, but only at a time where the ritual customs of the traditional Vedic society had lost their self-evidence.[99] This is not to say that the traditional Vedic ritual customs were abolished. On the contrary, they functioned as the psychological backbone and back-up of the newly developing norms and values in the *Law Books (dharmaśāstras)*, in striking contrast to the *Vedas* which, like Heesterman is quoted as saying, 'contain no positive injunctions that could be used directly as rules of conduct'.[100] The need to develop a codified body of norms and values related to human behaviour in general is also illustrated by Arjuna's failure to draw sufficient guidance from what 'we have heard repeatedly' (1.44). Apparently, Brodbeck notes, 'Arjuna, trying his best to let the *Śāstra* be his guide, . . . has received contradictory guidance and is thus thrown back upon his own resources with disabling effect'. Can Krishna's assurance that a life of devotion (*bhakti*) to Him is all Arjuna needs, provide sufficient practical guidance?[101]

Henotheism, the exclusive worshipping of one god only amidst many other gods, here takes the form of a complete surrender and total devotion (*bhakti*) by Arjuna to the one god Krishna. But its historical origin and function have not been understood in terms of a socio-political issue or context. Brodbeck explains the *Bhagavadgītā* in terms of a henotheistic solution to a moral crisis – the loss of the Vedic norms and values as practical guidance for proper behaviour, in a society of increasing individualism and its pressure on the individual's necessity to decide what ought to be done without knowing whether one actually does the right thing. Instead of offering an ethical handbook on how to act properly, the *Gītā* encourages the devotee to wholeheartedly dedicate all his actions to the one god, Krishna, without asking for practical guidance for normative behaviour. Without a normative Vedic background, it is incumbent upon the individual to decide what ought to be done, and this pressure on the individual explains Arjuna's moral crisis and psychic breakdown. Henotheism offers a way out of the crisis by taking away the moral pressure on the individual and replacing it with divine grace.

4 Conclusions

Regarding the societies to which the *Mahābhārata* epic and the *Gītā* refer explicitly or implicitly, one cannot say a lot with certainty because of the considerable difficulties the dating of these layered texts and their allusions poses. Three institutions feature prominently as sources of conflict and legitimation – the state, the family and religion.

In the earlier, narrative sections of the epic, society is depicted with reference to kinship relations and tribal chiefships, whereas in the later, didactic sections, oligarchies or kingdoms dominate the scene. Thapar therefore concluded that one can trace an institutional shift from clan-based to state-based political structures. The hierarchical order of society is reflected in the *Gītā*'s ideology of the four classes and the monarchical establishment of power is reflected in the Pāndavas' founding of a new capital in Indraprastha. Instead of being an inter-tribal conflict over succession, the Kurukshetra war should be understood as referring to a historical transition from a segmented type of society to a hierarchical type of society, Thapar suggested; and in the epic's picture, the earlier type of society is romanticized while the new type of society is met with a sense of insecurity. Hiltebeitel, then, stressed the socio-political context of the rise of empires and resistance to them in the form of an epic educating the king about the virtue of non-cruelty. Brodbeck drew attention to the link between the transition from a tribal, kinship group setting to a more differentiated society, on the one hand, and higher population densities due to the economic transition from pastoralism to agriculture, on the other hand. He suggested that the insider–outsider ideology having to give way to a more inclusive *karma* ideology explains why Arjuna is so concerned with the integrity of his kinship group whereas Krishna simply ignores the family issue.

Religion too is depicted as a source of conflict and legitimation, but less prominently so than the state and the family. The two main issues are, first of all, the structural tension between the two dominating classes, the priestly class of the *brahmins* and the ruling class of the *kshatriyas*, and secondly, the threat Buddhism and the loss of tradition are likely to have posed to the traditional religion and culture of brahminical Hinduism.

PART III: CROSS-CULTURAL COMPARISONS

1 Introduction

Several observations can be made regarding the similarities and differences between the socio-political and socio-cultural contexts of Greek tragedy, Shakespearean tragedy and Hindu drama discussed so far. Much more on the issues related to these contexts will be spellt out in the next chapters. Here, the focus will be on the historical origins and functions of the texts and what they represent socio-politically. The *main question* of this third part of the chapter will be – in what respects do or do not the socio-political aspects of Greek and Shakespearean tragedy have parallels in the *Mahābhārata* epic and the *Bhagavadgītā*?

2 Historical origins

2.1 The state as an institutional source of conflict

All the texts discussed in this chapter have emerged within historical contexts in which the state is being felt and presented as a main source of conflict.

The contents of the Greek tragedies reveal a shift from aristocracy to democracy. The form of the plays reveals a style of debating that reflects democracy as it was practised within the Athenian institutions. The basic socio-political conflict underlying early modern English society as it is expressed in Shakespearean tragedies such as *Hamlet* is not a conflict between aristocracy and democracy, but a politico-religious conflict between, first of all, monarchy and republicanism on the legitimacy of exercising state authority and secondly, between Roman Catholicism and Protestantism. The basic socio-political conflict underlying Indian society at the time that the epic genre becomes prominent seems to be the rise of empires and resistance to them. By the time of the epic's composition between the mid-second century BCE and the year zero, the old warrior order has already been replaced by empires that are morally reflected upon in the epic by reference to an imagined historical warrior order as charter for a better future, Hiltebeitel maintains. Instead of experiencing a transitional Greek conflict between aristocracy and democracy, Indian society has always been characterized by an ideological conflict or tension between aristocracy and priesthood, Biardeau claims.

The topic of legitimate rulership is a core motif in Greek tragedy, Shakespearean tragedy and Hindu epics alike, and seems to reflect a commonly shared recurring theme in historical periods of political transition.

2.2 The family as an institutional source of conflict

The family emerges as another institutional source of conflict at odds with politics and the state.

Aeschylus' Agamemnon sticks to his warrior duty and royal honour as commander-in-chief, at the expense of the life of his own daughter Iphigeneia, a case not unlike that of Arjuna, who also sticks to his warrior duty as commander-in-chief, at the expense of family members whom he sacrifices. The patricide by Oedipus and the incestuous marriage between Oedipus and his mother in Sophocles' *Oedipus Tyrannus*, and the fratricide by Claudius and the incestuous marriage between Claudius and his sister-in-law in *Hamlet* equal the fratricidal war and threat of caste mixture through intermarriage in the *Bhagavadgītā*. Greek tragedy reveals a shift from locating solutions to social conflicts in the order of the family (*oikos*) to locating them in the order of the state (*polis*). The family itself needs to be relocated within the frame of the city and its institutions. Royal families have lost their moral and socio-political legitimacy. In Shakespearean tragedy, the family and the state are two main sources of disruption of the traditional order and represent two socio-political battlefields for the same emotions of love and hatred.

In the case of the Hindu epic, Thapar and Brodbeck stress the transition from kinship-based chiefships to power-based kingdoms. Brodbeck sketches the transition from a tribal, kinship-based society in which the family constitutes the main demarcation line between insiders and outsiders, to a broader-based society in which the increasing population density is coped with by the introduction of an all-inclusive *karma* ideology, at the expense of the family. In the *Bhagavadgītā*, Arjuna may be concerned with the integrity of his kinship group, but Krishna simply ignores the family issue. The epic marks a shift from the family to the state as the organizing principle. This sounds strikingly similar to Hegelian interpretations of *Antigone*. If a comparison between the epic or the *Gītā* and *Antigone* on this point is justified, the difference between the two 'charters' is all the more striking. In the (Hegelian version of the) Greek case, a power shift from the family to the state is intertwined with the imposition of a privileged position of the man at the expense of the politically marginalized position of the woman – structural female dependence already occurs in the *Odyssey*. In the Indian case, it is not a conflict between the genders. It's a male's problem. The state imposes itself at the expense of the family, and the masculine warrior Arjuna cannot fulfil his family duties and his class duties simultaneously. Arjuna faces Hector's dilemma in the *Iliad*, having to leave his family behind without male protection or having to give up his male role as chief warrior.

2.3 Religion as an institutional source of conflict

Regarding the institutional role of religion, Greek tragedies, like Indian drama, but unlike English tragedies, were staged as part and parcel of annual religious city play-festivals honouring the gods and attended by the gods. They were staged against the religious background of fairly sinister myths about divine fate, immortal gods and doomed mortals. The exact meaning of these religious myths was under debate, but posed no reason for civil wars. In early modern England, public theatre had developed into a separate institution, relatively independent from religion and the state. No gods were honoured or attending. In that sense, the theatre had become a secular matter altogether. But religion and the state were nonetheless eager to interfere and to exercise censorship. For the Puritans in the city of London, the theatre was sinful and should be forbidden. For the theatre, religion was a constant threat. It was also a source of conflict in other respects. One of the basic socio-political conflicts was between Roman Catholic and Protestant approaches to ghosts, revenge, penitence, guilt, the afterlife and conscience. And the topic of legitimate rulership was considered a religious affair worthy of theological treatises and power struggles. Regarding religion as an institutional source of conflict in India, one may point to Biardeau, who argues that there has always been an ideological tension between priesthood (representing spiritual power) and aristocracy (representing material power). This basic conflict does not take the form of a historical transition from aristocracy to priesthood or from priesthood to aristocracy. It is presented as the structural and normative backbone of society by the dominant, that is, *brahminic*, culture of the Indian society.

The mixing up of priestly and aristocratic behaviour lacks religious legitimacy and marks a general decline in *dharma* (cosmic, social and moral order), according to the *Mahābhārata* epic's own interpretation. This sense of decline is indicative of historical changes both in the socio-political and in the religious domain. In the religious domain, brahminic orthodoxy faces a religious crisis. Orthodoxy is in need of promoting a new religious vision against the background of the challenge of the ascetic movements taking over the religious scene. Whereas Greek henotheism is, according to Versnel, symptomatic of undemocratic and totalitarian tendencies in Hellenistic society and culture, Hindu henotheism, Brodbeck basically suggests, is symptomatic of the loss in Indian society and culture of traditional Vedic norms and values that no longer provide sufficient practical guidance related to human behaviour in general.

3 Historical functions

The socio-political functions of the texts in their original historical contexts vary according to these contexts. In the case of Greek tragedy, tragedies defined Athenian civic identity by staging it publicly. They were also politically educational, by staging intrinsically democratic elements, such as discussion, calling to account, assuming responsibility, advocating alternative positions and displaying social tensions and conflicts between citizens, women and slaves. There is much disagreement about the exact socio-politically critical and subversive features and functions of tragedy in general. Taken as a whole, tragedy legitimized the Athenian political system, which favoured the democratic rights and practices of its citizens at the expense of the aristocracy, but also at the expense of the women and the slaves. But Greek tragedy simultaneously challenged these Athenian civic rights and practices from religious, moral and rhetorical viewpoints. The internal function of self-confirmation and consolidation of tragic plays for the Athenian *polis* was not meant to be broadened beyond the limited number of free male Athenian citizens.

In the case of Shakespearean tragedy, the main function of theatre plays was entertainment, both popular and royal entertainment, not religious entertainment. Shakespearean plays were not in a position to subvert or offend the political *status quo* of the English monarchy or the religio-political establishment in general. But as part of a relatively independent institution, Shakespearean plays are much more likely to have functioned in a challenging way than in a legitimizing way.

In the case of the Hindu *Mahābhārata* epic, Thapar argued that the epic does not legitimize the newly emerging monarchies but romanticizes the earlier tribal society while expressing a sense of insecurity in a period of socio-political transition. Hiltebeitel suggested that the core motif of the epic as a whole is the education of King Yudhisthira, who has to learn what it means to be(come) a righteous king. The epic has a politically educational function in the time of Magadha's metropolitan states. The *Bhagavadgītā* explicitly legitimizes the hierarchical *status quo* of the caste system and its caste duties. As a consequence, Krishna's teaching does not just take place on a battlefield that thus turns into a spiritual battlefield for the devotees of Krishna and for those who seek *dharma;* it also turns the battlefield as a 'field of *dharma*' or righteousness into a real battlefield for warriors who have the duty to fight wars.

5

Literary–cultural aspects

PART I: TRAGIC AND DRAMATIC ISSUES

1 Introduction

A fourth set of aspects of tragedy has to do with the tragedies' dealing with narrative sources and their cultural values in connection with the transition from the mythic and epic genres to the tragic genre. Is tragedy symptomatic of a shift from one set of cultural values to a different set of cultural values? Does tragic literature (re)present a different value system from epic literature? Do 'epic' values turn 'tragic'? If so, what does the discontinuity consist of? If not, what does the continuity consist of? We will also examine the question of whether a tragic hero is different from an epic hero because heroes embody the values of their cultures. Is the hero's use of language different? A related issue pertains to the extent to which tragedy marks a general shift in world view and view of man. A shift in the value system implies shifts in the world view and view of man. And what about the status of the individual in the value system? Is tragedy primarily about the outstanding individual, or is tragedy concerned with the community at large?

2 Mythic, legendary and epic stories as narrative sources

Is the literary–cultural past of Greek myths and epics crucial to the emergence of Greek tragedy? The historical origins of Greek tragedy are uncertain. Maybe, a Dionysiac cult-ritual enacted a Dionysiac cult-myth and developing tragedy, then turned its back on Dionysiac themes, as Rainer Friedrich and

Richard Seaford have it.[1] Whether with or without a cult-myth as its original subject matter, somewhere in time, a Dionysiac cult-ritual was combined with the ancient tradition of heroic myths.[2] It is primarily (not exclusively, cf. Aeschylus' *Persians*) on this body of myths that the Greek dramatists drew for their themes, their characters (especially heroes, but also gods) and their story patterns, as the Homeric epic, and later the lyrics had done before them. Although the ancient heroic myths were taken as more or less historical stories from their own remote past, they were not considered holy texts. Deviations from the mythical stories were allowed, provided they were not essential – changing the core elements would turn enemies (in myth) into friends (on stage), that is, tragedy into comedy (Aristotle's example of Orestes and Aegisthus in comedy leaving the stage as friends). Aristotle stresses the difference between a historian who presents what happened (facts) and a poet who presents what could have happened and might happen (possibilities).[3] Edith Hall notes that some of the myths, such as myths around King Theseus as the presumed founding father and protector of Athens, for lack of great local heroes, were actually invented; other mythical heroes, such as 'the Argive, Theban, and other non-Athenian heroes from the old epic cycle, while remaining central to tragedy, are often appropriated in order to become part of the Athenian past'.[4]

Can similar ways of appropriating the literary past be observed in the case of *Shakespearean* tragedy? The one link with the literary past that most of us would expect to be prominent, but which is not at all self-evident, is the presumed link between Shakespearean and Greek tragedy. Elizabethan tragedy, that is, was expected to be following Aristotelian rules and the *Latin* example of *Senecan* tragedy, at least if one had a neo-classicist taste. Sir Philip Sidney was an admirer of 'Seneca's style'. Senecanism was fashion. Raymond Williams explains, 'In Seneca, there is an important stress on the nobility of suffering and enduring misfortune, which provided a basis for the later transfer of interest to the suffering individual, away from the general action'.[5] Shakespeare may have read Seneca's Latin tragedies on Greek themes in their recent English translations. His theatrical contemporaries and predecessors certainly did. Although Shakespeare did not embrace Seneca's declamatory style, he never fully turned away from it. Lawrence Danson illustrates this with *Hamlet,* 'When Hamlet asks the players at Elsinore to give him a taste of their quality, he asks for a play he once heard—not a play to please the multitude, for "twas caviar to the general": it is a Senecan play about Pyrrhus, Priam, and Hecuba, and Shakespeare's pastiche displays his critical self-consciousness of the style'.[6] Sir Philip Sidney's neo-classicist claims are not Shakespeare's. Yet, Senecanism had an impact, also on Shakespeare's work. But Senecan tragedy is Roman, not Greek. It was Lessing who would start to claim Shakespeare as the real inheritor of the Greeks, as opposed to neo-classicism.[7] Although Lessing was wrong in assimilating Greek and Elizabethan tragedy, the Greek–Elizabethan identity is still widely taken for granted.[8]

Like the Greeks and Seneca respectively, Shakespeare used royal and imperial history, including its warrior ethic, as a primary source for both his 'history' plays and his 'tragedies'. He did not draw from epic literature as such, but drew from well-known stories about British kings and Roman emperors, which were no less related to a heroic society and its aristocratic and martial value system than epic literature itself. The British narrative sources are neither epic literature nor canonized collective memory of the English nation.[9]

This is not to suggest that certain narrative motifs cannot be much older. According to Bert O. States, who focuses on the interplay of plot and character, both *Hamlet* and the *Henry IV* plays are, to a striking degree, variations on the *epic* theme of the *education of the prince*, featuring, in each case, a prince who, for reasons of his own, hangs back from responsibility and spends himself in forms of behaviour that are socially errant or antic. In gross terms, Hamlet and Hal are in the same situation, the distinction resting roughly on the difference between the problem of killing a king and the problem of becoming one.[10]

Shakespeare, then, draws freely from his literary sources. He presents opposing sides and chooses historical topics, such as the civil wars preceding the Tudor dynasty. This is because he is concerned, not about historical accuracy, but about the meaning of these stories to his contemporaries. The stories would constitute a trial by fire out of which the early modern English nation would be reborn, as David Bevington argues.[11]

3 The questioning of tradition and the problematization of heroes

Jean-Pierre Vernant is one of many scholars who underscore the discontinuity between tragedy and its ritual and literary past. He argues that tragedy was innovative on an institutional level in having the city state present itself on stage for an audience of citizens. Also, it was innovative in being a new literary genre. Finally, it presented the old heroic value system not, like in epic and choral lyric, as a given model, but as subject to questioning and debate.[12]

The break with the literary past is striking indeed. Tragedy has transformed the telling of elaborate literary texts into the staging of succinct theatrical performances, and it has reinterpreted the meanings of mythic and epic contents. Peter Burian points out that the repertoire of legends from which tragedians drew their plots was limited (mainly the legends on Troy and

Thebes), and that the stories were adapted to a limited number of underlying plot patterns.[13] 'It follows', Burian goes on, 'that tragedy is not casually or occasionally intertextual, but always and inherently so'. This provides the spectators with a familiar frame of reference, and it supplies the poets with possibilities to 'direct or dislocate' audience expectations.[14] Tales already known to the audience and part of what Burian calls 'a system of tragic discourse' are being *recast* continuously:

> A play whose plot has become canonical, Sophocles' *Antigone*, appears to have had little in the way of literary precedents. Yet, even Sophocles cannot be said to have given the story its definitive form: we know that Euripides went on to write an *Antigone* in which the heroine survived to marry Haemon and bear him a son.[15]

The third point brought to the fore by Vernant, the *questioning* and debating by tragedy of the traditional heroic value system, is crucial in Christopher Gill's approach to tragedy's contents. Gill holds the view that the unconventional actions and attitudes of the 'problematic heroes' lead to extreme conflicts because their 'second-order reasoning' or 'reflective reasoning' clashes with the 'first-order reasoning' that accompanies the conventional norms.[16] 'First-order' reasoning is a *deliberative* type of reasoning. It provides practical reasons for applying normative rules of action in a specific case. It is of a rule-case or means-end type, as displayed in the Homeric deliberative monologues.[17] 'Second-order' reasoning does not take conventional expectations and normative rules and practices for granted in advance. On the contrary, this *reflective* type of reasoning, as displayed in Achilles' and Sarpedon's great speeches and in Greek tragedy, consists in reflection about the worthwhile human goals, rules and virtues, and about the ethical frame, the kind of interpersonal context and the kind of human life in which such goals, rules and virtues make sense.[18] What is problematic about the so-called 'problematic heroes' of Greek epic and tragedy, Gill argues, has to do with their situation, which provokes them into engaging in second-order reasoning and conventionally unacceptable behaviour.[19] The *tragic conflict* is a *conflict between conventional (pre-reflective) norms and post-conventional (reflective) norms*, between 'first-order' reasoning and 'second-order' reasoning,[20] and between the tradition and potential innovation of the value system they share.[21]

That tragedy can be seen as a tragic reinterpretation of mythic and epic material, and more specifically, that *mythic and epic heroes are transformed into tragic heroes*, can be illustrated. One example would be Goldhill's observations, in the previous chapter, on the story of Orestes who was presented as exemplary in a positive sense in Homer's *Odyssey,* but became problematic in Aeschylus' *Oresteia.*[22] Two other examples are Segal's interpretation of Oedipus and Jarcho's interpretation of Agamemnon.

Charles Segal considers the Oedipus myth, in its simplest form, a version of the myth of the hero, resembling the stories of Perseus, Jason, Theseus, Cyrus the Great, Moses, Romulus and Remus, Siegfried and others – a series of trials that the hero faces and overcomes triumphantly – except that Sophocles turns the triumph into a tragedy. On the one hand, Oedipus succeeds because he actually solves the riddle of who he is, and he has the courage to face the suffering that goes with it. On the other hand, Oedipus has gained his knowledge through painful effort, and his self-knowledge has revealed to him a blindness from within, rather than from without, that has caused his trials.[23]

Viktor Jarcho sketches a cultural development from Homer to Euripides in the ways human responsibility and decision making are presented.[24] In the *first phase*, in Homer's *Iliad*, Agamemnon is compelled to admit that Achilles' refusal, a refusal provoked by Agamemnon – to participate in the war – has led to the defeat of the Greeks and that something must be done urgently to rescue the situation. Because of that, Agamemnon is prepared to assume responsibility by offering material compensation for Achilles' damaged honour. But this admission is in no way to be equated with an admission of his guilt. Agamemnon ascribes the origin of his 'guilt' to higher powers (Zeus, fate, Erinys), which put wild blindness into his heart (*Iliad* 19, 86–90). In the *second phase*, in Aeschylus' *Agamemnon*, the Trojan War is an ambiguous case that fights for a just cause (Helena) against too high a price (victims). It is doubtful whether sacrificing Iphigenia in order to assure a successful outcome of the war is worth the crime. Since the law of worldwide revenge is descending upon Troy, the unlawful act becomes a necessity. But for a human being to reach the stage where he is capable of such a crime, he must be close to madness. That is why Agamemnon, at the moment of taking his decision, is portrayed as irrationally harbouring a strong desire for virginal blood and having evil thoughts (*Agamemnon* 214–23).[25] In the *third phase*, in Euripides' *Iphigenia at Aulis*, the sense of living in a rational world and of being responsible for one's actions is no longer present. In *Hippolytus*, *Heracles* and *Orestes*, Artemis, Theseus and Apollo had already taken away the burden of moral responsibility from the shoulders of the heroes, and the heroes had not protested – whereas Oedipus, Ajax or Daeanaera could have shirked their responsibility for the same reasons. According to Jarcho, the effort of the acting characters in *Orestes* manifests the socio-political context of the *polis* solidarity being destroyed and the individual being left to his own devices. The moral isolation of the individual could evoke either a pragmatic, egocentric reaction or an idealistic one. While *Andromache* was an example of the first option, *Iphigenia at Aulis* and Sophocles' *Oedipus at Colonus* were examples of the idealistic response. Iphigenia transforms from an innocent, protected and simple girl into a figure of unparalleled moral height, whereas Agamemnon has fallen back to the morally dubious level of avoiding any tragic choices and of confusedly trying to secure his vain career.

From the previous examples, one might conclude that the *watershed between epic literature and tragedy* is easily identifiable but, in fact, the reverse is true. The scholarly notion of 'the tragic' drawn from tragedy has, during the last centuries, been enlarged and is now also applied to Greek epic literature. But this is not new. In fact, it is very classical. Stephen Halliwell points out that in Plato's *Republic*, 'the tenth book's famous description of Homer as "teacher and leader of the tragedians" (595c 1–2), and "first of the tragedians" (607a 3), establishes that the Homeric epics themselves matter to Plato in this context primarily as texts which justify a tragic reading'.[26] Richard P. Martin explains that for Aristotle, 'drama' is 'as self-evident and singular an experience as film is for us', and that he compares it to epic only in order to make a point about drama – an opposition 'more akin to contrasting "film" and "the novel" taken as a whole'. Moreover, betraying 'the spirit of competitive dramatic production in Athens', Aristotle 'describes only partially "tragedy" or "epic" before taking up the *best* way of making both', and Homer offers the best epic poetry Aristotle can imagine, since it is most reminiscent of tragic drama.[27]

James M. Redfield offers a contemporary and fairly Aristotelian application of the notion of tragedy to Homer.[28] Whereas the ethnologist, describing an alien culture, 'must state the norm of that culture to an audience which does not know it', Redfield argues, 'the poet of fiction, by contrast, speaks to his own culture, to an audience which knows the norm but has not considered its implications. The poet investigates the norm in situations and in relation to characters where the norm implies dysfunction, . . . fails to prescribe the proper end or to furnish the necessary means'.[29] Redfield defines 'tragedy' as *all fiction which is an inquiry into the (dys)functioning of a culture by testing the limits of its virtues.* In contrast to a comic character, a tragic hero is expected to be morally and socially competent ('virtuous' and 'wise'), to adequately respond to situations, in accordance with the norms of his culture. In his capacity of excellent representative of his culture, he then surprises if he falls into vice and error. Apparently, under extreme circumstances, the resources that his culture provides to uphold the normative standards while facing these circumstances, prove inadequate. By showing the effects of these circumstances, the tragic poet tests the limits of his culture. Redfield, then, goes one step further by applying his extended notion of tragedy to *epic* literature.[30]

R. B. Rutherford and John Gould too, confirm Redfield's position on Homer.[31] Jacqueline de Romilly agrees with Redfield that Hector is a tragic hero. His story follows the scheme of a tragic fate, including the tragic reversal of happiness (victory) into disaster (death).[32] She does not offer a definition of tragedy that might include epic literature, but she explicitly considers Homer's *Iliad* closer to tragedy than to epics.[33] Michael Ewans subscribes to this viewpoint, 'The *Iliad* is demonstrably akin to the later genre of tragedy not just in the means used to evoke pathos, but in its feeling-tone or effect'.[34]

Does the similarity between a tragic vision of life in Homer's *Iliad* and a tragic vision of life in Athenian tragedies justify an interpretation in terms of historical continuity? Not necessarily. There is historical continuity in the sense that classical Greeks and contemporary scholars alike recognize the tragic character of Homer's epic and its follow-up in Athens' tragedies. But the historical causes or pressures for having a tragic vision of life are different. According to Joseph M. Bryant, 'while Agamemnon, Odysseus, and the Trojan war itself belong to the Mycenaean era, the institutional life represented in the epics is largely that of Dark Age Greece'.[35] The collapse of the Mycenaean order (around 1200 BCE) gave way to a violent culture of many small communities led and protected by their warrior aristocracy who could not guarantee security and were constantly exposed to death in battle. Bryant agrees with Max Weber that Homer's sketch of heroic fatalism (around 775 BCE) constitutes the introduction of the tragic vision in the West and that it can be explained sociologically as caused by a combination of the life-affirming disposition characteristic of the ruling strata whose sense of status and whose social functions pressure them to reject pessimistic resignation, 'coupled with a warrior's' inclination 'towards a religiously neutral fatalism'.[36] This specific historical context, in which state protection is lacking because state institutions themselves are absent, is worlds apart from a city state such as Athens organizing annual festivals, including tragedy competitions for its citizens.

In general, scholarly theories on the epic genre do not seem to go so far as to ascribe an inquisitive and testing function to epic. Martin, for example, writes in terms of an *articulating* function, 'to articulate the most essential aspects of a culture'.[37] In its function of articulation, epic has the ambition and potential to become a metonymy for culture itself, Martin concludes. I would join Redfield in pointing out that articulation itself, in the case of epic literature, serves cultural purposes such as the testing of values. But in *epic* literature, this testing function in general serves mainly *celebrating* and *legitimizing* purposes, whereas in *tragic* literature, this testing function serves mainly *questioning* and *critical* purposes. Epic literature varies when it comes to containing a certain degree of tragic tendencies, as the difference between the *Iliad*, a war epic, and the *Odyssey*, a travel epic in peacetime, illustrates.

But in Greek tragedy too, there is a limit to the actual degree of questioning. Hall points out that:

> Oedipus in *Oedipus the King* considers the possibility that his natural mother was 'a third-generation slave' (1062–3), and Ion fears that his mother was of servile or lowly birth (556, 1477), but in both cases their mothers turn out to have been aristocrats. In the case, however, of the never-free, slaves from birth, the tragic texts everywhere assume that the slave/free boundary is as fixed, natural, and permanent as the boundary between man and god. It was necessary to the perpetuation of institutionalised slavery to foster a belief in the *natural* servility of those born into the slave class, and no character in tragedy proposes abolishing slavery.[38]

Hall concludes that 'while tragedy can *envisage* the opposite social movement, from seeming aristocratic to actual servile birth status, it never actually happens'.

Although *Shakespeare*'s Elizabethan tragedy goes back to Roman instead of Greek tragedy, and cannot therefore be said to carry on the innovative and critically inquiring nature of Greek tragedy, it is equally innovative and critically inquiring in spirit. Like Sophocles' hero Oedipus, Shakespeare's hero Hamlet asks questions, as Adrian Poole notes.[39] Asking questions can reveal an inquisitive mind. But asking questions, in Shakespeare's *Hamlet*, does not just reveal an inquisitive mind. It reveals a critically inquiring mentality, a 'questioning spirit', Harry Levin states. He continues:

> What is more revealing, the word 'question' occurs in *Hamlet* no less than seventeen times, much more frequently than in any of Shakespeare's other plays. Recalling that it comes as the final word in Hamlet's most famous line, we may well regard it as the key-word of the play. . . . Furthermore, besides direct inquiry, there are other modes of questioning . . .. *Interrogatio* is the simplest mode, with the rhetorical question indicating its own response, or with the catechism preordaining its set replies. But when the answer is unforeseen, or when there is no answer—that is the kind of open question which *Hamlet* is more particularly concerned to pose. The play begins with such a question: 'Who's there?'[40]

Dubitatio, Levin's next mode of questioning, is less emotional and more deliberative. Doubting is a kind of deliberation with oneself, hesitating in the face of two possibilities. Hamlet's own preliminary analysis had taken the inevitable form of a sequence of questions that give him cause to pause, to suspend, to stop in order to deliberate with himself in a soliloquy, at every turning point in the labyrinth. 'Hamlet', Levin argues, 'is not so much a perplexing personality as he is a state of perplexity into which we enter, the very personification of doubtfulness'.[41]

The questions of a tragic hero take the form of a quest, or rather, the quest of a tragic hero takes the form of a question mark, Poole writes and adds:

> Tragedy is a way of asking questions to which there can be no satisfactory answers, and there can be no answers that would 'satisfy' because of the means through which the questions must be asked, through the very flesh and blood, the living and dying of the human beings who make, or make *up*, the questions.[42]

Tragedy turns epic heroes into anti-heroes. Shakespeare's *Hamlet* is even more innovative in that its hero Hamlet consciously turns himself into an anti-hero – he becomes an antic hero, someone who acts like a fool, who takes the role of an actor on stage. Hamlet becomes both an agent and an actor.[43] If Bernard Knox is right in ascribing a 'heroic temper' to Homer's Achilles and Sophoclean heroes – a 'heroic temper' being defined as 'stubborn independence of mind' and 'a determination to stick to a certain position, whatever the consequences' –, then Shakespeare's Hamlet matches the first part of the definition, but it is only too obvious that he lacks the determination to stick to a certain position. On the contrary, no sooner has he sworn revenge than he decides 'to put an antic disposition on' (I.v.172).

4 Tragic conflict as a clash of cultural values

Tragedy can be, among other things, about a clash of cultural values. Is tragic conflict, by definition, unsolvable because its clashing values are incompatible? Should tragedy be defined as the *unsolvable conflict between incompatible values?* From Hegel to Rosset, albeit in very different ways, the idea of an absolutely unsolvable conflict has been a persistent way of defining tragedy. Contrary to Hegel's moral interest is the Nietzschean approach of Rosset, 'the tragic teaches man first of all the "irreconcilable" and the "irresponsible" '.[44]

According to Isaiah Berlin, incompatibility means that, in life, not all values can be successfully combined with one another at the same time. The reason for incompatibility lies in limitations of (a combination of) space, time, means and resources. One cannot lead two lives at the same time. Incompatibility need not lead to difficult dilemmas if it is clear which of the values at stake is better or more important. A value conflict becomes a true dilemma when conflicting values are incommensurable, that is to say, equally compelling (ultimate) within a specific value system, but without a common higher value to refer to.[45] Even if a compromise is found and part of the conflicting values can be realized (and the pain eased), a price has to be paid as both conflicting values cannot be realized completely. A value conflict 'requires a choice that always entails a sacrifice'. The value conflicts that allow for no compromise and 'can be resolved only by a rigid either/or choice . . . are usually the tragic ones', Berlin suggests.[46]

Georg Friedrich Wilhelm Hegel focuses on ethical conflicts that appear intrinsically unsolvable, but because of that are full of progress.[47] Hegel uses tragedy to illustrate the limitations of a certain stage in the evolution of spirit. In Hegel's perception, the collective spirit of humanity is driven by a movement from consciousness to self-consciousness. Progress is achieved if a certain collective state of mind, a temporary mentality, the spirit of the age, is faced with internal limitations that necessarily give rise to a more complicated mentality, which includes the previous mentality, but also incorporates the consciousness of its internal limitations and realizes the necessity of going beyond it. Greek tragedy is understood by Hegel as symptomatic of a Greek mentality, which is conscious of moral conflicts between the human laws of society and the divine laws of the family and of the necessity to surpass them, but which does not contain the knowledge needed to actually overcome these ethical conflicts. To the Greek mind, Hegel contends, these ethical conflicts are inescapable and unsolvable, but also appalling and unbearable, urging the spectator to realize the necessity of transcending the standpoints that produced these conflicts by leaving behind the tragic Greek mentality and corresponding form of life itself.

For Paul Ricoeur too, tragedy illustrates certain kinds of conflict, particularly ethical conflicts. Robert Piercey points out two features of Ricoeur's early approach to tragedy. First, 'tragedy instructs us only as long as we remain within the tragic standpoint, and not, as Hegel would have it, when this standpoint is *aufgehoben'*. We learn from tragedy by identifying emotionally with its heroes. Second, while 'a tragedy can transform the emotions of its audience, . . . we should expect little else of it. . . . We are meant to gain a heightened appreciation of the seriousness of the conflict inherent in the human condition. We are not meant to learn how to avoid this conflict. . . . Tragic wisdom turns out to be a sort of "suffering for the sake of understanding"'.[48] From *Antigone's* identification of duty with what is immediate (as opposed to 'abstract') and individual (as opposed to 'general'), the source of the conflict, one may learn to appreciate the value of exercising *phronesis*, practical wisdom, 'to place less value on the narrow partisan commitments and more on deliberating well, on judging soundly about particular cases'. But this is much less a lesson about *doing* anything in particular than about changing 'our way of *looking* at moral principles that come into conflict'. Instructed spectators view moral principles no longer 'simply as precepts that bind categorically but as components of something larger'. But 'this conversion in outlook does not give rise to some new, higher-order norm'.[49]

Understanding comes at a price. The conflicts reveal equally compelling, but incompatible principles, and reason has to face the fact that it *cannot solve these conflicts rationally* by (dis)solving them on some higher level of understanding. Reason has to face its own inherent limitations. Moreover, it is not just the conflicts themselves, but also the conflicting interpretations that the tragic plays allow for as symbolic expressions, which reason has to face. Symbolic expressions not only reveal, but simultaneously hide their meaning. Reason has to face a clash between a conscious, surface meaning of plays and a deeper, unconscious meaning – the conscious one manifesting and hiding the unconscious one, 'Ricoeur claims that what really fascinates us about *Oedipus Rex* is a second, hidden drama. He argues that "on the basis of a first drama, a drama of incest and parricide, Sophocles has created a second, the tragedy of self-consciousness"'.[50]

What to hold of the idea of an *absolutely unsolvable* tragic conflict between irreconcilably clashing cultural values? Greek tragedy offers enough examples to refute this Romantic idea in its absolute form. Rösler came with a quite different interpretation of the *Antigone*, as we saw earlier on, and A. Maria van Erp Taalman Kip too offers several convincing arguments against the idea.[51] I agree that both Antigone and Creon take extreme positions, and that they have to pay for their extremism. But they do not pay a price because the conflict itself is unsolvable. If Antigone had not provocatively or compulsively repeated her funerary rite for Polyneices a second time, or if Creon had listened to Haimon, the conflict would not have escalated. The conflict *becomes* unsolvable, but it is not necessarily unsolvable in principle, and that is exactly what turns it into a 'tragic' conflict. It becomes a 'tragic' conflict under the conditions of the extremism of the main characters, in the case of Antigone and Creon, or under the extreme conditions of evil warfare among family members, in the case of Eteocles and Polyneices.

I would argue, however, that although the tragic conflict is not necessarily unsolvable, it is an *unavoidable* and *compelling* one. Even if there is a solution to the conflict, the solution is never an easy compromise. The tragic constellation is too extreme to allow for an easy way out. There is always a price to be paid, and it is paid in human suffering. No compensation can undo that.

Aeschylus' *Oresteia* could be taken as a good example. According to Goldhill, the dominant approach to the *Oresteia,* in which it is seen as moving from tragic conflicts to a legal resolution, is problematic in the sense that the resolution does not resolve the uncomfortable perception that Agamemnon's conflict, Orestes' conflict and Clytemnestra's conflict are, all of them, clashes of competing obligations.[52] Equally uncomfortable are the different meanings attributed to the shared notion of *dikē* (right, law, court action, justice). The talk of justice does not bring about a once and for all solution. Goldhill writes, 'Indeed, every character declares *dikē* to be on his or her side, makes a one-sided claim to this key evaluative term. In this way, tragedy explores how normal, political, evaluative language is used within social conflict, and becomes a source of social conflict'.[53]

Goldhill's interpretation of tragedy in terms of its *exploring* function indicates a *postmodern* approach to culture whereas Redfield's interpretation of tragedy in terms of its *testing* function indicates a *modern* approach to culture. A *modern* approach of culture either sees culture as a homogeneous and dominant mediator of norms and values imposing itself on all its carriers or sees culture as a controversial source of conflict encompassing innovative alternative subcultures and countercultures that *test* the dominant culture. A *postmodern* approach to culture sees culture as a heterogeneous field of possibilities for choice, negotiation and transfer that have to be *explored* constantly for lack of a dominant culture imposing them and because every possibility remains contingent and temporary instead of being once and for all.

5 The power of language

In epic literature in general, a hero not only excels by his doing of deeds, but also by his speaking of speeches. Words, once spoken, make a difference. In *epic* literature, *spoken language* is *powerful*. Spoken words, as in oaths, contain a magical power to actualize their own potential by being spoken. Words, once spoken, cannot be undone. They are deeds themselves, creating facts on the ground, political facts that may even block the best solution to a conflict. Spoken words have the same impact as deeds. They even have power over deeds, in the sense that the honour of a hero depends on his reputation, that is to say, on the ways in which his deeds are spoken about and will be recalled in the stories told about his heroic deeds. No less than his fame is at stake, that is to say, his name, his social identity. Speaking the truth is a crucial epic value. Keeping a promise, sticking to an oath is binding. The effectiveness of the curse of a truthful person is guaranteed. In this cultural value system, the language of spoken words is expected to be transparent, reliable and effective.

In *tragic* literature, *the powers and dangers of words in action* are *investigated*, Goldhill emphasizes in his writings on the language of tragedy.[54]

In Aeschylus' *Oresteia*, for example, Clytemnestra's tricky language is powerful in persuading and deceiving Agamemnon, whereas Cassandra's prophetic language is powerless in persuading anybody, since her gift from Apollo is always to tell the truth and never to be believed; Orestes' language is no less violently manipulative than his mother's.[55] The same words mean different things to different people. Language can be used to communicate, but also to manipulate, to persuade and to conceal. Tragic language draws from a mixture of registers, literary, religious, political and rhetorical alike, and it moves from one register to another during each performance. This dynamics, Goldhill explains, displays the polyvalence of words and the misunderstandings it generates. Thus, 'tragedy critically explores the public languages it mobilizes'.[56]

In his analysis of the heroic idiom of *Shakespearean* tragedy, James C. Bulman traces a development within the subsequent plays in Shakespeare's use of *heroic language*.[57] Shakespeare starts his career as a playwright who imitates the heroic conventions. He may, through his heroes, question the morality of a heroic tradition or the legitimacy of a heroic code, but his heroic characters do not. They are real heroes in the conventional sense of the word. In *Julius Caesar*, however, Brutus 'instructs his accomplices to counterfeit like actors'. But Brutus still tries to bridge the opening gap between acting and being. He tries to identify with the heroic code and align himself to the heroic role of liberator of Rome. Antony no longer does – his heroic idiom no longer defines his personality. His self-consciousness allows him to play roles and speak accordingly.[58]

This disengaged treatment of the heroic idiom had begun as early as *Richard III*, Bulman explains. Richard III, the first of Shakespeare's *ironic heroes*, 'measures his own villainy in direct proportion to his ability to deceive others with shows of conventional heroism'.[59] The first of Shakespeare's heroes to direct his irony *inwards* is Richard II, who 'fails to engage himself with a heroic ethos. . . . By thinking, he becomes the first of Shakespeare's "modern" tragic heroes', Bulman notes. Richard II 'feels obliged to defend his kingship verbally', but he knows that his claim is only a claim. 'His dilemma springs from his failure to be engaged with the roles he plays'. His moral concept of kingship is shattered by his *ironic self-awareness*.[60] Hamlet 'directs his irony both *outwards*, to the playing of roles for public consumption, and *inwards*, to his mode of self-apprehension. Hamlet would like to conceive of himself as a traditional revenger, passionately committed to his heroic purpose and able to use the diction of old plays unselfconsciously', but he is too conscious of it as a 'role'. 'He is a victim not so much of cowardice as of too much playgoing'.[61]

Bulman concludes that whereas in the early plays, the conventional heroes (Talbot, York, Titus) are admired, similar heroes in the middle plays sound archaic, 'Laertes defies the gods too patly; Fortinbras makes mouths at invisible events. Shakespeare withdraws sympathy from them in direct proportion to the conventionality of their characterization. In doing so, he indicates how far, too, he has withdrawn allegiance from the traditional heroic idiom that once served him well'.[62]

Shakespeare displays a thorough command of the traditional heroic idiom, but rejects it as an outdated means of representing tragic heroism. A cultural shift in world view and view of the human being underlies this rejection.

6 Historical shifts in world view and view of the human being

Vernant and Vidal-Naquet have suggested that Greek tragedy constitutes a historical phenomenon existing for only one century and marking the social *transition* at Athens from a society nurtured by a *traditional value system* based on the recognition of holy powers and on corresponding notions of given and imposed authority, such as 'the order of the world' and 'the justice of Zeus', to a society nurtured by a *new value system* that explored the scope and limits of human choices and responsibilities. In the beginning, at the time of Solon, the theatrical performances are highly controversial, because the 'heroic' past appears still too close, whereas by the time of Agathon, a young contemporary of Euripides, the need for debating the 'heroic' past is no longer felt – the dramatist invents his own plots.[63]

Do these developments indicate an increased *anthropological* interest at the expense of the *religious* interest? Vernant stresses that Greek tragedy defines the human being socially and religiously, as a hero representing traditional values under the cultural pressure of a just recently arisen city state. Aristotle, one century later, will be entirely anthropocentric in focus, lacking any sense of the role of the divine in tragedy, as Edith Hall points out.[64] Th. C. W. Oudemans and A. P. M. H. Lardinois do not agree with Vernant and Vidal-Naquet when it comes to identifying tragedy as the transitional stage between the previous 'archaic' world view and the later 'modern' world view. In their understanding, the ambiguous nature of the human being in Greek tragedy betrays the ambiguities of an archaic religious cosmology that differs radically from our own. Their point is that this cosmology of ambiguity is not limited to Greek tragedy, but also underlies Greek myth. They suggest an almost flawless continuity in Greek cosmology from Homer to Sophocles.[65] I do not think they put things in the right perspective. Neither they nor Vernant and Vidal-Naquet deny that the cosmology of the tragedians is primarily archaic. The issue is that the Greeks applied ancient cosmological categories (archaic cosmology) to *new* anthropological and socio-political problems – and, in doing so, brought about changes in world view too. Oudemans and Lardinois do not, in my opinion, sufficiently account for the crucial long-term changes in the Greek *view of the human being* from Homer to Aristotle, of which the tragic genre is so symptomatic. Fortunately, they do account for the crucial long-term changes in the Greek *world view* from Homer to Aristotle. But they play down the extent to which this cultural revolution applies to tragedy's religious changes from Aeschylus to Euripides as well.

Yet, there are indications that Greek tragedy does not become less religious, but indeed more impressed with the perception that gods and humans are worlds apart. Christiane Sourvinou-Inwood observes a *greater distance between deities and mortals* in Euripidean tragedies than in Aeschylean ones, and the same pattern of progressively greater distancing in Sophoclean tragedies. She combines this observation with her perception that a theatrical world in which gods mingle with humans on stage (smaller distance!) would have been experienced by the Greek audience as far more remote and as something from the heroic past than one in which gods do not appear at all or take the Euripidean form of divine epiphanies (greater distance!) that would have been exceptional, but realistic possibilities in the present-day religious experiences of the Greek audience. She argues that the smaller or greater distance between gods and humans is correlative with the greater or smaller distance between the world of the tragedy and the world of the audience. The greater the distance (in the course of the fifth century) between deities and mortals in the world of tragedy, the smaller the distance between the world of the tragedy and the world of the audience. Tragedy starts out as something close to remote sacred drama and develops into something close to everyday life, while fully remaining part of Athens' religious discourse, a discourse of religious exploration, without losing its religious scope or appeal. Euripides' disguised (!) gods and *dei ex machina* are no less religiously authoritative than divine characters in an Aeschylean play, but they presuppose more distance on stage between a deity and a mortal.[66]

The ancient Greek emergence of a new world view and view of the human being is, in turn, illustrative of a shift in focus within several cultures worldwide during the '*Axial Age*', a more encompassing and long-term shift from what Oudemans and Lardinois call a 'connective cosmology' to what they call a 'separative cosmology'.[67] The idea of an 'Axial Age' has been developed by Karl Jaspers.[68] Jaspers expounded the theory that the history of civilization had gone through a revolutionary period of specific cultural transformations in a number of major cultures, including Zoroastrian Iran, early Imperial China, ancient Israel, Greece, India and the Arabian Peninsula, a period of cultural breakthroughs from the emergence of Zarathustra onwards until the appearance of Muhammad. Jaspers called this revolutionary period the 'Axial

Age.' Karen Armstrong positions this cultural revolution against a backcloth of turmoil, migration, conquest and the shock of unprecedented aggression, as a spiritual revolution often occurring as a pause for deepening insight and liberating renewal between two imperial-style ventures.[69]

The cultural revolution consisted of the emergence, conceptualization and institutionalization of a basic tension between the mundane world and the transcendent world. A new type of intellectual elite developed and cultivated an awareness of the necessity to actively construct the world according to some idealist vision of a transcendent world underlying and ruling the mundane world from a qualitative *distance*. By independently propagating this idealist vision, the intellectual elite took a new attitude of standing back and looking beyond, of critical, reflective questioning of the actual and apparent, and of being sensitive to a reality that lies beyond that and differs sharply from the actual and apparent. The difference is thought of in terms of dichotomies, such as 'this-worldly' versus 'other-worldly', 'transient' and 'apparent' versus 'essential' and 'true', 'ritual' versus 'moral', 'habit' versus 'choice', 'material' versus 'spiritual', 'relative' versus 'ultimate.'

Since the world of experience had become a bigger one to discover and to conquer physically and mentally, the heavens were further removed from the earth now than they had been before. The distance between the human being and his *outer* world had increased, and simultaneously, the distance between the human being and his *inner* world had increased. The heavenly Will was less easy to implement not just because the heavens were further away now, but also because the depths of the soul were further away now as well. The gap between 'the realm of the transcendent' and 'the realm of the this-worldly' was felt as *a tension within the person*, as a longing for psychic, moral and spiritual fulfilment. For the first time in the history of religions, the inner human self had to be converted wholeheartedly (to the transcendent Will of God or Heaven represented by the mundane centre, or to the absolute Brahman or *nirvana*). Apart from collectively participating in the realms of the divine by attending the local rituals, individual hearts and minds had to be discovered and conquered in order to be saved. Collective participation became individual self-knowledge and conversion, empowerment became salvation, ideas became ideals, images became self-images, ritualists became believers. Stephen A. Geller stresses that the literary innovation consists of a new type of narrative linked to a new interest in personality in all its relations, in particular the issue of change in personality.[70]

In Greece, conversion was a Hellenistic phenomenon, not yet a fifth century BCE phenomenon. *Self-knowledge*, however, was already an issue in tragedy.[71] An 'axial' transition was also taking place in the field of Greek *law*, and the dramatists used their vocabulary to show its incoherence, its tensions and its ambiguities. Charles Segal writes that, at a time of intense interest in issues of causality, motivation and legality, *Oedipus Tyrannus* explored the shadowy areas between involuntary crime, religious pollution, moral innocence and the personal horror in feeling oneself to be the bearer of a terrible guilt.[72] These developments, I would argue, indicate an increase both in terms of *individualization* and in terms of *internalization*. The collective value system becomes a matter of personal commitment and psychological concern. The society, not the individual, is still at stake.

The demarcation lines between the archaic and the new world views and views of the human being are more difficult to draw than Oudemans and Lardinois suggest by putting (Aeschylean and Sophoclean) tragedy on one side of the dividing line. But a long-term cultural revolution took place. From Homer on, and cast in the religious language of an archaic world view, *a newly developing self-awareness of the human being* as a morally and individually responsible being in a broadened and deepened sense of the word gradually emerged, and the tragic genre is, more than any other genre, symptomatic of this historical period of socio-cultural transition. According to Kathleen M. Sands, the historical rise in ancient Greece of the tragic genre is an expression of the rise of a moral awareness of the fundamental contradiction between reality and ideality, between life and human beings as they are and life and human beings as they should be ideally. Sands sees this historical constellation repeated during the historical rise of the tragic genre in modern Europe.[73] Ruth Padel, focusing on tragedy's obsession with mutilating harm, violent damage, suffering and pain, epitomized in madness, links the typically tragic dealing with these themes to the emergence of tragic madness in different epochs:

> In many ways, it is not a continuous tradition. Tragedy expressed itself at specific moments: fifth-century Athens, Elizabethan and Jacobean England, seventeenth-century Spain and France. Some periods tried it and failed. For the Romantics, tragedy was the supreme goal they never reached (except, for a while, in Germany). Why should madness resurface in tragedy in these different epochs? Maybe one thing these societies share in common is this: that they were all, in different ways, poised on some momentary cusp between theological, or daemonological, and innovative scientific explanations for human pain.[74]

Padel thus joins Vernant and Vidal-Naquet in stressing a transitional clash between theological and anthropological views of man.[75]

As to historico-cultural shifts in world view and the view of the human being in *Shakespearean* tragedy, it marks an epoch in which the limits of moral responsibility are put to the test, especially in revenge tragedies. Hamlet's final peace of mind does not justify the conclusion that he is an unambiguously moral hero, Harry Keyishian asserts. Hamlet is confronted with the necessity to act, even at the price of his own moral contamination.[76] The revenge motif has the potential to examine, '. . . a number of significant social concerns: questions of suffering and identity; the extent and limits of personal responsibility, especially with regard to wrongs for which neither the state nor providence provides redress; the adequacy of human law and the legitimacy of the social order; the existence and nature of providence'.[77] Beyond that, he continues, revenge tragedy helps to cope 'with the question of how virtuous action can be taken in an evil world when that action itself must be devious, politic, or tainted with evil'.[78] Danson, in particular, holds that Shakespeare's tragic characters are morally 'mixed characters whose greatness is inextricable from the things that undermine it', who 'have already judged themselves more trenchantly than we can', and whose 'self-consciousness is a consciousness of the social or divine economies which limit . . . the self'.[79] The limits of the early modern subject and its moral autonomy are put to the test.

Joan Rees would agree that Claudius is a morally mixed lot, for though Claudius devotes himself to and becomes identified by Hamlet with an evil principle, he remains for the audience a good-looking man, no monster, but one with whom Gertrude could plausibly fall in love and one who is capable of giving love in return (IV.vii.13). But Rees is much less ambivalent when it comes to Hamlet's role in the plot as the moral hero who opposes Claudius and thus destroys evil in the end with an untainted mind, while Claudius and Laertes become increasingly unscrupulous and blood-minded.[80]

Hamlet's doubtfulness and vigorous questioning can be considered symptomatic of the *sceptic* spirit of the *Renaissance*. Doubt is 'the rhetorical pattern that articulates the philosophical outlook of skepticism', Levin writes.[81] The mood of uncertainty that characterizes *Hamlet* also characterizes the Elizabethan period.

According to Huston Diehl, the questions Hamlet tries to cope with are in part religious questions characteristic of 'the *questioning* spirit of early *Protestantism*' and its ambivalent relation to authority. Protestantism 'denies the legitimacy of traditional authority figures and yet insists on the authority of the world of God and celebrates the assurance of faith', nurturing 'both defiance and obedience, scepticism and certainty, doubt and faith'. Hamlet 'wrestles with the contradictory demands of competing authorities, including his dead father, his king (who is both his stepfather and paternal uncle), and his own conscience (which must answer to God the Father)'.[82] Studying at the Lutheran university of Wittenberg, Hamlet is portrayed as 'a youthful rebel striving to obey, a sceptic seeking certitude, an intellectual who acts on faith'.[83]

Hamlet's doubtfulness, then, can be considered symptomatic of the sceptic spirit of the Renaissance and of the questioning spirit of Protestantism, doubting all authority, except God's authority. What these two spirits have in common is the examination of reason and conscience. Both reason and conscience are important themes in *Hamlet*, and they are scrupulously scrutinizing and scrutinized in the play, in efforts to distinguish appearance from reality, illusion from truth, self-deceit and hypocrisy from sincerity. Harold Bloom calls Hamlet 'the hero of consciousness'.[84] He suspects that Hamlet, more than Luther, was the prime origin of Romantic self-consciousness.[85]

Unlike Murray, Jorge Arditi holds the view that it is precisely because Hamlet fails to wholeheartedly become a *role-player* in a profoundly new sense of the word, that his role-playing becomes madness and his madness a role. What exactly does Arditi mean by 'role-playing'? What was at stake when the Renaissance and the Baroque embraced the dramaturgical metaphor of 'role-playing' was nothing less than a *changed view of human beings* and their positioning in the new infrastructure of social relations, Arditi argues convincingly. People felt they were operating in the world as if they were acting on stage and initially they felt uneasy about it. The increased experience of interpersonal detachment and existential freedom prompted this unease, perfectly captured by 'the conception of society as a stage and of the person as a role-player'.[86]

In the first instance, the metaphor of role-playing refers to the person as *character* and not, as one might think, to the person as *actor*. 'Life in the world compares to the life of characters *in* a drama, not to the life of actors *outside* of the play, of people freely changing the personae they enact, moving at will from role to role, from stage to stage'.[87]

In the second instance, however, the metaphor of role-playing is no longer a metaphor, but a disturbing reality. *The person as a player of roles presupposes a radically detached individual,* enacting one role after another, moving freely from stage to stage. This goes far beyond 'simply complying with expectations, putting on appearances, or being constantly on a stage', Arditi argues.[88] 'It implies the existence of an individual who exists outside of any specific play', who lacks a fixed set of duties to perform and who has a relativizing world view. These implications are disturbing in the moral world of civility and of the princely politics of grace that characterized a Renaissance that was not yet familiar with a structural sense of interpersonal detachment and all too eager to compensate for the floating freedom of individuation with monarchical power claims and classicist authority claims. It was not until much later that people would get used to and feel comfortable with the relativizing idea and practice of interpersonal detachment, of being able to function properly without identifying fully with one's roles. I fully agree with Arditi and would just like to recall as evidence of these later developments the Baroque's fancying of the idea and practice of wearing wigs and attending masked balls.

The initially disturbing possibility of enactment of a multiplicity of 'often incommensurable scripts' by a detached individual who fears to lack spontaneity and authenticity and who fears to encounter hypocrisy everywhere, is exactly what *Hamlet* is about, Arditi continues. Instead of *complying with* and fulfilling *his duty*, Hamlet becomes aware of the disturbing consequences of *taking a role*, if everything can be a play and if every 'self' can be an 'actor'. Within the mental frame of the social order (*res civile*), being a detached individual implies the risk of being lost, alienated, on the border of madness; and being a madman implies playing a role, being 'not in madness, but mad in craft,' as Hamlet himself declares (III.iv.188–9). Hamlet's role-playing becomes madness and his madness a role, one of his many shifting roles.[89] Suffice it to add that, in the end, Hamlet embraces his role of nobleman (Murray's point) when he turns his dying thoughts to the princely authority of his Norwegian successor as the legitimate centre of political power, thus affirming the social order (Arditi's point). All tragic conflict is finally resolved. Or, is it?

The Renaissance and Protestant examination of reason and conscience indicate an awareness on the part of the early modern subject of the disturbing consequences of taking a role in society. In the historico-cultural reading of Christopher Pye, Shakespeare's heroes can be understood in terms of early modern subjectivity, against the background of the simultaneous emergence of new forms of theatre, of the market and of social identity. The literary–cultural context is a socio-economic one. In the modern era, products are exchanged on the basis of their use-value, not on the basis of their intrinsic value. Feudal and modern cultural values clash, at the expense of the feudal sense of intrinsic values. The modern marketplace reduces everything, its subjects included, to nothing intrinsically valuable. Both products and persons represent a fluctuating exchange value instead of having a positive content and value of their own.[90] The early modern subject is not a solid individual whose actions firmly shape the world, but rather a person whose sense of intrinsic value is annihilated during the transition from the feudal to the modern era. Starting from scratch, the only way to regain a sense of identity is to self-assert one's individual subjectivity as something new that can defy the world on the basis of one's own inwardness, Pye suggests. The new individual makes himself believe, not that interiority exists – for its existence as a separate inner world is at least already postulated by Augustine – but that 'interiority can give the subject leverage against his world'.[91] He convinces himself and others by producing the story of the discovery of the modern individual as a new and powerful phenomenon in history, but is aware of the fact that he embodies a disturbingly 'unstable point' of departure for his contingent initiatives.[92] The early modern subject compensates for that awareness by investing 'its energy in the very act of appearance. The modern subject has to sell itself, has to put itself on stage as a stage performer, in order to assert its exchange value as a theatrical commodity and as a socially recognized identity'. It is from the obsession with its own vanishing point – the Albertian perspective in art! – that the modern subject emerges as an individual, Pye argues. The modern subject defines itself in relation to its own negation.[93] That is why it loves theatre so much. Theatre offers to the modern subject the possibility of 'staging' itself 'explicitly as a foundational fiction', as much as selling itself as a starring individual, physically acting and on display. 'It is no coincidence that the era of the market was also the era of spectacle'.[94]

Early modern heroes such as Talbot in Shakespeare's *Henry VI, Part 1* have to make history by recovering and reconstructing it, for lack of exemplifying and embodying it, Pye claims.[95] It is not Talbot's reputation that is being recalled, but the story of his reputation, which is being recounted. Telling the story of his own past reputation makes the 'hero Talbot' to a great extent the product of his own staging as a hero, not so much as a self-made man, but as a renowned hero of the past. Modern heroes never fully recover from their sense of loss of history. Historical change has turned into contingent exchange.[96]

In *Hamlet*, the vanishing point of the hero, the moment of his disappearance in the plot beyond the gaze of the audience, is Hamlet's boat trip to England, Pye continues. Like in the case of Talbot, this turning point is not the point of no return, but precisely, the point of disappearance and return.[97] Hamlet's claim that 'the interim's mine' (V.ii.73) means being able to acknowledge the interim as his very condition, Pye argues. Before the message 'Rosencrantz and Guildenstern are dead' (V.ii.365) returns, Hamlet must have come to his own. But he comes to his own as an *interim hero* who, in his dying speech, acknowledges, 'I cannot live to hear the news from England'. (V.ii.348) By acknowledging the interim as his very condition, the modern subject knows too much, knows of its own limit as the very condition of its emergence and performance. He knows he should have been dead (in England) and he knows he will now die before the message of the death of his friends declaring him alive and kicking meets its deadline – a deadline which Hamlet had produced for himself. He had to 'act before the returning message would betray what he knew of the king's intentions'.[98] Everything emerges out of the single act Hamlet undertakes aboard ship, 'At once a suicidal gesture—a self-abnegation—and the sacrifice that establishes the possibility of an identificatory consolidation, the death of the messenger ultimately founds the possibility of Hamlet's identification not with another but with his own negation'.[99] Hamlet's substitution of himself for Rosencrantz and Guildenstern is not the last one in the logic of violent exchange. In fact, it clears the way for a staged duel between Hamlet and Laertes, whose relationship is a mixture of rivalry and idealizing identification. Again, Hamlet's identification is not with another, but with his own negation, 'I'll be your foil, Laertes', Hamlet says (V.ii.249).[100]

According to John Jeffries Martin, both the modern (Burckhardt) and the postmodern (Greenblatt) interpretations of the Renaissance self suffer from their genealogical agenda of wanting to present it as the origin of their own versions of the self. In line with Arditi and Pye, he emphasizes that Renaissance identities, unlike those of the seventeenth century, were often 'anxious identities, uncertain about the nature of the boundaries . . . between the inner and the outer "self"', and 'identity was *not* about individuality but rather explicitly about *the problem of the relation of one's inner experience to one's experience in the world*'. The Renaissance self, then, was neither primarily an inner self nor primarily a social self, but a problematic *relation* between one's *social* experience and one's *inner* experience.[101]

What are we, in this section, to make of that other self-produced 'interim period of time', the historico-cultural gap between the view of man in Greek tragedy and the view of man in Shakespearean tragedy? Williams explains that Greek tragic action was not rooted in individual heroes, but in a social and cosmic world that transcended them. He points out that 'we think of tragedy as what happens *to* the hero, but the ordinary tragic action is what happens *through* the hero'.[102] He observes, 'What we then see is a general action specified, not an individual action generalized. What we learn is not character but the mutability of the world'.[103] Medieval Christianity is hardly different in this respect. The Christian morality play *Everyman* represents a general action specified. Elizabethan tragedy marks the shift from the commonness of 'everyman' to the particularity of the individual who embraces the view that 'life itself is seen at its most intense in an individual experience'.[104] This individual experience does no longer coincide with the social status and duty that the early modern individual shares with his Greek predecessor. The modern tragic hero can even actively challenge and try to shape the social order to which he belongs. But he still belongs to it – Elizabethan tragedy is humanist tragedy, not bourgeois tragedy.[105]

What Williams has to say about the historical shift from the commonness of 'Everyman' (the common type, role, duty, fate) to the particularity of the individual (the particular experience that constitutes me) is strikingly illustrated by the sudden shift in the very first dialogue between Hamlet and the King and Queen (I.ii.72–106):

Queen:
    Thou knowest 'tis common. All that lives must die,
    Passing through nature to eternity.
Hamlet:
    Ay, madam, it is common.
Queen:
                    If it be,
    Why seems it so particular with thee?
Hamlet:
    'Seems', madam? Nay, it is. I know not 'seems'.
    'Tis not alone my inky cloak, good mother,
    Nor customary suits of solemn black,
    Nor windy suspiration of forced breath,
    No, nor the fruitful river in the eye,
    Nor the dejected 'haviour of the visage,
    Together with all forms, moods, shapes of grief,
    That can denote me truly. These indeed 'seem';
    For they are actions that a man might play.
    But I have that within which passes show —
    These but the trappings and the suits of woe.
King:
    'Tis sweet and commendable in your nature, Hamlet,
    To give these mourning duties to your father.
    But you must know your father lost a father;
    That father lost, lost his;
        . . .
    To reason most absurd, whose common theme
    Is death of fathers, and who still hath cried,
    From the first corse till he that died today,
    'This must be so'. We pray you throw to earth
    This unprevailing woe, and think of us
    As of a father.[106]

Is *Hamlet* primarily about the outstanding individual and therefore an exception, or is it concerned with the community at large? David Margolies holds the view that all Shakespeare's tragedies are about social disintegration.[107] In the case of *Hamlet*, the attention of the audience is drawn in favour of one character only, Prince Hamlet, because Hamlet's struggle with social disintegration takes place mainly in Hamlet's mind, perception, world view, asides and monologues. The court has good reasons to ignore his views and disqualify them as mad. The audience, however, is inclined to identify and sympathize with Hamlet's perspective because it has hardly any dramaturgical indications from the actions on stage to doubt his version of what is actually going on. The audience is attracted by and drawn into Hamlet's mind, which cannot speak for lack of a much-needed new language. Despite his verbal virtuosity, Hamlet suffers from a problem of *articulating* what is going on in his mind and heart. 'But it is the *[social!] content* of that consciousness, not its psychological structure, that is important', according to Margolies.[108] The tragic individual is a social being who suffers from his *social* isolation, whether he be Achilles, Oedipus or Hamlet. This aspect too is an element that Greek and Shakespearean tragedy have in common.

7 Conclusions

Tragedy deals with narrative sources and their cultural values in different ways from epics, but the distinction between the two is not clear-cut. Greek tragedy drew from a limited repertoire of ancient heroic texts (including Homer's epics!) and did so freely in the sense that deviations from the mythical and epic stories were allowed. The stories were often appropriated in order to become part of the imagined Athenian past. Contemporary Athens, after all, constituted the audience. Similarly, Shakespeare drew freely from his literary sources, especially the Roman tragedies by Seneca and the English chronicles on the history of the British Isles. These tragedies and chronicles were neither epic literature nor canonized collective English memory. The plays were meant to address contemporary English issues, not to reconstruct history. Shakespearean tragedy did not draw directly from Greek tragedy and cannot therefore be considered its inheritor, as Lessing mistakenly suggested.

Both Greek and Shakespearean tragedy presented the traditional heroic value system as a model to be questioned and explored critically. They shared the same inquiring spirit, and in that respect, Lessing is not mistaken after all. According to Redfield, this characteristic is not exclusively tragic, but also applies to Homer's epics, especially the *Iliad*. We saw why Greeks such as Aeschylus and Aristotle would, in all likelihood, have agreed. Redfield, then, defines 'tragedy' as 'all fiction which is an inquiry into the (dys)functioning of a culture by testing the limits of its virtues'. I have suggested that such testing can serve different purposes and that in epic literature, this testing function serves mainly celebrating and legitimizing purposes whereas in tragic literature, this testing function serves mainly questioning and critical purposes. Instead of using Redfield's modern terminology and speak of tragedy's 'testing' function, one may prefer Goldhill's postmodern terminology and speak of tragedy's 'exploring' function, but both are meant in a critical sense of the word. Whereas epic heroic language is powerful, reliable and binding, tragic heroic language is either less powerful or much more ambiguous, controversial, manipulated and manipulative. Both Greek and Shakespearean tragedy critically test or explore the limits of the power and reliability of heroic language.

Tragedy turns epic heroes into anti-heroes, in the case of Hamlet, even into an antic hero. The epic hero overcomes problems by solving riddles, gathering knowledge and learning from experience, the tragic hero generates problems by asking questions and making discoveries. Gill argues that what is problematic about the 'problematic heroes' of Greek epic and tragedy has to do with their situation, which provokes them into engaging in 'second-order' reasoning and conventionally unacceptable behaviour. Their tragic conflict is thus a conflict between conventional (pre-reflective, 'first-order' reasoned) norms and post-conventional (reflective) norms.

The occurrence of a tragic hero and his or her ambiguous language is symptomatic of wider historico-cultural shifts in world view and the view of man. Greek tragedy is an expression of increased individualization and internalization. The traditional collective value system remains a social affair, but in addition, it becomes a matter of personal commitment and psychological concern. Tragedy is indicative of long-term changes in the Greek view of the human being from Homer to Aristotle. A new self-awareness of the human being as a morally and individually responsible being develops. Sands sees tragedy, not just Greek, but also Elizabethan tragedy, as an expression of the traumatic rise of a moral awareness of the fundamental contradiction between reality and ideality. Elizabethan tragedy, I would add, constitutes a second wave not only of the tragic genre, but also of increased individualization and internalization. The sense of alienating distance between the social or outer world and the inner world has sharpened once again. The tragic hero is still a social hero who suffers from the gap between the individual and the community, but this time, in Elizabethan tragedy, his identity is not confined to his social status. His interiority provides the modern subject some leverage against his world, as Pye put it. The individual now initiates his own projects in the field of social relations. Williams pointed out that the tragic hero is now an individual human being who, from his own aspirations, from his own nature, sets out on an action that leads him to tragedy. Initially, he feels uneasy about his initiatives, as if acting on stage, for lack of being fully rooted in a given social structure. He faces new limits, both within himself and in a culturally unreliable world. The intrinsic values of feudalism and Christianity are replaced by the fluctuating values of the marketplace and of religious wars.

Should Elizabethan tragedy, then, be defined as the unsolvable conflict between incompatible (or incommensurable) values? Not necessarily. Values do not need to clash in order to produce a tragic conflict. It suffices that they fluctuate to a disturbing degree. What about Greek tragedy's values? These values too, fluctuate. Tragedy explores the fluctuating meanings of their terminology. Values that actually clash may nonetheless produce a tragic conflict that is solved and yet remains fully tragic because it is compelling. If a clash of values produces irreparable damage and is therefore considered unsolvable, it often is so not because the tragic conflict is unsolvable by definition, but because it has become unsolvable due to extreme conditions or positions maintained by the tragic heroes involved.

PART II: INDIAN AND HINDU ISSUES

1 Introduction

In this second part of the chapter, on Indian and Hindu issues, there will be a presentation of the ways in which the literary–cultural aspects that have been discussed are present or absent in the *Mahābhārata* epic and the *Bhagavadgītā*.

The first issue relates to the shift from the epic genre to the tragic genre. In Greece, even though Homer's epics remained the schoolbook texts for learning Greek, the epic genre lost its prominent place to the tragic genre. In India, the epic genre gained in importance and no tragic genre emerged to replace it. What happened? Did Indian literature develop other genres while coping with similar issues?

The second issue concerns the questioning of traditional cultural values. The Greek literary shift from the epic genre to the tragic genre was also a cultural shift from a conventional set of values to a post-conventional set of values. How are the traditional values being presented in the Indian material? How do the *Mahābhārata* and the *Bhagavadgītā* deal with conflicting values? Do they testify to a clash of cultural values that cannot be resolved, but only be suffered tragically? Is the epic systematically debating and questioning the boundaries and limits of the core values of the Hindu culture it (re)presents?

A third issue pertains to the occurrence of 'problematic heroes' within the epic genre. Epic heroes are usually expected to embody the traditional values of their cultures. Does tragedy's transformation of 'epic' heroes into 'tragic' heroes have parallels in the *Mahābhārata* and the *Bhagavadgītā*? And are there traces of wider shifts in world view and the view of man?

2 The epic's narrative sources and functions

The idea of 'epic' as 'a comprehensive totality incorporating whatever was worth retelling', articulating and potentially performing all aspects of culture within the basic institutional context of the festival is an idea that ancient and classical Greece have in common with latter-day India.[109] Cross-culturally, Richard P. Martin writes, the epic genre is expansive by nature, expanding praise poetry, tends to include other genres as well, like songs and proverbs, and can embody underlying myths; at festivals, it can be performed anywhere at any time in any form.[110]

In the Indian case, the arrangement and rearrangement of narrative sources culminating in the compilation of a comprehensive totality not only takes epic proportions, it also proves its validity and credibility as a genre. The epics are being held in high esteem precisely because they are mainly compilations of traditional material rather than original compositions. In Western culture, Freda Matchett explains, the word 'compilation' tends to have a somewhat negative meaning, and a 'mere compiler' is not particularly creative. Within the Hindu tradition, however, things are quite different:

> of the most prestigious figures in Hindu mythology is Vyāsa. He is the origin, humanly speaking, of the Vedas, the *Vedāntasūtra*, the *Mahābhārata* and the Purānas. He is *the* Arranger or Compiler: that is what his name, or to be more precise his title, means. For the Hindu, the act of arranging is in fact a form of creating, perhaps even the highest form. As Hindus see the cosmos, it is created and recreated in a never-ending cycle of great acts of arrangement and rearrangement. In contrast to the Christian idea of *creatio ex nihilo*, the Hindu tradition sees creation as the repeated differentiation of the unmanifest primordial materiality into a seemingly infinite number of forms which can be arranged into a variety of patterns, not only through re-creation (where the same patterns recur, as *Vishnu* 1.5.63–7 indicates), but also through the way in which various myths or cycles of myths can

arrange themes of figures in different sequences. It is this perception of the cosmos which gives to Hindu mythology its kaleidoscopic quality: the basic elements can be shaken up together time and again so that they fall into new configurations.[111]

Within a vast universe, things are constantly rearranged.

A major theme underlying the plot pattern of the *Mahābhārata* epic is that of a war between all the contemporary heroes of the age, resulting in a 'totalizing war precipitated by the overpopulation of the Earth personified', as Gregory Nagy recalls. Earth's complaint to Brahma that she is overburdened has the gods descend in order to remove the Earth's burden of demons who oppress the Earth's surface in the form of kings who wage war against each other, covering the Earth with armies and battles. 'The gods' decision to initiate a final war is correlated with their decision to initiate the incarnation of the five Pāndava heroes'. Nagy points to this epic theme as 'compelling evidence' for a common 'Indo-European heritage of the epic traditions about the Trojan War'.[112] Also, like the mortal Pāndava heroes, begotten by five corresponding immortal gods, the epic heroes in Homeric poetry 'can be defined simply as mortals of the remote past, male or female, who are endowed with superhuman powers because they are descended from the immortal gods themselves'.[113] Mortal heroes can nonetheless become immortal, but only after death. Due to this immortalization, a hero can be worshipped. Nagy recalls that the ancient Greek word *hērōs* refers not just to a dramatic character, but to a figure of cult, as do heroic figures like Arjuna, who is being worshipped in modern times in India, 'during local festivals featuring animal sacrifices and re-enactments—both epic and dramatic—of the hero's life experiences'.[114]

Epic literature is difficult to pin down. Martin argues that the epic genre has symbiotic ties with folklore, myth, and especially praise-poetry. Praise-poetry and epic have a kernel-and-expansion relationship.[115] Epic literature, as Romila Thapar understands it, is a specific genre of its own. The emergence of the *Indian epic* is traceable, Thapar explains, via the *dāna-stuti* (eulogies on gift-giving), *gāthā*, *nārāśamsī* (eulogies on heroes) to the *ākhyāna* (commemorating *rājās* and heroes) and the *kathā* (cycles of stories generally involving heroes). The *dāna-stuti* hymns scattered throughout the Rig Veda are eulogies on chiefs and deities – especially the god Indra – who act as chiefs, bestowing generous gifts on grateful bards and priests.[116]

Genealogy as a record of succession lay at the core of the epic tradition and linked epic to embedded history as well as to the *itihāsa-purāna* and later historical forms, Thapar claims. Genealogy is used by new groups in the ascendant to *legitimize* their power and claim connections with those who were in power earlier. Links were consequently sought in the post-Gupta period by new ruling families with the Sūryavamśas and the Candravamśa. The epics embodying the stories of these lineages were thus assured continuity.[117] The past that epic literature refers to, Thapar suggests, validates the present in the long discourses on what constitutes good government or the correct functioning of the *kshatriya* as king, perhaps best exemplified in the dying Bhīshma delivering the lengthy *mokshadharma* perorations, lying on his bed of arrows. In one way, this means righteous kingship is being idealized. In the didactic sections, monarchy is described as the ideal system. But that is not primarily because one is in need of a model, of a picture of ideal kingship. In the didactic sections, the existence of the state is taken for granted. It is for reasons of legitimization of the present that epic literature looks back nostalgically on a previous age.[118]

Hiltebeitel has credited Thapar for being 'the only scholar to his knowledge to have suggested a link between the experience of empire and the adoption by "Hindu" poets of an epic genre'.[119] But he does not share her conclusion that legitimate succession is the primary motif and legitimization of the *status quo* the primary function of the *Mahābhārata*. On the contrary, the core motif of the epic as a whole, he argues, is the *education of the king*, Yudhisthira, who has to learn throughout the epic what it means to be(come) a righteous king.[120] If the old warrior order is debated, it is in order to critically examine it not because it represents a still existing historical reality, but because it allows for the development of an educational charter of the future by which a king has learnt to behave as a righteous king.

Thapar and Hiltebeitel represent two opposite approaches to the epic as an integrated whole. These approaches influence their argument.

Those scholars who have an affinity with the tradition of historical criticism will stress the *chronological discontinuity* within the work as a whole, in particular the discontinuity between the narrative sections that are presumed to be older, and the didactic sections that are presumed to be younger. This approach allows for the interpretation that the earlier *narrative* sections present the traditional value system as a *given* model, whereas the later *didactic* sections tend to present the *questioning and debating* of these values. The epic as a whole would have gone through a long history of story-telling, writing and rewriting, interpolating and editing, which would not have contributed positively to the consistency of content and style of the work as a whole, but would have been expressive of many developments in Indian cultural history. Chattopadhyaya, Thapar and Katz are exponents of this interpretation.

Ruth Cecily Katz tries to combine a diachronic typology of the epic with a synchronic typology.[121] Diachronically, she considers the *Mahābhārata* to be halfway on the scale of Hindu sacred scriptures between the ritualistic *Vedas* ('archetypically Indo-European') and the devotional *Puranas* ('archetypically Hindu'), not just chronologically, but religiously speaking.[122]

Synchronically, Arjuna's personality traits – Arjuna being (one of) the main character(s) of the epic – are subdivided into three levels or types – Arjuna as hero, Arjuna as human and Arjuna as religious devotee.[123] The *heroic level* is the level of pure heroism, where heroes win justly and do not doubt their prowess; the link between *dharma* and victory is felt as automatic,[124] and there is a harmony between fate and effort. Arjuna's role is that of sacrificer.[125] The level of pure heroism allows for comparisons with other Indo-European/ Semitic examples because it draws on these older martial concepts of heroism, anterior to the extant epic and connected with a bardic oral tradition. The *human level* is the level of human vulnerability and ambiguity both in terms of morality and in terms of mortality. Heroism and humanity are presented as opposite poles – strength over against weakness, ruthlessly fighting over against disgust with war, sense of duty against emotional sympathy with the enemy, divinity against humanity. The tension between the heroic level and the human level culminates in the *Bhagavadgītā*. The tension is resolved on the *devotional level*, where Arjuna's heroic act of sacrifice is transformed into a heroic act of devotion. The devotional level is connected with a late stage of sectarian reworking, which introduces the epic's strand of Nara-Nārāyana mythology.[126]

In Katz's approach, these two typologies are closely related. The second typology (Arjuna as hero, as human and as religious devotee) is a synchronic typology – all three types are present simultaneously in the same epic text – which coincides with the first, diachronic typology (the *Vedas* as Indo-European, the *Mahābhārata* as both and the *Puranas* as Hindu). In this way, she tries to solve the tensions between diachronic and synchronic interpretations.

In my opinion, Katz's model is helpful in reconstructing the complexities of a problem to which there is no solution. Although I fully sympathize with her conviction that the epic bears marks of a development from earlier concepts of heroism to later concepts of devotion, I find her model of actually subdividing them into three types or levels somewhat artificial and not entirely convincing.[127] Tracing developments in such detail has so far proven impossible, but the overall impression, that literary and historical developments in the form and contents of the epic have taken place, is beyond scholarly doubt.

Those scholars who prefer the structuralist view will stress the *chronological continuity* within the work as a whole and keep the number of historical developments to a minimum. This approach allows for the interpretation that one core set of values is prevalent throughout the entire work, that the main story reflects ritual patterns, and that structural conflicts, ambiguities, inconsistencies and repetitions are perpetually returning in both the narrative and the didactic sections. The traditional value system, then, displays a *structural* pattern that is meant to be a solution, but is inherently problematic, and therefore much less of a given model than of a constant source of *questioning and debate*. Hiltebeitel and Heesterman are exponents of this tradition.

Those scholars who argue from the Hindu theological sense of time as expressed in the epic, will stress the moral *decline of the World Age* in desperate need of renewal by the cosmic intervention of Krishna, the degeneration of royal succession as a manifestation of the degeneration of an Age in which *dharma* and *adharma* are no longer opposites, but have started to fatally mix. The very substance of what the core values of *dharma* and *artha* stand for is, since then, a source of mixture and confusion, subject to debate and questions. Biardeau comes closest to this Hindu approach.

Scholars from all traditions could nonetheless agree in principle with the thesis that the *Mahābhārata*, not as a whole, but on the whole, assumes a value system that is not only presented as a given model, but also subject to questioning and debate. What does this value system look like?

3 Development and debate of a socio-religious value system

A coherent Hindu value system may be hard to identify, but the overall religious history of Hinduism testifies to several stages. At first, until around (very!) roughly 600 BCE, there was the ancient Vedic religion (called after the *Vedas*, its sacred ritual texts), which had a ritualistic approach to reality. Vedic priests addressed the gods by performing rituals, especially the fire sacrifice. The priests then speculatively cosmologized the sacrificial rituals while continuing to perform them. The idea was that ritual performance and the speculative knowledge related to its cosmic efficacy maintain the three worlds (earth, heaven, underworld). This earth, the social world, was part of the wider cosmic world, the world of nature, a natural and social order upheld by ritual performance and priestly esoteric knowledge. *Social values* were crucial.

From around 600 BCE onwards, ascetic movements started to break away from these Vedic ritualistic ideas and practices. Instead of fostering social values, they embraced the prospect of ultimate liberation from the bonds of the three worlds. Their idea was to leave behind entirely all worldly desires and cultivate inner spiritual growth in order to become one with the ultimate reality underlying the illusory appearance of the three worlds. *Ascetic values* and the goal of ultimate liberation from the cycle of rebirths gradually became crucial.

The striking thing about Hinduism as a religious culture is that it came to cultivate *both ideals simultaneously* – both sacrifice and renunciation, both ritual performance and cutting off the ritual connection for the sake of spiritual liberation, both the figure of the householder (performing the ritual) and the figure of the ascetic (renouncing the ritual), both social values and ascetic values.

Eventually, the idea of becoming one with the ultimate reality underlying the illusory world of appearances (again) took a more personalized form – personal devotion (*bhakti*) of one favourite god (amidst many gods) as the ultimate reality and driving force behind the universe. Social and ascetic values were still crucial, but they were now *devotionalized*. In medieval times, devotionalist movements would be organized into institutional 'sects'.

The *Mahābhārata* epic concentrates on three social values or 'goals' and one ascetic value of 'goal'. The social values or this-worldly goals are *kāma*, sexual desire and erotic pleasure, *artha*, material wealth, profit and interest, or purpose and anything good as a means to a purpose, and *dharma*, cosmic and moral order and duty.[128] The ascetic value or other-worldly goal is *moksha*, liberation from the cycle of rebirths.

Each of these values or goals was *legitimate in its own right*, not to be disqualified by higher values, but to be cultivated in their own specific fields. These specific fields were the areas of competence of specific groups of people. Cultivating the value of *dharma* had always been the specific ritual and intellectual competence of *brahmins*, and was therefore considered their particular goal in life. Likewise, cultivating the value of *artha* was the specific politico-economic and management competence of warriors and kings, and was consequently considered their particular goal.[129] Cultivating the value of *kāma*, erotic pleasure and satisfaction of (sexual) desire, was the particular competence of women, and thus their particular goal.[130] Cultivating the value of *moksha*, ultimate liberation from the cycle of rebirths, was the particular goal of ascetics. All these goals were valuable goals in their own right, represented by specific groups in particular, although not coincidal with these groups.

The notion of *dharma* expresses a sense of established order that relates to different levels of reality. On a *personal level*, it relates to the extent to which one fulfils one's social duties in life, primarily the duty of meeting the established role expectations of the fellow members of one's caste and sex. Not the pursuit of general principles, but the enactment of existing moral practices within one's own group of kinsmen is expected. A warrior should behave as such and fight when it comes to fighting instead of showing cowardice (*Gītā* 2.2 and 31). A male should behave as such and 'not act like a eunuch' showing 'this vulgar weakness of heart' (*Gītā* 2.3). And a king should behave as such and protect his kingdom and subjects against illegitimate and unjust rulers (*Gītā* 1.33). On a *societal level*, the notion relates to the extent to which the clan society upholds its hierarchical apartheid system of caste/race differences and its ancestral rituals (*Gītā* 1.40–44). On a *cosmic level*, the notion relates to the extent to which good prevails over evil and time takes its course in the creation and destruction of the world. The necessity of an established or given order on all these levels is presupposed.

In the classical (second century CE) treatises (*śāstras*) on social rules, norms and values, Gavin Flood writes, the purposes of man (*purushārthas*) are articulated as *a system of three goals*.[131] As one would expect, *dharma* is the most important purpose of human life in the *dharma-śāstras* (treatises on *dharma*) – 'When wealth and pleasure are pursued alone, outside of *dharma*, they lead to social chaos. This same idea is expressed in the *Gītā* where Krishna identifies himself with the desire in all beings which is not opposed to *dharma* (7.11)'.[132] In the twelfth chapter of the epic, Śāntiparvan or the Book of Peace (12.167), the five Pāndava brothers are having a discussion with the wise Vidura about which of the goals is most important. Vidura argues for *dharma* as the underlying principle of cosmic and social order, thanks to which everything else can thrive. Arjuna claims that order and pleasure rest on *artha*, pursuing one's interest, material wealth and profit. Bhīma favours *kāma*, desire in the sense of motivation, for without it, one would have no desire for worldly prosperity (*artha*) and for life in general, or attain liberation. Yudhisthira agrees with Vidura, but in practice, this is easier said than done.

The *fourth goal* of life, *moksha* (ultimate liberation), is a separate case, literally a 'goal apart' (*apavarga*) from the other three goals (*trivarga*), opting for an individual pursuit of spiritual liberation beyond the social world.

The three goals of *kāma*, *artha* and *dharma* constitute one pole, the one goal of *moksha* constitutes the other pole of that *fundamental bipolarity* that has become *the very structure of Hinduism*, according to Madeleine Biardeau.[133] The pole of the three goals is concerned with maintaining the three worlds (earth, heaven, underworld) whereas the pole of the fourth goal is concerned with leaving the three worlds behind entirely. A this-worldly value system, represented by the householder, is combined with a non-worldly value system, represented by the ascetic or renouncer.[134] The brahminical discourse that focused on *four core values* or goals in life (*purushārthas*) is basically a theological construction of the dominant notions that were current in different circles, but did not constitute a fixed system, Flood argues. It constitutes a general theory of human values, not just of moral values, Rajendra Prasad emphasizes. The theory is both descriptive and evaluative in nature and function, focusing on objectives both valued and valuable, partly because objectives are per definition objects of desire, desire favouring anything considered worthwhile, partly through the content and interrelations of the objectives, Prasad explains.[135]

The epic's Book of Peace demonstrates that a lot of *discussion* was going on as to which value or goal should be considered to prevail over the other goals. Although these discussions prove indecisive and, in that respect, illustrate that no fixed system of values existed in the epics, the debate simultaneously illustrates that efforts to turn core values at the time into a consistent hierarchy of values, are indicative both of a need for social coherence and of a recognition of social diversity on the religio-cultural level. This religio-cultural level of debating values or goals in life was traditionally dominated by the *brahmins* who had privileged access to all sources of advanced knowledge, including esoteric ritual knowledge, that is, authoritative knowledge. Their superior knowledge authorized them to function as lawmakers to their kings and to instruct them on the legitimacy of their pursuit of political goals. That is why the debate was mainly a brahminical affair and all the more authoritative – except that it was put into the mouth of the ruling warriors, which suggests that it was mainly a *kshatriya* affair.

Biardeau contends that the Vedic religion was reinterpreted in light of the renouncer's tradition, and the ideas of renunciation were reinterpreted by *bhaktas* (henotheistic religious devotees). The 'universe of *bhakti*' (devotionalism), which can already be discerned in the epic literature, but is systematized later in the Purānas, is made up of a cosmology expressing a *hierarchy of values* that places *bhakti* on top.[136] But in the end, *moksha* is the highest value. In fact, the value system is not a fixed one since, in the epics, the substance of the worldly values involved is constantly under debate. The primary reason for that given by the epics themselves is time – the *Mahābhārata* is a work of kingly instruction in an era of decline of *dharma* called the *Kali-yuga* (cf. 'Iron Age').[137] The Kurukshetra War, therefore, represents the eschatological crisis of an age that is in urgent need of the apparition of one of Vishnu's saving incarnations (*avatāras*), Krishna. That is to say, theologically speaking.[138] Historically speaking, according to Biardeau, the apocalyptic mood of the epic is a reflection of the threat Buddhism posed to the brahminic culture and influence, especially since its Buddhist imperial king Ashoka conquered Northern India.[139]

4 Epic heroes embodying traditional values

Biardeau agrees with Dumézil that the epic characters are types rather than individuals, 'meant to embody values and social functions rather than illustrate psychological truths'.[140] Yudhisthira, Arjuna and Bhīma are the three main brothers among the five Pāndavas, and Arjuna's character is a cross between Yudhisthira's contemplative and scrupulous character and Bhīma's brutal and amoral character. Yudhisthira represents the unworldly value of *moksha*, whereas Bhīma advocates the worldly value of *kāma*, its extreme opposite. Both are needed, but their extremism is to be kept within certain boundaries because 'the uncommitted attitude of Yudhisthira and the unchecked behaviour of Bhīma would lead to a disastrous "reign of the fishes"' (*matsyayāya*, the big fishes eating the smaller ones, the rule of the jungle).

The apparent irreconcilable opposition between them calls for a *mediation*, embodied by Arjuna in his role as ideal king, Biardeau claims.[141] All major values are involved – *dharma* in the personal form of Arjuna's caste duty and in the form of fighting a just war to regain legitimate kingship, *artha* in the form of Arjuna's class duty to wage war and in the form of pursuit of any of these major goals by use of the necessary means, *kāma* in the form of desire for the benefits of ritual sacrifice, and *moksha* in the form of yogic values related to renunciation of the benefits of Arjuna's sacrificial action in battle. Does Arjuna embody these values in such a way that their relationships represent an irreconcilable conflict, a *clash of values*, or does his character represent the perfect match between them? Biardeau sees Arjuna as the ideal mediator, embodying a type of *artha* that combines an element of *kāma* with an element of *moksha*. In the *Gītā*, she argues, Arjuna comes to embody *artha* perfectly since he takes up fighting, but a form of *artha* that lacks self-interest and that therefore includes balancing the opposition between *moksha*, in the sense of renouncing all action, and *kāma*, in the sense of desiring pleasure and the benefit of sacrificial action. The *bhakti* context also allows for the value of *dharma* to acquire a broader meaning by which it encompasses all goals, including even *moksha*, since the ascetic value of renouncing the worldly benefits of one's action becomes normative not just for the *brahmins*, but for all classes who act purely out of love for the one god.

Arjuna's performance of his warrior duty (*artha*) as his personal duty (*sva-dharma*) to serve the cosmic order (*dharma*) by serving his personal god (*bhakti*) indicates a religious breakthrough of *universalizing* and *democratizing* proportions, allowing all layers of society to gain access to the highest spiritual goal by (simultaneously) cultivating their own socio-religious status in society. It was the introduction of *bhakti* ('surrender' to the grace of one god, and the popular devotionalist movements practising this form of 'devotion') that brought about the democratization of religion by proclaiming the possibility of spiritual access to the highest religious goal of *moksha* for all kinds of groups within the society, not just for ascetics and *brahmins*, but also for warriors, workers and women, provided the group members individually surrender to the grace of one god and dedicate their hearts and duty-bound activities to the one god as an act of self-sacrifice. This new way of thinking implied the rearrangement of the previous hierarchy of values dominated by *moksha* on the other-worldly level and by *dharma* on the worldly level, by allowing the values of *artha* and *kāma* to be linked to the highest value of *moksha* directly. That is to say, by cultivating *artha*, a warrior did no longer just pursue a worldly goal, but in doing so, he would simultaneously strive for *moksha* by pursuing it in the context of practising *bhakti*. Within the context of practising *bhakti*, the value of *artha* was now a straightforward way of striving for ultimate liberation. Likewise, by cultivating *kāma*, a woman no longer just pursued a worldly goal, but would strive for ultimate liberation by dedicating her heart to loving the one god.

Despite these universalizing and democratic tendencies in Hindu devotionalism, Hindu values tended to remain, to a great extent, *status-dependent* and *caste-dependent* instead of becoming all-inclusive and universal. At the top of the hierarchy are the *brahmins*, who constitute the religious elite and intellectuals. It is the approval by the *brahmins* that creates legitimacy. The *brahmins* have made *ritual status* the core of their identity. It is their genius, Murray Milner Jr explains, to have avoided making the control of land and labour or the control of force the primary basis of their power, because these resources are the most alienable and easily appropriated by outside conquerors or upstart discontents, whereas the highly elaborate lifestyle, emphasizing ritual purity, is nearly impossible for outsiders to copy or appropriate. The *brahmins'* dilemma is how to translate their religious status into other resources, including wealth, without undercutting that status, Milner states.[142]

On the level of ideology or culture, four categories are prominent – the *brahmins*, the warriors (*kshatriyas*), the merchants (*vaiśyas*) and the labourers or producers (*śūdras*). But on the empirical or social level, only the *brahmins* and the *śūdras* are present in nearly every local area in India, while the other two are often unrepresented. That is because the warrior status and the merchant status are based on alienable resources whereas the religious status of *brahmins* is a relatively inalienable one – the same can be said negatively for the untouchables– and because the omnipresence of the *śūdras* is rooted in the indispensability of labour in an agrarian society.[143]

In the *epic* and the *Gītā*, the social issue of sticking to one's own duty (*svadharma*) is related to the fear of caste mixture (*varna*, 'class' or 'estate'), of mixed birth (*varnasankara*):

Devoted to his own duty,
A man attains perfection.

Hear then how one who is devoted to his own duty
Finds perfection:

By worshipping with his own proper duty
Him from whom all beings have their origin,
Him by whom all this universe is pervaded,
Man finds perfection.

Better one's own duty, though imperfect,
Than the duty of another well performed;
Performing the duty prescribed by one's own nature,
One does not incur evil.

One should not abandon the duty to which one is born
Even though it be deficient, Arjuna.
Indeed, all undertakings are enveloped by evil
As fire is by smoke.
[18.45–8][144]

The confusion or overlapping of being born of a mixed couple and the confusion or overlapping of *svadharma* – of *brahmins* behaving like *kshatriyas* or the other way around – are only two different aspects of one and the same fundamental disorder (*adharma*) in society, Biardeau writes.[145] That social categories and values *resist universal applicability* to all groups, despite their common *bhakti* access to ultimate salvation, has also been pointed out by Hiltebeitel, not only with regard to the value of *ahimsā*[146] or that of the highest *dharma*[147], but also regarding class mixture.[148] Regarding women and class mixture, Arti Dhand points out that:

> it is only high-class women who carry the potential to support or subvert the class structure, and therefore it is only their conduct that arouses indignation. Little concern exists for managing the sexuality of lower-class women . . . because their sexuality has no serious impact on the social class structure. Thus, in the Kaurava court, Draupadī's protestations of *pativratā*-hood are treated as pretensions, to be ridiculed and scorned (II.63.11–13).[149]

So far, then, the epic has debated the traditional values and their mutual relationships, presented them in heroes who embody specific values, and rephrased them within the framework of devotionalism. But does the epic question and criticize the traditional values? Does a clash of values occur? And if so, does a clash of values turn these epic values into tragic ones, and epic heroes into tragic heroes?

5 The problematization of heroes: Karna and Yudhisthira

If tragedy turns epic heroes into anti-heroes, two candidates for tragic heroism in the *Mahābhārata* epic present themselves as potential parallels, which have to be examined – Karna and Yudhisthira.

5.1 Karna

According to Julian F. Woods, the tragic anti-hero of the *Mahābhārata* is *Karna*.[150] Daniel H. H. Ingalls, by the way, testifies to a similar opinion, when he writes, 'The hero Karna of the *Mahābhārata* is tragic quite in the Western sense, and many of the Rajput ballads are tragedies in the same vein. Thus, the *bon mot* is falsified that India knew no tragedy until the coming of the British'.[151] Woods follows Biardeau's interpretation, although Biardeau seems to stress Karna's evil side.

Karna's life as a whole, we are told in the epic, has been planned before his birth in order to pave the way for the warrior caste to go to heaven (12.2.4–5). Karna, the illegitimate brother of the Pāndavas, was fathered by the sun god Sūrya and born to Kuntī prior to her marriage to Pāndu.[152] Born before Kuntī's marriage, he had been abandoned by her as an infant and raised by a charioteer, losing his *kshatriya* (warrior) status until Duryodhana elevated him to the kingship of Anga. The abandonment of Karna at birth and his adoption by lowly parents has parallels in many heroic life stories. Karna was raised outside the court, and does not know his true parentage (until 5.138ff.). But he too, like all the others (Pāndavas and Kauravas alike), has been instructed militarily by Drona (1.122.47). Karna had pretended to be a *brahmin* so as to be able to study with Rāma Jāmadagnya, the noted hater of *kshatriyas*. One day, however, when Jāmadagnya was asleep, Indra, disguised as a worm, bored into Karna's thigh. This Karna had suffered stoically, so as not to awaken his teacher, but when, upon waking, Jāmadagnya saw the wound, he realized that Karna must be a *kshatriya*, not a *brahmin* – only a *kshatriya* could have stood such pain without saying a word. He cursed Karna so that he would forget the divine weapon that Jāmadagnya had taught him. Karna was also cursed by a *brahmin* to have the wheel of his chariot fall into a hole in battle (8.29.31, 12.2.23ff.).

Karna turns out to be an excellent fighter. Arjuna takes Karna's performance during the tournament as a personal insult or challenge – he cannot stand to be matched, for he has already developed that pride which is essential to heroes (1.126.17). A battle begins between Arjuna and Karna, but is stopped when it is discovered that Karna cannot claim a noble lineage and therefore is no match for Arjuna. Duryodhana responds by crowning Karna king of Anga, setting him up against the Pāndavas, and creating with him a friendship and alliance that is to endure throughout the epic.[153] Katz comments:

> Karna is the key to Kaurava humanity. Although he is violent, and is often called sinful, since he is one of the four who 'did not shed a tear' when Draupadī was mistreated during the dice game (3.28.7ff.), it is generally clear that he is on the Kaurava side out of genuine friendship and loyalty toward Duryodhana, and because of his undeserved rejection by the Pāndavas, who do not realise who he is until after the war is over (11.27.6ff.). It is also stressed continually in the battle books that Karna is a fair fighter: in particular, he stands by his vow to Kuntī that he will slay none of the Pāndava brothers except Arjuna. Karna is, further, a paragon of generosity: the first step of his undoing, the loss of his earrings and armor, is the result of his inability to refuse anything to a *brahmin*; he must give up even his innate accoutrements when Indra, in brahmanic disguise, requests them (1.104.17; 3.284.12f.). The climax of the audience's sympathy for Karna comes when he is heard, just prior to his death, lamenting the fact that although righteous, he did not attain victory: 'Unable to bear these disasters, wringing his hands, railing, he [said]: 'Knowers of *dharma* have always said: "*Dharma* protects those devoted to *dharma*." Since my [wheel] sank today, it does not protect its devotees. I think *dharma* does not always protect.' Speaking thus, with horses and charioteer reeling, buffeted by blows from Arjuna's weapon and agitated in his actions due to a mortal wound, he again and again censured *dharma* in battle. (8.66.43–4) '.[154]

Karna's impending death had first been announced by Yama, the 'king' of the dead, just prior to Arjuna's sojourn in heaven (3.42.1ff.). Woods describes Karna facing impending disaster. Caught between his duty to Duryodhana and the realization that his cause is hopeless, a clash between effort and fate, he opts for the tragic path of loyalty to the one who has befriended him. When the hour of Karna's death draws near, Kāla (Time personified) approaches invisibly and, alluding to the curse, tells him, 'the earth is devouring your wheel'. 'Karna pleads for time, but Krishna has no compunction about urging a reluctant Arjuna to take this opportunity and finish him off. . . . A light is seen leaving the lifeless corpse to pass into the sun'.[155]

5.2 Yudhisthira

According to Alf Hiltebeitel, the main hero of the *Mahābhārata* as a whole is *Yudhisthira*, not Arjuna or Krishna.[156] Hiltebeitel uses the notion 'main hero' in a literary sense of the word. The notion 'main hero' does not refer to the virtue of heroism (*vīryam* or *śauryam*) because heroism (cf. *Gītā* 18.43) springs essentially from the warrior's nature. Heroism fits the warrior-yogi Arjuna rather than King Yudhisthira. For the king, it must be integrated among qualities pertaining to other dimensions. Royal duties and caste duties are not interchangeable.[157]

Yudhisthira is portrayed neither as an idealized hero nor as the ideal king. He looks much more like a *brahmin* who is inclined to non-violence and renunciation when it comes to waging war, and he looks possessed when it comes to playing a game of dice. Already before the war, the inner conflict Yudhisthira is struggling with is how to reconcile the conduct of *dharma* with ruling a kingdom. After the war, he is stricken with grief because of the loss of so many people and the weeping of the Kaurava women, and has to be consoled. In his opinion, *kshatriya* values like might, valour and wrath are causally connected to calamity and deadly extinction whereas an ascetic life of mendicancy is not (12.7.3–5).[158]

'One of the chief objects of the *Mahābhārata*', according to Hiltebeitel, 'is to instruct kings and other warriors in how to curb endless cycles of violence, particularly as such cycles effect and implicate *brahmins*'.[159] The one quality that Yudhisthira has to develop is the quality of non-cruelty (*ānrśamsya*).[160]

Crucially, in upholding the highest *dharma* of non-cruelty, Yudhisthira follows his *particular* warrior caste duty, not some universal ideal or value in general.[161] Like non-violence, non-cruelty is a principle that lies in its particularities rather than in any universality. Every caste and context has its own particular *dharma* that fits its conditions. The epic resists universalization.[162] Non-cruelty is non-violence tailored to the duties and constraints of a just king and warrior.[163]

After having listened to stories about non-cruelty, such as the story of Nala and Damayantī,[164] the story of the sage and the dog with the human heart[165] and the story of the *dharmic* hunter, Yudhisthira is put to the test three times. In the meantime, he begins his just rule displaying non-cruelty by protecting the war widows and mothers, as well as the poor, blind and helpless. Non-cruelty is a positive value signifying 'a fellow feeling, a deep sense of the other. It occurs often with *anukrośa*, to cry with another, to feel another's pain', 'commiseration'.[166] By the epic's end, Yudhisthira has lost his brothers and his wife. The only creature left is his devoted dog. About to enter heaven, he is told that he can only enter heaven if he leaves his dog behind. (The second test.) He refuses, out of non-cruelty, Hiltebeitel suggests. He has learnt his lesson and is rewarded for it – the devoted dog turns out to be his father Dharma, and they enter heaven together.

There are two aspects in Hiltebeitel's portrayal of Yudhisthira that support my conclusion that the epic depicts Yudhisthira as a tragic hero instead of a triumphant one. The first aspect concerns Hiltebeitel's stress on grief[167] and non-cruelty as characteristic of Yudhisthira's heroism. The highest *dharma* for king Yudhisthira is non-cruelty, related to protecting the war widows and mothers, the poor and blind and to a fellow feeling occurring often with *anukrośa*, to cry with another, to feel another's pain.[168] The second aspect has to do with Yudhisthira's never-ending search for *dharma*. Hiltebeitel has shown that in the end, the structural conflict is not resolved, because Draupadī's question to Yudhisthira on the essence and substance of *dharma* remains unanswered. Instead, the structural conflict is presented to the audience in a fictional form, that is to say, in a form that allows the audience to test its culture's virtues by reflecting on their limits, as Redfield would formulate it. The real battlefield is a culture facing itself and trying to come to terms with its own contradictory value system. On this point, Heesterman would fully agree.

6 Controversial values and problematic heroes

The second issue that was raised in the introduction to the second part of this chapter was about the historical occurrence of a cultural shift from a conventional to a post-conventional set of values. In my discussion of the issue, the focus was on social and ascetic values and on the notions of kingship and warriorship. But the answer to that second question, of how the Indian texts deal with conflicting values, had to include an answer to the third question raised in the introduction, the question pertaining to the occurrence of 'problematic heroes' within the epic genre. Let me start with the issue of whether the traditional notions of kingship and warriorship became the subject of much discussion, and then turn, without further notice, to the other issues as well.

The transition from chiefdoms into monarchies, and later from monarchies into empires and back again into monarchies, is likely to have changed the notion of kingship itself, its significance and legitimacy, not just its political reality. The meaning of the notions of kingship and warriorship would have been under debate, either directly, as in the philosophical tradition of political theories, such as the *Arthaśāstra* and the *Dharmasūtras*, or more indirectly, as in the narrative tradition of the epics. As Thapar indicates, the *Mahābhārata* has such philosophical sections within its narrative corpus. These are called the 'didactic sections' because within the context of the narrative, they are put into the mouths of characters who take up the role of teachers. The two most important didactic expositions are in the *Śānti-parvan* (Book of Peace) by Bhīshma and in the *Bhagavadgītā* by Krishna, respectively.

There are, however, many debates going on between characters in the narrative as such. The most important figure fuelling the debate about what it means to be a righteous king is the main king of the narrative, Yudhisthira. His behaviour as a king and his doubts about kingship are considered highly controversial by other main figures, such as his wife Draupadī, his brother Arjuna, and his narrator Vyāsa. The most important figure fuelling the debate about what it means to be a warrior is the main warrior of the narrative, Arjuna. His behaviour as a warrior and his doubts about warriorship are, likewise, considered highly controversial by Yudhisthira, on the one hand, and by Krishna, on the other. Thus, the extensive and ongoing debate about the significance of kingship and warriorship is already part and parcel of the *Mahābhārata*. The *Mahābhārata* can, therefore, be taken as a debate on some of the core phenomena of classical Indian society and culture, that is to say, on kingship and warriorship and on the wider values that are involved in their exercise.

Thapar's thesis that legitimization is the primary function of epic literature implies, ultimately, that critically examining the limits of the virtues of Indian culture is not the primary function of the *Mahābhārata*. Instead, debating legitimate succession serves the political function of legitimizing the *status quo* of the new system – the monarchy.

According to Hiltebeitel, however, if the 'old warrior order' is debated, it is in order to critically examine it. Both the main hero Yudhisthira and the value of *dharma* are controversial and the main focus point of the ongoing critical debate. In the *Gītā*, Arjuna is the one who, in his refusal to fight, once questions the inner consistency of the value system involved, and thus confirms the validity claim of each value involved in the clash of values. In the epic as a whole, Yudhisthira is the one who persistently questions the substance and validity of particular values – of *dharma* and *artha* – and thus, constantly questions the inner consistency of the value system. But in the case of Yudhisthira, he is not the only one. On the contrary, he is surrounded by others who object to his questioning, to his questionable answers or to his questionable behaviour.

Outstanding in this regard is one woman, Draupadī, his wife. She is, Hiltebeitel argues, the epic heroine whose role it is to question, to challenge the *(a)dharma* in general and Yudhisthira's authority in particular, especially during the dice game. Hiltebeitel refers to a striking parallel in Homer's *Iliad* brought forward by Mihoko Suzuki, who analyses the questioning role of Helen interrogating the authority of the epic's heroic code that scapegoats women in the name of men's heroic struggles.[169] The question 'What is the highest *dharma*?' or 'What is the essence of *dharma*?' is at the heart of the epic – not just *dharma* as an issue, but *dharma* as a riddle that provokes radical *questioning*, Hiltebeitel states. This is nowhere clearer than in the crucial case of Draupadī's question to Yudhisthira in the assembly hall. 'It is by appealing to *dharma* around a question that brings both overt and hidden questions to life that she can save herself and the Pāndavas'.[170] Hiltebeitel shows that Draupadī's appeal to *dharma* leads to some vigorous debates, but these never produce an answer to her question. Draupadī's question of what exactly *dharma* means as an ideal and in practice remains open to debate throughout the epic.[171] Dhand points out that Draupadī can question the negative consequences of men failing to live up to *dharma* because she herself embodies the uncritical ideal of *pativratā*, 'a woman who is sworn to her husband or lord/master', thus representing the traditional 'ideal woman', 'one who defies all the temptations that are endemic to the human condition and remains chaste, faithful, and exemplary in preserving domestic and social order'.[172]

The ways in which heroes and heroines are questioning and being questioned are diverse. They are a mixture of dialogue, philosophical instruction and narrative. The effect is that the problematic heroes are presented as grounding their problematic actions in 'second-order' reasoning, as Gill would call it, about the basic goals and values that should govern human action. If values are embraced, it is not because one is expected to embrace them, but because debate and insight have led to the conclusion that they deserve to be cultivated. In the *Gītā*, Krishna does not impose a list of virtues that has to be obeyed, but depicts a virtuous ideal that has to be interiorized if it is to be cultivated and practised. He leaves Arjuna some real scope for reflection and choice, 'Thus the knowledge that is more secret than all that is secret has been expounded to you by me. Having reflected on (*vimrśya*) this fully, do (*kuru*) as you wish (*icchasi*)'. (18.63) Gill would call Krishna's gesture an invitation to 'second-order' reasoning – an invitation to reflect before making a *reflective* choice. But whereas warrior values are freely debatable in the epic, Krishna's argument of the immortality of the self and of the ultimate identification of Arjuna's self with the eternal Self in the *Gītā* is not open to debate, Corstiaan van der Burg would add as a comment.

When it comes to the value system, Biardeau's account leaves the strong impression that all intellectual forces have gathered in order for the traditional value system to be justified and maintained against the pressures of heterodox ideologies, such as Buddhism, instead of being questioned and criticized. The internal rearrangement of the Hindu (*brahmin*-dominated) value system serves a defensive strategy. It should not be understood as a self-critical reappraisal of the current value system, let alone as a shift to a new value system.

The price being paid for the rephrasing of tradition consists of broadening the meaning of its core values so as to allow a *higher level of applicability* and relevance of the same values. This is indeed a price being paid because broadening the meaning of the core values makes the value system more abstract and, as a result, more vulnerable to being seen as irrelevant and easy to manipulate or ignore. The risk of irrelevance and pliability of the value system is felt precisely where its normativity should function smoothly – on the concrete level of boundaries between the castes being upheld, so that every group continues to fulfil its traditional duties properly according to expectation. In that sense, my use of the term 'abstract' is misleading. The broadening of the meaning of several notions does not make these notions more abstract – in the sense of principles being applied top-down – but makes the network of concrete and bottom-up connotations denser. More connotations, connections, links, relationships introduce a higher degree of applicability within more contexts *without necessarily leading to a clash of values*. It is likely to lead, in fact, to a symbiosis of values, provided people do not object to the closeness and simultaneity of different values as long as the caste boundaries are upheld. And this dual move is exactly what happens in the *Gītā* – on the one hand, bounded categories are opened up at the religious level, while on the other, the risk of unbounded categories is reduced at the practical level. On the one hand, the *Gītā* introduces full religious access to God for all classes (9.32); on the other, the *Gītā* considers Krishna the creator of the caste system (4.13) and considers the caste system the symbol of social order and stability (1.41–3). On the one hand, religious mobility is opened up; on the other, social mobility is blocked.

In order to understand what is going on, I take Heesterman's view – and by implication, do not follow Biardeau in this respect – that one should distinguish between the transcendent, on the one hand, and the sacred plus secular, on the other. From a transcendent point of view, support for the action is withdrawn because the Actor is located beyond the realm of action of the agent. From an immanent point of view, support for the action is sacralized because the action is located in the realm of caste duties and of devotional sacrifice. The sacralization of the impurity of acting violently by waging war implied a justification and legitimization of impure action, in general, as long as it was consistent with the performance of one's own caste duty, and of the impure activities of Hindu kings and warriors, in particular. What was 'meant for warriors in the epic', Biardeau concludes, 'has been conceived all along Indian history as valid for all other non-*brahmin* Hindus as well. . . . The brahminic model was not lost sight of but was generalised so as to fit all other groups of Hindu society including *śūdras*, women and all impure castes'.[173]

Karna and Yudhisthira are truly tragic heroes, as Hiltebeitel demonstrated for Yudhisthira. Can Arjuna be taken to be a tragic hero embodying the insoluble conflict between clashing core values of the Hindu culture? He definitely could, at the beginning of the *Gītā* before the Kurukshetra War has actually started. The problem Arjuna raises there, Biardeau argues, is one of values. But there is no sustained questioning on the part of Arjuna. Instead, he is receiving instruction and, after the instruction, the conflict has disappeared, or rather, has been shown to be a mere appearance. At first, Arjuna almost turned into a tragic hero. But after having received instruction from Krishna, he turns out to be a hero of triumph, and according to some scholars, an ideal king who embodies all the core values of Hindu culture in a balanced way.

Hiltebeitel contends that Krishna is simply one character within the epic as a whole and that, therefore, the *Gītā* represents only one position in the debate on values – the author Vyāsa leaves Arjuna behind and uses Yudhisthira for his development of the plot. Biardeau takes the *Gītā* to epitomize the message of the epic as a whole. Neither Hiltebeitel nor Biardeau considers Arjuna to be a tragic hero.

Biardeau and Heesterman agree that the epic, as a whole, and the *Gītā* in particular, epitomize Hindu culture. The epic and the *Gītā* embody the very structure of Hinduism – the dynamic bipolarity of upholding two ideals simultaneously, the this-worldly ideal of *dharma* (including *artha* and *kāma*) and the other-worldly ideal of *moksha*. What they do not agree on is the character of the synthesis. Biardeau depicts a balanced embodiment of all the core values of Hindu culture in the hero of triumph, Arjuna. Heesterman insists that the tension between the two poles of the bipolarity is too radical to be solved. The insoluble conflict between these clashing poles, which are upheld simultaneously, is the very conflict Hinduism manifests. It is the inner conflict of the Hindu religio-cultural tradition, whose *limits* are tested in the epic, and the *Gītā*. Heesterman's position is basically that the inner conflict is radically insoluble, that is, it is by definition a tragic conflict. Heesterman's position is, of course, the position of an outsider who does not believe that the synthesis can actually solve the conflict; his position is not that of a Hindu. A Hindu is much more likely to sympathize with Biardeau's depiction of a *brahminic* and a *bhakti* position.

This is strikingly illustrated by Ramesh N. Patel's Hindu philosophical interpretation of the *Gītā*. According to Patel, Krishna's message in the *Gītā* concerns the true identity of man, which is not created, but only discovered by action. His message implies a coping strategy in case of a value conflict, Patel contends:

> Just as true identity cannot be defined by particular actions or specific ends, true freedom cannot be restricted by particular contents or concrete values. True freedom means true independence from anything external to it. . . . A person whose total identity is a mere sum of multiple roles is

likely to break down when he or she cannot keep such roles from turning into a mutual conflict. . . . The only way to secure oneself against it is to liberate oneself from an identification with values that can conflict. . . . In fact, it is the passionate attachment to each of the conflicting values that brought about the situation and, if one's identity is made up only of these values, one has no resource at all for liberating oneself from them and re-considering them.[174]

Faced with an unsolvable clash of values, Krishna offers his solution in *Gītā* 18.66, 'Abandoning all duties (*dharmas*),/Take refuge in Me alone'.

7 Historico-cultural shifts in the view of the human being

The emergence of a newly developing self-awareness of the human being as a morally and individually (and spiritually!) responsible being in a broadened and deepened sense of the word within the ancient Indian culture was cast in the religious language of early Hinduism. Crucial in this development were the *Upanishads*. But in ancient India, it is the epic genre which is, more than any other genre, expressive of the long-term changes in the Hindu view of the human being, from the early *Vedas* to the philosophical doctrines of *karma* and *moksha*.

What human beings can do, in the early *Vedas*, is to try to please the gods with sacrifice and praise, but they cannot be certain of the impact of their human efforts. Woods points out that this human impact increases dramatically 'when the priests gain control of the gods by their knowledge of the ritual. A new sense of power thus emerges in the *Brāhmanas*, reinforced, in part, by a magical tradition that received orthodox approval in the *Atharvaveda*'. The sense of being in control of one's destiny is still limited, of course, first of all, by the fact that it only regards the priests, and secondly, because the priests, knowingly, still have to perform the sacrifice. 'The desires (*kāma*) themselves are one's own, but they are fulfilled not directly, but mediately through an esoteric knowledge of the general order of the world over which one would otherwise have little or no control'.[175]

Although accountable for what one does, the individual does not yet shape his own destiny, until the rise of the doctrine of *karma*, which holds each individual personally responsible for his own destiny, due to a causal connection between past behaviour and future conditions of that same person in previous, present and future lives. The human being no longer needs to please the gods or the priests, but needs to cultivate moral and spiritual self-discipline, if he is to develop the self-consciousness of a spiritual being who is rewarded for his self-discipline and self-knowledge. Woods states:

> The first textual evidence of a movement in this direction was the appropriation, by Varuna, of the role of dispenser of divine justice (for example, *Rgveda* 1.24.9). Other gods subsequently assumed this function. This line of development eventually led to the idea of the Divine Grace of Vishnu or Shiva as a reward for the conduct of the devotee.[176]

The eventual occurrence of the doctrines of *karma* and *moksha* indicates a late development not only of individual moral awareness, but also of the doctrine of individual rebirth and liberation from rebirths. All these doctrines are current in the epic.

Much earlier than the epic, the *Upanishads* mark the turning point. The collective and ritualist knowledge of Brahman in the *Brahmanas* is *individualized* by cultivating an ascetic lifestyle of retreat from society into the forest, and is *internalized* by identifying one's (deeper than individual) inner immortal self (*ātman*) with this all-sustaining cosmic Self (Brahman). On the one hand, the gap between the human being and his outer world has deepened. The outer world now includes an Ultimate Reality or Absolute Reality that is far beyond both the visible and the invisible worlds of the immanent realm. This transcendent Reality is called 'Brahman' – named after the power inherent in rituals. On the other hand, the gap between the human being and his inner world has deepened. The inner world of the individual now includes a cosmic permanent self that is far beyond the individual emotions, the mind and the ego of the psychosomatic empirical realm. This internal transcendent Reality is called *atman*. In the monistic world view and mystical experience of the *Upanishads*, individual and located consciousness is a manifestation of universal consciousness pervading the physical and psychosomatic world. Realizing the identity between one's immortal self and the cosmic Self is considered a liberating form of knowledge.

8 Conclusions

The first question that was raised in the introduction of this second part of the chapter was – did Indian literature develop other genres while coping with similar issues? The answer was that the epic genre is expansive by nature and that it succeeded in India to incorporate tragic tendencies.

The second and third questions were more difficult to answer. Put briefly, the epic contains much critical debate on the precise meaning of social and ascetic core values and on the tensions and correlations between them, especially in the didactic sections of the epic. The epic also features several outstanding 'problematic heroes' who embody these tensions. Scholars do not agree on the exact way in which the epic's dealing with conflicting values should be interpreted precisely because the process of reinterpreting controversial values and their importance in the value system takes place not just among the epic characters, but in the course of the epic's long history of formation as an epic. Nor do scholars agree to what extent the epic's function was to legitimize or to criticize specific conceptions of kingship and warriorship. More on these conceptions of kingship and warriorship can be found in the chapter on martial aspects.

PART III: CROSS-CULTURAL COMPARISONS

1 The rearrangement of narrative sources

Cross-culturally, as Martin observed, the *epic* genre is expansive by nature, expanding praise poetry, tends to include other genres as well, like songs and proverbs, and can embody underlying myths; at festivals, it can be performed anywhere at any time in any form. The *tragic* genre, on the other hand, staging succinct theatrical performances, tends to be compact and selective by evoking universalities in the form of a limited number of particularities and plots. However, its performances are even more theatrical than the bardic telling of epics. The idea of 'epic' as a comprehensive totality incorporating whatever is worth retelling, articulating and potentially performing all aspects of culture within the basic institutional context of the festival is an idea that ancient and classical Greece have in common with latter-day India, Nagy argued. My guess is that Elizabethans, instead of exploiting the idea of 'epic,' embraced the idea of 'theatre' or 'the arts'.

Matchett noted that the Indian epics are held in high esteem precisely because they are mainly compilations of traditional material rather than original compositions. For a Hindu, the act of arranging is, in fact, a form of creating. As Hindus see the cosmos, it is created and recreated in a never-ending cycle of great acts of arrangement and rearrangement. Biardeau assumes that the epic utilizes Vedic texts in a skilful manner, at once both very free and very savant. How does tragedy deal with its narrative sources? Although the ancient heroic myths were taken as more or less historical stories from their own remote past, they were not considered holy texts. Deviations from the mythical stories were allowed. Tales were being recast continuously. Sophocles' *Antigone* seems to have had a newly invented plot and Euripides' *Antigone* had Antigone survive, marry Haemon and bear him a son. Elizabethan tragedy was expected to follow Aristotelian rules and the Latin example of Senecan tragedy. Like the Greeks and Seneca respectively, Shakespeare used royal and imperial history freely.

There is no doubt about a historical link between the praise of chiefs or kings and the *epic* genre in general, even though Hiltebeitel did not see this link in the same way as Thapar did. Thapar explained how, via the eulogies on gift-giving and heroes, genealogy as a record of succession lay at the core of the epic tradition, legitimizing later rulers. Post-Gupta Indian ruling families sought links with the ancient Sūryavaṃśa and Candravaṃśa lineages. The epics embodying the stories of these lineages were thus assured continuity. Similarly, Greek *tragedy* attempted to develop a corpus of myths around the Athenian king, Theseus. Non-Athenian heroes from the old epic cycle are often appropriated to the Athenian past. One example of this Athenocentrism is Sophocles' *Oedipus at Colonus*. Shakespearean tragedy does not testify to such straightforward legitimation. It draws from British royal history for purposes of entertainment. Senecan tragedy was in fashion but, as Williams explained, in Seneca, there is an important stress on the nobility of suffering and enduring misfortune, which provided a basis for the later transfer of interest to the suffering individual, away from the general action.

According to States, both *Hamlet* and the *Henry IV* plays are variations on the *epic* theme of the 'education of the prince'. The core motif of the *Mahābhārata* too, is a variation on this epic theme, according to Hiltebeitel. King Yudhisthira has to learn throughout the epic what it means to be(come) a righteous king; but this much older narrative motif is used to articulate contemporary resistance to the much later rise of empires, he argued. Redfield warned that in Greek *tragedy*, the learning process of the hero is not dramatized, and he added, 'In tragedy the frequent event is not learning but discovery; the hero does not learn a lesson but finds out a secret'.[177]

In Greece and England, the epic genre lost its prominent place to the tragic genre, transforming the unlimited telling of stories into a theatrical performance of a limited repertoire of specific stories. In India, the epic genre was not replaced by tragedy, but absorbed a variety of genres and developments, including 'tragic' tendencies.

2 The problematization of heroes and their language

The second issue pertains to the occurrence of 'problematic' heroes in the epic and tragic genres. Do heroes turn 'problematic' in both genres? Does tragedy's transformation of 'epic' heroes into 'tragic' heroes have parallels in the *Mahābhārata* epic and in the *Gītā*?

In *epic* literature, in general, a hero not only excels by his doing of deeds, but also by his speaking of speeches. Spoken language is powerful. Words, once spoken, cannot be undone. *Tragedy* critically explores the public languages it mobilizes, Goldhill argued. Clytemnestra's tricky language is powerful in persuading and deceiving Agamemnon, whereas Cassandra's prophetic language is powerless in persuading anybody. In the conventional representation of heroism that Shakespeare inherited, heroes were heroes because they spoke and acted like heroes. Bulman showed that in Shakespeare, heroes no longer coincide with their idiom, and they are increasingly aware of the discrepancy between themselves and the idiom that defines the traditional role they try (and fail) to align themselves with. Despite his use of the heroic idiom, Richard II fails to engage himself with a heroic ethos. By thinking, he becomes the first of Shakespeare's 'modern' tragic heroes, Bulman claimed. In *Hamlet*, he argued, Hamlet directs his irony both outwards, to the playing of roles for public consumption, and inwards, to his mode of self-apprehension.

Tragedy reinterprets the meanings of mythic and *epic* contents. Goldhill showed how the story of Orestes is always told in Homer's *Odyssey* to be exemplary in a positive sense, whereas in Aeschylus' *Oresteia*, this key example becomes problematic due to a shift of focus, a focus on gender. Orestes becomes famous for matricide – instead of being famous for restoring order in his paternal house. Whereas for Homer, the answers to the conflicts of his narrative were to be located in the order of the *oikos*, for Aeschylus, the answer is to be found in the *polis*. Tragedy turns epic heroes into anti-heroes. Sophocles made the hero myth of Oedipus one of tragedy instead of triumph. As an inverted form of the hero myth, Oedipus's success at each stage really hides a terrible failure. The Aristotelian tragic hero is a virtuous and worthy man who falls into vice and error. Shakespeare's *Hamlet* is even more innovative in that its hero Hamlet consciously turns himself into an anti-hero – he becomes an antic hero, someone who acts like a fool, who takes the role of an actor on stage. Hamlet becomes both an agent and an actor.

If tragedy turns epic heroes into anti-heroes, triumphant heroes into losers, the tragic anti-hero of the *Mahābhārata* epic, according to Woods and Ingalls, is Karna – and his mother Kuntī is no less a tragic figure in her failing efforts to save all her sons simultaneously. The epic clearly has its tragic heroes. Does this also apply to its main heroes, Yudhisthira and Arjuna?

Yudhisthira and Arjuna belong to the five Pāndava brothers who incarnate (aspects of) gods intent on fighting the demons incarnated in the Kaurava cousins. The Pāndavas are expected to behave as representatives of the good as opposed to evil – to behave as virtuous and worthy men. But they fall into vice and error. They win the war by trickery and deceit, unlike Achilles, but very much like Odysseus. Katz has pointed out that the Pāndavas 'seem to be aware that their unworthy behaviour is questionable', but that they do not suffer from it and prefer to justify it (Odysseus is even proud of his cunning intelligence). Their trickery and deceit does not turn them into 'problematic heroes', it seems. But there is a difference between the *Iliad* and the *Mahābhārata* – 'The *Iliad* too contains a large number of deceitful actions by both sides, yet it does not dwell on them: in fact, Homer omits the pivotal deception of the war, the Trojan horse, from his account entirely'. The *Mahābhārata* 'concentrates more on such tricks, multiplies them, explores them from all angles, and disapproves of them at length, in a way the *Iliad* never does. Hopkins suggests that in the early heroic poems which, he felt, were incorporated into the *Mahābhārata*, such trickery was taken for granted, much as it is through most of the *Iliad*; only later did it become an object of great concern'.[178] It became symbolic of the Hindu conception of the epic's time – the deeply apocalyptic conviction that 'the time is out of joint'.

If Hamlet is at home in the world of thought and inaction, as States suggested, so is Yudhisthira. On the other hand, like Greek epic characters, Indian epic characters would have been judged by the dignity (devotion to duty) and the effect of their actions rather than by the state of their minds, embodying social functions and values rather than psychological truths, Biardeau presumed. If the tragic content of *Hamlet* is not in Claudius's crime, but in Hamlet's inability to devise a response – tragedy thus hypothetically testing virtues' limits – as Redfield remarked, so is the tragic content in Yudhisthira's inability to devise a response. Would it be too much to say that Yudhisthira, the way Hiltebeitel portrayed him, could be considered *a tragic hero?* He is certainly not an idealized hero. He is a hero who suffers from his struggle with the value of *dharma,* which he is supposed to embody as a king who wages war. He is not happy with the pyrrhic victory that the Kurukshetra War brings him, to say the least. In fact, the impression he leaves meets one of the core insights of (Redfield's) Aristotle into what tragedy is all about – both that virtue exists and that it is inadequate for happiness. The only problem with identifying Yudhisthira as a tragic hero in this sense of the word is his weakness of will as a gambler at dice games and also his inclination to renounce the moral world of duties altogether. He lacks that virtuousness that would convince a Greek tragedy's audience that worthy men exist in the first place.

And yet, Hiltebeitel portrayed him as basically a tragic hero in Redfield's sense of the word, unlike Achilles, but much like Hector, who remains within his community, but tests the limits of loyalty. Hiltebeitel pointed out that Yudhisthira repeatedly insists on placing moral ethics above those of one's own *dharma*, in particular, the warrior caste's duties as preached by Krishna to Arjuna in the *Gītā*, and that Sutton notes a sympathy on the part of the authors for the goodness of Yudhisthira. As a real hero, Yudhisthira is put to the test three times. But unlike Oedipus, he really succeeds in passing these tests by truly manifesting a new value, the value of non-cruelty. Unlike Sophocles' hero myth, this 'hero myth of triumph' does not turn into 'a hero myth of tragedy', as Segal would put it. Yudhisthira proves to have become truly virtuous. The structural conflict, thus, seems resolved by proclaiming the *dharma* of non-cruelty, which comes under the particular caste duties of a warrior, and by proclaiming Yudhisthira as its embodiment. This would imply that he is not a tragic hero after all, in Segal's sense of the word. I highlighted two aspects depicting Yudhisthira as a tragic hero instead of a triumphant one. The first aspect concerns Hiltebeitel's stress on grief and non-cruelty as characteristic of Yudhisthira's heroism. The second aspect has to do with Yudhisthira's never-ending search for *dharma*. Hiltebeitel has shown that in the end, the structural conflict is not resolved because Draupadī's question to Yudhisthira on the essence and substance of *dharma* remains unanswered.

Arjuna has his tragic moments, but he does not display a tragic character. One of his most tragic moments is, of course, the *Gītā*'s battlefield scene – the commander-in-chief, about to kill his relatives, refuses to fight, the chief warrior behaving like a eunuch or an ascetic. In certain respects, one is reminded of the refusal of the chief warrior Achilles. But this time, the refusal is at the very spot and moment of the battle about to be fought. Arjuna suffers from his awareness of the tragic dimension of the tragic constellation, like Hamlet. But his charioteer, Krishna, is in no tragic mood and takes over. Arjuna is encouraged to think of Krishna only, without the purity of his mind being affected by the crime he is about to commit under the pressure of extreme circumstances. Krishna's notion of heroism lacks any sense of tragedy whatsoever. Single-mindedness and peace of mind are at the heart of what true warrior heroism is about. In tragedy, the problem of the hero is a problem of 'rational' knowledge – the hero must continue to act while guided by an exact awareness of how little of his action is truly his own, Redfield observed. In the *Gītā*, this is not the problem, but the solution! The problematic Greek and Shakespearean heroes share with their Indian counterparts a heightened and tormented moral consciousness, but the

Indian burden of social responsibilities, instead of leading to social isolation, ignites an awareness of the degenerating force of time and an awareness of the transcendent existence of an eternal self beyond time. In the *Gītā*, Arjuna starts out as a 'problematic hero', but is persuaded to behave like a 'conventional hero', thanks to his awareness of the transcendent self and his conscious focus on God. There is no place left for 'problematic heroes' in the *Gītā*. Nor is the language of heroes being problematized in any way in the epic. Spoken language, as in oaths, remains powerful. Tricky language is used for trickery, not for exploring the ambiguities of language.

3 The testing of cultural values

How does tragedy deal with cultural values articulated in the narrative sources? Does tragic literature (re)present a different value system from epic literature? Do 'epic' values turn 'tragic'?

Redfield defined 'tragedy' as 'all fiction which is an inquiry into the (dys)functioning of a culture by testing the limits of its virtues'. In tragedy, we are surprised by vice and failure. The tragic content of *Hamlet* is not in Claudius's crime, but in Hamlet's inability to devise a response. The typical *tragic* hero is a morally and socially competent person who nevertheless responds inadequately to extreme situations, not like a worthy representative of his culture. This may be his own failure, but it also displays the limits of the cultural value system itself when applied to extreme situations. The applicability of the traditional values is no longer self-evident. Their validity becomes debatable. Cultural values are put to the test. I argued that in *epic* literature, which derives from aristocratic and royal praise poetry, this testing function, in general, serves mainly *celebrating* and *legitimizing* purposes, whereas in *tragic* literature, this testing function serves mainly *questioning* and *critical* purposes. Epic literature varies when it comes to containing a certain degree of tragic tendencies, as the difference between the *Iliad*, a war epic, and the *Odyssey*, a travel epic in peacetime, illustrates.

Although Shakespeare's Elizabethan tragedy goes back to Roman instead of Greek tragedy and cannot therefore be said to carry on the innovative and critically inquiring nature of Greek tragedy, it is equally innovative and critically inquiring in spirit. Like Sophocles' hero Oedipus, Shakespeare's hero Hamlet asks questions. He reveals a critically inquiring mentality, a questioning spirit, symptomatic of the sceptic spirit of the Renaissance and of Protestantism, doubting all authority, except God's authority.

Gill held the view that 'what is characteristic of the problematic heroes of Greek poetry is that their non-standard (and apparently 'unreasonable') actions and attitudes are motivated by reflective reasoning about the proper goals of a human life'.[179] The tragic conflict is a conflict between conventional (pre-reflective) norms and post-conventional (reflective) norms, between 'first-order' reasoning and 'second-order' reasoning, and between the tradition and potential innovation of the value system they share. This is exactly the kind of conflict and debate taking place in the didactic sections of the epic, notably in the twelfth Book of Peace (*Mahābhārata* 12.167) and the *Gītā*. This brahminical discourse, Flood argued, focuses on four core values or goals in life (*purushārthas*) and is basically a theological construction of the dominant notions that were current in different circles, but did not constitute a fixed system. The Book of Peace contains a lot of discussion as to which value or goal should be considered to prevail over other goals. These discussions prove indecisive and, in that respect, illustrate that no fixed system of values existed in the epics, but that the need for more coherence and reflection was felt. The popularity of the new religious movements called *bhakti* (surrender to the grace of one god) brought about a democratization of religion by proclaiming the possibility of spiritual access to the highest religious goal of *moksha* (ultimate liberation from rebirths) for all kinds of groups within the society. This new way of thinking implied the rearrangement of the previous hierarchy of values, dominated by *moksha* on the other-worldly level and by *dharma* on the worldly level, by allowing the values of *artha* and *kāma* to be linked to the highest value of *moksha* directly.

However, the internal rearrangement of the Hindu (*brahmin*-dominated) value system should not be understood as a self-critical reappraisal of the current value system, let alone as a shift to a new value system. It served a defensive strategy. The rephrasing of tradition consisted of broadening the meaning of its core values so as to allow a higher level of applicability and relevance of the same values – as long as the social caste boundaries were upheld. In the *Gītā*, I would argue, Arjuna is presented as initially a 'problematic hero' who nonetheless can be persuaded to abide by the conventional values of his tradition. His decision to take up arms following Krishna's 'second-order reasoning' is presented as a reflective moral choice to join the expected community values for reasons that presuppose a religious version of the new attitude of standing back and looking beyond. His and Yudhisthira's actions and attitudes are motivated by reflective reasoning about the proper goals of human life. The choices Arjuna and Yudhisthira are expected to make are preceded by and embedded in an elaborate ethical debate about conflicting values that put the traditional value system to the test. It is not the war as such that is debated. The debate surpasses an ethical discussion about waging a 'just war'. The debate is about conflicting values involved in engaging in a supposedly just war. It is the validity and consistency among the radically different and sometimes conflicting values within the value system whose limits are tested. In the *Gītā*, Arjuna is the one who, in his refusal to fight, once questions the inner consistency of the value system involved, and thus confirms the validity claim of each value involved in the clash of values. In the epic as a whole, Yudhisthira and Draupadī are prominent among those who persistently question the substance and validity of particular values – in their case, of *dharma* (justice) and *artha* as sources of royal authority – and thus, constantly question the inner consistency of the value system. One is reminded of Aeschylus' *Oresteia,* which raises the question of how *dikē* (justice) is to be defined, and of Shakespeare's tragedies, which raise the question of royal authority.

Tragedy can be, among other things, about a clash of cultural values. I argued that although the tragic conflict is not necessarily unsolvable, it is a compelling one. Even if there is a solution to the conflict, the solution is never an easy compromise. The tragic constellation is too extreme to allow for an easy way out. There is always a price to be paid. Does this argument apply to the Hindu value system as well? The striking thing about Brahminic Hinduism as a religious culture is that it came to cultivate two potentially clashing ideals simultaneously – both sacrifice and renunciation, both this-worldly, social values and other-worldly, ascetic values. All these values were valuable goals in their own right, represented by specific groups. Biardeau depicted a balanced embodiment of all the core values of Hindu culture in the hero of triumph, Arjuna. Heesterman insisted that the tension between the this-worldly pole and the other-worldly pole of the bipolarity is too radical to be solved. Yudhisthira illustrates Heesterman's interpretation – he identifies with the other-worldly pole while simultaneously accepting the this-worldly pole. The unsolvable conflict between these clashing poles that are upheld simultaneously is the very conflict that Hinduism manifests. It is the inner conflict of the Hindu religio-cultural tradition, whose *limits* are tested in the epic and the *Gītā*. Heesterman's position is basically that the inner conflict is radically unsolvable, that is, by definition a tragic conflict. A Hindu is much more likely to sympathize with Biardeau's depiction of a *brahminic* and a *bhakti* position.

Ricoeur suggested that tragic wisdom can be gained not from solving the conflict, but from dwelling within the conflicted situation. Tragic wisdom does not consist in a didactical teaching; it consists rather in a conversion in the manner of *looking* at the conflict. We are not expected to do anything in particular, but to change our way of looking at moral principles that come into conflict. Would Ricoeur's reading apply to the *Gītā*? Arjuna's conflict of loyalties between family duties and warrior duties is certainly a consideration. But Krishna's outlook brings about Arjuna's conversion in the manner of looking as well as in the manner of acting. Arjuna's conversion in the manner of looking is decisive but, in fact, it shifts from a tragic outlook to a non-tragic outlook. Krishna's outlook is binding and it gives rise to a new, higher-order norm. Therefore, the *Gītā* could never be 'tragic' in Ricoeur's 'aesthetic deliverance' approach of tragedy.

4 Cultural shifts in the view of the human being

The occurrence of 'problematic heroes' within the epic genre and the prominence of 'problematic heroes' in the tragic genre testify to major historico-cultural shifts in the view of man. The newly developing self-awareness of the human being as a morally and individually responsible being in ancient and classical Greece is indicative of the Axial Age, a cultural revolution involving an increased sense of distance between the transcendent (divine) and the immanent (human) realms, between the inner (psychic) and the outer (social) world, involving an increase of individualization and internalization. A similar emergence of a newly developing self-awareness of the human being as a morally and individually (and spiritually!) responsible being in a broadened and deepened sense of the word within the ancient Indian culture was cast in the religious language of early Hinduism. Although accountable for what he does, the individual does not yet shape his own destiny, until the rise of the doctrine of *karma,* which holds each individual personally responsible for his own destiny, due to a causal connection between past behaviour and future conditions of that same person in previous, present and future lives, we noted.

A second wave of increased individualization and internalization in Western Europe marked the early Modern Age. What the Greek hero and the Shakespearean hero have in common is that they are social beings who suffer from their social isolation, and that they have a heightened and tormented moral consciousness. The sense of alienating distance between the social or outer world and the inner world had sharpened once again. The tragic hero was still a social hero who suffers from the gap between the individual and the community, but this time, in Elizabethan tragedy, his identity was not confined to his social status. His interiority was thought to provide the modern subject some leverage against his world, as Pye put it. Arditi argued that during the Renaissance period, people felt they were operating in the world as if they were acting on stage, and they felt uneasy about it. The increased experience of interpersonal detachment and existential freedom prompted this unease, perfectly captured by the conception of society as a stage and of the person as a role-player. The person as a player of roles presupposes a radically detached individual, enacting one role after another, moving freely from stage to stage, lacking a fixed set of duties to perform. The *Gītā* too, presupposes a radically detached person, enacting one role after another, moving karmically from one body into the next, from one life into the next. In the Indian case, however, the sense of detachment is even more radical than in the modern Western case. It implies the existence of a de-individualized self who exists outside of any specific play. This is an eternal self beyond the individual, who always remains embedded in a fixed set of duties to perform despite his spiritually relativizing world view (*sub specie aeternitatis*). A tragic view of the human being is combined with a tragedy-free view of the eternally free self, whose individual materializations perform roles with which the self should not identify. A tragic view of the human being is simultaneously combined with and kept separate from a transcendent or spiritual view of man.

Hamlet's tormented self-consciousness is not purely psychological, but embedded in his failing social connections. It is not yet the degree of social isolation typical of heroes in liberal tragedy later on, Williams explained. In humanist tragedy, the tragic hero is still marked by a social status, embedded in the public order. He is, however, also different from and beyond it. The early modern subject is both status-determined and psyche-determined. Achilles and Oedipus are certainly psyche-determined in the sense of being fatally hot-tempered, but in the Greek culture oriented towards obtaining results, the focus is on the corresponding arrogant behaviour that has its status effects. Hamlet, obsessed with his status, is consumed by the very thought of status; floating in a world of social disintegration, his lack of social rootedness creates a tormented self-consciousness.

In both the ancient and classical Greek and Indian cases, the cultural move towards universalization, individualization and internalization had become noticeable in a deepened interest in self-knowledge at the expense of attendance to ritual, and in self-emptying sympathy, empathy with enemies, polluted outcasts and strangers, and universally shared suffering, at the expense of exclusive group boundaries and exclusive group solidarity.[180]

In both cases, the gods are interested in justice among human beings, but the gods feel no compassion.[181] The heightened ethical consciousness of moral values and their vulnerability turns humans into humane beings, but it does not turn gods into divine (in the sense of 'morally superior or perfect') beings. Mario Liverani offers an explanation for the Greek case, and maybe also for the Indian case, 'those societies that placed their ethical values in civil or royal codes, or in philosophical knowledge (as in the Greco-Roman world), were able for many centuries to maintain their traditional religion and their pantheon alongside, for "ceremonial" purposes'.[182] The Axial Age revolution does not ethicize the Greek and Hindu images of the divine the way it does in the case of Western monotheism. In India and Greece, I therefore suggest, traditional religion remains the framework of reference that allows for *a tragic view of man, not of the divine*, because the religious framing is based on a juxtaposition, not on a mutually responsive and personal relationship between human and divine partners. The Greek and Indian gods and humans share the same cosmos as their habitat, but gods and humans live apart together, according to different sets of rules. In the Greek case, (pre-Hellenistic) Greek *religion* remains untouched by the spiritual revolution of the Axial Age and its gap between the mundane and the transcendent. In the Indian case, Hindu *religion* is deeply touched by the Axial revolution, but this does not take the form of an ethicized image of the divine; on the contrary, it takes the yogic form of a radically de-ethicized image of the divine, allowing for a tragic view of the human being within the mundane realm and within the perspective of the immanent world, but also for a view of the human being as a player of roles, in some ways strikingly similar to Shakespeare's Hamlet.

6

Martial aspects

PART I: TRAGIC AND DRAMATIC ISSUES

1 Introduction

A fifth set of aspects of tragedy has to do with tragedies' dealing with martial values in connection with the transition from the epic genre to the tragic genre.

In this first part of the chapter, we will examine whether it is possible to draw demarcation lines between epic literature and tragedy when it comes to the martial values of warrior heroism. In what sense do these function as a traditional model? And to what extent do they become the object of testing the limits of a martial culture? What is the relationship between the victor and victim in epic and tragic warrior heroism?

A general use of notions such as 'martial culture' suggests that it is possible to perceive similarities between martial value systems in different societies separated by space and time. This is indeed the case, and will be demonstrated for the phenomenon of 'honour' in particular. However, efforts will be made to balance phenomenological descriptions with historical ones. The martial code of honour, for example, differs from age to age and from society to society. Striking a balance between similarities and differences among martial cultures constitutes a major challenge to their description in this chapter. But the parallels between martial aspects in Western and Indian epic and tragic literature are striking and their closer examination is worth making. Arjuna is as much imbued with martial values as Hamlet is, but their differences are equally telling.

The first part of the chapter presents the Greek and Shakespearean material. The second part, on Indian and Hindu issues, will present the Indian material. The third part will draw the necessary cross-cultural comparisons.

2 The heritage of a martial culture as a given model

2.1 *Martial culture in ancient and classical Greece*

Within world literature, *epic* literature is a genre of its own and assumes a value system of its own. It is related to societies ruled by chiefs, warlords or kings, and dominated by a corresponding martial value system – aristocratic, warlike, special-personality-focused, cultivating a sense of superiority.[1] This martial culture is used as a foil in both epic and tragic literature. In the *Iliad*, Seth L. Schein writes, Homer's heroes are great warriors who 'could not transcend death, the limit of the human condition, except through celebration in song by poets'.[2] The basic meaning of *timē*, 'honour,' is 'price' or 'value' in a tangible sense. Tangible victory in battle is 'beautiful–noble' (*kalon*), while tangible defeat is 'ugly–disgraceful' (*aischron*). The tangible mutilation of dead bodies does not just disfigure them, it makes them 'ugly' in the sense of destroying their honour, Douglas L. Cairns explains.[3] Fear of shame, concern for the (dis)approval of others, feeling and showing respect for others and concern for one's personal sense of honour, are all aspects of 'shame' (*aidōs*). The deliberate infliction of shame and dishonour is called 'pride' or 'arrogance' (*hubris*). Those who win tangible honours also receive honour conceived abstractly; from this, comes their *kleos,* 'glory and reputation', what is said about them near and far, even when they are dead. Cairns agrees with Adkins that the judgement is based on results rather than intentions.[4]

To be sure, in the course of the *Iliad*, Achilles comes to question and contradict the validity of the normative social value system. Cairns points out that competitive dimensions of 'honour' clash with cooperative dimensions of 'honour', and with the concept that battle comrades ('friends', *philoi*) share the obligation to accord each other 'respect', which is an aspect of 'shame' (*aidōs*).[5] His 'disillusionment enhances Achilles' tragedy and constitutes part of Homer's critical exploration of the nature and conditions of warrior heroism and of human life. Nevertheless, for Achilles and for everyone else in the poem, there is no real alternative. Life is lived and death is died according to this martial code of values: to be fully human—that is, to be a hero—means to kill or be killed for honour and glory', Schein states.[6] I would like to add here that whereas small-scale traditional societies imbued with martial values have a tendency to consider only their warriors as full members of the community, and military service as both a duty and a privilege, this is no longer the case in vast empires and imperial monarchies, such as China, Persia and Rome, where warfare is in the hands of a specialized elite, as F. G. Naerebout and H. W. Singor observe.[7]

Another important Homeric notion is *aristeia*. The European word 'aristocracy' derives from this very notion. Schein explains:

> *Aristeia* is a word used in later Greek for 'excellence' or 'prowess,' including, in particular, the excellence or prowess of a Homeric warrior when he is on a victorious rampage, irresistibly sweeping all before him, killing whomever of the enemy he can catch or whoever stands against him. . . . In Greek of all periods, the adjective *aristos,* 'best,' is the superlative of *agathos,* 'good,' but in the *Iliad,* whose world is a world of war, 'good' and 'best' mean 'good [or: best] in battle.'[8]

Prowess, valour and courage in battle are values related to 'manliness' (*andreia*). In turn, 'war is the prototypical scene for manifestations of courage and manliness' in ancient Greek sources, according to Ralph Rosen and Ineke Sluiter. Martial examples are prototypical of 'manly courage'. Manliness is related to an agonistic context, courage to a context of danger. By definition, cowardice (*anandria*) deserves disapproval, as much as manliness deserves approval. Male status is at stake. The expression of approval and disapproval, according to Murray Milner, Jr, is the distinctive source of status power.[9] Its prototypical representative in the *Iliad* is 'the aristocratic hero who single-handedly and furiously engages with the enemy'.[10] Achilles and Heracles are considered the best examples of heroic manliness. The very first word of the *Odyssey* is *andra*, man – Odysseus being famous for his cunning intelligence, a man very different from Achilles. Karen Bassi notes that cowardice is exemplified by historical examples while manliness is exemplified by epic heroes.[11]

The sixth- and fifth-century Athenian warrior ('hoplite'), however, has to balance personal against social and political concerns. His 'glory' arises from acts of manliness that are part of the common goals of military victory over an external enemy and of stability of the state. In Aeschylus' *Seven against Thebes* (717), Eteocles identifies as one of his five reasons for facing his brother that, as a hoplite, he cannot shirk his duty – a necessity grounded in the *polis* of Thebes, as N. J. Sewell-Rutter writes.[12] Homeric rage is replaced by hoplite *self-restraint*. Joseph M. Bryant points out:

> that the adoption of close-formation tactics coincides with a significant shift in meaning for one of the major virtues in the Greek moral code, *sōphrosunē*, a word originally signifying 'prudence' and 'shrewdness of mind' but that

henceforth came to mean 'self-control' and 'moderation'—precisely the traits a man hoped to find in the hoplites who stood beside him in the line, since it was their composure that literally shielded his life.[13]

Marcel Detienne is quoted as suggesting that the rise of the hoplite phalanx around 650 BCE brought about a secularization of speech within Greek warrior culture. The 'dialogue speech' that the warrior now needs 'as a tool to persuade and mobilize his peers' proves more efficacious than the 'magico-religious speech' of poets, diviners and kings; Peter T. Struck, then, observes a deeper tie between manliness and public speech, 'the field of martial endeavour, where peers win recognition for their manliness, as a precondition for the formation of public dialogue-speech', in the male space of the public arena.[14] Manliness and public speech were already linked up together in Homer's *Iliad* 9.443, where Phoenix is said to be 'a speaker of speeches, a doer of deeds'. To deliver a speech is to deliver a blow to the opponent. Gregory D. Alles observes that in the *Iliad*, the power of persuasion is a *social* power that depends on successful social interaction, and it is *relational* in the sense of residing in the social relationships that have to be mobilized in order to be obligingly influential.[15] The fifth- and fourth-century Athenian citizen's manliness was also defined by economic independence. Male slaves (skilled and paid) were seen as 'defective men', and hired employment was equated with slavery.[16]

Ancient Greek society did not abandon the martial value system of the 'heroic past' (the palace systems and kings with horse chariots of the Bronze Age) as imagined in the epic literature of the Dark Age of Iron (1200–775 BCE; *oikos*-based aristocrats with horses), but updated it under the democratizing influence of the introduction of *polis*-based hoplite infantry at the expense of cavalry (by the seventh and sixth centuries, aristocrats fighting *on* horses).[17] Aristotle's *Politics* (IV, 1297b 15–28) pictures a historical development from 'monarchy' to 'republic of the cavalry' to 'republic of the hoplites' to 'republic of the sailors'.[18] This picture shows an increasing militarization of the city state population of Athens. From the seventh century BCE onwards, it became simply one of the functions of the citizen to be a soldier. The warrior function in society was democratized. Everyone who could afford to equip himself with the requisite weapons (*hopla*) could join the troops, thus becoming a 'hoplite'. The heavy military equipment became cheaper in the sixth and fifth centuries BCE, but remained an elitist affair. This development influenced the martial value system, in the sense that the competitive heroism of the outstanding individual warrior and his personal fame was no longer idealized – apart from the cultural influence Homer's exemplary epic continued to exercise. Instead, the co-operative skills of soldiers to operate as a team and to sacrifice themselves for the sake of the common good were now cultivated.[19] Unlike naval warfare, hoplite warfare could do almost completely without specialized military leaders, until the time of the Peloponnesian War, when the state of war became more or less permanent. From the end of the fifth century BCE, tens of thousands of specialized or impoverished Greeks became mercenaries, who served as professional sailors and soldiers in the entire region, from the Persian Empire and Egypt to Sicily and among the Carthagians.[20] This phenomenon illustrates both the degree of militarization and the degree of alienation, because from the perspective of Greek free citizens, Greek mercenaries had come closer to being slaves serving a foreign tyrant than to being full members of their native communities exercising their duty as a right.

The high degree of militarization of Greek society may explain why the ancient Greeks were inclined to divide up their world between friends (*philoi*) and enemies (frequently, and in a general sense, *echtroi*, or, strictly militarily, *polemioi*). The Greek moral code of helping one's friends and harming one's enemies is an expansion of the concept of justice as retaliation, Mary Whitlock Blundell explains.[21]

In the Greek case, I am inclined to conclude, martial culture is not just used as a foil in both its epic and its tragic literature, it also reflects the norms and values of an increasingly militarized society. A martial ethos, albeit in an updated form, continues to function as a given model.

2.2 Martial culture in early modern England

For a start, a cross-cultural comparison with early modern England on the points of updating the martial norms and values and of the role of mercenaries and specialists overseas offers interesting insights into similarities and differences. During the mid-Tudor and early Elizabethan periods until 1585, the English aristocracy was largely demilitarized for lack of opportunities, or turned abroad to mainland Europe as gentlemen volunteers and officers in the professional armies of foreign princes and states, as Roger B. Manning points out.[22] Elizabeth I and James I were despised by the barons for seeking peace instead of war. At home, the Irish and Scottish aristocracies had retained their medieval martial traditions, engaging in private warfare (clan conflict, blood feuds, cattle raiding), where the principal motive was personal revenge rather than public warfare and political objectives. Abroad, the Irish, Scottish and English swordsmen joined professional armies whose greater efficiency was based on missile weapons instead of edged weapons and on military hierarchy instead of social hierarchy. On return to the British Isles, their military experience as veterans and mercenaries overseas reinforced the call not only for remilitarization (linked to a 'chivalric revival') back home, but also for the modernization of warfare. The aristocracies of the British Isles underwent a cultural change after their exposure to the martial ethos of mainland European aristocracies. As a consequence, the English aristocracy was remilitarized, and the Scottish and Irish aristocracies, which had never been demilitarized, came to appreciate the greater 'opportunities that service in the British army offered for honour, glory, and professional careers' by the end of the reign of the soldier-king William III (1688–1702), Manning states.[23]

But the transition from private combat (*duellum*) to public warfare declared by the authority of a sovereign or a state (*bellum*) was not just a technical affair, Manning continues. The martial norms and values too, would be updated. On the one hand, remilitarization reinforced a martial culture whose bearers came to regard courtier culture as effeminate. From reading Roman writers, British martialists learnt that military honour was more widespread in republics than monarchies. Also, prior to the civil wars, their own monarchs no longer shared their martial culture.[24] On the other hand, modernization of warfare meant that competitive pursuit of personal honour in battle could now endanger the cooperative achievement of collective victory instead of bringing it closer.[25] Warfare was no longer 'fought according to chivalric rules by noblemen and gentlemen who regarded their enemies as worthy opponents' and who regarded 'war as a ritual that served to emphasize their status and validate their honour rather than as an instrument to gain military and political objectives', as Manning puts it.[26] This conflict between social hierarchy and military hierarchy took time to settle in favour of the latter. 'The nobleman preferred hand-to-hand combat where he could display individual prowess, and he did not readily adapt to fighting as part of a group to secure agreed-upon military objectives. . . . On more than one occasion as late as the English civil wars, English peers offered to fight individual combats to determine the outcome of battle', Manning notes.[27] That the martial value system was also 'updated' in the sense of 'continued', is illustrated by a fashion that is crucial to the plot of Shakespeare's *Hamlet* – the cult of defending one's personal honour and taking personal revenge by duelling.[28] The fashion itself was new, but the face-to-face combat fought with edged weapons was rooted in time-honoured customs, and it remained an important means of nobly defending one's honour.[29]

Like the Greeks and Seneca respectively, *Shakespeare* used royal and imperial history, including its warrior ethic. He did not draw from epic literature as such, but drew from well-known stories about a society equally ruled by chiefs, warlords or kings, British kings and Roman emperors, and no less dominated by a corresponding martial value system than epic literature itself. What these narrative sources and their use have in common is that they are related to the warrior hero's code of honour.[30] Hamlet is obsessed with the duties of a nobleman, especially the duty to take revenge and not to be a coward.

But Hamlet was not the only one. 'All gentlemen of whatever rank, from princes to lords to plain gentlemen, were presumed to belong to the community of honour', and 'honour could be retained only by deeds', Manning argues.[31] The Tudor and Stuart monarchs sought to monopolize the granting of titles and armorial bearings – thus becoming the single source of honour(s) instead of a merely recognizing body – and to adjudicate disputes about points of honour through the College of Heralds.[32] Shakespeare's own father, the glover John Shakespeare, had applied to the College of Heralds for a coat of arms in 1575 or 1576, at the height of his wealth and prestige. This was an expensive procedure, which a person undertook not only to confer honour on himself, but also to enhance the status of his children and grandchildren – among whom William Shakespeare. It meant passing from the status of yeoman to the status of gentleman, from commoner to gentry. The key requirements were to live like a gentleman and to have studied at a university or to have held a civic office, and to pay the heralds' high fees. The application was just before John's dramatic downward slide began, was shelved and forgotten. Except that it seems not, Stephen Greenblatt suggests, to have been forgotten by his oldest son, William. Decades later, in 1596, the claim was reviewed and this time approved. Greenblatt comments:

> Most obviously, by helping his father complete the process, the playwright, in an act of prudential, self-interested generosity, was conferring gentle status on himself and his children. Will had by this time no doubt played gentlemen onstage, and he could carry off the part outside the playhouse as well, but he and others would always know he was impersonating someone he was not. He now had the means to acquire legitimately, through the offices his father had once held, a role he had only played. He could legally wear outside of the theater the kinds of clothes he had been wearing onstage. For a man singularly alert to the social hierarchy— and Shakespeare spent most of his professional life imagining the lives of kings, aristocracy, and gentry—the prospect of this privilege must have seemed sweet. He would sign his last will and testament 'William Shakespeare, of Stratford upon Avon in the county of Warwick, gentleman.' His heirs and their offspring would be ever further from the glover's shop and, for that matter, the playhouse; they would have the luxury of taking their gentility for granted and laying claim without irony to the motto that someone—again, in all probability, Will himself—had devised to

accompany the shield and crest: *Non sanz droict*. 'Not without right.' Is there a touch of defensiveness in that motto, a slight sense that the claim to gentlemanly status might raise eyebrows? If so, the insecurity would not belong to the impecunious glover but to his successful playwright son. For whatever John Shakespeare's problems—drink or foolish loans or whatever—he did in fact legitimately possess the social standing, through the offices he had held in Stratford, to lay claim to the status of a gentleman. Not so his son. There were few occupations for an educated man more stigmatized socially than player. That Shakespeare was acutely aware of the stigma can be surmised from the sonnets, where he writes that, like the dyer's hand, he has been stained by the medium he has worked in.[33]

William Shakespeare, 'gentleman' – a word used as early as 1200 to refer to a nobleman.

But there are important differences. Shakespeare's understanding of being a 'gentleman' marks only one particular stage in the long history of aristocratic notions of status and honour. Martial values had changed substantially, and have changed ever since, despite the 'continuity' of a martial culture within Western society. Martial value systems are strikingly similar worldwide in their focus on social status, honour and shame, excellence and reputation, male dominance and violence. But there is no historical continuity between, for example, Greek armies fighting the Trojan war, Athenian armies fighting Persian wars, Roman armies fighting Mediterranean wars, and medieval armies going on a crusade. During the Middle Ages, Frank Henderson Stewart writes, 'victory in battle was essential for the maintenance of honor'. But from the Renaissance onwards, 'the idea appeared that one who fought valiantly (but survived) might preserve his honor even in defeat'.[34]

The transformation of a Western martial code of honour *from chivalry into etiquette* accompanied the development from the status of nobleman to that of gentleman.[35] In the first instance, there was no difference between a 'nobleman' and a 'gentleman'. In the thirteenth century, *chivalry* was essentially the secular code of honour of a martially oriented aristocracy operating within the setting of a Christian society, Keen argues.[36] Treatises on chivalry, such as the one by Raymond Llull (around 1270), and courtly romances, such as the romance of *Lancelot* (1488), help to define the classical virtues of good knighthood – *prowess, loyalty, generosity, courtesy* (manners fitting to a court), *and franchise* (the free and frank bearing that is visible testimony to the combination of good birth with virtue).[37] The *church* had made efforts to limit the greed, injustice and irresponsibility of unrestrained violence. The *court*, however, was the decisive factor in bringing about a culture of chivalry.[38] In courtly circles, the furious warrior is expected to behave as a courtier who exercises *self-restraint* instead of brute violence if he is to assert his authority. In courtly circles, the passionate warrior is expected to feel as a courtier who shows refined *sensitivity* instead of possessive dominance if he is to attract the ladies at court. Women are no longer part of the warrior's booty. The warrior learns 'courtliness' or 'courtesy' (militarism and sociability among the nobles themselves). But courtly manners, although an essential precondition, are not yet courtly love. Courtly manners are based on external constraints, a matter of social conformity, whereas courtly love is based on internal erotic longing nurtured by idealizing a form.[39] But troubadour poetry is not about women. It is about the lover and his longings. *The warrior hero is not just civilized, but humanized* in the *chansons de geste*, Richard Barber observes. Man can become more noble through the love of another.[40]

In the sixteenth century, the value of chivalry underwent a transformation, with the advent of printing and the increase in secular education, Barber points out, 'The intellectual ferment that resulted was almost entirely artistic and secular. What marks off the gentleman from the knight is above all his critical appreciative attitude towards both politics and art, an attitude which permeates Castiglione's study of the new man, *The Courtier'*.[41] 'Civility' and 'civil manners' become attached to the centralizing powers of princes and monarchs, to the socio-political principle of a princely or monarchical 'grace' endowed with the force of a political and social ethics. Castiglione's self-fashioned grace (*sprezzatura*) is 'not only something to be learned and mastered but also earned from others—the prince, in particular' (cf. Macchiavelli's logical focus on the prince), Jorge Arditi notes.[42] In England, the Renaissance nobleman, sensitive to prowess, honour, duelling, love, art and verbal virtuosity, was embodied by Sir Philip Sidney as much as by his theatrical counterpart, Prince Hamlet. In *Hamlet*, it is Osric who is ridiculed for lacking the perfect balance between virility and sociability, being able to shy away from macho pretence, but not from effeminate mannerism.

The late-eighteenth-century notion of *etiquette* would involve *a disconnection of propriety from ethics*, Arditi argues. The word *etiquette* itself is telling, because it means 'little ethics', that is to say, it lacks any reference to absolute norms and values (cf. Lord Chesterfield's *Letters*). Instead, the aristocracy invents and reinvents its own etiquette by constructing behavioural similarity among its members. The late-eighteenth-century notion of etiquette is indicative of a displacement of power from the royal court to the multi-centred network of the aristocracy as a self-sufficient social group. The English gentleman, detached from any stable substance except his own deep sense of the integrity of the nobility as a group, would become its embodiment.[43]

3 Epic and tragic testing of martial values

3.1 Introduction

Epic and tragic literature do not just use martial culture as a given model, however. Martial values are tested in much the same way as traditional values in general are put to the test. Issues pertaining to status and honour, male dominance and violence, competition and cooperation, courage and self-restraint, loyalty and selfishness, being victorious and being a victim, will be discussed in some detail in the following sections.

3.2 The testing of martial values in ancient and classical Greek epic and tragic literature

What does 'manliness' (*andreia*) come to mean in the context of the Attic civil war? In Homer, it was a physical condition rather than an ethical one, but in Thucydides, the ethical and rhetorical quality of words such as 'manliness' is contested. Men (*andreioi* instead of *aneres*) are now defined by an abstraction (*andreia*). The Greek fifth century BCE is an age of civil war, the age of Aeschylus' *Seven against Thebes*, in which men take up arms against their own brother and in which 'manliness' is clearly a negative attribute, Bassi suggests.[44]

In Sophocles' *Oedipus Tyrannus*, Oedipus is faced with riddles and oracles. Such (and other literary) cases of divination, Struck argues, test his status and strength as a dominant male in the city.[45] The divine sign is an ordeal that has to be read well, and it turns out that the actual qualities needed for that are not some affiliation with the gods or a divine intelligence, but effective leadership, courage, and decisiveness, in short, manliness. Moreover, 'the protagonist's success in interpreting the oracle rests on his ability to make an effective public statement of its meaning to his peers'. Thus, he wins recognition for his manliness in the male space of the public assembly. Oedipus wins his position of dominant male by his masterly interpretation of the riddles of the sphinx. The following contest embodied in the oracles, often cast in martial terms, severely tests Oedipus' manliness. From being the 'first among men' (33), his failure to unravel the oracles by the end has lowered him to his final position as 'worst of men' (1433). This failure goes hand in hand with a failure of public speech. Instead of listening to his advisers, he accuses them of conspiracy and behaves like an arrogant tyrant unfit for democratic debate (873, 880–81).[46]

Bassi concludes that philosophical efforts in the fourth century to define the term 'manliness' can be read as a response to its ambiguous meaning in the fifth century. *Andreia* came to be regarded as only one aspect (physical prowess and courage) of the broader ideal of *aretē* (virtue), both translated into Latin as *virtus*. In the martial Roman Republic, physical prowess or courage, especially as displayed in war, remained the central element of manliness.[47]

The issue of *honour and status* is addressed in both epic and tragic literature. In Sophocles' *Philoctetes*, Neoptolemus must prove himself 'noble' (*gennaios*, line 51), his character being true to that of his aristocratic father. The reference to his 'nature' (*phusis*, lines 79–80, 88–9, 903–4) is not a reference to human nature in general, but to his noble birth and duty, Cairns emphasizes. *Noblesse oblige.* In living up to aristocratic standards, he is also being true to himself. To do what is not fitting is to abandon one's nature. 'Neoptolemus is forced to choose', not just between different friendship ties, but 'between co-operative and competitive aspects of his concern for honour', Cairns observes.[48] Homeric psychology is social psychology. But it is also sociology – since social isolation is a reciprocal process, it may tell us as much about the society as about Achilles, whose social isolation is *status*-determined, Redfield argues.[49] Society, at least from the Greek point of view, rewards nothing but adequate performance.[50] Greek tragedy presupposes a culture oriented towards obtaining results and it acts out its limits, according to Redfield.[51] In Sophocles' *Philoctetes* (79–85), Odysseus suggests to Neoptolemus that *success* in itself can secure a reputation for justice and piety, even if the means to that success involve the shamelessness of telling lies to one's *friends*. This is a shameless suggestion precisely because it is disrespectful of friends (battle comrades instead of enemies), Cairns argues. Odysseus knows he is a liar, but subjectively, he is not sensitive to the shame of lying to friends, and objectively, he manages to get away with it. Tragic heroes and their audience have more difficulty with it; to them, tangible success has its limits when it competes with friendship.[52] The moral issue of helping *friends* and harming *enemies* is presented from a multiplicity of ethical standpoints in tragedy, Blundell argues. 'Homeric warriors regularly gloat over their enemies—a fate the latter are anxious to avoid'. In Sophocles' tragedies, the distinction between helping friends (*philoi*) and harming enemies is put to the test. The pursuit of friendship (*philia*) may lead to different forms of conflict of loyalties. 'Conflict of loyalties', Blundell explains, 'arises most readily between the three main classes of *philoi*—familial, civic, and personal—whose *philia* is determined by different criteria, and who therefore embody competing types of claim'.[53]

What makes Homer's heroes great, noble and tragic, Redfield claims, is their 'capacity to act and at the same time comprehend themselves and their situation'.[54] Achilles has, as it were, been pushed over the edge; he looks back at culture from the outside. He becomes a social critic, even a satirist. Achilles' refusal of the warrior's role is an affirmation of the warrior ethic in the sense that Achilles claims the right to be praised and rewarded by the community for leaving the community, entering the anti-community of combat, and accepting the marginal status of the warrior. Agamemnon does not honour him as such, but as an inferior who should accept the compensating gift of a superior. This leads to Achilles' *re-evaluation of the heroic ethic*.[55] Achilles, after all, is the isolated individual who identifies with his warrior code of honour, risks his life for his community in return for honour, is denied the honour that the community owes him and is nonetheless called back to take up the warrior's role, but he is also the victim of his own extreme adherence to the warrior code of honour, who only finds himself again in his grief for the loss of his friend Patroclus, which makes him forget his anger over the loss of his honour by Agamemnon's shameful treatment.

Gill does not fully share Redfield's stress on Achilles' social isolation. Achilles' refusal of Agamemnon's gifts is based on their commonly shared value system, which they interpret differently. Agamemnon sees himself as the king and senior in birth who has the right to (re)distribute booty as he pleases, whereas Achilles sees them both as fellow chieftains who do not exchange gifts because they have to, in a calculated one-to-one exchange of so much cooperative combat for so many gifts, but because chieftains grant their fellow chieftains favours, noble acts of unforced generosity, as a free expression of their willingness to cooperate. By accepting them, Achilles would 'concede that Agamemnon is "more kingly" (*basileuteros*)'. Achilles would give up his status of independent chieftain. By refusing them, Achilles appeals to the shared value system of fellow chieftains and his claim to be one of them. Achilles and Agamemnon disagree on the exact meaning of 'the interpersonal context'.[56]

The really *tragic hero* in the Aristotelian sense is Hector, Redfield argues. Hector *tests the limits of loyalty*. He remains within his community. But he suffers from a conflict of loyalties of which he is fully aware.[57] The hero, if he is to live up to the principle of heroic balance, has to insist on his own greatness while preserving a proper modesty before the far-greater gods, as Redfield contends, or before the community and its cooperative moral standards (cf. Nestor!), as Cairns would argue.[58] Loss of this balance – as by Patroclus and Hector incapable of retreat[59] – is the characteristic heroic error.

In short, Achilles and Hector are two different embodiments of the same structural conflict between the ideals of the community and the limits of the individual warrior to meet these ideals on its behalf. Achilles is the isolated individual who falls victim to his own identification with (competitive dimensions of) the warrior code of honour. Hector is the family man and commander-in-chief, fully integrated within his community, who suffers from a conflict of loyalties. This structural conflict is not solved, but presented in a form that allows the audience to test its culture's virtues by reflecting on their limits.[60] The real battlefield is a culture facing itself and trying to come to terms with its own contradictory value system.[61]

Schein appreciates Redfield's position on Hector, but stresses the *tragedy of all heroes as warriors, of warfare*, and of Homeric life as such:

> The human situation in the *Iliad* might well be called tragic, because the very activity—killing—that confers honor and glory necessarily involves the death not only of other warriors who live and die by the same values as their conquerors, but eventually, in most cases, also of the conquerors themselves. Thus, the same action is creative or fruitful and at the same time both destructive and self-destructive.[62]

Further on, Schein is more specific about the tragic dimension of being human in this Trojan war:

> The tragic situation that became clear in the case of Simoeisios—that the only way for an individual to achieve greatness and meaning in life is by the destruction of other individuals engaged in the same pursuit—is clear also on the level of society. The aim of the war is to destroy a socially evolved human community just like the community that each Greek left behind him when he set sail for Troy. The prize of individual self-assertion and self-fulfillment is social annihilation. From the point of view that sees human beings as by definition social, the Greeks, cut off from their homes and families, are in effect less human than the Trojans. From a point of view that sees war as the only way for a human being—or rather, a human male—to exist meaningfully, the Greeks are more successfully, and therefore more fully, human than the Trojans.[63]

In Aeschylus' *Oresteia*, it is Agamemnon instead of Hector who faces the challenge of choosing between his martial code of honour as commander-in-chief and his family. Like Hector, Agamemnon chooses to sacrifice his family, his daughter Iphigeneia, literally. But both options lead to actions that 'shame' should inhibit. Sophocles' characters often have only a partial and biased grasp of what values such as 'shame' entail. The same value, Cairns observes, is interpreted differently, one kind of 'shame' is set against another, each interpretation suiting a character's partial interest.[64] Sophocles' Ajax, he argues, 'is much more extreme in his pursuit of honour than anyone in Homer', far too competitive to be sensitive to the cooperative dimensions of honour.[65] Ajax rejoices in the usual mockery of one's enemies, but includes his personal enemies Menelaus, Agamemnon and especially Odysseus. The mockery of one's enemies can, also in Ajax's imagination, take the shameless form of a refusal to allow one's enemies to be buried. Later, Ajax's own burial is refused by Menelaus and Agamemnon for the very same reason (of dealing with an enemy), but Odysseus turns out to have a different reading of the same code of honour.

Euripides presents the martial values critically. In *Phoenissae* (509–14), Eteocles, concerned for his honour, but also hungry for power and therefore unwilling to reconcile with his brother Polyneices, sees it as 'unmanliness' (*anandria*) to lose the greater share and get the smaller, and is ashamed that his brother should get what he wants by force. Cairns writes:

> Eteocles represents himself as concerned both for his own reputation and for that of his city, but his justification is couched in terms which reveal only selfishness; to say that it is *anandria* to give up the greater for the smaller share is to confuse greed with manliness, while his concern for the honour of Thebes barely conceals his reluctance to give up his privileges. What are understandable motives in Aeschylus and Sophocles are base and mean in Euripides.[66]

Whereas in Homer, 'shame' regarding others (friends, suppliants, guests) is often practised out of concern for the regard of others, in Euripides, it is more often out of concern for one's own honour.[67] Euripides' association of 'shame' with an educated upbringing already occurs in *Iliad* 6.441–6, but is recurrent in Euripides' plays.[68]

In Plato's *Phaedrus* myth of the soul's chariot, the nobler horse is a lover of honour, but checked by wisdom and 'shame', resists a debasing appetite, is obedient to the command of the charioteer, the discipline of reason. 'Spirit' (*thumos*) 'has its own desire' – the desire 'for honour', which 'must be educated to side with reason'; spirit supplies 'judgements about the honourable and dishonourable', reason 'about the better and the worse'. In Plato's *Republic* (439e–440a), Cairns explains, the example of Leontius' anger links anger to one's own honour and status – 'anger is typically seen as resentment of an affront'. This 'spirit' (*thumos*), which is connected with honour (*timē*), 'gives rise to ambition (*philotimia*, love of honour) and competitiveness (*philonikia*, love of victory)'. If 'spirit' were 'allowed to dominate', the ideal society would be threatened. 'Plato regards competitiveness and concern for appearances as attributes of the unfettered love of honour'. Reason should guide the love of honour. The perfect society cultivates the love of honour correctly, the imperfect ones do not.[69] Charles Taylor contends that in a warrior morality, the warrior is expected to be 'filled with a surge of energy', carried away by courage and strength seen as 'a kind of possession or mania' quite incompatible with Plato's 'reflective and self-collected stance of rational contemplation'. But, he continues, love of honour and glory is never set aside altogether, only discredited as a life goal and subordinated, and this is the proper role of Plato's 'spirit' (*thumos*) – to be the auxiliary of reason. Taylor adds that this function of 'spirit' is 'analogous to the warrior function in society, which should be properly subordinate to political leadership'. He considers Plato's subordination model a better model for what emerged in Western society than the containment model exemplified by the post-Crusade model of the Christian knight.[70]

In Greek epic and tragic literature, then, martial values are not taken for granted. They become as problematic as the heroes who are expected to embody them. Manliness turns out to be a source of (self-)destruction. A balance between competition and cooperation is lacking. The limits of loyalty become apparent. Friends are treated like enemies. Honour appears a less noble affair than it should be. Different tragic characters have different readings of the same code of honour. The warrior ethic is re-evaluated. Heroic action becomes tragic action because of the tragic hero's full awareness of the limits of his action.

3.3 The testing of martial values in Shakespearean tragic literature

Not until 1599 or thereabouts, David Bevington suggests, did Shakespeare begin to really deal with issues of doubt and moral relativism. Shakespeare's general scepticism included the martial values. *Troilus and Cressida* (1601) sees the Trojan War as one in which all values become suspect, the war itself being, in Thersites' mordant view, an argument about 'a whore and a cuckold' (2.3.71–2), with conflicts in the name of honour dissolving into conflicts of power, and with Hector senselessly losing his life as victim of a savage appetite for revenge that has gone out of control, as Bevington puts it.[71] Bevington adds, however, that Shakespeare sets ideas in debate, 'Troilus's belief in the relativity of values is set in opposition to Hector's insistence that "value dwells not in particular will"'.[72] Hector represents the conviction that inherent value exists, regardless of its instrumental, strategical or market value.

In the historico-political reading of Shakespeare by Alvin Kernan, the questions Hamlet tries to cope with are political questions against the background of the rise of the modern centralized state.[73] Establishing *a new monarchical order at the expense of the old feudal order* must have been on the mind of the king watching *Hamlet*, and although he may not have felt it to be *a clash of old and new values*, it certainly turned out to be as much a clash of cultures as it was a clash of political power interests. Kernan illustrates this by comparing Old Hamlet, the father-Ghost, with Young Hamlet, son and courtly Prince:

> Coming from what was still in many ways a feudal barony only beginning to take on the contours of a national state, James would have recognized at once the old-fashioned medieval warrior prince, Old Hamlet. Wearing complete armor, 'cap-a-pe', courteous, religious, and chivalrously concerned that women, no matter how base their conduct, not be physically harmed, the old king is an idealized composite of the chiefs of an older heroic age with the rulers of the more immediate feudal past, when kings like himself and Old Norway determined the fate of kingdoms in single combat conducted in front of their armies and honored their pledged word on the outcome. He is the old-style father as well as an old-style king—representing the individual's past, as well as the nation's—and the force of his energy and the certainty of his morality are menacing to son and subject alike, as he crashes his heavy battle-ax in fury on the Baltic ice and commands the younger Hamlet to honor the ancient code of blood revenge and murder the uncle who has killed his father.[74]

In Elsinore, as across Renaissance Europe, a new type of prince had come to power whose legitimacy went back only one or two generations at the most, like the English Tudors or the Valois and Bourbons of France, Kernan suggests:

> Legitimacy in the Danish state, as in the English, derives from several different sources: natural authority and battle courage in Old Hamlet, skill in statecraft and ruthlessness in Claudius, and legitimate descent plus intelligence and sensitivity in Prince Hamlet, who is Plato's philosopher-king. In young Hamlet is concentrated all that was most idealistic and optimistic in Renaissance humanism: he is a student at Wittenberg—the university of Dr. Faustus and Martin Luther—a critic of the arts and frequenter of the theater, a lover, and a poet. He is the ideal courtier, the *uomo universale* fashioned by Castiglione and so admired by Ophelia. . . . Hamlet can see and speak, as no one else in the play can, to the heroic past in the figure of the father-king, Old Hamlet, but the old sureties, particularly about blood revenge, are no longer real for him. Caught between two worlds, for most of the play Claudius is able to manipulate him easily, and although in the end Hamlet becomes the instrument for bringing Claudius to his death, he can never fulfill his early promise to become the philosopher-king of Denmark.[75]

Hamlet fears he is a coward. He wonders whether he is a coward, and what makes one think so. But, Murray says, he remains true to his self-image of a noble character, 'The one constant in all this, and it is a crucial one, is that Hamlet is always disposed to do what he *thinks* is noble'.[76] Following the dialogue with Osric, the play primarily emphasizes Hamlet's nobility. In killing the King, he acts 'with a sense of full justification', Murray states. 'He is noble in his exchange of forgiveness with Laertes, in his concern that Horatio should report his cause "aright", and in turning his dying thoughts to the future of Denmark (337, 344–5, 360–3)'.[77]

But the nobility is under *status pressure*, and the duel between Laertes and Hamlet is symptomatic of that status pressure. Robert N. Watson notices:

> Ambition, too, was a particularly alluring and dangerous sin in Shakespeare's society, where radical economic, technological, and theological changes had unsettled people from hereditary roles that dated back to medieval feudalism. For the many who migrated to urban centres, there was neither a safety-net to prevent starvation nor a glass ceiling to prevent social climbing—only a scramble for money, status, and favours from the powerful. While the subtle refashioning of inward identity provoked soliloquies, the rapid refashioning of outward identity provoked civil authorities—desperate to preserve traditional order—to punish upstarts and innovators (even high-ranking ones such as Essex and Norfolk). The conservative tendency of human culture must have been similarly punitive, in less official but more pervasive ways: in unsettled times, people reflexively conspire to ridicule new styles and penalize opportunists, and Elizabethan and Jacobean comedies (especially those of Ben Jonson) showed people doing so. Furthermore, in a society where status was so unstable, ambition often led to violent revenge, as duels over honour became an epidemic among the aristocratic elite.[78]

Thomas McAlindon does not just point out that 'Shakespeare's conception of nobility has its roots in the chivalric code, with its twin ideal of violence and civility, devotion to war and to ladies'; he also explains how this duality can be understood in terms of a model of nature as a dynamic system of interacting opposites (love and strife, concord and discord, order and chaos).[79] The warrior hero's *code of honour* consists of two virtues that may turn into two vices. The limits of both virtues are tested. Both virtues run the risk that the scale tips, especially if the boundaries between the two virtues overflow, resulting in a state of confusion. Balancing these two forces of human nature doubles the duty of the warrior hero, who is not just obliged to fight furiously on the battlefield, but also to conquer the hearts of the ladies at court by speaking eloquently and loving conscientiously. Hamlet's character too, McAlindon writes,

> reveals a fundamental dualism which in turn is related to the structure and dynamics of contrarious nature. Like Brutus, Hamlet is called upon to perform a violent act which the code of honour represents as his sacred duty. Martial valour is no more alien to him than it was to Brutus, the scholarly soldier. Being the complete Renaissance man, he is skilled in both tongue and sword, the arts of peace and of war; at the end, he demonstrates his complete superiority with the sword to his much lauded rival. The code of honour, however, with its characteristically exclusive identification of duty with violent action that takes no account of pity, human-kindness, and forgiveness, upsets the balance of his nature. And the disturbance in his nature is intensified by the fact that the violence to which he is driven by the honour code is accompanied by an intense personal hatred for his intended victim. Moreover, that hatred exists in a state of tortuous interaction with the instinct for love and compassion on which his character as a man of conscience and civility is based.[80]

'In the given circumstances', Hamlet 'becomes at times depressingly like the reckless and conscienceless heroes' he mocks in his lighter moments; thereby, he fails to live up to his own standards. His fearlessness shows him in possession of heroic quality, and his heroic achievement 'unites resolution and restraint, valour and humanity (or conscience), sword and tongue. Whether he accomplishes that in the end is open to question. . . . Before the end, however, Hamlet has been betrayed by the code of honour and martial violence to which the Ghost and the memory of his father have called him', McAlindon concludes.[81]

There is also the aspect of personal betrayal. That the code of honour is constantly being violated in the playworld of Elsinore, from the violent seizure of the throne by the brother of the legitimate king, the overhasty and incestuous marriage between Claudius and Gertrude, and the violating interrogation of Ophelia by Polonius, until the poisoning of the wine by Claudius and of the sword by Laertes, is not just a characteristic of the Danish court. It is a telling metaphor of social life at the time, as it could be recognized by Shakespeare's contemporary audience, Margolies argues. 'Community of values, the value of honour in particular, is disintegrating'. The word 'honour' loses its meaning. Words and values become hollow because the community sharing them itself disintegrates.[82] From *Hamlet* until *Timon of Athens*, the tragedies 'are all metaphors of social disintegration. Each succeeding tragedy. . . shows a social world at a further stage of decline'.[83]

In *I Henry IV,* V.i.129–41, Falstaff was 'the knight who fills the inherited forms of chivalry with a new individualistic content, and who reasons that honour is no more than a word', but Falstaff was presented as disreputable. 'In *Hamlet* however, the slippage between the customary meaning of the form and the actual content is more serious because the problem is endemic, not localised in particular individuals'.[84] Honour is reduced to form, and the pursuit of honour as one's social role and duty has been hollowed out by individualism. The royal court betrays a constant slippage between form and content, and a naturalization of corruption and complacency. This is embodied by the courtier Osric. He 'lacks individualising traits', but he is Laertes's accomplice in plotting Hamlet's poisoning. Behind his meaningless language, he is murderous. 'The problem is not that he uses language to *disguise* his meaning . . . but that the slippage of meaning allows him to *escape* personal responsibility', Margolies argues.[85] Hamlet's verbal virtuosity parries Osric's hollow language, but his verbal victory is of no avail. The value system represented in the language applied to the court is no longer operative, yet its language is. The reality has changed but the language has not. The gentlemen and women 'of worship' (the same root as 'worth'!) have a rank of honour, but lack the qualities deserving of honour. This contradiction between the two 'worships' ('His Worship the gentleman' versus 'worthy of being respected') has become a problem of definition, of defining reality (in)adequately:[86]

> Because the formalised understanding available in the play is like that of Polonius, tradition-bound and inhospitable to learning from actual experience, Shakespeare has no means of articulating values clearly; systematic understanding—ideology—in the play belongs to the 'enemy'. Shakespeare makes Hamlet carry alone the whole burden of opposition. Hamlet sees what is wrong but . . . he can go no further than rejecting the dominant culture, recognizing honour in the 'breach' without proposing an alternative.[87]

Prince Fortinbras is no improvement. His ambitious pursuit of honour is clearly at the expense of social well-being.[88] Honour is in decline. Hamlet embodies the disappointment, frustration, anger and bitterness evoked by the rotten state of the court and its complacency, hypocrisy, insensitivity and cynicism. He also embodies the disillusioned adolescent, whose idealistic view of the human being has been destroyed by harsh reality.[89]

In Shakespearean literature, then, the martial values of the old feudal order clash with the Machiavellian values of a new monarchical order, as Kernan pointed out. Faced with his feudally styled father, Hamlet fears being a coward. The chivalric code of honour that always had its twin ideal of devotion to war and devotion to the ladies now loses the balance between these two virtues of violence and civility. The honourable duty to take violent revenge, McAlindon suggested, upsets the balance of Hamlet's nature as a Renaissance courtier. But Hamlet is not just betrayed by the unbalancing potential of his martial code of honour. The personal betrayal that goes hand in hand with social disintegration constantly violates the code of honour at court as well as in the social world at large, Margolies argued. Honour is presented as a value still upheld in words, but no longer in deeds, and since there is no alternative language available, the decline of honour cannot be articulated clearly, in spite of the verbal virtuosity of the Renaissance courtier.

3.4 Victor and victim in warrior heroism

What, then, can be said in general about the relationship between victor and victim in warrior heroism? Is epic warrior heroism different from tragic warrior heroism?

According to René Girard, the difference between myth and tragedy is that *myth* focuses on the sacrifice as a real solution, whereas *tragedy*, even though the tragic plot will eventually turn to the same solution, is conscious of the violent character of the solution.[90] In the case of *Oedipus Tyrannus*, the disputes between Oedipus and Teiresias turn them into twins involved in an escalating spiral of accusations and potential violence, much like Eteocles and Polyneices later on. In the myth, the accusations of patricide and incest are ascribed to the supernatural gifts of the seer Teiresias, whereas in the tragedy, they are linked to the natural exchange of the verbal hostilities between them (*OT*, 357–8). Moreover, Oedipus is qualified as a *pharmakos*, as both a medicine and a poison, as both the saviour and the polluter of Thebes. Oedipus is the king made into a scapegoat of his kingdom. Tragedy unmasks the false difference between 'just' victors and 'guilty' victims by unmasking the 'guilty' victims as the victims of violent (guilty) scapegoating. Sophocles' *Antigone* is a striking example in case. Antigone and Creon are rivals who compete over the legitimacy of the heritage that the dead brothers Eteocles and Polyneices have left behind – a family in ruins and a state in ruins. Creon refuses the dead Polyneices his funerary rite because he committed treason. Antigone refuses Creon the right to blame only Polyneices by falsely playing Polyneices off against Eteocles. Creon falsely differentiates between the two brothers, and he appeals to a false identity of the unity of the state by founding it on a common violence against Polyneices. Through her public demand for a funerary rite, Antigone stresses the true identity between brothers and sisters, and she protests against Creon's scapegoating (isolating and marginalizing) of one brother only, thus unmasking Creon's policy as an illegitimate effort to build the state and its unity on the immoral violence of scapegoating. The polluted and polluting victim is not necessarily guilty. From Girard's approach, I would conclude that the cultural value of authorized violence is being questioned.

In epic literature, warrior heroism is normally about brave and harmful actions done to the enemy of the hero and his community. Ideally speaking, the hero is endowed with supernatural powers and identified as the victor. The name and honour of the hero draw from the winner's perspective of his military success and courage. The one factor that turns the epic hero into a tragic hero, in my opinion, is the *shift in perspective from a victor's perspective to a victim's perspective, from the perspective of gain and harming to the perspective of loss and suffering.* Homer's *Iliad* is an epic with strong tragic tendencies, extending feelings of compassion beyond the dividing line between friends and enemies. As Eli Sagan puts it, in Homer's *Iliad,* the feeling of pathos ripens because we care for both sides of the war. Homer, in fact, takes no sides.[91] In Aeschylus' *Agamemnon*, the Trojan War is no triumph of justice over injustice. Warrior heroes fight for a just cause (Helena) against too high a price in terms of victims. Suffering is not just on the part of the victims. Hector's wife and child are not just abandoned to their fate as war victims. Hector, the actor who abandons them, is fully aware of what he is doing and suffers from this fore-knowledge of the limits of his battlefield actions against Achilles. He has to endure the unintended consequences of his intended actions, but he suffers consciously. To that extent, the actor too is included in the victim's perspective. The tragic agent or actor is fully aware of the epic proportions of the counter-productivity of his supposedly triumphant actions and, in a way, becomes its first mental victim. *The victim's perspective encompasses both the actor or agent and the one acted upon*, I would suggest. The opposition is not simply between a classical actor identified as a responsible victor who harms others, and a non-actor identified as a victim who undergoes suffering. *The actor-oriented perspective is not to be confused with the victor-oriented perspective,* and the non-actor-oriented perspective is not identical to the victim-oriented perspective. It is within the victim-oriented perspective that both the actor or agent and the non-actor or the object of agency are potential or actual victims. The actor or agent is a victim of his own action because he brings about *unintended suffering*. In that sense, H. J. Heering can state that tragedy always includes unintended, yet inevitable guilt.[92] Intended action fails to correspond to unintended consequences. Freedom in the sense of responsibility fails to correspond morally to necessity in the sense of *force majeure*. The courage of the tragic hero consists in his capacity to endure the unintended consequences of his intended actions and to face up to his suffering from these consequences. But the non-actor or object of agency too, is a victim of the action in the tragic sense of the word because he endures *undeserved suffering*, suffering that lacks a moral correspondence between the destiny one deserves and the fate one suffers. Both actor or agent and non-actor or object of agency are victims in their own ways if they are to be seen as tragic, and both of them are tragic in their own ways if they are victims.

There are constellations, however, in which only one of them can be identified as the tragic victim. If a victim falls prey to an aggressor who brings about intentional harm, the victim is still the tragic victim suffering undeserved harm, but the aggressor is plainly malign or morally evil, not tragic. Unless the intentional harm inflicted by, say, Eteocles in Aeschylus' *Seven against Thebes*, is part of the inherited guilt of the Labdacid family. The family doom, which a family member inherits, then, includes a propensity to incur fresh guilt.

If the actor is a plainly malign aggressor, the tragic victim is tragic because he suffers undeserved harm, not necessarily because he reacts by offering a *tragic response*. What would a 'tragic response' consist of? In my understanding, it would be characterized by facing up to and enduring consciously, by reluctantly accepting as a matter of fact, the appalling reality of the harm (to be) suffered. Though the harm he faces is 'deserved', Eteocles' level-headedness too is an illustration of this tragic endurance. One's freedom would consist of the conscious recognition of one's necessity to acknowledge suffering and the impossibility to erase it. If the tragic victim who suffered undeserved harm is able to offer such a tragic response, he would show an attitude and state of mind indistinguishable from that of the tragic hero, whose courage consisted in his capacity to endure the unintended consequences of his intended actions. Whether one is responsible for a harmful event or not, one suffers consciously from one's response to it, or from the inevitability of one's response to it. Whether guilty or not, one's tragic response is a courageous response. What if one loses courage? One's condition of unintentional consequences or undeserved harm would still qualify as tragic, but one's response would not. Neither cowardice nor resignation can qualify as tragic responses if no clear sense of facing up to suffering is held alive. To that extent, there is always an element of mental resistance to evil and suffering in a tragic response, of fully acknowledging that evil is evil and suffering is suffering, even though a tragic response – unlike an angry response – is much closer to accepting evil and suffering than to resisting them.

The victim's perspective opens up a world of *suffering, sympathy and compassion*. Tragedy turns victorious heroes into victims who are recognizable to fellow human beings and therefore something to relate to. Achilles' social isolation has to do with the fact that he is the victim, not just of Agamemnon's shameful treatment, but of his own extreme adherence to the warrior code of honour. He only finds himself again in his grief for the loss of his friend Patroclus, which makes him forget his anger over the loss of his honour. In Sophocles' *Oedipus Tyrannus* (425 BCE), reason enables the audience to learn the lesson of suffering and compassion by gradually identifying with Oedipus, Karen Armstrong suggests.[93]

A similar shift took place in *Elizabethan* tragedy. In the reading of George K. Hunter, the medieval martial values had been christianized thoroughly by the heroic image of Christ as a patiently suffering martyr.[94] Despite the Christian heroic values becoming secular values, their reinterpretation allows them to survive from one age into another. How exactly does this metamorphosis come about?

Christian ethics cultivates the belief in a meek, humble, patient, selfless warrior. Dramatically speaking, Hunter suggests, a selfless, meek warrior in the midst of dramatic action reminds us of the gap between (passive) virtue and (active) character (Aristotle's doer). On stage, a protagonist who is selfless does not act, as is to be expected from a strongly marked individual character, but is 'a passive hero' who 'creates a blank space in the centre of the action', directing the attention of the audience to other selves elsewhere on the stage who compensate for the lack of action of the principal hero. A striking example is Jerome Bosch's painting *Carrying of the Cross*. 'The strength of the victim is measured by the energy of the victimizers; . . . this martyr demands these tyrants'.[95]

Tyrant drama is an important part of early Elizabethan tragedy, Hunter points out, due to the political context – political antagonist tyrants are set against apolitical Christian victims.[96] The *tyrant–victim opposition* is a stable one within the traditional framework of Christianity, setting the boundaries for politics. But it becomes unstable as soon as political values become independent from religious containment. Under these circumstances, the dramatist may be tempted to concentrate the drama on one extreme or the other, tyrant or martyr, Hunter argues. This is illustrated by Christopher Marlowe's *Tamburlaine the Great* (1587–8), the play that is often thought to be the first example of mature Elizabethan tragedy. Its martyr-victims do not pose a serious moral challenge to the tyrant-hero. But Renaissance culture demands an active heroic protagonist 'who can combine integrity of soul with a power of self-projection that had hitherto been the prerogative of the villain'. 'If Marlowe's *Tamburlaine* is a tyrant play without a martyr, Thomas Kyd's *The Spanish Tragedy* (c. 1585–90) is a martyr play without a tyrant', presenting Hieronimo as the martyr-hero who 'can afford to be wholly passive in the compensating knowledge that God is active', but who exchanges religious passivity for individual action. 'Hieronimo must reconcile the parts of both tyrant and martyr, be the betrayer and murderer (of the innocent Castile no less than the guilty Lorenzo), yet still be in command of the rhetoric of the suffering victim of undeserved wrongs. Kyd establishes a new relationship between tyrant and victim, presenting them as quasi-psychological polarities set up by a single mind rather than social polarities or religious opposites'. Kyd's hero, Hieronimo, considers himself to be a victim. He lacks a religious vocation, but obeys his inner voice telling him to cleanse the world by behaving like a tyrant. To the extent that Hieronimo is a martyr who has become a martyr to himself, the socio-political hero has become a psychological hero.[97]

The Shakespearean tragedies that, according to Hunter, most obviously pick up developments of Christian martyrdom as it appears in *The Spanish Tragedy* are *Titus Andronicus* and *Hamlet*. Hamlet is a 'good secular individual' who is forced to engage in damnable action due to 'principles outside the secular range'. Hunter concludes, 'And again our sense of necessary martyrdom is made valid not by understanding what the martyrdom is for but by learning to share the martyr's belief that it is necessary'.[98]

Hamlet as the *victim-hero* is the focus of Keyishian, but in a very different sense from Hunter's martyr-hero. As a *hero*, Keyishian sets Hamlet off against his father.[99] As a *victim*, however, Keyishian sets Hamlet off against his mother and his uncle, who 'break his heart for he must hold his tongue' (I.ii.158). Hamlet does not become a martyr because he starts out as an avenger of his father; he becomes a revenger because he starts out as a victim without recourse to justice. His very powerlessness turns him psychologically into a potential revenger. Revenge as a response to victimization turns Hunter's much more moral hero into a fully psychological hero who definitely has become a victim-hero because of a moral cause – he has been morally offended – but who decisively has to face the psychological consequences of the fact that he has no recourse to justice. Although Hamlet's psychic balance is a delicate one, he dies at peace with himself.

> He has upheld his own values: the aggrieved youth Laertes, who has also stumbled seeking revenge, forgives him for the death of Polonius; the philosopher Horatio says he died deserving a singing escort to heaven; and he has upheld his father's values as well: his successor Fortinbras grants him the burial rites of a soldier and a king.[100]

Laertes, Horatio and Fortinbras all invite the audience to sympathize with the mental suffering of this victim-hero Hamlet, one may conclude.

4 Conclusions

Epic literature is related to aristocratically ruled societies with a martial culture. Tragic literature has inherited this martial culture. Both epic and tragic literature use martial culture as a foil. A set of martial values does not just function as a given model, but also as something to be tested and updated. Male dominance and violence become problems instead of solutions. The shift in perspective, from a victor's perspective of gain and harming to a victim's perspective of loss and suffering, turns the epic warrior hero into a tragic warrior hero and demands attention for his victims as much as for himself as a victim of the situation. In ancient and classical Greece, the prominence of a martial ethos in tragic literature reflects the norms and values of an increasingly militarized society, and in early modern England, that of a remilitarization of the aristocracy. The English royal court and the gentry have their own versions of the martial code of honour. The re-militarized aristocracy revitalizes its martial culture and the royal court modernizes it. The old-fashioned English aristocracy tends to perceive the royal court as effeminate and cowardly. In Shakespearean literature, the martial values of the old feudal order clash with those of the royal court. But the royal court too, is severely criticized for being corrupt and hypocritical. Honour is in decline and the chivalric code of honour itself is under pressure. Competitive violence clashes with cooperative civility and the outer honour of glorious results clashes with the inner honour of virtuous respectability, in Greek tragedies as much as in Shakespearean ones. Despite the historical discontinuities between the Greek and Elizabethan martial cultures, the parallels remain striking.

PART II: INDIAN AND HINDU ISSUES

1 Introduction

If we go by the third criterion put forward by Vernant, Greek tragedy presented the old heroic value system not, as in epic and choral lyric, as a given model, but as subject to questioning and debate. Could the same be said of the *Mahābhārata* epic? Should the *Mahābhārata* be taken as an epic in the common, strict sense of the expression 'epic literature', as a genre of its own, related to societies in which the warrior code of honour is cultivated, or should it be taken as an epic in the sense of Homer's *Iliad*, as part and parcel of the tragic genre, related to societies in which the warrior code of honour is tested, questioned and debated? Several approaches seem possible. Different scholars offer different interpretations of the epic and its main heroes.

One way of mapping the scholarly debate is by arranging the scholarly approaches according to their main epic hero. Hiltebeitel focuses on Yudhisthira; Katz, who historicizes Biardeau, focuses on Arjuna; Malinar focuses on Krishna, and Brodbeck too, has an interesting approach to Krishna's instruction of Arjuna. In the previous chapter, on literary–cultural aspects, two sections in the second part were dedicated to 'epic heroes embodying traditional values' and 'the problematization of heroes: Karna and Yudhisthira' respectively. In the second part of the current chapter on martial aspects, we will begin with a section on 'the idealization of heroes: Arjuna and Krishna'. This section complements those two sections. The four warrior heroes discussed share two martial issues in particular – the issue of kingship in relationship to warriorship and the issue of changes in the concept of warrior heroism. The discussion of these issues results in two additional sections.

2 The idealization of heroes: Arjuna and Krishna

2.1 Arjuna

According to Madeleine Biardeau and Ruth Cecily Katz, Arjuna is *the* great hero. But is not Yudhisthira the great hero? Not really, they suggest. His inclination to passivity is often ridiculed by other characters, and he is said to behave more like a *brahmin* than like the *kshatriya* he really is. Not Yudhisthira alone, but Yudhisthira, Bhima and Arjuna, together, constitute the totality of Pāndava kingship – Yudhisthira supplies the *dharma*, Bhima and Arjuna supply the supporting warrior power.[101]

Arjuna's heroism is one of his three aspects. Katz subdivides Arjuna's personality traits into three levels or types – Arjuna as hero, as human and as religious devotee.

At *the level of Arjuna as a hero*, Arjuna's father is the god Indra, warrior-king of the gods, who represents the acquisition of kingly power by force and who explains Arjuna's magical fighting skills.[102] His burning of the Khāndava Forest (1.214–25) reflects an ancient *heroic ideal* – extreme violence in support of world order. Arjuna's and Krishna's wild and horrible behaviour is presented objectively, as self-evident and taken for granted; nor are their victims dwelt upon with sympathy.[103] The forest, after all, is the jungle; it represents chaos as opposed to order. Arjuna proves himself to be the best of all the warriors.[104] Arjuna's heroic (or kingly) role in the forest and on the battlefield may be characterized as that of the perfect sacrificer. Sacrifice was the ancient ideal task of the Indian king, whom Arjuna represents, for the sake of 'maintenance of world order'.[105] Arjuna's kingly role of sacrificer is also present after the war, during Yudhisthira's performance of the horse sacrifice, the greatest sacrifice a king can undertake.[106] Arjuna plays the role of the victorious hero, who has *dharma* on his side and whose epithet is *jaya* ('victory'), Katz argues.[107]

At *the human level*, however, Arjuna begins to morally question the warrior role, which was glorified at the heroic level. The key to humanization is vulnerability:

> In general such realization comes about only when a hero's humanity makes him vulnerable, after the fact, to negative results of his behavior. Good examples from outside the Indian context might be the humanization of Achilles after the death of Patroklos, or of Gilgamesh after Enkidu's death: the latter in particular undergoes a great change, from brute warrior to seeker after truth. . . . The human weakness that brings about regret in both these cases is friendship. Arjuna has a similar human weakness in the *Gītā* episode.[108]

Arjuna recognizes that his own *dharma* (*svadharma*, personal duty), the *kshatriyadharma* (warrior duty), which should work in support of eternal *dharma* (*sanatanadharma*), is not so neatly correlated with eternal *dharma,* as he might have assumed.

What makes the Kurukshetra War different from the Khāndava Forest battles is that it is a battle against human opponents. The destructive side of the 'sacrifice of war' is especially apparent when viewed from *the perspective of the victim*. The blood relationship between Arjuna and his enemies is very significant because 'it forces him to recognize their common humanity'. Later on, Arjuna is portrayed as mourner of his son, Abhimanyu. 'Here Arjuna is seen in the role of victim, like the women of the "Book of Women" '.[109]

In one sense, Katz argues, the *Gītā* episode marks another initiation in the hero's life – Arjuna's 'initiation into wisdom'. The expectation of reward, which surely exists at the heroic level, is to be discarded stoically. Thus, although a return to heroism is advocated, the change in attitude is significant. Arjuna's heroic behaviour is *humanized*. Like a hero's mortality, impasses of *dharma* are typical of the human condition, turning heroic acts into vulnerable and guilty acts.[110]

Like in Western doctrines of a 'just war', in the epic too, rules preceding and during the war have to be respected. The cause for starting or joining the war has to be a just cause, and the ways in which combatants should behave during the war have to be in accordance with specific rules of the *martial code of honour.* Both sides had accepted these rules before the war begins.[111] A moral awareness that the Pāndavas win the war by *trickery and deceit* is clearly there with the epic poets, but even the Pāndavas themselves seem to be aware that their behaviour is questionable in certain cases, although they justify it in various ways, often displaying a certain moral innocence or inconsistency.[112] Arjuna is often the central figure in a deceitful action, although Yudhisthira, Bhima and others also play their roles, and Krishna is as a rule behind the deceits, in his capacity as helper and adviser to the Pāndavas.[113] The necessity of turning to trickery to win a victory is not uncommon in heroic literature. But nowhere is trickery stressed as much as it is in the *Mahābhārata*, Katz points out.[114] This is because of the epic's obsession with *dharma*. Trickery by gods and demons is virtually taken for granted. Criticism of such trickery intensifies immediately, however, when the combatants are human beings. Why would human deceit be worse than divine deceit? According to Katz, 'the answer must have to do with the *Mahābhārata*'s keen awareness of the humanity of both perpetrator and victim' in the case of human deceit. The Kauravas, representing the demons in the battle between the gods and the demons, suddenly emerge as human victims. The Pāndava case 'no longer appears one-sidedly righteous, when their enemies no longer represent absolute chaos or evil'. Many Kaurava partisans are not at fault morally; they are fine men, righteously motivated, whom fate has placed on the evil side. The issue is *dharma*'s decline. For the *Mahābhārata* epic, uncertainty regarding *dharma* and moral ambiguity become a defining factor of the human condition. In the end, Arjuna's heroic powers desert him, and he dies a human death.[115]

At *the level of Arjuna as devotee*, the religious dimension of Arjuna that most strongly suggests that he should be taken as a role model, Arjuna's relationship to Krishna turns out to be a relationship of devotion to the Supreme King ruling the universe. Arjuna restores his threatened heroic potential, and transcends it, by his devotion to God. If he is semi-divine as Indra's son and partial incarnation, he is fully divine as Vishnu/Krishna's friend and devotee, Katz contends. Arjuna as devotee participates in Krishna's divine nature, she states unconvincingly. But Katz is very convincing in showing that while Arjuna may have his *tragic moments,* he does *not* display a *tragic character*, if by 'character', we mean the integrated version of what Katz has actually split up into three layers.

2.2 Krishna

According to Simon Pearse Brodbeck, the epic laments *the demise of the old warrior code of honour,* symbolized by the fact that the Pāndavas, the heroes, are only able to win the war by scandalously breaching the conventions of combat.[116] But Krishna's conception of warrior heroism in terms of action without attachment (*asakta karman*) is best understood against its initially *military background*. What Krishna asks from Arjuna on the battlefield is 'without the ordinarily expected payback, a certain attitude of single-mindedness in the person acting'.[117] Brodbeck writes:

> The idea is that whether or not one prevails in battle is beyond one's control, so it is premature and irrelevant to imagine one's glorious victory or miserable defeat: one must gird one's loins and do one's best, focused on the task with single *buddhi* [an awareness of the cosmic perspective on things], come what may. This idea may have included . . . Krishna Vāsudeva as the paradigm of such an attitude.[118]

Brodbeck explains this attitude of 'achieving and maintaining a mental approach to one's physical activity' by comparing them to similar experiences in the field of martial arts and top-class sport.[119]

I find his sporting analogy very helpful and persuasive. According to scholars such as Richard Frackowiak[120] and Dave Collins[121], the mental strength of exceptional sportsmen – say, David Beckham during a free kick – is related to the fact that they do not only practise physically on the practice pitch, but that they also practise mentally by visualizing the situation in their minds, on top of doing it in a real situation. To reach your peak, you have to do both. Visualization is the vital mental exercise needed to train a player to eliminate anxiety.[122] Simply by visualizing, a player can conquer his fear of failure, transporting his mental state into the 'zone', the ultimate mental state for any player. The 'zone' is typified by low levels of thought, low levels of effort, almost a 'letting go'. When a player is in the 'zone', time will fly, effort will be low, thoughts he has are thoughts of pleasure. It is almost as if the other players are moving in slow motion, it is easy to make decisions, you know what people are going to do, you are slipping into routine, with automatic thought processes taking over. The player does not have previous failures in his mind; he is mentally rehearsing the entire sequence of events in his mind; even before kicking the ball, he knows the result.

Arjuna is encouraged *to think of Krishna only*, (2.61) without the purity of his mind being affected by the crime he is about to commit under the pressure of extreme circumstances, Brodbeck points out. Krishna's martial art has 'much in common with the surviving oriental martial arts, all of which are psychological and philosophical as well as physical', he notes; Krishna:

> deplores actions which are motivated by desire for personal gain, and he introduces a variety of alternative motivational ideas: for the good of society, for the maintenance of the cosmos, for the love of God. Only by

acting on the basis of these external motivators will a person be able to maintain peace of mind. Krishna is able to back up this claim by explaining that, in fact, all action is externally determined, and that the impression of human agency is a delusion.[123]

Brodbeck remarks that 'if a *transferable* method of having such an attitude at will had been found, then sport would not be as interesting as it is. This suggests that the *Gītā* finds it hard to set forth a comprehensible and comprehensive description of what the attitude is and how it is to be attained' and maintained.[124] Brodbeck is reluctant to appeal to the mystical character of the state of mind Krishna is alluding to. What Krishna actually would have offered initially, he suggests, is a theory of 'action without attachment' that served the purpose of 'allaying fears of post-war trauma, before the soteriology of *moksha* was developed'.[125]

Krishna's notion of warrior heroism, no need to say, is lacking any sense of tragedy whatsoever. Single-mindedness and peace of mind are at the heart of what true warrior heroism is about.

In the *Bhagavadgītā*, Krishna is the ultimate solution to the problem of how to act, according to Angelika Malinar. *Krishna represents ideal kingship* and teaches it to Arjuna *as an alternative for both ascetic renunciation and unrestrained rulership*. Unrestrained rulership is represented by Duryodhana (in the Udyogaparvan), who sacrifices family ties for selfish interest in power by force. Since Krishna advocates sacrificing the family ties to the warrior's duty of exercising authority by the use of force, the illegitimacy of Duryodhana's position is anything but self-evident. Duryodhana claims that his traditional role of royal performer of the ritual sacrifice automatically bestows upon him the authority of the gods, and it is the warrior's duty to stick to his consecrated task of defending his territory by all means. Uncompromising steadfastness, after all, is the prime value of a warrior,[126] and the one value Arjuna fails to display. Arjuna's argument that the goal of warriorship does not make sense if the means of war destroys the very family it is supposed to offer the fruits of victory, and that this insight should lead to a peaceful refusal to actively engage in war, comes close to embracing institutional asceticism (abstaining from all [ritual] action by becoming an ascetic). Indifference is not necessarily the alternative to Duryodhana's warrior value of steadfastness or to Arjuna's fairly ascetic value of renunciation because indifference concerning the outcome of the war is an ambiguous value that can express both Duryodhana's self-interest without consideration for others or for his own life, and the disinterest of heroes and ascetics. The *Bhagavadgītā*, moreover, implicitly disqualifies

Duryodhana's self-interest as a form of blindness, and explicitly disqualifies Arjuna's disinterest as a form of confusion. Neither of them links action to knowledge in the proper way, neither of them escapes the problem of guilt. Neither of them succeeds in distancing himself from the entanglement of his self and the result of his actions. Action is linked up with blindness or confusion because it is linked up with desire.

One seemingly crucial (but ultimately, not decisive) value the *Bhagavadgītā* comes up with as an alternative is *self-restraint* or *self-control*. This notion requires closer investigation. The *Bhagavadgītā,* according to Malinar, draws its notion of self-restraint from the *yogic* concept of physical and spiritual self-discipline in combination with the *samkhya* concept of cosmic self-acting nature (*prakrti*). The real enemy in the war appears to be one's own desire, that is to say, the desire to relate to the fruits of one's actions as if these are the desirable fruits of one's desirous actions. Arjuna should come to realize that he is not the real actor of his actions, but that cosmic nature itself is acting through his actions, regardless of what Arjuna does or intends to do. This cosmic activity is thought of as a cosmic sacrificial process in the sense that the energy spent is necessary to guarantee the maintenance of the metabolic universe. Participation in this cosmic sacrifice would imply active participation in its purpose of upholding the universe while dissociating oneself from the self-interested desire to relate to the results of one's actions. This is exactly what *Krishna* is doing as the legitimate (*dharmic*) and independent (*yogic*) Lord of the universe. He reveals himself to Arjuna as the ideal self-restrained ruler upholding the universe by acting purposefully, according to his royal duty, without desiring any personal gain (results) from his sacrificial activity. Devoting one's actions to this self-detached king of the universe becomes the purest and most liberating duty a human being can fulfil.[127] Desireless self-discipline benefiting the well-being of the community (*lokasamgraha*) becomes a core value of the warrior code.

The conflict of *loyalties* (between the *kuladharma,* family duties, of a relative and the *svadharma,* caste duties, of a warrior) is transcended by becoming loyal to the one legitimate ruler of the universe. There is no return to the traditional family code. According to Malinar and von Stietencron, Duryodhana represents a new concept of power and rulership, which is based on *territory instead of family*.[128] The traditional kinship system of government of ruling royal families is replaced by territorially based centralized states. This new development had started in the fourth century BCE in Magadha, following the Persian example of the Achaemenides. Politically speaking, a kingship based on external expansion was much more powerful than its predecessors as long as it focused on external enemies. The unrestrained urge for expansion brought about a moral crisis, however, as to its legitimacy. At the latest, this crisis must have occurred when the expansion turned inward. *Self-restraint and self-detachment* were now proclaimed the *new warrior values,* which could transcend the new habits of unrestrained rulers without returning to the old family values of a ruling family system.[129]

3 The controversial issue of kingship

The extensive and ongoing academic debate about the significance of kingship and warriorship in Indian civilization reveals that, although certain cultural values are definitely involved in the reality and symbolism of kingship and warriorship, it is by no means evident exactly how each of these values relates to the other ones. The core values of *dharma* and *artha* are a case in point. No fixed system of values emerges from the debate, but no hopeless arbitrariness either, as Biardeau's and Hiltebeitel's reflections show. Kingship and warriorship definitely had a significant role to play in the reality and imagery of Indian history, its political theories and its epics.

As a historical reality, kingship was the fruit of an increasingly differentiated society, starting out as a patchwork of scattered lineage-based chiefdoms and ultimately developing into vastly expanded state systems which, in turn, could easily witness themselves being reduced to much smaller regional powers since no all-embracing state system could ever uphold the military, political and economic infrastructure needed to impose itself effectively in the long run.[130] Thapar suggests that the term *rājan* initially refers to a tribal leader whose legitimacy is based on birth and lineage, but later on extends to a notion of kingship that has a territorial link, including tax (*bhāga*, share) instead of just tribute (*bali*), and 'the wielding of *danda*, literally a rod, symbolising the coercive authority of the state. A *kshatriya* without *danda* would lead to total chaos and destruction. Such passages invariably draw on the *rāja-dharma* sections of the *Dharma-śāstras'*. This appeal to coercive authority is characteristic of monarchies:

> Clearly defined descriptions of monarchical functioning occur in the didactic sections as in the Śāntiparvan. Theories explaining the origin of kingship are characterised by the loss of utopia. The earliest time is the pristine golden age before the manifestation of pride, arrogance and oppression which results in a condition of evil. This is sometimes symbolised as a condition of drought echoing the earliest stereotypes linking rainfall with good government. A king is appointed by the gods in order to terminate the state of chaos. Such an appointment inevitably carries with it the sanction to use authority.[131]

The occurrence of a historical shift from kingship being based on external expansion and focused on external enemies to kingship being cut off from these raiding expeditions for material resources outside the king's primary domain is also a crucial issue for Jan C. Heesterman, but he would put accents differently from Thapar and Malinar.[132] According to him, the dilemma is that the king, in order to exercise power effectively, has to be part of the community and, in order to act with authority, has to be external to it. In the texts, *kingship* in general is not idealized, but considered *highly ambiguous*, both benignly protective and violently destructive. In order to legitimate his use of force, the king perpetually has to actually or ritually prove it. But for that, for his power and authority, he depends on others – on fellow chiefs and on the community at large, and also, of course, on the *brahmin* priests who perform in the royal ritual to his benefit. The royal ritual cycle, which includes a ritualized chariot drive or a ritualized cattle raid, should connect the settled agricultural community (*grāma*) and the outside world of the jungle (*aranya*) as two phases of an alternating cycle so as to establish his authority within the community from without. The ambivalence and danger of the royal ritual (*rājasūya*) is also documented in the epics. The royal ritual will lead to the Kurukshetra War, which is part and parcel of the royal ritual cycle.[133]

The historical, or rather, ritual shift came about when the ritual cycle, which was full of risk and under the constant threat of violent breakdown, was then thoroughly restructured by cutting up and destroying the cyclical concatenation, Heesterman suggests. The purpose was to break out of the endless cycle by establishing a new conception of the transcendent, and thereby of authority, which would not separate the sacred from the profane, but introduce a rift between the sacred and the profane, on the one hand, and the transcendent, on the other.[134] The *brahmin* priest who incorporated the values of asceticism within society came to represent absolute, *transcendent* authority cut off from the social world, while the *sacral king* came to represent the *social* world. The king would, consequently, have to *associate* himself with the *brahmin* in order to *legitimize* his rule, whereas the *brahmin* would have to *dissociate* himself from the king in order to remain *authoritative*.

Heesterman's position is very close to Biardeau's and Hiltebeitel's conviction that the Kurukshetra War has to be understood ritually, and also close to Hiltebeitel's conviction that the *Mahābhārata* is about breaking the cycle of violence. Heesterman does not, however, state that breaking the cycle of violence is the message that the epic teaches to Yudhisthira in order to educate the king, but rather that breaking the cycle of violence is a motif in the epic, which is symptomatic of a historical shift from pastoral raiding to agricultural taxing and trading, but simultaneously of a religious shift in dealing with the unsolvable conflict between power and authority, security and danger, balance and imbalance, kings and brahmins.

From Heesterman's point of view, Malinar's approach to the *Gītā* is fairly problematic in one respect. Heesterman writes:

> I do not entirely agree with Angelika Malinar. Krishna is not the ideal king. One may even wonder whether India knows such an ideal king. Even Rāma was, as a king, not able to be ideal. More than elsewhere, in the Indian civilisation kingship is dubious. A king, that is, lacks transcendent authority because he is and is supposed to be fully worldly. Krishna, however, is both above and outside the cosmos, and simultaneously encompasses the cosmos—a splits of which only he, not the king, no matter how ideal, is capable.[135]

Chakravarti Ram-Prasad comments similarly:

> Malinar's view of Krishna as the ideal king is highly problematic. First, there is the larger question of the very centrality of kingship in classical Indian thought, with mainly Western writers over-stressing it (as if kingship were not to a certain extent important to practically all pre-modern Christian culture). But even if we set that aside, Krishna is not to be so easily ascribed ideal kingship compared to Rāma; and this is certainly so within the tradition. His origins are as a princeling of a small state; his primary base, even after the establishment of a city-state in Dvaraka, is in the lowly cowherd clan of Yadavas; at no time does his formal intervention in the affairs of the cousins amount to royal action; it is as emissary, as cousin to both parties, and, elusively, as a transcendental presence, that he appears in the *Mahābhārata*.[136]

Apparently, most Western scholars agree that the *Mahābhārata* is a work of kingly instruction, but they do not agree on which character represents the ideal king (Biardeau: Arjuna/Yudhisthira; Katz: Arjuna; Hiltebeitel: Yudhisthira?; Malinar: Krishna), or they may even doubt whether the notion of 'ideal kingship' is a sufficiently reliable and unambiguous one to be focused upon (Heesterman, Ram-Prasad).

4 Changes in the concept of warrior heroism

If one takes one of the epic characters as one's main focal point for finding an answer to the question whether the *Mahābhārata* is critically examining the warrior code of honour, one realizes that different characters such as Yudhisthira, Arjuna and Krishna seem to represent different answers because they seem to represent similar functions differently – *the role of the king, the role of the warrior and the role of the hero.* When the martial value system is being questioned, both the royal value system and the warrior value system are implicated. But can these value systems be identified with each other and put in one?

Thapar argues that the traditional role of the warrior is being replaced, or rather, confiscated and consumed by the role of the king, who primarily focuses on *brahmins,* but also needs the heroism of the warrior stories as a means of *legitimizing* his exercise of force and his authority as a king. The heroic ideal of royal warriors, apart from honour and bravery, increasingly emphasized generosity in gift-giving and the ordering of sacrificial ceremonies, and thus access to wealth. It also implied the increasingly unequal distribution of that wealth in favour of priests and ritual occasions.[137]

Albeit from a different perspective, Thapar's position comes strikingly close to that of Heesterman who, on the one hand, sketches a king who remains bounded to his community and to his fellow chiefs as a *primus inter pares*, and on the other, describes a king who then turns to the transcendent authority of *brahmins* for his legitimization. And it is the very function of legitimization as put forward by Thapar, which paradoxically unites Thapar and Heesterman on the issue of downplaying the significance of ideal kingship as a model. What does Thapar's position on the topic of legitimization amount to? Thapar, in a way, takes the king of the inner frame of the epic, Janamejaya, as her main focal point for finding an answer. The notion of *ideal kingship*, she basically argues, is less important in epic literature than the notion of *legitimate kingship*.

According to Thapar, the Indian concept of *warrior heroism* dates from the time of pastoralism and from the subsequent time when agriculture began to take precedence over pastoralism. During the pastoralism of Rig Vedic society, cattle was the main asset, and cattle raids were common. '"Winner of cows" (*gojit*) is an epithet for hero (*Rg Veda* 3.47.4, 5.63.5, 6.31.3)'.[138] The tribal leader (*rājā*) in this pastoral society is called 'lord of the herd' (*gopati*), whereas later on, the king (*rājā*) will be called 'lord of men' (*nrpati, nareśvara*). In the early eulogies on heroes, the heroes are clan chiefs who are victorious in raids and generous to the bards.[139]

The next historical step, then, according to Heesterman, is that of a king who performs a ritualized cattle raid. Similarly, the *epic warrior* who undergoes his initiatory preparation in the forest and engaged in austerities (*tapas*), returns as a *consecrated warrior*. The epic warrior is consecrated to the extent that the war is part and parcel of the royal ritual. The epic battle is a sacrifice, a *sacrificium*, 'something made sacred', 'something consecrated'.

It is this concept of warrior heroism related to pastoral chiefs, ritually performing kings, and consecrated warriors, which is then being 'humanized', to borrow Katz's term. At some stage, she argues, the warrior hero is no longer a sheer victor, a hero of triumph whose victims are not dwelt upon with sympathy. It is, in fact, the war from the victim's perspective, as in the Book of Women mourning over all those warriors killed and all those women left behind, and in the portrayal of Arjuna as mourner of his son Abhimanyu, where Arjuna is seen in the role of victim, all of them recognizing the common humanity of both enemies and friends. The concept of warrior heroism has undergone a dramatic change, from the warrior hero as victor to *the warrior hero as victim*. In the second instance, within the devotionalist framework, the warrior hero offers his own self as a victim for the purpose of the whole world's good, thus imitating the Lord of the Universe who has incarnated on earth for the sake of the world's just order.

It is also at this stage that the warrior hero's violence is no longer taken for granted, but severely criticized in the epic. The martial value system of what is now presented as 'the old warrior order', personified in the persons of Vrddhakshatra (literally 'old warrior'), Jarāsandha and Bhīshma, is being replaced.[140] According to Alf Hiltebeitel, the battle is a sacrifice, but the problem with that is that 'the agonistic sacrificial paradigm lacks a mechanism for stopping the cycle of violence'.[141] As Yudhisthira tells Krishna, heroism is a heart-eating disease, and 'a peace won by the total eradication of an enemy is crueler than the heart-eating disease of heroism (5.70.55–6)'.[142] The recommended transformation is an *inner* one:

> As a virtue, *āhimsa* bears the ascetic imprint of the desire not to kill or harm creatures, which, in its ascetic framework, is a desire to overcome the desire for life. While the *Bhagavad Gītā* includes it in several lists of advocated virtues (10.5, 13.7, 16.2, 17.14), its purpose is to revitalize an ideal *kshatriya* who will fight to reestablish an *ārya dharma* convinced by such arguments, and particularly the second (action without the desire for fruits), fourth (death in battle as a ticket to heaven; 2.32), and fifth (the real self is unslain; 2.17–26). These are precisely non-Buddhist and non-Jain arguments: that *ahimsā* can be adjusted not only to the practice of sacrifice, but to the sacrifice of battle.[143]

Dermot Killingley's reading of the *Gītā* has the same tenor. Killingley points out that Arjuna's warrior heroism is being transformed by the ideal of the *yogic* person, but that this *yogic* ideal of detachment does not disqualify the warrior heroism inherent in Arjuna's warrior class identity.[144]

Killingley's argument could also be used to stress that the ideal of the saint (*yogi*) in the *Gītā* replaces the ideal of the warrior hero (*kshatriya*). Heroic warriors do not renounce the battle, but they do renounce the glory of battle. They fight truly for the *dharma* now and not for themselves. *Warrior heroism* is being *spiritualized*. However, the Indian concept of saintship is different from its Western counterpart. Indian heroes are like Indian saints – greater than life, but also different from real life; ideals but not ideals to identify with; representatives of a world different from daily life; of a transcendent world; exponents of the divine world and of a divine play; instead of counteracting and defying the human world; too transcendent, too different from the human world to be defying it.[145]

Hiltebeitel, then, confirms Killingley's reading of the *Gītā* by stressing the fact that the warrior's heroism is not disqualified, but revitalized on a different level. The level referred to is not just a moral level. It is not just about warriors learning how not to be passionate or cruel. The warrior's heroism is revitalized on a spiritual level. It bears the *ascetic* imprint of the *desire* to overcome the desire for life. That is to say, the framework for the ethicizing of the warrior's heroism is the metaphysical framework of Hindu spirituality. In Hinduism, *spirituality* covers everything that broadens the mind beyond the realm of this-worldly affairs. Overcoming the desire for life, in that sense, is as much a matter of desire as it is a matter of desirelessness for the fruits of this-worldly actions. The concept of warrior heroism is indeed both being humanized and being spiritualized.

It is within this spiritual framework that the concept of warrior heroism is being *ethicized*, that is to say, turned into a form of behaviour and mind-set, which is the expression of a *reflective* moral choice following an extensive debate about the rights and wrongs, pros and cons of a possible choice and its alternatives. The choices Arjuna and Yudhisthira are expected to make are preceded by and embedded in an elaborate ethical debate about conflicting values that put the traditional martial value system to the test. It is not the war as such which is debated. The debate surpasses an ethical discussion about waging a 'just war'. The debate is about conflicting values involved in engaging in a supposedly just war. It is the validity and consistency among the radically different and sometimes conflicting values within the value system whose limits are tested.

5 Conclusions

The *Mahābhārata* epic's set of martial values is based on a given model as the traditional heritage and is, at the same time, a source of controversy. It is controversial, first of all, because it is inherently violent, whereas violence is no longer taken for granted as a legitimate part of life in general and of royal rulership in particular. This has led to a humanization of the concept of warrior heroism that takes the victim's perspective seriously. It has also led to the ethicizing of the concept of warrior heroism – the expectation to behave as a warrior has become the object of value debates and reflective choices. Secondly, due to religious changes, first from ritualism to asceticism and then from asceticism to devotionalism, the concept of warrior heroism has been spiritualized, that is to say, yogically internalized (the inner world of the warrior hero has now become radically non-detached, attached neither to victory nor to defeat) and devotionally internalized (the inner world of the warrior hero has now become completely devoted to his Lord). This has led to a replacement of the old warrior order, or rather, to both a re-evaluation and a revitalization of the warrior hero's set of martial values and duties.

PART III: CROSS-CULTURAL COMPARISONS

1 Warrior class and martial culture

Epic literature is related to societies ruled by chiefs, warlords or kings, and dominated by a corresponding martial value system. Homeric literature is no exception to that rule. In the Indian epics too, the martial culture is used as a foil. Warriors, kings and (il)legitimate succession dominate the scene. Tragic literature too used this martial culture as a foil. Shakespeare used royal and imperial history, including its warrior ethic. He did not draw from epic literature as such, but drew from well-known stories about a society equally ruled by chiefs, warlords or kings, British kings and Roman emperors, and no less dominated by a corresponding martial value system than epic literature itself.

Ancient Greek society did not abandon the archaic martial value system, but updated it to suit a *military innovation*, the shift from cavalry to infantry, which had democratizing consequences. *Individual* combat became less important than *collective* discipline, and aristocrats became less important than they used to be, while commoners gained importance. Likewise, in early modern Europe, a military shift from cavalry to infantry and artillery had democratizing consequences. Chivalric culture fostered the individual display of prowess and valour, but modern warfare was becoming more impersonal in so far as it was determined by infantry and by considerations of policy, strategy and logistics.

Here too, historical developments would not lead to an abandonment, but to a modernization of the martial value system.

Small-scale traditional societies imbued with martial values have a tendency to consider only their warriors as full members of the community, and military service as both a duty and a privilege. In Homer, Schein stated, to be fully human means to kill or be killed in the pursuit of honour and glory. This is no longer the case in vast empires and imperial monarchies like China, Persia and Rome, where warfare is in the hands of a specialized elite, as Naerebout and Singor observed.

The warrior class of *kshatriya* (warriors and rulers) is clearly a separate segment of society cultivating its martial value of *artha* as its specific *dharma*. As a group, the warrior class is constantly being compared to the *brahmin* class. According to Biardeau, it is the class difference between *brahmins* and *kshatriyas* that constitutes the primary source of tension in the epic.

In classical Hindu India, it was *religious innovation* instead of military innovation that had democratizing consequences. Instead of the cavalry being overshadowed by infantry (and artillery), religious ritualism and asceticism came to be overshadowed by personal devotion (*bhakti*). This development, meant for *kshatriyas* in the epic, has been conceived during all of Indian history as valid for all non-*brahmin* Hindus as well. It gave every *svadharma* (personal duty) a religious content and an access to ultimate salvation.

But there is another religious element that influences cross-cultural comparisons between Europe and India – the dominance of religious asceticism in ancient and classical India, which has no counterpart in Europe. Ascetic renouncers in India would later become involved in martial arts. But originally, they had cultivated the value of non-violence, thus abandoning the martial culture. Whereas the Indian renouncers initially abandoned the warrior code, Armstrong argued, the Greeks were militarizing the entire *polis*, against the overall spirit of the Axial Age, but with an Axial twist:

> The hoplite army was a people's army, drawing on a larger proportion of the male population than ever before. And conversely, that meant that the people, the *demos*, were now essentially an army. In India, fighting had become the sole prerogative of the *kshatriya* class; warfare was now a specialized activity, from which the other three classes were barred. It was thus circumscribed and contained and, as the ideal of *ahimsa* took hold, was regarded increasingly as impure, tragic, and evil. But not so in Greece, which was going in the opposite direction. During the seventh century, the entire polis had become militarized. The citizenry had become an army, which could be mobilized at very short notice. This was a radical break with the past. Hesiod had suggested that it was time to abandon the traditional

heroic ideal; the hoplite army effected this severance. The individual warrior, yearning for personal glory, had become an anachronism: the new ideal was collective. The hoplite soldier was essentially one of a team. . . . Like the Axial ideal of *kenosis*, it promoted an ethic of selflessness and devotion to others. The difference was that this self-surrender was acted out on the battlefield in a savagely effective killing machine.[146]

I am not too sure that the selfless devotion of these Greek soldiers to their common interest can be likened to the Axial ideal of *kenosis*.

In ancient and classical Greece and in medieval and early modern Europe, *warriors and rulers* would have shared a sense of privilege and a claim to dominate *by nature*. The leading members of both groups were, on the whole, considered to belong to the same social class of aristocrats, known as 'nobility'. The 'nobility' of the nobleman meant, first of all, to have noble blood, to be of aristocratic descent, and therefore to claim the privilege to rule as a birthright. But to be a member of the ruling class always included the duty to fight. In Sophocles' *Philoctetes*, Cairns emphasized, Neoptolemus must prove himself 'noble' (*gennaios*), and the reference to his 'nature' (*phusis*) is not a reference to human nature in general, but to his noble birth and duty. Martial values, such as 'doing one's warrior duty', tend to be derived from a warrior's aristocratic 'nature' and 'noble birth', at least in epic and tragic literature. *Noblesse oblige* – nobility as a birthright, which implies the duty to strive for military fame. For many centuries, this was no less the case in Western Europe than in ancient Greece. The remarkable number of losses among (aristocratic) officers in the World War I illustrates the point that 'born to rule' meant 'born to fight'.[147] Those noblemen who did not actually fight should rule by holding an office. After free birth and military or princely service, to hold civic office, to have a wealthy style of living and to display generosity became equally valid qualities of a nobleman. A combination of public service and a wealthy style of living were sufficient grounds for Shakespeare's father to apply for the title of 'nobleman' and its accompanying coat of arms that William himself inherited, 'non sanz droict'. Agamemnon, I recall, was blamed for failing to display generosity towards Achilles. Also included in the *Gītā*'s list of noble virtues are the display of 'generosity' (*dānam*) and 'lordly spirit' (*īśvarabhāvaś*). Karna is a paragon of generosity – the first step of his undoing, the loss of his earrings and armour, is the result of his inability to refuse anything to a *brahmin*. In ancient India, both the warrior and the king belong to the same warrior class of *kshatriya*, and they do so by noble birth. Their noble nature is also their duty. The epic *kshatriyas* who behave like *brahmins* go against their own nature and duty, which is both personal and collective. The confusion or overlapping of being born from a mixed couple and the confusion or overlapping of one's own duty – of *brahmins* behaving like *kshatriyas* or the other way around – are only two different aspects of one and the same fundamental disorder (*adharma*) in society. 'By *dharma* beings are upheld apart (*dharmena vidhrtāh prajāh*)'.[148]

There was always a degree of tension, however, between *nobility* acquired *by birth* and *nobility* acquired *by merit*, by virtue of valour in battle. Already, the conflict between Agamemnon and Achilles bears the marks of this tension. Military service at court had always been a legitimate way of gaining princely or royal recognition and of thus acquiring a noble status in Western Europe. But in early modern Europe, the increasing power of sovereigns generated a new tension, which reflected both a power struggle between nobles and kings or princes, and a cultural conflict between martial and courtly values – the tension between 'nobility acquired by virtue of valour in battle' and 'nobility acquired by the princely grace of monarchs' – a distinction between 'native' and 'dative' honour. The martial culture of the swordsmen did not necessarily coincide with the courtier culture of the ruling elite. The role of the warrior was different from the role of the sovereign, prince or king. The interest of the military to cultivate a combative spirit and fight for honour and glory did not necessarily correspond to the interest of the court to cultivate a courtly spirit and be involved in politics.

This tension is acted out in the clash of cultures between the old-fashioned medieval warrior king, Old Hamlet, whose remembrance idealizes the heroic past, and the fashionable Renaissance philosopher-prince, Young Hamlet, whose lack of decisiveness discredits his noble blood and martial heritage. Old Hamlet is religiously pious and chivalrously concerned that women should not be physically harmed, as Kernan noted, whereas Young Hamlet has reasons to doubt religious truths and women's favours alike. The new monarchical order clashes with the old feudal order. The new court culture of a gracious prince clashes with the old martial culture of a warrior baron. Hamlet has to prove that he is a worthy son of his noble father, the legitimate king. He does so by killing the illegitimate king, Claudius. But in doing so, he fails to become the next legitimate king. In fact, he uses his newly acquired royal authority to vote (!) in favour of his violently occupying and thus illegitimate competitor Fortinbras, King of Norway, to become his legitimate successor. Ironically, this revengeful king – nothing personal, of course! – is the one who unrevengefully grants him the burial rites of a soldier and a king. A dead body, Hamlet finally embodies both a warrior and a king.

In the Indian epic, there is no difference between noblemen by birth and noblemen by bravery in battle. One is born into one's caste. 'Indeed, anything superior to righteous battle does not exist for the *kshatriya'*. (*Gītā* 2.31) Thus, one's destiny is to fight and it is defined by nature. Moreover, as Hiltebeitel put it, the epic resists universalization. Every class and context has its own particular *dharma,* which fits its conditions. There is no common human nature or shared universal ethics beyond one's own class. (Cf. *Gītā* 18.41, 45–8!)

What does the relationship between warrior and king look like? The duty to fight and the right to rule are related, but not identical. In the narrative sections, tribal warriors and their tendency to wage personal and limited wars as an honourable means to solve conflicts are prominent. Thapar argued that the notion of 'ideal kingship' is less important in epic literature than the notion of 'legitimate kingship'. In the didactic sections, monarchy is described as the ideal system. Righteous kingship is being idealized. The nostalgically depicted old warrior order with its tribalism and pastoral cattle raids has been lost and replaced by the kingly rule of new empires. A *kshatriya* is a born warrior. His first duty, Biardeau argued, is to be a protector of people, to fight for the sake of legitimate kingship; but also, to fight for the sake of the welfare of the world. In Biardeau's approach, the warrior and the king tend to coincide and culminate in Arjuna. Hiltebeitel and Heesterman stressed the differences between the warrior role and the kingly role. The king has more universal duties than the warrior, having to promote righteousness for every subject, not just for the victorious. Representing the community as a whole, the king draws his authority from beyond the realm of the battlefield, not just from victory in war.

To belong to the warrior class means, initially, to belong to a special community of individuals who are ready to kill and be killed for the sake of the larger community of state and society represented by the king. *Tragic* literature and tragic tendencies in epic literature act out the tensions between individual warriors or the warrior class as a separate group, and the larger community of state and society, represented by the king, *testing* the limits of the values involved. The *core values* at stake are intertwined – *loyalty, duty and self-sacrifice.*

In the *Iliad*, Achilles fulfils the duty of a warrior. He is even the best warrior, and a king in his own right, but 'his' king, Agamemnon does not treat him accordingly, denying him his due share in the war's booty, a woman, Briseis. Agamemnon thus risks a breakdown of the bond of loyalty between the individual warrior and the larger community, Redfield argued. Agamemnon tests the limits of Achilles' loyalty. Achilles refuses to continue his role as chief warrior on the battlefield, thus confirming the rupture between warrior and community. Gill pointed out that Achilles struggles with his loyalty to the warrior community at large (and with his need for personal fame), but not with his loyalty to the king, because he does not consider Agamemnon 'more kingly' than other fellow-chieftains like himself; on the contrary, he denies him his kingly status. In the case of Hector, the other tragic hero, the limits of loyalty are put to the test in a different way. Hector suffers a conflict of loyalties, between the royal chief warrior's duty to fight on behalf of the state and the community at large and the husband's duty to stay alive for the sake of his own family. In Aeschylus' *Oresteia*, it is Agamemnon, instead of Hector, who faces the challenge of choosing between his martial code of honour as commander-in-chief and his family. The pursuit of friendship (*philia*) may lead to different forms of conflict of loyalties. Conflict of loyalties, Blundell explained, arises most readily between the three main classes of *philoi* – familial, civic and personal – whose *philia* is determined by different criteria, and who therefore embody competing types of claim. In Sophocles' tragedies, the distinction between helping friends (*philoi*) and harming enemies is put to the test.

Likewise, the Indian martial value system of duty, loyalty, killing or being killed and the need for sacrifices, is not only presented as a given model, but also subject to question and debate. Thapar stressed the legitimizing function of the epic genre, not its critically questioning function. The narrative issue is, after all, legitimate succession to the throne. Malinar and Hiltebeitel, on the other hand, stressed a crisis of legitimacy. Malinar suggested that Duryodhana represents a new concept of power and rulership that is based on the (centralized state) territory instead of the (ruling royal) family. Counteracting the dangerous aspects of this development, self-restraint and self-detachment were now proclaimed the new warrior values that could transcend the new habits of unrestrained rulers without returning to the old family values of a ruling family system. Hiltebeitel argued that if the martial code of honour is debated, it is in order to critically inquire and question it, and thus develop a new value system for kings.

Whose loyalties are at stake? Arjuna's conflict of loyalties between a relative's *kuladharma*, family duties, and a warrior's *svadharma*, class duties, reminds us of similar loyalty conflicts of Homer's Hector and of Aeschylus' Agamemnon. In Arjuna's case, the conflict of loyalties is transcended by becoming loyal to the one legitimate ruler of the universe, Krishna, according to Malinar. Hiltebeitel portrayed Yudhisthira as basically a tragic hero in Redfield's sense of the word, unlike Achilles, but much like Hector, who remains within his community, but tests the limits of loyalty. Quoting Sutton, Hiltebeitel pointed out that Yudhisthira repeatedly insists on placing moral ethics above those of one's own *dharma*, in particular, the warrior class duties as preached by Krishna to Arjuna in the *Gītā*. The struggle that Yudhisthira suffers from is, then, the structural conflict between the expectation of the community, which depends on protection by its king as a warrior, and the limits of the warrior as a king to meet this expectation in the name of righteousness instead of using violence. In terms of the Indian value system, the warrior and kingly value of *artha* clashes with the kingly and warrior value of *dharma*. According to Heesterman, the dilemma is that the king, in order to exercise power effectively, has to be part of the community and, in order to act with authority, has to be external to it. In his view, kingship in general is not being idealized in ancient India, but considered highly ambiguous, both benignly protective and violently destructive.

2 Male dominance and courage, deeds and speech, violence and self-restraint

All the male heroes are expected to be courageous and dominant instead of cowards and weak or womanlike in situations of danger and conflict. Martial values, such as *manliness* and *courage* (and 'fear of being considered a coward'), are not just Homeric values, but continue to dominate Greek tragedies such as Sophocles' *Ajax* and *Philoctetes*. Manliness is related to an agonistic context, courage to a context of danger, Rosen and Sluiter explained. By definition, cowardice (*anandria*) deserves disapproval, as much as manliness (*andreia*) deserves approval. Its prototypical representative in the *Iliad* is the aristocratic hero who single-handedly and furiously engages with the enemy. Achilles and Heracles are considered the best examples of heroic manliness. Women like Briseis are taken to be part of a warrior's booty. Bassi noted that cowardice is exemplified by historical examples while manliness is exemplified by epic heroes. The sixth- and fifth-century Athenian hoplite, however, has to balance personal against social and political concerns. The classical Athenian citizen's manliness is also defined by economic independence. Struck pointed to the actual continuity between the Homeric battlefield and the Athenian democratic assembly – both remain fields of martial endeavour where peers win recognition for their manliness. Hamlet too, is obsessed with the fear of being a coward ('Am I a coward?' II.ii.568). Claudius discredits his grief by calling it 'unmanly' (I.ii.94). Hamlet's father is presented as a real man, an example that makes Hamlet's manliness seem doubtful. But Hamlet's father displays courtly sensitivity instead of possessive dominance regarding his wife's moral weakness. Women at court have become ladies to their gentlemen. Osric (V.ii.81–179) is the embodiment of the effeminate courtier, an example that makes Hamlet's manliness seem beyond doubt.

The manly courage of the tragic hero consists, in the case of Hector, Oedipus and Hamlet as much as in the case of manly women, such as Antigone and Clytemnestra, in their capacity to endure the unintended consequences of their intended actions and to face up to the suffering from those consequences.

Whether guilty or not, one's tragic response is a courageous response. What if one loses courage? One's condition of suffering from unintentional consequences or undeserved harm would still qualify as tragic, but one's response would not. Neither cowardice nor resignation can qualify as tragic responses if no clear sense of facing up to suffering is held alive. To that extent, there is always an element of mental resistance to evil and suffering in a tragic response, of fully acknowledging that evil is evil and suffering is suffering, even though a tragic response– unlike an angry response – is much closer to passively accepting evil and suffering than to actively resisting them.

Manliness and courage are also crucial to the *Indian* notions of warrior heroism (*śāuryam* and *vīryam* [cf. *vir-tus*!]), as is evident in *Gītā* 18.43:

Heroism, majesty, firmness, skill,
Not fleeing in battle,
Generosity, and lordly spirit
Are the duties of the *kshatriyas*, born of their innate nature.[149]

In the Virātaparvan, it was the main warrior Uttara who suffered an attack of cowardice, but was then instructed by his charioteer (Arjuna), his erstwhile eunuch dancing-master returning to his true warrior nature. In the *Gītā*, it is the main warrior Arjuna who behaves like a coward and a eunuch, unmanlike, according to his charioteer Krishna (2.2–3, 2.31). During his preparation for the war, Arjuna is engaged in austerities (*tapas*). Thus, he becomes a consecrated warrior. To be engaged in austerities in order to gather vital powers is a shamanistic form of asceticism that links asceticism to fertility, male potency and female force (*shakti*) through physical self-control (endurance of abstinence). This form of Indian asceticism is sometimes difficult to distinguish from the mystical form of Indian asceticism, which links asceticism to non-violence. Mahatma Gandhi's practice of non-violence was a combination of both.[150] Arjuna's manliness is also related to his skills as an archer in the agonistic context of having won his wife Draupadī as his prize in a tournament – bow bending as a marriage test is typical of Indo-European literature (cf. *Odyssey*) and includes sexual symbolism.[151] In the epic, the old warrior order, Hiltebeitel noted, is personified in the person of Vrddhakshatra, 'Old *Kshatriya*', in the boastful 'old baron' Jarāsandha, and in the father figure, Bhīshma, dying on his bed of arrows, literally 'the dying exemplar of the old *kshatriya* order', as Fitzgerald is quoted as saying.[152]

How does tragic literature deal with male dominance and the need to cultivate a readiness to face danger? It focuses on the tension between, on the one hand, the courage to face danger and the need and strength to use violent force, and the virtue of self-restraint, on the other. Tragic heroes are involved in highly ambiguous power struggles. In tragedies, those who are in power are not necessarily legitimate authorities whose male dominance need not be justified. In fact, their deeds do not match their claims. Neither Agamemnon in the *Iliad* nor Claudius in *Hamlet* represent the kind of moral authority needed to authorize their dominance. They behave like shameless males who want to dominate at any price, and possess the first lady as their asset. Sophocles' *Oedipus Tyrannus* depicts its hero, Oedipus as a dominant male who starts out as a winner, but ends up as a loser who lacks effective leadership, courage and decisiveness. In the fifth-century context of Attic civil war, the ethical and rhetorical quality of words like 'manliness' is contested. Bassi concluded that philosophical efforts in the fourth century to define the term 'manliness' can be read as a response to its ambiguous meaning in the fifth century.

In Homer, both the skilled use of *weapons* and the skilled use of *speech* are the skills of a man and a warrior, like in the case of Phoenix, who is called 'a speaker of speeches, a doer of deeds'. In the *Mahābhārata* epic, fighting with speech is one recognized form of fighting. One fighting with speech should be opposed with a counterpart who also fights with speech as his weapon.[153] Hamlet too, is skilled in *both sword and tongue*. The recurrence in martial cultures of this combination of manly weapon skills and manly speech skills in military battlefields and public arenas is striking. It does not necessarily indicate historical continuity. In the Indian case, fighting by speech must have had cultural roots in archaic small-scale societies, where the custom of settling a conflict by a public ritual contest of insults is widespread.[154] In the Greek case, Struck was able to suggest such a continuity. In Sophocles' *Oedipus Tyrannus*, Oedipus partly loses recognition for his manliness in the male space of the public assembly because he rhetorically fails to persuade others of his perception of the truth and behaves like an arrogant tyrant. In the early modern English case, as opposed to early medieval times, the discontinuity is evident. Hamlet is being stylized as a Renaissance nobleman, rooted in the revived thirteenth-century chivalric code, with its twin ideals of violence and civility, a self-restrained form of devotion to war and to ladies.

But the limits of both virtues are tested, McAlindon argued. Skilled in both sword and tongue, sensitive both to honour and to love, the code of honour prescribing reckless violence upsets the balance of Hamlet's nature, which simultaneously has to conquer the hearts of the ladies at court – instead of convincing the male peers – by speaking eloquently, writing poetry and loving conscientiously. Hamlet is betrayed by both ideals of the chivalric code. Margolies observed that the royal court betrays a constant slippage between form and content, embodied by the effeminate courtier Osric who, behind his meaningless language, is murderous. Hamlet's verbal virtuosity parries

Osric's hollow language, yet his verbal victory is of no avail. But again, Hamlet is also handicapped psychologically by his self-awareness of playing roles. The masculine role of unrestrained revenger that Laertes is all too eager to take upon him, without second thoughts, is not his. No sooner has he sworn revenge than he decides 'to put an antic disposition on' (I.v.172). Brutus too, in *Julius Caesar*, tries to make acting and being inseparable when he arranges Caesar's murder as a theatrical event. The tension he feels between aping heroic forms and knowing that those forms are, for him, counterfeit, makes him real in a way that no conventionally drawn hero, not even Caesar himself, could ever be, according to Bulman. But Brutus tries at least manfully to identify himself by the heroic forms he enacts. By contrast, Antony and Hamlet admit the disparity between acting or speaking and being.

A crucial difference between the Greek and the Indian uses of speech as a means of exercising authority and wielding the power of persuasion was pointed out by Alles. If applied here, one might argue that a Greek epic warrior depends for his power of persuasion on his successful interaction with others and on his capacity to mobilize existing social relationships, whereas an Indian epic warrior depends for his power of persuasion on his successful engagement in austerities (*tapas*) and on his capacity to mobilize the divine forces of nature. The crucial *Mahābhārata* epic debate on *dharma*, where a woman, Draupadī, challenges Yudhisthira and Duryodhana publicly in the Assembly Hall, is decided neither by male persuasion nor by female persuasion, but by Draupadī's capacity (due to her *dharmic* nature) to mobilize divine forces.

Real men are expected to be courageous, dominant and ready to take up arms. But the use of *violence* should be contained. The use of brute violence always had its limits imposed either by the collective disapproval of the community and the gods or by the authoritative rules of the ruling court, the city state courts and the Church. Achilles' uninhibited pursuit of vengeance in his maltreatment of Hector's body is strongly condemned as a lack of *self-restraint*, expressed in terms of a lack of shame. A god has to intervene in order to keep Hector's body intact. The hoplite virtue of *sōphrosunē* no longer refers to 'prudence' and 'shrewdness of mind', but to 'self-control' and 'moderation'. Aeschylus' *Oresteia* declares an end to the endless cycle of revenge by judiciary means and under divine auspices. The exercise of power through violent force cannot do without law and order. It must be restrained from without and from within. The medieval church had made efforts to limit the greed and injustice of unrestrained violence, but its containment approach had not been very successful. The courts became, Elias suggested, not the cause, but the core of a crystallization process that moulded martial self-understanding along courtly lines and courteous shapes, creating profiles and self-portraits of chivalry, courtesy and civility. The knight who had seen himself as a warrior hero ready to fight for his king now came to see himself as a courtier who remained ready to fight, but who was also a civilized nobleman and a self-disciplined gentleman sensitive to the favours of a lady. By the time of Shakespeare, both Sir Philip Sidney and Hamlet were expected to stylize themselves as embodiments of Renaissance noblemen, sensitive to prowess, honour, duelling, love, art and verbal virtuosity, that is to say, as embodiments of the natural grace of self-discipline, both in matters of war and in matters of love. Claudius even uses the expression 'nobility of love' (I.ii.110).

As pointed out by Dumézil and Katz, Bhima and Arjuna are two different types of warrior. The different manners in which they fight reflect the manners of their divine fathers, Vayu, the Vedic wind god, and Indra, the Vedic war god. Dumézil traces this division back to the hypothetical Indo-European prototype also reflected, for example, in the Greek distinction between Heracles and Achilles. The Vayu/Bhima type of warrior is, according to Dumézil, brutal, amoral and not particularly intelligent. The Indra/Arjuna type is more like a chivalrous knight caught up in a moral web of rules. Arjuna's and Krishna's burning of the Khāndava Forest seems to reflect an ancient heroic ideal – extreme violence in support of world order. The warrior violence in battle is being sanctioned by interpreting it ritualistically as a sacrifice, the 'sacrifice of battle'. It cannot be called *himsā* [violent] if this violence is not for the sake of killing, but intended as sacrifice.

One tragic way of testing the limits of the need to use violence is the introduction of the call for revenge. Revenge combines the need to use violence, the need to display manly courage and the need to restore justice, that is to say, to fight courageously for a moral cause with unlawful means under the conditions of a betrayal of law and order or an infringement on the code of honour. Achilles, Ajax and Hamlet feel wronged and their call for revenge has to cope with these aspects. But revenge is disproportionate by nature, doing damage as much as undoing it. Revenge is doomed to fail to restore the balance. The release of the violence needed tends to violate the need for self-restraint. Ajax does not show self-restraint (shame) in his efforts to physically violate and socially humiliate his 'enemies', especially his 'enemy' Odysseus – but his 'enemy' Odysseus does, in return. Hamlet acquires the manly courage needed, and also the self-restraint that goes with focusing on the target, but the collateral damage resulting from it defies law and order.

In ancient India, the influence of the non-violent ascetic movements of world renouncers, such as the Buddha, is felt everywhere in the epic, but especially in the way Yudhisthira's character is being presented and in Arjuna's refusal to fight. The traditional value of warrior heroism was under critique, Armstrong argued, both in the Greek and in the Indian cases, but not at all in the same way. In the Indian case, the sages of the Axial Age were abandoning their heroic code and reducing the god Indra, the archetypal Aryan warrior, to a lowly Vedic student. Instead, the sages turned to renouncing violence and renouncing the this-worldly realm in favour of the transcendent world. This ideal of non-violence and renouncement also penetrated the warrior class, whose ethos is reflected in the *Mahābhārata* epic.[155] Yudhisthira, especially, refused to interpret warfare as a ritual sacrifice necessary to restore order. He was inconsolable at the sight of its victims. There are innumerable passages in the epic that defend the warrior's vocation to fight and kill, including passages on the dubious role of Krishna, but fundamental doubts remain as to its legitimacy. The Axial spirit, after all, 'desires the welfare of all creatures and of all the worlds'. One of the chief objects of the *Mahābhārata*, according to Hiltebeitel, is to instruct kings and other warriors in how to curb endless cycles of violence, particularly as such cycles effect and implicate *brahmins*. The particular *dharma* of kings must include not only the means to violence, but also the means to its appeasement. The king cannot renounce violence, but must learn non-cruelty. Non-cruelty is non-violence tailored to the duties and constraints of a just king and warrior. It indicates a humanization of the concept of warrior heroism and an ethical cultivation of radical self-restraint. Achilles' and Ajax' maltreatment of dead bodies was strongly condemned as a lack of self-restraint, expressed in terms of a lack of shame. In the *Mahābhārata*, it is Duryodhana's mistreatment of Draupadī's body during the dice game scene that is seen similarly as a shameless lack of self-restraint. Malinar saw Duryodhana as the epic character who represents unrestrained rulership, who sacrifices family ties for selfish interest in power by force. Duryodhana's uncompromising firmness is disqualified as a form of blindness. His lack of self-restraint is a lack of *yogic* virtues, a lack of physical and spiritual self-discipline, and it is a form of greed, of unlimited desire. Krishna's desireless self-discipline, she argued, becomes a core value of the new warrior code. Killingley pointed out that Arjuna's warrior heroism is being transformed by the ideal of the *yogic* person, but that this *yogic* ideal of detachment does not disqualify the warrior heroism inherent in Arjuna's warrior class identity. The concept of warrior heroism is, in fact, being spiritualized, not just ethicized, was my conclusion.

Brodbeck suggested that Krishna's conception of warrior heroism in terms of action without attachment (*asakta karman*) is best understood against its initially military background. What Krishna asks from Arjuna on the battlefield is a certain attitude of single-mindeness in the person acting, without the ordinarily expected payback. Biardeau's account left the strong impression that all intellectual forces have gathered in order for the traditional martial value system to be justified and maintained against the pressures of heterodox ideologies, such as Buddhism, instead of being questioned and criticized.

3 Status, honour and shame

To belong to the warrior class means to belong to a community of honour. The larger community praises and honours individual warriors or the warrior class as a separate community for fighting on behalf of the larger community by committing violent, anti-communal actions, Redfield explained. The fragile relationship between the warrior(s) and the larger community is maintained by honour. The warrior is motivated by honour and, in return for honour, he risks his life for his community. Girard stressed that lack of difference means chaos and disintegration, especially for traditional cultures based on role inequality and social hierarchy. Each time Yudhisthira wants to give up war and his kingship, and renounce this world, he is suspected to be more like a *brahmin* than a *kshatriya*. It is the approval by the *brahmins* that creates legitimacy. The *brahmins* have made ritual status the core of their identity. The particular *dharma* of the warrior class is *artha* ('wealth', 'material interest', 'aim or purpose in general', 'anything good'). The status of a nobleman is connected with the privilege of wealth, but also with the duty to acquire and distribute wealth. *Noblesse oblige*. War for Arjuna is the core of his own duty as a warrior.[156]

Warriors should behave in accordance with specific rules of warrior chivalry. Both sides in the epic have accepted these rules before the war begins. Some similarities with European rules are striking. Homer's and Sophocles' heroes can be beaten by the tongue (public speech) instead of some physical weapon. Hamlet too, beats his adversary, Osric, by verbal virtuosity. Likewise, in the epic, one fighting with speech should be opposed with speech. This rule also reminds us of another striking similarity – warriors fight each other on an individual basis. A chariot warrior is to be fought by a chariot warrior, an infantry man by an infantry man. The competitive dimension in the pursuit of honour and status is not lacking either. One should not kill someone who is unsuspecting or in distress, but only fight an opponent whose equal status is worthy of being challenged. A battle begins between Karna and Arjuna, but it is stopped when it is discovered that Karna cannot claim a noble lineage.

Tragic literature tests the warrior's code of honour. In Achilles' case, the denial of his honour by Agamemnon violates Achilles' sense of honour, of being worthy of publicly privileged treatment and tangible wealth. Achilles' dilemma is status-determined. He has to be competitive, Cairns (and Redfield) noted, and insist on his own greatness while preserving a proper modesty before the community and its co-operative moral standards embodied by Nestor, who mediates in the status competition between Achilles and Agamemnon. But Achilles also blames Agamemnon for failing to be cooperative, generous as a fellow chieftain, Gill observed. Sophocles' Ajax, Cairns argued, is much more extreme in his pursuit of honour than anyone in Homer, far too competitive to be sensitive to the cooperative dimensions of honour. Ajax does not show any shame in his efforts to shame the 'enemies' among his 'friends', whereas his 'enemy' Odysseus does. Sophocles' characters often have only a partial and biased grasp of what values such as 'shame' entail. Neoptolemus is doomed to fail when forced to choose between competitive and cooperative dimensions of honour. Whereas in Homer, 'shame' regarding others (friends, suppliants, guests) is often practised out of concern for the regard of others, in Euripides, it is more often out of concern for one's own honour, Cairns observed. Concern for lofty values, such as honour and shame, is cultivated for selfish reasons.

Due to the instability of Shakespeare's new urban capitalist society, Watson argued, the nobility suffered from status pressure. In a society where status was so unstable, ambition often led to violent revenge, as duels over honour became an epidemic among the aristocratic elite. The duel between Laertes and Hamlet is a case in point. At the Danish court of Elsinore, the code of honour is constantly violated. Margolies described how honour is reduced to form, and the pursuit of honour as one's social role and duty has been hollowed out by individualism. The gentlemen and women 'of worship' have a rank of honour, but lack the qualities deserving of honour.

According to Brodbeck, the Indian epic laments the demise of the old warrior code of chivalry, symbolized by the fact that the Pāndavas are only able to win the war by scandalously breaching the conventions of combat. Unlike Hamlet who, as McAlindon suggested, is being betrayed by the code of honour, the Pāndavas betray it.

Hamlet's circumstances are not just status-determined. Jones was right when he stressed the difference between Aeschylus' Orestes and Shakespeare's Hamlet – Orestes is isolated by his *status*-determined circumstances, Hamlet by his *psyche*-determined circumstances. Only for himself, Hamlet *thinks*, Denmark is a prison, 'Why, then 'tis none to you. For there is nothing either good or bad but thinking makes it so. To me it is a prison'. (II.ii.248–50) The bond that unites the hero with others is violently shattered by personal betrayal, a social cause with psychic effects. Hamlet's social isolation is both status-determined and psyche-determined, but the focus is on the psyche, to an extent unprecedented in the tragic genre. His ironic self-awareness undermines his ability to wholeheartedly embrace the heroic roles of revenger, warrior and king that he is expected to play, not as roles, but as his very duty, right and noble nature. In *Richard II*, the king fails to engage himself with a heroic ethos. Richard's dilemma springs from his failure to be engaged with the roles he plays. His moral concept of kingship is shattered by his ironic self-awareness. Instead of complying with and fulfilling his duty,

Arditi observed, Hamlet becomes aware of the disturbing consequences of taking a role, if everything can be a play and if every 'self' can be an 'actor'.

Neither Bhīshma nor Yudhisthira identifies with his warrior role. Both Richard II and Hamlet spring to mind in their failure to engage themselves wholeheartedly with their roles. Yudhisthira, especially, is prepared to quit his role as king. Krishna, however, sticks to the own duty of Arjuna's warrior role. But Krishna does so in a way strikingly similar to that of Hamlet – by separating the self from its identification with its roles, by practising mental disengagement. The differences are equally striking. In Hamlet's case, mental disengagement leads to social isolation and alienation, in Arjuna's case, to social participation and recognition. Hamlet suffers from his lack of identification with his roles, whereas Krishna envisages a mental state that is beyond role identification and suffering. Hamlet sees his mental disengagement partly as reminiscent of the Stoic ideal of indifference represented by Horatio, but for the greater part, he sees it as his failure to embrace this or any other role, that is to say, as a problem instead of a solution. Krishna sees the lack of identification with a role as the ultimate solution not just on the military battlefield, but on the spiritual battlefield. Hamlet becomes both an actor and a play-actor, Arjuna becomes neither. Both Hamlet's and Arjuna's problems are not just status-determined, but also psyche-determined; Krishna's solution is spirit-determined or self-determined.

Martial values such as 'honour' and 'shame' are core values in martial value systems, but they are not exclusively martial, unless 'honour' is identified with 'bravery' or 'prowess' and with 'victory in battle', and 'shame' with 'cowardice' and 'defeat in battle', as is often the case in Homer's *Iliad,* but not in Greek tragedy in general. This difference between Homer's epic and Greek tragedies suggests a gradual development from a 'results culture', which focuses primarily on visible performances and tangible consequences, to a 'reflective culture', which includes a focus on intentions and problematic additional circumstances. A similar development can be traced in Western Europe, as Stewart explained. Victory in battle remained essential for the maintenance of honour until the Renaissance, when one might preserve one's honour even in defeat. This suggests a gradual development from a focus on outer aspects of honour (power, prestige, reputation, wealth) to a focus on inner aspects of honour (personal integrity, moral virtues, honourableness).

In line with the martial traditions to live and die for honour and glory, Hamlet's name must be established by stories glorifying his name. Horatio is asked to spread Hamlet's noble reputation by telling his story. But, as Lee argued, it is a story *manqué*. In Talbot's case, it is not his reputation that is being recalled, but the story of his reputation that is being recounted. In Hamlet's case, it is neither of them. It is just the story of his court experiences that will be told

(V.ii.343, 373–79) as if court were a battlefield and courtly life a battle, as if acts of revenge for domestic crimes are the same as heroically killing an enemy in battle – an implied, but impossible, similarity in Electra's talk of establishing a reputation for 'manliness' when killing her mother in Sophocles' *Electra*, according to Bassi.

Victory in battle is no longer a source of honour, but a matter of trickery. War itself is criticized as a source of impurity and an evil, instead of being a purifying sacrifice. Bhīshma, himself a warrior-sage and an authoritative grandfather to all warriors involved, argues that even victory in battle is simply an evil.

Despite the universalizing and democratic tendencies in Hindu devotionalism, *Hindu* values tended to remain, to a great extent, status-dependent and caste-dependent instead of becoming all-inclusive and universal. The extent to which the Indian culture was a culture oriented towards obtaining results can be deduced from the fact that one was expected to be identified and judged by the 'fruits of one's action'. Arditi, quoting Worthen, noted that *Hamlet*, among other things, is a play about taking a role. Could the same be said of the *Gītā*? Krishna is repeatedly appealing to Arjuna's presumed sense of honour and fear of shame, while recalling that it is the duty and glory of a warrior to fight instead of incurring evil and disgrace (*Gītā* 2.31–38). But more important are Krishna's references to *yogic* indifference, which make results such as 'victory in battle' something not to be concerned about, 'having become indifferent to success or failure'. (*Gītā* 2.48)

4 Victor and victim in warrior heroism

Epic warrior heroism is normally about brave and harmful actions done to the enemy of the hero and his community. Ideally speaking, the hero is identified as the victor. The name and honour of the hero draw from the winner's perspective of his military success and courage. The Indian epic warrior heroism is, in the first instance, very similar to that in Homer. In their heroic burning of the Khāndava Forest, Arjuna's and Krishna's display of extreme violence is not condemned, nor are their victims deplored. At the heroic level, Katz argued, the prowess of Arjuna, whose epithet is *jaya* ('victory'), brings victory, and victory is what counts in a war. Victory or death is seen as the duty of a warrior (5.133.11).

The one factor that turns the epic hero into a *tragic* hero, in my opinion, is the *shift in perspective from a victor's perspective to a victim's perspective*, from the perspective of gain and harming to the perspective of loss and suffering. In Aeschylus' *Agamemnon*, the Trojan War is an ambiguous case – warrior heroes fight for a just cause (Helena) against too high a price in terms of victims. Tragedy turns victorious heroes into victims who are recognizable to fellow human beings, and therefore something to relate to. The recognition of suffering evokes compassion. At some stage in the epic, Katz suggested, the warrior hero is no longer a sheer victor. Arjuna refuses to fight out of disgust with the destructive side of the war. Unlike the Khāndava Forest battles, the Kurushetra War is a battle against human opponents. In this war, human deceit is worse than divine deceit, according to Katz, because of a keen awareness of the humanity of both perpetrator and victim.

Suffering is not just on the part of the victims. The victim's perspective encompasses both the actor or agent and the one acted upon. The opposition is not between a classical actor identified as a responsible victor who harms others, and a non-actor identified as a victim who undergoes suffering. The tragic actor or agent is a victim of his own action because he brings about unintended suffering. Hamlet is confronted with the necessity to act, even at the price of his own moral contamination, Keyishian noted. There are constellations, however, in which, if a victim falls prey to an aggressor who brings about intentional harm, the victim is still the tragic victim suffering undeserved harm, but the aggressor is plainly malign or morally evil, not tragic. In these constellations, the tragic victim is tragic because he suffers undeserved harm, not necessarily because he reacts by offering a 'tragic response', by facing up to and enduring consciously, by reluctantly accepting as a matter of fact, the reality of the undeserved harm suffered.

Achilles' social isolation has to do with the fact that he is the victim, not just of Agamemnon's shameful treatment, but of his own extreme adherence to the warrior code of honour. He only finds himself again in his grief for the loss of his friend Patroclus, which makes him forget his anger over the loss of his honour. Blundell indicated that Homeric warriors regularly gloat over their enemies– a fate the latter are anxious to avoid. Achilles' 'sweet' anger (*Iliad* 18.109), provoked by injury, stimulates the desire for sweet revenge. But there is also, as Sagan put it, the ripening in Homer's *Iliad* of the feeling of compassion for both sides to the war in which Homer takes no sides between friends and enemies. Remembering his own father, Achilles returns the body of his most hated enemy Hector to Hector's father, Priamus.

The tyrant–victim opposition in Elizabethan tragedy before Shakespeare is too simple to be fully tragic, too close to a categorical tyrant–victim opposition. Hamlet, on the other hand, is suffering from his expected role as a revengeful victor and sees himself rather as a victim of that victor role, 'O cursed spite, that ever I was born to set it right'! (II.i.188–9). Moreover, disappointed in his mother, he is a victim without recourse to justice. As Keyishian pointed out, his very powerlessness turns him psychologically into a potential revenger.

That is to say, even if he is victorious in his revenge, his revenge draws from victimization, his power from powerlessness.

According to Girard, the difference between myth and tragedy is that myth focuses on the sacrifice as a real solution, whereas tragedy, even though the tragic plot will eventually turn to the same solution, is conscious of the violent character of the solution. In the case of *Oedipus Tyrannus*, Oedipus is the king made into a scapegoat of his kingdom. Tragedy unmasks the false difference between 'just' victors and 'guilty' victims by unmasking the 'guilty' victims as the victims of violent (guilty) scapegoating. In Sophocles' *Antigone*, Creon falsely differentiates between the two brothers, and he appeals to a false identity of the unity of the state by founding it on a common violence against Polyneices. Through her public demand for a funerary rite, Antigone stresses the true identity between brothers and sisters, and she protests against Creon's scapegoating (isolating and marginalizing) of one brother only, thus unmasking Creon's policy as an illegitimate effort to build the state and its unity on the immoral violence of scapegoating. The polluted and polluting victim is not necessarily guilty.

The Kauravas, although demonic, suddenly emerge as human victims. The Pāndava case is no longer one-sidedly righteous Their 'enemies' no longer represent absolute chaos or evil. Morally speaking, the Kaurava 'enemies' are hardly to blame. Fate is more to blame, having placed them on the evil side. It is the human opponent who brings out a human reaction in Arjuna. It is, in fact, the war from the victim's perspective, as in the Book of Women mourning over all those warriors killed and all those women left behind, and in the portrayal of Arjuna as mourner of his son Abhimanyu, where Arjuna is seen in the role of victim, all of them recognizing the common humanity of both enemies and friends. The concept of warrior heroism has undergone a dramatic change, from the warrior hero as victor to the warrior hero as victim.

And yet, this is not at all Krishna's response to Arjuna's profound pity (*Gītā* 1.28, 2.7) and eyes filled with tears (2.1). Krishna, 'almost bursting out in laughter' (2.10), admonishes the dejected Arjuna not to mourn for any being (2.11, 2.25–27, 2.30). Instead of teaching Arjuna compassion, Krishna instructs him to disqualify his pity as an unstable and impure emotion – unless it is the unintended and purified by-product of his mental surrender to Krishna's saving lordship over the universe.

Yudhisthira, however, as Hiltebeitel pointed out, had already, after his coronation in Hāstinapura, begun his just rule protecting the women who lost their husbands and sons in battle, as well as the poor, blind and helpless. The highest *dharma* for king Yudhisthira is non-cruelty, related to protecting the war widows and mothers, the poor and blind and to a fellow feeling occurring often with *anukrośa*, to cry with another, to feel another's pain, commiseration.[157]

7

Psycho-ethical aspects

PART I: TRAGIC AND DRAMATIC ISSUES

1 Introduction

A sixth set of aspects that is intimately connected with tragedy is its focus on the moral and psychological weight of human intentions and actions. Different issues related to this set of psycho-ethical aspects will be presented in order to depict the complexity of the matter at hand. The *main question* will be – how are human actions and human intentions linked in tragedy?

In the historical context of ancient Greece, the Greek tragedies were a new literary genre, highly controversial in the beginning for their critical discussion of traditional values and for their courage to explore the moral and psychological weight of human intentions and actions in the (opaque) 'light' of divine intention and action. Since the Greek tragedies do not constitute a homogeneous unity, different interpretations may draw on different plays and put the same issue differently. Some have called Greek tragedy the dawn of moral consciousness in the West, or the dawn of Western will. In what sense?

In the historical context of early modern England, Shakespearean tragedies were part of a wave of plays called 'tragedies' by contemporaries. The category 'tragedy' does not refer to a clear-cut dramatic genre because contemporaries also used the categories 'history' and 'comedy' without always being very specific about the differences between these categories. But again, these plays deal with the moral, psychological and also religious weight of human intentions and actions, though hardly at all with interfering divine intentions and actions, apart from some incidental reference to divine providence.

Shakespeare's *Hamlet* became a key symbol of modern man acting, but lacking action despite intention. Is that rightly so?

For each cultural case – be it Greek, Shakespearean, or (later on) Hindu – similar issues relating to the psycho-ethical aspects will be discussed – 1. The nature of the moral conflict; 2. The nature of the psychic conflict; 3. The relations between action, knowledge, and desire; 4. The degree of self-knowledge.

But we will start this chapter, as another way of introducing the theme, with one general theory of tragedy that is particularly relevant to these issues.

2 K. M. Sands' theory of tragedy

Some of the issues to be discussed have been crucial for defining what tragedy is all about. The inevitability of a moral conflict between two incompatible moral values, the opposition between necessity and freedom, and the tragic error or mistake, are among the most well-known ways of defining the 'tragic' dimension in tragedy. One general theory that explicitly defines tragedy in terms of these issues will be addressed now – that of Sands. Sands' recent contribution is very inspiring, in my opinion. Parts of it were presented in the chapters on narrative aspects (Part I Section 6.1) and literary–cultural aspects (Part I Section 6). Presenting her theory here allows for another insight into the broader scholarly debate among specialists in the field of tragedy studies. General theories of tragedy that are primarily linked to the issue of world views embedded in plot patterns were addressed in the chapter on narrative aspects, while general theories of tragedy pertaining to audience response were presented in the chapter on artistic–communicative aspects. Hegel's 'psycho-ethical' theory of tragedy was explained in the chapter on socio-political aspects.

'Tragedies', Kathleen M. Sands holds, 'record the fundamental contradiction between reality and ideality: life is not as it should be; we are not as we should be. . . . In repudiating some part of reality, some part of ourselves, tragedies convey a prereflective, negative moral judgement'.[1] The difference between tragedies and morality plays, however, is that tragedies convey negative moral judgements about ourselves, the world or the gods without relying upon metaphysical warrants such as divine justice, the natural order, the ultimate Good. Sands defines 'tragedy' as 'the necessity of making moral judgements that are existentially but not metaphysically absolute'.[2] The existential grounds on which to build our lives may not be absolute grounds, they are no less moral grounds. Tragedies are not just about catastrophes, but about *moral catastrophes*. The catastrophes are 'not just of innocent suffering but of innocent fault'. This motif of the 'tragic fault' is a typically tragic notion expressing the ultimate brokenness of the world and of ourselves. The moral imperfection of the world and of ourselves is something we are conscious of, the birth of moral consciousness, but also something we suffer from, a traumatic discovery. Sands describes the fundamental contradiction between reality and ideality (ideals about ourselves, the world, nature, the gods) as 'the birth trauma of moral consciousness'.[3]

There is always suffering in the contemplation of morality because morality is never perfect, and yet, in tragedy, one does not give up on the ideal of moral perfection. Moral perfection or wholeness does not exist. It can only be partial and provisional. We suffer from that insight. The very awakening of our moral consciousness goes hand in hand with a sense of loss. The dawn of moral consciousness is at once the shattering of the moral and rational order in our world and acts. Tragedy is much less a world view than it is a shattering of world views, a loss of belief in ultimate justice and universal order. But tragedy is also the renewed and sharpened awakening of the desire for ideals despite the full recognition of their ultimate loss. Tragedy is not simply an expression of fatalism, resignation and melancholia. It is an affirmation of values. To stand against the world and ourselves is at once to affirm the world and to affirm our value as human beings.

Sands' theory is helpful in highlighting the psycho-ethical aspects of both Greek and Shakespearean tragedy. A closer look at the Greek and Shakespearean material itself is also needed, of course, in order to properly examine the issues raised.

3 Moral conflict

The *Greek* tragic conflicts are not between forces within man himself, Jean-Pierre Vernant argued.[4] Tragedy does not primarily refer to an inwardly torn man, but to a man defined socially and religiously, as a hero representing traditional values under the cultural pressure of a just recently arisen city state. The new literary genre of tragedy has as its main theme *the moral weight of human action*. According to Vernant, participation in Attic politics implied involvement in making decisions but, more than that, it revealed a growing consciousness of being individually responsible for the way city affairs were carried out. Responsibility came to include the intention of the agent or actor; the individual became a legal subject in his own right.[5]

Tragedy marks the dawn of Western will, one may argue. But neither the individual nor his inner life showed enough consistency and autonomy to constitute the modern type of I-conscious subject who is at the centre of his decision making and of his actions. What the ancient Greeks meant by 'intention' remained vague and imprecise. It lacked the hard core of consistency and autonomy that we call 'will'. The very concept of a faculty within the human being that develops a policy by consulting its own willingness and that imposes its decisions by actively determining the external situation had not yet arisen.

Instead, the focus was upon actions. Actions were considered to have a stronger impact than the agents, the agents being the facilitators of the actions that made their impact beyond the grip of the agents.[6] The *results of actions* were considered much more objective than the intentions accompanying them. In Sophocles' *Oedipus Tyrannus* (895: *praxeis*), 'it is the deed that counts, not the motive', R. P. Winnington-Ingram notes.[7] On the one hand, the individual agents were now shown on stage to be engaged in considering options, in weighing the pros and cons against each other, in taking deliberate action, in assuming responsibility, in feeling guilty about committed crimes; on the other hand, they were shown to be exposed to the quirks of fate and the plans of the gods, which turned out to be much more decisive than the powerless decisions of human mortals. Tragedy, according to Vernant, problematizes the human being as acting being (agent or actor), disturbingly interrogating *man's relationships to his own actions*.[8] On the one hand, the tragic agent or actor is guilty since he is the responsible cause of his actions; on the other hand, the tragic agent is the victim of fate and the gods, possessed by a *daimon,* who makes his mind insane. As to the notion of *guilt,* tragedy combines the ancient concept of wrong-doing in terms of blemished mistake, of misstep, of mental derangement brought about by divine contagion, by demonic forces, in the form of a family curse, of blindness or of ignorance, with the fifth-century concept of wrong-doing in terms of conscious mistake, of intentional decision, of deliberate choice. Tragedy combines these two concepts as distinct and often opposing, but inseparable and sometimes collaborating aspects. The tragic notion of guilt is, for that reason, an inherently ambiguous one, much like the notion of human action itself.

I would explicitly extend 'actions' to include 'speech acts', that is, publicly spoken words.[9] Morality is first of all a matter of visibility, audibility and social results. In a context of honour, publicly saying something or leaving something unsaid is nothing less than an act which produces its effect.[10] Both the results of the actions and the reasons stated count, even if the reasons stated do not convince others. Michael Trapp, in his response to Helene Foley's interpretation of *Antigone*, points out that neither Creon nor Antigone nor Haemon succeed in communicating their respective moral convictions.[11] He sees a problematization not simply of civic values and discourse, but of moral deliberation in general, and sets this in turn against a picture of the nature of tragedy that stresses the medium's dedication to 'thinking the uncomfortable thought'.

The *Shakespearean* tragic conflicts are sometimes very much about religious world views, but always about *moral* responsibilities, about the moral and religious status of human action and knowledge as debatable issues to be raised and problematized, not just publicly, but also internally as a psychological debate between one's very own reason, will and heart. The best example remains *Hamlet*. It focuses on the moral and religious weight of human intentions and actions.

The moral weight of human intentions now becomes a complicated matter because both thought and action have as many motives as they have reinforcing consequences. A core element of tragedy is restated in psychological terms. There is a sharpened shift in focus *from human actions to human intentions*. The real *conflict* is not so much between a Christian world view and a nobleman's ethic as it is *between Hamlet's reflections and his actions*, it seems. But Hamlet is facing a moral dilemma, which could be stated in just these terms, as a conflict between a Christian world view and a nobleman's ethic. Hamlet is faced with the conflict between taking revenge on behalf of his father and thereby killing his uncle and being damned eternally for it, and taking revenge on behalf of his father and thereby fulfilling his duty as the loyal son, whose code of honour demands the restoration of justice and the removal of the stain that casts a slur on the reputation of the royal family and the state. In this version, the moral dilemma consists of a conflict between religious and cultural values.

But there are other ways of stating the moral dilemma that Hamlet is facing. One example would be in terms of a comment made by Robert N. Watson, 'Hamlet expresses concern that God has forbidden suicide, but not that God has forbidden revenge. In any case, Hamlet's situation is ambiguous, since he pursues not only a personal vendetta on behalf of his family, which Elizabethan commentators condemned, but also official justice as a prince of the state, which they tended to approve'.[12] In this version, the moral dilemma, or at least one moral dilemma, consists of a conflict between primarily cultural values.

If, however, the moral dilemma is stated in terms of revenge or no revenge, it takes the form of a question – *To act or not to act*, or rather – To act immorally or not to act and be moral. Whichever way you look at it, Hamlet is facing a moral dilemma.

4 Confusing conflict and deliberate response: A matter of knowledge or will

In tragic conflicts, a moral dilemma is easier stated than understood. How exactly do action and reflection interact? How is the (re)action being motivated? What precise role does the intention play, according to Greek and Shakespearean contemporaries themselves?

Vernant stresses the ambiguity of the combination of blemished mistake and conscious mistake and implicitly signals both its continuity and the shift in emphasis from blemished mistake to conscious mistake, from the ancient to the classical concept of wrongdoing. But the classical concept is not the modern concept. The Greek notion of human action is understood, according to Vernant, in a rather intellectualistic way as a matter of *knowledge*, not as a matter of *will*. The Socratic and Platonic idea of wrongdoing as a form of ignorance instead of unwillingness speaks volumes.[13] Wrongdoing is primarily a mistake of the mind, a fatal blindness. For Aristotle, knowledge, like ignorance, depends on external objects being presented to the mind as good or being perceived as desirable for the soul. The crucial point here is that the movement of both the deliberating mind and the desiring wish is caused by an external object or goal that orientates the behaviour of the individual, but does so from the outside. There is no internal faculty spontaneously and autonomously wanting something that may not yet even be there in the outside world, let alone a willpower imposing its own projects by acting them out. The *intentionality* of the tragic agent or actor, then, according to Vernant, is not acting voluntarily or involuntarily, but eagerly (*hekōn*) or in spite of himself (*akōn*). The necessities of internal character and external fate constitute the objective condition of the human soul and mind, allowing no subjective freedom for an independent will to be at the centre of moral decision-making.[14] Nevertheless, a sense of moral responsibility has broken through. But it is much more about necessities and compliance with necessities than it is about freedom of choice and expression.

Bernard Williams, in his discussion of the Greek notion of the *will*, points out both the continuity and the discontinuity between Homer, Plato, Aristotle and the Kantians. Homeric characters certainly have a will to endure suffering and a capacity for deliberation and for self-control. Williams suggests 'that the strangeness of the Homeric notion of action lies ultimately in this, that it did *not* revolve around a distinction between moral and nonmoral motivations'. What Kantians miss in Homer, he suspects, is a Kantian 'will that has these two features: it is expressed in action, rather than in endurance, because its operation is supposed itself to be a paradigm of action; and it serves in the interest of only one kind of motive, the motive of morality'.[15]

Plato, he continues, seems to have invented the idea that the basic theory of action itself is a theory that must be expressed in ethical terms. In this theory, 'the functions of the mind or soul, above all with regard to action, are defined in terms of categories that get their significance from ethics'. Williams writes:

> This is an idea that is certainly lacking in Homer and the tragedians. . . . It seems that once the gods and fate and assumed social expectations were either no longer there or no longer enough to shape the world around human beings, Plato felt it necessary to discover the ethically significant categories inside human nature, and at the most basic level: not just in the form of a capacity for ethical knowledge, as Socrates had already thought, but in the structure of the soul, at the level of the theory of action itself.[16]

In the ethicized psychology of Plato's *Republic*, in his tripartite model of the soul, the only reasons Plato can think of for the soul to act upon coherently, are good reasons, that is to say, moral reasons, rational concerns that aim at the good. They are imposed upon the desires that conflict among themselves, by a distinctive part of the soul that should control the desires – reason. Kantians consider this model a crucial step in the right direction but 'find the(ir) "will" still absent from Plato'.[17] Still absent from Homer and the tragedians is Plato's idea that a psychic conflict between opposite states of mind or desires implies a corresponding division in the soul between opposite parts of the soul.[18] Plato maintains that giving in to temptation is not voluntary (*hekōn*), but forced by the strength of one's appetite, despite having the right opinion that it is bad to give in, Richard Sorabji points out. Aristotle will argue that giving in to temptation is voluntary because no external force is involved, but only a desire internal to the soul.[19] Williams explains that *Homer* uses the words *hekōn,* which very often means 'intentionally' or 'deliberately', and *aekōn,* which means 'reluctantly' or 'against one's will' or 'contrary to what one would otherwise want', that is to say, Homer had a notion of *intention*, and also a notion of action done reluctantly, but not necessarily unintentionally.[20]

Christopher Gill too, clarifies the difference between a Greek and a Kantian understanding of moral deliberation and conflict. In the *Kantian* psycho-ethical model, 'the moral response involves, or implies, an act of "autonomy", or self-legislation, by which the individual agent binds herself to universal principles'.[21] Rational will, the locus of moral agency, is distinguished sharply from desires, impulses and passions. Moral decisions express the kind of rationality that abstracts both from the communal relationship in which the individual agent participates and from those emotions and desires that are not validated by the universal principles that the agent's rationality recognizes. Reason tends to become identified with moral reason, whereas passion tends to be disqualified as non-moral. The Kantian 'weakness of will' is understood to mean 'the failure of rational, moral will to exert its "strength" over emotions and desires'. In the *Greek* psycho-ethical model, *emotions and desires are 'belief-based',* closely interrelated with beliefs and reasoning in the sense of deliberation.[22] Psycho-ethical conflicts, therefore, are not analysed in terms of a conflict between a (weak) rational will and a (strong) non-rational passion, but in terms of a conflict between two sets of belief-plus-reasoning plus the emotions and desires correlated with these respective beliefs. If a conflict is confusing, it is because two sets of belief-plus-reasoning are considered to be clashing.[23] The emotions and desires that go with them are assumed to reflect these competing beliefs. The 'weakness of will' (*akrasía*) is understood to be the internal conflict of someone whose character and reasoning have not been *fully* shaped by the norms of his ethical community.[24]

In the chapter on literary–cultural aspects, we saw that Gill goes one step further than this virtually Greek (*emic*, insider's) way of presenting the matter. He holds the (*etic*, outsider's) view that tragic actions and attitudes are motivated by reflective reasoning about the proper goals of a human life. The tragic conflict is a conflict between conventional (pre-reflective) norms and post-conventional (reflective) norms, between 'first-order' reasoning and 'second-order' reasoning, and between the tradition and potential innovation of the value system they share.

The *Shakespearean* dilemma that Hamlet faces is a confusing dilemma. To act (immorally) or not to act (and be moral), is that the question? The many soliloquies that suggest a strong *appeal to reason* seem to exploit the human capacity for reasoning in order to state and restate the dilemma(s) Hamlet is facing. Like his tragicomic 'shadow anatomist' Polonius, Hamlet is very consistent in his use of logical reasoning.

According to Harry Levin, Hamlet faces *two dilemmas* – the problem of what to *believe* and the problem of how to *act*.[25] The problem of what to believe is raised by the problematic assumption of the traditional belief in ghosts, while the problem of how to act is raised by the problematic assumption of the traditional code of revenge. Whether good or evil prevails in this world seems to hinge on Hamlet's assessment of the Ghost. Whether or not Hamlet should act upon the Ghost's command to take revenge seems to hinge on Hamlet's sense of kin solidarity, which 'runs counter to both the Catholic and Protestant religions'.[26]

Hamlet tries to cope with these and other dilemmas by *reasoning*. The seven soliloquies[27] are as many deliberations of Hamlet with himself, hesitations before alternatives:

The method preferred by Renaissance logicians—which does not differ greatly from the selective procedures used today by so-called mechanical brains—was the dichotomy, which chopped its subjects down by dividing them in half and subdividing the resultant divisions into halves again. The result may be bracketed into a diagram of the sort that we find in Robert Burton or Petrus Ramus. Thus, if we leave aside the unpromising consequences of 'not to be', the proposition 'to be' entails two possibilities: 'to suffer', and—if we flinch from that for the moment—'to take arms . . .' What follows is, once more, a bifurcation. How we may end our troubles by opposing them is equivocal; our opposition may do away with them or with ourselves. This deflects us toward the alternative, 'to die', and if that is truly the end, if death is no more than a sleep, we are back in the dreamless realm of 'not to be'. But if, instead of oblivion, there are dreams; and if those dreams are nightmares, comparable to the worst sufferings of this life; then we are impaled upon the other horn of the dilemma—'to suffer . . .', 'to be . . .'.[28]

The dilemma Hamlet is facing, as stated by the Fourth Soliloquy, appears to be an *ontological or metaphysical dilemma* instead of a moral one – *To be or not to be*. Or does it? The doubter's mode of dialectic, Levin argues, leads him back – through complementary semi-circles – to his binary point of departure:

Hamlet seeks the essence of things in a world of phenomena, where being must be disentangled from seeming; and since the entanglement is a personal one, perhaps a sword is the only means of escape. The ontological question becomes an existential question, and the argument shifts from metaphysics to ethics.[29]

The main dilemma appears to be an *existential dilemma*, about how to deal with life's suffering. The dilemma, as stated by the Fourth Soliloquy, is whether to act or not to act upon 'the slings and arrows of outrageous fortune' and 'take arms against a sea of troubles and by opposing end them'. (III.i.58–60) William Kerrigan and Watson too, point out that the dilemma Hamlet is facing is *whether or not to embrace a Stoic attitude*. Watson suggests that the question 'To be or not to be' may not mean 'Should I commit suicide?', but rather the question Hamlet goes on to consider – 'Should I survive by stoically accepting wrongs, or die performing revenge?'[30] Kerrigan suggests that the night motif stands, among other things, for *revenge*, whereas Horatio stands, not so much for restraint as for *indifference*. But both are *Senecan* in origin.[31] At the time, Stoicism was considered a moral counterforce to strenghten vulnerable heroes whose self-control had to be achieved in the face of the transforming power accorded to the passions, Gail Kern Paster argues.[32] In the play, Hamlet admires Horatio for his Stoic attitude, but:

> Horatio is an onlooker of the tragic action. His constancy and rationality are easily attained—even in such troubled times. For Hamlet, such constancy signifies mostly as a behavioural ideal that he can only admire from a distance. Thus, if Horatio is an exemplar of Renaissance Stoicism, Hamlet himself stands as critique of Stoicism's political relevance and viability in a state founded on usurpation through murder. The passionlessness so admired by the Stoics does not serve as the springboard to action for a son obligated to feel and revenge his father's murder.[33]

According to Paster, 'it would be reductive to read Shakespeare's tragic protagonists merely in terms of a struggle between reason and passion . . . But this struggle did in fact preoccupy the moral philosophers of early modern Europe and helped to set the terms for their understanding of human choice and agency'.[34]

The necessity of taking revenge is likely to include the necessity of building up a sufficient degree of engaged *passion*, of investing emotional energy into the *willingness* to commit a murder. However, this creates the risk of unrestrained passion or rage. Hamlet seems incapable, capable neither of indulging in passionate revenge (reasoning instead of acting) nor of restraining it as soon as it is set into motion (raging like a madman).

Watson points out that the popularity of tragedies of revenge at the time can be understood against the background of the new phenomenon of urban capitalism. Both revenge and ambition are symptomatic of the terrifying instability of the new urban capitalist economic system whose essence was to encourage, but also punish ambition.[35] While referring to Kerrigan, Watson links ambition to a cultural shift in the meaning of the notion of desire. Shakespeare's 'period seems to have invented a new and *inexhaustible* kind of ambition*—and defined it as *fundamental to human nature*. Against a classical and medieval notion of *desire* as finite, seeking its own end in satisfaction, Renaissance culture came to advocate a Romantic and *modern notion of desire as an infinite regress*, willing to invent further goals in order perpetually to forestall its own demise in stasis'.[36]

Thomas McAlindon too, points to the Renaissance conception of human nature, and to the way it differs from the Christian conception, when he stresses that the issue is not about a *vertical* battle between angelic and bestial dimensions of human nature, but about the *horizontal* overflowing of boundaries. Hamlet no longer displays a fine balance of forces within boundaries. His natural capacity for love 'can flow by way of grief into a hunger for revenge that knows no bounds; or by way of jealousy into hatred'. It is the intricate relationship between love and the call to violence and hatred that characterizes Hamlet's *tragic* situation, McAlindon states.[37] His 'instinct for love and compassion', as McAlindon calls it, sheds a revealing light on the limits of *reason* in Hamlet's dealing with revenge. Reason is limited by *feelings* that reason cannot account for. So-called cowardice, justified fear, modest doubt, reason, melancholic thinking, to see feelingly – these aspects constitute that state of mind which, if allied to pity and human kindness, is at the very heart of what is called *conscience*, McAlindon suggests.[38] McAlindon mentions three implications. First of all, the notion of 'conscience' is related to responsibility, not freedom. Secondly, the notion of 'conscience' is related to responsibility to oneself, not to others; it is 'con-science', the knowledge one has of oneself as a witness to oneself. Thirdly, the notion of 'conscience' springs from a combination of reason and love.

Harold Bloom would not agree (or could agree to the permanent loss of Hamlet's capacity to love):

Despite his passion in the graveyard, we have every reason to doubt his capacity to love anyone, even Ophelia. He does not want or need love: that is his lonely freedom, and it provokes the audience's unreasoning affection for him. Shakespeare's wisdom avoided the only fate for Ophelia that would have been more plangent than her death-in-water: marriage to Hamlet-the-Dane.[39]

Is Hamlet's confusing conflict, in the end, a matter of knowledge or of will, of thinking or willing, of reason or passion? A. D. Nuttall concludes that Hamlet's problem is not 'weakness of will', but 'disjunction of the will' – 'The very act of mental willingness has assumed a strangely separate existence and has become disengaged both from the normal corroborative emotions and from action'.[40] Hamlet's reflexive consciousness has destroyed the unity of thought and action. Mental willingness is out-thought and un-done by afterthoughts, and thinking is making Hamlet ill instead of willing.[41]

Nuttall points to Hamlet's role-playing and delivering of melodramatic speeches to himself (such as 'Now could I drink hot blood' [III.ii.390 or 397]) when he is alone, and suggests that 'Hamlet must be using this black-revenge style to practise upon himself'. Whereas for Richard II, role-playing is 'a means of evading action', for Hamlet it is 'a desperate attempt to galvanise muscles that are inert', as Nuttall puts it.[42] This is acting not for lack of action, but for the sake of action: by creating, from the outside in, a real emotion, exactly like the actor who is moved to tears by his own reciting of a speech about Hecuba (II. ii.500–80), not by being possessed by a Greek god.

This rhetorical power of delivering dramatic speeches clearly makes an appeal to the imagination. But in Hamlet's case, the inner world of the imagination becomes a disturbing world apart, a world of thinking in which an imagined reality is hardly distinguishable from unreal dreaming:

Hamlet: Denmark's a prison.
Rosencrantz: Then is the world one.
Hamlet: A goodly one; in which there are many confines,
wards, and dungeons, Denmark being one o'th'worst.
Rosencrantz: We think not so, my lord.
Hamlet: Why, then 'tis none to you. For there is nothing either good or bad but thinking makes it so. To me it is a prison.
Guildenstern: Why, then your ambition makes it one. 'Tis too narrow for your mind.
Hamlet: O God, I could be bounded in a nutshell and count myself a king of infinite space, were it not that I have bad dreams.
Rosencrantz: Which dreams indeed are ambition. For the very substance of the ambitious is merely the shadow of a dream.
Hamlet: A dream itself is but a shadow.
Rosencrantz: Truly; and I hold ambition of so airy light a quality that it is but a shadow's shadow.
Hamlet: Then are our beggars bodies, and our monarchs and outstretched heroes the beggars' shadows. Shall we to th'court? For, by my fay, I cannot reason.
[II.ii.243–64][43]

Hamlet's reasoning is, in fact, superior to anything Rosencrantz and Guildenstern can think of. They basically postulate the inexhaustible desire of ambition, which starts out as an unrealistic dream that can never be satisfied. Its materialization can only be a pale shadow of what an ambitious man had set out to achieve. Hamlet postulates that there is something really rotten in the state of Denmark. What is bad about Denmark is objectively bad if measured according to the Stoic confident world view of having to live a personal moral life in an impersonal rational cosmos. Stoically speaking, living a moral life means living according to the laws of nature that reason enables you to distinguish. The line 'For there is nothing either good or bad but thinking makes it so' (II. ii.248–9) is originally meant to express reason's capacity, if free from passion, to distinguish between good and bad. It is a Stoic commonplace instead of an expression of ethical relativism. 'But', Nuttall argues, 'when Hamlet appropriates Stoic language to himself, all this [confidence in the objectivity of reason and of a moral universe] is gone'. Stoicism is subjectivized. The exertion of reason becomes 'a way of denying rather than truly representing reality' – 'Hamlet means that *he* can see that Denmark is a wicked kingdom in which he is confined. Denmark is bad. But then whimsically he allows that this should be a subjective view—others might assess the situation differently'.[44] Hamlet struggles with the epistemological difficulty of separating dream (unreal 'shadow') from reality. His highly imaginative, but sceptic thinking haunts him like a nightmare. The inner world of subjective assessments drifts away from the outer world of objective hold, from the inside out when the passionate dream of ambition turns into a pale shadow of itself in reality, and even more so from the outside when reality itself turns into a dream, and a bad dream at that.

From this section dealing with the role of desire, passion, will, intention, beliefs, reasoning and confusion in the process of facing a moral conflict, it has become clear that the moral conflict is also experienced as a psychic conflict. But in what terms did the Greeks and the Elizabethans perceive a moral conflict to be a psychic conflict? Was there a coherent vocabulary at their disposal to describe the psychological aspects of human nature and decision making?

5 Psychic conflict

5.1 The vocabulary for attitudes of mind and heart

The ancient Greek vocabulary for attitudes of mind and heart does not constitute a system of categories. Crucial to its understanding is the perception of the emotions or feelings in relation to normal consciousness, as Ruth Padel summarizes eloquently:

> Emotion is something coming at you from outside. When thought of physiologically, emotion is air and liquid bubbling within, swelling the entrails. Emotions do not belong to individuals. They are wandering, autonomous, daemonic, outside forces. . . . Greek tragedy represents normal consciousness as an inner and outer multiplicity. You experience feelings as you experience the nonhuman outside world: gods, animals, the weather coming at you, random and aggressive. Feelings are other in self. Your own inwardness, the inner equipment with which you feel and think, is multiple too. This equipment, like your feelings, is in some sense divisible from you. In Homer, someone's *thumos*, spirit, "commands" him to act. You may act "willingly with an unwilling *thumos*." In tragedy too, innards

can be differently impulsive from their owner. They may know more. They sing or prophesy. They move, tremble, knock against each other. "Heart kicks *phrēn*".[45]

'Tragic language presents all emotion as inner movement', Padel explains. 'Greek poetry speaks of passion, especially anger, as dark boiling turbulence: an inner storm darkening the innards. . . . Organs swell and blacken in passion'. Passion is an intensification of consciousness and its darkness. Passion can take the form of anger, rage, fury, madness, because passion disturbs the normal emotional state of mind.[46]

My earlier emphasis on action and public expression of reasons as opposed to psychological character and supposed motive should not lead to absolutizing the opposition, however, in the sense that one only needs to account for actions, effects and explicit reasons, as if motives were lacking if not explicitly stated. In fact, in tragedy, the characters on stage who judge each other by their respective reasons and by the effects of their acts, go beyond that by claiming that they understand the minds of the persons involved well enough to make their judgements whereas this claim is often denied or neglected by others, as Goldhill points out. What goes on in the minds of the characters is something the characters themselves argue about. The public, masked personae of tragedy do not suggest a Victorian novelist's focus on idiosyncrasies of personality, but 'there is a considerable focus on the words which express an internal existence, attitudes of mind, disposition' of these personae.[47] The term for attitude, *phronema*, derives from *phronein*, which in *Antigone*, 'moves from "to be of a particular disposition of mind", to "to think" and "to be wise" '. But, Goldhill suggests, how the term is meant to be taken depends on its appropriation by the respective characters, who use the term strategically to oppose the accusations of others as to their states of mind, or use terms of attitude, such as 'senseless' and 'mindless', strategically to position the actions of oneself and others. In Goldhill's view, there seems to be no stable vocabulary of mind and attitudes in Greek tragedies because such a vocabulary is itself used strategically by the characters in order to blame and fight each other, for social purposes, not for the purpose of picturing interiority.[48]

The *Shakespearean* vocabulary for attitudes of mind and heart seems fairly stable because it draws on the classical *physiology of humours*. Hamlet calls himself 'a dull and muddy-mettled rascal' (II.ii.564). The expression 'co-mettled' suggests low birth and betrays its rootedness in the Elizabethan physiology of humours – blood (passion) and judgement (reason) are not equally co-meddled.[49] The Elizabethan physiology of humours goes back to that of classical antiquity. Good blends are produced by the right food, drink, climate and daily activities. Galen (129–*c.* 210 CE), quoting carefully selected passages from Plato, Aristotle and Hippocrates, applies the thesis that psychological capacities follow bodily blends not only to the intellect, but to emotional traits and to emotions.[50]

The part of the humours theory best known is the classification of emotional traits into four types – choleric, sanguine, melancholic and phlegmatic. This classification of emotional traits in physiological terms relates the humours to the four elements in the ancient Greek understanding of nature – fire, water, earth and air. Fire (hot and dry) would be associated with being furious – the choleric temperament (hot-tempered; irascible; *cholē*, bile; *cholas*, intestines; *cholos*, anger, resentment; *cholera*, illness of the bile). Water (cold and moist) would be associated with being torpid or sluggish – the phlegmatic temper (detached; very calm; *phlegma*, mucus or slime causing diseases). Earth (cold and dry) would be associated with being down – the melancholy temper (depressed; *melas*, black, plus *cholē*, bile). Air (hot and moist) would be associated with being fiery and combined with too much blood – the sanguinary temperament (violent; *sanguineus*, bloody, blood-rich); 'sanguinary' (violent) is not the same as 'sanguine' (cheerful, lighthearted). A perfect balance between these physical substances or fluids would guarantee harmony, that is to say, health, and being 'good-humoured' or 'in a good humour' instead of 'ill-humoured' or 'in a bad humour'.

Hamlet too, when he refers to his emotions and states of mind, refers to them in terms of bodily fluids and humour, such as a cold and bloodless liver and a lack of bitter choleric humour – 'For it cannot be/But that I am pigeon-livered, and lack gall/To make oppression bitter' (II.ii.573–4). Even his statement, 'But I have that within[,] which [sur]passes show' (I.ii.85) should be understood, Paster suggests, to refer to a *corporeal* interiority. Paster argues that *the modern separation of the psychological from the physiological had not yet occurred* when it comes to the language of self-experience.[51] Paster, in fact, uses the same metaphors as Padel to describe 'inwardness' in terms of 'embodiments' – 'In a model of the human body expressing the cosmos, emotions cross the bodily interior as winds cross the earth. They are part of the material substance of a self continually moved and threatened with change by forces within and without the body'. There is 'a correspondence between inner and outer, body and cosmos, emotions and weather'.[52]

5.2 *Reasoning and madness*

Tragedy is deeply concerned with decision making. In all the extant plays of Aeschylus, a decision is central, N. J. Sewell-Rutter notes.[53] Certain plays focus on the deliberations explicitly revealed or debated before the decisive act itself: Aeschylus' *Seven against Thebes* and *Agamemnon*, Sophocles' *Ajax* and *Philoctetes* and Euripides' *Phoenissae,* among others. Deliberation is crucial. And it is linked to *reason*. Reason can be a tool for cruel and perverse action. Yet, it can compel an audience to feel compassion, Karen Armstrong argues. She draws attention, first of all, to *the dark side of reason* itself, as put on stage in 431 BCE, when Euripides' *Medea* was presented at the City Dionysia.[54] In revenge, Medea killed Jason's new wife, his father and the sons Medea herself had borne Jason. But unlike former heroes, Medea was not acting under the orders of a god; she was driven by her own stringent reason. Reason was becoming a frightening tool. It could, if skilfully used, find cogent reasons for cruel and perverse actions. After all, for the Greeks, logic was not coolly analytical, but fraught with feeling. Armstrong then draws attention to the Greek discovery of *the humane side of reason*:

> Reason could compel an audience to feel compassion for people who might seem to have no claim on their sympathy. Euripides continued the tragic tradition of reaching out empathically to the 'other', even towards Medea and Heracles, who had committed such unspeakable acts. At the end of *Heracles*, Theseus offered the polluted, broken man his sympathy. When he led Heracles offstage, the two heroes had their arms around each other in a 'yoke of friendship', and the chorus lamented 'with mourning and with many tears. . . For we today have lost our noblest friend.' These words instructed the audience to weep too. This was Dionysian *ekstasis*, a 'stepping out' of our ingrained prejudice and preconceptions to an act of compassion that, before the play, might have seemed impossible.[55]

Deliberation in tragedy is also linked to *madness*. Sewell-Rutter explains how Aeschylus' treatment of Eteocles' decision is very different from Euripides' treatment. Euripides highlights the brothers' consent, instead of one man coming to a self-destructive decision. Is Aeschylus' Eteocles mad? According to the Chorus, he is in the grip of 'wrathful spear-raging infatuation' (686–7) and 'a savage desire' (692). He and his house are beset by 'Erinys' (699–700) and 'a *daimon*' (705). The family curse is palpable, and divine causation is everywhere. Is it a god (*daimon*) that motivates his decision? Eteocles 'identifies five reasons for facing Polyneices' (653–719), three entirely human motivations and two divine ones. The divine motivations (Apollo hating his family, and his father's curse) 'are not threats or oracles or prophecies of the kinds that press upon Agamemnon' (at Aulis) 'and Orestes' (who steels himself). His decision is very different from theirs. No one, man or god, is pushing Eteocles, except Eteocles himself. He must face his brother, both because of his father's inexorable curse and because of his character. He does not express a free will, but displays 'a curiously voluntary compulsion', as Sewell-Rutter puts it:

> The compulsion under which Eteocles labours is neither more nor less than the compulsion of his being Eteocles, son of Oedipus, and grandson of Laius. Neither here nor in the other passages that we have considered is there any trace of a problem of free will that would be recognizable to the modern philosopher. What we have found, however, is a delicate and intriguing play of subjective and objective necessity—of *constructed* necessity. Eteocles, like other tragic characters, makes his compulsions for himself in a process of appropriation.[56]

To ascribe an emotional impulse (like self-blinding) to a *daimon* or god is commonplace in Homer and Aeschylus. But, Winnington-Ingram points out, in Sophocles' *Oedipus Tyrannus*, Oedipus' self-blinding is unprophesied by Apollo's oracles. Yet, Oedipus ascribes his self-blinding to his own hands *and* to Apollo as its actor (1329–31). This is, according to Winnington-Ingram, not because Apollo represents divine foreknowledge of what is destined to happen, but because of Apollo's link with self-knowledge. On Apollo's temple was inscribed the motto *gnothi sauton*, 'know yourself'. Apollo is the divine power (*daimon*) that presides over Oedipus' self-discovery.[57]

The tragic conflict is often put in terms of an argument (!), of pro and contra arguments between antagonists like Antigone and Creon, or Oedipus and Tiresias. But reason seems as unsettled as the conflict itself since the argument easily turns into anger or even madness. How do reasons and intentions relate to the psychic conflict as a disposition of mind?

Williams discusses Telemachus' mistake of leaving a door open and Agamemnon's claim that the gods intervened by making him *mad* for a while. Telemachus was in a *normal state of mind* when he made his mistake; he was his usual self and can be held responsible for things he did unintentionally; Agamemnon too recognizes that his action was the cause of what happened; that is why he must make up for it; but he claims that when he took Briseis from Achilles intentionally, he did so in a blinded state of mind; he was not his usual self. Agamemnon is not dissociating himself from his action, but dissociating his action from himself (from his usual self). Williams concludes that cause, intention, state of mind and response are the basic elements of any conception of responsibility, and that there are many ways of interpreting and relating them.[58] Normally, cause and response are linked according to the rule that the response should be applied to a person whose action was the cause of the harm. In the case of *Oedipus Tyrannus,* the act of killing Oedipus' father, the cause, had attracted pollution, a supernatural effect, in the form of Thebes' pestilence; the person who had *done* the killing had to be killed or banished simply because he *did* it. In modern societies, supernatural effects will be left out of the judicial consideration, but the link between action and response will be taken into consideration. In the case of *Oedipus at Colonus,* the terrible thing that *happened to* Oedipus, through no fault of his own, was that he *did* those things, Williams points out. The Chorus' response was pity, 'aroused not just by what he later suffered but by what he did'.[59]

Oedipus' response of blinding himself was self-imposed, not an act of duty or obligation, but of regret. 'There are two sides to action, that of deliberation and that of result, and there is a necessary gap between them', Williams states. 'It is in the nature of action that an agent's regret cannot be eliminated by partitioning one's life into some things that one does intentionally and other things that merely happen to one'. 'Regret must governed, in good part, by results that go beyond intention'. Oedipus thereupon blinds himself, but later thinks this act was excessive, Ajax commits suicide, and Heracles too, having killed his children in his madness, chooses suicide. But in Euripides' *The Madness of Heracles,* he is talked out of it, sustained by 'the friendly support of Theseus and by the thought that suicide was a form of cowardice'.[60] The tragic responses of the responsible agents remain *open to debate,* Williams concludes.

Goldhill points out that the focus on transgression in and through particular states of mind is especially important in Sophocles.[61] Sophocles' depiction of Ajax' *madness* on stage, and Ajax' 'deception speech', which leads the Chorus and Tecmessa to think that their lord has given up his intention to suicide, are striking examples of Williams' conclusion that the tragic responses remain open to debate – both Ajax' state of mind and the relation between mind and action are questioned. Ajax' state of mind is questioned because it is difficult to reconcile the different descriptions (in the play) of Ajax' mind into a single consistent picture of previous sanity, temporary insanity, and later recovery, and in terms of the interrelations of madness and sight. Also, the responsibility of the goddess Athena, the external control of Ajax' mind, is set in tension with the extensive vocabulary of internal decision-making (Vernant's definition of 'tragic man'). Ajax' 'deception speech' contains lines whose meaning is ambiguous and obscure when spoken by Ajax, but understood as transparent and univocal when listened to by the Chorus.[62] 'Access to Ajax's mind', Sewell-Rutter agrees, 'is constantly problematized. Is Ajax sane at any point, and if so, when? But above all, . . . what is he going to do next?' Speculation about his state of mind is 'of paramount importance' because 'it is on this deliberation . . . that the fortunes of so many others depend'.[63]

Madness (*mania*) is seen in terms of excessive passion and violence, divine hatred and punishment, pollution and skin disease, Padel explains.[64] Passion has a disturbing impact on both mind (*phrenes* or *phrēn*) and behaviour. Passion, especially anger, distorts one's mind and makes one act badly. Passion, like divinity, changes things, inside and outside, and both in Greek tragedy and in Greek medicine, change is seen as a cause of suffering. Madness is not seen in the nineteenth-century fashion as a secret presence, latent and individual to the self, but as *a visible, temporary and disturbing invasion* of the normal state of mind and the innards by some external force whose disturbance of the emotions has a violently striking effect on the mind and behaviour of the person.

The inner movement of a disturbed mind consists of wandering astray, off-track, displaced, out of its right place, 'out of his mind', Padel continues. Madness is violent inner movement that involves inner damage and loss of control. Simultaneously, the outer movement of a mad person like Io is forced into wandering, embodying the connection between mad and abroad, as opposed to sane and home. Madness takes place outside the community, in isolation, alienation and loneliness, losing home or not being able to return home. The outer movement of a disturbed mind initiates a perverted view of things and crime. The inner movement and the outer movement run parallel, she points out. Both are movements aside and astray, de-viations, de-railments, de-lirious (*de*, 'out of', *lira*, 'the furrow'). These movements take place in the mind *and* in the body. The *ekstasis* ('being out of place', 'stepping out') is a 'stepping out' of normal sense and behaviour. It is not a shamanic soul journey for the sake of healing, or a mystical ecstasy for the sake of reunion of the soul with the divine. *The soul does not depart from the body. Both depart from the right place.* Greek madness does not separate mind and body, but dislocates both within their own socio-mental and socio-physical landscapes. The mind does not leave the body and wander somewhere else, Padel explains. What happens is a restless wandering of mind and body, both lost in their respective landscapes.[65]

Madness is dangerous. Even more so than passion and divinity, it threatens the boundaries between the human and non-human. Madness is a contagious sign of destructive divine attention that may itself attract further destruction and pollution. Madness is like a (temporary) disease, a plague spreading and attracting divine anger. Where contact is intensely important and also potentially contagious and damaging is not in sex but in hospitality, Padel observes.[66] Madness and disease have physical as well as divine causes and cures. In the fifth century, physiology is inseparable from daemonology. Feeling is represented as the movement of liquid and air inside, and as the movement of *daimon* in you. Madness is black angry inner flood and is caused by the gods.

Being caused by the gods, madness may also become Cassandra's or Dionysus' bacchic gift of prophecy. Madness is related to blackness, darkness, blindness, perverted vision and loss of consciousness, but it may also be related to sharpened sight, true vision, heightened consciousness. Whether one sees truly in madness depends on the gods' intention in sending the madness. Seeing what normal people cannot see is shared by madmen and prophets alike. But no one in tragedy *wants* to see daemons like Erinyes (Orestes) or Dionysus as a bull (Pentheus). No one wants to be mad, to see madly. No maddened person gains from his relations with divinity.[67]

Madness plays a crucial role in Greek tragedy. Padel explains why. First of all, *madness articulates the issue of cause and effect*. Madness has two possible stages – it may cause crime, or punish it. The so-called *atē*-sequence is Homeric background to tragedy's uses of madness. *Atē* means 'harm', 'damage'. Its function in Homer is to invoke a damage-chain.[68] Harm as cause is connected to harm as consequence. Together, they constitute a sequence of causal damage causing damage. The inner unseen harm (mind damage, erring mind) – which may be caused by divine anger – causes the outward, visible harm (error, crime) – which may cause divine punishment. Whereas Homer uses the damage-chain to articulate the ambiguities of cause and effect, tragedy uses madness, Padel argues. Tragedy bases its whole structure on the damage-chain (*atē*-sequence), enacting and exploring the world-damage damaged minds do. Madness in Greek tragedy may cause crime, or punish it, because it is *violent* damage, to mind, to outward appearance, to behaviour. Violence is generative, ripples out, begetting more of itself, moving from violent mind to violent act, and on to larger destruction.[69]

Secondly, *madness articulates the issue of truth from pain*. Madness produces truth out of pain. The pain is physical agony, grief, or simply being on the point of death. An Athenian slave's testimony was not believed unless he was tortured. Physical pain also accompanied prophetic possession. The innards were 'knowing' and 'prophesying' (cf. entrails divination).

Thirdly, *madness articulates the issue of truth from abnormality and illusion*. Truth comes from the edge of the normal, where people do not usually go, only extra-vagant and ec-centric people, and where illusion and reality meet and clash, such as in the theatre.[70]

Madness plays a crucial role in *Dionysus*' theatre. Tragic madness mirrors three of *his* aspects, Padel argues.[71] First, his *violence*. Dionysus connects the interior violence of madness with violence performed on stage (cf. Seneca!) and in the world. Second, his interest in *illusion, disguise, mask*. Madness involves taking illusion for reality. Feigned madness is another feature of *both*

Greek and Renaissance tragedy. Even Odysseus feigned madness to avoid the Trojan war draft. Hamlet's madness, interpreted as proving him 'mad for love', is tested. What he told Ophelia 'was not like madness'. Once it is seen through, Hamlet is in danger, Padel suggests. Third, his *outsider status*, being a foreign god of wild madwomen on mountains.

For Greek tragedy, madness was a curse, 'an imposition from outside'. For the *Renaissance*, 'the *outstanding* person has special blackness *within'*, Padel explains. First, within. 'Madness is something wrong within, not from outside. You must get it out: purge the black bile, exorcise the demons'.[72] Then, outstanding. Humanist writers on melancholia, like Ficino, Montaigne and Burton, introduce the *new* idea that black Saturn, the source of madness, is in fact also the source of *genius*. All great men are melancholics. Their internal darkness, their black bile, has to be seen, from now on, as *a potential for* bestial madness, badness and *human greatness*. Padel writes, with Marlowe's *Doctor Faustus* in mind:

> Tragedy had to deal with blackness, inside and out, the black of badness and madness, and did so brilliantly. It is the color of *Hamlet* and *Macbeth*. But black was tragic differently now: it marked a potential for greatness. The black of broken potential, lost personal greatness, belongs with our chaotic ideas of the tragic today, but it was Elizabethan tragedy, not Greek, that brought it about, exploring the blackness of human potential lost.[73]

In Shakespeare's *Hamlet*, Hamlet's appeal to *reason* may be straightforward in his soliloquies, in his behaviour, it is highly ambiguous, since he has decided 'to put on an antic disposition' (I.v.172). Is his antic disposition a sign of *madness*, or is it a cover-up of a motif beneath the surface of his behaviour, that is, a sign of strategically hiding his plotting of revenge? Claudius is not convinced by Polonius' diagnosis that Hamlet is mad. But he uses it for political purposes as an excuse to have him removed from the court – a matter of national security. This political use is, in fact, a response in kind to Hamlet's own political use of madness as a way of protecting himself against Claudius' attempts to find out what Hamlet knows. Levin argues that it is feigned madness, but that real madness, as the abandonment of reason, is a constant danger throughout the play.[74] When Hamlet takes off his antic disposition, in the Closet Scene, it is difficult for him to convince Gertrude that he is sane.

Both positions *could* easily be reduced to a *comic* level – the plight of the man who is generally misunderstood and the pose of the man who deliberately invites misunderstanding, Levin continues. *Hamlet* abounds in what – if it were an Elizabethan comedy – might have been designated as errors or suppositions, misconceptions contrived and coincidental. Even the Ghost raises the question of a possible disguise, and Polonius dies a martyr to mistaken identity.[75] Taking the comic level seriously as one aspect of the play, and arguing from the comic perspective, Levin arrives at the conclusion that this play too, like the others that Shakespeare was writing at this period, has its *fool*'s part; and, in view of its pervasive concern with death, it seems appropriate that this particular fool should have been dead and buried for 'three-and-twenty years' – the skull personifying Yorick, the late king's jester. Conspicuous by his silence, it is Yorick's skull that becomes a mark of identification for Hamlet. In fact, 'in his mortal absence, his former playfellow wears the comic mask. Hamlet . . . becomes *a court jester*'.[76] 'Hamlet', Levin concludes, 'is re-enacting the classical *eiron*, the Socratic ironist who practises wisdom by disclaiming it. More immediately, Shakespeare was dramatizing the humanistic critique of the intellect, as it had been propounded by Erasmus, to whom life itself was a kind of comedy', and to whom self-criticism was a premise that enables man to criticize others because the fools think they are wise, but the wise man knows himself to be a fool.[77]

Bert O. States approaches *Hamlet* from the point of view that humans perceive 'character' in things, and especially in fellow human beings.[78] Character is not identical to the total sum of character traits, but to the way these character traits hang together.[79] In Hamlet, the pattern of behavioural change is more radical than in any other Shakespearean character. Hamlet tends to store energy and release it, like a simple condenser, as States puts it. Hamlet's *melancholy* is something brought on by (recent) events: 'I have, of late, but wherefore I know not, lost all my mirth' (II.ii.295–6). The condition of melancholy explains Hamlet's moods swinging 'back and forth' from intense excitement, anger, or irascibility – in a word, cruelty – to deep depression. The condition of melancholy is a dysfunction or illness that the Elizabethans would approach medically as a poor mixture of the 'body humours'.[80]

States is not the first and only author to have come to this conclusion. A. C. Bradley had already explained Hamlet's self-absorbed (no Ophelia in his monologues!) wavering, bitterly self-reproaching and sudden self-reasserting attitude in terms of melancholy.[81] According to States, in the Elizabethan idea of a mixture of body humours, the *sanguine–melancholy polarity* represents the extremes of mental 'motivation': stability and instability, health and sickness.[82] Melancholy is the primary response to the loss of a sanguine faith in the accountability of the world. What States is suggesting here is that the Elizabethans, and the Greek ancients before them, did not take the harmony between the four humours as the ideal norm for health, but privileged the sanguine as the principle of health through which deviations from the norm can be ramified.[83]

If melancholy is the primary response to the loss of a sanguine faith in the accountability of the world, Hamlet is the melancholy character who lost his original sanguine character before the plot has him enter the stage. Ophelia's lament (III.i.153–63) describes Hamlet's character then and now, and the gap between the two.[84] In his advice to the players, what Hamlet is preaching in his master-class on acting (III.ii.1–53) does not simply represent a Renaissance theory of acting, but a manifestation of his original sanguine character. Horatio becomes a 'shadow' Hamlet, the visible sign of Hamlet's sanguine self. Hamlet makes a good actor, putting on the antic disposition. But 'there is a *confusion* in Hamlet: the antic disposition is both put on and not put on, at once a device and an outlet'. This confusion is due to his melancholy, which acts out his nostalgic effort to restore 'his distance from the world and, more importantly, from his own social self, or the part of his identity that he can never inhabit again: the sanguine side of his disposition'.[85]

'A good part of his stage-life consists in defining the sanguinity of the nature around him against the deep loss of his permanent exile from it'. Or rather, States observes, it consists in anatomizing it. 'Hamlet is a *melancholy anatomist*, animated by *a struggle of reason and madness, order and fragmentation*— driven, on the one hand, to define and to "set down" in his tablets "all the uses of the world" and, on the other, to chaos or suicide'. Anatomy reduces a body to order by turning it into a heap of fragments; anatomy is 'a paradoxical strategy for revealing order that actually "decays" order in the process', as Devon Hodges has it (according to States). Anatomy and melancholy are both an effect of loss – the loss of meaning, constancy, coherence, truth, love. 'A melancholy sense that something is lost propels a desire to conduct an anatomy' which itself, in turn, creates loss. The melancholic anatomistically searches the world for what has been lost in a way analogous to the fury with which one might recognize everything in the house while looking for the car keys – reason chasing madness, and vice versa.[86] In anatomizing the world, States observes, Hamlet has a 'shadow' Hamlet very different from Horatio – Polonius, known for his long-windedness and his spying. 'If Claudius is given to the oxymoron and Hamlet to the pun, Polonius' characteristic verbal strategy is *enumeratio*', thereby 'reducing a body to order by turning it into a heap of fragments'. (Ironically, it is Polonius who, in his unequalled enumeration style, gives a strikingly accurate description of Hamlet's melancholy, that is, of the general stages in a depression and its consequences!)[87] But Polonius does so compulsively and carries it 'monomaniacally into the conduct of daily life until he dies of it'. He literally shadows Hamlet, 'and in shadowing him falls into a thematic parody of his own habits. For Polonius' indulgence in wordplay—in "art" at the expense of "matter" (II.ii.95)—is but the comic prolongation of Hamlet's philosophical wordplay and scruple hunting, or "thought" at the expense of "action"' and 'advancement' in meaning, States suggests.[88] But whereas Polonius is a tragicomic figure stabbed to death through the fatal character flaw of his obsession with spying, Hamlet is a tragic figure. His difficulty is that in anatomizing the world, 'he confronts the entire range of value and can, until the end, find no clear place in it for himself'.[89] Hamlet's difficulty (in States' version of it), is his very tragedy, and it is a psychic one.

6 Self-knowledge

The previous sections have shown the disturbing extent to which tragic conflicts are psycho-ethical in nature. One wonders whether, faced with such psycho-ethical conflicts, tragic characters will ever gain some form or degree of self-knowledge from their traumatizing experiences. The issue of self-knowledge will be explored briefly in this section.

Moral achievement relies on both action and reflection. Moral choices demand deliberation and conscious reflection, that is, a certain *degree of knowledge*. But human vision does not have the power to establish certainty. Tragic knowledge is constituted by the recognition that *reason faces its limits* when confronted with the blinding excessiveness of passionate madness, but also when confronted with the lacking, on the part of finite mortals, of a complete overview of their destinies and the workings of time. Absolute knowledge is clearly beyond human reach.

Redfield claims that 'the central ethical' (not 'moral' in the sense of choosing between good and evil!) 'problem of the hero is thus a problem of rational knowledge: the hero must continue to act while guided by an exact awareness of how little of his action is truly his own'.[90] It is the special privilege of the tragic hero that he meets his own limits (death) in the fullness of reflective self-knowledge.[91] This holds for both Hector and Achilles. In the story, it means delay. Fullness takes time to complete, and to be realized by the audience. Not just the fullness of self-knowledge, but also the fullness of action – 'Error is known by its consequences, and the tragic pathos is evoked, not by the fact of error, but as the meaning of error is experienced through consequences'.[92]

Sophocles' *Oedipus Tyrannus* remains the most outstanding example of the dramatists' exploration of the importance of human knowledge and responsibility in an ambiguous world order. According to Claude Calame, *Oedipus Tyrannus* enacts a shift from verbal knowledge to visual knowledge.[93] Whereas verbal knowledge and physical sight lead to suppositions, visual knowledge and physical blindness give access to truth. The entire prologue plays on the theme of sight. A narrative reversal takes place on two levels – first, human knowledge directed by the questions of a creature simultaneously divine, bestial and feminine, is replaced by divine knowledge, which becomes the object of human questioning; secondly, knowledge based on words is replaced by knowledge based on sight; the Sphinx episode serves as a negative example of the nature of true knowledge. Oedipus' self-blinding provokes an ironic reversal of the initial desire for knowledge and for face-to-face inquiry. Richard Buxton's response to Calame calls into question the sharp opposition made by Calame between supposed knowledge and real knowledge.[94] According to Buxton, in the world of *Oedipus Tyrannus,* clear statements can be both true and false, human and divine. There is no certain access to the domain of truth and divine will. One simply cannot know. The divine world is opaque.

Segal too considers Sophocles' play dominated by anxiety, uncertainty, lack of control and the problem of self-knowledge.[95] The plot unfolds as the recovery of lost knowledge and a lost past. By introducing the hero's hesitation at the moment of discovery, Sophocles makes the truth emerge as a deliberate act of will. The story-pattern of riddle and decipherment appeals to our desire for knowledge. Segal calls the play 'the first detective story of Western literature'. He considers the play a tragedy not only of destiny, but also of personal identity, of searching for origins and meaning. It dramatizes the lonely path of *self-discovery*. Segal goes on by saying that knowledge in *Oedipus Tyrannus* is the reverse of that in Aeschylus' *Prometheus Bound*, where Prometheus' gift to (technological) man is allowing man not to foresee the day of his doom. *Prometheus* takes us to beginnings still marked by man's primordial struggle with nature for survival. *Oedipus* describes the tragedy of humanity at a later stage, when *a reflective awareness of the world within* becomes more important than domination of the world outside. This post-Promethean knowledge is tragic rather than technological; it is a knowledge that looks to ends and ultimate reality rather than to means and immediate goals.[96] What Padel said about madness also applies to Oedipus' self-knowledge – it articulates the issue of truth from pain.

If tragedy developed from choral song, Page duBois suggests, the occurrence of a single character standing out from the chorus marks the emergence of a Western sense of 'character', the *persona* carved out in the separation of an individual from a collective.[97] She agrees with Charles Segal that there is a parallel between the invisible space on stage concealed behind doors and gates (the gates of the palace, of the mouth, or of the body), and the invisible graphic space of the tragic poet's text (hidden in the performance) – the inner life of the self does not appear on the stage, but in the behind-the-stage implied by the invisible text. Segal is quoted as saying that 'this interplay between interior and exterior space parallels the increasing awareness of the interior realm of the psyche, the individual personality'. DuBois objects to the modern phrasing in terms of 'awareness' and replaces it with a postmodern phrasing in terms of 'construction' of the self:

> Rather than see this as an increasing *awareness* of something already existent, as Segal and Bruno Snell do, I would argue that in tragedy we are witnessing the *construction* of that self, that interiority, that individualism, in a process concomitant with Athenian democratic ideology concerning equality and the interchangeability of citizens.[98]

In *Shakespearean* tragedy, notions such as 'self-knowledge', 'self-awareness' and 'self-construction' all seem highly relevant in the case of Hamlet. But *self-knowledge and self-consciousness are not to be confused.* Self-consciousness can mean something quite different from self-knowledge. Does Hamlet achieve self-knowledge?

Harold Bloom praises Hamlet for a capacity of self-consciousness, for 'his genius, which is for consciousness itself', for his 'astonishing gift of awareness'.[99] Bloom's modern Hamlet is clearly only a genius of modernity in retrospect. Margreta de Grazia recalls the fact that 'Hamlet's deep and complex inwardness was not perceived as the play's salient feature until around 1800', and for good reasons. Hamlet, she argues, is a very down-to-earth character who is attached to the inheritance of his land, to the soil of his estate, but also to the soil of the graveyard and to the dust of his body's fate after death. 'The greatness of persons as well as of nations is measured by the expanse of their terrain' and 'A hamlet is a cluster of homes: a kingdom in miniature'. Precisely because Hamlet is dispossessed by the Danish court, he feels deprived and injured. It is his material dispossession, not his gift of awareness that affects what goes on inside Hamlet and that determines the plot of the play.[100] To me, de Grazia's argument is also convincing in the light of Shakespeare's biography. William's preoccupation with material wealth, ownership of the company and investment in a house and land back home are well-known. Shakespeare would have been very sensitive to 'man's relation to land, from graves to estate to empire'. And yet, the virtuosity of Hamlet's soliloquies has convinced me that, with hindsight, the early modern context is tangible in more than one respect.

The crucial breakthrough in *Hamlet* did not involve developing new themes or learning how to construct a tighter plot, Stephen Greenblatt argues, but developing an intense *representation of inwardness* called forth by a new technique of radical *excision of the motive*.[101] By removing or obscuring the motive that makes the initiating action of the story make sense, refusing to provide himself or his audience with a familiar, comfortable rationale, Shakespeare could reach something immeasurably deeper. Substantially reducing, as a literary means, the amount of causal explanation and of explicit motivation that accounted for the action that was to unfold, enabled the creation of a strategic opacity. But the creation of opacity as such was not the point. Taking out a clear motivation allowed Shakespeare to shift his attention to a description of the inner life of human beings, to an unprecedented representation of tormented inwardness. In the years after *Hamlet*, Shakespeare wrote *Othello* and *King Lear*. Again, in *Othello,* he refused to provide the villain Iago with a clear and convincing explanation for his behaviour, and in *King Lear* too, Shakespeare eliminated the motive – Lear sets up the love test so that he can divide the kingdom, while the play opens with characters discussing the already drawn up map of the division.[102]

States argues that the *psychological depth* in Hamlet's character is brought about by *recurring gaps* between the motive thrust upon him (revenge) and his delay to act upon it, between other characters and Hamlet's overreaction to them (intensity), between his words and his actions, and between circumstantial evidence and watertight evidence. These gaps are filled up with Hamlet's or other characters' speculations about the reasons for that, or even only filled up with Hamlet's anatomizing description of the issue instead of reasons and explanations.[103] It is the very undecidability of these gaps in the interplay of represented parts that allows for as many psychological and other interpretations of Hamlet as the bridging of these gaps suggests necessary.

John Lee agrees with States that the theory of humours offers *a vocabulary of interiority* that describes how a person's inner life works. Yet, Lee points out, it does so *in common, impersonal terms*, and in physiological terms at that, not in psychological terms. Similarly, 'soul' recalls 'the place in which Claudius locates Hamlet's possibly fertile melancholy. Used some forty times in *Hamlet*, it has many meanings but, although again an interior term, it lacks any sense of psychological or other individuation'. One of the few questions that Hamlet might be expected to ask at various moments throughout the play, but never asks, Lee observes, is 'Who am I?' 'His questions are of the "what" not "who" variety'.[104] Lee argues that the meaning of Hamlet's 'that within' (I.ii.85) remains vague. 'It could refer to his "melancholy" or to his "immortal soul"'. 'Surpassing show', it either betters show, or goes beyond show, and so is indescribable.[105]

Lee criticizes States for using the concept of the gap to explain Hamlet's interiority in terms of character and of psychological depth because it has no place for change. Besides, it is left to the literary critic's personal choice to decide which traits of Hamlet's character are dispositional, and which traits are aberrations and therefore not traits. Moreover, the psychological depth of Hamlet's character cannot plausibly be argued to stem from gaps.[106] If I am not mistaken, Lee's criticism over-interprets States' remarks on recurring gaps as if States uses 'gap' as an (inadequate) concept to picture interiority, whereas States uses it much more in Greenblatt's sense of technical excision of motive, thus creating a lack of pictures of interiority, and creating a desire for pictures to fill the gap, instead of creating 'gap' as a picture.

Lee's alternative draws from George A. Kelly's *Psychology of Personal Constructs* and Charles Taylor's *Sources of the Self*.[107] What Kelly's approach helps us to recognize in Hamlet's soliloquies, Lee argues, is how such general constructs ('to be–not to be', 'seems–that within', etc.) are capable of expressing individual difference and how they constitute a unique personality, in much the same way as 'fixed-role therapy encourages clients to represent themselves in new ways, to behave in new ways, to construe themselves in new ways, and thereby to become new people'. In the case of Hamlet, 'the attempt to do so borders on madness', because his haunting past makes 'Hamlet question his previous ways of construing his family and society'. The Ghost's confirmation of the murder of Old Hamlet actively 'murders the Prince's past, by proving Hamlet's knowledge of the world false'. But a wholesale reconstruction is easier to state than carry out. With the Ghost's arrival, Hamlet states his wish to 'cast off all his old values, experiences, and beliefs, founding a new construction of the world on the Ghost's commandment':[108]

> Yea, from the table of my memory
> I'll wipe away all trivial fond records,
> All saws[109] of books, all forms, all pressures past
> That youth and observation copied there,
> And thy commandment all alone shall live
> Within the book and volume of my brain.
> [I.v.98–103][110]

Lee points out that 'it is as a commonplace book, here, that the Prince conceptualizes his mind. . . . Commonplace books provided storehouses of *rhetorical knowledge*, memory-banks. They provided a way of anatomizing literature, . . . a means of breaking down the information contained within a literary work into constituent parts and then of storing it, with the purpose of facilitating its retrieval and later use within one's own arguments or thoughts'.[111] Polonius exemplifies its use, particularly in his farewell to his son Laertes.[112] 'The commonplace book, then, was not only an image for the mind but an image of the sixteenth-century rhetorical mind', Lee concludes.[113]

Rhetoric, as a field of tactical self-presentation and socially instrumental knowledge, was bound to structure the way in which Renaissance persons thought. Shaping thought, it was bound to structure them internally, to shape persons' constitution of the world and of themselves. But this could be considered either positively or negatively, Lee points out. The Renaissance *image of* the human being as Proteus, as *a fluid shape-changer*, multiform son of the Ocean, linked water, language and human nature together in a positive sense. Shakespeare's Hamlet, however, dramatizes the troubling aspects of this Protean, rhetorical sense of the self. Aware of rhetoric's powers, Hamlet is also aware of its deceits and tricks.[114] Disillusioned with rhetoric, Hamlet declares he will wipe away this rhetorical system and body of knowledge that has filled his mind and that constituted the sixteenth-century rhetorical sense of self, Lee states.[115]

In Lee's own words, 'Kelly's theory provided a model for seeing and describing interiority not as an expressive gap, but as *a verbally constructed possession.* In this way', Lee argues, 'by focusing on the possessed nature of interiority, as opposed to its directly expressed nature, the absence of our contemporary vocabulary for the description of interiority was not seen to be an insoluble problem'. Taylor's theory provides Lee with a means of making Kelly's construct theory descriptive both of historical change and of relative degrees of innerness.[116] According to Taylor, every person feels the need to ask questions about what are their moral goods and in what relation he or she stands to those goods. The 'self' is the point of perspective by which one's *relationship to one's values* is *articulated.* The 'self' is not identity's equivalent, but an area within identity, specifically verbal, and bound up with the interpretation of actions and events.

If applied to *Hamlet*, Hamlet is offered the bipolar construct 'particular–common' by Gertrude and Claudius, to which Hamlet responds by putting forward the quite different construct 'seeming–that within' (I.ii.68–86), and later on, the construct 'the world–to me' (I.ii.134, II.ii.249–50, II.ii.308).[117] The point is, however, that Hamlet's *constructs* keep on *collapsing* their terms. His soliloquies and conversations make clear that the clarity of a single perspective never remains available to him for long. They are like diary entries, capturing the immediacy of each day as it comes, and addressing the diarist only.[118] The soliloquies, in their repetitive return to the same object of description, Hamlet himself, become a form of autobiography, creating the story that is his life.

But Hamlet's efforts at *self-exploration* are much closer to the autobiographic *Essays* of Montaigne than to the *self-mastering* thoughts of Descartes. 'What Montaigne discovered in his interior was a landscape of terrifying inner instability. . . . The repetitive nature of the essay is the formal device by which Montaigne represents the truth, as he sees it, that life is not being—"essence"—but becoming—"passage"'. Part of that passage is the essay itself – a literary form of self-creation that is constitutive of one's inner world. 'Hamlet's repetitions, his soliloquies, are essays which share in Montaigne's techniques. They are his attempts to capture himself, showing his frustration at his inability to capture a solid picture of that self'.[119] Hamlet does not achieve self-fashioning (too instrumental) or self-mastery (too stable and certain). Instead, he achieves self-exploration, self-mapping and self-creation. His self is a story, but it is a *tragic* story because, while being forced to make up his own narrative', he fails 'to find an identity or story that will express him'.[120] As Hamlet lies dying, he regrets not being able to tell his story and he begs Horatio, his 'recorder', to tell his story instead. (V.ii.330–1, 340–43)

> There is no sense in which the Prince has arrived at self-knowledge. There is no point at which the Prince tells us what he has learnt about himself. All the questions that he has raised remain. Indeed, his musings over the nature of man continue.[121]

This tragic outcome would only boost Hegel's conviction that the spirit of the age was destined to move beyond tragedy's psycho-ethical conflicts in order to solve them and achieve self-knowledge, that is to say, self-produced self-consciousness and self-mastery.

7 Conclusions

In tragedy, there are many ways in which human actions and their consequences are linked to human intentions, but these links are always problematic. Should one ascribe a character's actions to his or her intentions, to a *daimon*, to a demon, to the gods, to fate, to a family doom, to oracles, to incompetence, to arrogance, to lack of knowledge, to circumstances, to bad luck? Often, characters and audiences alike are confronted with a confusing combination of causes and consequences. This confusion is particularly striking when it comes to decision making. Faced with moral conflicts and their immoral consequences, the danger of madness is never far away.

In Greek tragedy, there is a shift in focus from actions to intentions. A culture traditionally focused on visible results and divine interventions discovers the equally compelling weight of human motives as human causes of actions and their consequences, and the disturbing gap between intended actions and unintended consequences. In Shakespearean tragedy, there is a sharpened shift in focus from actions to intentions and a sharper distinction between the world of actions and the world of intentions compared to Greek tragedy. The moral dilemma is restated as a problem that has to be solved both ethically and psychologically. The problem is not just intended actions and unintended consequences. Hamlet considers his unintended stabbing of Polonius 'no matter', as nothing more than collateral damage and well-deserved anyway. The problem is action *and* thought, how to act and how to acquire the certain knowledge needed to bridge the gap between thought and action. Much like Descartes' problem in his *Discours de la méthode*, Hamlet's problem is no longer primarily the religious authorization of revealed truth and traditional wisdom, but the methodological acquisition of rational certainty and the gap between his mind and the material world of his actions. Both action and thought now have as many motives as they have reinforcing consequences, too many for the self-proclaimed court spy Polonius to be detected. Sophocles' Oedipus too, like a real detective, methodologically acquires the reasonable certainty needed to find the murderer, but what he discovers is a truth revealed by the oracles and by the seer, Teiresias, whose religious authority he had disputed.

The psychological weight of human intentions and actions is felt as an integral part of the tragic conflict. Greek and Shakespearean tragedies confirm Sands' thesis that the very awakening of the Western moral consciousness goes hand in hand with the shattering experience of the moral imperfection of the world and of human beings themselves. Wrongdoing, Vernant explained, is no longer considered exclusively as a blemished mistake, but also as a mistake of the mind, as a fatal blindness or ignorance and, Gill would add, as a confusing clash of two sets of beliefs. Oedipus achieves self-knowledge, but it is tragic in nature – it hurts because it is truth extracted from pollution and pain. Hamlet does not achieve self-knowledge and that too, is a tragic form of self-consciousness – it hurts because Hamlet fails to tell the story that could be claimed to be his own. In both cases, the self-awareness implies social isolation. Whatever truth is found or lost, its discovery or loss emerges from pollution, pain and the moral brokenness of the world and its inhabitants' entanglement in it.

What the Greek and Shakespearean vocabularies for attitudes of mind and heart have in common is that the modern separation of the psychological from the physiological had not yet occurred in the field of terminology. The availability of language regarding self-experience is limited. The post-tragic Greek theory of humours describes interiority in common, impersonal terms and is still applied in Shakespearean tragedy. No vocabulary beyond the vague reference to 'that within' is at Hamlet's disposal to distinguish his type of person from his personal self-experience as a unique individual, and while asking the typical 'What am I?' question, he never asks the modern 'Who am I?' question. A difference between Greek and Shakespearean tragedy pertains to the use of a vocabulary for attitudes of mind and heart. The Greek tragic characters, Goldhill suggested, use their vocabulary strategically for social purposes, not for purposes of picturing interiority. Despite his lack of a modern vocabulary for interiority, Hamlet's reflections on action and thought testify to the fact that he suffers from the modern separation between the outer world of behaviour and the inner world of thought. But this observation of Hamlet's early modernity is with hindsight. Hamlet's deep and complex inwardness was not perceived as the play's salient feature until around 1800, and for good reasons, as de Grazia pointed out.

PART II: INDIAN AND HINDU ISSUES

1 Introduction

In the historical context of classical India, the *Mahābhārata* epic and, in particular, the *Bhagavadgītā* section within the epic took up, summarized and harmonized a debate on the moral, psychological and religious weight of human action that had already been going on for centuries, ever since the *Upanishads* had made an effort to redefine the relationship between acting and knowing. But in offering a comprehensive summary and harmonization of the debate, the *Bhagavadgītā* became a sacred scripture of its own in that it gradually emerged as the only authoritative Hindu treatise on the moral and religious status of human action. Partly due to a number of authoritative medieval and modern commentaries, the *Gītā* finally became a key symbol of Hindu culture and religion in modern times.[122] Commentaries on it, in turn, became the philosophical context of the text, allowing access to its Hindu interpretations in much the same way as Aristotle's treatise on tragedy and comedy, the *Poetics*, did for the Western interpretations of tragedy and comedy.

In this second part of the chapter on psycho-ethical aspects, the focus will be exclusively on the *Gītā*'s view of human nature. The *Gītā* presents Arjuna's tragic conflict as a psycho-ethical conflict in need of a spiritual solution. This spiritual solution is offered by Krishna's teaching, which consists of complicated philosophical and theological reasoning aimed at convincing Arjuna to view things differently. The *main question* will be – how are human action and human intention linked in the *Gītā*? The Indian and Hindu issues addressed are similar to the ones discussed in the first part: 1. The nature of the moral conflict; 2. The nature of the psychic conflict; 3. The relations between action, knowledge and desire; 4. The degree of self-knowledge.

2 Moral conflict

Arjuna, on the battlefield of Kurukshetra, faces a moral dilemma. On the one hand, Arjuna is expected to fight because it is his duty as a nobleman to defend his kingdom by force against illegitimate rule and to protect both the king's subjects and the principle of justice from being submitted and violated by his unlawful opponents on the battlefield. There is no doubt that Arjuna is about to fight for a just cause, the cause of justice to be done to the rightful ruler, Yudhisthira, and his subjects. On the other hand, Arjuna is expected to fight a deadly war involving the killing of some of his own kinsmen, affectionate friends, respected elders and revered teachers.

Facing the killing of kin and a deadly war, he suddenly hesitates. The medieval commentator Rāmānuja, as G. W. Kaveeshwar points out, mentions three causes for Arjuna's dejection – affection for blood relations, intense pity and a concern about good and evil.[123] Rāmānuja regards familial affection as the chief cause, whereas Kaveeshwar stresses the concern about good and evil. This discussion will be pursued later on.

Like Kaveeshwar, M. M. Agrawal stresses that Arjuna is primarily facing a moral dilemma and that Arjuna 'follows a whole lot of solid *moral* reasons for the shift in his attitude'.[124]

In the first instance, the moral dilemma consists of a *conflict of social loyal-ties*: the simultaneous necessity and impossibility of choosing between the warrior code not to neglect one's duty and the family code not to kill a relative. But *the moral dilemma is simultaneously a religious dilemma*. It is a religious duty to respect the family and its continuity, especially for the sake of the ancestors who depend on the ritual offering of *pinda* for their status as spirits.

In the second instance, the moral dilemma consists of a *conflict of cosmic proportions*. The battle is between good and evil. The battlefield of the Kurus is called the 'field of *dharma*' or 'field of righteousness'. This qualification interprets the battle as the universal battle between good and evil, between the just ones and the unjust ones. The Kaurava clan, led by its king Duryodhana, are the unjust ones, because they have cheated during the dice game with Yudhisthira, the noble king of the Pāndava clan, who is nevertheless too weak a king to protect his kingdom and family from falling into the hands of

Duryodhana, whose lust for power has proven to be uncompromising and inconsiderate of the consequences for others. This makes Arjuna realize that his righteous battle against evil brings about even more evil and a breakdown of the very moral order (*dharma*) he is supposed to defend. In that sense, it is a lost battle either way. The moral dilemma is a real dilemma because, either way, *dharma* is violated. Nevertheless, Krishna calls the war *dharmayuddha* (righteous battle), and salutary for Arjuna's own *dharma* (2.31), a gateway to heaven (2.32).

The notion of *dharma* is a complicated one. Recalling the discussion in the chapter on literary–cultural aspects, it expresses a sense of established order that relates to different levels of reality. On a *personal level*, it relates to the extent to which one fulfils one's social duties in life, primarily the duty of meeting the established role expectations of the fellow members of one's caste and sex, not the pursuit of general principles. On a *societal level*, the notion relates to the extent to which the clan society upholds its hierarchical 'apartheid' system of caste/race differences and its ancestral rituals. On a *cosmic level*, the notion relates to the extent to which good prevails over evil and time takes its course in the creation and destruction of the world. The necessity of an established or given order on all these levels is presupposed. But the possibilities of its realization on all levels and in each and every respect simultaneously are in serious doubt. Several dharmic values are at stake. The moral dilemma exists precisely because the *conflicting dharmic values* cannot be brought under one overriding principle, because the only overriding principle eligible is *dharma*. The simultaneous necessity and impossibility of choosing one of the dharmic values at the expense of other ones reveals that it is not so much Arjuna facing a personal problem, but much more *dharma* itself undergoing a crisis on the *practical level* of its imminent enactment.

The practical level is crucial in one respect – it focuses on the *actions and their results*, their objective 'fruits', not on the agents and their intentions, their good will. The agents are considered 'sinners' insofar as the results of their actions are considered 'sinful', not vice versa. Arjuna's consideration of the (undesirable) consequences, therefore, has to be taken as of crucial moral importance, not just as of psychological importance in the sense that it expresses fear of the future. It is the objective consequences of his actions that make Arjuna morally accountable. The actions themselves, in the objective sense of the word, ought to be right (*kārya*). The *kārya* aspect (of rightness) is a characteristic of the act itself.[125] Despite Arjuna's highly emotional response to the situation, his emotions do not count, morally speaking. What counts are the actions and their results, not Arjuna's sincerity and authenticity. To fight or not to fight, *to act or not to act,* that is the question. That is to say, to act *right(eous)ly*.

3 Confusing conflict and emotional response: A matter of desire or emotional appraisal

3.1 Arjuna's state of mind

How should Arjuna's emotional response be interpreted? Arjuna's emotional response is one thing; Krishna's interpretation of that response is another. Krishna immediately opposes 'the wise one' to 'the deluded/confused one' (*Gītā* 2.13), defining 'the wise one' in *yogic* terms as constant in pain and pleasure (2.15), and Arjuna as one who should not mourn (2.25–27), who is like the irresolute (2.41), like the ignorant ones (2.42), like those full of desires (2.43), in danger of being attached to inaction (2.47), and easily carried away by the turbulent senses that generate attachment, anger, delusion, loss of memory, destruction of discrimination and eventually, a man's loss (2.60–63). In short, Krishna interprets Arjuna's emotional response in terms of confusion (*moha*) and clinging (*sangas*). From a *yogic* point of view, Arjuna is suspected to suffer from the two 'original sins' that Hinduism shares with Buddhism – ignorance or blindness (*avidyā*), and desire or attachment (*kāma*). But this *theological* diagnosis seems more inspired by the proper emotional response than by Arjuna's actual response.

Kaveeshwar expressly distinguishes the notion of *moha* (bewilderment, confusion) from the notion of *kāma* (desire), and thus from the connotation of attachment.[126] The point he is making is that *kāma* (egoistic attachment) is not at the root of Arjuna's psychological crisis; despite the fact that the central idea of the *Gītā* is often said to be related to the elimination of *kāma*, Arjuna's initial state of mind cannot be used as its first illustration.

Nevertheless, according to Kaveeshwar, though Arjuna's confusion had not been caused by egoistic attachment, the latter had not been permanently uprooted from his mind. In fact, Arjuna himself concedes that he had approached the battlefield due to the attraction for royal pleasures (*Gītā* 1.45). It was when it occurred to him that the war would deprive him of the true good that he shrunk. Thus, even though the passion of egoistic longing was not actually operative in his mind at the moment, when he objected to the war, there was no guarantee against its future appearance. Hence, Krishna having first advised Arjuna to wage war, went on to subsequently preach the elimination of egoistic attachment for his permanent good.[127]

Apparently, Krishna's preaching goes one step further than is necessary at that moment. Kaveeshwar tries to present this extra step as a necessary one but, in my opinion, he is not very convincing in his effort. He artificially links the others' desire for royal pleasures to Arjuna's disgust of the war in terms of cause (desire) and effect (disgust), thus smuggling into his argument the external presence of desire as a constant potential danger for Arjuna's inner state of mind.[128]

My own position is that, among other issues, as a minor issue, the issue of desire is implicitly (disgust) and even explicitly (*Gītā* 1.45 – greed for the pleasures of kingdom) present in the story itself right from the beginning but is subsequently – that is, in Krishna's response to Arjuna – exploited and elaborated upon extensively in the teachings of Krishna, who reflects on the event in a didactical way by instructing Arjuna in one particular direction. This position is confirmed by Dermot Killingley's analysis:

> The Bhagavadgita abounds in words for desire, pleasure, enjoyment, wish, will, attachment, longing, and love.[129] Some of these words, such as *lobha* ('greed'), have moral connotations, but most of them are morally neutral. Passages referring to the opposite of desire—hatred or disgust—are also relevant; so are those on equanimity or indifference (*samatva, sāmya*). This is one of the recurrent topics of the poem. The yogi is characterised by an equal attitude to pleasure and pain (2.38, 6.32, 12.18), and to things that other people would consider desirable and undesirable: cows and dogs, or gold and clods or stones (5.18, 6.8). The topic of desire is prominent not only in the teachings given by Krishna to Arjuna, but in the narrative form of the poem. Arjuna's dilemma, which is the starting-point of this frame, is expressed in terms of desire. On the one hand, Arjuna desires power (1.33, 1.45), and so do his opponents (2.5c), and on the other hand, he does not desire enjoyments, victory or life itself if they are achieved at the cost of killing his kinsmen and elders (1.32, 2.5–8).[130]

However, the issue of Arjuna's desire is not *narratively* presented as the source of the dramatic situation. It is Krishna's diagnosis that *didactically* interprets the dramatic situation in terms of desire.

On the *narrative* level, Arjuna seems to display *pity, grief* and maybe *fear.* Unfortunately, Kaveeshwar's monocausal reasoning reduces the notion of (Arjuna's) pity (*krpā*) to self-pity, and the notion of (Arjuna's) grief (*śoka*) to fear of sin. At the root of Arjuna's mood, he claims, there cannot be but one cause only – the fear of committing a sin by killing his kinsmen at his own hands and the unbearable prospect of being tainted with blood for no sensible reason.[131] In my understanding, Kaveeshwar's type of reasoning represents a reduction both of the appraisal of the complexity of the situation that elicits differing emotions and of the complex variety of forms that the emotional response can take. Let me try to explain why, by inserting a brief interlude on Nico H. Frijda's theory of emotions, which clarifies the links between situation and emotional response and, in doing so, sheds more light on Arjuna's state of mind – and body. (§3.3) It also sheds more light on the relationship between an emotional response and a deliberate response. (§5)

3.2 Nico H. Frijda's theory of emotions

According to Frijda, specific emotions correspond to specific forms of appraisal of the same complex situation and to specific modes of dealing with the situation. Each emotion corresponds to a different appraisal of the situation – a different 'situational meaning structure' – and is characterized by it. If a situation of danger is seen as one of threat that one doubts can be countered, it produces fear; if as one that is a willful obstruction, it produces anger; if as a challenge that can be met, it produces enthusiasm and eagerness.[132]

Frijda happens to illustrate his 'intimate correspondence thesis' by choosing *loss* as an example of 'major and stable situational aspects' and *grief* as an example of 'response to the major and stable aspects'.[133] In his description of some appraisals of the situation, Frijda also turns to sadness and grief:

Sadness and grief correspond to the situational meaning structure of emptiness or barrenness; that is, to the explicit absence of something valued. Loss, of course, is one of the most distinct forms, and 'pining' a word designating orientation toward something explicitly absent. . . . Absence pertains not only to loss of a person: There is grief upon the loss of an ideal once cherished. It need not even pertain to loss; there exists grief concerning absence that never was filled: a love affair that never managed to become what it could have become, or an unhappy childhood recollected. Of course, these can be construed as losses, of hopes and of opportunities.

For absence to truly constitute grief, it must possess the property of finality: the notion that absence will be forever. Without finality there is misery or distress or anger. Anger upon loss indeed appears to function as a means to ward off realization of finality: 'I wish there was something I could blame,' to quote again one of Parkes's subjects.

The term *absence* here means absence of some intentional object, some object of interest. Such absence may extend to the world as a whole, and in fact every grave personal loss tends to rob the entire world of its color. To the extent that absence spreads beyond a specific focus and global emptiness takes over, grief turns into depression. In depression (meaning the mood, not the clinical syndrome) there is no object serving as focus for behavior or nonbehavior. There is, however, a situation with a meaning structure; only that situation is the world as a whole, and situational meaning structure invests it in global fashion. That structure is barrenness and isolation.[134]

Frijda argues that what triggers grief is loss of a thing of importance, whatever the thing and whatever the reasons for its importance – that is, the concerns. What elicits emotions, then, are constellations of events relevant to concerns. Emotions result from match or mismatch between events and concerns.[135]

Frijda also discusses the emotion of fear.[136] He does not object to Aristotle's description of fear as the 'sense of impending evil'. Its corresponding situational meaning structure is a situation of threat combined with the element of uncertainty about the issue (outcome) or about the 'ability to cope'. Fear is the uncertain expectation of the presence of 'negative valence' (something possessing intrinsic aversiveness) or of the absence of 'positive valence' (something possessing intrinsic attractiveness), over which there is insufficient control, but which is modifiable; its degree corresponds to the measure of closure and urgency of the situation. If the situation of threat is seen as transitory, fear will take the form of protective effort; if escape is possible and if the threat is more than protective behaviour can handle, fear will take the form of escape effort; if the threat is seen as a combination of features to a point where no behaviour is possible, no fearful behaviour will be shown except trembling and being sleepless, and the emotional experience will merely consist of persistent awareness of impending evil.

Frijda has very little to say about pity and compassion, but what he has to say is worth noting for my disagreement with Kaveeshwar. According to Frijda, unselfish emotions like compassion, pity, suffering when seeing others suffer and joy upon their success or escape from danger, rest, in part, upon a specific, probably innate, sensitivity for distress expressions in others that serve as releasers of care-giving behaviour; in part, they derive from the individual's own concerns, either directly through what the other means to him or by proxy, through empathy or identification.[137]

3.3 *Psychic conflict*

Let us now return to the *Gītā* and apply some of Frijda's insights. The opening scene of the *Gītā* has Arjuna express several emotions and several concerns. Rāmānuja mentions three causes for Arjuna's dejection – affection for blood relations, intense pity and a concern about good and evil. Rāmānuja regards familial affection as the chief cause, whereas Kaveeshwar stresses the concern about good and evil in the sense of fear of committing a crime. In my opinion, the story itself does not allow for a systematization or hierarchical classification of emotions, but depicts a constellation that encompasses a whole range of complicated emotions. Maybe, all of us are right in our own ways. But suppose we take Frijda's ideas on the emotions of grief, depression, fear and pity (or compassion) as our frame of reference for interpreting the opening scene, what pattern would become visible in that case?

Arjuna's *grief* and *depression* are referred to in the body-language and terminology of *Gītā* 1.28, 1.47, 2.1, 2.8 and 2.10 – to literally and mentally sink down, to collapse, despondency, eyes tear-filled, sorrow, grief. From the linking of grief to a withering of the senses in 2.8, one may infer that Arjuna's mouth becoming parched in 1.29 is also linked to the emotion of grief in 1.28. Grief and depression respond to a corresponding situation(al meaning structure) of barrenness, absence and loss. The explicit absence of something valued can be the absence of either a person or an object of interest. In the case of Arjuna, it is both.[138] Arjuna is about to lose everything of value to him, including the value of his life if he survives.

Arjuna's *fear* is nowhere referred to in the terminology. Some of the body-language can be taken as an expression of fear, if it is not taken as an expression of grief, shocked indignation, protest and bewilderment. Krishna blames Arjuna for being a coward. This suggests fear of fighting, not fear of committing a crime. Arjuna does not take up this argument and continues instead to enumerate his objections while Krishna does not take up Arjuna's argument of committing a crime and continues instead to blame Arjuna for being confused. The situation of danger is seen by Arjuna as a situation of threat that he strongly doubts can be countered. Because of that, one may infer that his appraisal of the situation definitely produces fear. Arjuna sees evil signs and has a strong sense of impending evil, but there is no explicit mention of fear. Arjuna's appeal to the sight of evil signs and of an evil outcome can be understood as expressions of protest, of arguments against the war, instead of being expressions of fear. Since the situation should be otherwise, it produces indignation (at the very thought of killing the revered gurus of great dignity, in 2.4–5, for example), protest (killing kinsmen is clearly against family law and authoritative oral tradition, in 1.38–44, and Arjuna makes an appeal to these in order to raise a strong protest), and bewilderment (2.7), but no anger. The desirelessness of Arjuna to fight seems much less a form of depressed listlessness than a form of protest – 'I do not wish!', 'I shall not fight!' The situation of threat is hardly seen as modifiable and the catastrophic issue is virtually certain, whereas 'fear' includes the element of uncertainty about the issue (outcome) or about the ability to cope with an event that is modifiable, but over which there is insufficient control. The situation of threat is seen as virtually inescapable and final, and the only forms of escaping Arjuna can think of are depression as a defence mechanism, which allows for withdrawal from active involvement in the situation and for time to recover from the first shock, and praying to his guru Krishna for instruction as a defense mechanism, which allows for even more time and for a transfer of responsibilities to the guru who must now tell him what to do and take the decisions for him. The prospect of being about to commit a crime is very much present in Arjuna's mind and, no doubt, produces fear, but nowhere such a 'fear of sin,' as Kaveeshwar calls it, is mentioned. The prospect of going to hell is depicted as a real threat in 1.44, and as such there is good reason for it to be feared. What Arjuna is explicitly uncertain about is the answer to the question whether to fight or not to fight is the right thing to do, for, in 2.6 he says that, 'we know not which of the two were better for us'. In this sense, the fear of choosing evil and of committing a crime is an important aspect of Arjuna's emotional make-up. But in the depiction of the opening scene, the emotion of fear is overshadowed by the emotions of grief and pity.

Arjuna's *pity or compassion* is referred to in the body-language and terminology of *Gītā* 1.28, 2.1, 2.7 and 2.11 – overwhelmed with utmost compassion, eyes tear-filled, pitying these fellow human beings. Pity responds to a corresponding situation in which someone else's fate is at stake; that fact shapes the pitying subject's appraisal of his own situation; the other person's situation forms part of it, in a sort of recursive manner that releases care-giving behaviour, in part because of some innate sensitivity for distress expressions in others, in part because of the direct emotional significance of the other person for the subject concerned, or through empathy and identification. Pity or compassion is by definition an unselfish emotion to the extent that it is the other person's fate that is at stake, but it can be a selfish emotion to the extent that the pitying subject cannot separate his own fate from the other person's fate. It is hurting to see this other person being hurt; it is even more hurting to bring about the very hurting of this other person being hurt. The sight or foresight of such an emotionally significant person being hurt releases a strong readiness to practise care-giving behaviour. This is exactly what happens to Arjuna who testifies to the emotional significance of his kinsmen, teachers and friends, and to the sheer impossibility of doing the exact opposite of practising care-giving behaviour, namely, killing at his own hands those whose fate is at stake while being unable to emotionally separate his own fate from theirs. In brief, waging this war would mean losing everything and committing a terrible crime, but it would also mean self-destruction, being hurt unbearably, emotional suicide, self-loss.[139]

4 The vocabulary for attitudes of mind and heart

Kaveeshwar's interpretation of Arjuna's problem also makes use of the very terminology for attitudes of mind and heart that is abundantly available in the *Gītā* itself in the chapters 14, 17 and 18.[140] This *physiological vocabulary* has later been systematized and elaborated by the classical school of thought known as *sāmkhya*. The same terminology is still used in modern interpretations, as Kaveeshwar's case illustrates. Before applying it to Arjuna's problem, I shall explain the terminology as it has been developed in its classical reading because the classical reading has been very influential and allows for a deeper insight into the psychological potential of this traditional Indian cosmology describing human nature in terms of nature in general.

In classical *sāmkhya* thought, the envisaged terminology, known as the theory of three *gunas*, is part of its encompassing concept of nature as moving matter (*prakrti*). Nature is determined by the *gunas* ('strands') or 'cosmic constituents' and by time. The *Gītā* too, uses these categories. The basic idea is that all parts of nature contain varying proportions of three physiological constituents or *gunas*.[141] These three *gunas* or physiological 'qualities' determine the character of things. The character of things, including that of human beings, is thought of as not only physical, but also moral and mental (attitudinal), in very much the same way the English word 'character' is used for both the 'salient form' and the 'distinctive way of being' of something. That is to say, the moral and mental make-up of human beings and other parts of 'primal nature' are understood as basically physical qualities that take the shape of moral behaviour and mental attitudes.[142]

Feelings are indicative of worldly experience and, for that very reason, cannot be indicative of ultimate freedom, which is the higher goal of the human being in classical *sāmkhya* – spiritual aloofness (*kaivalya*).[143] There is no reference whatsoever in the *Gītā* to the *sāmkhya* ideal of spiritual aloofness (*kaivalya*). The ways in which the *Gītā* conceives of the goal of the human being are dealt with later on.[144]

The three basic constituents out of which everything is woven are:

1 *Sattva guna*: brightness in the sense of light, purity, rightness, goodness, illumination, knowledge and wisdom. It is buoyant, illuminating and produces pleasure. Its colour is white.[145]

2 *Rajas guna*: energy in the sense of fire, restless activity, ambition, strong feelings, lusting, insatiability, gluttony, attachment, jealousy,

envy, hatred, maliciousness, foulness. It is mobile and stimulating. It is that power of nature that affects and moves the other two constituents.[146] It is the principle of motion that produces pain. Restless activity, feverish effort and wild stimulation are its results. Its colour is red.

3 *Tamas guna*: inertia in the sense of darkness, stolidity, torpidity, sluggishness, sleepiness, tiredness, forgetfulness, old age, depression, sorrow, hunger, thirst, fear, ignorance, delusion, stupidity. It is heavy and enveloping.[147] It produces apathy and indifference. Its colour is dark.

The nature of a thing is determined by the preponderance of a particular *guna*. Things are called good, bad or indifferent; intelligent, active or slothful; pure, impure or neutral, on account of the predominance of *sattva*, *rajas* or *tamas*, respectively. Each thing is composed of all three *gunas*, which are present either actually or potentially. In some things, one *guna* predominates, in others another, but they are all present. There is a constant movement inherent in the *gunas* themselves, the tendency of each *guna* being to gain supremacy over the other, a dynamism not being caused by anything external. Nature (*prakrti*) is not only complex and all-pervasive; it also evolves or undergoes change perpetually, either in the manifest form of evolution (*sarga*) or in the latent form of dissolution (*pralaya*).

If one applies the *guna* categories to the caste system, the character of *brahmins* is presumed to contain a high proportion of *sattva guna*, and because of that, *brahmins* are teachers and priests, that is to say, specialists in knowledge and wisdom. The character of *kshatriyas* is presumed to contain a high proportion of *rajas guna*, and that is why *kshatriyas* are warriors by nature, that is to say, energetic, ambitious and focused on action and the acquisition of honour and wealth. According to Śankara,[148] the character of warriors originates from *rajas guna* mixed with *sattva guna*, whereas the character of *vaishyas* or merchants and craftsmen (wealth producers) originates from *rajas guna* mixed with *tamas guna*, while the character of *śūdras* or labourers is presumed to contain a high proportion of *tamas guna* with a small admixture of *rajas guna*. The *Gītā* too, is very outspoken in this regard:

The duties of the *brahmins*, the *kshatriyas*, the *vaishyas*,
And of the *śūdras*, Arjuna,
Are distributed according to
The qualities which arise from their own nature.

Tranquility, restraint, austerity, purity,
Forgiveness, and uprightness,
Knowledge, wisdom, and faith in God
Are the duties of the *brahmins*, born of their innate nature.

Heroism, majesty, firmness, skill,
Not fleeing in battle,
Generosity, and lordly spirit
Are the duties of the *kshatriyas*, born of their innate nature.

Plowing, cow-herding, and trade
Are the duties of the *vaishyas*, born of their innate nature.
Service is the duty of the *śūdras*,
Born of their innate nature.
[18.41–4][149]

Applying these *guna* categories to the four classes identifies the social differences between the classes as natural ones. The hierarchical order of the caste system, then, symbolizes and manifests the natural order (*dharma*). This suggests a static order. In the *Gītā*, the suggestion of a static order is turned into a prescript (18.45–8). Modern interpreters of the *Gītā*, however, have pointed out that the *guna* theory is not just meant to explain complexity and diversity, but also change, as A. V. Rathna Reddy illustrates.[150]

The *gunas* are thought of in the *Gītā* mainly in terms of their influence on a person's character and behaviour.[151] It is the state of the individual's *guna* configuration at death reflecting one's lifetime of *karmic* actions that determines the new birth, as Krishna explains to Arjuna in 14.14–15:

If the embodied soul dies when *sattva* reigns, he attains to the pure worlds of those who have the highest knowledge. The one dying in *rajas* is reborn among people who are given to acting; while one expiring in *tamas* is born among the witless.[152]

If one applies the *guna* categories to the character of Arjuna, one realizes that in the *Gītā* the terminology is only in the second instance used for describing the problem Arjuna's struggle represents. Primarily, it is used for describing the solution, a solution that will be discussed later on. My point here is that the same terminology could also be used to describe the problem. The problem is that *Arjuna's response is tamasic whereas it should be rajasic*. It should be *rajasic* insofar as Arjuna is a *kshatriya* or warrior who is presumed to have a high proportion of *rajas guna* and act accordingly – energetic, ambitious and focused on action and the acquisition of honour and wealth. Krishna, basically, blames him in the first instance for disregarding his honour as a warrior, for lacking courage, for demonstrating bewilderment (confusion) instead of brightness, for showing apathy and restraint instead of ambition and initiative. In the second instance, Krishna moves beyond the argument of Arjuna behaving *tamasically* (instead of behaving *rajasically*) by developing a complicated argument that identifies *rajas guna* as part of the problem, not of the solution. This argument links *rajas guna* negatively with action in the expectation of some 'fruit' (reward or punishment), *karmic* action generated by desire, passion and anger, instead of linking *rajas guna* positively with warrior virtues (3.37, 2.62–63). There will be more on this argument later on.

5 Confusing conflict and deliberate response: A matter of reasoning

An emotional response to a situation is more immediate than a deliberate response. Thus, there is something odd about Krishna *blaming* Arjuna for being overwhelmed by certain emotions. Blaming Arjuna for being overwhelmed by certain emotions is the negative, reverse side of making an *appeal to emotions*. Apparently, there is a degree of choice and responsibility in having these overwhelming emotions instead of other ones. Again, Frijda can shed some light on the matter. He explains how every emotion has its advantages and disadvantages.[153] The point is that the advantages of certain emotions over others explain emotional persistence because these emotions fulfil strategic functions such as avoidance, self-protection, disengagement and time for readjustments, and are consequently preferred and cultivated. Emotions, after all, are forms of response that could and would be otherwise if the appraisal of the situation were a different one and if other forms of response were preferred. There is room for manoeuvre on the battlefield of appraisals and emotions. One can be blamed for both.[154]

Krishna blames Arjuna not only for being fainthearted – which is clearly in the domain of emotions – but also for being confused – which is more in the domain of appraisals. There is a huge difference between *Arjuna's confusion* (*moha*) here and *Yudhisthira's* previous obsession with dicing, which was hardly distinguishable from *madness*.[155] Despite Krishna's doubts about the lucidity and firmness of Arjuna's deliberations, Krishna's powers of persuasion make an *appeal to reason*. Apparently, Arjuna still has a reasoning capacity that can be addressed. His deliberations cannot be dismissed as sheer blindness. Arjuna does have a point. In fact, the problem is that he has several points. His reasoning capacity generates equally good reasons for both horns of the moral dilemma. That is precisely, Agrawal argues, why one should not be puzzled when Arjuna feels remorse. The conflict of loyalties is a conflict of internalized values, and therefore a psycho-ethical conflict.[156] What Arjuna's mind or reason does not generate is the kind of knowledge necessary to solve the moral problem itself. If a solution to the conflict is to be found, it would, as a consequence, have to solve the dilemma both on a psychological and on an ethical level. The dilemma is, after all, being described in terms of threatening to bring about a lack of happiness, both collective (1.37) and personal (1.46).

6 Reasoning towards a spiritual solution: A matter of action, desire and purity

6.1 Reasoning as part of the solution

The solution Krishna comes up with is neither a psychic nor a moral nor a rational one, but beyond that. What Krishna has to offer is a spiritual solution.

It takes Krishna quite some time to lead Arjuna all the way from his psycho-ethical problem to its spiritual solution. Krishna turns out to be a sophisticated counsellor and a teacher acquainted with the major spiritual traditions of ancient India. In fact, most of the *Gītā* is dedicated to *restating the dilemma* in such a way as to encompass and integrate or transcend all previous philosophical and theological debate on action and knowledge in the Indian religious realm at the time.

Rhetorically speaking, Krishna begins with pointing out the impermanence of existence and the dualism between the mortal body (*deha*) and the 'embodied one' (*dehī*), the immortal soul or self (2.13–30). Besides, it is the duty and glory of a warrior to fight instead of incurring evil and disgrace (2.31–38). It is the (short-term) destiny of warriors who fight that they gain access to heaven (2.32).

But from then onwards, Krishna begins to focus on the notion of action. It becomes the (long-term?) destiny of anyone who acts according to Krishna's teaching to avoid rebirth and to be one with Krishna. *The focus has shifted from Arjuna's war action to action in general*. In order to grasp the gist of Krishna's sophisticated position, first we need to understand the Vedic approach to action (Brahmanism), and then move on to the influence of the ascetic movements (Śramanism), thus following the historical developments within the ancient and classical Indian religious tradition. In chronological terms, it may be helpful to keep in mind that, roughly speaking, the Vedic, pre-Hindu (1200?–600? BCE) religion ritualistically addressed first the gods, then the sacrificial fire itself, cosmologizing it; subsequently, the early Hindu (roughly 600–200 BCE) *Upanishads* and the ascetic movements (Hindu, Buddhist and Jain ones) internalized the ritual of sacrifice; eventually, the classical (150–0 BCE?) and medieval *Mahābhārata* epic and the *Bhagavadgītā* devotionalized and both demilitarized and remilitarized the concept of sacrifice, which is crucial to the concept of action.[157]

6.2 The Gītā's first line of reasoning: Ritual and sacrificial action

The ancient Vedic notion of action (*karman*) was primarily understood in a ritualistic way as a matter of determined (motivated) performance and of promising results, and *wrongdoing* as a matter of polluted performance and of damaging results. Action was primarily thought of as *ritual action*, and ritual action meant sacrificial action. *Gītā* 3.13–15:

Good men eat the remnants of sacrifice
and are cleansed of all impurities.
The wicked, who cook merely for themselves,
partake of evil.

From food, creatures arise.
Rain produces food.
Sacrifice brings rain.
Cultic work is the root of sacrifice.

Cultic work comes from the Divine,
the Divine from the one supreme, subtle sound.
Hence the Divine, although omnipresent,
is ever established in the sacrifice.[158]

This Vedic notion of action is presupposed throughout the *Gītā*[159]. Nowadays, we have action movies and adventure holidays to make us feel that we live life to the full; in traditional cultures, full participation, real action meant ritual, sacrificial action. *Gītā* 4.31b:

A man who does not sacrifice
has no part in this world. How could he enter the other?[160]

In fact, in the Vedic world view, the creation of the world had started with the creation of the founding sacrifice.[161] Mankind (*purusha*) has been created from 'Man' as the first sacrificial animal (*pashu*).[162] *Gītā* 3.10 explicitly refers to this sacrificial origin of mankind:

> Having created mankind along with sacrifice,
> Prajāpati, (the Lord of Creatures) anciently said,
> 'By this (i.e. sacrifice), may you bring forth;
> May this be your wishfulfilling cow.'[163]

Life and order must be won out of their opposites, sacrificial death and destruction, as Jan C. Heesterman puts it.[164] In the chain of ritualist cosmological identifications, the sacrifice, Prajāpati, *purusha*, man, life and death, sacrificer and sacrificial victim, become interchangeable.

In a Vedic ritual, what counts are the correct performance of the ritual, the purpose of the ritual, and the corresponding result. The purpose can be ceremonially fixed by the occasion or period, but it can also vary according to the personal motives of the one who expects to benefit from the performance of a particular ritual. This expectation of a specific reward as a result of performing a specific ritual is part of a wider package – ritual as such constitutes and regulates the worldwide give-and-take correspondence between benefactors and beneficiaries, between causes and effects, between surplus and debt, between action and reaction, between production and consumption in the cosmic process of *natural (and cultural) exchange*. Through sacrifice, we give back to the universe, or to the gods, what we have taken for our enjoyment. This is expressed in terms of food and the payment of debts; *Gītā* 3.11–12:

> Please the gods by sacrifice
> and they must make you prosper.
> While you and the gods sustain each other,
> you will reach the highest good.
>
> Sustained by sacrifice
> the gods will fulfill your desires.
> Only a thief consumes their gifts
> without giving to them.[165]

Sacrificial gifts are obliging in both directions of the social exchange. Theft is referred to as egoistic consumption, keeping for oneself what one is obliged to share, lack of balance, appropriating a disproportionate part of the profit from a shared transaction. It is the perfect traditional description of 'taking bribes' and 'corruption' – an unbalanced give-and-take. Sacrifice is the opposite of theft. Sacrifice, ritual action is mutually binding.

As such, it not only establishes the link between the production and consumption of the world, but it reproduces this connection constantly, thus linking these connections together to form an endless *chain of binding interaction*. Ritual action makes the world go round, keeps things going. Without ritual, the order of the universe would stop functioning properly, would stagnate, would fall back into chaos. Without ritual, the world order (dharma) cannot be maintained and enjoyed. The world order is upheld by constantly enacting it, by practising it. The *purpose* of ritual coincides with the purpose of the world order, and the performer of ritual participates in its purpose by enacting it.[166] In fact, the concept of 'purpose' establishes a link between ritual and desire. The *Gītā* too (3.10), calls 'sacrifice' the wish-fulfilling cow, the mythical cow that grants all desires. A sacrifice is performed in order to gain a reward, such as long life, the birth of a son or a secure place in the worlds beyond death. Desire is thus the motive of ritual action, and of righteous action in general (*Laws of Manu* 2.2–5; cf. the *Īśa Upanishad*, 1–2), according to Killingley.[167]

But it is not just the purpose of the ritual that counts. The correct performance too is crucial. In order to perform a ritual correctly, one has to have proper knowledge of the 'established liturgy' (*vidhi*). Knowledge of the Vedic ritual injunctions is the specialism and privilege of the priestly class of brahmins. They prevent people from making a wrong use of ritual. Their *action is linked to knowledge*, that is to say, action is linked to expert knowledge, which draws on the revealed knowledge of the Vedas, the sacred tradition of the eternal past.

Both *ritual action (sacrifice)* and *social action (duty)* are understood as a matter of purity. In the Vedic tradition, represented by the brahmanic position, purity is primarily a property of the ritual action and social action as such, not of the ritual actor or social actor who accompanies the actions by performing them. The purity of the action is measured by the correctness of its prescribed ritual performance – the keyword here is 'sacrifice' – or by the fulfilment of its expected role performance – the keyword here is 'duty' – and these are fairly objective (intersubjectively shared and perceivably controlled) criteria.[168]

Arjuna is about to attract indelible *impurity*. He is about to actively bring impurity on himself and on his community, and he has only himself and his community to blame. That is to say, he belongs to two opposing communities simultaneously and has to abide by two conflicting rule expectations. Family opposes warrior class, and the family code opposes the warrior code. What is right and what is wrong in this conflict? Either way, he will violate one of them, will pollute one of the groups and will have to blame himself for it, according to the 'objective' criteria of the community and of the visible impact (results) on that respective community.

Arjuna's choice in favour of non-action is not a solution to the problem of purity and impurity because failing to fulfil the role expectations of the warrior class would bring about indelible shame. Krishna's choice in favour of action is not a solution either because it would violate the family laws. Unless his action can uphold or restore some form of purity that annihilates the impurity involved. Arjuna opts for limiting the damage by trying not to be involved actively, but only passively, and by asking Krishna to instruct him about the exact criteria for right and wrong, good and evil deeds. Krishna answers that it is possible to perceive a constellation in which the contagious link between polluting action and personal (im)purity is lacking.

Along the *first* line of reasoning, Arjuna's moral indignation and depressed inactivity are taken as expressions of the impure desire for rewards of (ritual, sacrificial) action. Whether moral or immoral, good or bad, Arjuna is blamed for doing actions for personal gain, thus expressing selfishness and desire. Instead, he should participate in the universe by conforming to his duty as a warrior in the same way as ritual action upholds the world order because it behaves accordingly (sacrificially) by nurturing the food chain that the world order is. The food chain of the natural world has two characteristics in common with the exchange of gifts in the social world – their dynamic structure is cyclical and it transcends the agents participating in it. Humans and gods participate in the creative activity of the universe and, in doing so, they uphold it by nurturing it. Ritual sacrifice is the one activity where man's true involvement in the universe takes place. Performing one's caste duties is its worldly counterpart. Both cover the pursuit of *dharma* (cosmic order) and of *lokasamgraha* ('holding-together of the world/s', 'world-sustenance'), the greater goal of sustaining the cosmic order of the universe, the long-term cycle of the exchange of nature as a whole. Sacrifice is not just a social transaction of gift exchange, but a natural cycle of food exchange.[169]

In some parts of the broader narrative plot of the *Mahābhārata* epic, this Kurukshetra war is pictured as a *ritual sacrifice*.[170] Military action becomes a sacrificial ritual performance. The implication is that it turns warriors into ritually consecrated warriors. It does so if the warriors accumulate the cosmic creative power of heat (*tapas*) – and thus fire – which is the effective power of both the sacrifice and the sun, during the initiating consecration. According to Biardeau, transforming each of Arjuna's violent actions, beginning with war, into a sacrifice is also the underlying sense of the year of living incognito prior to the war. It corresponds to the period of consecration for the sacrifice – the war being the sacrifice *par excellence* for the warrior who offers himself as victim (self-sacrifice, *ātmayajña*) with the hope of substituting his enemy for himself – substituting one human victim for another.[171]

The *scope of action* has, as a result, been *widened,* but ritual action is still the point of departure.[172] According to Kees W. Bolle, '"activity" in the *Gītā* and in the entire Vedic-Brahmanic tradition can best be seen as a series of concentric circles. The center is the paradigmatic detached activity of God Himself. . . . The circle around this center, God, is the ritual of men, each group characterized by its function' (four castes or *varnas*). 'The ordinary, worldly activity of people makes up the next circle'.[173]

So far, then, in the debate about the link between action and desire, the *Gītā* seems to favour Brahmanism by widening the scope of ritual action and sacrifice. But things are more complicated in the *Gītā* than what can be said about ritual action and sacrifice. The *(first) line of reasoning* that links ritual action, sacrifice, warrior action in battle and action in general, may be new in the sense that the Vedic notion of *ritual action* in sacrifice has been enlarged, it still operates within the same logical framework of ritual action, not within the Upanishadic and Buddhist logical framework of *non-action* or *desireless action.*

6.3 The Gītā's second line of reasoning: Desireless action

From within the Vedic religion, ascetic tendencies developed into charismatic movements of full-time ascetics who renounced practising ritual altogether, in order to achieve the extinction of action as such. Why would ascetics or renouncers (*śramanas, samnyāsins*) strive for non-action? It takes a broader framework to answer that question.

During the second half of the first millennium BCE, the cultural history of India was witnessing an increased sense of gap or *distance* between the human being and his surrounding world. This heightened sense of estrangement transformed the perceived visible *outside world* into a world of *illusionary appearance,* and the perceiving *inner world* of the mind and heart into a world of *clouded ignorance.* Ritual action, then, came under attack. The ascetic movements took the most radical position in considering ritual action *unessential* because, in their view, ritual belongs to the outer world of mere appearance. They also considered ritual action *a bondage* because it belongs to the outer world of binding interaction. This bondage is ascribed to the newly developed law of *karma* that imports that each act, turning back on its agent or actor, automatically generates its own reward (merit) or punishment (demerit) in this or a next life (of that very agent or actor). The ideal of the renouncer is to be liberated from life altogether, rebirths included.[174] In short, *action became linked to cosmic forms of ignorance and slavery*, and was consequently disapproved of.

Within ancient India, there were now two dominant religious ideologies and, indeed, social groups – ritualistic Brahmanism and ascetic Śramanism.[175] While the focus of Brahmanism was on the priestly performance and knowledge of ritual and social behaviour enjoined by the Veda, the authoritative revelation, Śramanism emphasized the authority of individual experience and rejected the violence involved in the sacrifice; its focus was on asceticism and meditation in order to achieve a form of spiritual liberation, variously conceptualized in different Śramana traditions, but generally regarded as a liberation from action and the cycle of rebirth.

At first sight, linking action to knowledge (Brahmanism) and ignorance (Śramanism), respectively, may seem similar to Vernant's Greek notions of action and wrongdoing. But such a seeming similarity would give a wrong impression. The crucial difference is that both the traditional Vedic and the new ascetic notions of ritual action are (slightly) less a matter of knowledge than they are *a matter of desire*.[176] The link between ritual action and desire is established by the concept of 'purpose' (*samkalpa*), 'which is both the intention or determination to perform a ritual and the expectation of a specific reward as a result of it. *Samkalpa* is an essential element in Vedic ritual, and any vows or rules of restraint one may undertake result from *samkalpa* also (Manu 2.3)'.[177]

Yet, the new ascetic notions of ritual action are also very much *a matter of knowledge* because the state of bondage is not the result of a moral 'fall', but of an epistemological lapse into ignorance.[178] Madeleine Biardeau explicitly speaks of 'an anthropology of desire', but this desire is intertwined with knowledge, knowledge of the object whose acquisitive perception[179] elicits the desire to grasp it. After having discussed Bhima's praises of desire (*kāma*) in Book 12 of the *Mahābhārata* (Chapter 167), Biardeau shows its consistency with the psychology expressed by the later philosophical systems, in particular Nyāya and Mimāmsā. *Action does not express man, it only reveals his egoistic desire*.[180] Under the influence of Śramanism, then, later Brahmanism develops the logical option that action can be linked to desire in a negative way.

In short, *knowledge is intrinsically linked to action by desire, and action is a manifestation of desire* for an object or result known to be good in itself. In terms of Biardeau's scheme – perception (empirical knowledge) leads to aimed reward (desire), leads to intention (inclination to act), leads to intended act, leads to intended result, leads to generated merit, leads to rebirth for harvesting the reward. As a person desires, so does he act. For early Brahmanism, this *link between action and desire* is likely to be something *positive*, whereas for Śramanism, it is always something *negative*. Later, Brahmanism holds an ambivalent view. How does the *Gītā* take a position in this debate?

The crucial point of departure in the world view of the *Gītā* is that the bondage of *karma* and rebirth is closely associated with action – the general idea being that action leads to bondage whereas absolute knowledge leads to freedom – but that *bondage is caused by desire rather than by action itself*. This leads to a different understanding of the nature of sacrifice. According to *Gītā* 3.9, sacrifice (*yajña*) is the one kind of action that does not bind because it is free from attachment:

> It is true, this world is enslaved by activity,
> but the exception is work for the sake of sacrifice.
> Therefore, Son of Kuntī, free from attachment,
> act for that purpose.[181]

A critical commentator such as Killingley may reinterpret this 'non-attachment' as 'not the absence of desire but the presence of a motive which lies outside the person who acts',[182] yet he adds that ritual sacrifice is not undoing the bondage caused by desire because it is not performed without intention or purpose (*samkalpa*) whatsoever. And the 'intention' of the agent or 'purpose' of the action inevitably comes with some thought of the fruit or outcome of the action. World-sustenance (*lokasamgraha*) contains its own intrinsic desirability. A radically critical commentator such as Simon Pearse Brodbeck is adamant:

> I argue that the only alternative to thinking of one's actions in terms of fruits is not to think of them at all. Although this idea is barely intelligible, at least as regards one-off actions such as participation in the *Mahābhārata* war, and although the text does not admit that this is what it must perforce mean by *asakta karman* [action without attachment, *LM*], I suggest that *asakta* actions are psychologically void and only describable in terms of *yajña, dharma* or *lokasamgraha* from an external viewpoint. I show that *yajña* fails to explicate the mental attitude that Krishna is keen for Arjuna to adopt, because the text cannot find a bridge between the traditional, cosmic and external meaning of the term, and the new, internal meaning which Krishna implies.[183]

Christopher G. Framarin, however, argues that one can have a goal without having a desire linked to that goal if the goal is based on a normative belief that the action is the right thing to be done, regardless of its outcome. The classical connection in the Hindu schools of philosophy between beliefs, desire, action and results, according to which beliefs generate desire and desire generates action to obtain results, assumes that desire is a necessary condition of action. But, Framarin suggests, this is not always the case. At times, like in *Gītā* 3.25, one should translate words such as *cikirshā* as 'goal' or 'intention' or 'motivation' instead of 'desire'. We cannot act without a goal – at least not intentionally – but we can act without a desire in the sense of 'a disposition toward joy and disappointment depending on the outcome'.[184]

The *Gītā*'s *second* line of reasoning is by no means secondary. On the contrary, it represents the *Gītā*'s primary message, which is widely understood to be its main response to ascetic tendencies to renounce action altogether. But in order for the *Gītā* to be able to come forward with its own notion of *desireless* action, it has to make a philosophical detour. This detour draws on Upanishadic and early Sāmkhya and Yoga ideas of dualism between the psychosomatic individual and the immortal self. It focuses on the agent of action in the spiritual context of realizing ultimate freedom, and combines Upanishadic and early Sāmkhya and Yoga ideas with Bhakti ideas, while applying them to the material context of waging war. In order to acquire a deeper understanding of the *Gītā*'s view of man, we need to elaborate on the philosophical argument and its ingredients in some detail, before continuing the second line of reasoning.

6.4 Philosophical heritage: Inherited ideas on action, body and consciousness

It is evident that a substantial part of the philosophical ideas of the *Gītā* is derived from or inspired by the *Upanishads,* but it is not entirely clear to what extent. Chandradhar Sharma writes, 'Tradition also supports this view when it makes Shrī Krishna a cow-herd milking the celestial milk of *Gītā* from the *Upanishads* pictured as cows, Arjuna acting as a calf, for the sake of the wise'.[185] In the *Gītā* itself, there is one explicit reference to *vedānta*, the thought expressed in the *Upanishads* (and later, one of the classical schools of philosophy based on it), in 15.15, where Krishna says, 'I am the author of the Vedānta and the knower of the Vedas'. The *Gītā* thus draws part of its authority as a sacred scripture from its closeness or claimed closeness to the *Upanishads*.

The *Upanishads* represent the ascetic tradition on the level of philosophy, stressing ultimate freedom, absolute knowledge and monistic identity of the immortal self with the Absolute, in a tentative rather than in a systematically consistent way. The *Upanishads* are a collection of esoteric texts that cover a long period in time (roughly 600–200 BCE) and reflect a *shift* in philosophical outlook away *from collective ritualist knowledge to individual mystical knowledge.* Both the *individualization* and the *internalization* of religion are characteristic of the ascetic movement of Śramanism.

Previous to the *Upanishads*, the *Brāhmanas* had already turned their attention away from ritual action as such, in favour of the knowledge needed to equate the power of the *mantras* (*brahman*) inherent in ritual action with the sustaining cosmic power of the sacrifice and of the universe. This ritual knowledge became an esoteric form of priestly knowledge that was considered effective and therefore powerful even without the actual performance of the ritual, by being performed mentally.[186] This mental performance would, from that time onwards, lead to the long-lasting Indian tradition of mystical practice (*yoga*), while the esoteric knowledge of identities and correspondences between microcosmic ritual and the macrocosmic universe would lead to the long-lasting Indian tradition of speculative theory (philosophy). By the time of the *Upanishads*, this knowledge of *brahman* was *individualized* by cultivating an ascetic lifestyle of retreat from society into the forest, and was *internalized* by identifying one's (deeper than individual) inner immortal self (*ātman*) as this all-sustaining cosmic Self (*brahman*). Realizing this identity between one's immortal self and the cosmic Self was considered a liberating form of knowledge. It freed the human being from the bondage of action, not just of ritual action, but also of moral (good) and immoral (evil) action.

How can knowledge *liberate* the human being from the bondage of action? First of all, this esoteric knowledge is *universal knowledge*, knowledge of the universe and of the nature of man, not just knowledge of the proper performance of ritual. Secondly, it is *purified knowledge*, part and parcel of the purity of the ritual and the truth about the universe. But it is now also considered as being characterized by detachment, free from desire. That is why it is liberating. Pure knowledge can liberate because it is free from desire. That is to say, if knowledge is power because it is capable of establishing mental contact between the human being and reality, mystical knowledge is transformative power because it generates mystical experiences by transforming impure mental contact with reality into pure contact with reality, both in action, speech and thought. Pure knowledge has the power to establish immediate access to real truth and true reality without any interference of desirous elements. Pure knowledge is liberating knowledge not because it knows about chains and liberation from chains, but because it has the power to actually eliminate desire and break the chains of action and existence. The binding power of action is broken by eliminating from it the dimension of desire, of motive, of attachment, of choice, of the intention that is inherent in all good and evil action. Pure or absolute knowledge brings about non-action, that is to say, removes desire as the driving force and source of action, whereas ignorance or blindness (*avidyā*) brings about binding action, that is to say, instils the action with a motive, an intention, a desire that thus generates either merit or demerit, but in both cases, binding *karma*. *Karma* is binding in the sense that each act leads to its own reward or punishment, either in this life or in a next life. Consequently, it automatically leads to rebirth, whereas pure knowledge leads to neither merit nor demerit. Pure knowledge breaks the causal chain of (re)births and thus leads to ultimate liberation from the cycle of rebirths and suffering.

Within the Upanishadic framework, the *scope of action* is *limited instead of widened*. The point of departure here is *no longer ritual action, but renunciation of action*. Action is limited to worldly, binding action, whereas absolute knowledge enables spiritual freedom from such worldly bondage, thus destroying the enslaving chain of actions, rebirths, and suffering (from time). Instead of focusing on temporary action, the *Upanishads* focus on timeless being. The question no longer is – 'Do we act properly and meritoriously?', but 'Who am I truly and ultimately?' This way of thinking leads to a metaphysical gap between worldly action and desire, on the one hand, and ascetic non-action and absolute knowledge, on the other. In the case of the *Īśa Upanishad*, it leads to a combination of renunciation and worldly activity in the synthesis of giving up only all thought of reaping any personal benefit from activity in the world.[187] Upanishadic freedom is understood in terms of ultimate freedom, that is, true freedom, not in terms of worldly activity. Worldly activity may consist of doing things that involve choices, but such human initiative (*purushakāra*) is rooted in the slavery existence of the empirical self (*jīva*) or ego (*ahamkāra*) whose true freedom is effectively blocked by its identification with various dispositions and impulses.

Another concept from the *Upanishads* that finds its way into the *Gītā* is the *dualism of matter (nature) and consciousness (self)*. This dualism reflects the *yoga* practice of imposing discipline on the senses, the mind (*manas*) and the intellect *(buddhi)*. Yoga notions of dualism are developed in the late *Upanishads* (after 500 BCE), such as the *Katha Upanishad*, the *Śvetāśvatara Upanishad* and the *Maitrī Upanishad*. Yoga practice operates on the premise that the senses, the mind and the intellect, all belong to matter, and that the higher powers of the body complex can control the lower ones. On this level, there is no dualism because everything is considered part of the body complex.[188] The dualism is not between body and mind, but between embodied consciousness and disembodied (or de-individuated) consciousness (or self).[189] The intellect can, by means of understanding, control the mind, while the mind, acting as a rein, can control the senses. In the *Katha Upanishad* (I.3.3–9), the self is said to ride in the body as a passenger rides in a chariot, his journey determined by the charioteer's control; in turn, the body being compared to the chariot is driven by the charioteer (the intellect that judges and takes decisions), who uses the reins (the mind) to control the horses (the senses).[190] In the Śvetāśvatara Upanishad, the yoga interest in bringing the body to rest and releasing the self from the phenomenal world of nature is combined with knowledge about this phenomenal world of nature. Here, the brahman is manifested in three modes – the Lord, the self (purusha) and nature (prakrti). Nature is referred to, among other things, in terms of the three gunas (I.4, V.5, 7, 12–13, VI.2–4, 16), but the gunas are only mentioned, not elaborated upon. Yoga is the means by which the self can be extricated from nature.

A difference between the early Upanishads and the late Upanishads is the increasing influence of theism, Thomas J. Hopkins explains.[191] Whereas the goal of the early Upanishads is to become one with the Absolute beyond name and form, the late Upanishads reflect the increased importance of personal gods by introducing a much greater interest in the personal aspect of brahman.[192] Directing one's thoughts and feelings to this all-powerful and unchanging Lord, uniting with him through meditation, one loses attachment to the ephemeral and deluding world and one is able to see the god's physical form (mūrti), a mental image of God hidden within man's self.[193] Hopkins writes:

> As the āranyakas and early Upanishads had internalised the fire sacrifice by emphasising its mental performance, so the late Upanishads now internalised images. What had, in both instances, been expressed by means of external physical symbols was now expressed by mental performance in meditation. The two were, moreover, brought together in the Śvetāśvatara Upanishad by a conjunction of their most essential characteristics: meditation using the syllable om, the sound essence of the Vedic sacrifice, led to the appearance of the mūrti, the visual essence of non-Vedic image worship.[194]

Being allowed to see the god's physical form (mūrti) is crucial in the Gītā too because this is exactly what happens to Arjuna in the supremely revealing scene described in Chapter 11 – Arjuna asking to see Krishna's universal form, Krishna giving Arjuna a celestial eye and allowing him to see Krishna's form as Time.

As to the early sāmkhya and yoga ideas, in the Gītā, the terms sāmkhya and yoga do not yet refer to the systematic schools of philosophy, although both terms were to become the names of the later two dualist schools of philosophy.[195] If indeed anticipating these later developments, the Gītā is full of certain early sāmkhya and yoga ideas or of a sāmkhya-yoga style of thinking, especially in Chapter 13. In the Gītā, the term sāmkhya refers to the spiritual method of realizing ultimate reality by means of reflection and 'right (i.e., dualist) knowledge' (samyak khyāti or jñāna), while yoga refers to the spiritual method of realizing ultimate reality through disciplined contemplation or meditation.

Like the *Śvetāśvatara Upanishad*, the *Gītā* is well-acquainted with and makes use of a view of (material) nature (*prakrti*), which describes the processes of nature in physiological terms. The *Gītā* even uses the same terminology (*prakrti*, *avyakta*), but does not necessarily mean the same thing as the later classical *sāmkhya-yoga* philosophy.[196] According to Chandradhar Sharma, in the *Gītā* the words *prakrti* and *avyakta* mean 'the unmanifest power of God'.[197]

The natural world (*prakrti*) is a world of change. Motion is inherent in it in the form of *rajas*. But motion is not animation yet. As the source of the animate world, it is unconscious. Unlike the classical Greek notion of nature (*phusis*), the classical *sāmkhya* notion of nature (*prakrti*) is not animated nature, but moving matter. It has to be presumed that it exists together with the unchangeable principle of consciousness or spirit (*purusha*) that animates the material world by bringing about awareness of the world. The cosmic universe has to consist of a combination of these two eternal principles.[198]

The most striking difference between this type of Indian philosophy and its Western counterparts is that the *sāmkhya* concept of *consciousness* or *spirit* is *passive* – purusha without *prakrti* is lame – and the concept of *matter* or *nature* is *active* – prakrti without *purusha* being blind, but in motion – whereas Western concepts ascribe some form of creativity or transformational capacity to spirit instead of matter. Typically, in classical *sāmkhya* thinking, the design that is found in nature, particularly in the living body, is explained as pointing not to the designer, but to one who profits by the design, as M. Hiriyanna points out.[199] There is no need of a designer, of a creator god. The design is pleasing to the witness who is conscious of the design. The eye-contact between the witness and moving matter being witnessed triggers their mutual entanglement. Contact implies exposure and experience, and experience means awareness of events – one way of defining consciousness. Lack of discrimination leads to fatal identification by the transcendent self with what is going on in nature, and thus to an impure, confused consciousness, whereas dualistic, discriminative knowledge leads to mental separation and liberation from nature.[200]

The second striking difference between typical *sāmkhya* thinking and its Western counterparts is the rootedness of *sāmkhya* thinking in the practice of *ritual purity*, an insight I owe to Axel Michaels.[201] Purity, Michaels explains, is defined by the fact that something is *not mixed*. This applies to castes, subcastes, family groups, but also to the entire physical and psychic world, the cosmos, the gods and even trees and stones. Mixture comes about through contacts (touching, feeding, greeting and otherwise) and through temporary and spatial changes, shifts and transitions. *Contact and change are detrimental to purity.* Conversely, impurity is best avoided by lack of contact and by lack of movement, for example, by identifying with the unmixed, unalterable and therefore immortal Vedic sacrifice. This way of thinking is also manifest in the *guna* theory of the *sāmkhya* philosophy. The original matter of nature (*prakrti*) loses its state of highest purity by starting to move. It starts to move because it comes into contact with spirit (*purusha*). Contact means – fatal contact. The 'Fall' is *not moral,* as it is in Christianity, *but ritual.* It is the contact that brings about the occurrence of individual properties ('names and forms'), whereas being in itself is amorphous and without properties. Being static and without contact means being pure, whereas moving means being mixed and thus impure. Even the gods, who are by definition interactive with other gods, are due to their contacts, already qualified by properties and thus no longer absolutely pure. *Individuality is a form of impurity brought about by contact.* Neither the classical *sāmkhya* school of thought nor the classical *yoga* school of thought are focusing on the evolution of all the manifestations in the phenomenal world. Their crucial focus is in the opposite direction, on the attainment of ultimate freedom beyond the phenomenal world. The only really interesting principle in the phenomenal world, therefore, is the principle that leads back to and is in direct contact with the Absolute – the *eternal* self as opposed to the *sentient, embodied* self.[202]

6.5 *The Gītā's second line of reasoning: Yogic action*

In the *Gītā* too, Krishna puts forward the argument of the immortal self or soul that cannot perish along with the body (2.13–26). Put in perspective, in the other-worldly perspective of asceticism, that is, Krishna's late Upanishadic and early *sāmkhya* type of argument is not just a casual first effort to convince Arjuna of returning to fighting, by simply relativizing worldly life and death *sub specie aeternitatis.* This argument is not just meant to relativize the worldly stakes of fighting a war, but to absolutize what is at stake, metaphysically speaking – *the identity of the self as opposed to the identity of the individual* (2.12). That is to say, there is more to it than the opposition between the mortal body and the immortal soul (self, spirit, *dehin*). *The self is not just separated from the body, but also from the desired effect of action* (2.19). In Krishna's argument, the opposition between the eternal self and the embodied individual is linked to the Upanishadic and Buddhist framework of non-action or desireless action. One might argue that Krishna's point is that the eternal self is not at stake on the battlefield, but Krishna's argument runs in the opposite direction – at stake is Arjuna's lack of full awareness of the eternal self. Arjuna's problem, according to Krishna, is *delusion,* that is to say, lack of ultimate knowledge (2.13, 17, 19, 21, 25). True knowledge would allow Arjuna not just to perceive the opposition between the eternal self and the embodied individual, but to transform his concept of action. A transformation of his concept of action would enable him to separate the desired action of the embodied individual from the desireless action of the eternal self.

How is such a separation brought about and how is it to be conceived of? Again, the basic outlook is ultimate freedom. Seeking ultimate liberation from the cycle of births, deaths and rebirths is the number one priority in life. Ultimate freedom is achieved by realizing absolute knowledge, that is to say, by radically transforming one's *state of mind*, so that pure consciousness is (re)established. Pure consciousness is free from the impurity of desire, thus eradicating the root of suffering. Simultaneously, this ultimate state of desirelessness or detachment must be linked to worldly action as its underlying state of mind. Instead of withdrawing from all worldly action by cultivating radical non-action, a solution suggested by a lot of *Upanishads*, Krishna preaches radically desireless action (*nishkāma karma*).

By definition, this notion of desireless action takes the form of not attaching to the fruit (reward or punishment) of one's action, so that the inclination to act (intention) does not emerge in the first place. There is no room left for one's desire for reward or result. That is to say, *there is no mind-set that allows the mind of the agent to identify with the purpose of the action*, neither in terms of the intended effect nor in terms of the motive. The identity (the immortal self) of the psychosomatic agent is radically cut off, both from the deliberations preceding the action and from the consequences resulting from it. In the knowledge that the identity of the agent is radically different from the action, the agent performs the desireless action. Human action thus performed seems a matter of knowledge, not a matter of will. Desireless action is supremely tranquil action, the spontaneous action of a *yogi* who is absorbed in meditation, as in *Gītā* 2.55–56:

> The Blessed Lord spoke:
> When he leaves behind all desires
> Emerging from the mind, Arjuna,
> And is contented in the Self by the Self,
> Then he is said to be one whose wisdom is steady.
>
> He whose mind is not agitated in misfortune,
> Whose desire for pleasures has disappeared,
> Whose passion, fear and anger have departed,
> And whose meditation is steady, is said to be a sage.[203]

My suggestion that desireless action is not a matter of will should be nuanced on the basis of 5.23:

> He who is able to endure here on earth,
> Before liberation from the body,
> The agitation that arises from desire and anger,
> Is disciplined; he is a happy man.[204]

Desireless action is not a matter of will in the sense of desire, but it is a matter of will in the Greek sense of disciplined endurance and perseverance (16.1; cf. 2.14), and it is a matter of knowledge in the Hindu sense of consciousness manifesting a disciplined state of mind (*buddhiyoga*[205]) and containing absolute knowledge (*jñāna*).

In classical *sāmkhya* terms, desireless action is 'animated' action, action (passively) inspired by (or rather, witnessed by) the inactive spirit of pure knowledge. Ramesh N. Patel, who offers a *sāmkhya* style of philosophy of the *Gītā*, notices that the interesting point to see is how quickly Krishna passes from the question of killing to the issue of the identity of the killer and then to his point about the true or ultimate identity of any agent engaged in any action that is important to the agent. The initial treatment of Arjuna has two aspects, one that is moralistic–therapeutic and the other, which concerns deep existence. The depth–existential aspect rapidly asserts itself over a quick pass over the moralistic–therapeutic aspect. The reason for Krishna's speedy pass is that Arjuna's problem only seemed to be, and was really not, about morality.[206]

Patel introduces a term that indicates remarkably well that the eternal self in the individual is not an individual itself, but the non-individual power that 'animates' the individual by turning individual – 'the embodied immutable individuator'. Patel's terminology implies, in fact, something profoundly un-Western, which is that the whole idea of individuality as something positive is to be left behind in favour of a notion of identity that becomes less and less individual the closer it gets to its true original identity. *The individual has to radically de-individuate (or de-individualize)*. Being embodied means being alienated from one's eternal self. But alienation is not just due to embodiment. The condition of self-alienation is not lifted if the spirit leaves the body. The spirit should also leave behind its traces of individuality in order to coincide with the eternal self.[207]

Since *the true identity* is already there and was always there, it *is not created, but only discovered by action*, that is, by action that is appropriate to such discovery. Krishna also shows ways and means for its discovery. They imply specific disciplined courses of action. But a course of such action has to be rooted in true identity. True identity cannot be defined by any number or types of actions. In sum, Patel writes, one may say that *the Gītā rejects identity in action and recommends action in identity.* Because no particular action or end can define the essential individual, it is inappropriate to speak of such action or end as the true identity of the individual.[208] Men become, in fact, individuals by their striving (their karmic activity), but deep down, they are not individuals in their being (their spiritual essence). Krishna urges Arjuna to give up his embodied striving and instead to be pure in body and mind.

If the immortal self (*dehin*) is essentially passive, functioning as 'an inactive witness which is presupposed whenever there is consciousness of anything',[209] the true identity (*dehin*) of the psychosomatic agent is itself inactive. So who or what activates the agent, if his agency cannot be ascribed to the immortal self who is 'the embodied one' (*dehin*)? Who or what makes the body move? The *samkhya* answer to that is *prakrti*, material nature. Nature brings forth motion patterns in the material world of humans and other agents. The killing agency that people assume they have, then, must be ascribed to nature. This *samkhya* answer is indeed one of the options Krishna uses as an argument to pull Arjuna away from his illusion that he is truly in charge of his own actions. The other two options, Time and Krishna Himself, will be explored later on.

Self-identification with the action is the fatal error leading to the illusion of a mistaken identity – not a moral error, but a metaphysical one. From a Western perspective, the question arises whether such a radical separation between the metaphysical identity of the agent and the moral character of the action is possible. After all, the agent cannot be called the actor if he cannot in any way be *identified with* the action as *his* action. The agent or actor may, of course, claim in some cases that his action was not his intention. He may distance himself from the consequences of his action by maintaining that his action was unintended or that its results were beyond his intention. In those cases, the agent does not himself *identify with* his action. But even in those cases, Bernard Williams would argue, people are held more or less accountable for being, as a matter of bad luck, doomed destiny, or moral debate, the performer or executer of the action's results.

This is not the *Gītā*'s approach. *The Gītā, instead, radically separates ultimate freedom from social responsibility, and then combines them.* While responsibility (in the sense of being accountable to one's group for living up to its social expectations of one's devotion to duty) is a moral issue, freedom is a metaphysical one. Responsibility plays a crucial role on the social level of worldly activities, whereas freedom means being freed from these worldly activities altogether on the spiritual level of cosmic identity with the Absolute (*brahman*). The ultimate freedom of one's eternal self (*ātman* or *purusha*) remains detached from the social responsibility of one's empirical self while allowing the empirical self to fulfil its specific caste duties and to identify with them on the social level of worldly activities. Krishna's metaphysical concept of desireless action enables him to widen the scope of pure knowledge to include pure action. Moreover, the concept of desireless action has the capacity to include ritual action, sacrifice and warriors fighting a war. Arjuna can now be convinced of becoming the ultimate freedom fighter in the metaphysical sense of the word, but simultaneously, he can become the supreme example of social responsibility. Equipped with the weaponry of spiritual knowledge and material military arms, Arjuna can embody the ideal combination of ultimate freedom and social responsibility. There is no talk of 'individual freedom' in this context, for two reasons. First of all, real freedom is ultimate freedom instead of freedom on the social level of the relationship between community and individual. Secondly, real freedom is the ultimate freedom of the eternal self whose identity is intrinsically cosmic and de-individualized. Only from the worldly perspective can the pursuit of ultimate freedom be perceived as individual, that is to say, as the initiative of an individual to leave the community behind and become an ascetic.

Yet, metaphysically *allowing* the empirical self (Arjuna) to take up its social responsibilities in the knowledge that the eternal self remains free from its binding power is one thing, encouraging and even *calling for* the empirical self to take up arms and fight is a different matter. What urge could there be, metaphysically speaking, to actually fulfil one's warrior duties and fight? If the direction of the ascetic argument is other-worldly – ultimate freedom being freedom *from* social responsibility – can this other-worldly direction convincingly make a turn of 180 degrees and be used for this-worldly purposes? The *Gītā's* positive answer to this set of questions is developed along two lines.

One way of approaching the issue is by focusing on the notion of sacrifice and on the character of the warrior. The *second* line of reasoning, which focused on non-action or desireless action, is now *linked* to the *first* line of reasoning, which focused on ritual action.

Earlier on, we noticed that the concept of *sacrifice* has to be understood in a wider sense. The epic's great battle, the Kurukshetra War, is pictured as a ritual sacrifice. Military action becomes a sacrificial ritual performance. The implication is that it turns warriors into ritually consecrated warriors. It does so if the warriors accumulate the cosmic creative power of heat (*tapas*), which is the effective power of both the sacrifice and the sun during the initiating consecration. But this preparatory consecration (in the forest), having been internalized, has become a *yogic* preparation that is characterized not just by austerities (*tapas*), but by mental detachment. The *yogic* preparation for the war leads to the idea that an inner conquest is required to assure victory in the external combat of battle (*Mahābhārata* 5.34.52–55, 12.69.4–5), Biardeau argues. The sacrifice Arjuna performs becomes an act of *yoga*, marked by one-pointed concentration (*ekāgra*) on the task at hand. In this manner, the notion of sacrifice is internalized to become a new ideal of conduct.

Turning warriors into ritually consecrated warriors is not the only implication. Sacrificial action is a specific category of action related to the give-and-take logic of the food chain of nature, which sacrifice upholds by nurturing it. Through sacrifice, we give back to the universe, or to the gods, what we have taken for our enjoyment. Only a thief consumes the gifts of the gods without paying back what he is indebted to them (3.11–12). Sacrificial killing, therefore, is not robbing people of their lives, but giving the universe or the gods what one owes them. A sacrifice is a gift. As a gift, it is meritorious within the Vedic logic of early Brahmanism. Within the ascetically tinged logic of later Brahmanism, it will become all the more meritorious if given without the expectation of favour in return. *If a sacrificial gift is given without the expectation of favour in return*, an alternative option opens up – the option that the sacrificial gift is beyond merit and demerit, free, without desire and therefore without *karmic* bondage. This is exactly what 3.9 opts for – that sacrifice is the one kind of action that does not bind. In the *Gītā*, one's duties should be performed as a sacrifice to the god(s), a free gift to the god(s) who sustain(s) the universe. To refuse one's duties is as much an act of selfishness as the performance of duties with the hope of reward. The ascetic virtue of altruistic generosity consists in giving disinterestedly without expecting return gifts, but also of allowing the ascetic not to accept (binding!) gifts. Ascetic gift-giving and gift-receiving lacks that obliging reciprocity of social participation precisely because (thus) the ascetic stands outside the community as its transcendent, dissociated ideal. This characteristic makes the ascetic the most worthy recipient of gifts in a culture where a gift (*dāna*) should be given to a worthy recipient.[210] The rise of a moral of liberality, of disinterested giving – the pure gift – needs to be seen in the context of the rise of ascetic practice, Michaels points out.[211] Also, the idea of life as an obliging gift that can never fully be returned in kind, but only celebrated in gratitude seems characteristic of the three monotheistic religions, yet alien to the Indian tradition.[212]

The *Gītā* also puts this teaching in terms of the *guna* theory. In the *Gītā*, both the disinterestedly offered sacrifice and the disinterested gift are, in fact, not so much a sign of merit, but of a *sattvic* person. *Gītā* 17.11–12 and 17.20–21 respectively:

Sacrifice which is offered, observing the scriptures,
by those who do not desire the fruit,

concentrating the mind only on the thought 'this is to be sacrificed';
that sacrifice is *sattvic*.

But sacrifice which is offered
with a view to the fruit, Arjuna,
and also for the purpose of ostentation;
know that to be *rajasic*.[213]

The gift which is given only with the thought 'it is to be given',
to a worthy person who has done no prior favor,
at the proper place and time;
that gift is held to be *sattvic*.

But that gift which is given grudgingly,
with the aim of recompense
or gain, with regard to fruit,
is considered *rajasic*.[214]

Killingley points out the extraordinary use of the *guna* vocabulary:

> So far, the *guna* theory seems to point to no more than an intelligent, far-seeing self-interest. But some passages about the *gunas* go further. For instance, while the *rājasik* person gives with the expectation of favours in return, the *sāttvik* person gives because it is right to give (*dātavyam iti*, 17.20–21). Similarly, while the *rājasik* person performs worship with a view to its rewards or fruits, the *sāttvik* person worships because it is right to worship (*yastavyam iti*, 17.11). The *Gītā* thus rejects Manu's view that all action is motivated by desire. Rather, it holds that the highest form of action is motivated outside the agent, in the categorical imperatives of *dharma*.[215]

Sacrificial actions and ritually consecrated warriors are, in a reasoning along these lines, characterized by their manifestation of ultimate detachment. The ideal of desireless action and the ideal character of a warrior (being detached) are expressed in terms of the *guna* theory.[216] If *tamas* is Arjuna's problem, *rajas* is not his solution, as one would expect from a warrior, but *sattva* is. The solution does not so much occur on the level of *artha* as it does on the level of *dharma*.

This teaching implies a reinterpretation of what cultic action consists of. But it also sets forth the age-old customs that should be practised (*dharma*). Cultic action is to be performed, except that one should perform cultic action without counting on a reward.

6.6 The Gītā's third line of reasoning:
Devotional action

Another way of approaching the issue is by focusing on the devotion of Lord Krishna as the all-powerful personal god within whose unifying being, the eternal Self (*purusha*) and nature (*prakṛti*) merely form separate parts (15.7, 10.42b, 7.6, 9.17, 14.3–4, 9.7–8). The individual devotion of one god among many as one's personal and only god is called 'henotheism' in Religious Studies and *bhakti* in Hindu theology. In historical terms, it marks *a shift within Hinduism from monism to theism*. The *bhakti* approach transforms the cosmic Absolute of the early *Upanishads* (*brahman*) and the embodied immutable individuator of Patel's *sāmkhya* thinking (*purusha*) into the one personal god who should be venerated. Personally worshipping one god exclusively is a disciplined practice called *bhakti yoga*. It focuses on *devoted action*. As such, it constitutes a *third line of reasoning*, which is linked to the *first and second lines of reasoning*. In fact, the three lines of reasoning are sometimes intertwined to such an extent that it is justified to consider the *Gītā* a work of theological synthesis.

In 2.61, the *karma yoga* approach, which links action to the desireless tranquillity of the *yogi* who controls his senses, is combined with *bhakti yoga*, which links action to the exclusive focus on Krishna:

> Restraining all these (senses),
> Disciplined, he should sit, intent on Me;
> He whose senses are controlled,
> His wisdom stands firm.[217]

By combining *karma yoga* with *bhakti yoga*, the devoted action of the devotee is supposed to manifest the same desirelessness or non-attachment that the *yogi* manifests. This is possible if the devotee (*bhakta*) is conceived of as meditating on and surrendering everything to God, including the desire for, and attachment to, the consequences of all action. *Gītā* 3.30:

> Deferring all actions in Me,
> Meditating on the supreme Spirit,
> Having become free from desire and selfishness,
> With your fever departed, fight![218]

Bhakti devotional practice is also combined with ritual action and sacrifice (9.26, 27, 34, 18.65). This enables the ritually consecrated warrior to dedicate his sacrificial action in battle to the one god as the addressee of his sacrificial gift. Krishna becomes the supreme goal of the devotee's action (11.55).

Most of all, *bhakti* is a devotional practice in which the devotee submits to the one god as his saviour god who delivers him from the cycle of rebirths, that is to say, as the one god who intervenes with his grace for the sake of the devotee's ultimate liberation (*moksha*) (12.6–11). In the case of Krishna, this divine intervention coincides with his intervention in the course of history for the sake of *dharma*, since Krishna has taken up the role of Vishnu.[219] The Vishnu incarnation is believed to intervene in times of decay (*adharma*) in order to restore the good in the world (4.7–8). In this way, Krishna–Vishnu himself acts without desire for the fruit of action (4.14a). Comprehending this enables Arjuna, the supreme devotee-warrior, to act without being bound by actions (4.14b).

Thus, the ideal person is the *yogi* who is devoted to God and dear to God (12.14–20) and who acts without desire for the fruit of action. The devotee is called to see God as the centre of all actions, so that one can be a renouncer (*samnyāsin*) while still acting because action is cast off (*sam-ny-as*) on to God (3.30, 18.57). The devotee should not act for himself, but for God, making his actions acts of worship and furthering God's aims – the welfare of the world, and the devotee's own salvation. Lord Krishna, in turn, as the centre of all actions, is himself the exemplar of the *yogi*. But:

> even God, who is the exemplar of the *yogi*, does not act in a totally unmotivated way. He does not act to fulfil any needs of his own, since he has none (3.22). Yet he continues in action as an example to others (3.23f), and the *yogi* should do the same, both to avoid confusing others (3.26), and for the maintenance of the world (3.20, 25). Besides maintaining the world in being (10.42), God acts in two specific ways: he takes birth in the world in order to rescue the righteous, destroy evil-doers and establish *dharma* (4.8), and he returns the love of his devotees (12.14–20). In Arjuna's case, Krishna returns his love by instructing him (10.1), by showing him his universal form (11.54), and finally by promising that Arjuna will reach God (18.65). In loving his devotees, God breaks his own rule of holding no one either hateful or dear (9.29; cf. 9.4f). In this too he is the exemplar of the *yogi*, who has no desires (5.3; 12.17), yet is devoted to God.[220]

Crucial here is the fact that the saving God of the *Gītā*, Lord Krishna, is cast in the neutral colours of yogic asceticism. *His incarnation* could be understood as *the intervention of a self-absorbed sacrificer, but not as a form of divine self-sacrifice*. Through total war, he is sacrificing the current universe for the sake of a new universe; he neither sacrifices himself nor identifies with the victim; on the contrary, as a *yogi*, he dissociates himself from his sacrificial performance. Self-sacrifice seems typical of asceticism, but it is not, in that it sacrifices everything redundant to the self, but for the sake of the transcendent self, according to Michel Hulin.[221]

7 Self-knowledge

Moral achievement relies on both action and reflection. Moral choices demand deliberation and conscious reflection, that is, a certain *degree of knowledge*. But human vision does not have the power to establish certainty. Absolute knowledge is clearly beyond human reach. Or, is it?

In the *Gītā*, it is absolute knowledge that makes the difference, also on the battlefield. It enables access to ultimate freedom, not to social responsibility, in the first instance. But how does a mortal human being like Arjuna acquire access to absolute knowledge in the first place? Arjuna's failure does not just consist in lack of will-power (weakness of the will), but in ignorance, lack of self-knowledge.

In Plato's philosophy, Charles Taylor explains, reason is the capacity to see the right order; reason is a matter of perception, of *vision*, of grasping the vision of the natural order and acting accordingly, that is to say, virtuously. Vision, reason and virtuous action go hand in hand – except that they do not automatically lead to 'external success'. Lack of vision, ignorance and vicious action also constitute a sequence; ignorance and vice are undone by vision, by a vision of the Good or Truth. 'Reason reaches its fulness in the vision of the larger order'. It is 'not a matter of internalizing a capacity' of vision, but a matter of 'conversion', of 'turning the soul's eye around to face in the right direction', towards the truth and away from illusion, as Taylor puts it.[222] On the *narrative* level of the plot of the *Gītā*, in Arjuna's case too, ignorance is undone by *vision*, by a philosophical picture taught by his *guru* Krishna and by a revealing vision of the agency of the Lord of the Universe, his *god* Krishna. At first, this vision is transmitted along the traditional paths of teaching (Krishna as *guru*), but then Krishna replaces his didactical and imaginative traditional teachings with an actual vision that takes the palpable form of an overwhelming appearance (Krishna as Lord of the Universe) and which commands personal surrender.

In the *Gītā*'s *teachings*, however, on the *philosophical* level, one of the traditional Hindu methods of acquiring absolute knowledge is called the 'Way of knowledge' (*jñanayoga*). This is one of the options recommended by the *Gītā*. It envisages a liberated state of mind through advanced meditation, that is to say, the *internalization of the capacity of vision*, a shift inwards from viewing to knowing. This shift inwards is already depicted in the oldest *Upanishad*, the *Brhad Aranyaka Upanishad*, in *BU* 4.3,[223] where Yājñavalkya teaches Janaka, the king of Videha, how the self (*ātman*) is that transcendent inner light of a person that witnesses the person, thus travelling through the person's outer world of the senses lit by sun, moon, fire and voice, the realm where one is awake, then travelling around in the transitory world, where the person creates for himself an entire world as his pleasure ground, the realm of dream, before retreating into the other world, where nothing from what he sees when he is awake or dreaming follows him, the serene realm where as he sleeps, he has neither desires nor dreams; in this serene realm, the self is a light without objects, consisting of knowledge oblivious to everything within or without, a seer left with his capacity to see.

In the West, Taylor argues, the epistemological shift from looking outward towards the objects to looking inwards towards the seer's inner capacity to see, can be traced in Augustine's writings on memory, search for knowledge and love of God. Augustine directs our focus onto the activity of striving to know, and off the objects (Plato's) reason knows. He takes a first-person perspective – I see 'that God's is the power sustaining and directing this activity', 'the Master within' directing my activity of striving to know, the One behind my eye, God as 'the most fundamental ordering principle in me'.[224]

In both cases, the shift from looking outward to looking inward leads to the religious discovery of being empowered to see – in the case of Yājñavalkya, by the person's transcendent self within that witnesses the person's inner and outer worlds and is his transcendental light and desirelessness (equalling the fulfilment of all desires); in the case of Augustine, by the person's transcendent God within who directs the person's outlook and desire (good will through divine grace) and is his transcendental light and love.

At this stage, I would like to point out several things. First of all, the West reached this kind of internalization with regard to self-knowledge around the early fifth century CE; India reached a similar kind of internalization around the seventh to sixth centuries BCE. This *difference in time* might, of course, suggest that India was simply one thousand years ahead in time. But such a comparison assumes that all cultures follow the same evolutionary development at a different pace. A cross-cultural comparison should stress, instead, that even if this is the case, *the cultural contexts* of similar processes of internalization with regard to self-knowledge *differ substantially*. This can be illustrated by my second point – the role of desire is a different one. In the Augustinian case, desire is embedded in the *social context* of a love relationship between God and man; in the Indian case, desire is embedded in the *ascetic context* of an individual relationship between the true self and its desirelessly contemplating presence in a person. Thirdly, the *Gītā's teachings* recall this mystical and epistemological shift by recommending the Way of knowledge as one legitimate approach to ultimate liberation, but the *Gītā's plot* sidetracks this shift from looking outward to looking inward, by turning to a revelatory vision of Krishna as the Master of the Universe directing one's outward activity, as one's decisive source of knowledge. The *Gītā's* philosophical concepts and its plot pattern do not necessarily confirm each other. Moreover, Krishna preaches an additional option that turns out to be the final one – the Way of submission or surrender (*bhaktiyoga*). *Bhakti* devotion aims at a personal experience of the one God. This Way of personal devotion opens up, in turn, the possibility of a new shift from looking outward to looking inward, in the form of henotheistic or monotheistic mysticism.

On the narrative level of the *Gītā*, the one god turns out to be Krishna. And Krishna does not just preach this message to Arjuna, He also allows Arjuna a personal experience of Himself as the one god. This *bhakti* experience is exactly what happens to Arjuna while being taught by Krishna. According to the *Gītā*, Chapter 11, Krishna shows him his divine physical form (*mūrti*), in much the same way as is suggested by the late *Upanishads*. The devotional approach is an emotional approach. *Feelings of devotion and love* play an important role in the relationship between Krishna and his devotees. Krishna repeatedly states, 'He who is devoted to me is dear to me'. (11.44, 12.14–20) In the *bhakti* experience of the devotee, such feelings mediate and accompany the experience of God. But the crucial turning-point in the *bhakti* experience is that God takes the initiative, in an act of grace that expresses his divine feelings of love for the devotee, to reveal himself to the devotee as the supreme Self. The devotee reaches at his personal knowledge of God because God makes himself known to his devotee. Krishna does so verbally. His verbal revelation awakens in Arjuna the desire to actually see the cosmic appearance of the Lord of the Universe. He is allowed Krishna's appearance by Krishna's grace. Arjuna is unable to see Krishna with his natural vision: Krishna has to endow him with a divine eye to see the divinity (11.8). *Bhakti* knowledge turns out to be *revelatory knowledge*. That is to say, the *Gītā* makes the truth emerge as a deliberate act of revelation on the part of Krishna, not of Arjuna. This revelatory truth is not a wise advice. It is simply overwhelming. It disarms Arjuna's unwillingness to fight, elucidates his mind and liberates his heart from the burden of potential guilt feelings and depression. Arjuna does not arrive at his conclusions through a rational and investigative search for the truth. He is taught the truth by his spiritual teacher, and he is shown a vision by his spiritual teacher as the Lord of the Universe. As the truth breaks through, it overrules the empirical knowledge of mortal human beings. It is more than Arjuna can bear. Arjuna is terrified.

For Arjuna, the revelatory knowledge turns out to go far beyond moral issues. His very existence and essence, his true identity is involved in the revelation. Knowledge turns out to be *self-knowledge*. For Arjuna, the question is no longer whether to fight or not to fight, but whether *to be or not to be*, that is to say, to be or not to be *truly immortal and act accordingly*. Not ethics, but anthropology turns out to be the true issue. Ethics is grounded in spirituality and ontology. Matters of action and non-action are grounded in the spiritual identity of the agent. *The Gītā offers a theory of human action within the framework of a religious anthropology* that focuses on the immortal de-individualized self. The main thrust of the argument is that if Arjuna's spiritual self does not attach to and identify with (the results of) his action because it knows of its own immortality and transcendence, the spiritual actor remains separated from the actual action of the agent.

8 Conclusions

The theory of the three *gunas* that provides the *Gītā*'s psycho-physiological vocabulary for attitudes of mind and heart is also used to describe nature in general in terms of types of movement and variety, as opposed to the immortal Self that is temporarily caught up in the worldly embodiment of individual human beings. On the worldly level, human nature is inherently desirous and ignorant, attached to the world of the senses and blind to the spiritual truth of ultimate liberation. Tragic conflicts are taken for real, but they are ultimately illusions nurtured by desire and ignorance. On the worldly level, the discrepancy between intended actions and unintended consequences constitutes moral dilemmas that cannot be solved morally. The moral and psychological weight of human intentions, actions and their consequences is a source of depression and confusion, if one is to go by Arjuna's breakdown on the battlefield.

Their religious weight, however, is a different story altogether. On the one hand, to a mind undisturbed by desires and afterthoughts, human intentions, actions and their consequences weigh nothing whatsoever because the ultimate Self is not involved in their execution. On the other hand, to a mind single-mindedly focused on the only ultimate Actor ruling the universe, human intentions, actions and their consequences weigh what they are worth as free sacrificial gifts of devotion to the one God who destroys and recreates righteousness and world order by the grace of His supreme intervention.

Arjuna's conflict is a tragic conflict in Hegel's sense of the word – a social conflict between two 'rights' or 'truths' that cannot be solved unless it is transcended and transposed to a higher level of rights or truths. Arjuna's conflict of loyalties between family duties and warrior class duties is not solved on the worldly level, but on the spiritual level. On the worldly level, the family duties simply lose out to the warrior duties, for no convincing reason. The outcome could have been in the opposite direction.

The conflict is interpreted by Krishna, in more abstract terms, as the dilemma whether to act or not to act. Along the described three lines of reasoning, Arjuna's dilemma whether to act or not to act is restated several times:

Along the *first* line of reasoning, his moral indignation and depressed inactivity were expressions of the impure desire for rewards of (ritual, sacrificial) action. Whether moral or immoral, good or bad, Arjuna was focused on doing actions for personal gain, thus expressing selfishness and desire. Instead, he should show indifference and act without desire.

Along the *second* line of reasoning, Arjuna's dilemma was reinterpreted in terms of the dilemma of choosing between ritualistic Brahmanism and ascetic Śramanism, of having to make a choice between action and non-action, and in terms of confusing the psychosomatic individual with the immortal Self. Arjuna's depressed resolve not to act was then a choice in favour of the ascetic's renunciation of action altogether. Instead, he should renounce the results of his disciplined action, but not action itself, mentally discriminating between the metaphysical identity of the agent and the actual action in ways the knowledgeable *yogis* and the Upanishadic or *samkhya* philosophers are familiar with.

Along a *third* line of reasoning, Arjuna's dilemma was restated as an expression of his ignorance regarding the theological truth about who ultimately is in charge in the universe and who should be the one addressee of all his actions. Instead of withdrawing, Arjuna should devote all his actions to Krishna as a devotional sacrifice, for the benefit of Krishna's plan with the universe (*dharma*) and for the sake of his own ultimate liberation (*moksha*).

Krishna's restatements of the original conflict are reinterpretations that transcend the tragic nature of the conflict and also move away from the Hegelian equality between the terms of the conflict – to act or not to act initially becomes to act selfishly or to act indifferently, a transformation clearly in favour of (*yogic*) indifference. The next move reinterprets the conflict in terms of a choice between ritualistic action versus ascetic non-action, again, a choice that favours one of the two options – in this case, the ritualistic action of orthodox Brahmanism, albeit in the form of a compromise with asceticism, since non-action is to be practised mentally. The third reinterpretation offers a choice between devotion to the one Ruler of the universe versus ignorance regarding this theological truth. That is to say, gradually, no dilemma is left to cling to. The conflict disappears by transcending it spiritually and viewing it in the light of eternity.

Krishna's response is worlds apart from Sands' view of tragedy as a birth trauma – the awakening of moral consciousness as a phenomenon that goes hand in hand with a sense of loss of belief in ultimate justice and universal order. In fact, Krishna almost bursts out in laughter at the scene of Arjuna's breakdown. The breakdown itself, however, and the tenor of the epic as a whole suggest the applicability of Sands' view of Western tragedy to the Indian epic. In India too, historico-culturally speaking, the awakening of this ethically reflecting type of moral consciousness brought forth a corpus of literature full of stories of problematic heroes and suffering victims and abundant with ethico-religious debates on the nature of *dharma*. Arjuna's breakdown refers to a moral breakdown of the traditional socio-cosmic order. Krishna's teachings restore confidence in that traditional order by putting it in (a transcendental) perspective. Psycho-ethical conflicts may hurt, but they have to be faced with the equanimity of a *yogi*. The performance of one's duties may hurt, but it has to executed with the dedication of a devotee. The mental suffering of a disturbed mind is purified and replaced by the calm and concentrated vision of cosmic truth. Cosmic truth does not emerge from pain. The pollution of an immoral act, of an impure intention or of an unintended consequence is purified and replaced by the dedication of all actions, intentions and results to the one and only real Actor of the universe. Cosmic action does not emerge from pollution, but from destructive and re-creative cleansing. Self-knowledge is achieved by transcending the world of pain and pollution, not by leaving behind the world itself, but by leaving behind all desire and ignorance.

PART III: CROSS-CULTURAL COMPARISONS

A sixth set of aspects that is intimately connected with tragedy is its focus on the moral and psychological weight of human intentions and actions. Several cross-cultural observations can be made regarding these psycho-ethical aspects, in particular, regarding the *main question*, that is to say, regarding the various ways in which human actions and human intentions are linked in the texts that have been discussed.

1 Moral dilemmas, actions and intentions

According to Vernant, participation in Attic politics implied involvement in making decisions but, more than that, it revealed a growing consciousness of being individually responsible for the way city affairs were carried out. Responsibility came to include the intention of the agent or actor. The results of actions were considered much more objective than the intentions accompanying them. In Sophocles' *Oedipus Tyrannus* (895: *praxeis*), 'it is the deed that counts, not the motive', Winnington-Ingram noted. On the one hand, the individual agents were now shown on stage to be engaged in considering options, in assuming responsibility, in feeling guilty about committed crimes; on the other hand, they were shown to be exposed to fate and the gods, which turned out to be much more decisive than the powerless decisions of human mortals. Tragedy, Vernant argued, problematizes the human being as acting being (agent or actor), disturbingly interrogating man's relationships to his own actions. On the one hand, the tragic agent or actor is guilty, since he is the cause responsible for his actions; on the other hand, the tragic agent is the victim of fate and the gods, possessed by a *daimon* who makes his mind insane, is even innocent in the sense of being a victim of his own ignorance, in the case of Sophocles' Oedipus, not even collaborating by their own wicked acts to their own downfall, as do Aeschylus' heroes, according to Winnington-Ingram.

In Shakespeare's *Hamlet*, the moral weight of human intentions now becomes a complicated matter because both thought and action have as many motives as they have reinforcing consequences. A core element of tragedy is restated in psychological terms. There is a sharpened shift in focus from human actions to human intentions. Divine intentions are considered by one character only, by Hamlet, and only to the extent that 'heaven' or 'providence' can restore order, and punish Hamlet and Claudius. The real conflict is between Hamlet's reflections and his actions, it seems. But Hamlet is facing a moral dilemma that could be stated in terms of a conflict between a Christian world view and a nobleman's ethic. It could also be stated in terms of a private family vendetta as opposed to a public state affair, as Watson argued. If, however, the moral dilemma is stated in terms of revenge or no revenge, it takes the form of a question – To act or not to act, or rather – To act immorally or not to act and be moral. Whichever way you look at it, Hamlet is facing a moral dilemma.

Arjuna too, on the battlefield of Kurukshetra, faces a moral dilemma. On the one hand, he is expected to fight a righteous war and to fight because it is his duty as a nobleman to defend his kingdom by force against illegitimate rule. On the other hand, Arjuna is expected to fight a deadly war involving the killing of some of his own kinsmen, affectionate friends, respected elders and revered teachers.

In the first instance, the moral dilemma consists of a conflict of social loyalties – the simultaneous necessity and impossibility of choosing between the warrior code not to neglect one's duty and the family code not to kill a relative. But the moral dilemma is simultaneously a religious dilemma. It is a religious duty to respect the family and its continuity, especially for the sake of the ancestors who depend on the ritual offering of *pinda* for their status as spirits. In the second instance, the moral dilemma consists of a conflict of cosmic proportions. The battle is between good and evil. The battlefield of the Kurus is called the 'field of *dharma*' or 'field of righteousness'. But Arjuna's righteous battle against evil brings about even more evil and a breakdown of the very moral order (*dharma*) he is supposed to defend. The moral dilemma is a real dilemma because, either way, *dharma* is violated. It is undergoing a crisis on the practical level of its imminent enactment.

The practical level is crucial in one respect – it focuses on the actions and their results, their objective 'fruits', not on the agents and their intentions, their good will. The agents are considered 'sinners' insofar as the results of their actions are considered 'sinful', not vice versa. What counts are the actions and their results, not Arjuna's sincerity and authenticity. To fight or not to fight, to act or not to act, that is the question. That is to say, to act right(eous)ly. But Krishna teaches Arjuna how to intentionally withdraw his focus on the results of his actions, to resist a straightforward acceptance of the values of a culture oriented towards obtaining results, and to purify his consciousness from its social and moral weight. Does this intended transformation turn Arjuna into another Rāma, the purely virtuous hero in Vālmīki's *Rāmāyana,* whose dharmic actions have catastrophic social consequences? Not exactly. Gregory D. Alles compares Rāma to Achilles, 'Achilles epitomizes a consequentialist ethic: he is virtuous because he gets things done. To this extent, Homer's *aretē* resembles Machiavelli's *virtu.* Rāma epitomizes a categorical ethic. It identifies right action apart from, even despite, the consequences of action. To this extent, his *dharma* resembles Kant's duty'.[225] In Vālmīki's *Rāmāyana,* that is, Rāma's virtuous actions directly express his hidden, inner nature, regardless of the catastrophic social consequences. His personal human nature generates virtuous actions without necessarily bearing virtuous fruits. Rāma's actions are considered dharmic by virtue of the inner nature that they manifest, not by their results in terms of social impact, as is the case with Achilles and Oedipus. But Arjuna's case is different from Rāma's. Arjuna's dual nature is that of a warrior whose *dharma* calls for impure action, and that of a deeper Self whose pure nature is beyond action.

The most striking aspect that all three cultural cases have in common is *a shift in focus from human action and results to human intention and reflection.* This tendency to internalize enhances the weight of human intention at the expense of human action. The exact character of this increase of the importance of the inner world of human nature at the expense of the outer world differs considerably, however.

What the Greek case and the Hindu case have in common is that the starting point and focus is not on intentionality as such, but on action and the results of action. In the first instance, the Greek and Hindu action are judged by their visible results, not by the intentions accompanying them. Human nature is, first of all, embedded in empirically traceable material and social relations. It is within this material and social setting that a growing consciousness of individual responsibility and of inner struggle occurs. The human being discovers that his individual intention does not necessarily coincide with the social effects of his action, and he starts to suffer mentally from the discrepancy between action and intention. Man increasingly identifies with his inner world of good intentions and intended goals of action. But he cannot deny that this enhanced sense of inner responsibility does not remove his socially expected responsibility for the objective results of his action even if these results go against his best intentions. In fact, the more he identifies with his goals of action, the more he suffers from the gap between his intended goals and the actual results of his action. Moral responsibility comes to explicitly include the intention of the agent or actor. Reflection comes before action. Arjuna's sincere hesitation to fight reminds one of Sophocles' *Oedipus Tyrannus*. Segal wrote:

Oedipus swings between fear and hope as he encounters unknown figures from the past, first the Messenger and then Laius' Herdsman. Oedipus will now have to make the final decision, whether to cross the hairline from uncertainty to certain knowledge (1169–70). By introducing this hesitation at the moment of discovery, Sophocles makes the truth emerge as a deliberate act of will.[226]

In the case of the *Gītā*, Arjuna's hesitation marks the opportunity for ample deliberation and consultation, in order to make a final decision.

Man's suffering from the gap between intention and action is less a matter of damaged reputation and shame than of an increased sense of sin and guilt, to the extent that inner individual responsibility is becoming more dominant than socially expected responsibility.[227]

The Shakespearean case of *Hamlet* too, reveals a shift in focus from human actions and results to human intentions and reflection, and to the extent that the aristocratic life style and warrior code of honour expect Prince Hamlet to act and to stand by the results of his actions; there is hardly any difference between the starting point of traditional Greek and Indian culture and that of early modern martial England. The weight of the results of man's actions weighs heavily. Does the difference lie in the way *Hamlet* deals with this moral weight of human action? Like the *Gītā*, *Hamlet* is as much about non-action as it is about action. Like the *Gītā* in the second instance, *Hamlet* is explicitly about intentionality as such. The nature of human intention itself is analysed and discussed extensively by both Hamlet and Krishna. Intention (determination, readiness) is linked up with man's inner identification with the goals and results of his actions, and opposed to cowardice. In this respect, both the *Gītā* and *Hamlet* reveal a much higher degree of internalization than Greek tragedy. Both texts are extremely radical in articulating the problematic character of intentionality. The inner world is a confusing world. Who or what is guiding whose intention? How is the intention in contact with the action? Whose intention underlies whose action? If a virtuous man *acts* differently from a vicious man, may external success, may the *fruits* of his action still escape him, as Greek philosophers such as Plato and Aristotle thought? What *Hamlet* and the *Gītā* have in common is that focusing on the intention should lead to action, not to inaction. The action is not the arbitrary by-product of the intention, but the intended product, regardless of its fruitfulness.

The main difference between *Hamlet* and the *Gītā* is the status of the problem of intentionality. In *Hamlet*, intentionality is problematized, but not systematized, let alone solved. The thought of an envisaged action is imbued with many motives and afterthoughts. Intentionality appears as a source of confusion instead of focus, and *Hamlet* does not offer a coherent treatise, a psycho-ethical theory of action, to clarify the problem of intentionality. Bernard Williams pointed out that Homer and the tragedians lacked Plato's ethical theory of action, and he added a historico-cultural explanation:

> It seems that once the gods and fate and assumed social expectations were either no longer there or no longer enough to shape the world around human beings, Plato felt it necessary to discover the ethically significant categories inside human nature, and at the most basic level: not just in the form of a capacity for ethical knowledge, as Socrates had already thought, but in the structure of the soul, at the level of the theory of action itself.[228]

The causes provided in Williams' explanation are no different from the ones characteristic of the rise of the ascetic movement of Śramanism in the Indian culture of the Axial Age – the internalization and individualization of religion around the time of the *Upanishads*, a shift away from collective ritualist knowledge to individual mystical knowledge. My suggestion, then, is that the *Gītā* as a historico-cultural development and as a genre, although not a philosophical or theological treatise as such, is much closer to a psycho-ethical theory of action which, like those of Plato and Aristotle, has made up its mind about the rationally (or reasonably) accessible nature of action and intentionality, including moral guidelines on virtue and a spiritual solution to its problems, than it is to tragedies, even to tragedies such as *Hamlet* that explicitly problematizes intentionality, but does not systematize or solve it.

2 The nature of action and wrongdoing

2.1 Knowledge and ignorance

Tragic heroes are wrongdoers who are blamed and pitied for their wrongdoing. Greek tragedy, Vernant argued, combines the ancient concept of wrongdoing in terms of *blemished mistake*, of misstep, of mental derangement brought about by divine contagion, by demonic forces, in the form of a family curse, of blindness or of ignorance, with the fifth-century concept of wrongdoing in terms of *conscious mistake*, of intentional decision, of deliberate choice. Wrongdoing, then, becomes a personal mistake of the deliberating mind, a limited perception of mortals, sheer ignorance typical of humans. Tragedy combines these two concepts as distinct and often opposing, but inseparable and sometimes collaborating aspects. The concept of the blemished mistake belongs to the religious world of divine contagion, and to a Greek culture oriented towards obtaining results. The concept of conscious mistake belongs to the social world of human responsibilities and of deliberate choices. Both of them have blindness or ignorance as the primary cause of wrongdoing. The *Gītā* draws from a similar combination of concepts of wrongdoing. On the one hand, the ancient Vedic notion of action (*karman*) was primarily understood in a ritualistic way as a matter of determined (motivated) performance and of promising results, and wrongdoing as a matter of polluted performance and of damaging results. Action was primarily thought of as ritual action, and ritual action meant sacrificial action (3.13–15). On the other hand, Arjuna is instructed in order to make a reflective choice (18.63), in the full awareness of the eternal self.

Some similarities between classical Greek and Indian epistemology are striking. What they seem to have in common is the idea of action as a matter of knowledge, and wrongdoing as a form of ignorance, including the concept of knowledge and ignorance as being triggered, through the senses, by an external object or goal. Knowledge and ignorance, then, are object-dependent or perception-dependent. Knowing originally derives from seeing, wisdom from the vision of seers, ignorance from blindness. The view is internalized and becomes vision. The *Vedas* lead to the *Upanishads*. Hopkins summarized this by stating that, as the *Āranyakas* and early *Upanishads* had internalized the fire sacrifice by emphasizing its mental performance, so the late *Upanishads* now internalized images. What had, in both instances, been expressed by means of external physical symbols was now expressed by mental performance in meditation. Being allowed to see the god's physical form (*mūrti*) is crucial in the *Gītā* too, because this is exactly what happens to Arjuna in the supremely revealing scene described in Chapter 11 – Arjuna asking to see Krishna's universal form, Krishna giving Arjuna a celestial eye and allowing him to see Krishna's form as Time.

In Gill's Greek psycho-ethical model, emotions and desires are 'belief-based', closely interrelated with beliefs and reasoning in the sense of views and deliberation. An anthropological opposition between passion and reason is lacking. If a conflict is confusing, it is because two sets of belief-plus-reasoning are considered to be clashing. The emotions and desires that go with them are assumed to reflect these competing beliefs. Beliefs are expressed and observed in visible behaviour. One's acts reflect one's beliefs. The Greeks would have had recognized Arjuna's confusion as a matter both of clashing views plus corresponding emotions and reasoning *and* of clashing duties, that is to say, of corresponding behaviour. The Greeks would not have understood Levin's splitting up of Hamlet's dilemma into two dilemmas – the problem of what to believe and the problem of how to act. His problem of what to believe is raised by the problematic assumption of the traditional belief in ghosts, while his problem of how to act is raised by the problematic assumption of the traditional code of revenge. But his problem goes deeper than that. It presupposes a gap between thought and action, between 'mind' and 'matter', between the inner world and the outer world. Greek madness is seen as mad behaviour in the outside world, modern madness as internal darkness, Padel observed. The early modern vocabulary is still drawing from much older sources that do not yet assume a separation between the inner and outer worlds. Early modern madness has to be 'purged' or 'exorcized'. But in modern terms, this means that it has to be forced to leave the inner world of a disturbed mind and body and to enter the outer world of behaviour and action. Thought is no longer automatically expressed in action. The world of thought and the world of action have become separate worlds. A similar degree of separation or dualism is found in the *Gītā*.

Bernard Williams concluded that there are always two sides to action, that of deliberation and that of result, and that there is always a necessary gap between them. Sewell-Rutter suggested that tragic characters like Eteocles bridge the gap by deliberately constructing objective and subjective necessities. This can also be seen in the deliberations of Indian epic characters. In the case of Yudhisthira, before the dice game, he effectively absolves himself of blame, claiming that the Placer and fate compelled him to gamble. Yet, after the dicing, he fulsomely accepts blame and responsibility, pointing out to Bhima that, afflicted by a gambling mania, he (Yudhisthira) had lost self-control. So, while he had no choice but to accept the challenge to a dice match, the outcome of which was predetermined, nevertheless once it started, he himself chose to continue participating in it – it was his own temporary breakdown in self-control that drove him on to such a disastrous end, Hill noted.

2.2 Passion and madness, ambition and indifference

What the ancient Greeks seem to have in common with the classical Indians is the concept of 'will' in terms of 'endurance' and 'self-restraint', as opposed to the Kantian modern concept of 'will' which, Williams explained, is expressed in action for moral purposes, rather than in endurance for all kinds of purposes. *Gītā* 2.14 comes to mind:

> Physical sensations, truly, Arjuna,
> Causing cold, heat, pleasure, or pain,
> Come and go and are impermanent.
> So manage to endure them, Arjuna.[229]

If the *Kantian* 'weakness of will' is understood to mean the failure of rational, moral will to exert its 'strength' over emotions and desires, the *Greek* 'weakness of will' (*akrasía*), Gill argued, is understood to be the internal conflict of someone whose character and reasoning have not been *fully* shaped by the norms of his ethical community. Interestingly, the *Gītā* offers a striking example of that. Krishna blames Arjuna for his 'weakness of heart' or 'base faintheartedness' and 'lack of strength' or 'weakness' in the sense of 'impotence' (2.3), and opposes vices such as these to the *endurance* of *yogic* self-discipline, which resists the temptations of the senses, even 'without will' (*avaśas*), by prior practice (6.44) and by 'indifference' to worldly objects (6.35). Krishna also blames Arjuna for his delusion, that is to say, for his lack of full awareness of the eternal self, of ultimate knowledge, and instructs him so that his mind is fully shaped by the spiritual ideals and social norms of his community – traditional conformity to normative expectations and compliance with necessity instead of modern freedom of choice and expression.

Hamlet's lack of engaged passion and willpower to turn intention into action is something for which Hamlet reproaches himself. This might sound similar to Krishna's reproach of Arjuna for his faintheartedness. After all, Arjuna is expected to be *rajasic* – energetic, ambitious, focused on action and the acquisition of honour and wealth. But the context is a different one.

Within his social context, Arjuna is expected by significant others to live up to his caste duty and pursue the goals of his warrior caste wholeheartedly, that is, energetically, with the ambition of a typical fighter. Within Hamlet's social context, that is also the case. But within Hamlet's psychological context, Hamlet expects himself to be able to face up to both his father's expectations – his father being reduced to a virtual chimera and a memory – and his own afterthoughts that are, in fact, so numerous that they overrun the memory of his father's expectations. Hamlet's deliberating mind and desiring wish are much more triggered and nurtured by the inner world of his self-consciousness than by the outside world. In the case of Arjuna and Oedipus, their self-consciousness is determined by what others tell them, not by what they tell themselves. The only thing Arjuna and Oedipus need to do is to show a willingness to listen. In the case of Hamlet, he is mainly listening to his own reasoning precisely because he does not want to go mad from listening to the lies and hypocrisies of the outside world. McAlindon pointed out that Hamlet's notion of conscience is related to responsibility to oneself, not to others, and to one's knowledge of oneself as a witness to oneself.

Some differences between classical Greek and Indian epistemology are as striking as the similarities. This is already implicit in the difference between ancient Greek 'endurance' and *yogic* self-restraint. The source of the *yogi*'s self-restraint is his lack of desire. Greek action and wrongdoing are a matter of knowledge and ignorance, but it takes many centuries before Plato's opposition between conflicting opinions-plus-appetites and reason develops into the full-fledged struggle between passion and reason of Renaissance Stoicism in *Hamlet*. Indian action and wrongdoing are, even before the *Upanishads*, a matter of knowledge intertwined with desire. Biardeau explicitly spoke of 'an anthropology of desire'. Desire is the Indian missing link between knowledge and action. Knowledge of the perceived object elicits the desire to grasp it and act accordingly. Action does not express man, it only reveals his egoistic desire, Biardeau explained. The Indian struggle is not between passion and reason, but between attachment and spiritual knowledge. Egoistic desire generates an impure heart and mind, including reason. Hamlet tries to cope with his dilemmas by reasoning, but the power *and* weakness of his passionate reasoning borders on madness instead of imposing order. In the Indian perception, passion cannot be restrained by reason, but both passion and reason can be restrained by restraining the senses, and this discipline (*yoga*) can lead to a disciplined state of mind (*buddhiyoga*).

According to Kerrigan, Shakespeare's period has invented a new and inexhaustible kind of ambition – and defined it as fundamental to human nature. Against a classical and medieval notion of desire as finite, seeking its own end in satisfaction, Renaissance culture came to advocate a Romantic and modern notion of desire as an infinite regress, willing to invent further goals in order to perpetually forestall its own demise in stasis. Plato too, stresses the unlimited (insatiable) nature of desire, but his desire is ruled by reason, which is more comprehensive and therefore more fundamental to human nature than desire; also, Plato's reason or desire do not invent goals, but find them. The Hindu goals of the human being are also to be found, not invented. But what the Hindu and the English Renaissance cultures seem to have had in common is the importance they ascribe to desire as an infinite and potentially omnipresent force dominating human nature, to be balanced by self-control and *yogic* or Stoic indifference. If Arjuna must be indifferent to his killing, Hamlet must be indifferent to his revenge.

Ancient Greek conceptions of emotion, feeling, passion are as *physiological* as their Hindu and English counterparts. Emotion (mind and heart) is not located in the head, but in the innards. The ancient Greek vocabulary for attitudes of mind and heart does not constitute a system of categories. Emotion is something coming at you from outside. When thought of physiologically, emotion is air and liquid bubbling within, swelling the entrails. Emotions do not belong to individuals. They are wandering, autonomous, daemonic, outside forces, Padel explained. Greek tragedy speaks of passion, especially anger, as dark boiling turbulence, an inner storm darkening the innards. Organs swell and blacken in passion. Passion is an intensification of consciousness and its darkness. Passion can take the form of anger, rage, fury, madness, because passion disturbs the normal emotional state of mind. In the vocabulary of Shakespearean tragedy too, as Paster argued, emotions cross the bodily interior as winds cross the earth. They are part of the material substance of a self continually moved and threatened with change by forces within and without the body – a correspondence between the inner and outer, body and cosmos, emotions and weather.

States argued that Hamlet is the melancholy character who lost his original sanguine character. He thus runs the risk of becoming mad, like Ophelia. Levin argued that Hamlet's antic disposition is feigned madness, but that real madness, as the abandonment of reason, is a constant danger throughout the play. However, from the comic perspective, Hamlet plays the fool who becomes a court jester. This is worlds apart from Ajax's or Heracles' madness imposed by the gods. Hamlet's madness is risky, but self-imposed role-playing.

Padel pointed to the crucial role of madness in articulating the issue of cause and effect – whether your madness has human or divine causes is open to debate (and likely to have both), but you pay for what you do, even if you do not know what you are doing. In Indian thought, the doctrine of *karma* plays a crucial role in articulating the issue of cause and effect. The similarity between Greek madness and Indian *karma* is that you are paid for what you do. In the Greek case, payment means punishment; in the Indian case, it means punishment or reward – but it can never mean ultimate liberation. In a way, one might argue that *karma* has a touch of tragic action – the action is something that goes on and on and on, beyond one's immediate control or intention. But *karma* has too much potential for improvement of the future situation to be really tragic. The main difference is that *karma* is based on *desire as attachment*, whereas tragic madness is based on *desire (passion doubled) as violence*. This anthropological difference constitutes one of the most fundamental differences between the tragic Western views of the human being and their Indian counterparts.

2.3 Action and identity

What the Hindu and the English Renaissance cultures have in common is the fact that they understand feelings (emotions) and attitudes in terms of a systematized physiology of categorized humours – in the Hindu case, *sattva guna, rajas guna, tamas guna;* in the English case, choleric, sanguine, melancholic and phlegmatic, both related to a material mixture of fire, water, earth and air. By using these standardized physiological vocabularies, persons are approached as *types of person* and things as bearers of characteristics. The character of things, including that of human beings, is thought of as not only physical, but also moral and mental (attitudinal), in very much the same way the English word 'character' is used for both the 'salient form' and the 'distinctive way of being' of something. That is to say, the moral and mental make-up of human beings and other parts of 'primal nature' are understood as basically physical qualities that take the shape of moral behaviour and mental attitudes, as Dasgupta remarked. Types or characters are half-way between particulars and universals. The *Gītā* uses the *guna* categories to maintain caste differences. Hamlet has great difficulty in expressing what in particular goes on in his interiority, beyond the embodied states of being that occur both on the microcosmic and on the macrocosmic levels of nature. His *particular experiences* seem too particular to be expressed in typological terms. Raymond Williams drew a comparison between the medieval morality play *Everyman* and early modern English tragedy, constituting a historico-cultural shift from a gathering of life in terms of common and formal categories to one in terms of the particularities of concrete experiences. Life itself is now seen as at its most intense in an individual experience. In early modern tragedy, an individual action is generalized, whereas previously, in Greek tragedy and in

Christian morality plays, a general action was specified, Williams explained. In the *Gītā* and epic too, a general action is specified. Dramatically speaking, Greek and Indian narratives focus on types, their actions and statements, not on individual persons whose particular experiences constitute their unique identities.

Theologically or philosophically speaking, however, the difference between these Greek and Indian types could not be larger. What goes on in the minds of the Greek characters, Goldhill observed, is something the characters themselves argue about. Yet, it is ultimately presumed to be something *individual* in the sense that a character's true identity is ultimately his personal identity. This personal identity is expressed in his (speech) actions. Arjuna's true identity, on the other hand, is ultimately beyond his own individual personality. Arjuna's individual personality is expressed and embodied in his actions (*karma*). In his *karma,* he becomes an embodied individual. But this individual personality has to be cremated physically and to be purified spiritually, has to *de-individualize* in order to gain the ultimate freedom of the true self. Hamlet has to *de-socialize* in order to experience 'that within'.

Likewise, Polonius' wise advice to Laertes, 'to thine own self be true' (I.iii.78), is poles apart from Krishna's wise advice to Arjuna to destroy the ego-inflated illusion, 'I am the doer' (3.27). Krishna dissociates Arjuna's action from Arjuna's true self. Hamlet represents an entirely different case when it comes to the *dissociation of action and identity*. His lack of passion to become fully engaged in his duty to take revenge is not just a matter of faintheartedness, but of the inability to identify with his duty. His inability reveals a fundamental disconnection between his beliefs and his actions, between the freedom of his thoughts and the responsibility of his actions, between his self-consciousness and his roles, at the expense of the latter. He feels more obliged to his 'inner self' than to his 'outer roles'. But he is not able to connect them. His planned actions lack the motivation needed to get things done, and his vast ambitions lack the self-evident goals needed to believe in them. 'Our thoughts are ours, their ends none of our own'. (III.ii.232) Hamlet does not willingly embrace this disconnection between his state of mind and (the results of) his actions, as Arjuna seems to do; on the contrary, he tries hard to bridge the gap and identify with his actions. Philosophically speaking, he turns the Hindu solution to the problem upside-down, but psychologically speaking, he comes as close to the Hindu solution as one gets under the conditions of early Western modernity by withdrawing into his inner self – he de-individualizes his duties as 'only roles' to be played on the stage of life, but he individualizes 'that within which surpasses show' (I.ii.85).

The fundamental difference between Greek and Hindu views of the human being mentioned above (individual vs cosmic identity) is connected to one other fundamental difference. While Greek (and Shakespearean) views of the human being presuppose the near *identity of responsibility and freedom*, Hindu views of the human being presuppose the near *opposition between responsibility and freedom*, in the sense that a Hindu's freedom of choice is a worldly affair as opposed to 'his' spiritual freedom as a pure state of mind-and-being beyond all worldly affair.

Krishna dissociates Arjuna's action from Arjuna's true self, and presents Himself as the true Actor behind all actions in the universe. This configuration may sound similar to that of Agamemnon who, claiming that the gods made him blind or mad temporarily when taking Briseis, is not dissociating himself from his action (he actually *did* it), but dissociating his action from himself (it was not *his usual self* doing it), in Bernard Williams' analysis. This apparent similarity between Agamemnon and Arjuna brings out several differences. First of all, the theological concept of Krishna as the doer behind all actions refers to something structural, not to something accidental or incidental. That is to say, Krishna's action is equivalent to the functioning of fate, whereas divine intervention in Agamemnon's case is equivalent to the occurrence of fortune. Secondly, Agamemnon claims to have been possessed temporarily by the gods who took over his mind, which was infused with delusion, blindness and madness, whereas Krishna claims to be the doer in Arjuna's actions, not in his delusion and decision making. In fact, Krishna claims to undo Arjuna's delusion and decision making by the power of His illusion (*Gītā* 18.60–61). Thirdly, Krishna can be said to do a lot of reasoning in order to convince Arjuna, and a lot of teaching in order to educate his thinking, which suggests a strong appeal to reason instead of madness. Fourthly, Krishna makes an even stronger appeal to the single-mindedness in meditation and devotional practices. Arjuna is invited to empty his mind from the input of the senses and to focus his mind on Krishna only, instead of being carried away forcibly (as Agamemnon is suggesting):

> The turbulent senses
> Carry away forcibly
> The mind, Arjuna,
> Even of the striving man of wisdom.
>
> Restraining all these senses,
> Disciplined, he should sit, intent on Me;
> He whose senses are controlled,
> His wisdom stands firm.
> [*Gītā* 2.60–61][230]

However, Krishna presenting Himself as the true Actor behind all actions in the universe does lead to an overdeterminism reminiscent of Greek tragedy in which, Goldhill suggested, the sense of the boundaries of a personality in terms of responsibility for personal action is always being questioned in the overdeterminism of divine causation of psychological and physical action.

3 Self-knowledge

Tragic knowledge is knowledge about the vulnerability of the human condition. *Greek and Shakespearean tragic truth emerges from pollution, moral brokenness and pain.* In Greek tragedy, Padel argued, madness articulates the emergence of truth from pain. Truth about the human condition emerges from the experience of human suffering. It does not benefit the tragic characters who suffer from madness, but their audience. Madness also takes illusion for reality, thus reinforcing the audience's awareness that both the human power of reason to establish moral transparency and the divine power of oracles and prophecy to establish past or future certainty are beyond human control. Greek madness draws its prophetic truth from the mind's daimonic possession. Shakespearean madness draws its ingenious truth from melancholic blackness. Christian folly draws its simple truth from the soul's purity. Hindu wisdom draws its cosmic truth from the vision of Vedic seers and from the undisturbed state of mind in pure meditation. *Hindu cosmic truth is never produced out of pain. Only karmic truth, Yudhisthira's wisdom of non-cruelty, emerges from pain.* No Hindu truth emerges from madness. Madness does not play a significant role in the epic, to my knowledge. It is surely never, as it is in the early Renaissance, a *speculum*, 'mirror', where human nature sees its own self-hurt.

But many tragic characters do not fall victim to madness. One of them, Oedipus, beats everybody when it comes to solving daimonic riddles and using his reasoning capacities to trace the murderer of Laius. Oedipus' successful self-discovery leads to complete self-knowledge. But it also brings social death, mental darkness and physical blindness. His genuine desire for knowledge turns out to be fatal.

In the Hindu case, does Arjuna acquire sufficient knowledge to make a moral decision? In fact, he acquires far more than that. He acquires absolute knowledge, and absolute self-knowledge at that. But this is not the fruit of his reasoning capacities. It is thanks to Krishna's grace. Krishna not only preaches the Way of submission to the one god (*bhaktiyoga*); He also reveals Himself as the one god who holds Arjuna's destiny in a cosmic vision. His revelatory knowledge allows Arjuna access to experience Krishna as the one Lord of the Universe and to experience himself as a mere instrument of Krishna's divine agency. That is to say, unlike *Oedipus Tyrannus*, the *Gītā* makes the truth emerge as a deliberate act of revelation on the part of Krishna. This revelatory truth is not a wise advice. It is simply overwhelming. It disarms Arjuna's unwillingness to fight, elucidates his mind and liberates his heart from the burden of potential guilt feelings and depression. It makes him 'cross the hairline from uncertainty to certain knowledge' in a way very different from that of Oedipus. Arjuna does not arrive at his conclusions through a rational and investigative search for the truth. He is taught the truth by his spiritual teacher, and he is shown a vision by his spiritual teacher. Unlike Oedipus, Arjuna is not making a final decision to face the truth for himself. Yet, in both these cases, the truth is hidden from its witnesses, who dwell in confused ignorance or blindness. And as the truth breaks through, it overrules the empirical knowledge of mortal human beings. It is beyond their imagination. It changes their entire perception of the world, either positively or negatively.

For both Oedipus and Arjuna, the revelatory knowledge turns out to go beyond moral issues. Their very existence is involved in the revelation. Knowledge turns out to be self-knowledge. But there is one tremendous difference. *Whereas the revelatory knowledge is religiously saving knowledge in Arjuna's case, it is religiously dooming knowledge in Oedipus' case.* Whereas true knowledge leads to a decisive release from time, mortality, unhappiness and suffering in the Hindu case, in the Greek case, true knowledge leads to a decisive immersion in time, mortality, unhappiness and suffering. In both cases, however, true knowledge, or revelatory knowledge, is religious knowledge. For Oedipus, his dramatic conflict becomes tragic as it necessitates for its resolution the suffering of the protagonist, yet in terms of a world view that grounds the ethico-political in the divine, as Friedrich put it. Winnington-Ingram pointed out that Oedipus recognizes Apollo as the divine power that has led him to know himself, in accordance with the motto 'Know yourself' on Apollo's temple in Delphi. For Arjuna, the question is not anymore whether to fight or not to fight, but whether to be or not to be, that is to say, to be or not to be truly immortal and act accordingly. Not ethics, but anthropology turns out to be the true issue. Ethics is grounded in spirituality. Matters of action and non-action are grounded in the spiritual identity of the agent. The *Gītā* offers a theory of human action within the framework of a religious anthropology that focuses on the immortal de-individualized self.

In the case of *Hamlet*, Bloom praised Hamlet for a capacity of self-consciousness, not to be confused with self-knowledge. According to Lee, Hamlet's attempts to capture himself show his frustration at his inability to capture a solid picture of that self. Hamlet does not achieve self-fashioning (too instrumental) or self-mastery (too stable and certain). Instead, he achieves self-exploration, self-mapping and self-creation. His self is a story, but it is a tragic story. As Hamlet lies dying, he regrets not to be able to tell his story and he begs Horatio, his 'recorder', to tell his story instead. There is no sense in which the Prince has arrived at self-knowledge. There is no point at which the Prince tells us what he has learnt about himself. All the questions that he has raised remain. His musings over the nature of the human being continue. The religiously dooming knowledge of divine punishment does not preoccupy Hamlet too much, but there is *no religiously saving knowledge* in sight. In this regard, Britain and India are foreign countries to each other – they do things differently there.

8

Religious aspects

PART I: GREEK AND SHAKESPEAREAN ISSUES

1 Introduction

A seventh set of aspects that is intimately connected with tragedy in general, and with Greek tragedy in particular, is its focus on the religious weight of human and divine intentions and actions.

Some of the issues related to religious aspects have already been addressed within the context of other aspects, such as the ironic tension between the cosmic level of the immortal gods and the earthly level of the mortal humans (Chapter II); the religious character of Greek and Indian drama; the secular character of Greek and English tragic literature and the spiritual character of Hindu epic literature (Chapter III); the socio-political connections and tensions between religion and the state in the Greek, English and Indian cases (Chapter IV); the historical occurrence of a gap between the ethicized view of the humane and the un-ethicized view of the divine in the Greek and Indian Axial Age and also of henotheism and religious conversion in the Hellenistic Greek and Hindu *bhakti* cases (Chapter V); the concept of divine intervention in the Greek case of madness and in the Hindu case of renewing world order, and religiously saving or dooming self-knowledge (Chapter VII).

Two specific issues related to the religious aspects will be discussed in this chapter – the issue of the relationship between fate, fortune, freedom and responsibility, and the issue of divine intentions and interventions. The *main question* of the chapter will be – what is, according to the Western and Indian texts under consideration, the impact of superhuman powers, such as fate and the gods, on human actions and human intentions? Again, the chapter consists of three parts, the first part being dedicated to the Greek and Shakespearean material, the second part to the Indian and Hindu material and the third part to the cross-cultural comparisons. We will start this first part by introducing one general theory of tragedy that is relevant to the issues mentioned.

2 H. J. Heering's theory of tragedy

Although H. J. Heering's approach is very close to that of Sands, he does not define 'tragedy' in terms of the contradiction between reality and ideality, but in terms of the unbearable *tension between (human) freedom and (supernatural) necessity* and in terms of the mutual violation of freedom and constraint, an assaulted freedom in constraint and an assaulted constraint in freedom.[1] Human freedom is assaulted because it constantly has to take into account the violating impact of the constraining structure of reality; constraint is assaulted because human freedom permanently tries to assert itself at the expense of constraints.

Heering stresses that the unfortunate contradiction between ideal and reality is not tragic as such. Man's active involvement in bringing it about turns the contradiction into a tragic one. Man's greatness derives from his freedom, from his capacity to bear true responsibility, and man's inevitable, unintended guilt derives from his unavoidable confrontation with true necessity or constraint, from his incapacity to avoid his moral involvement in the world – his very greatness – being turned against him by the overpowering and unfathomable force of necessity, and leads to his fall. But 'tragic guilt' is different from 'ethical guilt'. No tragedy without ethics. Yet, 'ethical guilt' leaves room for manoeuvre for compromise, for a way out, forgiveness, conversion, a new start, unexpected love ties, whereas 'tragic guilt' is theatrical, featuring rigid characters, lonely isolation, absolute choices between pure evils, immutable structures, undoubted principles and undisputable convictions, a closed circuit of limited time and space.[2]

Heering points out that Heaven remains silent for Oedipus, that the human being may have his ideals, but that he cannot appeal to an ideal reality. He faces dark necessity, no way out of his ordeal, no window of opportunity, no moral universe in which he participates. Oedipus' blindness turned into Sophoclean *self*-knowledge does not make the *universe* intelligible or accessible. Greek tragedy is a matter of transgressing the border-crossing, of excess (*perissa, hubris*) instead of access. But, in fact, this transgression goes both ways, is interference in both directions, violating both the human sphere and the sphere of divine order and fatal necessity. Fate penetrates the human sphere of freedom, the human being penetrates the fatal sphere of necessity.[3] The tragic occurs on the border between human existence and its environment where engaged human beings face their limits and experience *the discrepancy between human existence and the surrounding world* – as their responsibility and failure, as Christianity adds emphatically, according to Heering.[4]

3 The necessity of fate and the moral order of nature

Greek fate (*moira*) is a spontaneous unfolding of divine or daimonic power (*daimon*). Fate can take the form of 'destiny', of 'the fates' (*moirai*) or of an individual's lot (*moira* or *daimon*), as Winnington-Ingram explains.[5] Redfield points out that a reference to *moira* (fate) or to some related term usually carries two implications: (1) the event is seen as significant; (2) the event is seen as unavoidable. The inevitability 'is attached to the particular event, not to a general deterministic system; for in such a system particular events would lose their significance'. 'Fate, however, is not a condition among many; it is the sum of all the conditions of action at the moments when those conditions combine to give events a definite direction and form' – it has *become* inevitable in the process of taking a definite form.[6] In this sense, fate is nature, is the order of the world. Michael Ewans too, stresses the absence of predestination in the Greek notions of fate and destiny (*moira, aisa*). The hero's *moira* takes shape along with the gradually unfolding events.[7] Fate is *event-related* and thus *plot-related*, and takes its final shape only after the alternatives have been narrowed down to their final option.[8] Inherited guilt, curses and Erinyes, which often serve to explain why a catastrophe occurs, are not to be confused with the workings of fate in the sense that certain things simply must happen. In tragedy, fate is not as important as one might expect, Sewell-Rutter suggests. The *epic* genre is much more apt to allow fate to play a prominent role, because in epic, there is an ongoing narrative from the past to the present and an authorial voice (Homer, Herodotus) that sees 'with the benefit of hindsight that some event did happen in the past . . . within some causal nexus', whereas *tragedy* 'represents events in the present tense'.[9]

Aeschylus depicts fate as a process that 'is inevitable but far from unintelligible', and ultimately 'part of divine justice', while Sophocles stresses the unintelligibility of fate.[10] Charles Segal states:

> What we mean by calling *Oedipus Tyrannus* a tragedy of fate might be more accurately phrased as Sophocles' sense of the existence of powers working in the world in ways alien to and hidden from human understanding.

Karl Reinhardt . . . . : 'For Sophocles, as for the Greeks of an earlier age, fate is in no circumstances the same as predestination, but is a spontaneous unfolding of daimonic power.' The play leaves it an open question whether Laius, Jocasta, or Oedipus might have prevented the fulfillment of the prophecies if they had simply done nothing: not exposed the infant, not consulted Delphi . . ., and so on.[11]

Williams too takes his examples from Sophocles. Can we say that if Oedipus had stayed at home, he would still have grown up to kill his father? How does the necessity of Ajax's decision combine with the prophet's words to make the rescue attempt necessarily useless? There is simply no answer to that question but that is exactly the point:

The special feature of supernatural necessity is that there is nothing relevant to be said about ways in which things might have gone differently . . .. This is not at all how it is with human affairs when an outcome is, for familiar and natural reasons, inevitable; we can explain its inevitability, and to explain it involves understanding how, in just these ways, things might have gone otherwise. . . . Supernatural necessity in the sense of ancient tragedy is . . . a special element in the world, a presence that has to be inserted into it. Sophoclean tragedy has a power to make this insertion compelling, by concealing the fact that there is no particular way in which it comes about.[12]

Williams compares this kind of supernatural necessity to an effective agent but, as he puts it, 'this agent, unlike the Homeric gods with their individual schemes, has' *no style, no character,* 'no characteristics except purpose and power'; he notes, 'There are no distinctive ways in which his purposes come about, and so, once such a purpose has been set, there is nothing to be said about alternative circumstances in which it would not be realised or would be realised by a different route'.[13] Dramatic necessity, the indeterminacy of fiction, can help us to understand supernatural necessity:

The play represents to us an outcome, together with such things as failed attempts to prevent it, with such power and in such a chain of significance as to kill speculation about alternatives. By compelling our attention and directing our fears to what it presents as actual, tragedy may leave us with no thought, and no need of a thought, about anything else.[14]

In *Shakespearean* tragedy, supernatural power 'operates in complete consistency with the contrarious dynamics of nature', according to Tom McAlindon, who examines Shakespearean tragedy in the light of his central claim that the ancient model of *natural order as a dynamic system of interacting opposites* had a much more profound effect on the Renaissance interpretation and representation of tragic experience than did the related notion of universal hierarchy. 'Pre-modern cosmology construed the world not only as a hierarchical structure of corresponding planes but also as a dynamic system of interacting, interdependent opposites'. The *two pre-modern conceptions* were combined. From *a hierarchical perspective*, the world was a stratified arrangement of earth, water, air and fire, each placed above the other in accordance with its degree of lightness or 'nobility'. From *a contrarious perspective*, 'every scale or degree was constructed from opposites'.[15]

The hierarchical arrangement of the elements was not thought to alter the fact that they *are* opposites with an entirely *natural* desire to combat each other. It is mainly from Empedocles' doctrine 'that nature is governed by both Love and Strife, by sympathies and antipathies', that 'the notion of the world as a system of concordant discord or discordant concord' derives. 'Every pattern of harmonious order, every structure of identity is, of its very nature, susceptible to violent transformation: all of a sudden, bonds collapse, things decline to their confounding contraries, and confusion prevails'. The *forces of chaos are intrinsic to nature* and its functioning. *This includes human nature* because the microcosm of human nature operates on identical principles as the macrocosm of nature. 'The contrarious model insistently implies that disorder, aggressive egoism, and blind passion are not just blemishes on nature caused by sin and the Fall, but are as natural as order, altruism, and reason'.[16]

What McAlindon is suggesting, then, is that the pre-modern cosmological tradition offered two world models and their possible conjoining. When conjoined, priority of emphasis could be given to one of them. McAlindon also suggests that Shakespeare's understanding of nature was fundamentally pre-modern,[17] and favoured an emphasis on the contrarious model.[18] Shakespeare's conscious and systematic exploration of the 'tragic experience' refers to contradictions of a trans-historical nature – they are about the *nature* of human nature and about the experience of psychic and interpersonal *chaos*.[19]

Elusive though it is, *Hamlet* reveals a pattern that has its roots in Shakespeare's conception of the contrarious cosmos and double nature. 'Fratricide and incest have initiated a state of psychological and social chaos in which the opposites of love and hatred, pity and fury, friendship and war, marriage and funeral, workday and 'holyday', day and night are wholly confused'.[20] The 'metamorphous and paradoxical nature of human nature' is demonstrated by Hamlet's revenge which, as Shakespeare learnt from Kyd's *Spanish Tragedy*, 'generates hatred from grief-stricken love' as 'fire from tears' (water). The distinction between 'natural' and 'unnatural' is blurred (I.ii.87, 103–4 and I.v.12, 25, 81).[21] Hamlet's struggle with love and hatred reflects the working of nature, not the workings of fate. One would have to turn to *Macbeth*'s Weird Sisters to experience a sense of dark fate in Shakespearean tragedy. But these witches operate in complete consistency with the dynamics of nature, McAlindon pointed out two pages ago. The Weird Sisters detect an inversion of the natural order. Like the Delphic oracle in Sophocles' *Oedipus Tyrannus*, Shakespeare's Scottish witches merely predict. Human beings create the fulfilment of their predictions, as Ewans points out.[22]

4 The free and gradual appropriation of fate

Tragic action presupposes, in fact, that the human level and the divine level are sufficiently distinct to be opposing each other, but simultaneously, the two levels must appear inseparable in order to have a really *tragic* action, according to Jean-Pierre Vernant.[23]

The opposition between *necessity and freedom,* or between *fate and freedom*, is misleading inasmuch as the opposition itself consists of a complex of factors. Emese Mogyoródi, for example, 'agrees with Dodds in considering the "necessity versus freedom" debate a debate about false alternatives'.[24] She makes differentiations for both the notion of freedom and the notion of fate. As to the notion of freedom, she describes *free choice* as '*a gradually unfolding decision* instead of one made prior to action'. Antigone's original impetus needs to be 'recognized' by Antigone 'and assented to in order to constitute a choice'. Antigone 'thus becomes the *"accomplice" of an elusive force* that remains hidden until the encounter with a diametrically opposed attitude and decision', as Mogyoródi puts it. 'Such a description of choice allows for a far less conscious agent', a factor which 'is intimately related to the crucial determinants of the tragic, that is, to *hamartia* (error), *peripeteia* (reversal), and *anagnōrisis* (recognition)'. The tragic character of Antigone's choice consists of her *gradual appropriation of the family doom*. Antigone exposes herself to the fate of the family, and by accepting this external necessity as her own fate, she chooses freely to 'join in with the alien force' and to be determined by the inevitable. The family fate, thus, is no longer an alien force, but becomes her own inalienable fate. For her sister Ismene, who does not actively join in, the family doom does not become her personal fate because she does not engage in it actively. *Suffering as such does not suffice to merit the title of 'the tragic'.* Her fate is a sheer *fatum*, an external force determining her life, not a tragic fate in the sense of her own appropriated and thus inalienable portion in life. Antigone's freedom consists of giving up her freedom by embracing her fate.[25]

This, in turn, means that her deed is not merely a transgression, but an act that induces a tragic fate. That is because necessity or determination would not be activated or reinvigorated without the heroes' willingness to assert their freedom – 'The real complicity of freedom and necessity consists in the paradox that without the act of "appropriation", necessity does not manifest itself with all its mythical profundity'.[26] By forging her own fate, Antigone re-enacts the common fate of the Labdacids from which Ismene excludes herself.

Interestingly enough, as Stephen Halliwell points out,[27] Plato's rejection of 'the tragic world view' is based on his notion of 'the tragic' as a sheer *fatum*. His metaphorical extension of 'tragedy' to life as such (*Philebus* 50b, *Cratylus* 408b–d, *Laws* 7, 817b1–8) does turn the notion of 'the tragic' itself into a philosophy in embryo. This tragic world view, Plato argues, should be rejected (*Republic* 2–3, 10).[28]

Like fate, freedom and choice are the culmination of a gradually unfolding process. Their mutual interaction turns the significant events either into a success story or into a tragedy. Tragedy is considered tragic, first of all, to the extent that it takes interlocking causation and time for a fate to take its full shape. A sudden turn of events, a sudden happy end or unhappy end is considered neither fatal nor tragic. Additionally, *fate becomes tragic to the extent that fate uses and depends on intentional acts of free choice for its enactment*, that is, for enabling necessity to transform freedom into the very source of inevitable suffering, loss of freedom and destruction. Sophocles' *Antigone* and *Oedipus Tyrannus* are among the best examples of the dramatists' exploration of the importance of human action and responsibility in an ambiguous world order. The counterproductive outcome of human acts of moral excellence is clearly beyond human control.

Human action does not have the power to enforce its most noble and moral intentions. It is in the power of supernatural necessity. But this does not mean that human beings do not have *freedom*. 'Human beings are metaphysically free in the sense that there is nothing in the structure of the universe that denies their power to intend, to decide, to act, indeed to take and receive responsibility', Williams states. 'When someone is constrained actually to do something, the typical situation is that there is an imposed choice. . . . Freedom stands particularly opposed to those constraints that are intentionally imposed by other agents or actors'.[29] While Platonic and Kantian 'ultimate freedom' presuppose an all-criticizing *characterless self*, Greek fate and chance presuppose *a characterless supernatural necessity or a characterless chance* (social reality), Williams writes.[30] Sophocles' shaping necessity is transformed into the uncertainties of an unnerving chance by Euripides and Thucydides, but this loosening of the sense of a supernatural necessity does not change the tragic human condition as presented by Sophocles. The question is not whether or not a supernatural necessity exists, but whether or not a shaping necessity contributes constructively to human beings' moral aspirations. 'Sophocles and Thucydides', Williams argues, 'are alike in leaving us with no such sense'.[31]

In *Shakespearean* tragedy, as McAlindon presents it, it is not the workings of fate that the heroes are facing, but the workings of *nature* and its intrinsic forces of chaos. These *forces of chaos* do not just occur in the outside world, but also *within human nature*. They can have a *constraining influence* too. If *love* drives Hamlet to the extreme point where opposites are confused, it also seems to inhibit him there, preventing him from becoming another Pyrrhus or Laertes in the quest for revenge.

McAlindon considers love the crucial affect in Hamlet's behavioural pattern. If this claim is justified, the way love is simultaneously credited and discredited as love by Claudius (in his effort to urge Laertes to action) is all the more interesting:

> Not that I think you did not love your father,
> But that I know love is begun by time,
> And that I see, in passages of proof,
> Time qualifies the spark and fire of it.
> There lives within the very flame of love
> A kind of wick or snuff that will abate it,
> And nothing is at a like goodness still;
> For goodness, growing to a pleurisy,
> Dies in his own too-much.
> [IV.vii.109–17][32]

Love is credited as a real phenomenon, but at the same time, it is discredited as temporal (caused by time) and unbalanced (excess of one Galenic humour). Anthony Gash comments:

> What it [Claudius' language, *LM*] claims to observe is a law in mental or psychological events which follows the same causal logic as physical processes. Starting with an example from chemistry (the candle flame) it ends with the biological language of 'plurisy', an excess of one humour, in this case blood, causing sickness. But this apparently scientific language is also internally in dialogue with the language of religion (love) and ethics

(goodness). In describing love and goodness as it does, this way of talking assumes that they are caused rather than causing, objects of knowledge rather than the causes and conditions of knowing. It is easily forgotten that it was an ancestor of this approach against which Socrates and Plato had reacted and which spurred Plato to enunciate the alternative model of knowledge which we now call philosophy, as distinct from natural science. . . . In Claudius' speech it is precisely this mysterious claim which is ignored or rejected, when love is portrayed as being subject to the same laws of growth and decay as any temporal phenomenon. That Shakespeare thought of Claudius' naturalism as in dialogue with the Platonic-Christian tradition is indicated by the formulation of his early and less sophisticated Machiavel, Richard III, who mocks 'this word "love" which greybeards call divine' (3 Henry VI, V.vi.81). And in one of his sonnets, Shakespeare takes the side of the greybeards by setting his love beyond the cause and effect sequences which determine and explain so much human behaviour, representing it as *sui generis* rather than caused or motivated.[33]

McAlindon and Gash point out, in fact, that Hamlet does not go along with Claudius' appeal to 'reason' in the sense of 'recognition of necessity or fate as identical to natural order, as opposed to chaos'. Right from the beginning, Hamlet refused to join Claudius' manipulative use (for political purposes) of 'reason' in the sense of 'recognition of universal laws of nature':

> 'Tis sweet and commendable in your nature, Hamlet,
> To give these mourning duties to your father.
> But you must know your father lost a father;
> That father lost, lost his; and the survivor bound
> In filial obligation for some term
> To do obsequious sorrow. But to persever
> In obstinate condolement is a course
> Of impious stubbornness. 'Tis unmanly grief.
> It shows a will most incorrect to heaven,
> A heart unfortified, a mind impatient,
> An understanding simple and unschooled.
> For what we know must be, and is as common
> As any the most vulgar thing to sense,
> Why should we in our peevish opposition
> Take it to heart? Fie, 'tis a fault to heaven,
> A fault against the dead, a fault to nature,
> To reason most absurd, whose common theme

Is death of fathers, and who still hath cried,
From the first corse till he that died today,
'This must be so'. We pray you throw to earth
This unprevailing woe, and think of us
As of a father.
[I.ii.87–108][34]

The one emotion that dominates the play, grief, is simultaneously credited and discredited as grief by Claudius, whose recognition of necessity is a strategy to eliminate the tragic experience of chaos and to eliminate a recognition of tragic fate. In Claudius' perception, the show must go on. In Hamlet's perception, there is the entire inner world of sincere feelings that cannot be neglected even though it cannot be seen and shown in the outer world of the court. Hamlet does not describe it, but refers to it in indirect terms as '"that within" which surpasses show'. *Instead of appropriating Claudius' transparent necessity of the natural order or, for that matter, a Greek, obscure necessity of fate, Hamlet seems to appropriate the obscure chaos of human freedom.* Hamlet's incidental reference to the Christian idea of providence comes across as one among many religious and secular ideas clashing, and as far less important than the secularized idea of fortune.

5 Fortune

Unlike fate, *fortune* plays a minor role in Aeschylus' and Sophocles' tragedies as compared with Euripides' tragedies. Fortune is more related to the accidental ups and downs within life than to a coherent 'spinning' of the thread of one's life as a whole towards a final destiny taking shape gradually. The arbitrariness of fortune concerns 'the accidental', that is, the additional, less essential aspects of life. *If fate is a matter of necessity, fortune is a matter of contingency.* Contingency means 'logical possibility without necessity', in the Aristotelian sense; 'ontological actuality without necessity', in the medieval sense, Kees Vuyk explains.[35] In the Greek case, fortune (*tychē*, chance) was taken to be 'the cause of chance events—events that one could not or did not calculate and that do not fit into a regular pattern', as Gábor Betegh puts it, 'While fate (*moira*) determines one's course of life as a whole, fortune tends to be responsible for singular events of varying importance. The connotations of the word were originally more positive, but by Hellenistic times it regularly had the pejorative meaning of blind, impersonal, arbitrary chance'.[36] Luck became less a matter of good luck than of bad luck, and entirely independent of human initiative. *Luck is a matter of inexplicable chance*, in Robert C. Solomon's terminology.[37]

Renaissance thinking about fortune opposes reason to passion. According to Bert O. States, the Passion's Slave Speech addressed to Horatio directly following the advice to the players (III.ii.66–97) plays Horatio off against the old schoolfriends, Rosencrantz and Guildenstern, who are repeatedly linked to *fortuna* and fortune-hunting, whereas Horatio is linked to *virtù*.[38]

In Hamlet's Passion's Slave Speech, *fortuna* and *virtù* appear as 'blood and judgement' (*passion* and *reason*):

> And blest are those
> Whose blood and judgement are so well commeddled
> That they are not a pipe for Fortune's finger
> To sound what stop she please. Give me that man
> That is not passion's slave, and I will wear him
> In my heart's core, ay, in my heart of heart,
> As I do thee.
> [III.ii.78b-84a][39]

'The speech is a return, in thin disguise, of the very advice Hamlet has been giving the players', States argues. 'That is, it translates the theory of acting into the sphere of human conduct. Horatio is to the perfect actor as Rosencrantz and Guildenstern are to the ambitious clowns who pad their roles to steal laughs'.[40] But the virtue Hamlet speaks of here – the happy marriage of passion and reason – is the very virtue Hamlet manifestly lacks.

Fortuna and *virtù* are key concepts in High Renaissance thinking, as also in the political thinking of people such as Niccolò Machiavelli.[41] Lauro Martines explains why. The question of relations between *virtù* (talented will) and Fortune had been discussed in the fifteenth century, but then, *virtù* could be seen as the victor, especially in discussions set among the dominant social groups. After the outbreak of the Italian Wars, the *topos* invaded political reflection as well as literature and moral thought:

> The dynamic aspect in Machiavelli's vision of politics is in the shifting opposition and union between *virtù* and *fortuna* and in the conflict between the State and the antisocial beast in man. *Virtù* is talented will power in great political affairs, the stuff of leadership and success. It may belong to individuals as to collectivities. *Fortuna* is the sum of forces lying beyond *virtù*—forces hostile, neutral, or helpful, but always changing. In its changes, *fortuna* may include or at any moment exclude the antisocial vices, but *virtù* can never really include the beast in man, for when the prince elects to partake of the beast in order to accomplish a political end, the choice is a rational one, made to serve the ends of the state. If in *The Prince* Machiavelli emphasizes relations

between *virtù* and *fortuna*, in *The Discourses*, looking to the political health of collectivities, he gives more emphasis to relations between *virtù* and political corruption (*virtù* gone decadent). In fact, these contrapuntal pairings were a formulation of the overwhelming question for Italian society: could the ruling classes rule? How much real control had they over political processes, over events, over the environment, over the peninsula's forthcoming destinies?[42]

The main antitheses in the idealized solutions of sixteenth-century Italian thinkers, Martines writes, are these – reason–passions, *virtù–fortuna*, man–beast, elites–multitudes, rich–poor, State–ambition (individual egotism), civil society–anarchic nature, law–violence, order–disorder.[43]

More needs to be said about the notion of *fortune* if one is to fully understand the discontinuities between the respective world views and views of the human being in Greek tragedy, in medieval Christian ideas about tragedy, and in Renaissance tragedy, but also their impact on the very definition of tragedy. George Steiner explains how a *medieval* distinction between tragedy and comedy in terms of *plot pattern* only (no dramatic performance, just 'a certeyn storie') was intertwined with the Christian *world view*, but lost its medieval directness. He points to Chaucer's medieval definition of 'tragedy' as:

> a narrative recounting the life of some ancient or eminent personage who suffered a decline of fortune toward a disastrous end.[44] That is the characteristic medieval definition. Dante observed, in his letter to Can Grande, that tragedy and comedy move in precisely contrary directions. Because its action is that of the soul ascending from shadow to starlight, from fearful doubt to the joy and certitude of grace, Dante entitled his poem a *commedia*.[45]

Steiner puts Chaucer's definition of tragedy in terms of fortune as the decisive plot pattern in perspective:

> Chaucer's definition derives its force from contemporary awareness of sudden reversals of political and dynastic fortune. . . . But the rise and fall of him that stood in high degree was the incarnation of the tragic sense for a much deeper reason: it made explicit the universal drama of the fall of man. . . . It is in a garden also that the symmetry of divine intent places the act of fortunate reversal. At Gethsemane the arrow changes its course, and the morality play of history alters from tragedy to *commedia*. . . . Of this great parable of God's design, the recital of the tragic destinies of illustrious men are a gloss and a reminder.[46]

Raymond Williams too, has some very helpful insights into the crucial changes from one culture to another.[47] In *Greek* tragedy, the action was at once *public* and *metaphysical*. The action was of ruling families belonging to a legendary past, intermediate between gods and men. In *Senecan* tragedy, there is a stress on the *nobility of suffering* and *enduring misfortune*, which provided a basis for the later transfer of interest to the suffering individual, away from the general action. In medieval *Christian* ideas about tragedy, the emphasis is on the *fall of famous men* who begin in 'prosperity' and end in 'adversity'.[48] This reveals, firstly, a shift of meaning from *change of fortune* to *fall*, reminiscent of the Fall. That is to say, it is expressive of a Christian notion of *fortune as an agency of providence*. Secondly, it reveals a shift from Aristotle's 'happiness and misery' to 'prosperity and adversity'. That is to say, the Christian notion of fortune increasingly refers to *this-worldly success as opposed to other-worldly striving*. It becomes a sin to trust to fortune in the sense of seeking worldly success instead of seeking God. Fortune is put outside any general and common human destiny. The worldly wheel of Fortune is a sinful option one should not get involved in the first place. A dualism between this-worldly and other-worldly striving tends to coincide with *a split between fortune and providence*. Under the pressures of 'the alienation of feudal society', Williams argues, the emphasis on 'a general condition became so attached to a single particular case—the fall of princes—that the general reference to tragedy became largely negative' and limited to princes, no longer at once public and metaphysical, but social (rank as an isolated condition) as opposed to metaphysical. In *Renaissance* tragedy, the medieval emphasis on the fall of princes is combined with a new interest in the methods and effects of tragic drama, governed by considerations of noble dignity and decorum. Rank in tragedy became important because of its accompanying aristocratic style. The idea of tragedy ceased to be metaphysical and became *critical*. Fortune became a *secularized* notion, and the action-oriented Aristotelian 'change of fortune' became the person-oriented *individualistic* notion of 'change in the hero's fortunes'.

Whereas States links fortune and virtue to passion and reason, respectively ('blood and judgement' in Hamlet's Passion's Slave Speech), Joan Rees links both *time* and *fortune* to the power of *custom* and the weakness of *passion* and *purposes*, and opposes them to *conscience*.[49] Rees argues that Hamlet seeks to stimulate the impulse to action, but that this impulse is always in danger of dying from the lethargy of custom (III.iv.161–70) and that all human passion weakens as new impressions supervene because of the effect of time and circumstance upon feelings and intent. Circumstances changing (time and fortune), human purposes are infirm.[50]

6 Divine intentions and interventions

The role of the gods in human morality is a persistent problem for the Greeks. Do the gods enforce human morality, share it, ignore it? Blundell concludes that it is a problem solved, if at all, in a variety of ways.[51] Vernant's religiously focused suggestion that Greek tragedy, by definition, presupposes a conflict between the human level and the divine level, may therefore have to be viewed with more nuance. Conflict of social loyalties often relates to the human level only, when individuals are competing for honour, when competitive and cooperative dimensions of honour are clashing, or when claims of different 'friends' (*philoi*) cannot be smoothly reconciled.[52] Zeus himself, at the beginning of Homer's *Odyssey* (I.32ff.), suggests that mortals, instead of being justified to blame the gods for the evils that befall them and instead of assuming responsibility for their own actions, often sow the seeds of their own misfortunes and 'have sorrows beyond what is ordained'.

In Greek religion, Jon D. Mikalson argues, there are three major areas of *divine intervention* – fertility and health, protection and prosperity.[53] But divine intervention is not easily identified. The word *daimon* often indicates an unidentifiable deity, but it may also, like *theos*, refer to a specific god. Later on, *daimones* became thought of as inferior deities. The word *daimon* could also mean 'fortune' or 'one's personal fortune', but it never meant a cult deity, just a cause of what happened. Mikalson explains how Sophocles makes use of these meanings of *daimon* in *Oedipus Tyrannus*. The movement from unidentifiable cause to identified deity supports Oedipus' movement from ignorance to understanding. Sophocles does not link Oedipus with *daimones* until the king begins to realize that he may have murdered Laius. (815–6) The *daimon* that afflicts Oedipus is increasingly personalized as peculiarly that of Oedipus (1193–6, 1300–2, 1311), and is finally identified, even as a specific cult deity (1327–30).[54] Padel points out another important difference between *daimon* and *theos*:

> As a general rule, *theos* and *daimōn* seem to suggest two different ways of regarding gods. *Theos* denotes something separate from human beings, something out there, in itself. It may watch you closely but anything it does is done from afar. *Daimōn*, it has been argued, is divinity that moves in: the nonhuman in the human. It is divinity getting its hands dirty, wading into human lives. Close, active, involved. The same god, therefore, may be called *theos* and *daimōn* at different moments.[55]

The taking of omens presumes that the gods had foreknowledge of the outcome of battles. But were the gods thought to determine this outcome?

In Aeschylus, they were; in Sophocles, reference to the gods' determining the outcome is not to be found, and in Euripides, they are scarce, Mikalson concludes.[56]

In one respect, there is a huge difference between popular religion and the literary religion in tragedy. In popular religion, 'the gods' are held responsible for everything good and desirable – but not for misfortune. For misfortune, people blame fortune (*tychē*), a *daimon*, or fate. In tragedy, 'the gods' too are blamed for evil, albeit rarely specific gods worshipped in an Athenian cult. In tragedy, the gods are more hostile and less forgiving than those in popular religion.[57]

In both life and tragedy, the gods would punish violators of divine laws. Profane areas outside the realm of piety, and therefore alien to the gods' functions, could be linked to the gods by taking oaths. But there is little evidence that the personal justice or morality of the gods was a concern in popular religion, where people did not expect the gods to be just or moral in ways identical to those of mortals.[58] Padel writes:

> Divinity guards and enforces human morality, but is not bound by the rules it imposes. Divinity is a source of contradictory orders, punishing you for obeying one according to the logic of another. Divinity issues prohibitions (do not kill your mother), forces you to break them, then punishes you for breaking them.[59]

In tragedy, gods in conflict with other gods normally do not meet face-to-face, but through human relations. Human relations are the battlefield or courtroom for gods fighting gods – not demons but *daimones*, divinities. *No god* protects humans from the demands made upon them by another god, or *cares* that his stake in humans – his jealous protection of his own rights and honours – means that these humans are in danger of offending another god, Padel argues.[60]

No tragedian suggests any *divine* contributions to early moral or legal life. Sophocles' 'Ode to Man' in the *Antigone* (332–75) lists all forms of cultural progress as *human* achievements. The gods did not create the human moral or legal code.[61]

If the gods did not create a just order, do they maintain it? In Greek *literature*, Mikalson suggests, characters assert that the gods are, or should be, just.[62] Aeschylus makes Zeus *the* protector of justice, 'but he does so for the sake of justice, not for the benefit of Zeus'.[63] When in Sophoclean tragedy the gods play a role, it is against the background of a cosmic order that is divine, just and regulated, but remote and obscure. *The eternal laws of the cosmic order are the sacred laws of nature that must be upheld.* Any infringement is taboo, brings about potential chaos, and must be undone by purifying ritual means, by blood revenge, by expiatory exile. Sophocles' *Oedipus Tyrannus* starts with the polluting effects of a yet unknown violation of the city of Thebes' purity, the plague. Men, animals, crops, all participate in the contamination that is unleashed by the revenging power of cosmic justice. It is explained by the divine oracle of Delphi, which also offers a ritual cure – 'drive out the murderers of Laios', further specified by the seer Teiresias. After that, the divine recedes, and human choices lead to the revelation of the truth. Oedipus learns that he will kill his father and marry his mother, but nobody learns why that should be. Silence about the ultimate motivation for the destiny prophesied for Laius and Oedipus makes the Sophoclean divine inscrutable, Robert Parker argues.[64] Ewans points out that, 'nonetheless, even Teiresias and Apollo *could* be wrong: both locaste and the elders actively contemplate this possibility towards the midpoint of the drama, and the elders are appalled by it (897ff.); for a time, Oedipus has no doubt that they *are* wrong'.[65] In Sophocles' *Antigone*, the seer Teiresias reveals to Creon that Creon's refusal to respect Polyneices' sacred burial rituals has caused the divine curse that Creon will lose his child because of his mistakes, and that the sacrificial offerings of Thebes will not be accepted by the gods. The cosmic balance has to be restored.

The gods participate in this cosmic order and sustain it, they do not create it. Zeus may be referred to as its representative (cf. the final line of Sophocles' *Trachiniae*). In *Oedipus Tyrannus* (738, 863–82, 903–5, 1198), Zeus' presence suggests an all-embracing, timeless moral order that provides a cosmic frame for human suffering, beyond the immediate agency of Apollo. Zeus' immortal rule contrasts with the shifting, unstable role of Oedipus. The attributes of Zeus' order (absolute power, eternity, purity, celestial remoteness) do not necessarily constitute a comforting vision; they are exactly antithetical to those revealed in the mortal protagonist, Segal states.[66] He continues:

> It is, of course, tempting to identify the second stasimon's vision of timeless gods with Sophocles' own, for it is the grandest, most abstract, and most philosophical view of divinity enunciated in the play. But a tragic chorus also has its place within the unfolding dramatic action, and this chorus' understanding deepens as the tragic events unfold to its view. These events will soon include Oedipus' discovery of a new kind of human strength, a strength in which he can 'bear' man's suffering of the woes of life (1415). In this new, human strength he demonstrates that the blood ties that have created his terrible pollution also carry with them the bonds of love, pity, and compassion (1417–1514). The remote gods of the second

stasimon, with their pure, celestial laws, are untouched by such stains of mortal generation; but they seem equally untouched by the human qualities of love and pity that are engendered along with the children.[67]

The ethical consciousness of moral values and their vulnerability turns humans into humane beings, but it does not turn the anthropomorphic gods into compassionate beings. Parker formulates carefully:

the logical structure of theodicy in Sophocles frequently seems to be of a restricted and negative form: in *Trachiniae* 'it is not the case that Zeus abandoned his son for no reason to a horrible death', or in *Oedipus at Colonus* 'it is not the case that the gods let Oedipus die unregarded', and so on. What is adduced, in a way found in the other tragedians too, is a mitigation or limitation of suffering or a compensation for it, and these mitigations and compensations serve to blunt the sharpest of men's complaints of divine cruelty and neglect. But too much remains unexplained and unknowable for strong positive claims about divine justice, still less about divine benevolence, to be possible.[68]

In my understanding, the non-moral characteristics of the Greek gods are no exception to the rule that in polytheism, gods embody forces of nature, and forces of nature are by no means necessarily moral forces. Take a force like strength. If strength appears to manifest itself beyond human proportions, it is considered divine, the work of a god. But how does *tragedy* deal with divine strength? In Sophocles' *Ajax* (89–120), Padel notes, Athena, goddess of reason, war and strategy, has made Ajax mad while Odysseus stands by, watching. Ajax is now busy savagely torturing animals, in his madness thinking that he is torturing his enemy, Odysseus. Meanwhile, Athena turns to the real Odysseus and points out to him the *divine strength* gods are capable of in making men mad like this. Odysseus answers that *he* is impressed, not with the divine strength demonstrated, but with the *human weakness* of all human beings, himself included.[69]

In *Shakespearean* tragedy, Hamlet is impressed by humankind's ambiguous human nature, 'in action like an angel, in apprehension like a god' – but dust too, that is to say, both lofty soul and down-to-earth matter (II.ii.302–7).[70] What is his impression of the Christian concept of God, divine intention and divine intervention?

Supernatural power (witches, ghosts, providence) operates in complete consistency with the dynamics of nature, as McAlindon observed. Apart from Claudius' efforts to escape divine punishment by trying to repent through prayer, divine intentions are considered by one character only, by Hamlet, and only to the extent that 'heaven' or 'providence' can restore order, force Hamlet to kill someone and punish him for doing so. (III.iv.175–7) Hamlet has a sense of providential involvement in human affairs. In Hamlet's mind, providence, revenge and timing are intertwined because they are all related to the necessity and reality of a moral universe, according to Harry Keyishian. Western religious culture 'furnishes the metaphysical underpinning for Shakespeare's account of the urge to revenge' because the Judeo-Christian tradition holds the conviction 'that evil will be punished eventually'.[71] Further on, Keyishian reiterates his own point that divine providence has always played a consoling role, but starts in Shakespeare's time to be questioned even among Christian believers.[72]

David Bevington points out that the philosophical debate on 'faith in divine providence' versus 'scepticism regarding providence' already takes place in *Hamlet* itself. Shakespeare stages the debate by having Hamlet disagree with Horatio, not just on the issue of the Ghost's insistence that Horatio and Marcellus swear to keep their vows of silence and Hamlet's proclamation that 'there are more things in heaven and earth, Horatio/Than are dreamt of in your philosophy' (I.v.166–7), but also on the issue of the extent to which providence shapes the story of revenge soon coming to its close. Hamlet is sceptical of many things, but eventually he remains a Christian who believes in 'a divinity that shapes our ends' (V.ii.10) and in 'special providence' (V.ii.214). 'Let be' (V.ii.218), he counsels Horatio. This 'readiness' sounds close to Horatio's stoic attitude but, Bevington argues, there is a huge *difference between Hamlet's Christian stoicism* that places all events in the hands of providence *and Horatio's Roman stoicism* that sees chance, instead of providence, at work in history. Bevington observes the irony that, whereas Hamlet sees his story in terms of serving heaven's purpose of punishing who deserve punishment, Horatio – who is asked by Hamlet himself to tell Hamlet's story – interprets Hamlet's story very differently, in terms of 'accidental judgements', 'casual slaughters' and 'mistaken purposes' (V.ii.375–8), that is to say, in profoundly sceptical, secular and ironic terms. Bevington concludes that 'Shakespeare, with his characteristic delight in debate, offers us a dual explanation in which the alternatives are mutually incompatible'.[73] What Bevington calls Hamlet's and Horatio's 'stoicism' strikes me as a shared attitude that seizes opportunities. This is different from modern risk-taking adventurers and calculators of probability, whose lost (early modern) sense of timing as a matter of moral responsibility has been replaced with a newly gained (modern) sense of opportunism.

According to McAlindon, one very important feature of Shakespearean tragedy is the role of *time*. 'Time is the measured movement of the material world and discloses a cyclic pattern of binary and quadruple opposites: day and night, spring and autumn, summer and winter. Man himself' in the Renaissance 'is conceived as a temporal microcosm', the parts of the body being connected with the heavenly bodies. 'Like any powerful ruler, Time can seem both terrible and reassuring. It signifies change, decay, and death', but also, being cyclical, order and constancy. In Renaissance culture, *time is associated with justice* whereas injustice is associated with haste. Timeliness is a behavioural ideal, held to be a prerequisite for all action that is effective, socially proper and just. In Shakespearean tragedy, 'the deeds which generate the tragic action are *untimely or mistimed* in the sense that they are dilatory or (much more often) either rash or cunningly swift'.[74]

Initially, Claudius' speed is a source of chaos, but it also counterpoints Hamlet's wavering between delay and fatal rashness. 'For Hamlet, everything takes on the dimension of time, and the time is out of joint. His inability to reshape it becomes for him a problem of when to act. He is troubled by memory, which keeps consciousness in time, and is a prerequisite for truth to self and to others—for resolution and constancy'. His sense of providential involvement in events makes him alter his attitude to time. 'It is not for him to create or even to identify the opportune moment for action: it will come to him, and "the *readiness* is all" (V.ii.215)'. The hero, working at last *in conjunction with* time, and beyond that with *time's order of justice*, puts an end to the confusion that his mighty opposite has created, or does so in part.[75]

Bevington's and Keyishian's topic of 'scepticism regarding providence' and McAlindon's topic of 'readiness in conjunction with time's order of justice' should not go unnoticed. In my opinion, these topics can be understood even better if viewed within the broader historical context of an *early modern* increase in subjectivity and reflectiveness.

The *pre-modern world view* presumes a given world order, which mankind (as a collective) is expected to join. Man's insertion is part and parcel of the whole. Man expects to find his goal in life, not to invent it. Man is destined to fit into the order of time. The time is not normally out of joint, and if it is, it will turn to normal again. The world order is in order, constitutes a moral order. Man has to be in conjunction with time's order. If the human being fails to join the existing world order, he fails his destiny, is out of place, marginal, led astray by the greater gods or taken away by the larger passions. His subjective influence and input are limited, and not the main part of what is happening anyway. This is the stuff of *ancient tragedy*. The ancient tragic hero's guilt is more passive than active, more a form of suffering endurance than of conscious acting – if set off against the modern tragic hero's guilt.[76]

The *modern world view* presumes a world order that men (as individuals cooperating according to a social contract) are expected to construct.

On the surface, there is no difference between medieval aristocrats displaying decorum and Renaissance aristocrats cultivating decorum, as we saw earlier on.[77] But in my understanding, there is a difference in views of human nature and action. The Renaissance aristocrats combine their aristocratic style with an aesthetic interest in methods of writing tragedy. That is to say, whereas medieval aristocrats displayed decorum in order to *confirm* their status, Renaissance aristocrats had an interest in form because to them, form displays one's capacity to *shape* reality, to impose one's style, to leave one's mark. The self-shaping Proteus was one of their favourite Greek gods. Renaissance aristocrats had an aesthetic interest in methods of writing tragedy for its *effects* on the audience. Also, the human being has to be ready to seize accidental opportunities as time passes by. Time becomes a matter of timing, of turning time in one's favour. The modern tragic hero's guilt is more self-made than passive, more a form of conscious acting than of suffering endurance, more the result of personal responsibility than of inevitable fate, more his own product than his predetermined destiny, less driven by the greater gods and the larger passions than by his own character and choices, less fitting into a given moral order than projecting his own utopia. Subjectivity and reflexivity are the stuff of *modern tragedy*. Modern man does not suffer from divine necessities, but from coincidental accidents, contingencies and collateral damage of joint ventures. That, Johan Taels notices, is the stuff of *comedy*.[78] Is modern tragedy, then, closer to a comic world view? Taels' answer to this question also sheds light on the early modern relationship between scepticism, providence and timing.

Schiller, Hegel and Kierkegaard, he argues, are representatives of a decisive shift in favour of the modern world view. The interesting thing is that this historical shift leads Hegel to prefer comedy to tragedy, whereas it leads Kierkegaard to prefer tragedy to comedy. What they have in common, Taels explains, is their modern awareness of reflectiveness. The early modern struggle between passion and reason culminated in the Enlightenment victory of reason over passion, and in the early Romantic idealization of passionless detachment. In Hegelian thought, passionless detachment takes the form of abstract reflectiveness, takes the form of a full consciousness finally floating freely above the struggling history that nature produced on its way to full-fledged self-consciousness. In short, it takes the form of a *panoptic comic world view*. Hegelian aesthetics declares the art form of *comedy* the highest artistic genre because its speculative achievement to develop a reflective point of view enables the Spirit to reach higher grounds than the ethical battlefields of history and tragedy. Panoramic comedy represents the superior understanding of detached reflectiveness and metaphysical laughter.

Kierkegaard is not amused. He suffers from a *tragic world view*. He prefers tragedy to comedy because his reflexivity does not liberate him from history's struggles. On the contrary, it plunges him even more into its failures – or rather, into its contradictions. Taels points out that Kierkegaard translates Aristotle's 'failure' or 'error' (*hamarteima*) as 'contradiction', thus (after Lessing) broadening the moral scope of the 'tragic' and the 'comic' to an existential scope that is not necessarily moral or religious. What the 'tragic' and the 'comic' share is contradiction. What separates them is pain or lack of it. Abstract reflectiveness leads to painless detachment, but concrete reflectiveness leads to passionate suffering, and our concrete existence leaves us no choice, but to acknowledge in our minds and hearts that there is no mental or speculative way out of our responsibility and guilt by cultivating a comic consciousness of absolute freedom. The more Kierkegaard reflects on his concrete existence, his reason serving his passion, the more his 'thoughts are bloody', to quote Hamlet, and painful.

However, Taels suggests, *the (post)modern world view tends to be comic, not tragic, precisely because of its increased reflectiveness*. This modern reflexivity is, in turn, intensified by the omnipresent powers of the mass media covering history from a bird's-eye view, exercising the power of panoptic knowledge, flexible focus and rapid shifts of attention, thus enhancing the detached attitude typical of postmodern comedy and scepticism.

But *postmodern comedy and scepticism* are different from *early modern comedy and scepticism*, Taels points out. Early modern comedy and scepticism are deeply moral and social. Early modern scepticism concerns established authorities, traditional customs, the past, but it does not yet fully doubt the moral and social order of the world. Early modern man is sensitive to an appeal to his subjective determination, a conscious readiness to actively shape his destiny, to become more self-reliant for lack of traditional authorities and out of individualistic ambition. Despite his metaphysical and political doubts, he still strives to be in conjunction with time's moral order. But the timing and the readiness are now up to himself; he has to make up his own mind. In this respect, and in postmodern retrospect, *Hamlet* presents a *tragicomic world view*. Hamlet makes up his mind not just about the existence of ghosts and the truth of the Ghost's word, but also about his timing and his readiness to be an instrument of divine punishment and providential planning. Hamlet eventually succeeds in joining time's moral order by actively shaping his destiny. But the excessive killing that goes with it is as much about destroying destinies as it is about shaping them, a tragic outcome that only fuels Horatio's neo-Stoic scepticism regarding divine providence. Horatio's last word is 'chance'.

7 Conclusions

The human level of mortal intentions and actions and the divine level of immortal power, purpose and intervention are deeply interconnected in Greek tragedy. The divine level has different faces and dimensions, varying from characterless impersonal fate to characteristically personal gods, from triggering human action through oracle predictions (*Oedipus Tyrannus*) to taking over human action through madness (*Ajax*), from being a transparent force of justice (Aeschylus) to being an obscure power in the background (Sophocles), from unfolding the increasingly unavoidable necessities of fate to following the arbitrary up-and-down contingencies of fortune. The gods are blamed for evil, they lack compassion and they are more hostile and less forgiving in Greek tragedy than they are in Greek popular religion. The gods maintain the sacred laws of nature they have not created.

The human level of intentions and actions in Greek tragedy is a mixture of divine constraint and human freedom and of prophesied pressures and human responsibilities. Heering's theory of tragedy is confirmed in current readings of the Greek material such as Mogyoródi's. Human decision-making is tragic because one's gradually unfolding decision is not distinguishable from one's gradual appropriation of fate as one's own inalienable destiny. Free choice becomes the other side of the coin of fate, using and depending on intentional acts of free choice for its enactment.

In Shakespeare's *Hamlet*, the workings of fate have been replaced by the workings of nature, on the one hand, and the workings of fortune and providence, on the other. What goes on at the microcosmic level of human nature reflects the dynamic forces of nature at the macrocosmic level. If nature is governed by both Love and Strife, so is Hamlet, McAlindon argued. Hamlet's tragic situation, then, is characterized by his inner conflict of love and conscience versus the call to violence and hatred. Instead of appropriating Claudius' transparent necessity of the natural order, Hamlet seems to appropriate the obscure chaos of human freedom. And instead of embracing Horatio's sceptic version of neo-Stoic fortune, Hamlet seems to embrace a sceptic version of Christian providence.

Several differences pertaining to the religious weight of divine and human action can be observed between Greek and Shakespearean tragedy. In Greek tragedy, fate and the gods are prominent whereas fortune is marginal; in Shakespearean tragedy, it is the other way around. Raymond Williams explained that in Greek tragedy, human action is at once public and metaphysical, while in Renaissance tragedy, action is still public, but no longer metaphysical, and sudden change is the enactment of a person-oriented fortune instead of action-oriented fortune. Taels pointed out that both ancient and early modern tragedy abide by the religious belief that the human being ultimately operates within the limits of a moral world order of divine justice, even if this is not experienced as such. The difference is that the ancient hero expects to find his goal in life and to join the existing world order, whereas the early modern hero tries to invent his goal in life and to actively shape the existing world order according to his ambition, shaping time's order by timing one's seizure of opportunities instead of enduring time's order of constraining necessities and fatal consequences.

PART II: INDIAN AND HINDU ISSUES

1 Introduction

What is the impact of superhuman powers, such as fate and the gods, on human actions and human intentions according to the Indian texts under consideration? In several respects, the *Mahābhārata* epic is very different from the *Bhagavadgītā* section within the epic when it comes to the issues of causal agency, of human freedom, responsibility and effort in the face of fate, time, fortune and divine intentions and interventions. The position of the *Gītā* on these issues will therefore be presented in a separate section (6) after the sections presenting the epic's views and concepts. For my phrasing of these views and concepts, I rely heavily on Peter Hill's study, which was published in 2001, in the same year as Julian F. Woods' equally valuable study on the same topic.[79]

2 The epic on the gods' intentions and interventions

If one goes by the epic's creation myths, Hill argues, it is only the three great gods Brahmā, Śiva and Vishnu – who are before and beyond the triple-world – that really matter. Normally, *the great gods* broadly direct and influence human affairs in accordance with their own purposes and ends, most especially the preservation of order.[80]

In the epic's creation myths, 'good, truth, virtue and, most of all, order, are only perceivable qualities if they exist in contrast with evil, untruth, non-virtue and most of all chaos. Likewise, gods are only distinguishable entities if they can be contrasted with demons'. However, the contrasts are not black and white, for these opposed categories are also interdependent in that you could not have one without the other.[81] Having said that, if the fragile triple-world is to prove a viable creation, some minimum standard of order is required, not just in the form of a set of rules, but in the form of a constant intervention of the great gods to predetermine the broad outline of events for the sake of preserving that order. And *the human being plays a supporting role* in that:

> We may conclude that the central drama in Epic mythology is the eternal conflict between gods and demons, who represent (though they do not originate) the forces of *dharma* and *adharma*, order and disorder, and less directly good and evil. What part does mortal man play in this cosmic conflict? Man is certainly not a principal participant but he does play a supporting role of great importance for the gods. For the sacrificial offerings of men alone sustain the strength of the gods in their struggle. Men and gods are natural allies in the struggle against the demons and the forces of *adharma*. They exist in a symbiotic relationship of mutual advantage which is well attested in the Epic.[82]

The central drama in the background is the *cosmic conflict between gods and demons, not between gods and men*.

Only in certain contexts is man's lot perceived as entirely predetermined, but interestingly, the agent of predestination is invariably not a great god directly, but a personalized abstraction – either the Placer (*dhātr*) or the Ordainer (*vidhātr*), Hill explains.[83] *The predetermining powers* of the divine Placer are *explicitly discussed* and referred to by some of the epic's main characters, such as Yudhisthira and Draupadī during their exile. Draupadī considers the Placer as 'a wrathful, malevolent and vindictive puppet master worthy only of the contempt of the mortal marionettes he manipulated' (3.31.24–36). Yudhisthira 'dismisses it as heresy (*nāstikyam*)', since her arguments 'repudiated the doctrine of *karma*, and more importantly they undermined all reason for adherence to *dharma*'. Yudhisthira argues that human acts are meaningful, that there must be a connection between action and reward, and that 'man is not the powerless puppet of a capricious Placer, for the blameless Placer merely distributes rewards in accordance with the acts of men'. Draupadī, in turn, 'partly agrees by admitting that there are other factors involved in acts than just the Placer' and that human acts yield a reward. In her view, 'the Placer assigns man's lot according to his *karma*'. Yudhisthira holds the view 'that man is wholly in charge of his own destiny'. (3.32–3)[84]

3 The epic on fate, time and fortune

According to Hill, 'it is within the context of death, destruction, catastrophe, and gross turns of fortune, that the effects of *fate* (*daiva*) and *time* (*kāla*) are most readily seen' and called upon.[85]

That *fortune* plays a crucial, but virtually invisible role in the epic's plot pattern has been shown by Hiltebeitel.[86] The wife of the five Pāndavas, Draupadī, plays a central role in the ups and downs of fortune. The goddess of Prosperity, Śrī, is incarnate in Draupadī. If Prosperity embraces a king, his kingdom will thrive; if she leaves the king for some other king, the decline of the kingdom will be his 'portion' of fortune. Śrī is the source of the king's sovereignty, provided the monarch is omni-virtuous (energetic, speaking the truth, not breaking or misusing vows, etc.). The ultimate or temporary downfall of kings such as Yudhisthira is thus dependent upon the presence of a set of qualities, non-moral and moral alike.[87]

The word 'portion' indicates that fortune comes, in fact, under the long-term workings of *fate* (*daiva*). When Duryodhana had resented Yudhisthira's wealth and royal ritual to inaugurate his Assembly Hall and claim kingly sovereignty, he had said that 'fate is supreme and human effort pointless' (2.43.32), but simultaneously, he and his uncle Śakuni had planned to overthrow Yudhisthira's throne by proposing a dice game. Julius Lipner concludes, 'So, under the guise of fate, namely the dicing match, they will attempt to manipulate fate to their advantage'.[88] Moreover, the approval of his father Dhrtarāshtra had been a combination of asking advice, making his own decision and claiming that the dice game would for sure have been ordained by fate, since fate is supreme, and would be blessed by the gods. (2.45.53–7) *The ups and downs of fortune*, in the epic, are thus considered *a matter of fate*. In the chapter on narrative aspects (Part II Section 3.3), it was pointed out that Śakuni and Duryodhana are incarnations of Dvāpara and Kali, personifications of cosmic world epochs (*yugas*), which themselves carry the names of the throws of the Indian dice.

Fortune may be fickle by nature, but what is the nature of fate? Hill writes:

In some contexts fate and Time are inscrutable and purposeless, but yet in other contexts they display a more moral dimension. Equally, in various contexts fate and Time are considered to be all-powerful and ineluctable, predetermining all events and actions: in this context resignation and detachment are normally recommended as the only adequate response to the crushing power of fate. But just as often fate comes across as a force that determines the broad outcomes while leaving the minutiae to human action: in this context performance of duty and preservation of honour are often recommended as the appropriate response to fate's contrary directions. Occasionally, too, the view is offered, or acted upon, that fate as a force can be made favourable or even overcome. However, what is missing from the Epic is any detailed critique of the nature of fate as a force. The broad image that does come across from the text is that of struggling humanity, in all its variety, attempting to accommodate itself before a supernatural order perceived as an impersonal power which metes out life and destiny less as a right than as a tenuous privilege.[89]

Sometimes, fate is seen as 'a force that impartially drives both sides in the war to destruction', but 'at various points, fate is specifically considered to be working in favour of the Pāndavas and against the Kauravas'. *Different characters hold different views.* 'Often time and fate exercise their destructive potential by deluding and perverting the judgement of the participants, driving them on to acts of folly'.[90]

4 The epic on karma

The 'law of *karma*' refers to the concept that the actions of an individual generate automatic effects that are undergone by the very individual who generated them. This law of cause and effect is an individual affair. It is a moral mechanism that works within one and the same life or from past existences to future existences. What happens to the individual is not due to the gods or fate, but to *karma* discharging its battery of consequences within the subsequent lives of that individual, who is thus fully responsible for its own destiny.

In theory, others cannot benefit from the individual's positive *karma*. Neither can they take away or undo someone else's negative *karma*. But whereas some sections of the epic demonstrate a strict interpretation of the law of *karma*, Hill observes, other sections incorporate the abrogation of sin and the transfer of sin and merit. The epic's considerable preoccupation with ways of avoiding the consequences of sin – by invoking a god to release from sin, by expiations and mortifications, by the generation of *tapas*, by devotion, by sacrifice, by the giving of gifts, by pilgrimage and by listening to meritorious teachings[91] – instead of facing up to them, goes against the strict *karmic* sense of direct and unavoidable responsibility.[92] The difference between a strict interpretation and a loose interpretation of the law of *karma* seems to be infused[93] by the difference between the this-worldly (*pravrtti*) approach of brahmanism and the other-worldly (*nivrtti*) approach of asceticism.[94] The other-worldly individualistic approach prefers the (newer) strict (non-transference) model of *karma*, whereas the this-worldly social approach embraces the (older) looser (transference) model, Hill claims.[95] What all the epic's major teachings on *karma* share, regardless of their different approaches, is a concern with man's ultimate capacity to control his own destiny. 'Nevertheless, the basis of their commitment to human action is fundamentally different'.[96] The *this-worldly* tradition wants to promote the active adherence to duty, whereas the *other-worldly* tradition wants to promote the active liberation from bondage. Most of the time, the epic's outlook is this-worldly and probably, Hill suggests, the strict interpretation of the law of *karma* is therefore largely ignored in favour of the meaningfulness of social action and 'allowing the abrogation of sin, and the transfer of sin and merit'.[97]

'It is not infrequent for *karma* to be called upon to explain *misfortune* or a reverse of circumstances', Hill points out; 'Mārkandeya consoles the grieving Yudhisthira along these lines at a particularly low point during the Pāndavas' exile', the exile being the fruit of a lost game of dice, a true reversal of fortunes.[98] In those cases, Hill explains, reference to the law of *karma* is consoling because it implies reference to a universal moral order beyond current human control. It has after all a deterministic side, which 'could easily come to seem like any other impersonal force beyond the current individual's control'.[99] Rarely do the epic characters blame themselves for their misfortune by referring to their *own* actions in previous lives.[100]

5 The epic on fate and human effort

How do fate and human action intertwine? There are no systematic attempts to distinguish between the two realms and determine the interaction. Basically, fate is accepted and fatalism is rejected:

> It is sufficient to maintain that both play a part. In truth, these analyses are what could be called the common sense view of fate and human exertion; and this is suggested by the frequent appeal to agricultural illustrations. From the simple observation of a peasant on the soil, common sense dictated the view that on the one hand there were uncontrollable external forces at work which could assist or destroy all mortal endeavours, and that on the other hand success in life depended on human exertion, even if it did not guarantee the desired result. To this extent, Epic narrators accepted fate but rejected full fatalism. The simplicity of the analyses, it needs to be

noted, may trouble us more than the Epic narrators, for the most important conclusion from their discussions would seem to be that whatever the particular combination of factors, human beings must act, and in particular they must act to fulfil their *dharmic* duties.[101]

There are two key events in the epic's central story line that spark off a deepening of the *debate on the notion of individual responsibility* – Dhrtarāstra's culpability for the family feud, and Yudhisthira's participation in the dice match. In the case of Dhrtarāstra's role, 'the epic bards never satisfactorily resolved the problem whether causal agency and responsibility lay with the individual actor, external forces, or alternatively some particular combination. . . . As the epic bards came and went over the centuries and added their views to the text, the apparent "contradictions" in the text', Hill suggests, 'took on the nature of competing interpretations of which they were fully aware.[102] . . . they may have preferred to leave the debate open'.[103] In the case of Yudhisthira, before the dice game he absolves himself of blame, claiming that the Placer and fate 'compelled him to gamble. Yet, after the dicing, he fulsomely accepts blame and responsibility', pointing out to Bhima that, afflicted by gambling mania, he (Yudhisthira) had lost self-control. So, 'while he had no choice but to accept the challenge to a dicing match the outcome of which was predetermined, nevertheless once it started he himself chose to continue participating in it . . . it was his own temporary break-down in self-control that drove him on to such a disastrous end'.[104]

Brodbeck too, draws attention to the tone of the debate, which he characterizes as 'legalistic' and 'tragic' alike:

These discussions often take place in a conventional, legalistic tone. It is important to note that these theories of human action do not all explicitly deny individual freedom and responsibility: they can be seen as adducing additional factors that may constrain choice and therefore reduce culpability. It is only occasionally that the notion of individual freedom is doubted in its entirety. What is doubted, however, is the potency of the individual in the face of superpersonal forces. It is emphasised that, even having done all within one's power to achieve x, y may still happen instead. This frustrating but ever present fact is the axis around which the *Mahābhārata*, *qua* tragedy, resolves. The debate is one about the extent of constraints, but these are constraints on outcomes of activity, not on what one does or tries to do. Krishna has much sympathy with the acknowledgement of powerlessness: the limited potency of the individual is the basis of his proposed *yogic* psychology of action.[105]

The tragedy of human powerlessness does not pertain to man's intentions or actions, but to their consequences in the face of superhuman powers of constraint.

6 The Gītā on fate, time, Krishna's predestination and human action

Although the issue of fate, predestination and human action is much debated in the *Mahābhārata* as a whole, it cannot be argued that the issue is of prime concern for the author(s) of the *Gītā*, according to Hill.[106] At the level of the mortal individual, the characteristics (*gunas*) of material nature (*prakrti*) lead to certain sorts of personalized motion patterns or behaviour patterns. It is material nature that is the active, but itself impersonal principle, also in psychosomatic man; *Gītā* 3.27:

> Actions in all cases are performed
> By the qualities of material nature;
> He whose mind is confused by egoism
> Imagines, 'I am the doer.'[107]

Brodbeck points out the implications:

> The individual person does not add anything to the run of events by acting under his or her own mental volitions: all such volitions have sufficient external causes, after all, and it is more fitting to say that the individual person is a phenomenal part of the run of events, a contingent by-product, and to describe his or her volitional impressions as effects, rather than causes, of changing reality. Human bodies are provided by the world: equally so are the mental causes of action, and thus the actions themselves. The *Bhagavadgītā*, in its search for a hermeneutical stance on human action, has thrown off all anthropocentrism to analyse action as pure event, as motion of things. The perspective is one of physics and cosmology. It is rigidly deterministic. This perspective is illustrated in different ways by the text. The true explanatory nexus of events, the event-potency which works through people and 'their actions', is given in different places as *prakrti*, *brahman*, and Krishna. In each case it is stressed that people do not make themselves act, but are made to act.[108]

Hill notes that, as an agent of action, the psychosomatic individual is neither completely free nor completely bound. The ability to act as a free agent or actor is constrained, but not eliminated, by one's inherited *guna* structure and the law of *karma*.[109] The *guna* structure is on the level of material nature. But the individual has a dual nature, which is both material (psychosomatic) and spiritual. Hill comments:

> The *Gītā's* concern is undoubtedly more with the spiritual side of mortal man than the material. Therefore, it is not surprising that on the questions of action and freedom, the *Gītā's* views are much more consistently and closely thought out on the position of the soul (Spirit) than on the position of the phenomenal individual (Nature). The soul [Spirit, *LM*], the *Gītā* insists, does not and cannot act, and likewise it is eternally free. The fact that it appears to act, and to be bonded and limited, is merely the greatest delusion of all. In its essence the soul is immutable, limitless and free.[110]

Because of its stress on surrender to Krishna as Lord of the universe, the *Gītā* is more preoccupied with God's grace than with mortal man's effort. It is through love and devotion and God's grace that the *yogi* attains the ultimate goal of Krishna himself, not through knowledge acquired by individual effort.[111]

Krishna is both radically transcendent and energetically immanent. 'While all is divine and unified in God, nonetheless Spirit, Nature and the Supernatural Personality of God are all treated as separate and distinct parts of the one whole. It is the Supernatural Personality of God . . . that becomes immanent and active in the ever-changing world of Nature ("the Perishable") and Spirit ("the Imperishable") (15.16–17)'.[112] Whereas Krishna's transcendent aspect is entirely beyond action, his immanent aspect is working on behalf of the universe. Krishna is not just the overseer (9.10) of *dharma*, but directs the processes of material Nature (*prakrti*) – the *gunas* and Time – by means of his creative power (*māyā*).[113] In *Gītā* 18.59, it is Arjuna's own material nature that compels him to fight; in *Gītā* 18.60, it is his own *karma*, born of his own material nature; in *Gītā* 18.61, it is Lord Krishna's power of illusion (*māyā*):

> The Lord abides in the hearts
> Of all beings, Arjuna,
> Causing all beings to revolve,
> By the power of illusion, as if fixed on a machine.[114]

The imagery of Krishna causing all beings to 'move' or 'revolve' as if fixed on a machine is very close, I would suggest, to the Chinese notion of fate as a turning wheel, 'perfectly predictable insofar as it is', like a cycle, 'both regular and repetitive', as Lisa Raphals puts it. If my suggestion of a similarity between the Hindu metaphor and the Chinese Wheel of Fate is justified, there is an important difference with the Western Wheel of Fortune:

> The Wheel of Fortune that is such a powerful metaphor of luck in the West has a completely opposite direction from the Chinese metaphor. The Chinese 'wheel of fate' is a wheel in constant motion and regular recurrence; the Western Wheel of Fortune turns and then comes to rest. The force of this metaphor is an arbitrary and unknowable point at which the wheel will stop.[115]

Krishna is energetically immanent in the world through his direction of the *gunas*, but also as *Time*. (11.23–30) Time is not seen as an impersonal mechanism, but as a predetermined result of Krishna's destructive activity. *Gītā* 11.32–33:

> The Blessed Lord spoke:
> I am Time, the mighty cause of world destruction,
> Who has come forth to annihilate the worlds.
> Even without any action of yours, all these warriors
> Who are arrayed in the opposing ranks, shall cease to exist.
> Therefore stand up and attain glory!
> Having conquered the enemy, enjoy prosperous kingship.
> These have already been struck down by Me;
> Be the mere instrument, O Arjuna.[116]

While the *Gītā*, as a whole, is not ultimately pantheistic, parts of it are strongly so in tone because, as Hill puts it, 'the phenomenal individual is swallowed up in God. . . . The most pantheistic of all sections in the *Gītā* is found in Chapter 10', even though panentheism prevails (10.42). 'An awed Arjuna asks Krishna to recount the manifestations of his power, by which Krishna pervades the universe'.[117] The answer contains striking verse lines, such as 10.36a – 'Of those who cheat (at gambling), I am the dicing'. Hill comments:

> Significantly, Krishna is identified as the dicing of those who cheat, which in the context of the *Mahābhārata* must mean that the fraudulent game of dice that lost Yudhisthira his kingdom and led to the destruction of God's enemies was a product of the manifestation of the divine power in the universe, and not of the meaningful actions of the individual participants.[118]

The conclusion that Katz reaches as to the acknowledgement of fate in the *Gītā*, is that 'the *Gītā*, rather than advocating the employment of heroic effort against fate (a strategy that cannot succeed for humans), favors submission to fate and its transformation at the level of devotion; this is its most impressive teaching to Arjuna'.[119]

Brodbeck concludes that the acknowledgement of fate in the *Gītā* seems, instead of discouraging human action, 'to facilitate human action by stripping it of its psychological drawbacks'. After all, fate is, by definition, far beyond human efforts to defy or elude it and leaves human agents no choice, but to take it for (divinely) granted.[120] The human being must become aware of the power of fate and then realize that, if you cannot beat it, you'd better join it, and join it actively. The power of fate and the powerlessness of human action make a successful joint venture if man's consciousness is attuned to their inevitable collaboration, that is to say, attuned to being 'the mere instrument' (11.33) of fate.

7 Conclusions

In the epic, the cosmic conflict is between gods and demons, not between gods and men. Men play a supporting role on the side of the gods by sacrificing to the gods. The cosmic conflict between gods and demons is fought out on earth, however, by men apparently fighting a just cause against other men who support chaos and injustice. The earthly conflict is between men and men, with the predetermining powers of the gods (including the divine Placer, personalized fate) in the background influencing the human conflict, either by intervening directly or by shaping the course of events in the long term. The god Śiva is associated with the dice game and with the threat of chaos, whereas Krishna (the god Vishnu) is conspicuously absent from the dice game scene, leaves nothing to chance and counterbalances the destructive impact of Śiva.

The difference between divine (*daiva*) predestination by personal gods and divine predestination by the impersonal forces of fate (*daiva*), time (*kāla*) and fortune (*śrī*) is not always clear. Nor is the difference between fate, time and fortune, since short-term ups and downs of fortune are considered part of the long-term workings of fate and time. A regular reversal of fortunes determines the plot pattern down the generations of the Kuru lineage, each generation witnessing glory and decline. Yudhisthira's dice game and ensuing exile constitute one such turning point. A fatal throw of the dice substitutes one better world epoch in the cosmic cycle of time for another worse epoch. Time is more a destructive power than a re-balancing one in the epic. An appeal to *karma* is not a popular way of explaining one's own misfortune because that would mean blaming oneself; but it is a way of explaining reversals of fortune with reference to a universal moral order beyond current human control. *Karma* has a touch of tragic action in the sense that the action is something that goes on and on and on beyond one's intention or control. The extent to which human action can make a difference is subject to debate – different characters hold different views. Fate is accepted, but fatalism is rejected.

In the *Gītā*, fatalism is accepted. The god Krishna reveals himself as time destroying the current universe in order to renew it. The earthly conflict between men and men is predestined to be self-destructive. Human action is considered to be part of the material world of nature (*prakrti*), not of the spiritual world of the eternally free Self (*purusha*). The material world of nature works according to the interaction between the three *gunas* and its motion patterns, including the behaviour patterns of human nature. The vocabulary of the *gunas* presupposes a material nature that is inherently active (auto-mobile), yet not consciously targeted; there is no personal mover moving the motion. The *Gītā* uses this vocabulary to stress that the human being is not the actor in charge of his own action. Human action is part of human nature, that is to say, subject to the workings of material nature. But the *Gītā* introduces the god Krishna as the one Actor who rules over nature and intervenes in the material world for the sake of recycling it through time. Human action, embodied in Arjuna, becomes the mere instrument of divine predestination.

PART III: CROSS-CULTURAL COMPARISONS

The cross-cultural comparisons drawn in the third part of this chapter also present an answer to its *main question* – what is, according to the Western and Indian texts under consideration, the impact of superhuman powers, such as fate and the gods, on human action and human intention?

1 Divine fate, time and fortune, human destiny and freedom

The Greek and Hindu texts share very similar concepts of *fate*. Fate is a more or less impersonal, divine or daimonic power that can be crushing and virtually all-powerful, but also a force that determines the broad outcomes while leaving the minutiae to human action. Its inevitability is attached to a significant and particular event, not to a deterministic system, such as in the case of predestination. Fate is the sum of all the conditions of action at the moments when those conditions combine to give events a definite direction and form – it has *become* inevitable in the process of taking a definite form. *After* his consent won by persuasion, Philoctetes' *very last* words acknowledge the role of fate (*moira*). This is his own conclusion with the benefit of hindsight. To illustrate Ewans' point that destinies take the form of 'if *x*, then inexorably *y*' in Greek tragedy, in the sense that a hero's destiny takes shape along with the gradually unfolding events, not simply by an accident analogous to the throw of the dice, but by choosing *x* as an action, I quote Hill about the role of the Placer (personified fate):

> After Duryodhana had been struck down in the battle of clubs with Bhima, Yudhisthira is again impressed by the controlling power of the Placer. Yudhisthira approached his fallen foe, and with tears in his eyes said: 'Assuredly it was ordained by the great-spirited powerful Placer that we should wish to afflict you, and you us, O foremost of the Kurus.'[121]

Hill would probably emphasize the word 'again' in the previous quote, but I would like to stress the word 'After' instead, in order to make Ewans' point here. Fate is a gradual unfolding of divine or daimonic power in retrospect. Fate is event-related and thus plot-related, and takes its final shape only after the alternatives have been narrowed-down to their final option. Fate is linked up with long-term cosmic time and order. This order is not necessarily a moral order. It can be inscrutable and purposeless. In Greek tragedies and Hindu epics alike, different characters hold different views on fate. In the *Mahābhārata* epic, faced with fate, there is not much room for human action. It can join fate, but it cannot really go against it. It can accommodate itself before this supernatural order perceived as an impersonal power that metes out life and destiny less as a right than as a tenuous privilege, according to Hill. The *Gītā* (11.33) seems to favour full submission to fate as all-devouring time, complying with fate unconditionally instead of defying it mentally – in the sense of affirming life as worthwhile despite its suffering. The Kurukshetra War is a necessity and Arjuna is made to recognize its inevitability. Arjuna's awareness of its necessity and his share in it makes him a tragic character at the start of the *Gītā*. Krishna's power of illusion through his direction of all-devouring time is like the workings of fate, but it is unlike the obscure fate of Sophoclean tragedy. Krishna's destructive activity through time is not seen as obscure or close to chaos (*adharma*). It is seen as a predetermined catastrophe for the sake of a renewal of cosmic order (*dharma*), as a fate whose necessity makes sense.

The most disturbing aspect of the elusive force of fate is that it can turn human agents into its accomplice. Supernatural necessity manifests itself with all its mythical profundity by using human free choices for fatal purposes. It would not turn tragic, if it would be activated or reinvigorated without the heroes' willingness to assert their freedom, Mogyoródi explained. The tragic choices (gradually unfolding decisions) of tragic heroes consist of their gradual appropriation of a fateful outcome that is either not known or not wanted, or both. It is within the context of death, destruction, catastrophe and gross turns of fortune that the effects of fate (*daiva*) and time (*kāla*) are most readily seen and called upon, Hill noted. The characters involved in the central plot almost never contemplate their own actions and fortunes in terms of past and future *karma*. Although *karma* is, in theory, a tidy solution, Hill concluded, to the problem of fate and human action, its undoing was that it placed the destiny of the individual in his own hands, and by and large, that burden proved too onerous. In general, I would suggest when focusing on *karma* and *moksha*, if repeated reincarnation is a Hindu's fate (temporal necessity), ultimate liberation is his destiny (eternal freedom), whereas death is a Greek's destiny (eternal necessity) and the time of death his fate or allotment of life span (temporal necessity).

How do Hindu fate and human action intertwine? There are no closely reasoned attempts made to demarcate the boundaries between fate and human effort, Hill observed. It is sufficient to maintain that both play a part, as is suggested by the frequent appeal to agricultural illustrations. But Arjuna faces the necessity of a fatal war *and* still has to act upon it *and* behave well *and* at the same time not get involved mentally. Without resisting or defying his fate, the situation is not tragic, but miserable or horrible. Arjuna is aware of the fatal necessity of war and his part in it, but he does not resist or defy his fate. Mentally, he does not appropriate fate as his personal choice by considering himself fate's agent. Mentally, he is not involved in his fate, but is absolutely free. As the embodiment of human action, he is merely fate's instrument, the passive instrument of divine predestination. Thus, at the end of the *Gītā*, he is no longer a tragic hero, and the constituents of his tragic situation have been split up into a field of action, a divine soul (the 'knower'), and the active vehicle as mediator. Arjuna is encouraged to accept his fate, but think of his destiny and keep the two apart.

In *Hamlet*, there are some serious and also sceptical references to divine providence ('Heaven') as a guiding force in an ultimately moral order of cosmic justice and time. In Renaissance culture, McAlindon explained, time is associated with justice whereas injustice is associated with haste. Timeliness is a behavioural ideal, held to be a prerequisite for all action that is effective, socially proper, and just. In Shakespearean tragedy, the deeds that generate the tragic action are untimely or mistimed. For Hamlet, the time is out of joint. We already noted that winning the epic war by trickery became symbolic of the Hindu conception of the epic's time as Time's lack of order of justice – the deeply apocalyptic conviction that 'the time is out of joint'. Hamlet tries to 'set it right'. Does Arjuna try to 'set it right'? The striking difference between Arjuna and Hamlet is that Arjuna's problem is *whether* to act, whereas Hamlet's problem is *when* to act. Both try to act in conjunction with time's order of justice. But in Arjuna's case, time is devouring the universe, Arjuna is frightened, and he is forced to comply. In Hamlet's case, time is, on the one hand, similarly devouring, if one goes by Yorick's skull, as Kerrigan explained it. According to Kerrigan, we recall, Hamlet's final mood of calmness in Act V.ii has the preceding graveyard scene as its clue. Meditating on death's attack on the integrity of the body, Hamlet's realization that there is death after death, that death is one hell of a revenger, relieves the pressures on Hamlet's tormented state of mind in his struggles with intentionality. Time as McAlindon explained it, is on the other hand more inviting, more a matter of timing, of time to be seized, and Hamlet is more ready to be involved in time than Arjuna, 'The readiness is all'. (V.ii.213–8) However, Bloom pointed out that Hamlet, when accepting his duel with Laertes, is in a defiant mood, declaring 'We defy augury!', but that his defiance is not easy to characterize. Was Hamlet convinced of winning against the odds? Was he consciously embracing his destiny of being doomed to die, becoming the accomplice of fate by asserting his freedom? Does he leave it to chance? Both Arjuna and Hamlet suffer from the burden of doom in their destiny, from their 'cursed spite'. But while Arjuna has to comply with his fate, Hamlet has to seize his destiny as his opportunity. Instead of appropriating Claudius' transparent necessity of the natural order or, for that matter, a Greek, obscure necessity of fate, Hamlet seems to appropriate the obscure chaos of human freedom. Hamlet's incidental reference to the Christian idea of providence comes across as one among many religious and secular ideas clashing, and as far less important than the secularized idea of fortune. Rees noticed the idea that all human passions weaken as new impressions supervene because of the effect of time and circumstance upon feelings and intent. Circumstances changing (time and fortune), human purposes are infirm; the Player-King proclaimed, 'Purpose is but the slave to memory' (III.ii.198). Hamlet is troubled by memory, which keeps consciousness in time, as McAlindon explained. Arjuna has to keep consciousness out of time.

Unlike fate, *fortune* is more related to the accidental ups and downs within life (short-term) than to a coherent 'spinning' of the thread of one's life as a whole towards a final destiny, taking shape gradually (long-term). In the

Greek case, while fate (*moira*) determines one's course of life as a whole, fortune (*tychē*, chance) tends to be responsible for singular events of varying importance. The connotations of the word were originally more positive, but by Hellenistic times, it regularly had the pejorative meaning of blind, impersonal, arbitrary chance. Fortune plays a minor role in Aeschylus' and Sophocles' tragedies. In the Indian epic, fortune (the goddess Śrī) plays a crucial (but invisible) role comparable to fate – fortune relates to the fickle rise and fall of kings.

In Shakespearean tragedy, fortune is everywhere while fate has virtually disappeared. That is to say, the workings of nature have taken over from the workings of fate. Despite serious and also sceptical references to providence in *Hamlet*, the explicit focus of the play seems to be on fortune, and how to respond to it with reason, dignity and *virtù*. *Virtù*, Martines explained, is talented willpower in great political affairs, the stuff of leadership and success. It may belong to individuals as to collectivities. *Fortuna* is the sum of forces lying beyond *virtù* – forces hostile, neutral or helpful, but always changing. In its changes, *fortuna* may include or, at any moment, exclude the antisocial vices, but *virtù* can never really include the beast in man. The main antitheses are reason–passions, *virtù–fortuna*, man–beast, elites–multitudes, rich–poor, State–ambition (individual egotism), civil society–anarchic nature, law–violence, order–disorder.

There are no references in *Hamlet* to Hamlet and his father as belonging to a doomed royal lineage, as is the case with the Tantalid and Labdacid families in Greek tragedy and the Kuru family in the Indian epic. The *misfortunes* of the Tantalids, Labdacids and Kurus seem to come from the long-term workings of *fate*'s necessity, instead of coming from the short-term workings of fortune's contingency.

The inherited taint of familial guilt in Aeschylus' *Oresteia* is not avenged and thus expiated in later generations, it gets worse. Agamemnon's crime is weightier still than his father's crime. This is an ascending rather than a descending sequence, Sewell-Rutter observes.[122] The son inherits not just guilt, but a propensity to incur fresh guilt himself. Crime begets crime. Eteocles is willingly fratricidal. The internecine fratricide is both what the two brothers fully intend to do and also the fulfilment of Oedipus' curse. Aeschylus and Euripides present the battle between Eteocles and Polyneices as arising, in part, from Oedipus' curse on them beforehand, and thus as the outcome of familial disaster informed by supernatural causal determinants. Sophocles, however, reduces the weight of supernatural causation by removing the family curse (which invokes divine punishment) as a preliminary cause in the catastrophic history of the royal house, thus shifting the focus away from divine interference, on human affairs. Supernatural causation (curses, the Erinyes, inherited guilt) and familial dysfunction are both present, but they are not neatly connected. Sophocles does not share the Aeschylean preoccupation with doubly (divinely and humanly) motivated action, Sewell-Rutter argues.[123] In *Oedipus Tyrannus*, the fickle rise and fall of a king and of human greatness in general is a matter of arrogance (*hubris*), the Chorus suggests piously, as Winnington-Ingram observed.[124] The moralizing Chorus is afraid that Oedipus may abuse his royal power and suffer disaster. If Oedipus becomes arrogant, then he must fall and suffer at the hands of the gods or divine order is at an end, they argue in an Aeschylean way. But disaster comes upon him through things done before ever he became king, and things not done out of arrogance, not even 'intellectual pride'. The Chorus may be offering a pious explanation of Oedipus' imminent downfall, but their explanation turns out to be the wrong explanation in Sophocles' plot pattern, Winnington-Ingram argued. Oedipus' downfall was due to simple ignorance.

In the Indian epic, during each generation, the Kuru family, this time headed by a blind (!) king, seems doomed to fail in securing a legitimate succession to the throne. The wife of the five Pāndavas, Draupadī, plays a central role in the ups and downs of fortune. She is really Śrī, the goddess of prosperity who is incarnate in Draupadī, Hiltebeitel explained. The rhythm of time is her only regulative principle. Her fickleness coincides with a 'pessimistic' view of time. If Prosperity embraces a king, his kingdom will thrive; if she leaves the king for some other king, the decline of the kingdom will be his 'portion' of fortune. Śrī is the source of the king's sovereignty, provided the king is 'omni-virtuous' (energetic, not breaking or misusing vows, etc.). The ultimate or temporary downfall of kings such as Yudhisthira is thus dependent upon the presence of a set of qualities, non-moral and moral alike. Draupadī is Yudhisthira's last stake in the dice game, and he loses her. It is not infrequent for *karma* to be called upon to explain *misfortune* or a reverse of circumstances. Mārkandeya consoles the grieving Yudhisthira along these lines at a particularly low point during the Pāndavas' exile, the exile being the fruit of a lost game of dice, a true reversal of fortunes. In those cases, reference to the law of *karma* is consolating because it implies reference to a universal moral order beyond current human control, Hill argued. If in the hands of Śiva dicing reflects the increase of *adharma* (lack of order and justice), the loss of 'prosperity', and an intoxicated aloofness to matters of gain and loss, there is a clear contrast with Krishna, who leaves nothing to chance, as Hiltebeitel observed. Biardeau pointed out that Śakuni and Duryodhana are incarnations of Dvāpara and Kali, personifications of cosmic world epochs (*yugas*), which themselves carry the names of the throws of the Indian dice. The ups and downs of fortune are thus considered a matter of fate.

2 The gods

What is the role of the divine, of the gods, of God? And what does religion contribute in terms of problems or solutions?

In one respect, Mikalson explained, there was a huge difference between Greek popular religion and the literary religion in tragedy. In popular religion, 'the gods' were held responsible for everything good and desirable – but not for misfortune. For misfortune, they blamed fortune (*tychē*), a *daimon*, or fate. In tragedy, 'the gods' too are blamed for evil, albeit rarely specific gods worshipped in an Athenian cult. In tragedy, the gods are more hostile and less forgiving than those in popular religion. In both life and tragedy, the gods punish violators of divine laws, but they care more about their own honour than about human destinies. No tragedian suggests any *divine* contributions to early moral or legal life. Sophocles' 'Ode to Man' in the *Antigone* (332–75) lists all forms of cultural progress as *human* achievements. Aeschylus makes Zeus *the* protector of justice, but he does so for the sake of justice, not for the benefit of Zeus. When in Sophoclean tragedy the gods play a role, it is against the background of a cosmic order that is divine, just and regulated, but remote and obscure. The eternal laws of the cosmic order are the sacred laws of nature that must be upheld. Any infringement is taboo. The gods are participating in this cosmic order and sustaining it, not creating it. The ethical consciousness of moral values and their vulnerability turns humans into humane beings, but it does not turn the anthropomorphic gods into compassionate beings. Parker noticed in tragedies 'a mitigation or limitation of suffering or a compensation for it'. The gods are not blamed outright for being cruel and negligent. 'But too much remains unexplained and unknowable for strong positive claims about divine justice, still less about divine benevolence, to be possible'.[125] In Sophocles' *Ajax* (89–120), Padel noted, Athena points out to Odysseus the *divine strength* gods are capable of in making great men such as Ajax mad. Odysseus answers that *he* is impressed, not with the divine strength demonstrated, but with the *human weakness* of all human beings, himself included.

In Shakespeare's *Macbeth*, the Weird Sisters detect an inversion of the natural order. These witches, like the Delphic oracle in Sophocles' *Oedipus Tyrannus*, merely predict, whereas human beings create the fulfilment of their predictions, Ewans suggested. In *Hamlet*, the appearance of the ghost, like that of the witches in *Macbeth*, is a divine response from 'Heaven' to human disruption of the natural order of the realm ('Something is rotten in the state of Denmark'). No other divine intervention is alluded to. Supernatural power (witches, ghosts, providence) operates in complete consistency with the dynamics of nature, as McAlindon observed. But this is not to say that the

Christian God has withdrawn from the minds of the main characters. In fact, the threat of divine punishment is much more real than the hope of divine reward or forgiveness. The immoral actions of murder, incest and revenge weigh heavily, religiously speaking. The sacredness of blood revenge is in doubt, or even outright sinful. Moreover, there is the problem of what to believe, as Levin pointed out, and this is a dangerous problem in a period of religious conflict between Roman Catholics and Protestants. Doubt has penetrated the pious minds of believers whose convictions are no longer self-evident. As to the solution, Christianity has to compete with the more or less secular option of Stoicism. Hamlet is facing the dilemma whether or not to embrace a Stoic attitude of indifference to his revenge. Eventually, Hamlet develops a sense of providential involvement in events that alters his attitude to time and offers him a real solution on the level of action – the readiness to work in conjunction with time. Hamlet and Laertes may forgive each other at the very end, but both depend no less on God's forgiveness of their killings, and there is no indication that God will actually forgive them.

Like the Greek gods, Krishna is not a compassionate god in the *Gītā*. He explicitly dismisses Arjuna's grief as a faintheartedness and is not mourning with the mourners, as mortals such as Yudhisthira do with the Kaurava women, and the Chorus with Oedipus. Like the Greek gods, Krishna intervenes for the sake of the maintenance or restoration of cosmic order. Even if men do not necessarily determine the outcome of battles, their common battlefield is the 'field of justice'. The battlefield of Kuru, *kurukshetra*, is called the battlefield of *dharma*, *dharmakshetra*, and Lord Krishna determines its outcome. The Hindu battle takes place against the background not only of time's order and renewal, but also of the cosmic struggle between gods and demons. While in Greek tragedy, human relations are the battlefield for gods to fight other gods, in the Hindu epics, human relations are the battlefield for gods to fight demons.

Arjuna's problems with intentionality and action, and Krishna's solution to them, operate in different spaces – the solution is not the opposite or contrary of the problem. Arjuna is not asked to change his intentions, shifting from one intention to another, but, in the *yoga* sections, to give up on the idea of intentionality altogether when it comes to the fruits of his action, or, in the *bhakti* sections, to set his mind on Krishna as a transcendental point of reference beyond the field of action. The closest one gets to that in *Hamlet* is Hamlet's speculations on Yorick's skull, following Kerrigan's interpretation. Equipped with a peaceful and ready mind, he will avenge his father, but need not plan a Senecan atrocity because the task of total revenge in the form of death after death is something he can leave to Kerrigan's 'plotting God of Christianity', whose curse will handle the really rough stuff. Likewise, Lord Krishna, appearing as time devouring the universe in the *Gītā*, will handle the really rough stuff. Arjuna, like Hamlet, has to cultivate the readiness to work in conjunction with time, to embrace the initially chaotic (devouring), but ultimately orderly (just) fate provided by a providential God, unlike Sophocles' Oedipus, who has to embrace the blind(ing) fate of a dark and only remotely just cosmos.

Krishna's trickery in the epic may appear to join the forces of injustice and chaos (*adharma*), but Krishna's tricky interventions, Hiltebeitel explained, leave nothing to chance. In fact, Krishna combines the two roles that Segal described for Zeus and Apollo in *Oedipus Tyrannus*, with Apollo as the immediate agent or actor and Zeus as the remote, pure, eternal and absolute power beyond that. Krishna counterbalances the cosmic imbalance brought about by Shiva's dice games. Together, Shiva representing the cosmic movement and dynamics of nature to the point of imbalance, chance and chaos, and Krishna representing balance, necessity and restoration of the cosmic order, are strikingly similar to McAlindon's description of the Renaissance concept of nature as governed by antipathies and sympathies, the forces of chaos being intrinsic to the natural order. In *Hamlet*, Old Hamlet's and Claudius' references to a personal God who punishes sinners compete with references to a secular concept of impersonal nature.

3 Human transgression of vertical and horizontal boundaries

The human transgression of boundaries takes different forms in different traditions, along a variety of *vertical and horizontal axes of relationship*, between the human and the divine, between humans among each other, and between order and chaos.

Prudence is called for. It would be too simplistic to state that Greek tragedy is focused on, say, 'arrogant pride' (*hubris*) and on the vertical axis between humans and the gods, whereas Shakespearean tragedy is focused on ambition and the horizontal axis between higher social status and lower social status. For a start, Greek tragedy has shifted theologically from a focus on the vertical axis (Homer's *Iliad* and Aeschylus) to a focus on the horizontal axis (Sophocles and Euripides). In Sophocles, Winnington-Ingram noticed, *hubris* is not the cause of Oedipus' downfall, but what the pious Chorus speculates to be its cause – the gods punishing Oedipus for his presumed misuse of power. Their Aeschylean theology looks for explanations along the vertical axis of humans provoking divine wrath. But Sophocles' Oedipus transgresses the limits of his human knowledge of the divine until this ignorance backlashes. Along the vertical axis between the human and the divine, a gap between them opens up. Along the horizontal axis of human relationship, the breakthrough of knowledge reveals social chaos instead of social order, and it brings about status reversal and status loss. Sophocles' *Antigone* too, if we go by Steiner's Hegel interpretation of the play, operates along both the vertical and the horizontal axes. And so does Homer's *Iliad*. Redfield stressed its vertical axis, while Cairns stressed the horizontal axis. The hero, if he is to live up to the principle of heroic balance, has to insist on his own competitive greatness while preserving a proper modesty before the far-greater gods, as Redfield contended, or before the community and its co-operative moral standards (cf. Nestor!), as Cairns would argue. Loss of this balance – as by Patroclus and Hector incapable of retreat – is the characteristic heroic error.

The Greek word for 'ambition', *philo-timia* ('love of honour'), has positive and negative connotations. It should not be confused with *hubris* in the sense of 'overweening ambition' and 'deliberate infliction of shame and dishonour'. The Shakespearean word 'ambition' in *Hamlet* II.ii.251–61 has negative connotations, causing bad dreams and claustrophobic depression, being related to early modern notions of inexhaustible desire and passion, of status instability and social chaos. Like its counterpart 'revenge', ambition lacks the capacity to balance things. Ambition is on the side of individual egotism, fortune, violence and disorder, as opposed to the state, *virtù*, law and order. Such a Shakespearean notion of ambition represents a transgression of boundaries that operates mainly on the horizontal axis of human relationships. Even if it triggers divine punishment (the vertical axis), Hamlet's surrender of his ambition into the hands of divine providence meets with Horatio's neo-Stoic scepticism (the horizontal axis). McAlindon pointed to the Renaissance conception of human nature, and to the way it differs from the Christian conception, when he argued that the issue is not about a vertical battle between angelic and bestial dimensions of human nature, but about the horizontal overflowing of boundaries. Hamlet no longer displays a fine balance of forces within these boundaries.

The *Mahābhārata* notion of ambition too, is on the side of (Duryodhana's) individual egotism – lack of self-restraint, violence and *rajas guna* at the expense of the community at large. But ambition is not a core issue in this epic, just one of many ways of violating the cosmic order. Moreover, the vertical axis between humans and the gods is very different in the Hindu epic from the one in Greek tragedy. This is because its epic heroes, despite their mortality, are nonetheless (partial) incarnations of gods and demons who fight each other. On the vertical axis, there is no obscuring gap between humans and gods, but a fluid transformation. The human battle between epic heroes on the social level (the horizontal axis) embodies the supernatural battle between gods and demons on the cosmic level (the vertical axis). Humans do not oppose gods, gods oppose demons. The human transgression of boundaries, therefore, is always a violation of both the social and the cosmic order, or rather, of one and the same socio-cosmic order (*dharma*). In this case, the distinction between a vertical axis and a horizontal axis may meet with difficulties.

All these texts share the religious belief that human and divine action takes place against the background of a universal order whose rules, boundaries and workings cannot be ignored without someone suffering fatal consequences. Abidance by these painful boundaries becomes the crucial issue. Dwelling at these borders is as much a source of existential pain as is their fatal crossing. Facing the borders, but recognizing the human powerlessness to bring about a bridging of gaps generates as much suffering as does the actual transgressing of borders. This is why Heering carefully concluded that the tragic occurs on the border between human existence and its (human and divine) environment, where engaged human beings face their limits and experience the discrepancy between human existence and the surrounding world.

9

Concluding observations regarding views of the human condition

1 Introduction

Our story draws to a close. It took several journeys to cross from one culture to the next and back again. But to call it a 'story' seems ill-taken. The closed structure of a coherent story is lacking. Rather, our journeys have generated an accumulation of observations. In this respect, they seem to resemble Marcel Proust's *A la recherche du temps perdu,* whose overall story line is less important than the sequence of panels actually painted. In our case, each panel dealt with one cluster of aspects of tragedy, its related views of the human condition and its related definitions of tragedy. The panels are complementary to one another.

The major key question guiding this study was – in what respects can the *Mahābhārata* epic's and the *Bhagavadgītā*'s views of the human condition be called 'tragic' in the Greek and Shakespearean senses of the word? The underlying interest was primarily in tragic views of the human condition, not in tragedy as such. Since tragic views of the human condition are primarily embedded in the plots of tragedies, we had to turn to the phenomenon of tragedy to examine its main aspects. Seven clusters of aspects were identified. A detailed description of each of the seven sets of aspects was meant to provide enough of a hold to look for parallels in seemingly similar Indian texts and contexts, enabling seven frames for a cross-cultural comparison of specific anthropological issues. Which anthropological issues have been raised and compared? And what has been concluded with regard to Western and Indian views of the human condition and human nature?

2 Narrative aspects

What, then, is the impact of these narrative aspects of tragedy on the views of human nature that emerge from such tragic narratives?

First of all, Greek, English and Indian epic and tragic narratives alike bring to the fore the vulnerable side of human nature. Death is just one force that reduces human greatness to nothing. Humans easily become victims of the human condition, that is to say, of being entangled in a world of superhuman forces, such as time and the gods. They easily lose what is precious to them despite their best intentions. If this can happen to great men such as Oedipus, it can happen to anyone, as Easterling paraphrased the chorus' response. The unrelenting search of human mortals for knowledge and justice may be highly virtuous, but beyond invisible boundaries, this search is doomed to become terribly counterproductive. Boundaries are like the nerves of the nervous system – not respecting them disrupts the irritated natural order. A moral order is inherent in (human) nature, but it is disrupted. Being human implies acting within limits that are set by an unknown sense of human proportions. Humans have great expectations of life and compelling expectations of their duty in life, but they are rarely capable of coping with either bringing about disappointment or suffering it. In the face of harsh truth and death, human beings may be able to stick to their sense of honour and dignity, but in the face of losing their honour, people turn dangerously vindictive or mad.

Secondly, these Greek, English and Indian narratives intensify the dark side of human nature that is either released after the breakdown of social and cosmic order, or is itself the source of evil, leading to illicit transgression and contaminating the established order. The interaction between the human condition and man's response to it is considered to have its own dynamic, to follow its own time mechanism of increasing necessity and impending destruction.

Thirdly, the tragic focus of the narratives severely limits the possibility that other aspects of the human condition or other sides of human nature are taken seriously. Tragic narratives emphasize that under extreme circumstances, such as (the threat of) war, the human condition is not a humane condition. More often than not, the human condition is in a critical state, conflicts are always extreme and solutions are never adequate or final. Humans suffer much more (deeply) than they enjoy the pleasures of life. Day-to-day conditions are considered too superficial to reveal what the human condition and human nature are all about. Happiness and harmony are the exception, suffering and conflict are the rule in life. The focus of tragic narratives on extremity and transgression imposes severe restrictions on viewing reconciliation, equilibrium and the joys of everyday life as equally telling and valid aspects. In this respect, the Hindu arrangement of plot patterns and human destinies is very different from Western tragedy. The Indian epic is no different from the Greek and English stories, except that it adds an alternative perspective that views human nature as, in essence and ultimately, belonging to a cosmic realm entirely separate from these tragic conditions. The Indian epic has one border whose crossing changes the entire picture – the heavenly Ganges, the river of purification. Shifting to this cosmic level means leaving the mortal world of tragedy and suffering behind without transforming it. The plot's second ending frames the plot's first ending. Likewise, Arjuna's tragic recognition of his final destiny is juxtaposed to Krishna's vision of his ultimate destiny – to play his role in the renewal of the universe through its destruction without attaching to it. Again, Arjuna's final destiny and his ultimate destiny are juxtaposed, not opposed. This Hindu arrangement of plot patterns and human destinies is very different from Western tragedy.

3 Artistic–communicative aspects

Three formal aspects in particular have been the focus of this chapter on tragedy's artistic–communicative aspects – the literary genre, the audience response and the dialogues. What, then, is the impact of these artistic–communicative aspects of tragedy on the views of human nature that emerge from such tragic narratives?

First, human nature takes great pleasure in attending and judging theatre plays. In doing so, humans should not be surprised to find themselves in the company of the Greek and Hindu gods – in striking contrast to the Christian God of London's Puritans. Humans rejoice in playfully representing their reality on stage, and they are not the only ones. This pleasure includes watching evil and suffering. People feel both attraction and repulsion while watching human suffering and disaster. They leave their homes to watch characters break down, broken characters that on stage at least, States suggested, coincide with their doomed destinies.

Secondly, people are moved by the imitation of what fellow human beings are like. They can identify with their suffering in a generalized way, either because they recognize the actions and destinies of other human beings as similar (Aristotle) or because they see their emotions as similar (Sanskrit aestheticians) to their own. The ideal human judge in Greek tragedy is 'one who has much experience of suffering' (*talapeiros*), Lonsdale noted. The sharing of tears and suffering leads to universal empathy or sympathy (Aristotle's *to philantroopon* and Abhinavagupta's *sādhāranīkarana*) and bonding, enlarging a sense of common humanity that includes enemies. What human beings seem to learn from watching tragedies is to face and recognize the significance of human suffering, not how to cope with it – beyond ritually lamenting it. That is one reason why Krishna's instruction to Arjuna takes away from their dialogue all sense of tragedy.

Thirdly, human beings desperately need rituals as a coping strategy. Funerary rites, in particular, are needed at the end of a tragic outcome if the participants, characters and audiences alike, are to recover from the worst mental effects of death and loss. The need to formalize recovery is almost always visible in a ritual closure of tragedy, but even more sharply felt in the Sanskrit generic convention that a tragic mood effect is not allowed to last until the very end of a play or narrative. A tragic view of human nature is not allowed to emerge as the final truth about human beings in the Sanskrit epics. The narrative constraints of the genre prevent this from taking centre stage.

Fourthly, if people engage in dialogue, they are expected to be able to listen, to be open-minded and to benefit from the experience of being persuaded to change their minds. Humans are made for relationships, for accepting the gift of contact. But more often than not, human beings tend to engage in failing dialogues that mirror and reinforce their lonesomeness and social isolation. Inner dialogues are more like battles with the enemy than like making friends with oneself, more like the warrior and his charioteer fighting than like the two Upanishadic birds sitting on the same tree, one eating, one watching. Whereas epic literature depicts heroes who have battle comrades as friends, tragic literature depicts heroes as lonesome. Whereas epic heroes are engaged in riddle-solving dialogues, tragic heroes are completely bound up in failing dialogues. In the *Gītā*, Krishna and Arjuna have what one would nowadays call a 'constructive dialogue', which leaves no questions unanswered and has nothing tragic about it. In the epic, however, the uncomfortable dialogue between Draupadī and Yudhisthira leaves crucial questions pertaining to justice unanswered and their dialogue may be considered tragic because it hurts and finds no breakthrough. But even this dialogue does not end in social isolation; it just restates the riddle instead of solving it.

Fifthly, there is no sense of tragedy without the conscious engagement of human witnesses (characters and audiences alike) recognizing the tensions involved and suffering from that recognition. Humans are capable of viewing the human condition as tragic, but they do not automatically do so in cases that will be considered 'tragic' by an audience that expects a tragic constellation, but 'comic' by an audience that is prepared for a comic constellation. Aristotle was right in linking the form (genre) to the audience response (expectations), and the audience response to the contents of tragedy. Tragedy evokes different expectations from comedy, and these expectations are intimately connected to the norms of that society and to the extent to which human beings can be expected to live up to these norms. Tragedy works precisely because people bring their set of normative expectations and judge the actions of their fellow human beings accordingly. On the part of Greek and Elizabethan audiences, even an ironic attitude would have presupposed the existence of a moral order inherent in human nature as part of nature in general.

4 Socio-political aspects

What do these cross-cultural comparisons tell us about the views of human nature emerging from the socio-political contexts underlying the texts?

First of all, human beings belong to groups, in particular to their kinship group, to their gender, to their social class, and to their friends and allies, whether they like it or not. Individuals belong to communities, not to themselves. The Hegelian opposition between the 'individual' and the 'community' is not universally recognized, in contrast to the opposition between one's own community and other communities. People do not take their belonging and group boundaries for granted, but are prepared to challenge them.

Secondly, a distinction between the domestic sphere of the family household and the public sphere of the state is taken for granted, but its allocation to women and men respectively is not, because of the implications for the power struggle between the sexes. The family household is understood as patriarchal by nature. Women, children and slaves are seen as dependent by nature. The woman should stay at home, but the man should 'come home' (*nostos*, homecoming) to restore male order. Men are expected to be in control of both the domestic and the public sphere simultaneously. If they are not, male authority and the moral stability of both spheres are in danger. The public sphere is considered more powerful than the domestic sphere because public actions have a wider impact and display more independence. The public sphere is felt to be rooted in the private sphere, more than the other way around, but it appears to be based on male power and the cosmic order.

Thirdly, social conflicts are inherent to human nature, yet highly problematic. Human beings are, by nature, social and political animals, as Aristotle argued. Their need to cooperate is not without the constant threat of conflicts. The natural capacity of humans to solve conflicts is limited by lack of power, choice, knowledge, change, improvement, balance, justice or peace, and their semi-divine capacity to solve extreme conflicts is extremely limited.

Fourthly, human beings create institutions such as the family household, the state, and religion, which are credited for organizing their social lives. These institutions solve social conflicts by legitimizing certain sets of rules and role models. Tragedy has it that more often than not, these institutions themselves lose their legitimacy and become sources of social conflict. Greek epic heroes are socially rooted in their families. Greek tragic heroes, however, witness their homes uprooted. Homecoming is no longer the solution to their social problems. The family itself needs to be relocated within the frame of the city state and its institutions, Goldhill explained. Shakespearean tragic heroes are no longer psychologically rooted in their families. Both the family and the state are represented as corrupt institutions. Indian epic heroes are socially rooted in their families and their participation in society is clan-based. Even if political power is no longer based on kinship ties, it is still legitimated by these family ties. In this respect, there is no difference with Greek and Shakespearean tragedy – Yudhisthira and Duryodhana depend no less on royal blood lines than Creon and Claudius. In Greek tragedy, a power shift from the family to the state is presented in terms of a simultaneous power shift from the woman to the man. This gender conflict plays no role in the Indian case. Arjuna's dilemma is similar to Hector's dilemma – Hector has to give up his male protection of the family he really cares for in favour of his male role as chief warrior.

5 Literary–cultural aspects

What does the epic and tragic dealing with narrative sources and their cultural values in connection with the transition from the mythic and epic genres to the tragic genre reveal about views of human nature?

First, human nature can be described in terms of a limited number of core values, of fundamental goals or purposes of human life. In Greek tragedy and the Hindu epic, man is meant, by nature, to stay within the limits of the cosmic order, to respect divine and social taboos, to honour the gods and men according to their status. Men are born in order to pursue the goals and fulfil the purposes that suit the nature of the group(s) to which they belong. A prince is born to become king and is meant to rule. A servant is destined to serve. This professional destiny is more explicit in the Hindu epic than it is in Greek tragedy, and in Shakespearean tragedy, it is abandoned. But in the Hindu epic, the core values and purposes of each group are only valid on the this-worldly level. In the end, *moksha* is the ultimate goal. Why are human beings on earth? In order to ultimately rid themselves of the bonds that keep them linked to their earthly and heavenly existence so that they will never ever again return to this earth or to heaven, but dissolve into the oneness of the undifferentiated universe. On this other-worldly level, tragic conflict as a clash of cultural values does not exist and it does not ultimately define human nature.

Secondly, human beings are embedded in cultural value systems whose internal arrangement of values is neither consistent nor fixed, whose applicability is debatable, and whose implications can become problematic to such an extent that solutions cannot undo the problems without a price being paid in the form of human suffering. Human beings appropriate the value system of their own culture by listening to exemplary stories, and they test the value system by listening to disturbing stories about its contradictory implications (e.g., justice implying pursuit of revenge implying commitment of a crime implying injustice), but also by reflecting upon, debating and questioning the applicability and validity of the core values involved. Core values or basic goals such as 'justice' (*dikē*, *dharma*) are more or less debatable; their applicability and even the range of their validity are not self-evident.

Thirdly, the values and goals are considered both inherent to human nature and virtues, that is to say, a human potential that must be cultivated in order to become fully human, but simultaneously a human potential that cannot be realized by sheer mortals.

Fourthly, both the ancient Greek and the ancient Indian emergence of a new view of man are illustrative of a shift in focus within several cultures worldwide during the Axial Age, a period of cultural revolution consisting of the emergence, conceptualization and institutionalization of a basic tension between the mundane world and the transcendent world. By independently propagating an idealist vision of a transcendent world underlying and ruling the mundane world from a qualitative distance, the intellectual elite took a new attitude of standing back and looking beyond, of critical, reflective questioning of the actual and apparent. From the Axial Age onwards, actions and speeches were motivated by reflective reasoning about the proper goals of life, as Gill would put it. The proper goals of human life were now ideas and ideals that had to be debated instead of being taken for granted as that which is expected.

Fifthly, there is a sense of unease about the (increased) distance between man and his outer world. Man cannot trust his senses in a world of appearances. Man cannot trust the gods in a world of hidden order and alienating distance between men and the gods. Divine spoken language can be obscure. Human spoken language is unreliable when it comes to speaking the truth, and dangerous when it comes to rhetorically persuasive power. In tragedy, man is portrayed as being forced to make agonizing choices in an unstable universe of ambiguous values. In Greek tragedy, this unstable universe is identified as the cosmic world of interaction between fate, the gods and humans. In Shakespearean tragedy, this unstable universe is identified as the social world of power struggles, status relations, ambition, greed and hypocrisy. In the Hindu epic, this unstable universe is identified as the moral decline of a degenerating World Age. In Greece and India, the Axial Age revolution leads to a tragic view of man, not of the divine, but in India, this tragic view of man is combined with a separate transcendent view of man. In fact, in many ways, the Hindu distance between man and his world is greater than the Western distance between man and his world because the Indian gap between this-worldly immanence and other-worldly transcendence is structurally more radical than in Western world views and views of human nature.

Sixthly, there is a sense of unease about the (increased) distance between man and his social world. Man cannot take his social values for granted in a world full of conflicting group loyalties. Individualization implies personal responsibility, but also social isolation and social death. The Hindu distance between man and his social world (individualization) consists of a more radical separation and juxtaposition of one's social responsibility as a caste member and one's individual freedom as a spiritual being. Arjuna as a spiritual being is taught not to identify with Arjuna as a social being. Kings are valued as more representative of 'man in general' than their subjects because it is inherent to their royal nature to be representative of their communities and because their action has more impact than that of their subjects. A general notion of human nature hardly exists on the social level of particular group distinctions, but it exists on the religious level as the distinction between humans and the gods, between mortals and immortals. Human beings collectively constitute one social category, that of 'mortals', as opposed to the gods. This social identity creates a sense of belonging to 'man', of sharing the same vulnerability, but also the same ambivalence about being the 'Oedipal outcome of the Sphinx's riddle'.

Seventhly, there is a sense of unease about the (increased) distance between man and his inner world. Man feels extremely disturbed when being forced to perform his social duty in a state of mind and heart that inhibits him from identifying fully and automatically with his duty as his destiny. One's duty becomes one's role, different from one's soul. The shift from complying with one's duty to taking a role implies a detached individual who faces freedom of choice and risks madness. The gap between 'the realm of the other-worldly' and 'the realm of the this-worldly' is felt as a tension within the person, as a longing for psychic, moral and spiritual fulfilment. The interiority of an individual person is now expected to grow in knowledge and virtue, to convert, to transform, to become self-aware or enlightened. The exact sense of interiority differs in each cultural case. In the Greek case, it consists of a sharpened awareness of personal responsibility for social affairs backlashing under the influence of fate. In the Shakespearean case, Pye observed the often fearful recognition that interiority can give the subject leverage against his world. The sense of personal detachment from the social world is expressed in the view of man as a player of roles (or performer of duties), both in the Shakespearean and in the Indian case. In the Indian case, interiority consists of the awareness of an eternal self cut-off from *karma*-bound individual agency and its performance of social duties.

6 Martial aspects

What does the epic and tragic dealing with martial values reveal about views of human nature?

First, human beings have a need for recognition. Public recognition is related to honour and status, lack of public recognition is related to shame and negligibility. In traditional cultures, human dignity is defined in terms of honour, that is to say, in terms of public social identity and representativeness. Human beings are representatives of their social functions. Their roles imply duties and privileges. People identify with role models. Aristocrats are more worthy of respect than commoners and are taken more seriously. In Shakespearean tragedy, aristocrats take themselves more seriously. In the Indian epic, there is no common human nature or shared universal ethics beyond one's own class (of aristocrats, in this case).

Secondly, both epic and tragic literature use martial culture as a foil and martial values as human ideals to be cultivated and tested. Nobility is acquired by birth in Greece, England and India alike. The acquisition of wealth is its privilege and generosity, its corresponding duty. Loyalty is put to the test in many different contexts, but Achilles, Hector, Neoptolemus, Antigone, Aeschylus' Agamemnon, Clytemnestra, Hamlet, Gertrude, Brutus, Arjuna and Yudhisthira all face conflicts of loyalty, albeit not always on the battlefield. Another recurrent martial value is the duty to fight, a value to be distinguished from the equally recurrent right to rule. Warriorship and kingship are intertwined, but their distinction remains a source of status conflicts in both Western and Indian literature. The difference between martial culture and courtly culture is sometimes represented as a clash of civilizations in Shakespearean plays as well as the Indian epics, between the brute force and unlimited revenge of the traditional order and the self-restraint of the modern order. Martial values such as manliness, courage and the fear of being considered a coward are found consistently in Western and Indian epic and tragic literature, from Krishna blaming Arjuna to Claudius blaming Hamlet. The *Iliad*, the *Mahābhārata* and *Hamlet*, all contain the idea that a man's skilled use of speech equals a man's skilled use of weapons. The duty to fight is subjected to rules if it is to be honourable. Achilles facing Hector, Odysseus facing Philoctetes, Claudius facing Old Hamlet, Laertes facing Prince Hamlet, Duryodhana facing Draupadī and Krishna facing the Kauravas shamelessly lack the respect they ought to pay to their opponents or lack the courage to fight them on equal terms. The martial code of honour is put to the test. This exploration includes the tension between the competitive and the co-operative dimensions of honour and the tension between the outer aspects of honour (results, status) and the inner aspects of honour (virtues, worthiness). Hamlet suffers mentally from his lack of identification with his martial role of bloody revenger, whereas Arjuna is taught complete detachment from identification with his martial role as a means of fighting without mental suffering.

Thirdly, warrior heroism has been cultivated as a human ideal worldwide in cultures that are engaged in waging wars. But the cultivation of warrior heroism as a human ideal has undergone substantial historical changes within each respective culture. In small-scale traditional societies, such as Homer's Greek society, to be fully human and to be a full member of society means to fight as a warrior on behalf of one's community. Military service is both a duty and a privilege. This noble ideal of warrior heroism is lost in vast empires and imperial monarchies where warfare becomes the specialism of a professionally trained elite. The Indian culture, however, constitutes an exception to the rule. It stuck to a social ideology that differentiates between four social classes, assigning the military function to one specialized class only – the ruling class of nobles. This Indian concept of four exclusive classes already occurs in *Rigveda* X (roughly 1200–900 BCE), and the emergence of vast Indian monarchies and empires (400–200 BCE) did not change this social ideology. Everywhere, the contents and appreciation of warrior heroism as a human ideal were subject to historical periods of militarization, demilitarization and modernization of warfare. In ancient and classical Greece, the increasingly militarized society modernized (democratized) its martial culture. Greek epic literature tested its limits and tragic literature questioned its values. In early modern England, the remilitarized aristocracy revitalized its martial culture and the royal court modernized it. Shakespeare's tragic literature questioned its values. In India, the royal courts modernized the Indian martial culture by centralizing and restraining the power of regional chiefs. But martial culture remained an exclusively aristocratic and royal (*kshatriya*) affair. It was not democratized. Its martial values were questioned, however, for spreading violence and cruelty. The ideal of warrior heroism was internalized yogically and presented as the capacity of a warrior hero to fight single-mindedly without being attached to outer results, such as victory and defeat. It was also internalized devotionally and presented as the capacity of a warrior hero to think of his God only without dedicating his thoughts, actions and results to anybody else.

Fourthly, in tragedy, human ideals are sources of disappointment and evil. Manliness turns out to be a source of (self-)destruction. A balance between competition and cooperation is lacking. The limits of loyalty become apparent. Friends are treated like enemies. Honour appears a less noble affair than it should be. Hamlet embodies the bitterness evoked by the rotten state of the court and its hypocrisy. He also embodies the disillusioned adolescent whose idealistic view of man has been destroyed by harsh reality. As Margolies put it, there is, in *Hamlet,* a feeling of loss. Man gained human dignity by being placed directly below the angels in the Great Chain of Being, 'in apprehension how like a god', as Hamlet said, but that vision must be abandoned. 'To be fully human', once a noble ideal, has become honoured dust, Yorick's skull. Above all, in tragic literature and in epic literature with tragic tendencies, the unrestrained exercise of violence and revenge is questioned. Even restrained violence and wars are often condemned as pure evil, especially in some sections of the *Mahābhārata* epic, but not in the *Bhagavadgītā*. The victim's perspective (focusing on human suffering and loss) takes over from the victor's perspective (focusing on power and gain). Victims and enemies are no less fellow human beings to identify and sympathize with than victors and battle comrades. The Indian epics and the Greek and Shakespearean tragedies testify to a humanization of the concept of warrior heroism and an ethical cultivation of martial self-restraint. Only in the Indian case, these humanizing and ethicizing tendencies, which are typically tragic tendencies, are combined with religious tendencies to yogically and devotionally spiritualize the concept of warrior heroism.

7 Psycho-ethical aspects

What are the moral and psychological weight of human intentions and actions, and how are human actions and intentions linked in these tragic and epic stories?

First, a shift in focus from human action and its consequences to human intention and reflection is common to the Greek, Shakespearean and Indian cases alike. In the Greek and Hindu cases, the starting point and focus is not on intention, but on action. Nonetheless, the Hindu case shares with the Shakespearean case a much higher degree of analysis of the nature of human intention and a much higher degree of man's potential for inner identification with his actions than the Greek case.

Secondly, wrongdoing, in Greek tragedy and in the older layers of the Hindu epic, is understood in terms of pollution and blindness or ignorance, in terms of blemished mistake and conscious mistake. In those cases, there is no separation either between thought and action – beliefs, confusion and emotion are expressed and observed in visible behaviour. This traditional starting point and focus has changed radically in the *Gītā*. In this respect, the *Gītā* and the Shakespearean case represent a substantially higher degree of separation between the inner world of thought, intentions and conscience and the outer world of action, behaviour and results ('fruits'). Despite the lower or higher degree of distinction between the inner and outer worlds, they all make use of physiological vocabularies to picture interiority.

Thirdly, in neither the Greek nor the Indian case is doing or wrongdoing understood in terms of the deliberate choice of some autonomous will imposing its rationality on desires or passions. The Greek and Indian notions of 'will', or rather, 'weakness of will', stress endurance, self-restraint and willingness to conform to the expectations of the community instead of stressing personal initiative and universal rationality. The Indian struggle is not between passion and reason, as in Shakespeare, but between attachment and spiritual consciousness. Strikingly similar in the Indian and Shakespearean cases, however, are their notions of desire as inexhaustible and, in that sense, infinite. In the Shakespearean case, human desire in the form of infinite ambition invents its own goals, whereas in the Hindu case, the goals of man are not invented, but found. In both cases, human desire has to be balanced by self-control and *yogic* or Stoic indifference. In the Greek linking of cause and effect, articulated by tragic madness, madness is based on desire as violence, while in the Indian linking of cause and effect, *karma* is based on desire as attachment. Greek madness is seen as mad behaviour in the outside world, modern madness as internal darkness, Padel observed.

Fourthly, in Greek and Indian epic and tragic literature, an agent or actor is a type of person and a general action is specified. In Shakespearean tragedy, however, an agent or actor is a particular individual and an individual action is generalized. In the Indian case, the individual's true identity is a de-individualized transcendent Self, while in the Shakespearean case, the individual's true identity is a de-socialized immanent self. In Krishna's dissociation of action and identity, the identification with one's social role is presented as an expression of a confused state of mind and of ignorance. In Hamlet's dissociation of action and identity, the lack of identification with one's social role is presented as an expression of a confused state of mind and of a lack of passion. Greek and Shakespearean views of man presuppose the near identity of responsibility and freedom, whereas Hindu views of man presuppose the virtual opposition (actually, the juxtaposition) between (social and immanent) responsibility and (individual and ultimately de-individualized, transcendent) freedom.

Fifthly, Greek and Shakespearean tragic truth emerges from pollution, moral brokenness and pain. This also applies to the tragic truth of the Indian epics, except that this *karmic* kind of truth is not considered decisive. Crucial in the Indian case is cosmic truth, and Hindu cosmic truth is never produced out of pollution or pain. In Arjuna's case, Krishna's revelatory knowledge is religiously saving knowledge, whereas in Oedipus' case, Apollo's and Teiresias' revelatory knowledge is religiously dooming knowledge. In Hamlet's case, religiously saving knowledge is an object of theological speculation and of philosophical doubt. In the Hindu case, self-knowledge means absolute knowledge and ultimate liberation; in the Greek case, self-knowledge means self-discovery and the recognition of human fragility; in the Shakespearean case, self-knowledge means self-exploration and doubting oneself.

8 Religious aspects

The religious aspects of tragedy touch upon the tensions and interactions between human freedom and supernatural necessity, fate and fortune, and upon the issue of divine intentions and interventions. What is, in our tragic and epic stories, the religious weight of human intentions and actions in the face of divine intentions and actions?

First, in Greek tragedies and Hindu epics alike, different characters hold different views on the impact of fate. In the *Mahābhārata* epic, faced with fate, there is not much room for human action. It can join fate, but it cannot really go against it. There are no closely reasoned attempts made to demarcate the boundaries between fate and human effort. Supernatural necessity manifests itself by using human free choices for fatal purposes, thus turning human freedom into a source of tragedy. Both Arjuna and Hamlet suffer from the burden of doom in their destiny. The striking difference between Arjuna and Hamlet is that Arjuna's problem is whether to act, whereas Hamlet's problem is when to act. Arjuna is aware of the fatal necessity of war and his part in it, but he does not resist or defy his fate. Mentally, he does not appropriate fate as his personal choice by considering himself fate's agent. He is encouraged to accept his fate (temporal necessity), but to think of his destiny (eternal freedom) and keep the two apart. Both Arjuna and Hamlet try to act in conjunction with time's moral order. But while Arjuna has to comply with his fate, Hamlet has to seize his destiny as his opportunity. Instead of appropriating Claudius' view of the transparent necessity of the natural order or, for that matter, a Greek, obscure necessity of fate, Hamlet seems to appropriate the obscure chaos of human freedom as an integral part of nature. The workings of Greek fate are replaced with the workings of Renaissance nature. Its intrinsic forces of chaos and order do not just occur in the outside world, but also within human nature. Hamlet's readiness to seize the opportunity provided by Providence indicates an active and self-shaping appropriation of destiny that 'defies augury' beyond anything that Greek tragedy would consider possible. Greek characters are expected to endure time's order, not to shape it. Despite references to Providence in *Hamlet*, the explicit focus of the play seems to be on fortune, and how to respond to it with reason, dignity and *virtù* (talented will power in great political affairs). There are no references in *Hamlet* to Hamlet and his father as belonging to a doomed royal lineage, as is the case with the Tantalid and Labdacid families in Greek tragedy and the Kuru family in the Indian epic. The misfortunes of the Tantalids, Labdacids and Kurus seem to come from the long-term workings of fate's necessity, instead of coming under the short-term workings of fortune's contingency. But humans take an active part in their own misfortune – Yudhisthira's prosperity depends on Draupadī who embodies Śrī, the goddess of Prosperity. She is the source of the king's sovereignty, provided the king is 'omni-virtuous'. The ultimate or temporary downfall of kings such as Yudhisthira is thus partly dependent upon the presence of a set of non-moral and moral qualities. Draupadī is Yudhisthira's last stake in the dice game, and he loses her.

Secondly, the Greek gods punish violators of divine laws, but they care more about their own honour than about human destinies. No tragedian suggests any *divine* contributions to early moral or legal life. Sophocles' 'Ode to Man' in the *Antigone* (332–75) lists all forms of cultural progress as *human* achievements. The ethical consciousness of moral values and their vulnerability turns humans into humane beings, but it does not turn the anthropomorphic gods into compassionate beings. The Greek gods participate in this cosmic order, not creating it, but sustaining it by punishing infringements. Likewise, in *Hamlet*, the Christian threat of divine punishment is much more real than the hope of divine reward or forgiveness. The immoral actions of murder, incest and revenge weigh heavily, religiously speaking. Old Hamlet's and Claudius' references to a personal God who punishes sinners compete with references to a secular concept of impersonal nature. The Hindu battle takes place against the background not only of time's order and renewal, but also of the cosmic struggle between gods and demons. While in Greek tragedy, human relations are the battlefield for gods to fight other gods, in the Hindu epics, human relations are the battlefield for gods to fight demons. The Greek, Shakespearean and Indian examples all share the religious belief that human and divine actions take place against the background of a universal order whose rules, boundaries and workings cannot be ignored without someone suffering the fatal consequences.

Thirdly, the human transgression of boundaries takes different forms in different traditions, along a variety of vertical and horizontal axes of relationship, between the human and the divine, between humans among each other, and between order and chaos. For Homer's *Iliad* and Greek tragedy, Redfield and Vernant stressed the vertical axis, while more recently, Cairns and others pointed out the prominence of the horizontal axis. Shakespearean tragedy relates the human transgression of boundaries, most notably to negative notions of ambition and limitless desire that operate mainly on the horizontal axis of human relationships, even if they trigger divine punishment (vertical axis). They represent, McAlindon suggested, not a vertical (Christian) battle between angelic and bestial dimensions of human nature, but a horizontal (Renaissance) overflowing of boundaries, a lack of balance of natural forces within human boundaries. In the Hindu epic, there is no gap between humans and gods (vertical axis), but fluid transformation and human embodiment of the divine. Human transgression of boundaries is always a violation of both the social order (horizontal) and the cosmic order (vertical). Humans do not oppose gods, humans are part of a socio-cosmic order that includes gods who oppose demons.

9 The ever-changing bird's-eye view

The underlying question of this study was whether, in the end, Indian views of the human condition are very different from Western views of the human condition. The answer sounds like stating the obvious – it depends on the specific anthropological issues raised. What makes things highly complicated, however, is the actual identification of the exact similarities and differences. In some specific respects, the Greek and Shakespearean cases are more similar to each other than to the Indian case; in some other respects, the Greek and Indian cases are more similar. In other respects, the Shakespearean and Indian cases are more similar. Different cultures have different styles of highlighting the shared dimensions of human nature and these are hard to pin down.

Carefully developing detailed descriptions and comparisons is what brought about the change. Gradually, horizons broadened in all directions. Increasingly, the unknown became known and the well-known lost its self-evidence. Eventually, central points and patterns in an enriching variety of cultural landscapes could be spotted. These landscapes did not merge into one single pattern. Nor did the observations merge into one single view. And yet, a broadening of horizons beyond one's own horizon took place, and the comparative approach allowed for more precise observations than general statements on these matters tend to contain. In the course of this study, some striking patterns of similarity and difference could be seen in the fields below and the roads uphill, lighting up according to the ever-changing bird's-eye view that seeks to disclose cultural landscape patterns across boundaries back and forth. Gliding silently over the fields, flying across one cultural landscape to the other and back again, they became strangely familiar.

Notes

Chapter 1

1 Douglas Allen, *Structure and Creativity in Religion: Hermeneutics in Mircea Eliade's Phenomenology and New Directions*. The Hague: Mouton Publishers, 1978, 205.

2 Benson Saler, *Conceptualising Religion: Immanent Anthropologists, Transcendent Natives, and Unbounded Categories*. Leiden: E. J. Brill, 1993. Some exemplars of a natural language category, in the judgement of ordinary speakers of a language, are deemed better examples, or more prototypical, than others. Users may differ in their judgements, but in general, it is feasible to draw from their examples several indications for determining the more clear-cut elements operating within the pattern of a family resemblance type of definition. Moreover, according to Saler, the same phenomenon may pertain to several categories, though perhaps in different degrees of what he calls 'judged goodness of fit'. That is to say, the same phenomenon may be a strikingly good or clear example of one category and, at the same time, be a bad example of a different category. Whereas an essentialist approach insists on precisely fixed boundaries, a prototype approach makes use of the examples that are considered clearer than other ones.

3 The Western cultural background of categories such as 'religion' – a category which draws from Christianity and Judaism as 'among the most prototypical' (Saler, *Conceptualising Religion*, 208) examples of what we mean by 'religion' – could be used to disqualify the category as too ethnocentric. Interestingly, Saler takes ethnocentrism not only as a historical fact but also as a productive springboard for entering the intercultural stage of comparative research. Some amount of ethnocentrism (not to be confused with superiority!) is practically unavoidable as a cognitive starting point in the search for transcultural understandings, so why not acknowledge it and make a virtue of necessity? All categories, not just Western categories, are historically developed practical tools that can be of great analytical use as long as they are capable of improvement and enlargement. In order to make comparisons, what one needs is *initial orientation*, and that is precisely what clear examples provide. What one also needs is the capacity to relativize the sharply drawn boundaries around one's categories.

4 Cf. Saler, *Conceptualising Religion*, 259: 'In extending the category label
to certain phenomena among non-Western peoples, we are claiming
some similarity to what we deem an important aspect of human life in
the West. We generally claim or imply, moreover, that we do so because
of apperceived similarity: that is, we do not create the similarity simply by
extending the term, but that we apply the term because we discern some
similarity.' Cf. also 262: 'Making comparisons is a process of discriminating
and organizing similarities and differences, and it is always guided by
assumptions that include standards.'

5 Bernard Williams, *Shame and Necessity*. Berkeley, Los Angeles, London:
University of California Press, 1994, 213 note 33: 'Ann Norris Michelini
offers, in *Euripides and the Tragic Tradition*, Madison, 1987, ch. I, a valuable
history of Euripidean interpretation, including the observation (pp. 49–51)
that the installation at the beginning of the nineteenth century of Sophocles
as the finest expression of the fifth century and the downgrading of
Euripides, who had for centuries been the most popular of the tragedians,
was itself part of the self-definition of the modern as opposed to the
classical.'

6 George Steiner, *The Death of Tragedy*. London: Faber and Faber, [1961] pb
1982,⁵ 188ff. Raymond Williams, *Modern Tragedy*. (Stanford, Calif: Stanford
University Press, 1966) Ontario: Broadview Press Encore Editions, 2001,
28–30.

7 Among themselves, the scholarly positions may, of course, yield
contradictory impressions. To some degree, such multi-vocality adds to
the credibility of the ongoing debate because less voices are silenced. But
at some point in the debate on any issue, if and when *coherent patterns
of understanding* arise at a more general level, from a bird's eye view,
conclusions, albeit preliminary ones, can be drawn. Depending on how
general or how detailed the perspective is, the scholarly positions may or
may not diverge.

8 I tend to make the cut between a general focus and a focus on details
where it makes a good comparison because my main concern and guiding
principle is that I gather a sufficient number of pieces of the puzzle to
answer the cross-cultural question – in what respects can the *Mahābhārata*
epic's and the *Bhagavadgītā*'s views of the human being be called 'tragic'
in the Western sense(s) of the word. Although I intend to do justice to each
scholarly position in the debate on any of the issues, what is needed for
viable overall comparisons is a more general picture of the most important
patterns structuring or colouring the anthropological issues, not too strong
a focus on the details and diversities within the scholarly debate.

9 Comparison depends on *balancing* convincing scholarly interpretations
on both sides of each issue, just as much as it depends on analysing the
similarities and differences between the ways in which each issue is raised
in each culture. The scholarly feedback draws its authority from the fact
that it remains in constant touch with the texts and contexts concerned.
Its perspectivism is not entirely arbitrary. Its 'arbitrariness is limited by its
responsibility to the data', as Wendy Doniger (*The Implied Spider: Politics*

and Theology in Myth. New York: Columbia University Press, 1998, 37) puts it.

10 Cf. Doniger, *The Implied Spider*, 76: 'The comparatist is part scientist, part artist, but this is seldom acknowledged'. cf. Douglas R. Hofstadter, *Gödel, Escher, Bach: An Eternal Golden Braid*. New York: Basic Books, [1979] 1999, 641–719, esp. 695.

Chapter 2

1 Philip Edwards, 'Introduction', in: *Hamlet, Prince of Denmark*. Updated edition, ed. Philip Edwards. Cambridge: Cambridge University Press, (2003), 1–32.

2 The sin of incest is due to Iocaste, who tried to thwart fate and murder her own son. This was the reason for adding the divine penalty of incest in the version of the oracle told to Oedipus (752–7) to the divine penalty of patricide in the version of the oracle told to the parents (676–8).

3 Michael Ewans, 'Patterns of Tragedy in Sophocles and Shakespeare', in: M. S. Silk (ed.), *Tragedy and the Tragic: Greek Theatre and Beyond*. Oxford: Oxford University Press, (1996) pb 1998, 438–57, at 441.

4 John Peck, Martin Coyle, *How to Study a Shakespeare Play*. (1985) Second edition. Hampshire/New York: Palgrave, 1995, 52.

5 Ewans, 'Patterns of Tragedy in Sophocles and Shakespeare', 441. Cf. Hugh Lloyd-Jones, 'Ritual and Tragedy', in: Fritz Graf (Hrsg.), *Ansichten griechischer Rituale. Geburtstags-Symposium für Walter Burkert*. Stuttgart/Leipzig: B. G. Teubner, 1998, 280.

6 Ewans, 'Patterns of Tragedy in Sophocles and Shakespeare', 443–5, 453 note 16.

7 Ewans, 'Patterns of Tragedy in Sophocles and Shakespeare', 449–50. Ewans' essay includes a brief, but very to-the-point, discussion of the question of whether the plot pattern should be called 'religious', on page 450, stressing the religious character of the central imagery of order and disorder.

8 Joan Rees, *Shakespeare and the Story: Aspects of Creation*. London: The Athlone Press, 1978, 171–4. What one might *expect* on the basis of the first scene is a *political conflict*: that the two young sons of the two dead kings (King Hamlet of Denmark and King Fortinbras of Norway) will be taking up the quarrels of their fathers and that the audience is being prepared for a political and dynastic struggle. But in the second scene, Claudius's first speech draws immediate attention to the *family situation* of the royal house, whereas the third scene deals with the *love relationship* between Ophelia and Prince Hamlet.

9 Harry Keyishian, *The Shapes of Revenge: Victimization, Vengeance, and Vindictiveness in Shakespeare*. New York: Humanity Books, (1995) 2003, 52–67.

10 Keyishian, *The Shapes of Revenge*, 54–5.

11 Ibid., 56.

12 Peter Burian, 'Myth into *muthos*: the shaping of tragic plot', in: Easterling (ed.), *The Cambridge Companion*, 178–208, esp. 181–3. Ger Groot, 'Ramkoers: Antigone tegenover Kreon', in: Paul Vanden Berghe, Willem Lemmens, Johan Taels (eds), *Tragisch: Over tragedie en ethiek in de 21e eeuw*. Budel: Damon, 2005, 17–41, esp. 23, argues that reconciliation takes place on a different level, not between the main characters, but on the level of knowledge and the recognition of one's destiny, between a character and his or her insight into the inevitability of limits, pain, contradictions, and the ambiguities of life itself.

13 Burian, 'Myth into *muthos*', 182.

14 Robert N. Watson, 'Tragedies of revenge and ambition', in: Claire McEachern (ed.), *The Cambridge Companion to Shakespearean Tragedy*. Cambridge: Cambridge University Press, 2002, 173: 'Hamlet expresses concern that God has forbidden suicide, but not that God has forbidden revenge. In any case, Hamlet's situation is ambiguous, since he pursues not only a personal vendetta on behalf of his family, which Elizabethan commentators condemned, but also official justice as a prince of the state, which they tended to approve. Shakespeare employs such ambiguities to prevent the audience from seizing on a simplistic moral view of the protagonist's dilemma, which must be irresolvable if it is to be fully tragic'. Whether a tragic conflict is unsolvable by definition or not is an issue that will be dealt with later on.

15 Thomas McAlindon, *Shakespeare's Tragic Cosmos*. Cambridge: CUP, (1991) 1996, 111–13, 125.

16 John Lee, *Shakespeare's* Hamlet *and the Controversies of Self*. Oxford: Oxford University Press, 2000, 182. On John Lee's approach, see more extensively the chapter on psycho-ethical aspects, Part I Section 6.

17 Burian, 'Myth into *muthos*', 187–9. The *retribution pattern* is organized around punishment for past offences. It may involve conflict between gods and mortals, with the mortals' challenge to divine supremacy leading to their destruction. The *sacrifice pattern* entails conflict between the needs and desires of the individual and those of a community in crisis, resolved in favour of the community through the willing participation of the sacrificial victim. The *supplication pattern* involves a triangular confrontation – a suppliant or group of suppliants, pursued by an implacable enemy, seek and obtain protection from a ruler who must then defend them, by force if necessary. The *rescue pattern* enacts a struggle whereby the principals, unexpectedly reunited, defeat a common foe and work out their own salvation. In the *return-recognition pattern*, conflict arises from the central character's ignorance of his own true identity. By labouring against inner and outer opposition to establish that identity, he is able to reclaim his proper inheritance.

18 Charles Segal, *Oedipus Tyrannus: Tragic Heroism and the Limits of Knowledge*. New York: Twayne Publishers, 1993, 12.

19 Burian, 'Myth into *muthos*', 189–90.

20 The theme of *retaliation* is prominent in Sophocles' *Ajax* and *Electra*. (Cairns, *Aidōs*, 227–49.)

21 Simon Goldhill, *Aeschylus: The* Oresteia. (1992) Second edition. Cambridge: Cambridge University Press, 2004, 20–33. There is no straightforward transformation from *dikē* as revenge to *dikē* as legal justice; the language of *dikē* is too intricate and opaque for that, he argues.

22 *Poetics*, 11 (1452a, 22–6).

23 Bernd Seidensticker, '*Peripeteia* and Tragic Dialectic in Euripidean Tragedy', in: Silk (ed.), *Tragedy and the Tragic*, 377–96, esp. 378–81.

24 Groot, 'Ramkoers: Antigone tegenover Kreon', 17–41. The first episode presents Creon versus the guard; the second episode shows Creon versus Antigone, and Creon versus Ismene; the third episode features Creon versus Haimon; the fourth episode shows Creon versus Antigone; and the fifth episode presents Creon versus Tiresias. Structurally, the second and the fourth episodes correspond to each other because, here, Creon and Antigone oppose each other; the first and the fifth episodes also correspond to each other because, here, Creon is confronted with two non-family members who are each other's opposite poles – the selfish and pragmatic guard, on the one hand, and the unselfish and visionary Tiresias, on the other hand. This structure of oppositional patterns pushes the third episode to the fore as dramatically crucial to the whole turn of events. How does Creon respond to Haimon's efforts to persuade his father? At first, Creon is willing to listen. But Haimon makes a tactical mistake by referring to Antigone's support by the people – a small but fatal mistake (*hamartia*) because Creon, who was about to be persuaded, slides back into his previous position.

25 Burian, 'Myth into *muthos*', 181.

26 Peter B. Murray, 'Hamlet,' in: *Shakespeare Criticism Yearbook* 37 (1996), 241–68; To explain the dynamics of Hamlet's behaviour, Murray also looks for the consequences that reinforce it (246).

27 Murray, 'Hamlet', 246–7.

28 Murray, 'Hamlet', 259–60: 'Hamlet's perception that death brings human greatness to "base uses" moves him to a deep sense of loss that he counters with irony: "O that that earth which kept the world in awe/Should patch a wall t'expel the winter's flaw" (208–9). These lines do not express an acceptance of death that frees Hamlet to act but a tragic prince's concern with death as the destroyer of human greatness. Paradoxically, Hamlet's disposition as tragic prince has displaced concern for the soul, choked off compassion for the loss of song, and provoked scorn of petty worldlings'.

29 Clément Rosset, *La philosophie tragique*. (1960) Paris: Presses Universitaires de France, 1991.

30 Rosset, *La philosophie tragique*, 7–22.

31 David Margolies, *Monsters of the Deep: Social Dissolution in Shakespeare's Tragedies*. Manchester/New York: Manchester University Press, 1992, 59–60.

32 Rees, *Shakespeare and the Story*, 170–2.

33 Anthony Brennan, *Shakespeare's Dramatic Structures*. London/New York: Routledge, (1986) pb 1988, 105–6; 129ff. The two key scenes of the play are the enacted-murder play scene (III.ii.1–284) and the final sword-play scene (V.ii.1–392). Brennan points out that both scenes are public entertainments, and both scenes are traps, plays-within-plays. The rhythms of the two entertainments have much in common. Each scene divides into four similar phases: 1. Anticipation of the entertainment (3.2.1–86; 5.2.1–213); 2. Prologue to the entertainment (3.2.87–129; 5.2.214–68); 3. The entertainment as trap (3.2.130–260; 5.2.269–347); 4. A commentary on the results of the entertainment as trap (3.2.261–84; 5.2.348–92). Page 33: 'The method of anticipation, building up suspense, reaching the climactic trap, and then unfolding the consequences of the trap, are the same in each case'. 'Shakespeare has made a deliberate link', Brennan suggests on pages 37–8, 'between the trap which Hamlet sets to surprise Claudius and the trap which, as a consequence, Claudius eventually sets to surprise Hamlet. An indispensable cue for the connection is the placing of the King and Queen on their seats in the same position, the positioning of Horatio as an observer and the general grouping of attendant courtiers in the same positions on each occasion'. The 'totally different consequences' of these structurally similar scenes 'are related to the two different temperaments of the men who organize the entertainments' – Hamlet has the action of murder imitated only, while Claudius has it for real.

34 Brennan, *Shakespeare's Dramatic Structures*, 134, 133 resp.; 136: 'It is an irony of the structure of the play that in the first half the spies which are sent to ensnare Hamlet are used by him to maintain his secret and his freedom. In the second half the antic disposition which has acted as protection for Hamlet is used by Claudius to maintain the secret and to pack him off to England. . . . Hamlet and Claudius play out their roles now not for each other but for the public'.

35 Brennan, *Shakespeare's Dramatic Structures*, 32. Everything leads to Hamlet's test in the play-within-the-play. Brennan, on page 33, observes, 'The moment Hamlet resolves his own uncertainty Claudius is able to do the same. Thus the action builds up again in a long rolling wave to the moment when the two characters, who had discovered the danger each poses for the other in the middle of the play, take their final pass at acting on the knowledge they had then acquired'. Page 37: 'Claudius who had to watch in horror the enactment of the poisoning of his brother, watches helplessly the poisoning of the wife he had won in that treachery'.

36 Brennan, *Shakespeare's Dramatic Structures*, 140–1.

37 Bert O. States, *Hamlet and the Concept of Character*. Baltimore, MD/ London: The Johns Hopkins University Press, 1992, 110, 168; 111–12: 'In this, the play is rather like *Waiting for Godot*, to which it is often compared. At some point it dawns on you that Godot is a red herring and that the real drama is the drama of "the middle"—that is, of waiting, rather than of arrival and confrontation, or that the auxiliary arrivals are indeed the relevant arrivals. . . . *Hamlet*, like *Godot*, is a special case of a middle that is devoted to problematizing its ending by preaching, so to speak, a philosophy of impasse. It is one thing for a work to delay its conclusion in the interest of telling a good story, another to pursue so self-consciously the problem of concluding'.

38 Keyishian, *The Shapes of Revenge*, 2–3, 24.

39 Ibid., 6–7.

40 Ibid., 4; cf. 52, 80.

41 Aristotle, *Poetics,* (1453a, 30–9).

42 Cf. also Gregory Nagy, 'The Epic Hero', in: John Miles Foley (ed.), *A Companion to Ancient Epic*. Malden, MA/Oxford, UK: Blackwell Publishing, 2005, 71–89, esp. 80: 'In the *Odyssey*, as I observed earlier, *nostos* is not only a "homecoming" but a "song about homecoming"; Odysseus achieves *kleos*, "glory", by way of successfully achieving a *nostos*, "song about homecoming". Whereas Achilles has to choose between *nostos* "homecoming" and the *kleos* "glory" that he gets from his own epic tradition (*Iliad* 9.413), Odysseus must have both *kleos* and *nostos*, because for him his *nostos* is the same thing as his *kleos*. Once again we see an active complementarity between the Homeric *Iliad* and *Odyssey*'.

43 A. Maria van Erp Taalman Kip, *Bokkenzang: Over Griekse tragedies*. Amsterdam: Athenaeum-Polak & Van Gennep, 1997, 73–4.

44 A. Maria van Erp Taalman Kip, 'The Unity of the *Oresteia*', in: Silk (ed.), *Tragedy and the Tragic*, 119–38, at 132.

45 Cf. Bernard Williams, *Shame and Necessity*. Berkeley, CA/Los Angeles/ London: University of California Press, 1994, 148–9: 'Euripides was famously called by Aristotle "the most tragic of all poets" but if this is appropriate, it is in the sense that his plays had a powerful theatrical effect, rather than that he presented tragic agency in its purest form'. 213 note 35: '. . . cf. the use of *tragikos* to mean "high-flown" . . .'.

46 Cf. Peter Szondi's definition of 'the tragic' as 'a dialectical modality of impending or actual destruction', in: Peter Szondi (ed.), *Versuch ueber das Tragische*. Frankfurt a/Main, 1961, 209.

47 Viviana Cessi, *Erkennen und Handeln in der Theorie des Tragischen bei Aristoteles*. Frankfurt a/Main: Athenäum, 1987, 263–74.

48 Cf. Michael Trapp's phrasing: 'a picture of the nature of tragedy that stresses the medium's dedication to thinking the uncomfortable thought'. (Michael Trapp, 'Tragedy and the Fragility of Moral Reasoning: Response to Foley', in: Silk (ed.), *Tragedy and the Tragic*, 80) and '*aporia*, the unsettling inadequacy of human resources to deal with circumstance, is central to tragic experience'. (Trapp, 'Tragedy and the Fragility of Moral Reasoning', 82) Redfield, *Nature and Culture in the Iliad*, xv–xvi: 'Dignity of bearing we associate particularly with the tragic poets, perhaps because tragedy deals not only in truth but in harsh, uncomfortable truth. . . . We call this vision "tragic" for two reasons, which have to do with the harshness of the truth stated and with the dignity of the man who states it. Man, in the vision of a Weber and a Freud, is confined by the conditions of his nature and his history, irremediably subject to the contradictions of his own existence. He has, however, the power to reflect upon these conditions and to understand them, and he has the power to teach this understanding'.

49 Cf. Richard Seaford, 'Something to Do with Dionysos—Tragedy and the Dionysiac: Response to Friedrich', in: Silk (ed.), *Tragedy and the Tragic*, 292, on the ending of the *Oresteia*: 'There is no doubt that the ending of the *Oresteia* answers the questions, however much *we* may dislike the answers, the way they are arrived at, or the very idea of questions being answered. But at the same time Vernant is right to say that anxiety persists. The Furies, who have created such havoc in the trilogy, are still there'. Adrian Poole, *Tragedy: Shakespeare and the Greek Example*. Oxford/New York: Basil Blackwell, 1987, 15–53, esp. 38, agrees and compares the persistent 'initiate fear' of Aeschylus' *Oresteia* to the 'anxiety of hope' in Shakespeare's *Macbeth*: 'The trilogy ends with "the initiate fear", of fearful/hopeful apprehension, now become the burden and the basis of a whole community, indeed of civil community itself. It belongs to everybody. Similar fears and hopes afflict the ending of *Macbeth*'.

50 Nicole Loraux, La voix endeuillée: Essai sur la tragédie grecque. Paris: Gallimard, 1999.

51 Keyishian, *The Shapes of Revenge*, 6–7.

52 Johan Taels, 'Het komische lot van het tragische in de (post)moderne media', in: Vanden Berghe, Lemmens, Taels (eds), *Tragisch*, 165–84, esp. 175. (Johan Taels, 'Laughing Matters: The Unstoppable Rise of the Comic Perspective', in: Arthur Cools et al. (eds), *The Locus of Tragedy*. Leiden/Boston: E. J. Brill, 2008, 299–318).

53 Keyishian, *The Shapes of Revenge*, 67.

54 Keyishian, *The Shapes of Revenge*, 79: 'In moving to resolve *Hamlet* and the Gloucester subplot of *King Lear*, Shakespeare has tried to deproblematize the revenges of Hamlet and Edgar by casting them as servants of higher authorities. I think he has not quite succeeded, and that is fortunate, because we would not still be engaged as strongly with these works if he had. The enlistment of providence on behalf of a philosophy of passivity does not answer all the questions raised by deep engagement with the revenge theme: in the overwhelmingly interrogative tone of *Hamlet* and the final devastation of *Lear*, many will continue to see the issues raised by revenge as surviving the playwright's efforts to bring them to closure'. Cf. 67.

55 William Kerrigan, *Hamlet's Perfection*. Baltimore, MD/London: The Johns Hopkins University, (1994) 1996, 122–51.

56 Kerrigan, *Hamlet's Perfection*, 131–2, 123.

57 Ibid., 136–8; cf. 146–7.

58 Kerrigan contends that this calm is not quite the mysterious indifference envisioned by Harold Bloom. Bloom himself points out that Hamlet's indifference is not clear-cut indifference. The word 'detachment' does not seem the proper word for the mood Hamlet displays when accepting the duel with Laertes, Claudius's own murderous mousetrap, according to Harold Bloom, *Hamlet: Poem Unlimited*. New York: Riverhead Books, 2003, 85: 'Detachment toward his dilemma is all but absolute in the new Hamlet: "We defy augury". Defiance is scarcely detachment, but Hamlet's defiance is not easy to characterize'. Cf. 89–91, 141–2.

59 Kerrigan, *Hamlet's Perfection*, 139.

60 Ibid., 151.

61 Rees, *Shakespeare and the Story*, 192.

62 At this stage, what comes to mind is McAlindon's observation that 'The conception of natural order which guides Chaucer . . . and Shakespeare (in all his work), that of a precarious balance of contrary forces, insistently implies that comedy (love and union) is potential tragedy, and that tragedy (division and violence) is comedy *manqué*'. ((1991) (1996), 10) Steiner would wholeheartedly agree and call it 'tragicomic', but the disadvantage of Steiner's terminology is that it cannot distinguish between tragic comedy (which is primarily comic) and comic tragedy (which is primarily tragic); this is because his terminology refers to one world view instead of several genres.

63 Paul Ricoeur, *Finitude et culpabilité. Livre II: La symbolique du mal*. Paris: Aubier/Éditions Montaigne, 1960, 153–332 (Deuxième Partie: Les 'mythes' du commencement et de la fin). In the *'drama of creation' type*, the origin of evil is coextensive with the origin of things in the sense that it is the original 'chaos' which the god struggles with by means of his act of creation. Creating means combatting chaos, fighting it by establishing a beneficial order. Creation is identical to salvation. Ritual is the re-enactment of the original act of creation, a ritual repetition of the original combat. This type implies a 'dramatic' world view, even though Ricoeur doesn't call it thus explicitly. In the *'creation completed' type*, the fall of man into sin, the biblical 'adamic myth', appears as an irrational event within the original setting of a perfect creation, in need of a new act of salvation, not a repetition of the original act of creation. Salvation becomes a matter of history, of unrepeated events, whereas creation becomes just a matter of staging cosmically the historical drama in time of future developments on the world stage culminating in an eschatological battle in which evil will be completely destroyed. This type implies an 'eschatological' world view. In the *'tragic' type*, the god seduces man, blinds him and leads him astray. Error becomes inseparable from human existence itself. Although the tragic hero does not commit the error, he is guilty of it. Since his error is inevitable, he cannot be pardoned for it. Salvation is a matter of aesthetics on the part of the spectator who is liberated aesthetically by recognizing the human condition as his own. Salvation consists of freedom coinciding with well-understood necessity. This type is seen by Ricoeur as a transitional type between the myth of chaos as part of the drama of creation and the myth of the fall of man. It implies a 'tragic' world view. In the *'myth of the banned soul'* type, the destiny of the soul is to have come from elsewhere, to have gone astray and entered the body and the material world as a place of temporary exile, a sort of fall from which the soul should release itself again through redeeming knowledge. Ricoeur calls the world view implied 'orphic' or 'gnostic'.

64 Ricoeur presents his typology statically at first, but finally introduces a personal commitment to the second type. On the basis of his personal belief in the revelatory character of the second type, the biblical 'adamitic myth' and the 'eschatological view on history', he suggests a dynamics of myths that transforms the four types of myths into an interplay of forces, the second type at the centre creating a field of force in which the Greek 'tragic' type is closest to the 'adamitic myth' type, and the Orphic 'myth of the banned soul' type the most remote one. The other myths are presented as complementary myths that reveal the reverse side of the 'adamitic myth', revealing related or additional truths that are confirmed by the 'adamitic myth'. Cf. 291.

65 George Steiner, *The Death of Tragedy*. London: Faber and Faber, (1961) pb 1982,[5] 11–12.

66 Steiner, *The Death of Tragedy*, 12–13.

67 Ibid., 16.

68 Steiner, 'Tragedy, Pure and Simple', in: Silk (ed.), *Tragedy and the Tragic*, 534–46, at 540: 'The Shakespearean sense of reality, of man's works and days, is conceptually and pragmatically tragicomic. Shakespeare *knows*, in every fibre of his compendious being, that a child is being born next door, a birthday celebrated below stairs, in the very instant of the murder of Agamemnon or the blinding of Oedipus. He *knows*, overwhelmingly, that the facts of the world are hybrid, that desolation and joy, destruction and generation are simultaneous. The sum of the extant is never in one key, it is never one thing only'.

69 George Steiner, ' "Tragedy," Reconsidered', in: *New Literary History* 35 (2004), 2–3: 'Fallen man is made an unwelcome guest of life or, at best, a threatened stranger on this hostile or indifferent earth (Sophocles' damning word, dwelt on by Heidegger, is *apolis*). Thus the necessary and sufficient premise, the axiomatic constant in tragedy is that of ontological homelessness—witness this motif in Beckett, in Pinter—of alienation or ostracism from the safeguard of licensed being. There is no welcome to the self'.

70 Terry Eagleton, 'Commentary', in: *New Literary History* 35 (2004), 157–8. Eagleton made the same point in Terry Eagleton, *Sweet Violence: The Idea of the Tragic*. Malden, MA/Oxford: Blackwell Publishers, 2003, 36–40, 57.

71 Eagleton, *Sweet Violence*, 1–2.

72 Ibid., 31, 60.

73 Eagleton, *Sweet Violence*, 37. Tragedy differs from the more brittle forms of teleology in that the injurious remains injurious; it is not magically transmuted into good by its instrumental value. The 'exchange-value' of the action, the renewed life to which it may lead, is not allowed to cancel its 'use-value'. (39) Eagleton considers Hegel's teleology and conception of truth tragic because Hegel's philosophy looks the negative in the face and tarries with it, presenting *Geist* itself as a tragic hero. But this tragic hero recovers (his self-identity) and transcends the tragic opposition in a way that diminishes the tragic retrospectively (41–3).

74 H. J. Heering, *Tragiek: Van Aeschylus tot Sartre*. 's Gravenhage: L. J. C. Boucher, 1961, 202, 204.

75 Heering, *Tragiek*, 208.

76 Ibid., 211, 203.

77 Ibid., 216–17.

78 Kathleen M. Sands, 'Tragedy, Theology, and Feminism in the Time After Time', in: *New Literary History* 34 (2004), 43.

79 Keyishian, *The Shapes of Revenge*, 63.

80 Ibid., 57 and 54 respectively.

81 Ibid., 63–4.

82 Ibid., 64–7.

83 Steiner, *The Death of Tragedy*, 324, 331–41ff. Steiner nonetheless sticks strongly to his postulate that theological assumptions and values are inherent to tragedy and the tragic. In the Greek deities, the Ghost in *Hamlet*, their proximity is palpable. Also, the secular closure of Shakespearean plays is not entirely closed to transcendence, Steiner contends, 'Scotland will blossom after Macbeth's death, Cassio's régime will benefit Cyprus, Fortinbras looks to be a sounder ruler than Hamlet would have been'. (Steiner, ' "Tragedy", Reconsidered', 5–7; see also 12).

84 Stephen Greenblatt, *Shakespearean Negotiations: The Circulation of Social Energy in Renaissance England*. Oxford: Clarendon, 1988.

85 Murray, 'Hamlet', 259–60.

86 Taels, 'Het komische lot van het tragische', 171–8 (Taels, 'Laughing Matters', 304–11).

87 Claire Colebrook, *Irony*. London/New York: Routledge, (2004) 2006, 1–8; 7: 'Until the Renaissance, irony was theorised within rhetoric and was often listed as a type of allegory: as one way among others for saying one thing and meaning another. When the Greek and Latin descriptions of Socrates became available to Renaissance writers, irony was still not what it was to become for the Romantics (an attitude to existence). Irony was a rhetorical method'.

88 Taels, 'Het komische lot van het tragische', 168–70 (Taels, 'Laughing Matters', 301–4).

89 Shakespeare, *The Tragedy of Hamlet*. Ed. Spencer, 51: 'But howsomever thou pursues this act, / Taint not thy mind' (I.v.84–5a).

90 Thomas G. Rosenmeyer, 'Ironies in Serious Drama', in: Silk (ed.), *Tragedy and the Tragic*, 497–519.

91 Rosenmeyer, 'Ironies in Serious Drama', 504.

92 Ibid., 512.

93 Ibid., 505.

94 N. J. Lowe, 'Tragic and Homeric Ironies: Response to Rosenmeyer', in: Silk (ed.), *Tragedy and the Tragic*, 520–33, esp. 524.

95 Lowe, 'Tragic and Homeric Ironies', 525. On irony in the *Iliad*, see also Seth L. Schein, *The Mortal Hero: An Introduction to Homer's* Iliad. Berkeley, CA/ Los Angeles: University of California Press, 1984, 29–30; on human role-playing and disguise in tragedy, see also Burian, 'Myth into *muthos*', 196–7.

96 McAlindon, *Shakespeare's Tragic Cosmos*, 15–16.

97 Harry Levin, *The Question of Hamlet*. London/Oxford/New York: Oxford University Press, 1959, 104–5.

98 Bloom, *Hamlet*, 144.

99 Sands, 'Tragedy, Theology, and Feminism', 41–61. More on her theory of tragedy in the chapters on literary–cultural aspects (Part I Section 6) and psycho-ethical aspects (Part I Section 2.2).

100 Sands, 'Tragedy, Theology, and Feminism', 42.

101 Ibid.

102 Sands, 'Tragedy, Theology, and Feminism', 42–3.

103 Ibid., 57–8.

104 In the tragic area of failing affection, Rosset discusses Proust's *Un amour de Swann*. The tragic area of discovering the inherent meanness of man is illustrated by referring to the works of Balzac.

105 P. E. Easterling, 'A show for Dionysus', in: P. E. Easterling (ed.), *The Cambridge Companion to Greek Tragedy*. Cambridge: Cambridge University Press, (1997) 2003,[5] 36–53, esp. 52–3.

106 Fiona Macintosh, 'Tragic Last Words: The Big Speech and the Lament in Ancient Greek and Modern Irish Tragic Drama', in: Silk (ed.), *Tragedy and the Tragic*, 414–25.

107 Kerrigan, *Hamlet's Perfection*, 145.

108 Ewans, 'Patterns of Tragedy in Sophocles and Shakespeare,' 441.

109 Peck, Coyle, *How to Study a Shakespeare Play*, 52.

110 Rees, *Shakespeare and the Story*, 178–84.

111 Watson, 'Tragedies of revenge and ambition', 164.

112 'Constitutes' or 'is situated in': the *Bhagavadgītā* has long been regarded as an interpolation.

113 James L. Fitzgerald, 'India's Fifth Veda: The *Mahābhārata*'s presentation of itself', in: Arvind Sharma (ed.), *Essays on the Mahābhārata*. Leiden/New York: E. J. Brill, 1991, 154: 'The prestige of Sanskrit in "medieval" India, and the relative stability of its being written down may have made this version of the *Mahābhārata* the single most determinative factor in the general *Mahābhārata* tradition'.

114 The eight initial chapters of the complete episode predict the death of Bhishma and the mourning it causes. According to J. A. B. van Buitenen, *The Bhagavadgītā in the Mahābhārata*. Chicago, IL: The University of Chicago Press, 1981, xi, they therefore justify Arjuna's loathing of being a party to it, and thus provide the setting and the occasion of the *Gītā*.

115 The *Gītā* retakes one crucial scene that has already taken place, namely, the surprising revelation of Krishna as the supreme ruler of the universe, which proves decisive in convincing Arjuna to rejoin the battle. If Krishna had already revealed himself as the divine ruler in a previous book of the epic, how can we explain that in the sixth book of the epic, Arjuna does not recognize Krishna as such right from the start?

116 A. K. Ramanujan, 'Repetition in the *Mahābhārata*', in: Sharma (ed.), *Essays on the Mahābhārata*, 420–1, admits that a text like the *Mahābhārata* is much more of a living and ongoing tradition than of a fixed and finished text. But he goes on to say that most traditional Hindus would never have been able to remember and recall in great detail this enormous epic if the epic had lacked an underlying narrative structure.

117 Ruth Cecily Katz, *Arjuna in the Mahābhārata: Where Krishna is, There is Victory*. Columbia: University of South Carolina, 1989, 258.

118 Irawati Karve, *Yugānta: The End of an Epoch*. Poona: Deshmukh Prakashan, 1969, 16.

119 James L. Fitzgerald, 'India's Fifth Veda: The *Mahābhārata*'s Presentation of Itself', in: Sharma (ed.), *Essays on the Mahābhārata*, 156 note 12.

120 Alf Hiltebeitel, *Rethinking the Mahābhārata: A Reader's Guide to the Education of the Dharma King*. New Delhi: Oxford University Press, 2002, 204.

121 Hiltebeitel, *Rethinking the Mahābhārata*, 197: 'If one vows to kill snakes, one shouldn't kill lizards by mistake. This problem overlaps with the wider problems of maintaining distinctions between castes, and between gods and humans. As Yudhisthira puts it, war reduces everyone to acting like dogs. It is when the *dharma* of caste breaks down that the "law of the fishes" (law of the jungle, *LM*) takes over. Caste mixture and confusion are the great dread of the *Bhagavad Gītā*, and of countless other epic passages. At the root of the Pañcāla cycle of violence is the confusion of caste (and other categories) between Drona and Drupada'.

122 Hiltebeitel, *Rethinking the Mahābhārata*, 118.

123 Ibid., 202.

124 Svargārohanaparvan, 18.1.1–10.

125 Hiltebeitel, *Rethinking the Mahābhārata*, 273.

126 Ibid., 210.

127 Ibid., 273–4.

128 Ibid., 277.

129 Alf Hiltebeitel, *The Ritual of Battle: Krishna in the Mahābhārata*. (New York: State University of New York, 1990) Delhi: Sri Satguru Publications (Indian Books Centre), 1991, 95–6.

130 Jan C. Heesterman, *The Inner Conflict of Tradition: Essays in Indian Ritual, Kingship and Society*. Chicago, IL: The University of Chicago Press, 1985, 123–4: 'Now the epics—both the *Mahābhārata* and the *Rāmāyana*—show exactly the same paradigm of cyclical alternation between *grāma* and *aranya* (the settled agricultural community (*grāma*) and the outside world of the jungle (*aranya*), *LM*). Both the Pāndavas and Rāma are forced to leave throne and realm and go out on a life of adventure in the wilds and return only after they have successfully come out of a long series of dangerous battles and ordeals. In both cases, the departure is connected with the aspersion. Rāma is cheated out of his already arranged unction. In the *Mahābhārata*, Yudhisthira, the leader of the Pāndava brothers, has the royal ritual performed but is then also cheated out of his realm in a game of dice forced upon him by his opponent, Duryodhana. Though the dicing game follows Yudhisthira's royal ritual, it does so without interval, and comparison with the ritual texts makes clear that it actually belongs to the royal ritual. It is not surprising, then, that the royal ritual is considered in the epics to be particularly dangerous. When the deceased father of the Pāndavas has his wish that Yudhisthira perform the royal ritual transmitted by the sage Nārada, the latter takes the opportunity to point out the dangers of this royal ritual, which will lead to the destruction of the warriors in the great Mahābhārata war—an idea that is later repeated by the sage Vyāsa, as well as on other occasions. So the royal ritual is directly linked to the tragic war, or rather, we might say that the war is part and parcel of the royal ritual cycle. We saw already that the *Aitareya Brāmana* has the aspersion followed by war and conquest, after which another consecratory sacrifice, the horse sacrifice, is performed. Similarly, the Pāndavas as well as Rāma perform on their triumphant return the horse sacrifice, which in the case of the *Mahābhārata* is given as an expiation for the catastrophal bloodshed'. See also 28ff.

131 Jan C. Heesterman, 'Epic Narrative and Sacrificial Ritual: A Note on the Royal Consecration', in: Eli Franco and Monika Zin (eds), *From Turfan to Ajanta: Festschrift for Dieter Schlingloff on the Occasion of his Eightieth Birthday*. Bhairahawa, Rupandehi, Nepal: Lumbini International Research Institute, 2010, 389–98.

132 Julian F. Woods, *Destiny and Human Initiative in the Mahābhārata*. Albany, NY: State University of New York Press, 2001, 31.

133 Is it fate (necessity) or fortune (chance) to win or lose a game of dice? Duryodhana and his maternal uncle Śakuni resent the prosperity of the Pāndavas and plan to take it away from them by challenging them to a game of dice. Julius Lipner, *Hindus: Their Religious Beliefs and Practices*.

London/New York: Routledge, (1994) pb 1998, 198ff., observes that Duryodhana first states that fate (*daiva*) is supreme and human effort pointless, but that he and Śakuni, who is an expert at gambling and never loses a game of dice, then plan the gambling challenge, and concludes that, under the guise of fate, namely the dice game, they attempt to manipulate fate to their advantage. When asked to approve of the plan, Duryodhana's father, the blind king Dhrtarāstra, 'knowing the evils of gambling', assents to it nonetheless, and makes fate and the gods responsible for its outcome, thus covering up his passion for his son Duryodhana (*Mahābhārata* 2.43.32– 2.45.57). Likewise, his equally weak and passive counterpart Yudhisthira covers up his addictive passion for gambling by appealing to fate (2.51.16).

134 Hiltebeitel, *The Ritual of Battle*, 143–91, esp. 156.

135 Ibid., 152–6, 163–5.

136 Ibid., 80–1.

137 Hiltebeitel, *The Ritual of Battle*, 73, 85, 100, 112. On Krishna and Draupadī, 227–8.

138 Hiltebeitel, *The Ritual of Battle*, 81, 86ff.

139 Ibid., 100.

140 Katz, *Arjuna in the Mahābhārata*, 155–96.

141 Hiltebeitel, *The Ritual of Battle*, 97.

142 Cf. *Gītā* 9.7.

143 Madeleine Biardeau, *Le Mahābhārata: Un récit fondateur du brahmanisme et son interprétation*. Paris: Editions du Seuil, 2002, Vol. I, 133–4; Hiltebeitel, *Rethinking the Mahābhārata*, 152 note 82; Woods, *Destiny and Human Initiative in the Mahābhārata*, 20.

144 Woods, *Destiny and Human Initiative in the Mahābhārata*, 7–8. In *Mahābhārata* 1.54–61, the Pāndava–Kaurava war is the sole reason for the gods' descent (*avatāra*) – they descend in order to remove the Earth's burden of demons who oppress the Earth's surface in the form of warrior kings who cover the Earth with armies and battles.

145 Biardeau, *Le Mahābhārata*, Vol. I, 160.

146 As a collective, all the warriors are re-absorbed into heaven instead of being saved or doomed on an individual basis. Cf. Biardeau, *Le Mahābhārata*, Vol. I, 135.

147 Biardeau, *Le Mahābhārata*, Vol. I, 97–161; Vol. II, 753–83.

148 Hiltebeitel, *Rethinking the Mahābhārata*, 158–61, suggests that the movement of the Naimisha Forest holy sages is an ascending movement of heavenly stars through the night.

149 Hiltebeitel, *Rethinking the Mahābhārata*, 166. He adds that the epic's emphasis on the relentlessness of time also finds theological expression in the *Gītā's* revelation that the deity is himself the totality of time. To identify Buddhism as the main rival in the background is in line with Biardeau.

150 The contrasts between order and disorder, good and evil, gods and demons, 'are not those of black and white', Peter Hill, *Fate, Predestination and Human Action in the Mahabharata: A Study in the History of Ideas.* New Delhi: Mushiram Manoharlal Publishers, 2001, 101–2, explains, 'for these opposed categories are also interdependent in that you could not have one without the other'. This makes the created triple-world not just a 'mixed bag of virtues and vices' but deeply fragile and in need of 'a minimum standard' to counter the constantly threatening forces of disorder. 'In the epic view, the order of the triple-world is at best a precarious balance between two powers of cosmos and chaos'.

151 John Gibert, *Change of Mind in Greek Tragedy.* Göttingen: Vandenhoeck & Ruprecht, 1995, 21.

152 Jan Assmann, *The Search for God in Ancient Egypt,* Ithaca, NY/London: Cornell University Press, 2001, 68–9 (*Ägypten: Theologie und Frömmigkeit einer frühen Hochkultur.* Stuttgart: Kohlhammer, 1984–85). These premodern meanings of 'dramatic' correspond to Ricoeur's use of the term in his 'drama of creation' type of mythical imagery concerning the origin and end of evil, as discussed previously (Part I Section 4).

153 Hiltebeitel, *Rethinking the Mahābhārata,* 204.

154 Lourens Minnema, 'Polytheistic and Monotheistic Patterns for Dealing with Religious Pluralism,' in: *Studies in Interreligious Dialogue* 12/1 (2002), 63–74.

155 Madeleine Biardeau, *Hinduism: The Anthropology of a Civilization.* Delhi/ Oxford: Oxford University Press, 1989, 32–40 (Engl. trans. of *L'hindouisme: Anthropologie d'une civilisation.* Paris: Flammarion, 1981, 40–7).

156 See the chapter on literary–cultural aspects.

157 Heesterman, *The Inner Conflict of Tradition,* 108–27.

158 There are striking examples of the juxtaposition of the linear pattern and the cyclical pattern in Hindu literature. Heesterman writes: 'One of those examples is the battle of the god Indra against the dragon Vrtra. At the moment Indra is about to kill the dragon, Vrtra says: "Do not kill me, you (Indra) are now what I (am)". No less striking is Kautilya's conception of the would-be conqueror and his opponents: both circular (the conqueror, surrounded by his opponents, around that the circle of his allies, then the allies of his enemy, and so on) and linear (the conqueror straight opposite his opponent, from behind the ally of his enemy, his own ally from behind his enemy, etc.). The conflict thus never ends. That the two schemes are conflated is also evident from the mixing of two sets of terms, in accordance with the circular and the linear pattern. Another example is Yudhisthira on his arrival in heaven where he finds his opponent Duryodhana'. (Quotation from a personal letter of Heesterman to the author, January 19th, 2005).

159 V. S. Sukthankar, *On the Meaning of the Mahābhārata.* (Bombay: The Asiatic Society of Bombay, 1957) Delhi: Motilal Banarsidass, 1998, 62ff.

160 Hiltebeitel, *The Ritual of Battle,* 41–3.

161 Ibid., 41–2.

162 Freda Matchett, Krsna: Lord or Avatāra? The Relationship between Krsna and Visnu in the context of the avatāra myth as presented by the Harivamśa, the Visnupurāna and the Bhāgavata-purāna. Richmond, Surrey: Curzon Press, 2001, 44–64.

163 Cf. J. W. Worden, *Grief Counselling and Grief Therapy: A Handbook for the Mental Health Practitioner.* Third Edition. New York: Brunner/Routledge, 2001, 25: 'I will use the term *mourning* to indicate the process which occurs after a loss, while *grief* refers to the personal experience of the loss. Since mourning is a process, it has been viewed in various ways, primarily as stages, phases, and tasks of mourning'.

164 *Gītā* 2.11; translation from G. W. Kaveeshwar, *The Ethics of the Gītā,* Delhi: Motilal Banarsidass, 1971, 9.

165 Hiltebeitel, *The Ritual of Battle*, 42.

166 Ramanujan, 'Repetition in the *Mahābhārata*', 424–6.

167 The irony contained in the eunuch–potent male reversal is addressed more explicitly by Wendy Doniger, *The Implied Spider: Politics and Theology in Myth.* New York: Columbia University Press, 1998, 15: 'Arjuna is living in disguise as an impotent transvestite dancing master, who offers his services as charioteer to a certain young prince, Uttara, giving as his reference none other than Arjuna himself, for whom, he says, he used to serve as charioteer. As the battle approaches, Uttara gets cold feet and doesn't want to fight; Arjuna tries to talk him into it, with a kind of parody of the speech that Krishna will give to Arjuna in the *Gītā*: "People will laugh at you if you don't fight". Reflexively, in the *Gītā* Krishna begins his exhortation by saying to Arjuna, "Don't act like an impotent transvestite; stand up!" (a line whose sexual double entendre was almost certainly unintended but may have operated on a subconscious level). In this proleptic parody, Prince Uttara jumps off the chariot and runs away, and Arjuna, in drag, his skirts flapping, runs after him (people who see him run say, "Gosh, he looks more like Arjuna than an impotent transvestite; that *must* be Arjuna")'.

168 Hiltebeitel, *The Ritual of Battle*, 114–40.

169 Ibid., 117–18.

170 Doniger, *The Implied Spider*, 7–9.

171 Ibid.

172 Doniger, *The Implied Spider*, 11–18.

173 Ibid., 14.

174 Ibid., 15.

175 Ibid., 18.

176 Ibid., 19.

177 Arjuna's last words in the *Gītā* are: 'My delusion is destroyed and I have gained wisdom/Through Your grace, Krishna./My doubts are gone./I shall do as You command'. (*The Bhagavad Gītā*, trans. Winthrop Sargeant, rev. ed. Christopher Chapple. New York: State University of New York Press, 1994, 734).

178 Katz, *Arjuna in the Mahābhārata*, 264.

179 Cf. Katz, *Arjuna in the Mahābhārata*, 228.

180 *The Bhagavad Gītā*, trans. Sargeant, 722.

181 However, the notion of 'play' (*krīḍā* predominantly in connection with
Shiva or *līlā* more in connection with Vishnu) as a theological metaphor
qualifying the activity of a creator god does not yet occur in the *Gītā* and
is only incidentally referred to in the epic (in the didactical treatise called
Mokshadharma). A 'theology of play' has not yet developed at this stage.
(Bettina Bäumer, *Schöpfung als Spiel: Der Begriff līlā im Hinduismus, seine
philosophische und theologische Deutung*. München: UNI-Druck, 1969,
24–34).

182 Cf. Richard H. Palmer, *Tragedy and Tragic Theory: An Analytical Guide*.
Westport, Connecticut/London: Greenwood Press, 1992, 72.

183 Another epic example is the rivalry between Sunjata, the lawful successor
living in exile, and his half-brother Dankarantuma, the unlawful king in the
West African *Sunjata* epic.

184 William Shakespeare, *The Tragedy of Hamlet, Prince of Denmark*. Edited
by T. J. B. Spencer, with an Introduction by Anne Barton. London: Penguin
Books, (1980) (1994) 2002, 89.

185 Seidensticker, '*Peripeteia* and Tragic Dialectic in Euripidean Tragedy', 379.

Chapter 3

1 Van Erp Taalman Kip, *Bokkenzang*, 39–45.

2 P. E. Easterling, 'From repertoire to canon', in: Easterling (ed.), *The
Cambridge Companion to Greek Tragedy*, 211–27. Wolfgang Rösler, *Polis
und Tragödie: Funktionsgeschichtliche Betrachtungen zu einer antiken
Literaturgattung*. Konstanz: Universitätsverlag Konstanz, 1980, 26–30,
discusses several factors and three intrinsic factors that have enabled
Greek tragedy to develop into a universalized and relatively timeless literary
genre – the spread of Hellenism throughout the Mediterranean and the
decontextualization of tragedy, the transition from an oral culture into a
writing culture, tragedy's ties with myth as its main source of contents,
tragedy's lack of clearly visible references to local circumstances and
historical persons, and its reasoning structure of developing an event
through argument and counter-argument. Edith Hall, 'The sociology of
Athenian tragedy', in: Easterling (ed.), *The Cambridge Companion*, 126,
explains tragedy's susceptibility to constant political reinterpretation in
modern theatre in terms of 'the tension, even contradiction, between
tragedy's egalitarian form—a truly democratic art form—and the dominantly
hierarchical world-view of its content'. More on the specific features of
Greek writing culture, Jan Assmann, *Das kulturelle Gedächtnis: Schrift,
Erinnerung und politische Identität in frühen Hochkulturen*. Muenchen:
C. H. Beck, 1992, 259–92.

3 Van Erp Taalman Kip, 'The Unity of the *Oresteia*', 119–38, at 132.

4 Lawrence Danson, *Shakespeare's Dramatic Genres*. Oxford/New York: Oxford University Press, 2000, 4.

5 Easterling, 'A show for Dionysus', 36–53.

6 Steven H. Lonsdale, *Dance and Ritual Play in Greek Religion*. Baltimore, MD/London: The Johns Hopkins University Press, 1993, 44–136, esp. 81.

7 Lonsdale, *Dance and Ritual Play*, 113, 61–9. While Dionysus is primarily associated with dance as a disruptive force, Apollo is associated with dance as an ordering force.

8 Lonsdale, *Dance and Ritual Play*, 67–8.

9 Another way of trying to identify what is 'tragic' about tragedy is by comparing tragedy to satyr play. Easterling, 'A show for Dionysus', 36–53, has made an effort to tackle the question what it was about tragedy as an art form that was particularly Dionysiac.

10 James M. Redfield, *Nature and Culture in the Iliad: The Tragedy of Hector*. Expanded Edition. Durham/London: Durham University Press, 1994, 83.

11 H. Gouhier, *Le théâtre et l'existence*. Paris: J. Vrin, 1997, 132: 'Le rire vient de l'idée de sa propre supériorité. . . . L'exemple classique est celui de l'homme qui tombe. . . . on trouvera au fond de la pensée du rieur un certain orgueil inconscient. C'est là le point de départ: *moi*, je ne tombe pas. . . '. This so-called 'superiority theory' assumes that if we are amused by something, we feel morally superior to it. From Lessing onwards, this approach will be replaced by the 'incongruity theory' of comedy, according to which the comic arises from contradiction, as Taels, 'Laughing Matters', 304, explains.

12 Rosenmeyer, 'Ironies in Serious Drama', 505f.: 'And when Northrop Frye distinguishes between comedy and tragedy—comedy sets up an arbitrary law and then organizes an action to break or evade the law; and tragedy presents the reverse process, of narrowing a relatively free life into a chain of causation—we seem to be looking at ironic descriptions of what happens, in its own ironic way, in the *Phaedo* or the *Timaeus*'.

13 Danson, *Shakespeare's Dramatic Genres*, 86–91.

14 Danson, *Shakespeare's Dramatic Genres*, 8–21. Cf. Alvin Kernan, *Shakespeare, the King's Playwright: Theater in the Stuart Court, 1603–13*. New Haven/London: Yale University Press, 1995, 31: '*Hamlet* is a tragedy of state, the type of play suitable for kings and courts, something worthy the dignity of the occasion and the noble audience'.

15 Danson, *Shakespeare's Dramatic Genres*, 25–9, 139, quotation at 28.

16 William Shakespeare, *The Tragedy of Hamlet, Prince of Denmark*. Edited by T. J. B. Spencer, with an Introduction by Anne Barton. London: Penguin Books, (1980) (1994) 2002, 85.

17 Danson, *Shakespeare's Dramatic Genres*, 19.

18 Redfield, *Nature and Culture in the Iliad*, 39–42.

19 Ibid., 42.

20 Ibid., 42–3.

21 Hall, 'The sociology of Athenian tragedy', 118; 119: 'Certainly by the second half of the fifth century the audiences of tragedy, like those of Shakespeare's day, were trained to appreciate both arguments and counter-arguments and the defence of even seemingly indefensible positions and unconventional points of view. Their mindset, their imagination, was inherently dialogic. A character in a lost Euripidean play said, "if one were good at speaking one could have a competition between two arguments in every case" (fr. 189 N²)'.

22 Goldhill, *Aeschylus*, 17–18.

23 There is one play that focuses on the power of persuasion: Sophocles' *Philoctetes*. According to Simon Goldhill, 'The language of tragedy: rhetoric and communication', in: Easterling (ed.), *The Cambridge Companion*, 141–5, Odysseus is committed to an instrumental view of language, where winning one's case is the only adequate criterion for speech-making – lying and deceit are part and parcel of his rhetorical skills and strategies. Neoptolemus, like his father Achilles, professes a strong distaste for verbal deceit, but is more or less persuaded by Odysseus to lie to Philoctetes.

24 Chapter on narrative aspects, Section 3.2.

25 Philippe Van Haute, 'Antigone, heldin van de psychoanalyse? Lacans lectuur van Antigone', in: E. Berns, P. Moyaert, P. van Tongeren (eds), *De God van denkers en dichters: Opstellen voor Samuel IJsseling*. Amsterdam: Boom, 1997, 172–91, esp. 186ff. In assuming his responsibility, he accepts his past as much as the cursed past of his Labdicide family. Teiresias succeeds in convincing Creon that he is confusing imaginary obedience to a woman (Antigone) with actual obedience to the dead (Polynices). (*Ant* 1068–73) It is as if Teiresias functions as the psychoanalyst that Jacques Lacan hints at in his interpretation, Van Haute suggests. Creon overcomes his fear of losing his masculine identity and assumes his responsibility for what happened. In doing so, Creon assumes a human greatness which Antigone lacks.

26 Burian, 'Myth into *muthos*', 178–208.

27 Burian, 'Myth into *muthos*', 200; 200–1: 'I summarise the scene beginning at line 1146, with particular attention to the thematics of speech. The old shepherd, realising that the garrulous messenger from Corinth may inadvertently reveal the awful secret of Oedipus' origins, *orders* him to be silent. Oedipus *countermands* his order and *threatens* punishment. The shepherd *asks* how he has erred, and Oedipus *reproaches* him for *refusing to tell* about the child of which the messenger has *spoken*. The shepherd attempts to allay Oedipus' suspicion by *alleging* that the messenger is *speaking nonsense*. Oedipus again *threatens* torture, the old man *begs* to be spared, Oedipus *orders* his arms to be twisted. Again Oedipus *asks*, and this time the shepherd *answers*, adding the *wish* that he had died on the day he gave up the baby. Another round of *threats* and *laments* leads to the further *question*, "Where did you get the child?", which the shepherd *evades* by the vague "From someone". To Oedipus' repeated *question*, the shepherd *answers* with a desperate *plea* to *ask* no more. But Oedipus *threatens* his destruction if he must be *asked* again, and he *admits* that the child was from the house of Laius. On the verge of the terrible recognition, Oedipus *asks* the final question, 'A slave, or one born of Laius' own race?' To the shepherd's *lament* that he is now about to *speak* the dread thing itself, Oedipus responds with one of the most memorable lines of the play (line 1170): 'And I to *hear*—but *hear* I must'.

28 Burian, 'Myth into *muthos*', 201. The tragic effect of tragic language has been analysed by M. S. Silk. He argues that on the evidence of Greek and Shakespearean tragedy, tragic language 'is propelled by a small set of irreducible determinants of which three seem to be of special importance: *compulsion, excess, and identity*. In concrete linguistic terms, tragedy tends to foreground *must* and *too* and the *name*'. (M. S. Silk, 'Tragic Language: The Greek Tragedians and Shakespeare', in: Silk (ed.), *Tragedy and the Tragic*, 465).

29 Victor Turner, *From Ritual to Theatre: The Human Seriousness of Play*. New York: PAJ Publications, (1982) pb 1992.

30 Cf. John Milton who writes in his *Areopagitica*: 'Assuredly we bring not innocence into the world, we bring impurity much rather: that which purifies us is trial, and trial is by what is contrary'. One is expected to be able to survive the 'trial' of deciding for oneself the difference between good and evil within the free (uncensored) Protestant scope of an emphasis on the progressive religious revelation achieved through 'trial', Anna Beer, *Milton: Poet, Pamphleteer and Patriot*. London: Bloomsbury, 2008, 171, explains.

31 Bloom, *Hamlet*, 9–11, 33, 55–6, 89–91, too, stresses the importance of theatricality for understanding Hamlet as a character with an actor's proclivities.

32 Jorge Arditi, *A Genealogy of Manners: Transformations of Social Relations in France and England from the Fourteenth to the Eighteenth Century*. Chicago, IL/London: The University of Chicago Press, 1998.

33 Margolies, *Monsters of the Deep*, 44–5.

34 Ibid., 52–6.

35 Brennan, *Shakespeare's Dramatic Structures*, 129–41, esp. 134–5.

36 Lee, *Shakespeare's Hamlet and the Controversies of Self*, 181–3, 199–206. Lee's views will be presented in more detail in the chapter on the psycho-ethical aspects, Part I Section 6.

37 Anthony Gash, 'The Dialogic Self in Hamlet', unpublished manuscript. Gash takes as his starting-point the view that the self is always already situated in a dialogic or dramatic relation to another person or persons, and that Wittgenstein was right in suggesting that our concept of the soul is clarified more by paying attention to our pre-reflective response to other people than by any so-called act of introspection. The Platonic analogy consists in the fact that the practice of dialogue and the new way of conceiving the self (psyche) are presented on a number of occasions as mutually guaranteeing each other.

38 The face-to-face relation between actor and audience, of the actor who looks back at me and in whose eyes I see myself, constitutes a dialogic subject–subject relation. But when I go to a play, Gash argues, I expect it to be staged in terms of a subject–object relation. I expect to see the behaviour of another person which I can identify as this or that, and on the basis of this 'knowledge' I will predict and judge, sympathize or disapprove. In fact, Gash observes, an audience's role in a play is likely to start out as Claudius' practice of spying: 'We'll so bestow ourselves that, seeing unseen,/We may of their encounter frankly judge' (III.i.33–4).

39 Gash (unpublished), 5: 'Hamlet's discourse refuses the symmetry of an "I" who is the mirror image of Guildenstern's implied "you". The subject of his utterances is not himself but his interrogator's language and ultimately the pattern of activity which that language expresses. The very first dialogue in which we encounter Hamlet after he has assumed his "antic disposition" shows the method in miniature: *Polonius:* Do you know me, my lord? (implication: why are you behaving oddly?) *Hamlet:* Excellent well, you are a fishmonger. (answering as if this were an unmotivated question, and thus shifting the focus back to Polonius and the purpose of his questions: fishing) (II.ii.173–4)'. Margolies, *Monsters of the Deep*, 65, offers an equally convincing interpretation of the Fishmonger dialogue based on the key motifs of 'honesty' and 'Polonius daughter' in the same dialogue, 'Hamlet wishes him as honest as a fishmonger. The argument becomes one of form and essence. Formally, it is ridiculous to see Polonius, the Chancellor, as a tradesman. This is part self-indulgent foolery on the part of Hamlet, and part identification of the essential Polonius as a bawd. A fishmonger relates to someone who keeps a stews, either a pond stocked with live fish that can be taken out for the table when desired or, metaphorically, a brothel. Polonius, in controlling the exercise of his daughter's affection for his own ends, is effectively a pimp, and thus fishmonger—but not openly, "honestly" so. The matter of honour signalled in "honest" is seen by Polonius in its formal aspect, his standing, whereas Hamlet is arguing an essentially dishonourable behaviour. Their agreement then is merely formal; at the essential level the differences remain unresolved'.

40 Gash (unpublished), 7.

41 Gash mentions the I-thou relationship between Hamlet and the Ghost ('Remember thee? Ay, thou poor ghost' I.v.95–7), between Hamlet and Yorick's soul behind his skull, and, in a way, between Hamlet and the player with whom he shares the narrative of the tragedy of the Trojan war on the boundary of recorded history. These genuine dialogues have in common, Gash points out, that shared memory is crucial, for it opens up a world of imagination beyond the 'prison of Denmark, the world and the mind' (II.ii.241–55). The dramatic structure of the play depends entirely on the audience knowing about this Other to the world of Elsinore and remembering it, regardless of their (dis)belief in ghosts. Hamlet's talking to a thing, Yorick's skull, is in fact an inversion of the common practice of mutual reification in the semi-dialogues that Hamlet encounters everywhere around him. The different degrees of reification and self-reification range from Osric, who because he is imitating a courtier can himself be mimicked without any remainder, to the infinitely more complex case of Ophelia whose obedience to her corrupt father makes her 'honesty' to Hamlet questionable. The dialogic point of Hamlet's response to Claudius' question 'Where is Polonius?' (IV.iii.31–6) is not, Gash observes, that Polonius is just a corpse, but rather that Claudius is only interested in that aspect of him – instead of being interested in Polonius' soul, that is, in Polonius as a person.

42 Heering, *Tragiek*, 186ff.

43 Heering, *Tragiek*, 79. Cf. Yudhisthira, left behind alone with his dog after the great war, faced with the choice between entrance into heaven without his dog and left on earth with his dog.

44 Palmer, *Tragedy and Tragic Theory*, 120.

45 Palmer, *Tragedy and Tragic Theory*, 129: 'True ambiguity admits no resolution; otherwise, we have only a state of temporary confusion rather than ambiguity. Because the vast majority of theorists discuss the end of tragedy in terms of attraction—the benefit or the source of pleasure—does this mean that we must see tragedy as passing through pain to pleasure or denying pain for pleasure? Only when a play allows the spectator to forget the painful process does the pain cease to color the attractive end. The Greeks, Shakespeare, and most other writers of tragedy include in the final scenes a reminder to reinforce the audience's memory of the element of repulsion. Encouraging this forgetfulness or lapse, as in comedy or melodrama, upsets the attraction/repulsion syndrome'.

46 Palmer, *Tragedy and Tragic Theory*, 137–8.

47 Cf. Noël Carroll, *The Philosophy of Horror or Paradoxes of the Heart*. New York: Routledge, 1990, 59–96.

48 Stephen Halliwell, *Aristotle's Poetics*. Chicago, IL: The University of Chicago Press, (1986) 1998, 350–6.

49 Stephen Halliwell, 'Plato's Repudiation of the Tragic', in: Silk (ed.), *Tragedy and the Tragic*, 332–49, esp. 342–3. According to François Chirpaz, *Le tragique*. Paris: Presses Universitaires de France, 1998, Plato and Aristotle did not want to hear what tragedy wanted to say – that human destiny is a terrible ordeal that man has to endure and cannot master by reason but which, if man is prepared to undergo the experience of intolerable suffering and live through it, will generate real, but hardly reassuring knowledge, the knowledge of understanding oneself as a human being, singular, but forced to accept this limited destiny as all there is to life. Man cannot remove the suffering by his reason (philosophy), but he can express it in words (poetry).

50 Martha C. Nussbaum, *The Fragility of Goodness: Luck and Ethics in Greek Tragedy and Philosophy*. Cambridge: Cambridge University Press, 1986, 378–94.

51   Charles Segal, 'Catharsis, Audience, and Closure in Greek Tragedy', in: Silk (ed.), *Tragedy and the Tragic*, 149–72, at 155.

52   Segal, 'Catharsis, Audience, and Closure in Greek Tragedy', 150–7, 167.

53   Ibid., 149–50.

54   Segal, 'Catharsis, Audience, and Closure in Greek Tragedy', 165: 'Aristotle's word for "humanity" in this sense is *to philanthroopon*, another rather controversial term. It has the specific meaning "moral sentiment" but may also include the wider meaning of "a general feeling of sympathy with our fellow mortals". Aristotle associates *to philanthroopon* closely with pity and fear in one passage (1452b38) and with "the tragic" in general in another (1456a21). This expansion of our sensibilities in compassion for others, I would suggest, is also part of the tragic catharsis. The most striking example of this broad sympathy in extant tragedy is Aeschylus' *Persians*, our earliest preserved play (472 BC), which re-creates in the theatre of the Athenians the tearful and pitiable suffering of their recently defeated enemies and invaders, the Persian king Xerxes and his army and family. This play foreshadows the reaching-out to the defeated and degraded hero, some fifty years later, in the endings of Sophocles' *Oedipus Tyrannus* or Euripides' *Heracles*'.

55   Margolies, *Monsters of the Deep*, 152–3.

56   Ibid., 153.

57   States, *Hamlet and the Concept of Character*, 44, 48, 21.

58   Ewans, 'Patterns of Tragedy in Sophocles and Shakespeare', 438–57, at 441; Watson, 'Tragedies of revenge and ambition', 160–81.

59   Segal, 'Catharsis, Audience, and Closure in Greek Tragedy', 150. On 162–3, Segal goes one step further by introducing a tension between a sense of 'closure' on the emotional level of theatrical experience and a sense of 'anti-closure' on the intellectual level of detached reflection. For Easterling, this introduction of a tension is one step too far.

60   Segal, 'Catharsis, Audience, and Closure in Greek Tragedy', 159.

61   Ibid., 158–9.

62   Shakespeare, *The Tragedy of Hamlet*. Ed. Spencer, 228.

63   P. E. Easterling, 'Weeping, Witnessing, and the Tragic Audience: Response to Segal', in: Silk (ed.), *Tragedy and the Tragic*, 173–81.

64   Easterling, 'Weeping, Witnessing, and the Tragic Audience', 177–8.

65   Easterling, 'Weeping, Witnessing, and the Tragic Audience', 178; Segal, 'Catharsis, Audience, and Closure in Greek Tragedy', 163.

66   Levin, *The Question of Hamlet*, 42. Bloom, *Hamlet*, 18, relativizes this observation when he points out the ironic discrepancy between Horatio's hope for an angelic chorus and a drum sounding its beat, a march of Norwegian soldiers replacing the wistful flights of angels.

67   Halliwell, *Aristotle's* Poetics, 350–2.

68 Shakespeare, *The Tragedy of Hamlet*. Ed. Spencer, 94.

69 In the Player's Speech, Hamlet 'rediscovers his own plight in the verbal painting. . . . The narrator, pious Aeneas, recalls him to his filial duty. The King his father, like Priam, has been slaughtered. The Queen his mother, ironically unlike Hecuba, refuses to play the part of the mourning wife'. (Levin, *The Question of Hamlet*, 147).

70 Levin, *The Question of Hamlet*, 151; 157: 'The Elizabethan conception of art as the gloss of nature was ethical rather than realistic; for it assumed that, by contemplating situations which reflected their own, men and women could mend their ways and act with greater resolution thereafter'. On 157–60, Levin argues that Shakespeare plays with the ambiguity of the verb 'to act', which alternates between 'doing' and 'seeming'.

71 Shakespeare, *The Tragedy of Hamlet*. Ed. Spencer, 89.

72 Gash (unpublished), 22–3.

73 Klaus K. Klostermaier, *A Survey of Hinduism*. Albany, NY: State University of New York Press, 1989, 62: '*Śruti* may be commented upon but can never be questioned. Its authority is undebatable. In theological debates, discussion is carried on only for the purpose of establishing the meaning of *Śruti*'. Cf. Gavin Flood, 'Sacred Writings', in: Paul Bowen (ed.), *Themes and Issues in Hinduism*. London/Washington: Cassell, 1998, 141: 'The vehicle of philosophical inquiry is almost always dialogue through a commentary on an authoritative text—the *Śruti* literature or some *smrti* literature, most notably the *Bhagavadgītā* and the *Brahma-sūtras*'. See also Lipner, *Hindus*, 23–194; Kim Knott, *Hinduism: A Very Short Introduction*. Oxford/New York: Oxford University Press, 1998, 13–26.

74 Lipner, *Hindus*, 74–6.

75 Cf. P. L. Vaidya, 'The *Mahābhārata*: Its History and Character', in: *The Cultural Heritage of India. Vol. II: Itihāsas, purāṇas, dharma and other Śāstras*. Calcutta: The Ramakrishna Mission Institute of Culture, 1953–62, 66, quoting *Mahābhārata* 1.56.33 ('whatever is here may be found elsewhere; but what is not here cannot be elsewhere'), a statement by Vaiśampāyana who is about to tell king Janamejaya the epic story and introduces it in these terms.

76 D. P. Chattopadhyaya, *Ways of Understanding the Human Past: Mythic, Epic, Scientific and Historic*. New Delhi: Centre for Studies in Civilizations, 2001, 24.

77 Gary A. Tubb, 'Śāntarasa in the *Mahābhārata*', in: Sharma (ed.), *Essays on the Mahābhārata*, 175.

78 Indira V. Peterson, 'Arjuna's Combat with the *Kirāta: Rasa and bhakti in Bhāravi's Kirātārjuniya*', in: Sharma (ed.), *Essays on the Mahābhārata*, 213 note 4.

79 Susan L. Schwartz, *Rasa: Performing the Divine in India*. New York: Columbia University Press, 2004, 4–5.

80 Shyamala Gupta, *Art, Beauty, and Creativity: Indian and Western Aesthetics*. New Delhi: D. K. Printworld, 1999, 5–66. On 32–3, Gupta points out that Bharata Muni's theory of *rasa* was meant to distinguish between

different dramatic genres, not between different literary genres. In the
history of Indian aesthetics, it became part not so much of the scholarly
debate on drama, but much more of that on language and poetry.

81 Daniel H. H. Ingalls, 'General Introduction, Sanskrit Poetry and Sanskrit
    Poetics', in: Daniel H. H. Ingalls (ed.), *An Anthology of Sanskrit Poetry:
    Vidyākara's 'Subhāshitaratnakośa'*. Cambridge, MA: Harvard University
    Press, 1965, 14.

82 Cf. Aristotle's sense of relative distance between audience and dramatic
    characters. Gupta, *Art, Beauty, and Creativity*, 48–9, explains that Bhatta
    Nāyaka had introduced the notion of 'generalization' (*bhāvakatva*) as
    the second function of words, and the power of generalization as the
    most important function of poetic language, 'the love of Rāma for Sītā
    . . . represents love in general without any reference to agent or object;
    rasa is an experience of grasping the generalized forms of emotions and
    feelings expressed by characters in drama and poetry who also represent
    the class of human beings in general'. Abhinavagupta (born 960 CE) later
    maintains in his own theory of 'universal sympathy' (sādharanīkarana) that
    the individual spectator or reader is 'a person gifted with the capacity to
    identify himself with the generalized emotions, on account of the latent
    impression of these emotions in his mind'. (Gupta, *Art, Beauty, and
    Creativity*, 52.) 'Those who have not experienced the feeling of love, for
    instance, and have consequently no impressions of experience left in them,
    as well as those who have no sense of community of human feelings, can
    never enjoy *rasa*'. (Gupta, *Art, Beauty, and Creativity*, 57; cf. 56.)

83 Schwartz, *Rasa*, 7–10, 23.

84 Tubb, 'Śāntarasa in the *Mahābhārata*', 171.

85 Gupta, *Art, Beauty, and Creativity*, 65.

86 Cf. Gupta, *Art, Beauty, and Creativity*, 58.

87 Chantal Maillard, 'The Aesthetic Pleasure of Tragedy in Western and Indian
    Thought', in: Mazhar Hussain, Robert Wilkinson (eds), *The Pursuit of
    Comparative Aesthetics: An Interface between East and West*. Aldershot/
    Burlington: Ashgate, 2006, 29–38, esp. 36–7.

88 Anand Amaladass, *Philosophical Implications of Dhvani: Experience of
    Symbol Language in Indian Aesthetics*. Institut für Indologie der Universität
    Wien, Sammlung De Nobili. Vienna: Gerold & Co, 1984, 79.

89 Gupta, *Art, Beauty, and Creativity*, 60–3.

90 Amaladass, *Philosophical Implications of Dhvani*, 121: 'In *rasa*-experience
    the external world, the *vyanjaka* (evoker, LM), evokes and at the same time
    controls, focuses and specifies the type of response in the experiencer.
    Rasa is a result of a dialogue between the reality outside and the actively
    responding experiencer'.

91 Amaladass, *Philosophical Implications of Dhvani*, 120.

92 The only criterion for *rasadhvani* is whether a sensitive poet or reader
    would consider a *dhvani*-interpretation significant or insignificant,

appropriate or inappropriate, adequate or inadequate, comparable to what the taste of wine tastes like to a connoisseur (*rasika*), a wine-taster who has a taste for wine. Anandavardhana makes a comparison with a connoisseur of music. (Amaladass, *Philosophical Implications of Dhvani*, 112–18, 193–4).

93 Translation by Tubb, 'Śāntarasa in the *Mahābhārata*', 175–6; see also trans. K. Krishnamoorthy, *Dhvanyāloka of Anandavardhana*. Critical edition with introduction, translation and notes. Dharwar, 1974, 275; trans. Daniel H. H. Ingalls (ed.), *The* Dhvanyāloka *of Anandavardhana: With the* Locana *of Abhinavagupta*. Translated by Daniel H. H. Ingalls, Jeffrey M. Masson, and M. V. Patwardhan. Cambridge, MA/London: Harvard University Press, 1990, 690; Amaladass, *Philosophical Implications of Dhvani*, 195.

94 Ingalls, 'General Introduction', 16.

95 *Dhvanyāloka* IV.5, quoted by Amaladass, *Philosophical Implications of Dhvani*, 168. See also trans. Krishnamoorthy, *Dhvanyāloka of Anandavardhana*, 276–7; trans. Ingalls, *The* Dhvanyāloka *of Anandavardhana*, 691–2. Cf. another passage, trans. Tubb, 'Śāntarasa in the *Mahābhārata*', 176: 'Likewise in the *Mahābhārata*, which has the beauty of a *kāvya* [poem] while being in the form of a *Śāstra* [treatise], the great sage [Vyāsa] has demonstrated that the creation of dispassion is the principal purport of his work, by composing a conclusion that produces a despondent feeling in response to the sorry end of the Vrshnis and the Pāndavas, and in doing so he has suggested that what he intended as the principal subject of his poem is the peaceful flavor [*shāntarasa*] and the human aim characterized by liberation [*moksha*]'. See also trans. Krishnamoorthy, *Dhvanyāloka of Anandavardhana*, 274–9; trans. Ingalls, *The* Dhvanyāloka *of Anandavardhana*, 690–3.

96 Tubb, 'Śāntarasa in the *Mahābhārata*', 184–5.

97 Ibid., 198.

98 Ibid., 172.

99 Amaladass, *Philosophical Implications of Dhvani*, 167.

100 Lyne Bansat-Boudon, *Pourquoi le théâtre? La réponse indienne*. Paris: Mille et une nuits, Librairie Arthème Fayard, 2004, 11. Cf. Schwartz, *Rasa*, 22.

101 Schwartz, *Rasa*, 22, 26–33.

102 Cf. also Catherine A. Robinson, *Interpretations of the* Bhagavad-Gītā *and Images of the Hindu Tradition: The Song of the Lord*. London/New York: Routledge, 2006.

103 Lipner, *Hindus*, 141f.

104 Richard Schechner, *Between Theater and Anthropology*. Philadelphia, PA: University of Pennsylvania Press, 1985, 117–211.

105 Freda Matchett, Krsna: Lord or Avatāra? The Relationship between Krsna and Visnu in the context of the avatāra myth as presented by the Harivamśa, the Visnupurāna and the Bhāgavata-purāna. Richmond, Surrey: Curzon Press, 2001, 4: 'Whereas Christians have been reluctant to use words like "appearance" or "manifestation" of their incarnate Lord, such ideas are implicit in the term avatāra, since it has associations with the theatre (rangāvatarana, "entering on the stage", is a word for the acting profession; rangāvatāraka is an actor). The avatāra is God appearing upon the world's stage, having descended from the highest level of reality to that of the trailokya (the triple world of devas, asuras and human beings) in order to perform some beneficial action, notably the restoration of the socio-cosmic order (dharma)'.

106 Cf. Bettina Bäumer, *Schöpfung als Spiel: Der Begriff līlā im Hinduismus, seine philosophische und theologische Deutung.* München: UNI-Druck, 1969; Matchett, *Krsna: Lord or Avatāra?*, 150–74. I would suggest that, on the one hand, Hindu theism is more occupied with establishing eye-contact with the gods through their images (*darshan*) and is in that respect more concrete than Western theism; on the other hand, Hindu theism is more abstract in its focus on ultimate liberation. Van Bijlert adds a personal observation on the notion of 'Hindu theism', 'Theism in Hinduism seems to be an instrument of ultimate liberation, not some absolute article of faith. Devotion to God is instrumental as is the belief in a God. Hindus can do without God if God is no longer necessary'.

107 Katz, *Arjuna in the Mahābhārata*, 215.

108 Madeleine Biardeau, *Etudes de mythologie hindoue. Vol. II: Bhakti et avatāra.* Paris/Pondichéry: Ecole française d'Extrême-Orient, 1994, 150–5, 271–85.

109 Hill, *Fate, Predestination and Human Action in the Mahabharata*, 147–52.

110 Hiltebeitel, *The Ritual of Battle*, 256ff.

111 Hiltebeitel, *The Ritual of Battle*, 257–9; cf. 167ff., 231f., 258–9: In *Mārkandeya Purāna* 5, the god Indra loses his physical force because he commits the sinful breaking of a 'friendship or warrior pact' with the demon Vrtra whom he slays.

112 Alf Hiltebeitel, 'Brothers, friends, and charioteers: Parallel episodes in the Irish and Indian epics', in: Edgar C. Polomé (ed.), *Homage to Georges Dumézil. Journal of Indo-European Studies.* Monograph 3 (1982), 85–111, esp. 88, 91–7.

113 Hiltebeitel, 'Brothers, friends, and charioteers', 92–3.

114 Ibid., 94, 97–9.

115 Hiltebeitel, *The Ritual of Battle*, 256f.

116 Ralph Marc Steinmann, *Guru-śishya-sambandha: Das Meister-Schüler-Verhältnis im traditionellen und modernen Hinduismus.* Stuttgart: Steiner Verlag Wiesbaden GMBH, 1986, 46–59, quotation at 278.

117 For explicit references, for example: *Chāndogya-Upanishad* 6.9, 6.12.

118 Steinmann, *Guru-śishya-sambandha*, 59–73, 279.

119 Axel Michaels, *Der Hinduismus. Geschichte und Gegenwart.* München: C. H. Beck, 1998, 101 (trans. into Engl. *Hinduism: Past and Present.* Princeton, NJ/Oxford: Princeton University Press, 2004, 87).

120 Steinmann, *Guru-śishya-sambandha*, 76, 280.

121 *Taittirīya-Upanishad* 1.11.2.

122 Steinmann, *Guru-śishya-sambandha*, 77–91.

123 Ibid., 80.

124 Cf. Steinmann, *Guru-śishya-sambandha*, 280.

125 *The Bhagavad Gītā*, trans. Sargeant, 202–3; cf. *Gītā* 18.67.

126 *The Bhagavad Gītā*, trans. Sargeant, 495.

127 Dermot Killingley, 'Enjoying the World: Desire (kāma) & the Bhagavadgītā', in: Julius J. Lipner (ed.), *The Bhagavad Gītā for our times*. New Delhi: Oxford University Press, 2000, 74: 'In Arjuna's case, Krishna returns his love by instructing him (10.1)'.

128 *The Bhagavad Gītā*, trans. Sargeant, 493–4.

129 Cf. on Arjuna's questioning: Angelika Malinar, *Rājavidyā. Das königliche Wissen um Herrschaft und Verzicht. Studien zur Bhagavadgītā*. Wiesbaden: Harrassowitz Verlag, 1996, 145–6.

130 Cf. Biardeau, *Le Mahābhārata*, Vol. I, 149: 'ce long dialogue quasi socratique, où Arjuna pose des questions et ne discute pas les réponses'.

131 Personal communication, Summer 2008.

132 Doniger, *The Implied Spider*, 12. One is reminded of Redfield, *Nature and Culture in the Iliad*, 41: 'Mythological solutions do not answer questions; they merely set them aside by shifting them to a level at which they cannot be answered. For this reason mythological answers cannot survive criticism; they presume, rather, the absence of criticism'.

133 Gregory D. Alles, *The* Iliad, *the* Rāmāyana, *and the Work of Religion: Failed Persuasion and Religious Mystification*. University Park, PA: The Pennsylvania State University Press, 1994, esp. 77–106; Gregory D. Alles, 'Verbal Craft and Religious Act in the *Iliad*: The Dynamics of a Communal Centre', in: *Religion* 18 (1988), 293–309; Gregory D. Alles, 'Surface, Space, and Intention: The Parthenon and the Kandariya Mahadeva', in: *History of Religions* 28 (1988–89), 1–36.

134 Alles, 'Verbal Craft and Religious Act in the *Iliad*', 297.

135 Ibid., 298.

136 It is, if one goes by texts like *Gītā* 18.61: 'The Lord abides in the hearts of all beings, Arjuna, causing all beings to revolve, by the power of illusion, as if fixed on a machine'. What that implies was already made explicit in 18.59–60: 'If, filled with egoism, you think, "I shall not fight", your resolve will be in vain; your own material nature (*prakrti*) will compel you. What you wish (*icchasi*) not to do, through delusion (*moha*), you shall do that against your will (*avaśas*, without will, against will, willy-nilly), Arjuna, bound by your own *karma*, born of your own nature (*svabhāvajena*)'.

137 Christopher Gill would call Krishna's gesture an invitation to 'second-order reasoning' an invitation to reflect before making a reflective choice.

138 David Damrosch, *What Is World Literature?* Princeton, NJ/Oxford: Princeton University Press, 2003, 4–5, takes 'world literature to encompass all literary works that circulate beyond their culture of origin, either in translation or in their original language'. He claims that 'world literature is not an infinite, ungraspable canon of works but rather a mode of circulation and of reading'. Cf. also his *How to Read World Literature*. Oxford: Wiley-Blackwell, 2009.

139 V. S. Sukthankar, *On the Meaning of the Mahābhārata*. (Bombay: The Asiatic Society of Bombay, 1957) Delhi: Motilal Banarsidass, 1998, 93–8.

140 Trans. Sarvepalli Radhakrishnan, *The Principal Upanishads*. London: George Allen and Unwin, 1953, 623–4. Hiltebeitel, 'Brothers, friends, and charioteers', 92, points out that in *Mahābhārata* 3.202.21–3, the soul is itself the charioteer.

141 Elizabeth A. Schiltz, 'Two Chariots: The Justification of the Best Life in the *Katha Upanishad* and Plato's *Phaedrus*', in: *Philosophy East and West* 56/3 (July 2006), 451–68.

142 Sukthankar, *On the Meaning of the Mahābhārata*, 99–100.

143 *The Bhagavad Gītā*, trans. Sargeant, 277.

144 Sukthankar, *On the Meaning of the Mahābhārata*, 100–1, 105.

145 Sukthankar, *On the Meaning of the Mahābhārata*, 103–8. On page 112, he also offers his answer to the question whether the *Gītā*'s plot fits in convincingly into the epic plot pattern as a whole. One reason why it does not fit in is the unrealistic character of the main scene which the *Gītā* depicts, of the charioteer teaching philosophy for eighteen chapters on the battlefield to the main warrior while the battle is about to start, 'A bizarre picture it seems, if we see in it only a warrior and his charioteer seated in their war-chariot occupying the centre of the battlefield and conversing about *Prakrti* and *Purusha*, *Sāmkhya* and *Yoga* and what not, when they ought to be discussing plans of war and questions of strategy. The grotesqueness of the scene vanishes, however, the moment we remove their masks and see who the persons participating in the discussion are. The key symbol is the chariot, a symbol which occurs in the *Upanishads*, in the *Mahābhārata*, and even in the dialogues of Plato. In the *Upanishads* the individual soul is described as the rider in the chariot of the body, while *Buddhi* is the charioteer. This has been improved upon in the *Gītā*, where the individual soul is still the rider, but the role of the charioteer has been taken over by the Supreme Self, who is beyond *Buddhi*, symbolized here as Bhagavān Śrī Krishna. This, as far as I can judge, is the only way of explaining the introduction of a lengthy philosophical discourse on the battlefield, just prior to the commencement of hostilities, which would otherwise remain a grotesque absurdity. . . . The precise spot selected in the poem for the discourse is also not without significance. Man is for ever poised between two opposing tendencies, between the up-going creative process (*pravrtti*) and the down-going destructive process (*nivrtti*), and he has to make his choice between them. When the perplexed mind knows not where duty lies, the self has only to commune with his own Self, since true knowledge in these matters is to be found within the self'.

146 Hiltebeitel, *Rethinking the Mahābhārata*, 215–39, esp. 218–19, 232–3.

147 Ibid., 233, 235.

148 Kees W. Bolle, *The Bhagavadgītā: A New Translation*. Berkeley, CA/Los Angeles: University of California Press, 1979, 256–7.

149 David R. Kinsley, *The Sword and the Flute: Kālī and Krishna, Dark Visions of the Terrible and the Sublime in Hindu Mythology*. (Berkeley, CA/Los Angeles: University of California Press, 1975) Delhi: Motilal Banarsidass Publishers, 1995, 65. Jayant Lele, 'The *Bhakti* Movement in India: A Critical Introduction', in: Jayant Lele (ed.), *Tradition and Modernity in Bhakti Movements*. Leiden: E. J. Brill, 1981, 13, comments on Kinsley's views.

150 Romila Thapar, *A History of India*. Vol. I. (1966) New Delhi: Penguin Books, (1990) 2000,[12] 109–35.

151 Matchett, *Krsna: Lord or Avatāra?*, 15–16, writes: 'The idea of a deity who embraces such values accords well with the democratization of religion brought about by the development of *bhakti* between the time of the Mauryas and that of the Guptas (roughly 200 BCE-300 CE). The Krsna of the *Gītā* had already declared that "women, *vaiśyas*, even *śūdras*" (*striyo vaiśyās tathā śūdrās*, BhG 9.32) were eligible to be his worshippers. Now in the *Harivamśa* Krsna himself lives as a young *vaiśya*, even though he is a *ksatriya* by birth. This marks the culmination of the process which Dandekar calls "the Krsnaisation of Visnu". From now on the image of the young cowherd dominates the Vaisnava imagination more and more. The *Bhagavadgītā* as the teaching of the *ksatriya* sage remains influential. But at the level of the imagination and the emotions it is Rāma who comes to be seen as God's representative in *ksatriya* terms. The figure of Krsna gains a more universal appeal than this, by incorporating *vaiśya* as well as *ksatriya* elements into his story'.

152 Although I tend to agree with Palmer that the more expansive epic form dissipates the simultaneity of constant attraction and repulsion – in my view primarily because Rosset's 'tragic mechanism' is clearly lacking, a lack which allows for arbitrary and sudden turns of events – I do not mean to deny that the plot pattern asserts both that virtue exists and that it is inadequate to happiness (Redfield's Aristotle-interpretation). Dialectic reversal does not play a part in the plot, however. It is not because of Rāma's actions backfiring at him but despite his actions that disaster prevails. Except for two crucial actions, that is, which are not presented as tragic choices. After having killed Ravana and liberated Sītā, Rāma is no longer separated from his wife. But his warrior code of honour forces him to wittingly ignore his feelings and to repudiate his wife twice for having lived in the harem of Ravana. These are moments where virtuous actions themselves (either Rāma's or Sītā's or both) lead to personal unhappiness. Sītā's personal innocence is of no avail. What counts are not their personal characters or their intentions, but the results of their actions. What counts is Sītā's objective trial by fire of innocence and her strict obedience to her husband. Within the frame of the plot, these proofs of integrity do not outweigh Ravana's objective infringement on her reputation – although they could have done so.

153 Keijo Virtanen, 'The Concept of Purification in the Greek and Indian Theories of Drama', in: Mazhar Hussain, Robert Wilkinson (eds), *The Pursuit of Comparative Aesthetics: An Interface between East and West*. Aldershot/ Burlington: Ashgate, 2006, 55–84, esp. 62.

154 Virtanen, 'The Concept of Purification', 74–7.

155 Edwin Gerow, 'Rasa and Katharsis: A Comparative Study, Aided by Several Films', in: *Journal of the American Oriental Society* 122/2 (April–June, 2002), 264–77, starts from the intimate connection between the intrinsic meanings or messages of works of art and their ends or purposes for the world outside. The Aristotelian link to the world outside the play, he argues, is not referential (by imitation) but functional (by symbolization). Poetry is not functional in the way carpentry is, being merely useful and immediately applicable, but in the way philosophy is, offering insight into human nature.

156 Gerow, 'Rasa and Katharsis', 266.

157 Ibid.

158 Schechner, *Between Theater and Anthropology*, 141: 'This view of the difference between causal chains and braided relations also helps explain why Western theater develops from crises that are then the business of the performance to resolve, while Sanskrit drama, and much contemporary Indian theater, "doesn't go anywhere". It's not supposed to go anywhere; it's not a "development-resolution" kind of drama but an expository, synaesthetic, and playful set of variations much more akin to the Indian raga system of music than to anything Aristotelian'.

159 Gerow, 'Rasa and Katharsis', 267.

160 Shubha Pathak, 'Why Do Displaced Kings Become Poets in the Sanskrit Epics? Modeling *Dharma* in the Affirmative *Rāmāyana* and the Interrogative *Mahābhārata*', in: *Hindu Studies* 10 (2006), 127–49.

161 Cf. Charles Taylor, *Sources of the Self: The Making of the Modern Identity*. Cambridge, MA: Harvard University Press, 1989, 127–42, esp. 134.

162 Taylor, *Sources of the Self*, 111ff.

Chapter 4

1 Georg Friedrich Wilhelm Hegel, *Phänomenologie des Geistes*, (1807) ed. E. Moldenhauer, K. M. Michel. Frankfurt a/M: Suhrkamp, 1986, 327–59 ('Der wahre Geist. Die Sittlichkeit'), 529–44 ('Das geistige Kunstwerk'). Cf. Renée van Riessen, *Antigone's bruidsvertrek: De plaats van de* Antigone *in Hegels denken over de vrouw*. Kampen: Kok, 1986.

2 George Steiner, *Antigones*. Oxford: Clarendon Press, 1984, 12–18, 31–5; Van Riessen, *Antigone's bruidsvertrek*, 20.

3 One duty opposes another, divine law opposes human law, piety opposes blasphemy, customs oppose legislature, inner imperative opposes outer law, testing the law through knowledge and reasoning opposes tyrannical wilfulness turned into arbitrary law, defiance opposes obedience, political crime opposes political punishment, rights of the dead and death oppose rights of the living and life. Moreover, the family opposes the state, the private hearth opposes the public forum, the particular opposes the universal, the woman opposes the man, the feminine opposes the masculine, natural opposes artificial, unconscious opposes conscious, the folk-world opposes the ruling elite, sisterhood opposes other blood ties such as parenthood, existence (being) opposes action, passivity opposes fight (struggle, war, *agon*), night time opposes daytime, immediacy opposes the distance of reason.

4 In fact, in a move towards self-fulfilment, Antigone acts out her potential for conflict. In Steiner's close paraphrasing of Hegel's thought and vocabulary (Steiner, *Antigones*, 30), Hegel argues that Antigone, willingly and fully conscious of what she is doing, defies Creon's law, suggesting that Creon's law is as much the blasphemous expression of tyrannical wilfulness and arbitrariness instead of universal rationality and morality, as Antigone's defiance of the law is the testing of the law through the blasphemy or sin of knowing, which reasons itself free from the law.

5 Steiner, *Antigones*, 34–5.

6 Ibid., 36–42.

7 Paul Cartledge, ' "Deep plays": theatre as process in Greek civic life', in: Easterling (ed.), *The Cambridge Companion to Greek Tragedy*, 3–35, quotation at 18.

8 Cartledge, 'Deep plays', 19–22.

9 Joseph M. Bryant, *Moral Codes and Social Structure in Ancient Greece: A Sociology of Greek Ethics from Homer to the Epicureans and Stoics*. Albany, NY: State University of New York Press, 1996, 69–72 and 119 (!); Jan Assmann, *Ägypten: Eine Sinngeschichte*. München/Wien: Carl Hanser Verlag, 1996, 152: 'Der ägyptische Begriff des *zoon politikon* ist von dem griechisch-antiken vor allem darin unterschieden, dass er weniger eine Fähigkeit zur, als vielmehr eine Angewiesenheit auf Gemeinschaft bezeichnet'.

10 Cartledge, 'Deep plays', 31.

11 On the worldwide phenomenon of city states and city state cultures and on Greek city-states in particular, see Mogens Herman Hansen and Frits Naerebout, *Stad en Staat: De antiek-Griekse* poleis *en andere stadstaatculturen*. Amsterdam: Amsterdam University Press – Salomé, 2006.

12 Nicole Loraux, *La voix endeuillée: Essai sur la tragédie grecque*. Paris: Gallimard, 1999.

13 Simon Goldhill, 'The audience of Athenian tragedy', in: Easterling (ed.), *The Cambridge Companion*, 54–68, quotation at 54.

14 Rainer Friedrich, 'Everything to Do with Dionysos? Ritualism, the Dionysiac, and the Tragic', in: Silk (ed.), *Tragedy and the Tragic*, 257–83, at 266. Joseph Rykwert, *The Seduction of Place: The City in the Twenty-First Century*. London: Weidenfels & Nicholson, 2000, 5, points out that 'the Greeks, who used the word *polis* for the city, used the very same word for a dice-and-boardgame that, rather like backgammon, depends on an interplay of chance and rule. The players' skill is shown by the way they improvise on the rule after every throw of the dice. If the analogy works', Rykwert argues, 'it would follow that we are agents as well as patients in the matter of our cities'.

15 Wolfgang Rösler, *Polis und Tragödie: Funktionsgeschichtliche Betrachtungen zu einer antiken Literaturgattung*. Konstanz: Universitätsverlag Konstanz, 1980, 8–23.

16 Cartledge, 'Deep plays', 22.

17 Heinrich Kuch, 'Gesellschaftliche Voraussetzungen und Sujet der Griechischen Tragödie', in: Heinrich Kuch (ed.), *Die griechische Tragödie in ihrer gesellschaftlichen Funktion*. Berlin: Akademie Verlag, 1983, 11–39.

18 Hall, 'The Sociology of Athenian tragedy', 93–126.

19 Ibid., 100–1.

20 Kuch, 'Gesellschaftliche Voraussetzungen', 37–8; Rösler, *Polis und Tragödie*, 25–6.

21 Spiro Kostof, *The City Shaped: Urban Patterns and Meanings Through History*. London: Thames and Hudson, (1991, pb 1999) 2001, 48.

22 Rebecca Bushnell, 'The Fall of Princes: The Classical and Medieval Roots of English Renaissance Tragedy', in: Rebecca Bushnell (ed.), *A Companion to Tragedy*. Oxford: Blackwell Publishing, 2005, 293–5, 300–1.

23 Dominic Shellard, *William Shakespeare*. London: The British Library/New York: Oxford University Press, 1998, 34.

24 Quoted from Edmund K. Chambers, *The Elizabethan Stage*. London: Oxford University Press, 1923, Vol. IV, 263.

25 Shellard, *William Shakespeare*, 34.

26 Ibid., 63–5.

27 Kernan, *Shakespeare, the King's Playwright*, 2.

28 Ibid., 9–10.

29 Steiner, *The Death of Tragedy*, 115–18.

30 'Toward the end of Elizabeth's reign', Kernan, *Shakespeare, the King's Playwright*, 10–11, explains, 'there was in England a Stuart party led by the earl of Essex that was pushing James VI, Stuart king of the Scots, as the successor Elizabeth stubbornly refused to name. In 1601, desperate at the loss of favor and income, (the earl of) Essex launched an abortive rebellion. His chief lieutenant was the earl of Southhampton, who was also Shakespeare's patron, . . . the person to whom Shakespeare's two erotic poems, *The Rape of Lucrece* and *Venus and Adonis*, were humbly dedicated. On the eve of the Essex rebellion, at the request of several members of the conspiracy', the Lord Chamberlain's Men staged in the Globe theatre 'his *Richard II* with its famous deposition scene, showing that despite Richard's stage protestations, "all the water in the rough rude sea" could actually "wash the balm off from an anointed king" (cf. III.ii.254–5). The censor had removed the deposition scene from the contemporary printed version, and its performance was clearly a treacherous act'. Queen Elizabeth later articulated her rage, pointing out to William Lambarde, 'I am Richard II, know ye not that?' Those involved were examined sharply. The players were exonerated from treason. The Earl of Essex went to the block, and the Earl of Southhampton was confined to the Tower, and released after James VI of Scotland had finally become the new Stuart king, James I of England in 1603.

31 Kernan, *Shakespeare, the King's Playwright*, xv–xvii.

32 Ibid., xx–xxi.

33 Ibid., 13.

34 Michael Hattaway, 'Tragedy and Political Authority', in: Cleare McEachern (ed.), *The Cambridge Companion to Shakespearean Tragedy*, Cambridge: Cambridge University Press, 2002, 103–22, esp. 104.

35 Cartledge, 'Deep plays', 5–8.

36 Seaford, 'Something to Do with Dionysos', 284–94, esp. 288–9.

37 Hendrik S. Versnel, *Inconsistencies in Greek and Roman religion. Vol. I: Ter Unus: Isis, Dionysos, Hermes: Three Studies in Henotheism*. Leiden: E. J. Brill, 1990, 36–7.

38 Seaford, 'Something to Do with Dionysos', 291–3.

39 Cartledge, 'Deep plays', 6.

40 Huston Diehl, 'Religion and Shakespearean Tragedy', in: Claire McEachern (ed.), *The Cambridge Companion to Shakespearean Tragedy*. Cambridge: Cambridge University Press, 2002, 86–102, quotation at 101. Note the tragic or ironic twist: Claudius turns out to be incapable of a remorse that restores the tragic sufferer to a condition of grace – a very un-Romantic approach to remorse, Steiner observes. (Steiner, *The Death of Tragedy*, 127–36, esp. 129.) Cf. Marlowe's *Dido*.

41 Watson, 'Tragedies of revenge and ambition', 160–81, quotation at 174.

42 Niccolò Machiavelli, *The Prince*. Translated with an introduction by George Bull. Harmondsworth: Penguin Books, 1982.

43 Hattaway, 'Tragedy and Political Authority', 106–10, quotations at 106 and 110.

44 Hattaway, 'Tragedy and Political Authority', 111–12.

45 Steven Shankman, Stephen Durrant, *The Siren and the Sage: Knowledge and Wisdom in Ancient Greece and China*. London/New York: Cassell, 2000, 19–48.

46   John D. B. Hamilton, 'Antigone: Kinship, Justice, and the Polis', in: Dora C. Pozzi, John M. Wickersham (eds), *Myth and the Polis*. Ithaca, NY/London: Cornell University Press, 1991, 86–98. The family is represented not just by the word *oikos* ('house'), but by the word *genos* ('lineage'), and this word, Hamilton contends, was already anachronistic in the fifth century. Yet, tragedy, no less than epic, was constantly showing royal lineages of the most undemocratic sort. Antigone, carrying out funeral rites for her brother, is acting as a kinswoman. But her ritual performance is not only that of a woman. She does both the mourning (the women's part) and the burial (the men's part), and her ritual contains the overtones of the epic funeral (cf. Patroclus' funeral in Homer's *Iliad*), that is to say, Antigone performs the function of the woman and warrior at once. This creates a conflict, or rather, a contest (*agōn*) between her and Creon, whereas Antigone's scale of affection in her valediction speech (905–12) indicates her closeness to her brother ('brother', *adelphos*, 'from the same womb') and her qualification as the one suppliant on behalf of her brother who is in a position to persuade Creon to give up his own stubborn position. Antigone's name reveals her function. *Anti-* can mean 'opposed to' *or* 'in compensation for'. The *gen-/gon-* is cognate with *genos* ('lineage') and *gonē* can even mean 'womb'. Antigone's action validates kinship based on the womb in compensation for its being dishonoured – she restores an equilibrium of honour to 'those from the same womb' (*autadelphoi*). The *polis* approves of her and honours her for it. On the other hand, Antigone is indifferent to Haimon, chooses virginity in death, opposes the massive burial associated with the funerals of the royal lineages, in short, opposes the bloodlines. In doing both, Hamilton argues, Antigone is an image of equilibrium and justice, but she also puts all women in their proper ritual place within the new *polis* and proclaims the power of the womb. We know that the legislation of Solon and Cleisthenes sets limits on funeral rites, having them take place indoors. This deliberate domestication might suggest that the *polis* destroyed the old aristocratic ways, but is it not just as plausible that the *polis* slowly integrated them into its own life? Rituals for the dead were not suppressed; they became 'familial'. While Aeschylus' *Seven against Thebes* had shown the two brothers of Antigone, Eteocles and Polyneices, kill each other, Sophocles shows Antigone, in the aftermath of their fratricide, redressing Creon's error and offering herself in sacrifice in order to reestablish the balance of justice in the *polis*, Hamilton suggests.

47   Judith Butler, *Antigone's Claim: Kinship Between Life and Death*. New York: Columbia University Press, 2000, 5–6.

48   Groot, 'Ramkoers: Antigone tegenover Kreon', 17–41.

49   Goldhill, *Aeschylus*, 41–9, quotations at 45–6 and 47 resp.

50   Hall, 'The Sociology of Athenian tragedy', 103–4.

51   Ibid., 106f.

52   Ibid., 109–14.

53   Wendy Doniger, *Splitting the Difference: Gender and Myth in Ancient Greece and India*. Chicago, IL/London: The University of Chicago Press, 1999, 133–203.

54 Hall, 'The Sociology of Athenian tragedy', 118, 125–6.

55 Peck, Coyle, *How to Study a Shakespeare Play*, 55–7.

56 McAlindon, *Shakespeare's Tragic Cosmos*, 111–12.

57 Ibid., 111; see also 125.

58 Kernan, *Shakespeare, the King's Playwright*, 40–3.

59 Aristotle, *Poetics*, 1462a.

60 Ibid., 1448a.

61 Ibid., 1449b.

62 Raymond Williams, *Modern Tragedy*. (Stanford, Calif.: Stanford University Press, 1966) Ontario: Broadview Press Encore Editions, 2001, 25.

63 Williams, *Modern Tragedy*, 21–2.

64 Williams, *Modern Tragedy*, 23–7, quotations at 21 and 23 resp. (See also the chapter on religious aspects (Part I Sections 5 and 6) for a discussion of the underlying view of human nature and action.) On the 'fall of princes' and the link between morality plays and political tragedies, see Bushnell, 'The Fall of Princes', 289–306. Steiner, *The Death of Tragedy*, 18–19, points out that Sidney's appeal both to authority and to reason is typical of neo-classicism, and that Sidney had been influenced by Castelvetro's influential interpretation of Aristotle.

65 Steiner, *The Death of Tragedy*, 194–5.

66 Steiner, *The Death of Tragedy*, 241; 243: 'In prose fiction, as D. H. Lawrence remarked, "you know there is a watercloset on the premises". We are not called upon to envisage such facilities at Mycenae and Elsinore. If there are bathrooms in the houses of tragedy, they are for Agamemnon to be murdered in'.

67 Steiner, *The Death of Tragedy*, 247. According to Steiner, *The Death of Tragedy*, 274, Georg Büchner's *Woyzeck* is the first real tragedy of low life. It repudiates the assumption implicit in Greek, Elizabethan, and neo-classic drama that tragic suffering is the sombre privilege of those who are in high places. Previously – except for Shakespeare's *King Lear* – , the griefs of the menial classes were meant to be laughed at.

68 Steiner, ' "Tragedy", Reconsidered', 9: 'From Aeschylus to Shakespeare, from Sophocles to Racine, high tragedy engages the (mis)fortunes of the privileged, of the princely, of a dynastic elite. The very rubric "tragedy" in its Senecan and medieval demarcation is that of "the fall of illustrious men". Tragedy argues an aristocracy of suffering, an excellence of pain'.

69 Steiner, ' "Tragedy", Reconsidered', 10.

70 Terry Eagleton, 'Commentary', in: *New Literary History* 35 (2004), 151–9, quotations at 158–9.

71 Eagleton, 'Commentary', 154. Cf. likewise Jos de Mul, *De Domesticatie van het Noodlot: De wedergeboorte van de tragedie uit de geest van de technologie*. Kampen: Uitgeverij Klement/Kapellen: Pelckmans, 2006.

72 Hall, 'The Sociology of Athenian tragedy', 96.

73 Steiner, *The Death of Tragedy*, 248.

74 Danson, *Shakespeare's Dramatic Genres*, 19.

75 D. P. Chattopadhyaya, *Ways of Understanding the Past: Mythic, Epic, Scientific and Historic*. New Delhi: Centre for Studies in Civilizations, 2001, 34, 49–50.

76 Romila Thapar, *From Lineage to State: Social Formations in the Mid-First Millenium B.C. in the Ganga Valley*. (Oxford: Oxford University Press, 1984) New Delhi: Oxford India Paperbacks 2000,[6] 132–41.

77 Romila Thapar, *Early India: From the Origins to AD 1300*. London: Allen Lane, The Penguin Press, 2002, 100.

78 Romila Thapar, 'The Historian and the Epic' (1979), in: Romila Thapar (ed.), *Cultural Pasts: Essays in Early Indian History*. New Delhi: Oxford University Press, 2000, 615; 626: 'Epic society as depicted in the narrative sections has little use for the storing of wealth and there is a constant urging that it be distributed. This would prevent the growth of the kind of economic surplus associated with intensive agriculture, well-established monarchical systems using this revenue and professional priests entirely dependent on the community for a living. But this picture derived from the narrative sections gives way to what appears to be a new economic situation in the didactic sections of the text. The change from a pastoral-cum-agricultural economy to one more intensively dependent on cultivation is most clearly seen in the pattern of gift-giving classified as *dāna*, and discussed in detail in the didactic sections, as for example in the *Anuśāna-parvan*. Two features are particularly noticeable: the material content of *dāna* changes from animal wealth and gold to include land and secondly there is a shift from a widescale distribution of wealth to the bestowal of wealth solely on the deserving *brāhmana*'. In her recent book *Early India*, 2002, 102, concerning the distinction between the narrative sections believed to be older and the didactic sections believed to be later, Thapar adds a warning: 'But even this is not invariably a reliable chronological divide'.

79 Thapar, 'The Historian and the Epic', 622: 'To the extent that the role of the senior kinsmen was crucial to the narrative of the epic, as for example in the decision to challenge the Pāndavas at a game of dice, it can be argued that the political form was closer to tribal chiefships than to absolute monarchies'.

80 Thapar, *From Lineage to State*, 132–5, quotations at 133 and 135 resp.

81 According to Hindu traditions, the class system began with the decline of *tapas* (ascetic heat). By way of explaining the origin of the *varna* system, the Vedic *Purusha-Hymn* is repeated in *Shānti-parvan*, 285.3ff. (Thapar, 'The Historian and the Epic', 623).

82 Recently, Thapar, *Early India*, 102, did not abandon her position in the debate.

83 Thapar, *From Lineage to State*, 140–1: 'What might have been an inter-tribal conflict over succession takes on the dimensions of the end of an epoch. This is precisely what it is; the end of the epoch of *kshatriya* (warrior, LM) chiefships . . . . The intrinsic sorrow of the battle at Kurukshetra is not merely at the death of kinsmen but also at the dying of a society, a style, a political form. The concept of the present as *Kali-yuga* (Iron Age, LM) combines a romanticization of the earlier society with the sense of insecurity born of a changing system'.

84 Hiltebeitel, *Rethinking the Mahābhārata*, 6–7.

85 Ibid., 15–18.

86 Ibid., 4.

87 Hiltebeitel, *Rethinking the Mahābhārata*, 180: 'The "old Kshatriya order" which the *Mahābhārata* envisions, and, as Fitzgerald says, often seems to loathe, probably had its only real historical foothold in the early post Rig Vedic period. As the early *Upanishadic* saying—"Where in the world are the Pārikshitas?"—indicates, it is long gone by then: well before the time of the epic's composition. In advocating the replacement of this old order, the *Mahābhārata* replaces and indeed rethinks an order defined by Vedic texts that no longer describe a current political situation. If the epic recommends a "transformation", it is, as Fitzgerald of course recognizes, an inner one; but it is not a political one over which current Kshatriyas—"legitimately" recognized as such in the epic or purānic sense—are in any way envisioned as contributors'.

88 Hiltebeitel, *Rethinking the Mahābhārata*, 178: 'I think the *sattra*-performing Brahmans (*sattra*: ritual session, LM) of the epic's outer frame are more likely to provide a key to its composition than Janamejaya, the king of the inner frame, who is probably no more than a great king from the past idealized as a royal audience. But even if the Mauryans, and Aśoka in particular, stand out in this imperial history, it is its relentlessness as a whole that seems to impinge on the epic poets'. Hiltebeitel follows Biardeau here: Jean-Michel Péterfalvi, Madeleine Biardeau, *Le Mahābhārata, Vol. I. Livres I à V*. Paris: Flammarion, 1985, 30.

89 Simon Pearse Brodbeck, *Asakta Karman in the Bhagavadgītā*. PhD thesis, School of Oriental and African Studies, London, 2002, 82ff.

90 For sociological reasons, Brodbeck, *Asakta Karman*, 82ff. and 111, distinguishes the ideology of ultimate liberation from rebirth (*moksha*) from the ideology of reincarnation and underlines that this ideology of ultimate liberation can be seen as a *subversive* move: one can escape reincarnation and binding action altogether.

91 Brodbeck, *Asakta Karman*, 87ff.

92 *The Bhagavad Gītā*, trans. Winthrop Sargeant, rev. ed. Christopher Chapple. New York: State University of New York Press, 1994, 79–81. On the family, women and sexual relations across classes in the *Mahābhārata*: Arti Dhand, *Woman as Fire, Woman as Sage: Sexual Ideology in the Mahābhārata*. Albany, NY: State University of New York Press, 2008, esp. 119–25.

93 Brodbeck, *Asakta Karman*, 100.

94 Madeleine Biardeau, 'The Salvation of the king in the *Mahābhārata*', in: *Contributions to Indian Sociology* 15/1–2 (1981), 75–97, quotation at 76.

95 Biardeau, 'The Salvation of the king', 79.

96 Biardeau, *Le Mahābhārata*, Vol. I, 97–161; Vol. II, 753–83.

97 Hill, *Fate, Predestination and Human Action in the Mahabharata*, 324–7.

98 Referring to Thapar's work, Hill, *Fate, Predestination and Human Action*, 324, points out *five changes* that occurred not just in India, but generally across the ancient world during the middle of the first millenium BCE, in order to explain the proliferation of rival sects: 'Politically these centuries saw the break-up of tribal based societies and the emergence of territorial based societies based increasingly on authoritarian forms of government and impersonal forms of state administration. The sense of alienation this instilled is perhaps best reflected in the Hindu theory of the "law of the fishes". To the growth of political authoritarianism may be added the emergence of substantial towns and cities with all the anonymity and alienation that goes with urban life. The growth of urbanisation, in turn, was based on the introduction of iron technology and the development of a sophisticated economic system. It was the use of iron, the extension of plough agriculture and the general intensification of agriculture that provided the economic base for the growth of towns. It also paved the way for major changes in agrarian structure with the emergence of large estates owned predominantly by individual *kshatriya* families. The criterion of wealth came to be based on land and money rather than on cattle which had been the measure of wealth and status during the Vedic period. These towns were also the natural home for a growing class of *setthigahapatis* or traders and financiers whose great wealth and importance were out of all proportion to the *vaiśya* status accorded to them by brāhmanical orthodoxy'.

99 Brodbeck, *Asakta Karman*, 136: 'With the evolution of the insulated (or, at least, unproblematically dominant) Vedic community into a more cosmopolitan society, social norms were now under threat from other ways of life: the community (and other communities) would only at this stage become conscious of many of its own traditions. In this situation, knowledge of normative behaviour was required in order that one be able to discharge actions without fear that one has somehow done the wrong thing: without a normative background it is incumbent upon the individual to decide what ought to be done, and the limited perspective that such an individual must base this decision upon precipitates an existential crisis involving desire, anger and *dukkha* (suffering, LM). The crisis is all the more severe if many of these decisions are the kind that, until recently, did not have to be made because a certain line of action was taken for granted, or because the situations demanding them (internecine wars, for example) simply did not arise'.

100 Brodbeck, *Asakta Karman*, 136.

101 Brodbeck, *Asakta Karman*, 137; Brodbeck continues: 'The invitation to offer all actions to the Lord, knowing that he is their author and the only true recipient of their benefits, that is, the attitude of *bhakti*, is not really an answer to the question of what to do: *bhakti* suggests that we do not ask the question in the first place, which is easier than un-asking it once it has been asked. The psychological pressure and the existential crisis remain the same, whether one is acting avariciously to ensure one's own benefit, or trying to bring the will of the Lord to fruition on earth. Either way, one does as one sees fit, and the trauma comes from feeling that one may be wrong about what is fit'.

Chapter 5

1 Friedrich, 'Everything to Do with Dionysos?', in: Silk (ed.), *Tragedy and the Tragic,* 272; Seaford, 'Something to Do with Dionysos', 284ff.

2 Kuch, 'Gesellschaftliche Voraussetzungen und Sujet der Griechischen Tragödie', in: Kuch (ed.), *Die griechische Tragödie,* 11–39; Van Erp Taalman Kip, *Bokkenzang,* 57–72; Lloyd-Jones, 'Ritual and Tragedy', in: Fritz Graf (Hrsg.), *Ansichten griechischer Rituale,* 271–95.

3 *Poetics*, 1451a 36–8 and 1451b 4–5.

4 Edith Hall, 'The sociology of Athenian tragedy', in: Easterling (ed.), *The Cambridge Companion to Greek Tragedy*, 101.

5 Williams, *Modern Tragedy*, 21.

6 Danson, *Shakespeare's Dramatic Genres*, 37–9.

7 Williams, *Modern Tragedy*, 28.

8 Why? See Williams, *Modern Tragedy*, 29–30.

9 The narrative sources that Shakespeare is likely to have used for his 'history' plays are Raphael Holinshed's *Chronicles of England, Scotland and Ireland* (expanded version 1587) and Edward Hall's *Union of the Two Noble and Illustre Families of York and Lancaster* (1548). See Danson, *Shakespeare's Dramatic Genres*, 104–6.

10 States, *Hamlet and the Concept of Character*, 159–60.

11 David Bevington, *Shakespeare's Ideas: More Things in Heaven and Earth.* Malden, MA/Oxford: Wiley-Blackwell, 2008, 43.

12 Jean-Pierre Vernant, 'Le dieu de la fiction tragique', in: Jean-Pierre Vernant, Pierre Vidal-Naquet (eds), *Mythe et tragédie en Grèce ancienne*. Vol. II. Paris: La Découverte, 1986, 17–24.

13 Burian, 'Myth into *muthos*', in: Easterling (ed.), *The Cambridge Companion*, 178–208, esp. 178–9.

14 Burian, 'Myth into *muthos*', 179.

15 Ibid., 184–5.

16 Christopher Gill, *Personality in Greek Epic, Tragic, and Philosophy: The Self in Dialogue*. Oxford: Clarendon Press, 1996, 181.

17 Gill, *Personality in Greek Epic, Tragic, and Philosophy*, 53–4, 133.

18 Gill, *Personality in Greek Epic, Tragic, and Philosophy*, 23, 177, 133–49. Both great Homeric speeches centre on the question of the kind of meaningful interpersonal context needed, but Sarpedon takes this context to be present whereas Achilles does not.

19 Gill, *Personality in Greek Epic, Tragic, and Philosophy*, 94ff.

20 Cf. Gill, *Personality in Greek Epic, Tragic, and Philosophy*, 23.

21 Gill, *Personality in Greek Epic, Tragic, and Philosophy*, 181.

22 Goldhill, *Aeschylus*, 41–9.

23 Segal, *Oedipus Tyrannus*, 70–4.

24 Viktor Jarcho, 'Die Weltanschauung des Dichters und die Verantwortung des Helden in der griechischen Tragödie', in: Kuch, 'Gesellschaftliche Voraussetzungen', 41–59. In putting forward one example only (Agamemnon), I admittedly describe Jarcho's argument in a highly reduced form.

25 Other readings of this crucial passage are possible. For example, if Agamemnon's free decision to go along with fate is rational, but followed immediately by madness – in which case Agamemnon remains fully responsible for his immoral decision. This is, in my opinion, a more convincing reading because Agamemnon starts out by making his decision and then gets 'the worst thought' – his decision drives him mad.

26 Halliwell, 'Plato's Repudiation of the Tragic', 340–1. Cf. also Nagy, 'The Epic Hero', 77.

27 Richard P. Martin, 'Epic as Genre', in: Miles Foley (ed.), *A Companion to Ancient Epic*, 12.

28 Redfield, *Nature and Culture in the Iliad*, 1994.

29 Redfield, *Nature and Culture in the Iliad*, 82. Redfield, xvi, emphasizes that tragedy is fiction, that is, not reality, but about reality. Mere conflict 'does not generate drama; mere conflict belongs to the realm of nature and can be appropriately settled by force. Drama arises within the sphere of culture and out of the ambiguities of cultural values and norms' (80).

30 Redfield, *Nature and Culture in the Iliad*, 83–5; see also 89: 'Let us remember that tragedy is an inquiry into the strengths and weaknesses of culture'.

31 R. B. Rutherford, 'Tragic Form and Feeling in the *Iliad*', in: *Journal of Hellenic Studies* 102 (1982), 145–60; John Gould, 'Homeric Epic and the Tragic Moment', in: Tom Winnifrith, P. Murray, K. W. Gransdey (eds), *Aspects of the Epic*. New York: St. Martin's Press, 1983, 32–45.

32 de Romilly, *Hector*, 41–4, 122–3, 99, 104–5.

33 de Romilly, *Hector*, 44: 'Quand on me dit: "Vous travaillez sur l'épopée", je suis toujours déroutée: pour moi, l'*Iliade* ressortit plus au genre tragique qu'au genre épique'.

34 Ewans, 'Patterns of Tragedy in Sophocles and Shakespeare', 438–40. See also Palmer, *Tragedy and Tragic Theory*, 137–8.

35 Bryant, *Moral Codes and Social Structure in Ancient Greece*, 15.

36 Ibid., 37.

37 Martin, 'Epic as Genre', 18.

38 Hall, 'The Sociology of Athenian tragedy', 112.

39 Poole, *Tragedy*, 89.

40 Levin, *The Question of Hamlet*, 20.

41 Levin, *The Question of Hamlet*, 67–74. Levin, 74, continues: 'His sense of certainty has been fatally ravaged, and with it his trust in others. They are even less sure of things than he is; Polonius obliges him by discerning three different animals in the same cloud; and Osric agrees that the weather is hot or cold, depending upon Hamlet's variable taste. In the absence of some external criterion, he searches within'.

42 Poole, *Tragedy*, 3.

43 According to Murray, 'Hamlet', 248–9, it is precisely because his action becomes too much the acting out of his feeling and thinking that he loses control of the situation. Hamlet takes up an antic role that reinforces itself by suggesting to Hamlet that he himself is in control because he is only playing a role. By playing this role, Hamlet gets entirely absorbed in the feeling and rhetoric that go with it, unable to see the full effect of the role on himself, culminating in the question 'Am I a coward?' (II.ii.566).

44 Rosset, *La philosophie tragique*, 23: 'le tragique enseigne d'abord à l'homme l' "irréconciliable" et l' "irresponsable" '.

45 Connie Aarsbergen-Ligtvoet, *Isaiah Berlin: A Value Pluralist and Humanist View of Human Nature and the Meaning of Life*. Amsterdam/New York: Rodopi, 2006, 13.

46 Aarsbergen-Ligtvoet, *Isaiah Berlin*, 14–15.

47 Georg Friedrich Wilhelm Hegel, *Phänomenologie des Geistes*, (1807) ed. E. Moldenhauer, K. M. Michel. Frankfurt a/M: Suhrkamp, 1986, 327–59 ('Der wahre Geist. Die Sittlichkeit'), 529–44 ('Das geistige Kunstwerk'). See also Mark W. Roche, 'The Greatness and Limits of Hegel's Theory of Tragedy', in: Rebecca Bushnell (ed.), *A Companion to Tragedy*. Oxford: Blackwell Publishing, 2005, 51–67.

48 Robert Piercey, 'The Role of Greek Tragedy in the Philosophy of Paul Ricoeur', in: *Philosophy Today* 49/1 (Spring 2005), 4–6.

49 Piercey, 'The Role of Greek Tragedy in the Philosophy of Paul Ricoeur', 9–10.

50 Ibid., 7.

51 Van Erp Taalman Kip, *Bokkenzang*, 74–7; Van Erp Taalman Kip, 'The Unity of the *Oresteia*', 133–5.

52 Goldhill, *Aeschylus*, 31.

53 Ibid., 33.

54 Goldhill, 'The language of tragedy', 127–50.

55 Goldhill, 'The language of tragedy', 139–40. Cf. Simon Goldhill, *Language, Sexuality, Narrative: The* Oresteia. Cambridge: Cambridge University Press, (1984) pb 2004.

56 Goldhill, 'The language of tragedy', 135–6.

57 James C. Bulman, *The Heroic Idiom of Shakespearean Tragedy.* Newark: University of Delaware Press/London, Toronto: Associated University Presses, 1985.

58 Bulman, *The Heroic Idiom*, 50–9; quotation at 55.

59 Bulman, *The Heroic Idiom*, 59–60.

60 Ibid., 63–7.

61 Bulman, *The Heroic Idiom*, 75–82; quotations at 77 and 79.

62 Bulman, *The Heroic Idiom*, 82.

63 See Jean-Pierre Vernant, 'Le moment historique de la tragédie en Grèce: Quelques conditions sociales et psychologiques', in: Jean-Pierre Vernant, Pierre Vidal-Naquet (eds), *Mythe et tragédie en Grèce ancienne.* Vol. I. Paris: La Découverte, (1986) 1989, 13–17, esp. 16–17.

64 Edith Hall, 'Is there a *Polis* in Aristotle's *Poetics*?', in: Silk (ed.), *Tragedy and the Tragic*, 296. Halliwell, 'Plato's Repudiation of the Tragic', 334 5, agrees.

65 Th. C. W. Oudemans, A. P. M. H. Lardinois, *Tragic Ambiguity: Anthropology, Philosophy and Sophocles' Antigone.* Leiden/New York: E. J. Brill, 1987, 1–28, esp. 1, 4, 23, 27–8.

66 Christiane Sourvinou-Inwood, *Tragedy and Athenian Religion.* Lanham: Lexington Books, 2003.

67 Their terminology is, in fact, very much to the point. An 'interconnected cosmology' is one in which human actions, especially human transgressions, have repercussions throughout the cosmos. For example, if I do not obey the chief of my tribe, my tribesmen's cattle may contract a disease. My boundary-crossing spreads pollution. Boundary-crossing is a source of powerful ambiguity, tabooing in a potentially negative or positive sense, embodying ambiguous power. A 'separative cosmology' is one in which ambiguity is avoided by introducing abstract distinctions between categories, such as transcendent and mundane, divine and human, ideal and practical, and by isolating dimensions. This 'separative cosmology' is usually considered typically 'modern', not just by Oudemans and Lardinois (who also refer to it as Cartesian), but even by Jaspers. Michael Walzer's telling description of liberalism in terms of 'the practising of the art of separation' is of interest here: 'Confronting this world, liberal theorists preached and practised an art of separation. They drew lines, marked off different realms, and created the sociopolitical map with which we are still familiar. The most famous line is the "wall" between church and state, but there are many others. Liberalism is a world of walls, and each one creates a new liberty'. (Michael Walzer, 'Liberalism and the Art of Separation', in: *Political Theory* 12/3 (August 1984), 315–30).

68 Karl Jaspers, *Vom Ursprung und Ziel der Geschichte.* München: Piper, 1949; cf. Günter Dux, *Die Logik der Weltbilder: Sinnstrukturen im Wandel der Geschichte.* Frankfurt a/M: Suhrkamp, 1982; S. N. Eisenstadt (ed.), *The Origins and Diversity of Axial Age Civilizations.* Albany, NY: SUNY, 1986; J. G. Platvoet, 'De wraak der "primitieven": Godsdienstgeschiedenis van Neanderthaler tot New Age', in: *Nederlands Theologisch Tijdschrift* 47 (1993), 227–43; Heiner Roetz, *Confucian Ethics of the Axial Age: A Reconstruction under the Aspect of the Breakthrough Toward Postconventional Thinking.* Albany, NY: SUNY, 1993; Shmuel N. Eisenstadt (ed.), *Multiple Modernities.* Piscataway, NJ: Transaction Publishers, 2002; Dominic Sachsenmaier, Shmuel Eisenstadt, Jens Riedel (eds), *Reflections on Multiple Modernities: European, Chinese and Other Interpretations.* Leiden/Boston: Brill, 2002; S. N. Eisenstadt, *Comparative Civilizations and Multiple Modernities.* 2 vols. Leiden/Boston: Brill, 2003; Johann P. Arnason, S. N. Eisenstadt, Björn Wittrock (eds), *Axial Civilizations and World History.* Leiden/Boston: Brill, 2005; Karen Armstrong, *The Great Transformation: The World in the Time of Buddha, Socrates, Confucius and Jeremiah.* London: Atlantic Books, 2006; Staf Hellemans, *Het Tijdperk van de Wereldreligies: Religie in agrarische civilisaties en in moderne samenlevingen.* Zoetermeer: Meinema, 2007; Frédéric Lenoir, *Petit Traité d'histoire des religions.* Paris: Plon, 2008.

69 Armstrong, *The Great Transformation*, 367: 'In China, the Axial Age finally got under way after the collapse of the Zhou dynasty and came to an end when Qin unified the warring states. The Indian Axial Age occurred after the disintegration of the Harappan civilization and ended with the Mauryan empire; the Greek transformation occurred between the Mycenaean kingdom and the Macedonian empire. . . . Even the Jews, who had suffered so horribly from the imperial adventures in the Middle East, had been propelled into their Axial Age by the terrifying freedom that had followed the destruction of their homeland and the trauma of deportation that severed their link with the past and forced them to start again. But by the end of the second century, the world had stabilized'.

70 Stephen A. Geller, 'The God of the Covenant', in: Barbara Nevling Porter (ed.), *One God or Many? Concepts of Divinity in the Ancient World.* Transactions of the Casco Bay Assyriological Institute, 2000, 310: 'Just as the Greeks used old cultic drama to explore human character and circumstance, so biblical religion wove the old Israelite traditions into a true history, a drama extended over the centuries and marked by a succession of real personalities. Biblical narratives show a deep involvement with and fascination with the issue of personality and its development. . . . With the possible exception of the final form of the Gilgamesh Epic, there is nothing like them in the ancient world. The patriarchal stories, the accounts of the careers of Saul and David, possess a vividness and psychological richness unparalleled in antiquity. The depths of the new concept of personality were being plumbed. The mystery of change in personality, how a given individual can become a different person, as, for example, Jacob and Joseph did, fascinates the biblical writers. That there was a singularity of person was the axiom of the new approach to the self, but the response of the inner world to the variety of circumstances to which it was subjected was a totally new area to be explored. The new doctrine of repentance developed by the prophets and accepted by covenant religion is another aspect of the problem of change of personality. Is the repentant sinner truly a new person? Can he really start over again? Such questions are the sort that arose'.

71 Gibert, *Change of Mind in Greek Tragedy*, 22–3: 'it turns out that within Greek tragedy there are formidable obstacles arrayed against change of mind. These may be divided roughly into the linguistic and the situational. Some of the words describing change of mind carry negative connotations or suggest that it is difficult and painful. At the same time, the voice of traditional morality is heard throughout tragedy, often directed against any kind of change and in favor of consistent excellence and unwavering adherence to lofty principles. Specific situations raise the stakes: tragic conflicts typically have a high public profile, many of them are cast as confrontations between enemies, and they all occur within a brief span of time. The first two of these are most serious impediments to change, threatening a character with "loss of face". Given what we know of Athenian society, we will not be tempted to describe these as merely rhetorical obstacles within a culture that actually worships change under the banner of self-improvement—a description that might fit the contemporary United States. That is an extreme comparison, but it raises an important point. If a character like Ajax (who despite his excess is at least comprehensible within his own culture) does change his mind, it remains to ask, "To what end?" In the 5th-century context, there is scarcely an ideology of religious conversion or salvation'.

72 Segal, *Oedipus Tyrannus*, 81. Goldhill, 'The language of tragedy', 132–3, observes: 'The Greek word *aitios* which means "responsible", "cause of", also means "guilty", and the verbal form *aitiasthai* means both "to find responsible" and "to prosecute" or "charge". There is in tragedy an integral association at the verbal level between the practice of law and the tragic world of conflicting responsibilities and decision-making. What is more, the political setting of many tragedies often requires its figures to engage in practical, political reasoning. So Creon in his first speech in the *Antigone* outlines an ideological position on duty and obligation in the *polis*'.

73 Sands, 'Tragedy, Theology, and Feminism', 57–8, also adds her postmodern comment: 'If tragedy is, as I have suggested, the birth trauma of moral consciousness, then it is not surprising that tragedy would reassert itself now. At the dawn of modernity, with the death or eclipse of God, morality was ingested and became humanism. In the dusk of modernity's many moral catastrophes, we can only hope, as Freud did for the melancholic, that we might come in some way to prefer ourselves to our ideals'. See also my chapter on psycho-ethical aspects (Part I Section 2).

74 Ruth Padel, *Whom Gods Destroy: Elements of Greek and Tragic Madness*. Princeton, NJ: Princeton University Press, 1995, 246–7.

75 Regarding Elizabethan and Jacobean England, Padel, *Whom Gods Destroy*, 227–9, sees the dominance of a religio-demonic view of madness which, by the seventeenth century and only among the educated, is being taken over by medical explanations for insanity – 'the beginning of a split within society, in attitudes to madness and divinity: a split made complete in the eighteenth century' when medical thought has removed God out of madness, but moralized it as the 'psychological effect of a moral fault'. Anyone now 'claiming divine or demonic visions is', medically speaking, 'mad'.

76 Keyishian, *The Shapes of Revenge*, 64, 67.

77 Ibid., 9.

78 Keyishian, *The Shapes of Revenge*, 9. According to Keyishian, 10, Catherine Belsey 'maintains that because revenge exists in the margin between justice and crime, it deconstructs the antithesis which fixes the meanings of good and evil, right and wrong, and poses political as well as moral questions. Revenge plays do not, she contends, resolve these issues; rather, they raise questions about divine, political, and personal authority—whether it is nobler to suffer in Christian patience or to take arms against secular injustices'. In revenge plays, 'Renaissance doubts and uncertainties concerning individual autonomy' were confronted: 'in the process of exploring the obligations and responsibilities of the subject in the implementation of divine and human justice, the revenge play contributed to the process of installing the subject as autonomous agent of retribution'.

79 Danson, *Shakespeare's Dramatic Genres*, 117.

80 Rees, *Shakespeare and the Story*, 184–5, 191.

81 Levin, *The Question of Hamlet*, 54; Levin, 54–5, continues: 'The well-ordered cosmos of Ptolemaic astronomy was being displaced by the planetary system of Copernicus, wherein the sun no longer revolved around the earth and man was no longer the center of creation. So Hamlet could write to Ophelia: "Doubt thou the stars are fire/Doubt that the sun doth move/Doubt truth to be a liar/But never doubt I love". (II.ii.116–19) As a poet who mixes cosmology with intimacy, Hamlet obviously belongs to the Metaphysical School. The purport of his stanza does not differ from the conclusion of Arnold's "Dover Beach", the affirmation that, in a universe of illusion and pain, the only true relationship is love. But Hamlet recants his love soon afterward, while Ophelia herself is enveloped from first to last in an astral nimbus of uncertainty'. One should add here that Hamlet's love is doubtful, but Ophelia's love is not. Ophelia loves Hamlet to the end and explains Hamlet's recantation by his madness. Hamlet's love is put to the test, not by Ophelia, but by Polonius, whose misuse of Ophelia is mistakenly seen by Hamlet as Ophelia's betrayal.

82 Diehl, 'Religion and Shakespearean Tragedy', 92.

83 Ibid., 93.

84 Bloom, *Hamlet*, 118–19.

85 Ibid., 143.

86 Arditi, *A Genealogy of Manners*, 86ff.

87 Arditi, *A Genealogy of Manners*, 89; he continues: 'In Cervantes and in the Shakespeare of *As You Like It* and *The Merchant of Venice*, there is only one stage, the world, and every person performs only one part within the play, that of his or her character'.

88 Arditi, *A Genealogy of Manners*, 86.

89 Ibid., 90.

90 One is reminded of some lines in Shakespeare's *Troilus and Cressida* 2.2.52–6: 'What 's aught but as 't is valued? But value dwells not in particular will. It holds his estimate and dignity as well wherein 't is precious of itself as in the prizer'.

91 Christopher Pye, *The Vanishing: Shakespeare, the Subject, and Early Modern Culture*. Durham/London: Duke University Press, 2000, 4–6.

92 Pye, *The Vanishing*, 14.

93 Here, Louise D. Derksen adds the comment that the subject also wants the performance to give it content, to be a mirror.

94 Pye, *The Vanishing*, 11 and 33 resp.

95 Pye, *The Vanishing*, 19–37.

96 Pye stresses the logic of socio-economic exchange, but even more so, the annihilating limits of this identifying logic of exchange. Revenge is such a form of exchange, substituting one person's death for another person's death. Revenge too, has its limits. Revenge is not able to make the world go round precisely because it is doomed to fail – its belated act cannot undo what has been done in terms of deaths and burials. Its return (benefit, profit) comes too late, as Talbot's revenge on Salisbury's dead body illustrates. See Pye, *The Vanishing*, 32–3.

97 Pye, *The Vanishing*, 111–12. On this trip, Hamlet is accompanied by Rosencrantz and Guildenstern, and by Claudius' death warrant. Hamlet takes this king's death warrant, and seals it with his father's model of the Danish seal – thereby ambiguously identifying himself both with the current king Claudius and with the previous king, his father. Pye interprets this 'sealing' psychoanalytically in a Lacanian sense of the word, as the dumb act of accession into the symbolic domain of language, of Hamlet's submission to the empty paternal signifier. That is to say, Hamlet becomes the messenger of the message, the 'seal' of sovereign identity, the self-assertive subject of his utterance and performance, the author of his story, the subject of his history. But he becomes this messenger by sealing off the dumb origin of the message. Thus, Hamlet sends Rosencrantz and Guildenstern to their death – thereby substituting himself for the other two, within a chain of violence in which the victim Hamlet becomes the agent Hamlet.

98 Pye, *The Vanishing*, 112; Hamlet 'remains fated to miss his own destiny' and his 'decisive encounter with his own limit' is, 'in Lacan's terms, an "encounter forever missed", as Pye, 114–15, puts it.

99 Pye, *The Vanishing*, 114. Pye's phrasing 'identification not with another' criticizes Girard's triangular mechanism of self-identification through mimetic rivalry and identification with another.

100 Pye, *The Vanishing*, 113–14. In Lacanian psychoanalysis, 'phallic' signifies 'that which lacks', the 'lost object' of desire, the 'series of lost objects'.

101 John Jeffries Martin, *Myths of Renaissance Individualism*. New Edition. Basingstoke: Palgrave Macmillan, 2006, 13–15.

102 Page duBois, 'Toppling the Hero: Polyphony in the Tragic City', in: *New Literary History* 35 (2004), 71, comes to similar conclusions, but her arguments are socio-historical and aesthetic: 'I want to point to just three ways in which Greek tragedy exceeds the individual character, the tragic hero, the great man or woman dear to the tradition: in its haunting by the slaves of ancient Greek society; in its access to mourning; and in its presentation of choral song that is necessarily collective, diverse, and heterogeneous'.

103 Williams, *Modern Tragedy*, 87–8.

104 Ibid., 88–9.

105 In *human tragedy*, the tragic hero is still marked by a social status, but also within and beyond it. In *bourgeois tragedy*, the gap between the private and public domain will replace rank, order and connection with class, amorphous society and separation. Human connection will still be possible, but only on an individual basis, in the form of humanitarian sympathy between private persons who do not share any positive conception of a common social order. In the late nineteenth century, *liberal tragedy* will even identify a false society and its constraining limits, to the extent of having the tragic hero suffer from total isolation and alienation, Williams, *Modern Tragedy*, 90–5, explains.

106 William Shakespeare, *The Tragedy of Hamlet, Prince of Denmark*. Edited by T. J. B. Spencer, with an Introduction by Anne Barton. London: Penguin Books, (1980) 2002, 21–3.

107 Margolies, *Monsters of the Deep*, 11.

108 Margolies, *Monsters of the Deep*, 66. Shakespeare, that is, has not yet found a dramaturgical solution to the problem of articulation, Margolies suggests. Polonius' asides (in the Fishmonger dialogue) and Hamlet's soliloquies are needed to make clear differences in perspectives, but they are not dramatic themselves; they indicate a weakness in Shakespeare's construction of the play, which he was able to overcome in *King Lear*. This tragedy was built around the same values and social critique as *Hamlet,* but he made the meaning visible through the action, so that the audience could judge for itself whether Lear was in touch with reality. (68ff.)

109 Nagy, 'The Epic Hero', 78–9.

110 Martin, 'Epic as Genre', 15–18.

111 Matchett, *Krsna: Lord or Avatāra?*, 3.

112 Nagy, 'The Epic Hero', 81ff., explains that in the ancient Greek Epic Cycle, specifically in the *Cypria*, the story of the overpopulation of Earth personified and of the solutions devised by the gods, describes as one solution a war to end all wars, destined to destroy the vast numbers of heroes who are overpopulating the earth. That totalizing war, according to the Cyclic *Cypria*, is the Trojan War. Alternative solutions include a cosmic cataclysm by way of floods and one by way of fire, recalling other parallels with cognate Indo-European traditions.

113 Nagy, 'The Epic Hero', 83–4.

114 Ibid., 85–6.

115 Martin, 'Epic as Genre', 17: 'As described by Africanists, praise-poetry is an allusive, highly compressed, and non-narrative evocation of the genealogies and successes of chieftains. Marked by often obscure, riddling names, brief references to events, and a repetitive, incantatory style, this genre is more widespread than epic, especially in southern and eastern Africa. Instead of a range on a spectrum, the praise-poem is a telescope: what is compressed in a style that imitates the instantaneous exultation of a client before his patron, in epic is expanded to fill out chronology, cause, and characterization. While praise (often in second-person address) is more direct and more lucrative, epic (usually third-person) is more lucid'.

116 Romila Thapar, 'Society and Historical Consciousness: The *Itihāsa-purāna* Tradition' (1986), in: Thapar, *Cultural Pasts*, 123–54, esp. 128. Both the *Mahābhārata* and the *Rāmāyana* had their earlier and perhaps more truly epic versions in what have been referred to as the *Rāma-kathā* and the *Bhārata* or *Jaya*. (130).

117 Thapar, 'Society and Historical Consciousness', 138; Romila Thapar, 'The Rāmāyana: Theme and Variation' (1982), in: Thapar, *Cultural Pasts*, 647–79, esp. 669.

118 Thapar, 'Society and Historical Consciousness', 132–3.

119 Hiltebeitel, *Rethinking the Mahābhārata*, 7.

120 Hiltebeitel, *Rethinking the Mahābhārata*, 4. See on the close connection between epic genre, social setting and the theme of the education of the king (discourse of an old adviser instructing a young prince): Richard P. Martin, 'Hesiod, Odysseus, and the instruction of princes', in: *Transactions of the American Philological Association* 114 (1984), 29–48.

121 Katz, *Arjuna in the Mahābhārata*, 1989.

122 Ibid., 5–6.

123 This subdivision serves as the framework for the book: Part I, Hero, 27–123; Part II, Human, 125–209; Part III, Devotee, 211–69.

124 Katz, *Arjuna in the Mahābhārata*, 243.

125 Ibid., 115, 117–18.

126 Ibid., 215–16, 218, 240.

127 For a critical review substantiating my own hesitations, see: Alf Hiltebeitel, 'Religious Studies and Indian Epic Texts', in: *Religious Studies Review* 21/1 (January 1995), 26–32.

128 In my opinion, there is a remote, but striking parallel in Plato's and Aristotle's notion of will or rational desire (*boulēsis*) for the good or the apparent good. Richard Sorabji, *Emotion and Peace of Mind: From Stoic Agitation to Christian Temptation*. Oxford: Oxford University Press, (2000) pb 2002, 323: 'The term "good" (*agathon*) in this context is used by Plato and Aristotle in a narrow sense, in contrast with honour and pleasure, which are the goals of the lower types of desire, *thumos* and *epithumia*. In some sense, however, Plato and Aristotle are ready to say that all desire, not just *boulēsis*, sees its objective as good in some way or other'.

129 One would expect the merchants (*vaiśyas*) to perform this economic role of accumulating wealth and profit. Instead, the cultivation of *artha* was particularly connected with the warriors and kings (*kshatriyas*), who were considered the legitimate possessors of the wealth of the land they had conquered by military and political means. In fact, the tradesmen and craftsmen are conspicuously absent in this brahminical value system, for cultivating the value of *artha*. This also applies to the *Gītā*.

130 Killingley, 'Enjoying the World', 67–79.

131 Gavin Flood, 'The Meaning and Context of the Purushārthas', in: Lipner (ed.), *The Bhagavad Gītā for our times*, 11–27, at 15: 'the *Arthaśāstra* refers to three aims, as do the *Manu Smrti*, and the *Bhagavadgītā* (18.34), where these are the legitimate pursuits of a man in the second or householder's stage (*āśrama*) of life, though these texts also discuss *moksha* outside the context of this system. In the *Śāstras dharma* is regarded as a human purpose, a human intention, though a higher human intention than profit or pleasure. "The knowledge of *dharma*", Manu says, "is enjoined for those who are unattached to profit and pleasure." Indeed, the hierarchy of the terms is reinforced by Manu's relating the goals to the three *gunas* or qualities which pervade existence, of lightness (*sattva*), passion (*rajas*), and darkness or inertia (*tamas*)'.

132 Flood, 'The Meaning and Context of the Purushārthas', 16.

133 Biardeau, *Hinduism*, 32–40 (Engl. trans. of *L'hindouisme*, 40–7).

134 Flood, 'The Meaning and Context of the Purushārthas', 21 and 20–1 resp.: 'The early *Mīmāmsakas* do not discuss *moksha*, and the *Dharmaśāstras* do not regard it as part of the system of the *purushārthas*, though they recognise its legitimate pursuit after the fulfilling of social obligations. But for the *Vedānta*, *moksha* is unequivocally the highest goal: the world-transcending liberation beyond *dharma* and the social world, attained by world renouncers. . . . By the time of Śamkara's commentary on the *Brahmasūtra* (ca. 8th century CE), *moksha* has been incorporated into the *trivarga* to form a 'group of four' (*caturvarga*). Here *moksha* surpasses the other purposes as the highest human value, though it is not recognised by the *Mīmāmsakas* until the eighth century with Kumārila. With addition of *moksha*, the *trivarga* is transformed into a system of three + one; it has become a set of four, the importance of which in Indian culture has been demonstrated by Malamoud and Olivelle. This transformation of the *trivarga* into the *caturvarga* and the supplanting of *dharma* and the other two purposes by *moksha*, suggests that a confluence of different value systems has occurred. Put simply, a Brahminical worldview in which the highest values are ritual and social responsibility, pleasure, wealth and worldly success, has incorporated a worldview in which liberation and the transcending of the social world takes precedence'.

135 Rajendra Prasad, A Conceptual-Analytic Study of Classical Indian Philosophy of Morals. (D. P. Chattopadhyaya (gen. ed.), History of Science, Philosophy and Culture in Indian Civilization, Vol. 12 Part 1) New Delhi: Concept Publishing Company, 2008, esp. 205–15.

136 Biardeau is less impressed with historical developments from one literary genre to the next than she is with its structural continuity. Her search for consistency throughout the *Mahābhārata* itself is conducted, according to James W. Laine, 'Hinduism and the Mahābhārata', in: *Wiener Zeitschrift für die Kunde Südasiens und Archiv für indische Philosophie* 30 (1986), 75–6, on the basis of a Lévi-Straussian structuralist approach that takes all versions of a story to be equally valid and locates the repeated pattern buried in the depth structure (logic of the changes) of the narrative.

137 The *Kaliyuga* yields, as it occurs at the end of a *kalpa* (mega-era), to a temporary dissolution of the universe called *pralaya*. In the epic, the cosmic dissolution takes the form of the Kurukshetra War. This brings victory of *dharma* over *adharma*, of good over evil, which clears the air for a renewed period of *dharma* called *Krita-yuga*. In the epic, the *Kritayuga* takes the form of Yudhisthira's ideal rule, according to Biardeau. Alf Hiltebeitel, 'Toward a Coherent Study of Hinduism', in: *Religious Studies Review* 9 (1983), 210, has some objections.

138 Madeleine Biardeau, *Etudes de mythologie hindoue. Vol. II: Bhakti et avatāra*. Paris/Pondichéry: Ecole française d'Extrême-Orient, 1994; idem, 'The Salvation of the king', 75–97.

139 Madeleine Biardeau, *Le Mahābhārata: Un récit fondateur du brahmanisme et son interprétation*. Paris: Editions du Seuil, 2002, Vol. I, 97–161; Vol. II, 753–83.

140 Biardeau, 'The Salvation of the king', 89.

141 Biardeau's *structuralist* approach to Arjuna is based on two premises. Her first premise is that the epic characters are types, rather than individuals. Her second premise is that Arjuna, not Yudhisthira, is the ideal king because of his special closeness to Krishna, the saving incarnation of the age, and to Indra, the king of the gods who has impregnated Arjuna's mother. In Biardeau's view, the cosmological *avatāra* myth is doubled by the epic myth of the *ideal king* whose model for actions and whose instructor on the terrestrial battlefield is the *avatāra* ('incarnation'). If Krishna is the actual saving incarnation of this age, then his bosom friend, cross-cousin and brother-in-law (by Subhadrā), Arjuna is the ideal king. (Madeleine Biardeau, *Etudes de mythologie hindoue. Vol. II: Bhakti et avatāra*. Paris/Pondichéry: Ecole française d'Extrême-Orient, 1994; idem, 'The Salvation of the king', 75–97).

142 Murray Milner, Jr, *Status and Sacredness: A General Theory of Status Relations and an Analysis of Indian Culture*. New York/Oxford: Oxford University Press, 1994, 65–70. Given the centrality of status in Indian culture, it is not accidental that India's lower social strata are 'outcasts' rather than prisoners, slaves, paupers, or the unemployed. Many societies have despised groups, but nowhere else has such an extensive and indispensable outcast group developed whose exclusion is so dependent on negative religious status (76).

143 Milner, Jr, *Status and Sacredness*, 76–8. Compared with the other castes, the merchant castes or *vaiśyas* constitute an ambiguous and anomalous category, according to Milner, 72–3.

144 *The Bhagavad Gītā*, trans. Sargeant, 706–9.

145 Biardeau, 'The Salvation of the king', 81.

146 Hiltebeitel, *Rethinking the Mahābhārata*, 202–9, esp. 207.

147 Hiltebeitel, *Rethinking the Mahābhārata*, 208; 204: 'By dharma beings are upheld apart (*dharmena vidhrtāh prajāh*)'.

148 Hiltebeitel, *Rethinking the Mahābhārata*, 197: 'There is a thread through these stories that has to do with classification, and the need to keep categories distinct. If one vows to kill snakes, one shouldn't kill lizards by mistake. This problem overlaps with the wider problems of maintaining distinctions between castes, and between gods and humans. As Yudhisthira puts it, war reduces everyone to acting like dogs. It is when the *dharma* of caste breaks down that the "law of the fishes" takes over. Caste mixture and confusion are the great dread of the *Bhagavad Gītā*, and of countless other epic passages. At the root of the Pañcāla cycle of violence is the confusion of caste (and other categories) between Drona and Drupada. And, from the standpoint of the story of the former Indras, it is the loss of distinction between gods and humans—and, we can now add, demons—that lies at the root of the whole *Mahābhārata* war'.

149 Arti Dhand, *Woman as Fire, Woman as Sage: Sexual Ideology in the Mahābhārata*. Albany, NY: State University of New York Press, 2008, 119–25, esp. 125.

150 Woods, *Destiny and Human Initiative in the Mahābhārata*, 43–6.

151 Daniel H. H. Ingalls, 'General Introduction, Sanskrit Poetry and Sanskrit Poetics', in: Daniel H. H. Ingalls (ed.), *An Anthology of Sanskrit Poetry: Vidyākara's 'Subhāshitaratnakośa'*. Cambridge, MA: Harvard University Press, 1965, 16.

152 V. S. Sukthankar points out that Karna's mother, Kuntī is no less a *tragic* figure. In an effort to prevent the war and save her other sons, the Pāndavas, she reveals to Karna his true identity and beseeches him tearfully to be reconciled with his half-brothers, but to no avail. The secret which Kuntī had wanted to preserve and which she thought she had skillfully buried, by severing her connection with her first child at its birth, had not been maintained. Sukthankar, *On the Meaning of the Mahābhārata*, 54, 'First she had to recount the story of her youthful indiscretion to her eldest son, Karna, whom she had wronged. She had hoped that by telling him the great secret of her little life, she could avoid the consequences of that act recoiling on her other sons, the five Pāndavas, whom she loved. In that she was destined to be disappointed, as Karna, in his turn, remained adamant, refusing, firmly but politely, to oblige her and make a scape-goat of himself. For her complete emancipation she had in the end to repeat the story with her own lips, after the death of Karna, to the surviving sons, in order that the last rites at least may be duly performed if the first had been neglected, in the pious hope that his life in the hereafter may not be a repetition of the hell in which he had lived on the earth. She had thus to acknowledge before the world her motherhood of the fatherless child after the death of Karna, which she had failed to do at his birth. Could anything be more silently tragic?'

153 The opposition between Karna and Arjuna reflects the natural opposition between sun and storm, and is emphasized by the fact that Karna's and Arjuna's respective fathers encourage and support them during their encounter at the tournament (1.126.23ff.). As Biardeau, 'Conférence de Mlle. Madeleine Biardeau', in: *Annuaire de l'École pratique des Hautes Études*. Cinquième section Sciences Religieuses 86 (1977–78), 143, points out, being the son of the sun god is not a curse per se – quite the contrary, since the regular course of the sun is necessary for the well-being of the world – but to be born out of wedlock and abandoned by his mother makes him out of the ordinary – he then becomes the replica of the dreadful sun which rises at the end of a cosmic period to destroy the world by fire.

154 Katz, *Arjuna in the Mahābhārata*, 172–3.

155 Woods, *Destiny and Human Initiative in the Mahābhārata*, 43–5.

156 Hiltebeitel, *Rethinking the Mahābhārata*, 46–7: 'This king has suffered from lack of comparability to Achilles. He cannot be the "real hero"—that Aristotelian cynosure whom an epic or tragedy is supposed to supply; he looks too Brahmanical, etc. But I will argue that he is the real hero, and also the "real king". Arjuna is ultimately a diversion. He forgets what he is taught and doesn't rule a thing. As we shall see, Vyāsa dismisses him by the end of the sixteenth book and saves everything for Yudhisthira, who remembers everything, at the end'.

157 Hiltebeitel, *The Ritual of Battle*, 195–7.

158 Yudhisthira tells Krishna that a peace won by the total eradication of an enemy is crueler (*nrśamsataram*) than the 'heart-eating disease of heroism' (5.70.55–6). (Hiltebeitel, *Rethinking the Mahābhārata*, 180 note 9. See also 66 on Nārada's question to Yudhisthira). Quoting Nicholas Sutton, *Religious Doctrines in the Mahābhārata*. Delhi: Motilal Banarsidass, 2000, 318, Hiltebeitel points out that Yudhisthira repeatedly insists on placing moral ethics above those of one's own *dharma* (*svadharma*) – in particular, the warrior caste's duties, as preached by Krishna to Arjuna in the *Gītā* (Sutton, 296), and as exemplified in Duryodhana (305–8). Sutton notes 'a sympathy on the part of the authors for the goodness of Yudhisthira' (320).

159 Hiltebeitel, *Rethinking the Mahābhārata*, 118. The particular *dharma* of kings must include not only the means to violence, but also the means to its appeasement. Not only must Yudhisthira be pacified after the violence of the war, but the cruel snake sacrifice (an endless vendetta against snakes!) of King Janamejaya (outer story frame), who is listening to the story of the pacification and education of king Yudhisthira (inner story frame), must be stopped and is stopped.

160 Hiltebeitel, *Rethinking the Mahābhārata*, 202. Non-cruelty is related to non-violence, each being proclaimed as the 'highest *dharma*'. But whereas non-violence is an other-worldly virtue, typical of the ascetic's way of renunciation, non-cruelty is much more in line with the epic's this-worldly outlook, which holds that total non-violence cannot be practised by the householder and the king. As a virtue, non-violence bears the ascetic imprint of the *desire* not to kill or harm creatures, of the desire to overcome life, Hiltebeitel claims.

161 Hiltebeitel, *Rethinking the Mahābhārata*, 203–4, explains: 'Lath mentions the impractibility of "total *ahimsā*" in the lives of householders and kings, and puts his finger on what is, I believe, the real nerve center in the epic poets' unease over *ahimsā*: its absolutism. The epic anticipates what Halbfass calls the 'major "philosophical" achievement' of the ritual exegesis of the *Pūrvamīmamsā*: "its method of shielding the Vedic *dharma* from the claims of philosophical, i.e., argumentative and universalizing thought, its demonstration that it cannot be rationalized or universalized within the framework of argumentative and epistemologically oriented thought, and its uncompromising linkage of *dharma* to the sources of the sacred tradition and the identity of the Aryan". This "eternal" Vedic *ārya dharma* treats *ahimsā* not as an absolute ascetic guideline for the monastic life; rather, as Bhīshma tells Yudhisthira: "The proclamation of *dharma* is done for the sake of the power of beings. What is connected with *ahimsā* would be *dharma*, that is certain. *Dharma* is (derived) from upholding, they say. By *dharma* beings are upheld apart (*dharmena vidhrtāh prajāh*). What is connected with upholding would be *dharma*, that is certain" '. An important point of debate among scholars is whether the value of non-violence started out as an ascetic value adopted by the *brahmins*, as Hiltebeitel assumes, or as a *brahminic* value shared by the ascetics.

162 Hiltebeitel, *Rethinking the Mahābhārata*, 207–8.

163 Ibid., 211.

164 Ibid., 215–39.

165 Ibid., 200–2.

166 Non-cruelty begins from a feeling of the 'absence of injuring men', including women, Hiltebeitel notes. It is 'a matter of the human heart that can expand

and contract as character and circumstances allow'. Hiltebeitel, *Rethinking the Mahābhārata*, 209–12, quotations at 212.

167 Hiltebeitel, *Rethinking the Mahābhārata*, 66–9.

168 Hiltebeitel, *Rethinking the Mahābhārata*, 213: 'While *ahimsā* tightens the great chain of beings, *ānṛśaṃsya* softens it with a cry for a *human* creature-feeling across the great divides'.

169 Mihoko Suzuki, *Metamorphoses of Helen: Authority, Difference, and the Epic*. Ithaca, NY: Cornell University Press, 1989; Hiltebeitel, *Rethinking the Mahābhārata*, 240 note 2: 'Cf. Suzuki 1989 on the "metamorphoses" of epic heroines beginning with Helen, and "woman as a figure that questions" (3). Given Homer's poetic voice and vision (40, 54–5), Helen in particular interrogates the authority of the epic's heroic code (28, 33) that scapegoats women in the name of men's heroic struggles'.

170 Hiltebeitel, *Rethinking the Mahābhārata*, 259–60.

171 Ibid., 240–77.

172 Dhand, *Woman as Fire, Woman as Sage*, 149; see also 160.

173 Biardeau, 'The Salvation of the king', 96–7; 97: 'Once the *kshatriya* gained access to salvation through his specific and impure activities, the generalisation became easy. Every sort of impurity could be sacralised and turned into *svadharma*. Nothing was left outside the realm of ultimate values, though at the same time the status of Brahmans remained unimpaired'.

174 Ramesh N. Patel, *Philosophy of the Gītā*. New York: Peter Lang, 1991, 64–5.

175 Woods, *Destiny and Human Initiative in the Mahābhārata*, 2.

176 Ibid., 3.

177 Redfield, *Nature and Culture in the Iliad*, 252 note 27.

178 Katz, *Arjuna in the Mahābhārata*, 155–96; quotations at 155 and 168–9.

179 Gill, *Personality in Greek Epic, Tragic, and Philosophy*, 181.

180 Armstrong, *The Great Transformation*, 227–42, 252–64.

181 For the Greek case, on justice, cf. Cairns, *Aidōs*, 126, 132–5, 239 note 81; on compassion, Armstrong, *The Great Transformation*, 110ff.

182 Mario Liverani, *Israel's History and the History of Israel*. London/Oakville: Equinox, 2006, 207.

Chapter 6

1 Cf. Assmann, *Das kulturelle Gedächtnis*, 274–5: 'Heldenepik ist die bevorzugte Gattung des kulturellen Gedächtnisses im Rahmen einer bestimmten Gesellschaftsform. Diese Gesellschaftsform ist *ritterlich*, d.h. aristokratisch, kriegerisch und individualistisch geprägt.

Zum Rittertum gehört, wo überall wir es auf der Welt antreffen, ein Superioritätsbewusstsein und ein besonderes, gewissermassen individualistisches Selbstgefühl, das sich wohl vor allem aus dem für die Pferdezucht notwendigen Landbesitz und aus der "übermenschlichen" Geschwindigkeit der Fortbewegung ergibt'. The term 'individualistic' in this context means 'outstanding', 'excelling', but *within* the community.

2 Schein, *The Mortal Hero*, 17. Schein, 69–70, continues: 'Homer's attitude toward heroism can be seen in the very word *heros*, which elsewhere denotes a figure worshipped in hero cults, but in the *Iliad* signifies a warrior who lives and dies in the pursuit of honour and glory. . . . Winning honour and glory, however, makes life meaningful not only because humans are mortal but also because of the social value system that is normative throughout the poem'.

3 Douglas L. Cairns, *Aidōs: The Psychology and Ethics of Honour and Shame in Ancient Greek Literature*. Oxford: Clarendon Press, (1993) 2002, 57. Frank Henderson Stewart, *Honor*. Chicago, IL/London: The University of Chicago Press, 1994, 21–5, suggests that we look at *honour as a right, the right to be treated as having a certain worth, a right to respect*. Honour is a *claim-right*, that is, a right that something be done by another. That which entitles one to honour, the source of honour, is not identical to one's honour. Moreover, honour is allocated according to certain rules, and different societies will apply different rules. Accordingly, one can claim or lose it.

4 Cairns, *Aidōs*, 74: 'Again, it appears that the judgement, whether that of one's own side or that of one's enemies, is based on results rather than intentions, and Adkins is therefore right to stress the importance of results in Homeric society, particularly in the warrior society of the *Iliad*, and particularly in the context of the individual's *aidōs* for the opinions of others'. Cairns adds, however, that this conclusion should be viewed with more nuance when it comes to the judgements of one's friends.

5 Cairns, *Aidōs*, 92–103. Stewart, *Honor*, 54–63, points out that in the major modern European languages and in Arabic, the word 'honour' covers both vertical and horizontal relations. Vertical honour (between unequals) and horizontal honour (between equals) both draw from a common underlying sense of respect and value. But the ancient and classical Greek notion of honour (*timē*) and the Latin word *honor* (and the medieval German word *êre*) had their uses in the context of vertical relations only, in terms either of group superiority-in-rank or of individual superiority-in-competition.

6 Schein, *The Mortal Hero*, 71.

7 F. G. Naerebout, H. W. Singor, *De Oudheid: Grieken en Romeinen in de context van de wereldgeschiedenis*. Baarn: Ambo, 1995, 134–5.

8 Schein, *The Mortal Hero*, 80.

9 Milner, Jr, *Status and Sacredness*, 22–8; Milner, Jr, 29–35, explains that status has two attributes. First, *status is a relatively inalienable resource; its distribution is limited*. Status is stereotyped (dis)approval, and is primarily located in other people's minds. To change your status, you must change other people's opinions. Appropriation of status works differently from appropriating property or social positions by means of force or wealth. Secondly, *status is a relatively in-expansible resource; its amount is limited.* It is a matter of the utmost concern for high status groups to keep their numbers as small as possible and to limit the accessibility for lower status groups to move upwards. On the acquisition of honour in Homer as a 'zero-sum game', in which any gain must be at the expense of another's loss, see: Cairns, *Aidōs*, 94 incl. note 141.

10 Ralph M. Rosen, Ineke Sluiter, 'General Introduction', in: idem (eds), *Andreia: Studies in Manliness and Courage in Classical Antiquity*. Leiden/ Boston: E. J. Brill, 2003, 8–9, 14.

11 Karen Bassi, 'The Semantics of Manliness in Ancient Greece', in: Rosen, Sluiter (eds), *Andreia*, 54. The absence of ambiguity in epic manliness may be due to rhetorical nostalgia, a product of cultural processes congruent with early state-formation, glorifying and displaying onto a rhetorical plane archaizing values (36–7).

12 N. J. Sewell-Rutter, *Guilt by Descent: Moral Inheritance and Decision Making in Greek Tragedy*. Oxford/New York: Oxford University Press, 2007, 160.

13 Bryant, *Moral Codes and Social Structure in Ancient Greece*, 90–1; cf. 93: 'The efforts of the Archaic war poets to transform martial *aretē* into a civic virtue were paralleled by the work of lawgivers in the domain of justice'.

14 Peter T. Struck, 'The Ordeal of the Divine Sign: Divination and Manliness in Archaic and Classical Greece', in: Rosen, Sluiter (eds), *Andreia*, 184.

15 Alles, *The Iliad, the Rāmāyana, and the Work of Religion*, esp. 77–106; Alles, 'Verbal Craft and Religious Act in the *Iliad*', 293–309.

16 Edward E. Cohen, 'The High Cost of *Andreia* at Athens', in: Rosen, Sluiter (eds), *Andreia*, 145–65.

17 Bryant, *Moral Codes and Social Structure in Ancient Greece*, 79–125, esp. 98, speaks of a 'redeployment of aristocratic excellences in the interest of the Polis'.

18 M. M. Austin, P. Vidal-Naquet, *Economic and Social History of Ancient Greece: An Introduction*. London: Batsford Academic and Educational Ltd., (1977) 1980, 207–8.

19 Peter Green, *A Concise History of Ancient Greece to the Close of the Classical era*. London: Thames and Hudson, (1973) pb 1981², 63: 'The psychological and political implications of this new civic defence force, in which farmers, merchants, well-to-do artisans and indigent aristocrats fought shoulder to shoulder for their community, were nothing short of momentous. Homeric individualism vanished overnight, and the whole concept of a chariot-borne monarch cheered on by the peasantry went with it. Most true-blue aristocrats, choosing social prestige over effective power, hived off into the small, costly, exclusive cavalry arm; since from

now on until Philip II's day (mid-fourth century) the issue of a battle was never decided by cavalry alone, they could no longer pose as their city's indispensable protectors. There was no democratic leveller to match the phalanx, where each man's shield defended his neighbour, and social distinctions went for nothing. The hoplites' collective achievement inspired a collective sense of pride. Here, if anywhere, we can glimpse the roots of the concept identifying the *polis* with its citizens'. For more recent insights on the elitist character of the hoplites until the fifth century BCE, see Henk Singor, *Homerische Helden: Oorlogvoering in het vroege Griekenland*. Amsterdam: Amsterdam University Press—Salomé, 2005, 109–37, esp. 116.

20 Austin, Vidal-Naquet, *Economic and Social History of Ancient Greece*, 131–41.

21 Mary Whitlock Blundell, *Helping Friends and Harming Enemies: A Study in Sophocles and Greek Ethics*. Cambridge: Cambridge University Press, 1989, 1–49.

22 Roger B. Manning, *Swordsmen: The Martial Ethos in the Three Kingdoms*. Oxford: Oxford University Press, 2003.

23 Manning, *Swordsmen*, 1–6.

24 Manning, *Swordsmen*, 7, 71–80, 119–20. The tournament became the central ritual of chivalry. (Richard Barber, *The Knight and Chivalry*. Revised edition. Woodbridge: The Boydell Press, (1970) 2000, 155–224.) It continued to be popular as a festival celebrating special occasions until the end of the sixteenth century, during the entire reign of queen Elizabeth I, featuring knights such as Sir Philip Sidney in 1581. But the personal enthusiasm for tournaments of King James I's eldest son Henry was by that time – he died in 1612 –considered unusual. (Barber, *The Knight and Chivalry*, 337–9.) The famous revolt of Robert Devereux, second Earl of Essex, against Queen Elizabeth I in 1601, has been termed 'the last honour revolt' and interpreted as the swansong of chivalric culture by Mervyn James. (Richard W. Kaeuper, *Chivalry and Violence in Medieval Europe*. Oxford: Oxford University Press, (1999) 2002, 299–300.) Even among the London crowd, Essex was popular as a paragon of chivalry. When his revolt failed, however, he soon abandoned the language and culture of autonomous honour, and adopted submission to the queen – honour was hers to distribute, not his to win in showy independence.

25 Manning, *Swordsmen*, 65ff.

26 Ibid., 5–6.

27 Ibid., 7.

28 Ibid., 193–244.

29 Jeroen Duindam, *Myths of Power: Norbert Elias and the Early Modern European Court*. Amsterdam: Amsterdam University Press, 1995, 47–8.

30 Manning, *Swordsmen*, 52: 'Shakespeare's history plays reveal much about what the playwright and his audience thought about honour. Ancient lineage and sound moral education conferred a predisposition to honour and yielded exalted rank and exceptional virtue (that is, valour). These qualities were necessarily manifested through displays of force, violence, and physical courage. A precondition of such exertions was martial prowess, and the best evidence of the quest for honour and glory was the testimony of wounds. As Shakespeare has Richard, third duke of York, demand of Edmund Beaufort, duke of Somerset, in *Henry VI, Part 2* (III.i): "Show me one scar character'd on thy skin:/Men's flesh preserved so whole do seldom win".

31 Manning, *Swordsmen*, 51. Stewart, *Honor*, 19–29, discusses the advantages and disadvantages of the so-called 'bipartite theory' of honour, the widespread theory that 'honour' has an external side to it – outer honour as reputation – and an internal side – inner honour as a personal quality, honourableness. The main problem is to specify how 'outer honour' and 'inner honour' relate. The tricky thing about honour is that one can lose it. But what exactly does one lose if one loses one's honour? The notion 'honourable' means 'that which makes one worthy of honour' (glorious, creditable) and/or 'being worthy of honour' (virtuous, respectable). Can one be honoured (recognized by the world) without being honourable (personally possessing valuable qualities), and can one be honourable without being honoured? In fact, one can. Honour draws from a variety of sources.

32 Manning, *Swordsmen*, 81ff.

33 Stephen Greenblatt, *Will in the World: How Shakespeare became Shakespeare*. New York/London: W. W. Norton and Company, 2004, 78–9.

34 Stewart, *Honor*, 35. Stewart, *Honor*, 69, suggests that in Western Europe, during the transition from high medieval to modern honour, three shifts took place – firstly, honour is originally something like prestige, but comes increasingly to be a right; secondly, that which gives one title to this right comes increasingly to be certain moral virtues; thirdly, an increase of reflexive honour sensitivity and practice (duelling) from the end of the sixteenth to the end of the seventeenth century.

35 Cf. the Confucianist transformation of the minor warrior aristocrats (*shih*) into the scholar-gentry and ideal gentleman (*chün-tzu*): Julia Ching, *Mysticism and Kingship in China: The Heart of Chinese Wisdom*. Cambridge: Cambridge University Press, 1997, 84–92.

36 Maurice Keen, *Chivalry*. New Haven/London: Yale University Press, 1984, 252.

37 Keen, *Chivalry*, 2–19, 156–61; Barber, *The Knight and Chivalry*, 47–64, 132–51.

38 But what kind of court? Any court that was able to impose *self-restraint* on the warriors it employed? Norbert Elias, *Über den Prozess der Zivilisation. Soziogenetische und psychogenetische Untersuchungen. Vol. I: Wandlungen des Verhaltens in den weltlichen Oberschichten des Abendlandes. Vol. II: Wandlungen der Gesellschaft. Entwurf zu einer Theorie der Zivilisation*. Frankfurt am Main: Suhrkamp, (1939) 1993–94, suggests (for the French *ancient régime*) that there is an intrinsic connection between the emergence of courts as exclusive centres of state-formation at the expense of the power of competing warlords – the stately courts monopolizing coercive force – and the cultural and psychological impact of the time the nobles were forced to spend at court, where they would learn, by means of etiquette, to regulate their behaviour, to show obedience to the prince or king and to show self-restraint. See also Robert van Krieken, *Norbert Elias*. London/New York: Routledge, 1998, 98, 105–6; Matthew Innes, ' "A Place of Discipline": Carolingian Courts and Aristocratic Youth', in: Catherine Cubitt (ed.), *Court Culture in the Early Middle Ages: The Proceedings of the First Alcuin Conference.* Turnhout, Belgium: Brepols, 2003, 59–76, esp. 75–6; Janet L. Nelson, 'Was Charlemagne's Court a Courtly Society?', in: Cubitt (ed.), *Court Culture*, 39–57; Martin Aurell, 'The Western Nobility in the Late Middle Ages: A Survey of the Historiography and Some Prospects for New Research', in: Anne J. Duggan (ed.), *Nobles and Nobility in Medieval Europe: Concepts, Origins, Transformations*. Woodbridge: The Boydell Press, (2000) pb 2002, 263–73, esp. 264ff.

39 Cf. Paul Moyaert, *Begeren en vereren: Idealisering en sublimering*. Amsterdam: SUN, 2002.

40 Barber, *The Knight and Chivalry*, 67–94, esp. 72.

41 Barber, *The Knight and Chivalry*, 382. Published in 1528, Baldesar Castiglione's *Il libro del Cortegiano (The Book of the Courtier)* met with wide approval, from England to Spain, and became the model for many later works on the education of a gentleman. Duindam, *Myths of Power*, 161, writes: 'Francis I (1515–47) took many Italians into his service and *Il Cortegiano* was a great success at his court. The courtier's essential quality had to be "natural grace". Any sign of effort or determination was out of place; a duel, a dance, or a conversation were all to be conducted with the same studied ease. Conversation became a parlor game'.

42 Arditi, *A Genealogy of Manners*, 110–11.

43 Ibid., 208–17.

44 Bassi, 'The Semantics of Manliness', 27–32, 56, and 38–40 resp.

45 Struck, 'The Ordeal of the Divine Sign', 169–74.

46 In Sophocles' *Electra* (975–85), Electra's talk of establishing a reputation for 'manliness' when killing her mother suggests that acts of revenge for domestic crimes are the same as (Hector's) killing an enemy on a foreign battlefield – an implied but problematic equation, according to Bassi. In Euripides' *Electra* (947–51), Electra is painfully aware of the absence of 'manly' epic heroes who have been replaced on the tragic stage by citizens playing them. (Bassi, 'The Semantics of Manliness', 40–3.)

47 Myles McDonnell, 'Roman Men and Greek Virtue', in: Rosen, Sluiter (eds), *Andreia*, 236.

48 Cairns, *Aidōs*, 250–9, quotation at 252.

49 Redfield, *Nature and Culture in the Iliad*, 20–5.

50 Ibid., 91.

51 Ibid., 263–4.

52 Cairns, *Aidōs*, 250–64.

53 Blundell, *Helping Friends*, quotations at 27 and 261–2 resp.

54 Redfield, *Nature and Culture in the Iliad*, 102.

55 Redfield, *Nature and Culture in the Iliad*, 104–7. Gill, *Personality in Greek Epic, Tragic, and Philosophy*, 114, summarizes Redfield's point eloquently. Cf. Bernard Williams, *Shame and Necessity*, 101: 'The necessity . . . that Ajax recognised, was grounded in his own identity, his sense of himself as someone who can live in some social circumstances and not others, and what mediated between himself and the world was his sense of shame. He, being a warrior under the heroic code, balanced that identity on a narrow base of personal achievement. So of course did Achilles and Hector in the *Iliad*'.

56 Gill, *Personality in Greek Epic, Tragic, and Philosophy*, 134–48, quotation at 144.

57 Redfield, *Nature and Culture in the Iliad*, 126: 'Hector is caught between household and city, between youth and age. He is both king and warrior; he is son and brother and also father and husband. In these contradictions the tragedy is latent. . . . As a free, choosing being, the hero looks to the future; as a mortal creature, he looks away from it. That is the inner contradiction of Hector's farewell to his wife. He leaves her to go toward action, heavy with consciousness of the limits of action. . . . The contradiction remains unresolved'.

58 Cairns, *Aidōs*, 48ff., 126, 132–5 and 239 note 81.

59 See also Jacqueline de Romilly, *Hector*. Paris: Editions de Fallois, 1997, 105.

60 The conclusion that the limits of the ancient Greek martial code of honour are being explored in Homer's *Iliad* is not meant to imply that Greek tragedy reflects its society in a straightforward way. Hall points out that, whereas in Athenian reality 'people could rise socially beyond birth-status', (Hall, 'The Sociology of Athenian tragedy', 99) 'in the tragic universe characters cannot improve upon the social status into which they were born'. (112) But one of the most frequent forms of 'tragic reversal' (*peripeteia*) is actually *status reversal*. 'Numerous characters, especially in plays treating the fall of Troy, lose previously aristocratic status and become slaves', a fate regarded as particularly more 'tragic' if suffered 'by those once free who have lost their freedom' than if suffered by those having 'been born into a whole life in servitude'. (111) 'The once-free, moreover, can regain their freedom. . . . Male characters who by accident of fortune lose high status also usually recover it, like Homer's Odysseus'. (112)

61 Gill, *Personality in Greek Epic, Tragic, and Philosophy*, 115–74, is largely in agreement with Redfield, but stresses the special reason the audience has for its sympathetic response. According to Gill, 123, 'structuralist analysis, with its focus on decoding the patterns of the work as a whole, is in danger of understating the central role of epic and lyric dialogue as a medium through which the audience engages with' the problematic heroes. To make his point, Gill focuses on Homer's Achilles and Euripides' Medea and the dialogical character and interpersonal context of their monologues.

62 Schein, *The Mortal Hero*, 71. For Schein's appreciation of Redfield's position on Hector, see Schein, *The Mortal Hero*, 192 note 4.

63 Schein, *The Mortal Hero*, 82.

64 Cairns, *Aidōs*, 215.

65 Cairns, *Aidōs*, 228–41, quotation at 228.

66 Cairns, *Aidōs*, 266.

67 Ibid., 272–3.

68 Ibid., 340–2.

69 Cairns, *Aidōs*, 381–92, quotations at 386–7, 383 and 390 resp.

70 Taylor, *Sources of the Self*, 117.

71 Bevington, *Shakespeare's Ideas*, 143–6.

72 Ibid., 175.

73 Kernan, *Shakespeare, the King's Playwright*, 1–2. 'There had been kings before the Renaissance', Kernan, 1, notes, 'but they had been in fact feudal lords who, with difficulty, maintained limited authority over groups of nearly independent barons, each ruling a duchy or march in his own right. Now divine-right monarchs appeared who claimed authority directly from God over all the areas of the civil and much of the personal life of all ranks of subjects. Codes of civil law that had a Roman basis favouring imperial power were introduced to compete with ancient legal arrangements developed in local circumstances to meet such community needs as the common law. Religion was reorganized along national lines, with the king as head of church and state. Standing professional armies under central control replaced bands of feudal retainers maintained and mustered by the old aristocracy in times of war'.

74 Kernan, *Shakespeare, the King's Playwright*, 34.

75 Ibid., 36–7.

76 Murray, 'Hamlet', 263.

77 Ibid., 263–4.

78 Watson, 'Tragedies of revenge and ambition', 160–1. On Essex, see note 24.

79 McAlindon, *Shakespeare's Tragic Cosmos*, 18–19.

80 Ibid., 102–3.

81 Ibid., 110–11.

82 Margolies, *Monsters of the Deep*, 6–7.

83 Ibid., 11.

84 Ibid., 49.

85 Ibid., 56.

86 It is disorienting not only because it is contrary to expectations, but also because it is nearly inexpressible: 'This is not a matter of irony, or meaning the direct opposite of what the words literally convey, but a slippage between word and referent, where expectation remains with the word but is frustrated in life'. (Margolies, *Monsters of the Deep*, 62). See also 63.

87 Margolies, *Monsters of the Deep*, 67.

88 Ibid., 47–8.

89 Margolies, *Monsters of the Deep*, 148–9: 'There is also in *Hamlet* a feeling of loss. The excellent image of human dignity expressed in the Great Chain of Being seems to be false. Man gained dignity by being placed directly below the angels in the Chain, "in apprehension how like a god" as Hamlet said, but that vision must be abandoned. Hamlet has to judge by what he sees before him and concludes: "what is this quintessence of dust?" (II. ii.306, 308). There is all the pain of adolescent disillusionment at a world gone bad'.

90 René Girard, *La violence et le sacré*. Paris: Grasset, 1972; René Girard, *Des choses cachées depuis la fondation du monde*. Paris: Grasset et Fasquelle, 1978; René Girard, *Le bouc émissaire*. Paris: Grasset, 1982; cf. Guido Vanheeswijck, 'Vijandige broers, verloren zonen. Halfweg tussen ethische bewustwording en mythische vergelding: de precaire positie van de tragedie volgens René Girard', in: Paul Vanden Berghe, Willem Lemmens, Johan Taels (eds), *Tragisch: Over tragedie en ethiek in de 21e eeuw*. Budel. Damon, 2005, 43–85.

91 Eli Sagan, *At the Dawn of Tyranny: The Origins of Individualism, Political Oppression, and the State*. (New York: Alfred A. Knopf, 1985) London: Faber and Faber, 1986, 81. Sagan sees this expansiveness of the feeling of pathos as crucial to all great epic poets.

92 Heering, *Tragiek*, 17.

93 Armstrong, *The Great Transformation*, 256: 'When he reached out to Ismene and Antigone, his distraught daughters, Oedipus forgot himself in sympathy for their plight. The chorus too was filled with terror, their dread so great that at first they could not look the mutilated man in the face. But gradually this spectacle of unspeakable suffering taught them compassion, their fear dissolving as they struggled to understand the depth of Oedipus's pain. They begin to speak tenderly to him, calling him "my friend" and "dear one" '.

94 George K. Hunter, 'Tyrant and Martyr: Religious Heroisms in Elizabethan Tragedy', in: Maynard Mack, George deForest Lord (eds), *Poetic Traditions of the English Renaissance*. New Haven/London: Yale University Press, 1982, 85–102.

95 Hunter, 'Tyrant and Martyr', 88.

96 Ibid., 89–91.

97 Ibid., 92–5.

98 Hunter, 'Tyrant and Martyr', 96. Hunter's exposition sheds an interesting light on the complexities of Brutus's character in *Julius Caesar* (note keywords like 'sacrificer', 'butcher', 'meek and gentle' in the two following quotes from the play!), but also makes one realize to what extent the plays themselves already stage our critical debate – a point made by Danson. Brutus is determined that his killing of Julius Caesar will not be a murder, but a justified, even a religious, sacrifice. 'Let's be sacrificers, but not butchers, Caius'. (II.i.166) But Brutus, the sacrificer, becomes the hunted victim of the pursuing spirit of Caesar in the second half of the play, Caesar's posthumous revenge. And in the first half, Brutus, the legitimate sacrificer, is already under critique within the play itself. Danson, *Shakespeare's Dramatic Genres*, 127: 'In *Julius Caesar*, mistake and mission are hard to separate because both the political issues and the characters' motives—those of Caesar and Antony, on the one hand, and Brutus, Cassius, and the conspirators, on the other—repel the reductiveness of moralistic judgements: one person's "noblest Roman of them all" is a "savage" in the judgement of another. And the play itself enacts our critical debates. So Antony, as if directly answering Brutus's claim to be a sacrificer but not a butcher, addresses the dead Caesar: "O pardon me, thou bleeding piece of earth,/That I am meek and gentle with these butchers" (III.i.257–8). The play enacts our critical divisions in another way as well, for in this odd version of revenge tragedy there is more than one mission and more than one revenge'.

99 Keyishian, *The Shapes of Revenge*, 57: 'Hamlet is in many ways his father's son: he, too, holds himself to high standards and strongly values physical courage, moral integrity, self-restraint, patriotism, loyalty, and respect for women (until they betray him). But Hamlet and his father are also crucially different in character and personality. For one thing, Hamlet is psychologically incapable of sharing his father's magnanimity toward Gertrude: her adultery seems to Hamlet as morally offensive as Claudius' fratricide. For another, while the Ghost's outrage is a product of his satisfaction with the probity of his life, his domestic virtues, the morality of his rule, and his glorious military achievements, Hamlet has no such confidence. At various points he characterizes himself as weak, morally flawed, and infirm of purpose; his mind is contaminated by feelings of impotence, self-doubt, and self-hatred; he is disillusioned, suspicious, and bitter in his dealings with others; and he is consumed by concerns we have no reason to suspect he has until he unexpectedly articulates them at some moment of tension. There is, as well, the problem presented by Hamlet's age. The young man the Ghost is asking to take vengeance upon a reigning monarch is still at university, needs parental permission to travel abroad, and can be subjected to a public and humiliating scolding before the assembled court. These differences underlie many of the psychological tensions Hamlet experiences and explain his restless oscillations from one stance to another: embittered observer and malcontent, Machiavellian strategist, man of passion, stoic, bloody homicide, moral guide, rationalist, and, finally, fatalist'.

100 Keyishian, *The Shapes of Revenge*, 67.

101 Katz, *Arjuna in the Mahābhārata*, 35–6: 'As pointed out most clearly by Dumézil in *The Destiny of the Warrior*, Bhima and Arjuna are two different types of warrior. The different manners in which they fight reflect the manners of their divine fathers, Vayu, the Vedic wind god, and Indra. Dumézil traces this division back to the hypothetical Indo-European prototype also reflected, for example, in the Greek distinction between Herakles and Achilles. The Vayu/Bhima type of warrior is, according to Dumézil, brutal, amoral and not particularly intelligent. The Indra/Arjuna type is, rather, a warrior knight, chivalrous, . . . caught up in a web of moral issues because he lives according to certain rules and regulations'.

102 Katz, *Arjuna in the Mahābhārata*, 44, states that the weapons he uses are named after deities whose particular powers they reflect. It is primarily by weapon usage that Arjuna incorporates into himself the various divine powers that are considered essential to kingship.

103 Katz, *Arjuna in the Mahābhārata*, 71–9. In one respect, the Khāndava story can be compared, according to Katz, 79–83, 'with the story of the battle of Gilgamesh and Enkidu together against Huwara (Babylonian version) or Humbaba (Assyrian version), the terrible spirit dwelling in the cedar forest, in the *Epic of Gilgamesh*. The image of two friends going together into the forest to prove their heroism for the first time parallels the image in the Khāndava story of Arjuna and Krishna proving their might in the forest', both battles constituting a rite of *warrior initiation* of their respective heroes. To regard the Khāndava episode as primarily initiatory suggests that Arjuna's main purpose in fighting Indra is simply to prove himself a man in his father's eyes. The episode of Arjuna's encounter with a Kirata ('mountain man'), who is the god Shiva in disguise, and his subsequent visit to Indra's heaven and fight against Indra's enemies, adds to the Indian definition of the hero, according to Katz, that in order 'to be a true Indian hero a character must be capable of great ascetic feats which will be at the root of his power'. (90–104) While the Khāndava Forest battle was against natural phenomena and animals, here the fight is against demons. In fighting these demon battles, Arjuna is performing the perfect Indra role of demon fighter. Since ascetic activity is ultimately an individual affair in the Indian context, Arjuna faces the journey and faces Shiva alone. 'Such lone activity is actually more typical of shamanic initiation than of warrior initiation'. (94) The forest exile culminating in the thirteenth incognito year may be viewed as a sort of consecration (*diksha*) for future action. Posing as a eunuch is a sign of heroic self-control that enables Arjuna to gather up his vital powers (a yogic task) for future use.

104 Katz, *Arjuna in the Mahābhārata*, 105.

105 Katz, *Arjuna in the Mahābhārata*, 116–17; 115: 'The metaphor of the Kurukshetra War as a sacrifice captures the central meaning of the epic at the heroic level, which is built upon the structural opposition of order and disorder, both represented by the imagery of fire and sacrifice. In simplest terms, order is represented by the rightly performed sacrifice, which gets out of control. In practice, however, the imagery becomes more complex, since even rightly performed sacrifice has its frightening and destructive aspect. . . . a "sacrifice of war" such as that at Kurukshetra may be viewed either as an effort to preserve order or as a scene of horrible destruction, or both. At the heroic level, however, the ultimate outcome is the preservation of order by the good, and the creative effort of the hero in the face of great odds is emphasized. Kurukshetra, "the field of the Kurus", is seen as the *dharmakshetra* ("field of *dharma*"), the field of world order (6.23.1 (*Bhagavadgītā* 1.1); 14.93.2)'.

106 Arjuna is chosen to oversee the major portion of this sacrifice, that is, to follow the sacrificial horse, which stakes out Yudhisthira's empire in all directions, and defend the horse during a prescribed period of wandering. Here, Arjuna takes the active role of warrior, not the relatively passive role of sacrificing king, although the fact that it is his wives who gather for the ceremony suggests that the epic visualizes him in the kingly role as well. (Katz, *Arjuna in the Mahābhārata*, 117).

107 Katz, *Arjuna in the Mahābhārata*, 117–18.

108 Ibid., 129.

109 Katz, *Arjuna in the Mahābhārata*, 131–8, quotations at 132 and 138 resp.

110 Katz, *Arjuna in the Mahābhārata*, 139–50.

111 Katz, *Arjuna in the Mahābhārata*, 186–7 note 1: 'When our battle is in progress, one fighting with speech should be opposed with speech. One who has left the midst of battle is by no means to be killed. And a chariot warrior is to be fought by a chariot warrior, a chief elephant by an elephant, a cavalryman with a horse, and an infantryman by an infantryman. . . . According to usage, with regard for heroism, according to one's power, according to age, having called out, one should strike, (but) not at one who is unsuspecting or in distress. One engaged with another, heedless or, likewise, with face averted, with weapons exhausted or without armour is by no means to be killed. One should by no means strike charioteers, bearers, weapon bringers, or sounders of kettledrums and conches'. (6.1.28–32) These rules are repeated, as a whole or in part, and with variations, throughout the battle books, and they also appear in the didactic books (12.96.7ff., 12.97.3).

112 Katz, *Arjuna in the Mahābhārata*, 155.

113 Ibid., 146–9, 166.

114 Katz, *Arjuna in the Mahābhārata*, 168–9: 'The Greeks were great admirers of cleverness, as many of their tales show, and even glorified an epic hero who was preeminently a trickster and master of disguise, Odysseus. The *Iliad* too contains a large number of deceitful actions by both sides, yet it does not dwell on them: in fact, Homer omits the pivotal deception of the war, the Trojan horse, from his account entirely'.

115 Katz, *Arjuna in the Mahābhārata*, 169–72, quotations at 171.

116 Brodbeck, *Asakta Karman*, 80.

117 Ibid., 13.

118 Ibid., 13.

119 Ibid., 13f., 212, 214.

120 Cf. Richard Frackowiak, James Rowe, Karl Friston, 'Attention to Action: Specific Modulation of Corticocortical Interactions in Humans', in: *Neuroimage* 17/2 (2002), 988–98.

121 Cf. Dave Collins, John Kremer, Deidre Scully, 'Psychology in sport', in: *Journal of Psychophysiology* 10/4 (1996), 350–1.

122 The movement in practice and in the mind, both activate the brain in the same brain part in the same rhythm, at least for two-thirds; visualizing in the mind is as good as physical practice as far as the activity of the brain is concerned. In one respect, visualization can do something that physical practice never can – on the practice pitch, there is no hostile chanting of opponents, but all that anxiety can be present in the brain when you visualize. If you are going to be aggressive in the real situation, be aggressive in your image; if you are going to be scared in the real situation, you should be scared in your mental image and overcome it in your mental image in order to perform accordingly.

123 Brodbeck, *Asakta Karman*, 99.

124 Brodbeck, *Asakta Karman*, 14; 13–14: 'As for Arjuna, despite his excellent performance during the battle, he does not appear to have become a permanent *karmayogin*: later in his life he claims to have forgotten what Krishna told him, and asks for a repeat, which Krishna himself admits he cannot provide properly (*Mahābhārata* 14.16)'.

125 Brodbeck, *Asakta Karman*, 87–112, quotation at 19; he continues by claiming that ' "ultimate liberation" would be modelled on "peace of mind".'

126 Malinar, *Rājavidyā. Das königliche Wissen um Herrschaft und Verzicht*, 77–8.

127 A link between the call for following Krishna's example of detached action and Arjuna as its kingly addressee seems to be suggested by Jacqueline Hirst, 'Upholding the World: Dharma in the Bhagavadgītā', in: Lipner (ed.), *The Bhagavadgita for our times*, 54: 'By following Krishna's example of detached action, the wise will continue to uphold the world, to act for *lokasamgraha*, the welfare or holding together of the world. Were Krishna not to give this example, people would neglect to act properly and chaos would ensue (3.23–25). . . . It is this whole teaching which is deemed the "most secret . . . knowledge of kings (or kingly knowledge—note, Arjuna, its value). It is *dharmyam*, easy to carry out, imperishable (9.1–2)." '

128 Malinar, *Rājavidyā*, 2–3, 69, 86.

129 Malinar and von Stietencron do not explicitly refer to Romila Thapar, but one quote from her earlier work may suffice to make clear that they could draw on it for their thesis that the traditional kinship system has a different relationship to territory and expansion than the subsequent centralized states: 'The breaking away of the segment of the clan was possible if there was enough land and other resources available in the vicinity. With the increase in numbers of *gana-sanghas* and kingdoms this became more difficult since in the case of the latter erstwhile frontier zones would have been claimed, protected and defended. The need to expand access to resources both in terms of fertile land and busy trade routes encouraged the conquest of neighbours. But the conquest of neighbours was through a systematic campaign as that between Magadha and the Vrjji confederacy, and not through sporadic raids. . . . Whereas the lineage system profited by intermittent raids and warfare, the state system required a limitation on locations given to warfare—the fields of battles and of campaigns—with a substantial area of stability and peace. This was necessary to prevent the disruption of agriculture and trade. Neighbours were therefore envisaged in a network of either hostile or friendly alliances'. (Thapar, *From Lineage to State*, 129).

130 John Keay, *India: A History*. London/New Delhi: Harper Collins Publishers, (2000) pb 2001.

131 Romila Thapar, 'The Historian and the Epic' (1979), in: Thapar (ed.), *Cultural Pasts*, 613–29, esp. 622–3; quotations at 623.

132 Jan C. Heesterman, 'The Conundrum of the King's Authority' and 'Kautilya and the Ancient Indian State', in: Heesterman (ed.), *The Inner Conflict of Tradition*, 108–27 and 128–40 respectively.

133 Heesterman, *The Inner Conflict of Tradition*, 123–4, quoted in paragraph 3.1 of the second part of the chapter on narrative aspects.

134 Heesterman, *The Inner Conflict of Tradition*, 124–5: 'As long as settled agricultural communities were limited in number and restricted in their resources, while wide expanses were left open, the alternation of settled life with nomadic raiding and transhuming expeditions to supplement meager resources may have been a reasonably effective proposition. However, with the growth and spread of settled agriculture, a different type of organization and a new conception of authority would have been needed. At any rate, the ritual reform gave a new answer to the problem of authority. The cyclical pattern of alternation between *grāma* (the settled agricultural community) and *aranya* (the outside world of the jungle) did manage to keep up the contact between this and the other world, between settled community and authority transcending it, but at a price of violence and insecurity. Authority and the settled life dependent on it remained all the time contingent on the uncertain outcome of the cycle of violence. We can readily understand the criticism which even the *Mahābhārata*, though still clearly showing the original cyclical pattern and even recommending death while facing the enemy as the "sacrifice of battle", has Bhīshma, himself a warrior-sage, level against war. Even victory in battle, Bhīshma convincingly argues, is simply an evil. The same idea seems to underlie the ritual reform, which as we have it in the texts, rules out violence and battle, reducing the last remnants of agonistic rites such as the chariot drive to innocuous, strictly ritualized affairs. In order to achieve this, it broke the cycle of violence. And by breaking the cycle, it opened the way to free authority and make it unassailably transcendent'. This is perhaps, Victor van Bijlert suggested in a personal comment in 2008, the real ancient starting-point of Hinduism as we know it.

135 Personal letter from Jan C. Heesterman on this issue, 15 May, 2001.

136 Personal email from Chakravarti Ram-Prasad on this issue, 13 June, 2001.

137 Thapar, 'The Historian and the Epic', 623–4; Thapar, *From Lineage to State*, 26.

138 Thapar, *From Lineage to State*, 24–31, 130–1; quotation at 24.

139 Thapar, *From Lineage to State*, 130–1.

140 Hiltebeitel, *Rethinking the Mahābhārata*, 181.

141 Ibid., 182 note 15.

142 Ibid., 180 note 9.

143 Ibid., 203.

144 Killingley, 'Enjoying the World,' 68.

145 *Constructions hagiographiques dans le monde indien—Entre mythe et histoire*. Sous la responsabilité de Françoise Mallism. Paris: Librairie Honore Champion, 2001.

146 Armstrong, *The Great Transformation*, 144–5.

147 Barbara Tuchman, *The Proud Tower: A Portrait of the World before the War 1890–1914*. New York: Macmillan, 1966.

148 Hiltebeitel, *Rethinking the Mahābhārata*, 204.

149 *The Bhagavad Gītā*, trans. Sargeant, 704.

150 Peter van der Veer, *Religious Nationalism: Hindus and Muslims in India*. Berkeley, CA/Los Angeles: University of California Press, 1994, 97.

151 Katz, *Arjuna in the Mahābhārata*, 58. On the ethics of sharing his prize with his four brothers, see Arti Dhand, *Woman as Fire, Woman as Sage*, 117–19.

152 Hiltebeitel, *Rethinking the Mahābhārata*, 181.

153 The 'insult contest' between Karna and his charioteer Śalya is a perversion that destroys Karna's energy (*tejas*). (8.27.18–27) (Cf. Hiltebeitel, *The Ritual of Battle*, 255).

154 Cf. 1 Samuel 17: Goliath's verbal challenging of the Israelites provokes an all-decisive one-to-one fight against David.

155 Armstrong, *The Great Transformation*, 138, 306–13.

156 Sovereignty is the core of Yudhisthira's royal duty.

157 Hiltebeitel, *Rethinking the Mahābhārata*, 213.

Chapter 7

1 Sands, 'Tragedy, Theology, and Feminism', 41–61; quotation at 43.

2 Sands, 'Tragedy, Theology, and Feminism', 52.

3 Ibid., 43.

4 Jean-Pierre Vernant, Pierre Vidal-Naquet, *Mythe et tragédie en Grèce ancienne*. Vol. II. Paris: La Découverte, 1986. See also Part 1 Section 6 on 'Historical shifts in world view and view of the human being' in the chapter on literary–cultural aspects.

5 Jean-Pierre Vernant, 'Ébauches de la volonté dans la tragédie grecque', in: Jean-Pierre Vernant, Pierre Vidal-Naquet, *Mythe et tragédie en Grèce ancienne*. Vol. I. Paris: La Découverte, (1986) 1989, 73; Segal, *Oedipus Tyrannus*, 81; Goldhill, 'The language of tragedy', 132–3.

6 Vernant, 'Ébauches de la volonté', 56, 72–3.

7 R. P. Winnington-Ingram, *Sophocles: An Interpretation.* Cambridge: Cambridge University Press, (1980) 2002[6], 202.

8 Vernant, 'Ébauches de la volonté', 70.

9 Cf. Phoenix in *Iliad* 9.443: 'a speaker of speeches, a doer of deeds'.

10 What comes to mind here are the references of Redfield, *Nature and Culture in the Iliad*, to John Jones and Aristotle; 24: 'For Jones . . . a character in tragedy is "significantly himself only in what he says and does". The themes of tragedy are therefore man in his social relations; the tragic action is external rather than internal, "situational" rather than personal'. and 26–7: 'Homeric poetry is a poetry of surfaces, that is to say, of social phenomena. For Aristotle (and, I think, for Homer) such poetry is precisely a poetry of character, for character is transparently visible in speech and action. . . . For Aristotle action has meaning only when it is responsible, that is, only when it is grounded on deliberate choice. We understand the choice when we see the act and when we hear the grounds of choice stated; action, in other words, is to be understood through its justifications and its results. From this way of seeing it, men are fully fit to judge one another, and we in the audience are fully fit to judge the figures who enact the imitated event. We see that these figures are not fully free; they must respond to the situation in which they find themselves. But we also hear them reasoning about their situation, and we see their reasoned acts transform the situation. We judge the character by his reasons and by the effect of his acts'. Simon Goldhill, 'Mind and madness', in: Simon Goldhill (ed.), *Reading Greek Tragedy.* Cambridge: Cambridge University Press, 1986, 172, agrees with Jones and Redfield to a great extent, when he remarks: 'The term translated by "character" is *ethos* and, while it certainly implies a set of attitudes or a particular disposition, there is an important difference between *ethos* and the common sense of "character". For *ethos*, as Jones says, "is without the ambition of inclusiveness". *Ethos* does not attempt, as "character" often does in modern usage, to express a whole personality or the make-up of a psyche'.

11 Michael Trapp, 'Tragedy and the Fragility of Moral Reasoning: Response to Foley', in: Silk (ed.), *Tragedy and the Tragic*, 80.

12 Watson, 'Tragedies of revenge and ambition', 173.

13 Vernant, 'Ébauches de la volonté', 55.

14 Ibid., 51–2.

15 Williams, *Shame and Necessity,* 21–49, esp. 36–41, quotations at 41.

16 Williams, *Shame and Necessity*, 42–3.

17 Cf. Sorabji, *Emotion and Peace of Mind*, 321: 'Instead of asking who invented *the* concept of will, I think it is more profitable to ask something different, since there is no one concept, and much less do we have an agreed concept nowadays. Rather, will is a desire with a special relation to reason and a number of functions associated with it. Some of these functions come in clusters. It is more illuminating to ask when these functions came together and who made the decisive difference. The functions include two important clusters, freedom and responsibility on the one hand and will-power on the other. My claim will be that both these clusters can be found early in Greek philosophy, and even in the same philosophical treatise, but totally dissociated from each other, and often connected with reason rather than with rational desire. It is a long time before all the elements get associated together. When they do get associated, yet other ideas previously instantiated in isolation join the group: the idea of perverted will and of will as ubiquitously present in all decisions. Once this history of clustering is clear, it will be the history that matters'.

18 Sorabji, *Emotion and Peace of Mind*, 304: 'In his earlier work, the *Phaedo*, he had distinguished only two conflicting things, body and soul, and had treated the soul as unitary. His conclusion in the *Republic* is that there are three kinds (*eidē*) and that they are in the soul. Later in the *Timaeus* (69 C-72 D) he will locate them in different parts of the body, so that they become three *parts* of the soul'.

19 Sorabji, *Emotion and Peace of Mind*, 308–9.

20 Williams, *Shame and Necessity*, 51: 'An action that a person does in this spirit, reluctantly, must be distinguished from an action that a person does unintentionally. Indeed the two things exclude one another: an agent in this situation is one who means or intends to do a certain thing but wishes he did not have to. In their typical uses, then, *hekōn* is not the opposite or contrary of *aekōn*: they operate in different spaces'.

21 Gill, *Personality in Greek Epic, Tragic, and Philosophy*, 7.

22 Gill, *Personality in Greek Epic, Tragic, and Philosophy*, 178–9: 'in Aristotelian and Stoic accounts of human action, motivation to action is analysed in terms of "deliberative desire", or of "impulse", based on conceptualization and inference; and those forms of analysis can be parallelled in the Homeric deliberative monologues'. Cf. Nussbaum, *The fragility of goodness*, 383: 'Aristotle, like Plato, believes that emotions are individuated not simply by the way they feel, but, more importantly, by the kinds of judgments or beliefs that are internal to each. A typical Aristotelian emotion is defined as a composite of a feeling of either pleasure or pain and a particular type of belief about the world. Anger, for example, is a composite of painful feeling with the belief that one has been wronged. The feeling and the belief are not just incidentally linked: the belief is the ground of the feeling. If it were found by the agent to be false, the feeling would not persist; or, if it did, it would no longer persist as a constituent in that emotion'.

23 Sorabji, *Emotion and Peace of Mind*, 309: 'The *Phaedrus* offers the very subtle idea that a false opinion can exist alongside a true opinion. In resisting sexual temptation, the charioteer, representing reason, may know that the temptation is wrong. But the worse of the two horses, representing appetite, speaks to the charioteer and "thinks it right (*axioi*) in return for its many labours to have a little enjoyment". (*Phaedrus* 255 E)'; 316: 'Augustine's recognition of two wills parallels Plato's recognition of two opinions, that of the bad horse that sexual indulgence is all right (*axioi*), and that of the charioteer that it is not. But Plato puts his contrast in terms of opinion, not of will'.; likewise, 313, on the Stoic position of Chrysippus. See also the chapter on artistic–communicative aspects, Part II Section 4.1, and the current chapter on psycho-ethical aspects, Part II Section 6.4.

24 Gill, *Personality in Greek Epic, Tragic, and Philosophy*, 233–6.

25 Levin, *The Question of Hamlet*, 105.

26 Levin, *The Question of Hamlet*, 23; see also 24. Cf. Greenblatt, *Shakespearean Negotiations*, 94–128.

27 Levin, *The Question of Hamlet*, 67–8.

28 Levin, *The Question of Hamlet*, 69. Watson, 'Tragedies of revenge and ambition', 172, offers a slightly different interpretation of the question 'To be or not to be' when discussing Ernest Jones' Freudian book *Hamlet and Oedipus*: 'Hamlet cannot kill Claudius because he identifies with him too much. All Claudius has done is fulfil precisely Hamlet's own oedipal fantasies: his guilt-ridden, subconscious desire to murder his father and then marry his mother. The problem with revenge is thus that it is inextricable from suicide, as the "To be or not to be" soliloquy suggests; the avenger now sees himself in the mirror. It is worth noting, however, that this most famous question in literature may not mean (as some people assume it does), "Should I commit suicide?", but rather the question Hamlet goes on to consider: "Should I survive by stoically accepting wrongs, or die performing revenge?" '.

29 Levin, *The Question of Hamlet*, 69–72.

30 Watson, 'Tragedies of revenge and ambition', 172.

31 William Kerrigan, '*Hamlet*'s Good Night', in: Kerrigan (ed.), *Hamlet's Perfection*, 51–2: 'The two contrary halves of this legacy descended to the Renaissance in separate traditions. It is part of the historical originality of *Hamlet* that the ethos of Senecan revenge tragedy should collide in its hero's soul with the ethos of stoic indifference. Prior to Shakespeare, the two Senecan traditions had rarely encountered each other. This collision is precisely what we behold in "O what a rogue and peasant slave am I!" and the other speeches of self-reproach. . . . But underlying this torrent of self-abuse, and the gallery of detested souls it generates, is this conviction: *I must be indifferent to my revenge*. Of course Hamlet does not consciously practise this stoic discipline. He would rather be Avenging

Night. But the indifference is implicit in his cynical wit, his constant sense of superiority to those purposeful souls with whom he converses, and most of all in his self-reproaches. Shakespeare seeded his soul with a mysterious and unwilled allegiance to *apatheia*'.

32 Gail Kern Paster, 'The tragic subject and its passions', in: McEachern (ed.), *The Cambridge Companion*, 144.

33 Paster, 'The tragic subject and its passions', 146.

34 Ibid., 149–50.

35 The very use of the word 'ambition' is striking in *Hamlet*, and telling, in my opinion. The young friends Rosencrantz and Guildenstern explain Hamlet's depressive ideas of Denmark as a prison and his bad dreams as indicative of ambition. The word itself occurs no less than three times in II.ii.251–61. The much older King Claudius' effort to repent in prayer is doomed to fail, for he is 'still possessed/Of those effects for which I did the murder,/My crown, mine own ambition, and my Queen' (III.iii.53–5).

36 Watson, 'Tragedies of revenge and ambition', 161 (italics, LM); William Kerrigan, '*Macbeth* and the History of Ambition', in: John O'Neill (ed.), *Freud and the Passions*. University Park, PA: Penn State University Press, 1996, 13–24. The phrasing may give cause to some misunderstanding. For example, Taylor, *Sources of the Self*, 116, points out that Plato constantly stresses the unlimited (unsatiable) nature of desire; but Plato and Kerrigan do not mean the same thing. For one thing, Plato's desire is ruled by reason, which is more fundamental to human nature than desire; also, Plato's reason or desire do not invent goals, but find them. For an interpretation of 'to thine own self be true' in terms of a Stoic ideal self, see A. D. Nuttall, *Shakespeare the Thinker*. New Haven, CT/London: Yale University Press, 2007, 192–3.

37 McAlindon, *Shakespeare's Tragic Cosmos*, 18–19 and 111 resp.

38 McAlindon, *Shakespeare's Tragic Cosmos*, 103, 112–13. Also, according to Rees, *Shakespeare and the Story*, 199, Hamlet asserts conscience: 'He will rouse the conscience of the king that he may choose damnation, rouse the conscience of the queen that she may be saved, and he continually examines his own conscience to see how things stand in his own soul. "Conscience doth make cowards of us all", he says (III.i.83), recognising that as a mortal man he cannot but be a sinner and that therefore his own risks in this drama of damnation are fearful. He must do the right things and do them, moreover, for the right reasons. At the end, his conscience is satisfied. The deaths of Rosencrantz and Guildenstern do not weigh upon him (V.ii.58); he has no further doubt that it is "perfect conscience" to kill Claudius and would be damnable to let him live to perpetrate further evil, and, finally and incidentally, he has roused the conscience of Laertes who had himself, egged on by Claudius, been near damnation. "Conscience and grace to the profoundest pit!", Laertes had exclaimed in Act IV, sc. v, "I dare damnation . . .", but conscience asserts itself at the end. As he recognises the virtue of Hamlet and the villainy of Claudius, he confesses and asks forgiveness'.

39 Bloom, *Hamlet*, 43–4.

40 Nuttall, *Shakespeare the Thinker*, 202.

41 Nuttall, *Shakespeare the Thinker*, 201–2: 'Coleridge accurately seizes something that is there in the text: "sicklied o'er with the pale cast of thought" (III.i.84), "thinking too precisely on th'event" (IV.iv.41). The most telling moment for Coleridge is a curiously disconcerting simile; Hamlet says that he will sweep to his revenge "with wings as swift/As meditation, or the thoughts of love" (I.v.29–30). "As swift as thought" is a common simile, for thought can in a second fly to the ends of the earth. But thought in the Prince of Denmark is an impediment, not a release. So Shakespeare interposes the retarding, polysyllabic word "meditation," and suddenly the phrase takes on the character of an inadvertent oxymoron. Coleridge was right. This book is about Shakespeare as thinker. Hamlet is Shakespeare's prime example of a thinker, and thought is making Hamlet ill'.

42 Nuttall, *Shakespeare the Thinker*, 198.

43 William Shakespeare, *The Tragedy of Hamlet, Prince of Denmark*. Edited by T. J. B. Spencer, with an Introduction by Anne Barton. London: Penguin Books, (1980, 1994) 2002, 77–8.

44 Nuttall, *Shakespeare the Thinker*, 193–4.

45 Padel, *Whom Gods Destroy*, 8, 13.

46 Padel, *Whom Gods Destroy*, 121, 49–50 and 66 respectively.

47 Goldhill, *Reading Greek Tragedy*, 174.

48 Ibid., 175–80.

49 Paster, 'The tragic subject and its passions', 146.

50 Sorabji, *Emotion and Peace of Mind*, 253–64; Owsei Temkin, *Galenism: Rise and Decline of a Medical Philosophy*. Ithaca, NY/London: Cornell University Press, 1973, esp. 17–19, 95–104.

51 Paster, 'The tragic subject and its passions', 143.

52 Paster, 'The tragic subject and its passions', 145 and 153 respectively.

53 Sewell-Rutter, *Guilt by Descent*, 162–71.

54 Armstrong, *The Great Transformation*, 254f.

55 Ibid., 255.

56 Sewell-Rutter, *Guilt by Descent*, 160–1.

57 Winnington-Ingram, *Sophocles*, 176–8. At 202–3, Winnington-Ingram describes how Oedipus behaves like an intelligent detective who uses reasoning and eye-witnesses to find out the truth. Oedipus has too much pride in his keen intelligence, and is fatally wrong in not realizing his own ignorance and blindness. The Chorus ascribes Oedipus' imminent downfall to arrogance (*hubris*), but 'intellectual arrogance' was the last thing that this piously moralizing Chorus would have had in mind anyway, Winnington-Ingram argues. Instead, the Chorus is afraid that Oedipus may abuse his royal power and suffer disaster. If Oedipus becomes arrogant, then he must fall and suffer at the hands of the gods or divine order is at an end, they argue in an Aeschylean way. But disaster comes upon him through things done before he ever became king, and things not done out of arrogance, not even 'intellectual pride'. The Chorus may offer a pious explanation of Oedipus' imminent downfall, but their explanation turns out to be the wrong explanation in Sophocles' plot pattern. Oedipus' impious acts drawing down the wrath of the gods were done in simple ignorance, not in pride of any kind.

58 Williams, *Shame and Necessity*, 55–6; 67–8: 'It is . . . a mistake to think that the idea of the voluntary can itself be refined beyond a certain point. The idea is useful, and it helps to serve the purposes of justice, but it is essentially superficial. If we push beyond a certain point questions of what outcome, exactly, was intended, whether a state of mind was normal or whether the agent could at a certain moment have controlled himself, we sink into the sands of an everyday, entirely justified, skepticism. . . . there is a problem of free will only for those who think that the notion of the voluntary can be metaphysically deepened. In truth, though it may be extended or contracted in various ways, it can hardly be deepened at all'.

59 Williams, *Shame and Necessity*, 69–71.

60 Williams, *Shame and Necessity*, 57–60, 68–74, quotations at 69–70 and 73.

61 Goldhill, *Reading Greek Tragedy*, 180ff.

62 Ibid., 191–3.

63 Sewell-Rutter, *Guilt by Descent*, 169–70.

64 Padel, *Whom Gods Destroy*, 1–164.

65 Ibid., 99–126.

66 Ibid., 145–53.

67 Padel, *Whom Gods Destroy*, 47–96. Socrates will later on prefer madness (*mania*) as the source of true *prophecy*, to human sanity (*sophrosunē*), the source of *augury* (divination). Democritus and Plato will connect poetic inspiration with divine frenzy (the Muses). Madness, in Plato's *Phaedrus*, lifts the soul to higher planes, to see truths inaccessible to the sane. It becomes sane to be mad. (82–9, 126–9). Erasmus' picture of Christ as a fool and Christianity as inspired madness will draw from Plato's *Phaedrus*; Christian folly is the simple soul seeing religious truths from purity, not from (Renaissance melancholic) darkness, Padel, 93, argues.

68 Padel, *Whom Gods Destroy*, 182–3.

69 Ibid., 174–96.

70 Ibid., 244–6.

71 Ibid., 239–41.

72 Padel, *Whom Gods Destroy*, 63 and 244 respectively.

73 Padel, *Whom Gods Destroy*, 64; 247: 'In the early Renaissance, madness is a *speculum*, "mirror", where human nature sees its own self-hurt'.

74 Levin, *The Question of Hamlet*, 113, draws our attention to the Closet Scene (III.iv.1–218): 'Hamlet reverses that outlook in a moment of hectic irony, by telling Gertrude to tell Claudius "That I essentially am not in madness,/But mad in craft". (III.iv.187–8). Madness, as the abandonment of reason, is a constant danger throughout the play, from Horatio's desperate warning against the Ghost (I.iv.69–74) through Hamlet's disingenuous apology to Laertes (V.ii.241–50). Yet Hamlet is clearly thoughtsick rather than brainsick—neurotic rather than psychotic, to state the matter in more clinical terms. In his battle of wits with Rosencrantz and Guildenstern, he is led to affirm that his "wit's diseas'd" (III.ii.333); but he has already come closer to the mark in characterizing himself as "mad north-north-west" (II.ii.397). He is, indeed, what circumstance has made him, a monomaniac. He can distinguish shrewdly enough between a hawk and a handsaw, or expatiate with lucidity and brilliance upon many another theme. But his obsession with his mother's marriage and his hostility against his uncle are forbidden themes which he may not harp on unless he is granted a certain license, not to say licentiousness. This "crafty madness" provides him with a means of expressing pent-up emotions, which are communicated to the audience through asides and soliloquies, but which can find no release until they reach the other characters through a sequence of sharply pointed *contretemps*. Thus his denunciation of feminine frailty, though its appropriate target will be Gertrude, first falls upon the bewildered ears of the innocent Ophelia, who thereupon concludes that he is mad'.

75 Levin, *The Question of Hamlet*, 120.

76 Levin, *The Question of Hamlet*, 124: 'So Hamlet, at the court where he cannot be king, must perforce be fool, an artificial fool pretending to be a natural. His assumption of foolishness is the archetypal feature of his story, as it has come down from primitive legend. In fact, his name derives from the Old Norse Amloði, which means "a fool, a ninny, an idiot"—and, more specially, a Jutish trickster who feigns stupidity. . . . Shakespeare, in refining upon such raw materials, utilized his mastery of those conventions which made the fool so strategic a figure on the Elizabethan stage. The comment of Gilbert Murray is penetrating: "It is very remarkable that Shakespeare, who did such wonders in his idealized and half-mystic treatment of the real Fool, should also have made his greatest tragic hero out of a Fool transfigured" '.

77 Levin, *The Question of Hamlet*, 124–5.

78 States, *Hamlet and the Concept of Character*, xiv. Character is as much the site of self-adjustment as it is the site of self-expression, States argues, because character is a strategic response to its environment while drawing from its own behavioural 'rootedness' and 'life-energy'. (States, *Hamlet and the Concept of Character*, 7, xviii, 20). If 'plot' can be taken as a horizontal phenomenon in the sense of a sequence of events that unfold in time and space, 'character' is a predominantly vertical phenomenon in the sense that it manifests itself as a repetition or as a self-continuation rather than as a change. The common terms 'character development' and 'character change' are confusing and even misleading. (8–18). 'There is nothing surprising in Hamlet when he stabs Polonius. He has been stabbing Polonius all along: all of his wordplay and irony in their earlier scenes being "little murders", rehearsals for this real murder'., States, 18, argues.

79 Cf. Margolies, *Monsters of the Deep*, 152: 'one of the elements of necessity is usually what in Aristotle's *Poetics* is called "character". This is not personality but what a person will or will not choose to do in circumstances where the choice is not obvious—i.e., it is essentially a person's principles'.

80 States, *Hamlet and the Concept of Character*, 63–6. States, 74–7, proposes a dialectical reading of the (Elizabethan!) humours as opposing or adjacent polarities. Thus, the choleric comes into existence by virtue of the phlegmatic, which is its natural opposite (as rest is the natural opposite of motion), and melancholy comes into existence by virtue of the sanguine, which is its natural opposite (as order is the natural opposite of confusion). Melancholy and phlegm, sitting next to each other, are sympathetically bound by the atmospheric attribute of coldness (having little spirit or inclination), in contrast to choler (the choleric) and blood (the sanguine) which are hot (vitality, aggressiveness); finally, phlegm and blood are moist (palpable, viscous, thick), whereas melancholy and choler are dry (sharp, unstable, thin). The choleric and the phlegmatic describe a dialectic polarity between hyperactive and hyperpassive, which concentrates on the sphere of the body; intellectual, spiritual or creative inclinations are virtually absent. Choler governs the will, the province of the irrational, of desire, violence, revenge, conquest, battle and manhood. An excess of phlegm signals a decline of both intellectual and purposive physical activity, of volition itself, signals a reduction to the domain of pure sensation, dullness and torpidity. The choleric/phlegmatic polarity represents the extremes of physical 'motivation' – pure instantaneous reactivity and pure continuous inertia.

81 A. C. Bradley, *Shakespearean Tragedy: Lectures on Hamlet, Othello, King Lear, Macbeth* (1904) London: MacMillan, (1957) 1960, 104–7.

82 It concentrates on the sphere of the mind – the *sanguine* is animated by the principle of *reason and sense (or belief)*, whereas the *melancholy* is animated by the principle of *imagination and vision (or desire)*. (States, *Hamlet and the Concept of Character*, 77–82) Melancholy 'is the principle of restlessness and sudden combination, the crucible in which the passions are "mixed" and heated to the point, usually, of perturbation. Its aspects are inconstancy (hence lunacy), isolation from the social order, and, as Frye notes, a boundless creative energy that is at once self-ish and self-transcendent—in sum, the stuff of which drama is made. Sanguinity is to psychological stability what 98.6 temperature is to bodily health: it is the seat of sociability, of man going cheerfully about his work and play, in what we might broadly call a cooperative world, insofar as sanguine people inhabit it, and thus it is the measure against which all men and women are judged' (84).

83 States, *Hamlet and the Concept of Character*, 83.

84 Ibid., 84–6, 190.

85 States, *Hamlet and the Concept of Character*, 186 and 199 respectively.

86 States, *Hamlet and the Concept of Character*, 190ff, quotations at 190–2.

87 *Hamlet* II.ii.146–51a: 'And he repelled, a short tale to make,/Fell into a sadness, then into a fast,/Thence to a watch, thence into a weakness,/ Thence to a lightness, and, by this declension,/Into the madness wherein now he raves/And all we mourn for'. Note the ironic 'we mourn' instead of 'he mourns'; if melancholy and tragedy are about mourning, who is actually mourning?! (Shakespeare, *The Tragedy of Hamlet*. Ed. Spencer, 72; see also C. J. Schuurman, *Stem uit de diepte: De mens en zijn bestemming in de symbolische taal der mythe*. Leiden: A. W. Sijthoff, 1970, 96).

88 States, *Hamlet and the Concept of Character*, 116–17.

89 Ibid., 200.

90 Redfield, *Nature and Culture in the Iliad*, 130–1; see also 133, 135–8 and 147.

91 Cf. Rosset, *La philosophie tragique*, 9; Chirpaz, *Le tragique*, 4, 20.

92 Redfield, *Nature and Culture in the Iliad*, 155. Cf. Rosset, *La philosophie tragique*, 16.

93 Claude Calame, 'Vision, Blindness, and Mask: The Radicalization of the Emotions in Sophocles' *Oedipus Rex*,' in: Silk (ed.), *Tragedy and the Tragic*, 17–37.

94 Richard Buxton, 'What Can You Rely on in *Oedipus Rex*? Response to Calame,' in: Silk (ed.), *Tragedy and the Tragic*, 38–48.

95 Segal, *Oedipus Tyrannus*, 71–2.

96 Ibid., 12–13.

97 duBois, 'Toppling the Hero', 75.

98 Ibid., 76.

99 Bloom, *Hamlet*, 118–19: 'What matters most about Hamlet is his genius, which is for consciousness itself. He is aware that his inner self perpetually augments, and that he must go on overhearing an ever-burgeoning self-consciousness. Only annihilation is the alternative to self-overhearing, for nothing else can stop Hamlet's astonishing gift of awareness'.

100 Margreta de Grazia, *'Hamlet' without Hamlet*. Cambridge: Cambridge University Press, 2007, with quotations at 1, 6 and 34 respectively.

101 Greenblatt, *Will in the World*, 323ff.

102 Greenblatt, *Will in the World*, 324, suggests a link with Shakespeare's life story: 'The excision of motive must have arisen from something more than technical experimentation; coming in the wake of Hamnet's death (Shakespeare's son Hamnet died in 1596, *LM*), it expressed Shakespeare's root perception of existence, his understanding of what could be said and what should remain unspoken, his preference for things untidy, damaged, and unresolved over things neatly arranged, well made, and settled. The opacity was shaped by his experience of the world and of his own inner life: his skepticism, his pain, his sense of broken rituals, his refusal of easy consolations'.

103 States, *Hamlet and the Concept of Character*, 45–9, 95–7, 101–2, 104–5, 118–19, 123, 130–1.

104 Lee, *Shakespeare's* Hamlet *and the Controversies of Self*, 155–6.

105 Lee, *Shakespeare's* Hamlet, 158; 160 and 188 resp.: 'The use of "self" does not provide direct evidence (of essentialist interiority) either'. Polonius' precept to his son, 'This above all: to thine own self be true' (I.iii.78), 'means nothing more than his reprimand, fifteen lines later, to Ophelia': 'You do not understand yourself so clearly/As it behoves my daughter and your honour'. (I.iii.96–7) 'To "understand your self" is the equivalent of "to know one's place" ', Lee points out.

106 Lee, *Shakespeare's* Hamlet, 165–71, 184–7; 186: 'To picture interiority as a gap is the equivalent of picturing interiority as a well; this equivalent image makes sense of, and is derived from, gap-critics' attachment to terms such as depth. Yet a gap is an unusual well; it is bottomless, having only sides. Its depth is unknowable—gap-critics would say profound. The possibility of that latter sense has suited critics who wish to protect and emphasize Prince Hamlet's inner life. To picture gaps as unsoundable wells makes clear that they cannot exist in a cumulative relationship to each other. More wells, contrary to Muir's and others' suggestion, do not equal deeper. Also, such a picture of interiority as a well is static. A well or gap cannot change; it either is there or it is not'.

107 Lee, *Shakespeare's* Hamlet, 171–92, 200–3. Kelly's model of 'man-the-scientist' rejects behaviourist approaches in characterizing man as an inherently active process, full of anticipation, constantly seeking 'ways to improve his ability to predict, control and render meaningful' the stream of life's events. 'Man, though a construct, is not a constructed product of the surrounding world but a constructor, a producer of himself'. (173–4) (A construct is a way of perceiving events, made up from an oppositional pair which contains a similarity-contrast comparison, for example, 'good-bad').

108 Lee, *Shakespeare's* Hamlet, 179 and 205.

109 Saws: (usually somewhat derogatory) wise sayings, platitudes.

110 Shakespeare, *The Tragedy of Hamlet*. Ed. Spencer, 52.

111 Lee, *Shakespeare's* Hamlet, 225.

112 Lee, *Shakespeare's* Hamlet, 226: 'Though Polonius' thinking, as it is seen in the play, is neither perceptive nor very wise, the precepts that he gives as a parting gift, though perhaps too many, are impressive. The commonplace system preserves acknowledged wisdom well (while at the same time tending to mould new experience into old categories). It explains the contradiction between Polonius' thoughts and the wisdom of his general advice, 'the seeming inconsistency' as Johnson put it, 'of so much wisdom with so much folly'.

113 Lee, *Shakespeare's* Hamlet, 226.

114 Ibid., 221–3.

115 Ibid., 209–26.

116 Ibid., 187, 213.

117 Ibid., 193–6.

118 Ibid., 199.

119 Ibid., 201–2.

120 Ibid., 205–6.

121 Ibid., 197.

122 Robert N. Minor (ed.), *Modern Indian Interpreters of the* Bhagavadgita. Albany, NY: State University of New York Press, 1986; Satya P. Agarwal, *The Social Role of the* Gītā: *How and Why.* New Delhi: Motilal Banarsidass, 1993; Eric J. Sharpe, *The Universal* Gītā: *Western Images of the* Bhagavad Gītā. *A Bicentenary Survey.* La Salle, IL: Open Court Publishing Company, 1985.

123 G. W. Kaveeshwar, *The Ethics of the Gītā.* Delhi: Motilal Banarsidass, 1971, 117–18.

124 M. M. Agrawal, 'Arjuna's Moral Predicament', in: Bimal Krishna Matilal (ed.), *Moral Dilemmas in the Mahābhārata.* Delhi: Motilal Banarsidass/ Shimla: Indian Institute of Advanced Study, (1989) 1992[2], 132–3: 'His initial response is highly emotional: "I do not wish to kill them, even for the gain of the kingdom of all the three worlds". (*Gītā* 1.35) But later he reasons from the point of view of self-interest. He says that he does not envisage any personal happiness at regaining the kingdom when all his near and dear ones have been killed. One cannot enjoy any gain at such a cost. "Having slayed my own kinsmen and so on, what shall I do with the kingdom and the pleasures of life?" (1.32) But there is much more to Arjuna's reasoning. There now follows a whole lot of solid *moral* reasons for the shift in his attitude. These reasons seem to be connected with a different moral theory from the one suggested in favour of his earlier decision to fight. . . . The battle is definitely going to destroy the clan, and such a battle is evidently sinful. Moreover, Arjuna who, unlike the Kauravas, sees the bizarre future consequences of the war has a further reason for avoiding the fight. . . . In the death of the elders and the gurus of the clan the structure of authority in the clan is destroyed. Then there follows the decline of moral order in the clan. From this decline comes the corruption of the women in the family. This, in turn, leads to racial/caste intermixture and impurity in the whole clan, which leads them all to hell. And, further, since they are no longer offering *pinda* to the deceased ancestors, they also suffer a fall in their spiritual status and perhaps remain in limbo. And, further, the numerous evils generated by racial/caste impurity lead to the destruction of the established caste morality as well as clan morality, that is, of the moral order in society as a whole. The decline of moral order in society brings ruin and unhappiness to all, sending all of them finally to hell. From the above account we can see now, while Arjuna's dilemma is partly based upon a conflict of sentiments and partly of prudence, it is primarily a *moral dilemma'*.

125 Cf. Kaveeshwar, *The Ethics of the Gītā*, 96.

126 Kaveeshwar, *The Ethics of the Gītā*, 56–7; see also 59–64.

127 Kaveeshwar, *The Ethics of the Gītā*, 74.

128 Kaveeshwar, *The Ethics of the Gītā*, 75: 'He was not deserting that war to satisfy any egoistic desire of his. And yet, that attachment had an indirect hand in generating the hatred for the war in his mind. Though not born out of *kāma*, that hatred was the result of his nausea for it. It was not merely the idea of a war against one's own people that was weighing upon his mind; along with it was also the idea that the war was being waged by the Pāndavas for the sake of their royal pleasures. And that made the entire situation absolutely intolerable to his mind. . . . He felt a loathing at the thought of the heinous extent to which their pursuit of *kāma* had brought them, and the very moment he turned non-egoistic! He uttered desperately that not to speak of the earthly kingdom, he no more felt a desire even for the mastery over the three worlds'. I agree with Kaveeshwar that Arjuna's mood of desirelessness – I would not call it a 'non-egoistic attitude' – at that moment is but a temporary upsurge and that his reason is not yet 'firmly established' (*achalā*) therein. What I consider unconvincing in Kaveeshwar's argument is that he explicitly speaks of emotions such as disgust and hatred on the part of Arjuna while simultaneously insisting on his purely *moha*-state of mind. *If Kaveeshwar wants to take Arjuna's feelings of disgust and hatred psychologically seriously, he should admit that the story itself may mention* moha *primarily, but also mentions utterances that depict feelings of disgust which are closely linked to* kāma. *After all, the Gītā offers a reflection on a dramatic scene full of emotions, not a purely philosophical treatise based on neatly defined distinctions between emotions.* The complex opening scene allows for more emotions than the one state of mind called *moha*. And these emotions may be closer to the issue of desire than Kaveeshwar would like them to be. The emotion of disgust or hatred, for example, can simply be interpreted as the other side of the coin of desire. Christopher G. Framarin, 'The Desire You Are Required to Get Rid Of: A Functionalist Analysis of Desire in the *Bhagavadgītā'*, in: *Philosophy East and West* 56/4 (October 2006), 606, describes 'desire' in terms of 'a disposition toward joy and disappointment—no matter how subtle— depending on the outcome'. Kaveeshwar himself stresses that *kāma* is both the desire for pleasure and the dislike for pain. Freud's 'pleasure principle' functions similarly. This implies that Arjuna's feelings of disgust and hatred are on the same level as the feelings of pleasure and greed, and since they are on the same level, disgust and hatred cannot solve the psychic conflict, but only perpetuate it. It also implies that the issue of desire – albeit not the primary issue of the opening dialogue which, according to Krishna in *Gītā* 2.2 is faintheartedness and in *Gītā* 2.11, 27, 30, 38 is grief – is present in the story itself right from the beginning, ready to be exploited and elaborated upon extensively in the teachings of Krishna.

129 Note by Killingley: 'Expressions in this semantic area include the nouns *kāma, sukha, bhoga, icchā, āśīs, samkalpa, sanga, rajas, rāga, anusvanga* (XIII.9), the verbs *icchati, kānksati, bhunkte*, and also the desiderative forms of verbs, compounds ending in *-artha* meaning 'having as one's aim', *-para* meaning "concerned with, intent on", and the use of the dative case to express purpose'.

130 Killingley, 'Enjoying the World,' 67.

131 Kaveeshwar, *The Ethics of the Gītā*, 137: 'That pity was not the outcome of personal affection or universal kindness. It was rather of the nature of a sense of shame or pity which one feels for himself, a lack of self-confidence, a feeling of utter helplessness, an attitude of self-condemnation. . . . This clarification of Arjuna's feeling of pity throws necessary light on the nature of his grief too. Actually his grief was concerned with the fear of sin in the killing of his kinsmen by himself'.

132 Nico H. Frijda, *The Emotions*. Cambridge: Cambridge University Press/Paris: Editions de la Maison des Sciences de l'Homme, 1986, 195.

133 Frijda, *The Emotions*, 195–6: 'When loss is, at a given moment, perceived from the perspective of its being something irrevocable, it induces sorrow and weeping; when it is perceived from the perspective of its being a condition that ought not be so, it stirs anger and protest. . . . Response to the major and stable aspects is called "grief", whether the precise response to full structure including variable aspects is that of sorrow, anger, or despair. The confusion—grief causes sorrow or anger—of course is precisely the same as that discussed earlier in connection with emotion definition by object or by action readiness mode. The relationship between situational meaning structure, as labeled, and action readiness change thus is not always strict. It is, however, always intimate. A given kind of action readiness change—abandoning striving, helplessness, in the case of grief—is the "logical" response to the major and stable features; and therefore that kind of action readiness change (grief, in fact) is the most "typical" response to grief'.

134 Frijda, *The Emotions*, 199–200.

135 Ibid., 278.

136 Ibid., 197–8, 216–17.

137 Frijda, *The Emotions*, 355. Frijda, 215, also mentions 'self-pity' when he argues that in some types of emotion, such as pity, compassion, and certain forms of jealousy, someone else's fate is at stake, and that fact in its complexity shapes the subject's situational meaning structure; the other person's situational meaning structure forms part of it, in some sort of recursive manner; the object in object fate can be someone else, but also one's own ego; self-pity is a point in case.

138 Arjuna sees loss of the valued lives of close kin and close friends in both armies, in 1.26–28. He sees the absence of any good resulting from slaying his own kinsmen, in 1.31. He sees no presence of any purpose or usefulness in gaining victory, the kingdom, and its pleasures, in 1.32–33, and the absence of any moral gain in 2.5. He stresses his desirelessness to fight, in 1.32–35. He sees the absence of any joy and happiness for himself after having killed his kinsmen, in 1.36–37. He depicts the prospect of total loss of family structures and family law, and of social and moral order, in 1.39–44, and the prospect of loss of the value of living altogether (of their own lives) after having killed the others, in 2.6. In Arjuna's appraisal of the situation, this battle is doomed to be a lost battle in every respect. According to 2.8, the prospect of a positive outcome is completely absent, and there is no sign that even a total gain on earth of rivalless, prosperous kingship and of overlordship of the gods would compensate for the loss and would therefore dispel Arjuna's grief. In 1.45, Arjuna comes to the desparate and regrettable conclusion that both armies are determined to commit a great crime, that is to say, he comes to the conclusion that the situation of impending evil has become irrevocable.

139 To the extent that Arjuna's own fate is inseparable from the fate of his kinsmen, pity may include self-pity. But *self-pity is not mentioned because, in my opinion, it is not the issue.* Arjuna does consider his personal happiness once, in 1.46, but this is not a major aspect of the opening scene, and it fits into the broader narrative opposition between 'Arjuna being unarmed personally' and 'Arjuna killing at his own hands': 'If the armed sons of Dhritarashtra/Should kill me in battle/While I was unresisting and unarmed,/This would be a greater happiness for me'. (*Gītā* 1.46) (*The Bhagavad Gītā*, trans. Sargeant, 84).

140 Kaveeshwar, *The Ethics of the Gītā*, 58–62, 74, 102–6.

141 The threefold nature of *prakrti* is considered to be a hypothesis deduced from the nature of the common things of experience by the aid of reason alone. (M. Hiriyanna, *Outlines of Indian Philosophy*. Delhi: Motilal Banarsidass, (1993) 2003³, 271–2).

142 Surama Dasgupta, *Development of Moral Philosophy in India*. Delhi: Motilal Banarsidass, 1994, 123–4.

143 Dasgupta, *Development of Moral Philosophy*, 128–9. Dasgupta mentions three kinds of feeling – pleasure, pain and the depressing. Chandradhar Sharma, *A Critical Survey of Indian Philosophy*. Delhi: Motilal Banarsidass, 2000, 154, mentions pleasure, pain and indifference, and further on, 157, pleasure, pain and bewilderment. Apparently, on the level of worldly experience and feeling, 'the depressing', 'indifference' and 'bewilderment' all come under the same category (of *tamas guna*).

144 See also Hiriyanna, *Outlines of Indian Philosophy*, 125–7.

145 Theos Bernard, *Hindu Philosophy*. Delhi: Motilal Banarsidass, 1999, 74–5, 92–3. Cf. *Maitrī Upanishad* 3.5 and Richard King, *Indian Philosophy: An Introduction to Hindu and Buddhist Thought*. Edinburgh: Edinburgh University Press, 1999, 168ff.

146 Bernard, *Hindu Philosophy*, 74.

147 Ibid., 74–5.

148 *The Bhagavad-Gītā.* With a commentary based on the original sources by R. C. Zaehner. Oxford: Oxford University Press, 1969, 393.

149 *The Bhagavad Gītā*, trans. Sargeant, 702–5.

150 A. V. Rathna Reddy, *The Political Philosophy of the Bhagavad Gītā*. New Delhi: Sterling, 1997, 101–2: 'the form of society of the *Gītā*, which is based on the psychological *gunas* of activity of castes, is not and cannot be of a static nature and form. . . . Social mobility and evolution are caused by the ascending psychological growth of *gunas* of the people. For instance, if most of the people are *tamasic* by nature, they will have a *tamasic* form of society, which is inactive, ignorant, isolated and enslaved. Swami Vivekananda, who branded the then Indian society as *tamasic*, deplored that the entire country looked like dead mutton, for there was no sign of activity in it. During his spiritual itinerary in India, he found that most of his countrymen were steeped in *tamasic* quality, that they were not aware of their sense of duty to the country and therefore its society remained backward and inactive. People have to overpower their *tamasic* quality of inactivity by cultivating the *rajasic* activity and the activity of *rajas*, in its turn, by the desireless action of *sattva guna*. As the form of social evolution of the *Gītā* is subject to the cultivating of the higher *gunas* of nature by the people, it differs from the Marxist materialistic interpretation, which denies the role of the psychological process of the involution of the *gunas* of nature in social evolution'. Van Bijlert adds a personal comment: 'Change, but what kind of change? Change should here be taken in conjunction with the concept of time: cyclical time or linear time'.

151 Killingley, 'Enjoying the World', 72–3, observes a clear pattern in the *Gītā* chapters 14, 17 and 18: 'In the lists of the examples of the effects of each of the *gunas* on a person in chapters 14, 17 and 18, a clear pattern emerges. If *sattva* predominates in a person's character, that person seeks and finds long-term satisfaction, even at the expense of short-term privation. The person dominated by *rajas* seeks and finds short-term satisfaction, and the person dominated by the third *guna*, *tamas* ("darkness"), is so lazy and stupid that he gets no satisfaction at all. The pattern is clear in the matter of food. The sāttvik person likes healthy, strengthening food which promotes happiness and satisfaction; the rājasik person likes strongly flavoured food which causes pain, misery and sickness, and the tāmasik person likes rotten food that has lost its taste and is past its sell-by date (*paryushita*; 17: 8–10). In general, *sattva* leads to long–term happiness that begins like poison and ends like nectar, *rajas* leads to short-term happiness that begins like nectar and ends like poison, and *tamas* leads to a happiness that is illusory in both the short and the long term, being merely the result of sleep, idleness and negligence (18: 37–9). So far, the *guna* theory seems to point to no more than an intelligent, far-seeing self-interest. But some passages about the *gunas* go further. For instance, while the rājasik person gives with the expectation of favours in return, the sāttvik person gives because it is right to give (*dātavyam iti*, 17: 20–1). Similarly, while the rājasik person performs worship with a view to its rewards or fruits, the sāttvik person worships because it is right to worship (*yastavyam iti*, 17: 11)'.

152 Trans. J. A. B. van Buitenen, *The Bhagavadgītā in the Mahābhārata*. Chicago, IL: The University of Chicago Press, 1981, 127–9.

153 Frijda, *The Emotions*, 429–31.

154 In *Gītā* 2.14, Krishna's appeal includes an appeal to 'will' in Bernard Williams' sense of 'endurance'. Apart from that, Arjuna should be 'resolved' (2.37).

155 Hill, *Fate, Predestination and Human Action in the Mahābhārata*, 307–8; Hiltebeitel, *Rethinking the Mahābhārata*, 242–3, 273–4.

156 Agrawal, 'Arjuna's Moral Predicament', 137–8: 'If, in a given situation, two different sets of reasons, both prima facie equally good, dictate two different obligations, and it is not possible to enact both, nor to eliminate one by reference to a higher-order principle, and yet in actual life one has to choose one, then it is clear that one has to suppress one's propensity to realize one in favour of the other quite arbitrarily. And, for this reason, one is likely to feel remorse. In such cases, as Williams rightly suggests, moral conflicts are like conflicts of desire. And further, he says, just as suppressing one desire in favour of the other one does of the former, by ignoring one moral obligation for the sake of fulfilling the other one has not really resolved the conflict. One has simply gone ahead despite the conflict. Thus, unlike conflicts of belief, in moral conflicts a moral "reminder" remains uneliminable and is shown by the fact that one feels remorse for not being able to carry out the ignored "ought". Now, Arjuna's conflict turns out to illustrate this point clearly. For, as Krishna suspects, Arjuna's primary motive in contemplating surrender is to give vent to his sentiments, and the cause of this lies in his attachments. True, Arjuna gives solid moral reasons in support of his revised attitude. But then, earlier, he had equally good reasons for contemplating killing the very same people whom he now thinks he cannot and should not kill. In adopting this new attitude, he has simply suppressed his earlier decision. But, as we have said, abandoning one horn of the dilemma in favour of the other does not dissolve the conflict. What, one might ask, *justifies* Arjuna's shift in his attitude? For simply stating a new set of reasons implying a contrary obligation does not show that his earlier reasons were morally inferior. And Arjuna has done nothing to prove that they are. . . . the fact that he adduces new reasons to justify his new attitude towards the war is secondary, and is itself determined by his sentiments. His reasons may be good reasons, but the ground for drawing upon a new set of reasons instead of sticking to the earlier ones is itself a-rational; it is rooted in his affections and fears. That is, his moral dilemma springs not simply from a conflict between two different sets of reasons, both valid in the situation, but also from an inheritance of conflicting values and their accompanying sentiments in his psyche'.

157 The complexity of the different layers of meaning that sometimes contradict each other and sometimes synthesize different strands of Indian thought also explains the complexity of meanings of the word for 'action', *karma*, in the *Gītā*. Arvind Sharma, *The Hindu Gītā: Ancient and Classical Interpretations of the Bhagavadgītā*. London: Duckworth, 1986, 82, notices: 'The word *karma* has been used in the *Gītā* in several senses. Thus it can mean (1) any act, (2) a sacrificial act, (3) *varna*-duties, or (4) acts of worship. Shankara has taken it in the second sense'.

158 Trans. Bolle, *The Bhagavadgītā*, 40–3.

159 The *Gītā* itself has a slightly different concept of action, but throughout the *Gītā*, knowledge of the elements and function of the ritual is assumed. Bolle, *The Bhagavadgītā*, 241: 'The beginning of chapter 6 reveals the living soul of a ritual religiosity, although the principal topic is renunciation. Verse 1: "That man knows renunciation and is disciplined who does the required cultic acts not counting on their results, not he whose sacrificial fire is extinct and who avoids all liturgy". The vocabulary is quite clear. In the Vedic and Brahmanic tradition, *agni*, fire, is not just fire in general, but the fire used for the sacrifice; the verb *kr* (from which *akriya*, "who avoids all liturgy" in the text is derived) means not only "to do" or "make" in general but "to perform ritual acts" '.

160 Trans. Bolle, *The Bhagavadgītā*, 58–9.

161 The world and mankind had originated from that primordial sacrifice, the sacrifice of the cosmic 'Man' or primal 'Person' (*purusha*) (*RigVeda* X.90). Its ritual re-enactment in the Soma or Fire sacrifice is related to the creation of the universe by the Lord of Creatures (Prajāpati), the main creator god of the Late Vedic hymns and Brāhmanas. Prajāpati first created Agni, the fire god of the sacrificial fire, but was used up in creating – by heating up, by self-cooking, by the creative power of *tapas*, the increase of heat – the universe and had to be restored by Agni in turn, with whom he was now identified. Thus, the sacrificer is equated with the sacrificial victim. Prajā pati's self-sacrifice is the sacrificer's prototype, embodying the nature of sacrifice – the sacrificer identifies with the sacrificial victim, that part of the sacrificer that defines him as such, and their identity in the purifying sacrificial fire buys the sacrificer free, dissociates the sacrificer from the impurity of the sacrificial victim. Identification and dissociation presuppose each other in the process of transformation that sacrifice is. The sacrificer is and is not the sacrificial victim, and their exchange enables renewal. Cf. Jan C. Heesterman, 'Self-sacrifice in Vedic Ritual', in: S. Shaked, D. Shulman, G. G. Stroumsa (eds), *Gilgul: Essays on Transformation, Revolution and Permanence in the History of Religions. Dedicated to R. J. Zwi Werblowsky*. Leiden: E. J. Brill, 1987, 91–106.

162 Cf. *Shatapatha Brāhmana* (700 BCE?) 6.2.1.18: 'a man (*purusha*) should be sacrificed first, for man is the first of the sacrificial animals (*pashu*)'.

163 *The Bhagavad Gītā*, trans. Sargeant, 167.

164 Heesterman, 'Self-Sacrifice in Vedic Ritual', 92.

165 Trans. Bolle, *The Bhagavadgītā*, 40–1.

166 Bolle, *The Bhagavadgītā*, 242: 'The word *samkalpa* is generally translated as "purpose". That is correct, but it is essential to keep in mind that it is in the first place the purpose *of the ritual.* The term occurs significantly in the ritual tradition. L. Renou, in his *Vocabulaire du rituel védique* defines *samkalpa* as "intention annoncée par le yajamāna d'exécuter un sacrifice" (the stated purpose of a sacrificer to perform a sacrifice). This stated purpose has its natural place at the beginning of a ritual; it is an official announcement: I am going to perform such and such a sacrifice. The ritual is man's true involvement in the universe. . . . Throughout the text, *karman* is a positive notion. It differs sharply from *karman* in Buddhism, where it becomes the inevitable law governing the infinity of existences, opposing the liberation one should strive for'.

167 Killingley, 'Enjoying the World', 71.

168 The correctness of ritual sacrifice and the fulfilment of social duty can be judged in terms of right and wrong by the community of village priests and by the community of village elders respectively. In a traditional village setting, ritual rules and role expectations are an integral part of the collective memory and consciousness of the village community. Not to act accordingly would be dangerous and shameful for the entire group. To act accordingly, however, means leading a safe and honourable life for the benefit of the entire community. These shared criteria are also 'objective' in the sense that they are to be applied to concrete, visible actions and their results. Attacks on family laws and group honour are highly concrete matters that have to be acted upon according to these 'objective' criteria, if one is to prevent the community from being tarnished and blemished forever, from being contaged with indelible impurity.

169 Historically speaking, the Vedic fire sacrifice had begun as a hospitality rite receiving and addressing the gods, but had then continued as a creative power in its own right, transforming the nature of sacrifice from a social exchange into a cosmic exchange. The fire or fire god (Agni) in plants was seen as offering himself to himself in fire.

170 As *ranasattra* in 3.242.14; as *ranayajña* in 5.57.12 and 5.154.4; and as *śastrayajña* in 5.139.29 (Critical Edition of the *Mahābhārata*, ed. V. S. Sukthankar. Poona: Bori, 1933–59). The role of this war as a ritual sacrifice being a crucial motif in the epic is a prominent theme in the works of Hiltebeitel and Biardeau, esp. Hiltebeitel, *The Ritual of Battle*, and Biardeau, *Etudes de mythologie hindoue. Vol. II: Bhakti et āvatara*, 60–3. Cf. Katz, *Arjuna in the Mahābhārata*, 113–18.

171 Madeleine Biardeau, 'Conférence de Mlle Madeleine Biardeau', in: *Annuaire de l'École pratique des Hautes Études: Cinquième section-Sciences Religieuses* 85 (1976–77), 165. The victim (*paśu*) is considered to be a mere substitute for the offering of the sacrificer's own self. Danielle Feller Jatavallabhula, 'Ranayajña: The Mahābhārata War as a Sacrifice', in: Jan E. M. Houben, Karel R. van Kooij (eds), *Violence Denied: Violence, Non-Violence and the Rationalization of Violence in South Asian Cultural History*. Leiden: E. J. Brill, 1999, 69–103; 97: 'the belief that the warriors slain in battle go to heaven automatically, without regard for their previous deeds, is possible only in the context of a war perceived as a sacrifice wherein their death is seen as a willing and dedicated self-sacrifice, like that of the sacrificial victims'.

172 Brodbeck, *Asakta Karman in the Bhagavadgītā*, 114, suggests a sociological explanation for the broadening scope of sacrificial action beyond its ritual context: 'This expansion of the notion of *yajna* beyond its old ritual context precipitates a new kind of responsibility into previously straightforward areas of human activity, and, by way of an example, I show that the *Dharmaśāstras* betray the increasing incidence of Arjuna-type existentio-behavioural crises in ancient India. Arjuna's plight illustrates the failure to find a systematic rationale for decision-making'.

173 Bolle, *The Bhagavadgītā*, 246; he continues, 246–8: 'It is obviously different from the prescribed, ritual acts. Nevertheless, the "ordinary" tasks of man derive from the cultic duty, and the Sanskrit language makes it possible to extend the discussion from one to the other smoothly. The *Gītā*, after all, is that episode in the great epic in which Arjuna, the warrior, commences with his doubts as to his "ordinary" duty; and the episode ends—after long instruction concerning ritual, renunciation, meditation, bodily yoga-techniques, love, and worship of God—with Arjuna taking up arms and performing his duty as a warrior. . . . We might speak of a radiation from divine activity to other activities farther and farther toward the fringes of the world. . . . The imagery of concentric circles or radiation toward the fringes is helpful as a reminder that the Indian world does not make the sort of radical separation between "the sacred" and "the profane" that we usually take for granted. The divine sphere and the human sphere are not contrasted after the manner of the biblical imagery of potter and pot (Isa. 45.9; Jes. 18.19). The genius of Christianity is to turn toward the world around it, not to turn in toward itself for fear of becoming polluted'.

174 Killingley, 'Enjoying the World', 79 note 5: '*Samnyāsa*, literally "throwing down, casting off", is the renunciation of all ritual actions, as well as all actions that have social and economic significance, in pursuit of liberation. The renouncer (*samnyāsin*) performs no rituals and lives apart from society. *Samnyāsa* is the practical outcome of the view that action, which in Vedic contexts often refers to ritual action, is binding'.

175 Romila Thapar, *Reinterpreting ancient India*. Delhi: Oxford University Press, 1993, 62–84.

176 Killingley, 'Enjoying the World', 72: 'Ritual theory classifies actions as periodical (*nitya*), occasional (*naimittika*), and optional (*kāmya*). It is the last, as their names implies, which are directly based on desire, since they are only performed by people who desire fruits from them. The *Gītā* does not use this classification explicitly, though it is used by Rāmānuja'.

177 Killingley, 'Enjoying the World', 71.

178 This process is outlined in a clarifying way by one of the *brahmins* accompanying the Pāndavas in the Kāmyaka forest (the name of which is associated with *kāma*, desire): 'When the six senses (*indriyas*) are focused on their respective objects (*vishayas*), the mind (*manas*), prompted by

habitual modes of thinking (*pūrvasamkalpa*, the thought processes of the past), is set in motion. With the mind provoked in this manner by the various objects of the senses, desire (*autsukya*) is born and action (*pravrtti*) is initiated. Then, being pierced by desire (*kāma*) amplified by the force of habit, with the arrows of the sense objects, he falls into the fires of greed (*lobha*) as a moth falls from its attraction to the light. Caught up in fun and feasting he finally sinks into the jaws of the great delusion (*mahāmoha*), and forgets who he really is. In this way, he falls into the cycle of rebirths, spinning about in womb after womb, (his mind) afflicted by ignorance (*avidyā*), inherited tendencies (*karma*) and want (*trshnā*). He cycles through the forms of existence from Brahmā to a blade of grass, born again and again in water, on land, or in the air'. (3.2.63–68) Trans. Woods, *Destiny and Human Initiative in the Mahābhārata*, 59; see also *Gītā* 2.62–63.

179 Cf. King, *Indian Philosophy*, 147: 'In the early *Upanishads* perception is explained in terms of the self (*ātman*) as an inner light which shines outward (through the eyes) and illuminates the objective world (e.g. *Brhadāranyaka Upanishad* 4.3.6). In his anthropological study of Hindu conceptions of seeing (*darśhan*) Lawrence Babb notes a similar model at work amongst contemporary Hindus: In the Hindu world "seeing" is clearly not conceived as a passive product of sensory data originating in the outer world, but rather seems to be imaged as an extrusive and acquisitive "seeing flow" that emanates from the inner person, outwards through the eyes, to engage directly with objects seen, and to bring something of those objects back to the seer. One comes into contact with and in a sense becomes what one sees'. (Lawrence Babb, "Glancing: Visual interaction in Hinduism", in. *Journal of Anthropological Research* 37 (1981), 387–401, esp. 396–7)'.

180 Biardeau, *Hinduism*, 70–2: 'The scheme set out by Nyāya—the Indian philosophical system which was constructed to serve as a basis and an exposition of logic—is more or less tacitly accepted by all the brahmanic systems: action is conceived as a kind of response by the subject to an external stimulus. Invariably the sequence is: knowledge leads to desire leads to inclination to act. There is no action that is not preceded by a desire, and the latter is never the desire to act, but desire for an object, for a precise result known to be good in itself. The knowledge which gives rise to the desire is often a perception; but this perception is of interest only inasmuch as it informs the subject of the present existence of an object within reach, which he knows in other ways to be good for him or useful to him (*artha*). Knowledge of the present object is inseparable from a whole halo of past experiences which gives it an index of value. . . . The brahmanic conception of action is so well expressed in this way that it reappears, in an even more systematic form, applied by Mimāmsā to the analysis of dharmic conduct. . . . It starts out from the self-evident datum—it is more than a postulate—that all action is painful, since it presupposes effort and fatigue. Therefore no one would ever act if he were not convinced that by this action he would obtain a good which would significantly reward the effort expended. Let us pre-empt the misunderstanding that is likely to arise in view of the widespread prejudice that the Hindu is "contemplative":

Mimāmsā certainly does not draw from contemplation its conception of action as painful. The Greeks in any case taught us that contemplation is the highest form of action. But the philosophers of Mimāmsā did not believe in contemplation, knowledge, the pursuit of the Absolute. . . . Action does not express man, it only reveals his desire, in the most egoistic sense of the term'. (Engl. trans. of *L'hindouisme: Anthropologie d'une civilisation.* Paris: Flammarion, 1981, 78–81).

181 Trans. Bolle, *The Bhagavadgītā*, 40–1.

182 Killingley, 'Enjoying the World', 72.

183 Brodbeck, *Asakta Karman*, 113.

184 Framarin, 'The Desire You Are Required to Get Rid Of', 604–17.

185 Sharma, *A Critical Survey of Indian Philosophy*, 37.

186 Thomas J. Hopkins, *The Hindu Religious Tradition*. Encino, Calif.: Dickenson Publishing Company, 1971, 30–5, 40; 50: 'the concept of mental performance of sacrifices brought about an integration of the personal and ritual aspects of *tapas*. Ascetic life in the forest was no longer a *preparation* for ritual activity; it *was* ritual activity, the "heating up" of the individual who was himself the sacrifice and the source of truth.'; cf. also 25–7.

187 Hiriyanna, *Outlines of Indian Philosophy*, 122.

188 Chakravarti Ram-Prasad, 'Saving the Self? Classical Hindu Theories of Consciousness and Contemporary Physicalism', in: *Philosophy East and West* 51/3 (July 2001), 381: 'The key idea about the conditions of consciousness comes down to this: consciousness requires embodiment. Common to the brahmanical (and Jaina) schools (and most Buddhist ones) is the thought that embodiment is a psychophysical complex, including both the gross body and its apparatus, sensory and mental. Crucially, the "mind" (*manas*) is understood as part of the body complex. All the schools talk of an "internal organ" (*antahkarana*), which is required to explain the undergoing of such states as pleasure, satisfaction, and frustration'.

189 The dualistic schools will stress the discontinuity between the self and consciousness as a quality possessed by the self, but quite distinct from the self and only manifested (functioning) when the self is embodied. The Advaita Vedānta school follows a monistic logic and therefore stresses the continuity between the self and consciousness as itself under certain conditions. Ram-Prasad (2001), 385: 'The self is a continuum only contingently individuated by psychophysical conditions, and its ultimate state is its de-individuation into that universal ground. The self, then, does not have consciousness as a quality; it simply *is* consciousness under certain conditions: 'there is no further conscious seer apart from the seeing' (*drstivyatirikto 'nyaścetano drastā*)'.

190 Elizabeth A. Schiltz, 'Two Chariots: The Justification of the Best Life in the *Katha Upanishad* and Plato's *Phaedrus*', in: *Philosophy East and West* 56/3 (July 2006), 451–68; 459: 'I argue that Yama's chariot image may also be read as providing a refutation of the life aimed at the satisfaction of sensual desires in favor of one that aims at wisdom (and does so without a startlingly positive evaluation of *mania*)'. and 461: 'While in each text the intellect is represented as the charioteer, its role is fundamentally different. In the *Phaedrus*, the function of reason is to harness the motivational energy of the horses and to contemplate the objects they identify, so that the whole chariot-soul may ascend to the forms. In the *Katha Upanishad*, the function of the intellect is to control the horses and utterly reject their objectives as valueless. Instead, the proper object of contemplation, and the proper beneficiary of service, is the royal passenger, the higher Self. . . . While Plato's chariot indicates the necessity of the desires (albeit desires carefully controlled), the Upanishadic chariot indicates a complete turning away from these desires'. See also the chapter on artistic–communicative aspects, Part II Section 4.1, and the current chapter on psycho-ethical aspects, Part I Section 4.

191 Hopkins, *The Hindu Religious Tradition*, 69–73.

192 The medieval term *nirguna brahman* for the impersonal aspect of the Absolute, 'Brahman beyond name and form', does not occur in the early *Upanishads*. The personal aspect of *brahman* is no longer a secondary, personalized aspect of the Absolute, but identified as a clearly defined personal god, like Rudra or Śiva as *the* Lord in the *Śvetāśvatara Upanishad*. The liberating knowledge of the Absolute beyond personal and impersonal attributes is replaced by or combined with the saving knowledge of the personal Lord who is present in one's own self and who produces nature by his magical creative power (*māyā*).

193 *Katha Upanishad* 2.22, and *Mundaka Upanishad* 3.2–3, have a doctrine of grace typical for *bhakti*: 'This *ātman* cannot be reached through insight or much learning nor through explanation. It can only be comprehended by one who is chosen by the supreme *ātman*; to such a person he reveals his form'. (Klostermaier, *A Survey of Hinduism*, 211).

194 Hopkins, *The Hindu Religious Tradition*, 72–3.

195 Sharma, *The Hindu Gītā*, 151: 'It is worth remarking that, although by the time the classical commentaries on the *Gītā* become available from the ninth century A. D., both Sankhya and Yoga were well-established schools of Hindu thought, yet none of the three great classical commentators —Shankara, Ramanuja and Madhva—fall into the trap of identifying these words with those schools. Madhva glosses *sankhyam* as *jnanam* and *yogah* as *upayah*, and even cites appropriate verses in support'.

196 Bernard, *Hindu Philosophy*, 72. See also M. Hiriyanna, *The Essentials of Indian Philosophy*. London: Unwin Paperbacks, (1949) 1978, 107–8.

197 Sharma, *A Critical Survey of Indian Philosophy*, 38.

198 Ibid., 153.

199 Hiriyanna, *Outlines of Indian Philosophy*, 279.

200 Gerald James Larson, *Classical Sāmkhya: An Interpretation of its History and Meaning*. (1979) Second, revised edition. Delhi: Motilal Banarsidass, 2005[4].

201 Axel Michaels, *Der Hinduismus: Geschichte und Gegenwart.* München: C. H. Beck, 1998, 358–61 (trans. into Engl. *Hinduism: Past and Present.* Princeton, NJ/Oxford: Princeton University Press, 2004, 326–9).

202 Bernard, *Hindu Philosophy*, 89: 'The Yoga system assumes the same cosmological doctrines as set forth in the Sāmkhya system. The only difference between the two is that the Sāmkhya system pertains to the universal condition of nature, and the Yoga system pertains to the individual condition of nature'.

203 *The Bhagavad Gītā*, trans. Sargeant, 140–1. A. L. Herman, *A Brief Introduction to Hinduism: Religion, Philosophy, and Ways of Liberation.* Boulder, CO/San Francisco/Oxford: Westview Press, 1991, 105–6, suggests that it is like the *karma*-neutral action of a *jīvanmukta*, of someone who has reached ultimate liberation while still living (2.55–7; cf. 5.16–23, 6.18–32, 12.13–20, 14.22–27, 16.1–3, 18.49–54).

204 *The Bhagavad Gītā*, trans. Sargeant, 265.

205 *Buddhiyoga*: discipline *(yoga* exercising restraint and thus allowing coherence, concentration, single-mindedness or unity/oneness to establish itself) of the mind (*buddhi*: intelligence, intellect, the capacity of the mind to gain insight beyond the senses (*indriyas*) and beyond thinking or thoughts (*manas*)), but also to judge the phenomena, not to be taken away by the diversity of sensorial impressions which invade thinking (*manas*) if the intellect (*buddhi*) lacks unity. Three helpful verses from the *Gītā* are 2.60–1 and 2.41: 'The turbulent senses/Carry away forcibly/The mind, Arjuna,/Even of the striving man of wisdom. Restrained all these senses,/Disciplined, he should sit, intent on Me;/He whose senses are controlled,/His wisdom stands firm'. (2.60–1); 'Here there is a single resolute understanding, Arjuna,/The thoughts of the irresolute/Have many branches and are, indeed, endless'. (2.41). *The Bhagavad Gītā*, trans. Sargeant, 145, 126. Cf. Malinar, *Rājavidyā. Das königliche Wissen um Herrschaft und Verzicht*, 138–40.

206 Patel, *Philosophy of the Gītā*, 54.

207 Ibid., 58.

208 Ibid., 60–3.

209 Brodbeck, *Asakta Karman*, 18.

210 Cf. Axel Michaels, 'Gift and Return Gift, Greeting and Return Greeting in India: On a consequential footnote by Marcel Mauss', in: *Numen* 44 (1997), 242–69, esp. 249 and 260–1. That the gift should be given to a worthy person is also testified to by *Gītā* 17.20, see next *Gītā* quotation.

211 Michaels, 'Gift and Return Gift', 242–69, esp. 252; 244f: 'Indeed India—or to be more precise, the legal notions based on the Dharmashastra—cannot be cited as an example for the obligation to reciprocate, not—and this is my point—because impurity is transmitted but because the theory of *dāna* arose in a period when any gift had to be measured against the highest soteriological goal, namely ascetic morality, and thus could only exist when the gift itself was ascetic—in short, when there was already a culture of open-handedness and generosity. Where this soteriological reference was lacking, there was, in India as elsewhere, the obligation to reciprocate or pass on the gift, but not only because of a special power in the gift but also because, as similar structures in greeting behaviour show, there are communicative obligations of a general nature (i.e., applicable beyond the context of giving and receiving) that require challenges to be responded to'.

212 Cf. Michaels, *Der Hinduismus*, 275: 'Es gibt daher keinen Dank im altindischen Opferwesen, nur ritualistisch bestimmte Reziprozität. Auch die Götter müssen opfern!'; Jacques Waardenburg, *Muslims and Others: Relations in Context*. Berlin/New York: Walter de Gruyter, 2003, 48–9, on the notion of gift; Jan N. Bremmer, *Greek Religion*. Oxford: Oxford University Press, 1994, 39, on the notion of gratitude.

213 *The Bhagavad Gītā*, trans. Sargeant, 644–5.

214 Ibid., 653–4.

215 Killingley, 'Enjoying the World', 72–3.

216 This approach seemingly contradicts or at least rephrases earlier verses such as 2: 45, where Arjuna is called upon to 'be without the three *gunas*', a call that is part of the first efforts of Krishna to convince Arjuna. But 2.45 refers to the Vedas. The items mentioned in 17.20–21 are also connected with the Vedas and sacrifice and thus classified according to the three *gunas*.

217 *The Bhagavad Gītā*, trans. Sargeant, 146.

218 Ibid., 187.

219 Sharma, *The Hindu Gītā*, 188: 'The recognition by Madhva of the identity of Vishnu and Krishna is of some scholarly significance. A distinguished Hindu scholar, the late Sir R. G. Bhandarkar, thought that Krishna was not yet identified with Vishnu in the *Gītā*, though he was soon afterwards. See his *Vaishnavism, Shaivism, and Minor Religious Systems*, page 13. But Krishna is directly addressed as Vishnu in XI: 24 and 30; and I do not believe that Vishnu can here mean "the sun". (Edgerton, Part II, p.31, n.2.)'.

220 Killingley, 'Enjoying the World', 74.

221 Michel Hulin, personal communication.

222 Taylor, *Sources of the Self*, 121–3; Kant will cut through the natural continuity from inner intention to external action by assuming a good will regardless of external action, Taylor explains.

223 Patrick Olivelle, *The Early Upanishads: Annotated Text and Translation*. New York/Oxford: Oxford University Press, 1998, 111–19.

224 Taylor, *Sources of the Self*, 136.

225 Alles, *The Iliad, the Rāmāyana, and the Work of Religion*, 45; cf. 38–9, 43–6, 98.

226 Segal, *Oedipus Tyrannus*, 72.

227 There are also differences, of course. Broadly speaking, the genius of Christianity is to turn toward the world around it, not like Hinduism to turn in toward itself for fear of becoming polluted, according to Bolle. Cf. also John Milton's moral judgement as emerging from his conscious self-exposure to moral impurity, as quoted in the chapter on artistic-communicative aspects, Part I Section 3.

228 Williams, *Shame and Necessity*, 43.

229 *The Bhagavad Gītā*, trans. Sargeant, 99.

230 Ibid., 145–6.

Chapter 8

1 Heering, *Tragiek*, 17–19 and 184 respectively; 184: 'die wederzijdse aanranding van vrijheid en gebondenheid, waarin wij de tragiek herkenden'.

2 Heering, *Tragiek*, 190–203.

3 Ibid., 29, 46.

4 Ibid., 216–17.

5 Winnington-Ingram, *Sophocles*, 150ff.

6 Redfield, *Nature and Culture in the Iliad*, 133, 135, esp. 270–1 note 5; quotations at 270 and 135 resp. Cf. Robert C. Solomon, 'On Fate and Fatalism', in: *Philosophy East and West* 53/4 (October 2003), 435–54, esp. 440–1: 'What an explanation in terms of fate adds to an explanation in terms of causes and antecedent conditions, in other words, is just this notion of significance'.

7 Ewans, 'Patterns of Tragedy in Sophocles and Shakespeare', 438–57, at 440; 441: 'The Greek gods represent . . . powers which are immanent both in mankind and in the processes of nature which surround the characteristic effect which we call "tragic", since it provides a vocabulary for expressing the role in life of elements beyond direct rational experience. These elements bind human actions together as action and consequence, and express the ways in which our *moirai* take shape. . . . in a world which lacked any concept of predestination or a mechanistic fate . . . Aeschylus and Sophocles made recurrent use of . . . methods to . . . achieve the gradual narrowing-down from an opening situation, in which a wide range of alternative possibilities is available, towards the point where a *moira* has taken its full shape'. 452 note 6: 'Adkin's analogy of the game of snakes and ladders (*Merit and Responsibility*, 19) is a helpful but partially misleading guide to the nature of *moira*. *Moirai* often take the form of "if x, then inexorably y"; but human beings do not land on x simply by an accident analogous to the throw of the dice: in Homer and in Greek tragedy, x is an action, which they choose to do'. 452 note 7: '. . . Xanthus sees Achilleus' death as inevitable–but only *after* the decision made in book 18, since he links it directly with Patroclus' defeat'.

8 Redfield, *Nature and Culture in the Iliad*, 133–5, 270–1.

9 Sewell-Rutter, *Guilt by Descent*, 149–50.

10 Winnington-Ingram, *Sophocles*, 159.

11 Segal, *Oedipus Tyrannus*, 77. H. S. Versnel, 'Thrice One: Three Greek Experiments in Oneness', in: Barbara Nevling Porter (ed.), *One God or Many? Concepts of Divinity in the Ancient World*. Transactions of the Casco Bay Assyriological Institute, 2000, 112–29, in his analysis of Herodotus' notion of fate points out that its conceptual inconsistency is a conspicuous characteristic of Herodotus' language and thinking which he shared with his contemporaries: 'All the same it remains fascinating that these multiple divergent and sometimes contradictory expressions in the passages of Herodotus are *not* presented as *different* or *variant* explanations in an explicit manner, let alone that their mutual compatibility or incompatibility is negotiated, discussed, questioned or denied'. (116) 'There is no systematization of the precise relationship between actions of personal gods and the all-embracing power of Fate: "im Schicksal sieht er das göttliche Wirken, ohne nach dem Verhältnis zwischen dem unentrinnbaren Schicksal und der göttlichen zu fragen" (Nilsson *ibid.*). Nor is there any *explicit* reflection on the precise relationship between freedom and responsibility in human action and the arbitrary omnipotence of "the gods". Numerous are the reports of events—especially catastrophic ones—that are prepared by the gods or the god, but enacted by man (7.8a I; 7.139.5; 8.109.3)'. (124) '"While Herodotus" "gods" may reflect either the arbitrary, or the moral or the mechanical principles of alternation or retaliation, Tuche is essentially an arbitrary and capricious power in accordance with her nature: Fortune, Luck, Chance'. (129)

12 Williams, *Shame and Necessity*, 145–7.

13 Ibid., 151.

14 Ibid., 146.

15 McAlindon, *Shakespeare's Tragic Cosmos*, 1–5, quotations at 2 and 5 resp., intends to correct the thesis of E. M. W. Tillyard that the Elizabethans 'saw the world as a stratified order where everything has its appointed place and identity' and that Shakespeare, in accordance with this pre-modern cosmology ruled by the principle of hierarchy or degree, 'always traced the cause of chaos of the disruption of hierarchy or violation of degree in the socio-political and the psychic spheres—to revolt against lawful authority, to the eclipse of reason and will by passion'. 'Ignored in this assumption', McAlindon argues, 'is the fact that the Tillyardian account of the Elizabethan world picture is seriously incomplete'.

16 McAlindon, *Shakespeare's Tragic Cosmos*, 3–10, quotations at 6–8; 6: 'The strife which forever agitates the opposites is kept in check, by the harmonizing force of love which binds them together in a fruitful union while upholding the justice of separate roles and identities. The whole order of life—unity, peace, and continuity—is founded on this bond of opposites, just as disorder, chaos, and death are caused by its collapse under the pressure of strife'. Since the bond of opposites 'is a projection on the universe of the natural law of reproduction, . . . the sexual, marital, and familial relationship' is frequent in the cosmic vision of 'the great writers of the Middle Ages and the Renaissance'.

17 McAlindon, *Shakespeare's Tragic Cosmos*, 4, uses the word 'traditional'.

18 McAlindon, *Shakespeare's Tragic Cosmos*, 8: 'Both in the Middle Ages and in the Renaissance, exponents of the religio-political status quo inevitably made much of the hierarchical model of the universe; it was a convenient way of naturalising the structure of feudal society. Shakespeare undoubtedly made use of it too; in my view, however, he found—like Chaucer, Kyd, and Marlowe before him—that the radically paradoxical notion of nature as a system of concordant discord or 'harmonious contrarietie', moved incessantly by the forces of love and strife, answered the facts of experience more truthfully'. Shakespeare's bias towards confounding contrariety, McAlindon, *Shakespeare's Tragic Cosmos*, 10, 25–55, explains, has as its literary background Thomas Kyd's *The Spanish Tragedy* and Christopher Marlowe's *Tamburlaine the Great,* but its original source of inspiration was probably 'the Knight's Tale', the first and most philosophical of Geoffrey Chaucer's *The Canterbury Tales*.

19 McAlindon, *Shakespeare's Tragic Cosmos*, 2; see also 21.

20 McAlindon, *Shakespeare's Tragic Cosmos*, 111, quotation at 125. The world of *Hamlet* is also a site of endless semiotic disorder. Everyone is moving through a labyrinth, through a maze of meanings, 'amazed', that is 'bewildered'. (113–14) 'The failure to match words and deeds, to fulfil his promise of revenge, gives rise to the phenomenon of uncertain identity: . . . who is true to himself? The 'inconsistencies are too palpable and too well accented by irony . . . to assume that they can be made fully intelligible. Hamlet . . . cannot be arrested in a unified image of "Hamlet" '. (114–15)

21 McAlindon, *Shakespeare's Tragic Cosmos*, 103.

22 Ewans, 'Patterns of Tragedy in Sophocles and Shakespeare', 447.

23 Vernant, 'Ébauches de la volonté', 72. Charles Segal, 'The Gods and the Chorus: Zeus in *Oedipus Tyrannus*', in: Charles Segal (ed.), *Sophocles' Tragic World: Divinity, Nature, Society*. Cambridge, MA/London: Harvard University Press, (1995) pb 1998, 189: 'Oedipus comes to exemplify that gulf between human *phusis* (inborn character, origins, human "nature" in both its physical and moral makeup) and the purity of the divine order'.

24 Emese Mogyoródi, 'Tragic Freedom and Fate in Sophocles' *Antigone:* Notes on the Role of the "Ancient Evils" in "the Tragic"', in: Silk (ed.), *Tragedy and the Tragic*, 358–76; quotations at 359, 362 and 369 resp.

25 Cf. Williams, *Shame and Necessity*, 132–5, on Aeschylus' *Agamemnon*: 'When he had decided and, as the Chorus says, "put on the harness of necessity", *anangkas edu lepadnon* (218), a violent frenzy overcame him. . . . Aeschylus does not say that Agamemnon submitted to necessity. . . . Agamemnon is said to have put on the harness of necessity as someone puts on an armour. . . . When Agamemnon "put on the harness of necessity", he decided he had to kill Iphigeneia. But there was another necessity lying behind his decision, of the kind with which we are now specially concerned: a necessity arising from supernatural forces that expressed themselves in the situation that called for his decision'.

26 Mogyoródi, 'Tragic Freedom and Fate', 370.

27 Halliwell, 'Plato's Repudiation of the Tragic', 332–49.

28 Halliwell, *Aristotle's* Poetics, 347, explains Plato's rejection: 'the Platonic contrast between two ultimate hypotheses about the world—the first that human lives are governed by external forces which are indifferent to, and capable of crushing, the quest for happiness; the second that the source of true happiness is located nowhere other than in the individual soul's choice between good and evil'.

29 Williams, *Shame and Necessity*, 152–4.

30 Ibid., 158–9 and 151 resp.

31 Williams, *Shame and Necessity*, 163; 163–5: 'Each of them represents human beings as dealing sensibly, foolishly, sometimes catastrophically, sometimes nobly, with a world that is only partially intelligible to human agency and in itself is not necessarily well adjusted to ethical aspirations. In this perspective the difference between a Sophoclean obscurity of fate and Thucydides' sense of rationality at risk to chance is not so significant. . . . Greek tragedy precisely refuses to present human beings who are ideally in harmony with their world, and has no room for a world that, if it were understood well enough, could instruct us how to be in harmony with it. There is a gap between what the tragic character is, concretely and contingently, and the ways in which the world acts upon him. In some cases, that gap is comprehensible, in terms of conflicting human purposes. In other cases, it is not fully comprehensible and not under control. That may be as true of social reality as of a world that contains supernatural necessities'.

32 Shakespeare, *The Tragedy of Hamlet*. Ed. Spencer, 181–2.

33 Anthony Gash, 'The Dialogic Self in Hamlet', unpublished manuscript, 19–20.

34 Shakespeare, *The Tragedy of Hamlet*. Ed. Spencer, 22–3.

35 Kees Vuyk, *Homo volens: Beschouwingen over de moderne mens als willende mens naar aanleiding van Nietzsche en Heidegger*. Kampen, 1990, 163–75.

36 Gábor Betegh, 'Moira/Tychē/Ananke̅', in: Donald M. Borchert (ed.), *Encyclopedia of Philosophy*. Second edition. Vol.VI. Farmington Hills: Thomson Gale, 2006, 319.

37 Solomon (2003), 451.

38 States, *Hamlet and the Concept of Character*, 188.

39 Shakespeare, *The Tragedy of Hamlet*. Ed. Spencer, 111.

40 States, *Hamlet and the Concept of Character*, 188.

41 Niccolò Machiavelli, *The Prince*. (1513) Harmondsworth, Middlesex: Penguin Books, 1982[2], 130–3 (ch. 25).

42 Lauro Martines, *Power and Imagination: City-States in Renaissance Italy*. (New York: Alfred A. Knopf, 1979) London: Pimlico, 2002, 311–15.

43 There is much overlapping and terms are movable, Martines continues on pp. 312 and 315: 'Reason may be contrasted with beast or with *fortuna*; rich—poor may be another form of elites—multitudes; State may stand against nature; and order could be used to sum up all the terms on the left-hand side. In the title of this part of the chapter, the antithesis "man against unreason" has been used as shorthand for the list as a whole. . . . *Fortuna* was the world of unreason, looming just beyond the power of human control, although now and then, quite inexplicably, its motions coincided with the needs of states and rulers. And so it was variously described as a tempest, a fickle goddess, blind chance, an occult force, a providential mystery. When Fortune was linked to the punishment of sin and therefore to the hidden motions of God, it was still put beyond the ken of human reason'.

44 Chaucer's *Prologue of the Monk's Tale* contains the famous medieval definition of tragedy: 'Tragedie is to seyn a certeyn storie,/As olde bookes maken us memorie,/Of hym that stood in greet prosperitee,/And is yfallen out of heigh degree,/Into myserie, and endeth wrecchedly'.

45 Steiner, *The Death of Tragedy*, 11–12.

46 Ibid., 12–13.

47 Williams, *Modern Tragedy*, 19ff., quotation at 23.

48 Williams, *Modern Tragedy*, 21, quotes Lydgate: 'It begynneth in prosperite/ And endeth ever in adversite/And it also doth the conquest trete/Of riche kynges and of lordys grete'. See also Bushnell, 'The Fall of Princes', 292–6.

49 Rees, *Shakespeare and the Story*, 196–201, esp. 199.

50 King Claudius takes up the topic of the effect of time and circumstance upon feelings and intent, when he asks Laertes how far he is prepared to go in avenging the murder of Polonius (IV.vii.109–22a). The Player-King too, addresses the issue comprehensively (III.ii.196–225) by stating that our decisions about what we are going to do depend entirely upon our being able to remember them afterwards (198), that it is inevitable that we forget to fulfil the promises we have made about actions that we ourselves have to perform (202–3), that for trivial causes grief turns to joy and joy turns to grief (209), that this world will not last for ever and so it is not strange that even our loves should change with our fortunes (210–11), that it is an open question whether love determines the direction of fortune or the other way round (212–13), that what we want to happen and what is fated to happen to us run in contrary directions (221), that our plans for the future are always overthrown (222), and that our thoughts are ours, but that their ends are none of our own (223). (Shakespeare, *The Tragedy of Hamlet*. Ed. Spencer, 118–20). Rees, 199, points out that 'the fire of love or anger (passion) does not last', that 'other impressions supervene', that 'the extraordinary emotion is overlaid by the ordinary, the customary', but that 'against the pressure exerted and the temptation presented by custom, Hamlet asserts conscience'.

51 Blundell, *Helping Friends*, 3.

52 For examples, see: Cairns, *Aidōs*, 2002, and Blundell, *Helping Friends*, 1989.

53 Jon D. Mikalson, *Honor Thy Gods: Popular Religion in Greek Tragedy*. Chapel Hill/London: The University of North Carolina Press, 1991, 54–64, 205. The literary convention of the occurrence of gods in bodily form to speak to mortals and prophesy the future in detail (*dei ex machina*) is unattested in classical popular religion. The Greeks practised divination, but they did not expect from oracles or seers detailed accounts of future events (64–8).

54 Mikalson, *Honor Thy Gods*, 22–9.

55 Padel, *Whom Gods Destroy*, 210.

56 Mikalson, *Honor Thy Gods*, 50, 213.

57 Ibid., 18–26, 206.

58 Cf. Liverani, *Israel's History and the History of Israel*, 207: 'those societies that placed their ethical values in civil or royal codes, or in philosophical knowledge (as in the Greco-Roman world), were able for many centuries to maintain their traditional religion and their pantheon alongside, for "ceremonial" purposes'. The Axial Age revolution did not ethicize their image of the divine, as it did with monotheism replacing polytheism and seeking direct means of contact between the individual and the divine while avoiding political and ceremonial mediation. In Greece, traditional religion remains the framework of reference that allows for a tragic view of man, not of the divine, because the religious framing is based on a juxtaposition, not on a mutually responsive and personal relationship between human and divine partners. The Greek gods and humans seem to share the same cosmos as their habitat, but they live apart together, according to different sets of rules.

59 Padel, *Whom Gods Destroy*, 214–15.

60 Ibid., 212–13.

61 Mikalson, *Honor Thy Gods*, 48, 219.

62 Ibid., 206–7, 218.

63 Ibid., 212.

64 Robert Parker, 'Through a Glass Darkly: Sophocles and the Divine', in: Jasper Griffin (ed.), *Sophocles Revisited: Essays Presented to Sir Hugh Lloyd-Jones*. Oxford: Oxford University Press, 1999, 11–30, esp. 14, 27.

65 Ewans, 'Patterns of Tragedy in Sophocles and Shakespeare', 444.

66 Segal, 'The Gods and the Chorus', 195–6.

67 Ibid., 197–8.

68 Parker, 'Through a Glass Darkly', 25–6.

69 Padel, *Whom Gods Destroy*, 68–9. Padel, *Whom Gods Destroy*, 26, also notes that Dionysus, the god of tragedy, has been described since the 1930s as a god of opposites, paradox, contradiction, but that he should not be considered more paradoxical than other Greek gods. Each killed *and* helped, urged on *and* punished, loved *and* hated in that area of human experience they controlled.

70 In Part I Section 4 of the chapter on psycho-ethical aspects, McAlindon pointed to the Renaissance conception of human nature and the way it differs from the Christian conception when he stressed that the issue is not about a (vertical) battle between angelic and bestial dimensions of human nature, but about the (horizontal) overflowing of boundaries.

71 Keyishian, *The Shapes of Revenge*, 5–6.

72 Ibid., 11.

73 Bevington, *Shakespeare's Ideas*, 151–4.

74 McAlindon, *Shakespeare's Tragic Cosmos*, 13–18.

75 McAlindon, *Shakespeare's Tragic Cosmos*, 120–5, quotations at 122 and 124 resp.

76 Hegel and Kierkegaard introduced similar ways of distinguishing between ancient and modern tragedy. Cf. Paul Vanden Berghe, 'Het tragische blijft toch altijd het tragische? Kierkegaard en Lacan over een moderne Antigone', in: Paul Vanden Berghe, Willem Lemmens, Johan Taels (eds), *Tragisch: Over tragedie en ethiek in de 21e eeuw*. Budel: Damon, 2005, 119–35 ('The Tragic is Always the Tragic: Kierkegaard and Lacan on a Modern Antigone', in: Arthur Cools et al. (eds), *The Locus of Tragedy*. Leiden/Boston: E. J. Brill, 2008, 181–95).

77 See Section 5 on Fortune, and also the chapter on socio-political aspects (Part I Section 2).

78 Whereas for Heering, *Tragiek*, 209–16, Hegel marks the beginning of the spread of a pan-tragic world view, to Johan Taels he marks the beginning of the spread of a panoptic comic world view: Johan Taels, 'Het komische lot van het tragische in de (post)moderne media', in: Vanden Berghe, Lemmens, Taels (eds), *Tragisch*, 165–84, and Johan Taels, 'Laughing Matters: The Unstoppable Rise of the Comic Perspective', in: Arthur Cools et al. (eds), *The Locus of Tragedy*. Leiden/Boston: E. J. Brill, 2008, 299–318.

79 Peter Hill, *Fate, Predestination and Human Action in the Mahabharata: A Study in the History of Ideas*. New Delhi: Mushiram Manoharlal Publishers, 2001; Julian F. Woods, *Destiny and Human Initiative in the Mahābhārata*, Albany, NY: State University of New York Press, 2001. Hill points out that there are several models or notions of causal agency operative in the epic: 1. The interference and predestination of the gods; 2. The impersonal workings of fate and time; 3. The law of *karma*. They all have some impact on human action, but their impact varies substantially, depending on the various outlooks the narratives take. In Hill's vocabulary, 'determinism' merely holds that all events are caused, for example by preceding events, whereas 'predestination' means events are fore-ordained or pre-planned by a personal god or gods, while 'fate' is the view that events are fore-ordained by some impersonal force or power in the universe. The line between 'predestination' and 'fate' in the epic is in practice not always clear. (Hill, *Fate, Predestination and Human Action*, 86, 197–8).

Cf. Solomon (2003), 443: 'Fatalism is the thesis that some even must happen, and no further explanation, notably no causal explanation, is called for. Determinism, by contrast, is the reasonably science-minded thesis that whatever happens can be explained in terms of prior causes and standing conditions (facts, events, states of affairs, internal structures, and dispositions, plus the laws of nature)'. and 447: 'Fatalism, traditionally conceived, insists on the necessity of the outcome, no matter what the causes may be. . . . the *what* of fate need make no specific commitments to any *how*'.

80 Hill, *Fate, Predestination and Human Action*, 124–64, 179.

81 Ibid., 110–14, quotation at 101.

82 Hill, *Fate, Predestination and Human Action*, 114. The higher (note: 'higher', not 'great', i.e., not Brahma, Shiva, Vishnu) gods 'also make periodic appearances' in the great battle at Kurukshetra, but 'the degree of their direct involvement is quite limited. Once the portions or fragments of the gods have become incarnated on earth in the form of the principal participants, the higher gods, with the possible exception of Indra, remain surprisingly aloof from the action. They also appear ignorant of the course of events. When all the celestials come to view the great struggle between Arjuna and Karna, heated disputes arise as to who will be victorious. A major contribution of the higher gods to the course of events is to make sure the Pāndavas are adequately equipped for the great battle' (119–22). Although the higher gods interfere pervasively and consistently in human affairs, 'they do not in any way play the role of agents of fate' by alloting the destinies of humans. They 'have become so involved in the affairs of the triple-world as integral participants that they can scarcely any longer stand aside and play the role of overseer or supervisor, which would be the minimum requirement if they were to act as agents of fate' (123–4).

83 Hill, *Fate, Predestination and Human Action*, 164–80.

84 Ibid., 168–79, quotations at 171–4, 176.

85 Ibid., 210.

86 Hiltebeitel, *The Ritual of Battle*, 143–91. See also the chapter on narrative aspects (Part II Section 3.2).

87 Hiltebeitel, *The Ritual of Battle*, 192–286.

88 Lipner, *Hindus*, 199.

89 Hill, *Fate, Predestination and Human Action*, 225.

90 Hill, *Fate, Predestination and Human Action*, 212; Hill continues: 'When Bhīshma finally fell, the event was so significant that both sides gathered around him and listen to him talk in favour of peace. However, despite the weighty words of the grandfather of the Pāndavas and Kauravas, they again issued forth for battle "impelled by time", and with "their minds overpowered by time" (*kālopahatacetasah*)'. The warrior heroes, especially the Kauravas, will perish because they have 'fallen under the power of time', are 'seized by time', are 'cooked by time' (209).

91 Hill, *Fate, Predestination and Human Action*, 43–59.

92 Ibid., 60–6, 71.

93 This holds true for both the few sections in the epic where the concepts of *karma* and rebirth are discussed philosophically in detail – the Uttarayāyā section of the *Ādiparvan* (Hill, *Fate, Predestination and Human Action*, 5–11), Mārkandeya's teaching and story in the *Āranyakaparvan* (11–21), the Mokshadharma section and Brhaspati's exposition in the *Śāntiparvan* (36–7, 21–4), Sanatsujāta's teaching in the *Udyogaparvan* (37–9), Krishna's teaching in the *Gītā* (322–57), and the Anugītā in the *Aśvamedhikaparvan* (24–9)—and for various circumstances narrative sections refer to (30–40).

94 Hill, *Fate, Predestination and Human Action*, 3–4, 66, 369.

95 Ibid., 66–7.

96 Ibid., 29.

97 Ibid., 40, 71.

98 Ibid., 14–15, 30.

99 Ibid., 72.

100 Ibid., 31–2, 40.

101 Hill, *Fate, Predestination and Human Action*, 242–3. Brodbeck, *Asakta Karman*, 184: 'Vassilkov (1999:24) suggests the following analysis: successful action depends on the conjunction of effort (*purushakāra*) and external factors (*daiva*), but the latter are unpredictable, and hence effort must always be made in case external factors facilitate success, failure being borne philosophically on occasions when they do not'. In the *Anuśāsanaparvan*, for instance, Yudhisthira asks Bhīshma which was the more powerful, fate or human effort. Bhīshma then recounts the history of a conversation between the great god Brahmā and the great sage Vasistha. Hill, *Fate, Predestination and Human Action*, 233: 'Having established the necessity of both fate and human effort in human action, Brahmā further explained that their effect was mutually reinforcing. "Even as a small fire, fanned by wind, becomes powerful, so fate, joined with human action, grows greatly. As a lamp fades through the diminution of its oil, so does (the influence of) fate with the decrease of (one's) acts". (6.43–44) Though the text does not entirely spell it out, presumably the idea is that if a man is fated to attain a fortune, then his fortune will be great if he exerts himself, but small if he does not. In short, the more one tries, the more fate will favour one'.

102 *Ādiparvan* 56.33 turns this into a virtue with its self-proclaimed intention of reflecting all points of view.

103 Hill, *Fate, Predestination and Human Action*, 292–301, quotation at 301.

104 Ibid., 307–8.

105 Brodbeck, *Asakta Karman*, 150–1.

106 Hill, *Fate, Predestination and Human Action*, 322–3.

107 *The Bhagavad Gītā*, trans. Sargeant, 184.

108 Brodbeck, *Asakta Karman*, 147. The individual's character (or *guna* configuration or 'own-being', *sva-bhāva*) covers factors which are fixed for each person (Arjuna was born a warrior) as well as factors that are continuously added through experience, maturity, or loss of memory, Brodbeck, 148, explains. He adds that Arjuna's character (*svabhāva*) is affected by Krishna's speech to such an extent that his decision is reversed.

109 Hill, *Fate, Predestination and Human Action*, 338–9. For the epic, Woods, *Destiny and Human Initiative in the Mahābhārata*, 57, seems to put a slightly different accent in this respect: 'Although not acknowledged in so many words, there is often a sense that *daiva* is a function of character'.

110 Hill, *Fate, Predestination and Human Action*, 351.

111 Hill, *Fate, Predestination and Human Action*, 339–41. Hill, 351–2, offers his diagnosis of the *Gītā*'s dealing with the problem: 'the problem of the nature of human action and human freedom is certainly one of the *Gītā*'s less successful parts. While the *Gītā* attempts to blend together the emphasis of *jñanayoga* and *karmayoga* on human action and freedom with the emphasis of *bhaktiyoga* on salvation through God's grace, this compromise is endangered by the *Gītā*'s obvious preference for *bhaktiyoga* alone. Even more, the *Gītā* endangers the position of *bhaktiyoga*, with its limited emphasis on human action and freedom, by so building up the position of its personal God that it destroys any position left for mortal man'.

112 Hill, *Fate, Predestination and Human Action*, 345.

113 Hill, *Fate, Predestination and Human Action*, 345–6. The word *māyā* occurs (only) in *Gītā* 4.6, 7.14–15, and 18.61. There is a difference between *maya* and *līla*. The scope constitutes the difference. The first notion relates to everything including the gods, the second notion to one god creating a world for himself.

114 *The Bhagavad Gītā*, trans. Sargeant, 722.

115 Lisa Raphals, 'Fate, Fortune, Chance, and Luck in Chinese and Greek: A Comparative Semantic History', in: *Philosophy East and West* 53/4 (October 2003), 537–74, esp. 561.

116 *The Bhagavad Gītā*, trans. Sargeant, 484–5.

117 Hill, *Fate, Predestination and Human Action*, 348–9.

118 Ibid., 350.

119 Katz, *Arjuna in the Mahābhārata*, 226.

120 Brodbeck, *Asakta Karman*, 150–1, 183–4.

121 Hill, *Fate, Predestination and Human Action*, 177.

122 Sewell-Rutter, *Guilt by Descent*, 22.

123 Ibid., 110–35.

124 Winnington-Ingram, *Sophocles*, 202–3; see note 57 in the previous chapter on psycho-ethical aspects.

125 Parker, 'Through a Glass Darkly', 25–6.

Bibliography

Aarsbergen-Ligtvoet, Connie, *Isaiah Berlin: A Value Pluralist and Humanist View of Human Nature and the Meaning of Life*. Amsterdam/New York: Rodopi, 2006.

Agarwal, Satya P., *The Social Role of the* Gītā: *How and Why*. New Delhi: Motilal Banarsidass, 1993.

Agrawal, M. M., 'Arjuna's Moral Predicament', in: Bimal Krishna Matilal (ed.), *Moral Dilemmas in the Mahābhārata*. Delhi: Motilal Banarsidass/Shimla: Indian Institute of Advanced Study, (1989) 1992², 129–42.

Allen, Douglas, *Structure and Creativity in Religion: Hermeneutics in Mircea Eliade's Phenomenology and New Directions*. The Hague: Mouton Publishers, 1978.

Alles, Gregory D., 'Verbal Craft and Religious Act in the *Iliad*: The Dynamics of a Communal Centre', in: *Religion* 18 (1988), 293–309.

— 'Surface, Space, and Intention: The Parthenon and the Kandariya Mahadeva', in: *History of Religions* 28 (1988–89), 1–36.

— *The* Iliad, *the* Rāmāyana, *and the Work of Religion: Failed Persuasion and Religious Mystification*. University Park, PA: The Pennsylvania State University Press, 1994.

Amaladass, Anand, *Philosophical Implications of Dhvani: Experience of Symbol Language in Indian Aesthetics*. Institut für Indologie der Universität Wien, Sammlung De Nobili. Vienna: Gerold & Co, 1984.

Arditi, Jorge, *A Genealogy of Manners: Transformations of Social Relations in France and England from the Fourteenth to the Eighteenth Century*. Chicago, IL/London: The University of Chicago Press, 1998.

Aristotle, *Poetics*. Edition Loeb Classical Library, *Aristotle: In Twenty-Three Volumes*. London: Heineman/Cambridge, MA: Harvard University Press, 1961.

Armstrong, Karen, *The Great Transformation: The World in the Time of Buddha, Socrates, Confucius and Jeremiah*. London: Atlantic Books, 2006.

Arnason, Johann P., Eisenstadt, Shmuel N., and Wittrock, Björn (eds), *Axial Civilizations and World History*. Leiden/Boston: Brill, 2005.

Assmann, Jan, *Ägypten: Theologie und Frömmigkeit einer frühen Hochkultur*. Stuttgart: Kohlhammer, 1984.

— *Das kulturelle Gedächtnis: Schrift, Erinnerung und politische Identität in frühen Hochkulturen*. Muenchen: C. H. Beck, 1992.

— *Ägypten: Eine Sinngeschichte*. München/Wien: Carl Hanser Verlag, 1996.

— *The Search for God in Ancient Egypt*. Ithaca, NY/London: Cornell University Press, 2001.

Aurell, Martin, 'The Western Nobility in the Late Middle Ages: A Survey of
    the Historiography and Some Prospects for New Research', in: Anne J.
    Duggan (ed.), *Nobles and Nobility in Medieval Europe: Concepts, Origins,
    Transformations.* Woodbridge: The Boydell Press, (2000) pb 2002, 263–73.
Austin, Michel M., and Vidal-Naquet, P., *Economic and Social History of Ancient
    Greece: An Introduction.* London: Batsford Academic and Educational Ltd.,
    (1977) 1980.
Bansat-Boudon, Lyne, *Pourquoi le théâtre? La réponse indienne.* Paris: Mille et
    une nuits, Librairie Arthème Fayard, 2004.
Barber, Richard, *The Knight and Chivalry.* Revised edition. Woodbridge: The
    Boydell Press, (1970) 2000.
Bassi, Karen, 'The Semantics of Manliness' in Ancient Greece', in: Ralph M.
    Rosen and Ineke Sluiter (eds), *Andreia: Studies in Manliness and Courage in
    Classical Antiquity.* Leiden/Boston: E. J. Brill, 2003, 25–58.
Bäumer, Bettina, *Schöpfung als Spiel: Der Begriff līlā im Hinduismus, seine
    philosophische und theologische Deutung.* München: UNI-Druck, 1969.
Beer, Anna, *Milton: Poet, Pamphleteer and Patriot.* London: Bloomsbury, 2008.
Berghe, Paul Vanden, 'Het tragische blijft toch altijd het tragische? Kierkegaard en
    Lacan over een moderne Antigone', in: Paul Vanden Berghe, Willem Lemmens,
    and Johan Taels (eds), *Tragisch: Over tragedie en ethiek in de 21e eeuw.* Budel:
    Damon, 2005, 119–35.
— 'The Tragic is Always the Tragic: Kierkegaard and Lacan on a Modern Antigone',
    in: Arthur Cools et al. (eds), *The Locus of Tragedy.* Leiden/Boston: E. J. Brill,
    2008, 181–95.
Bernard, Theos, *Hindu Philosophy.* Delhi: Motilal Banarsidass, 1999.
Betegh, Gábor, 'Moira/Tychē/Anankē', in: Donald M. Borchert (ed.), *Encyclopedia
    of Philosophy.* Second edition. Vol. VI. Farmington Hills: Thomson Gale, 2006,
    319.
Bevington, David, *Shakespeare's Ideas: More Things in Heaven and Earth.*
    Malden, MA/Oxford: Wiley-Blackwell, 2008.
The Bhagavad-Gītā. With a commentary based on the original sources by R. C.
    Zaehner. Oxford: Oxford University Press, 1969.
The Bhagavad Gītā, trans. Winthrop Sargeant, rev. ed. Christopher Chapple.
    New York: State University of New York Press, 1994.
La Bhagavad-Gītā suivie du Commentaire de Śankara (extraits), traductions
    d'Emile Senart et de Michel Hulin. Paris: Editions Points, 2010.
Biardeau, Madeleine, 'Conférence de Mlle. Madeleine Biardeau', in: *Annuaire de
    l'École pratique des Hautes Études.* Cinquième section Sciences Religieuses
    86 (1977–78), 143.
— 'The Salvation of the king in the *Mahābhārata*', in: *Contributions to Indian
    Sociology* 15/1–2 (1981), 75–97.
— *Hinduism: The Anthropology of a Civilization.* Delhi/Oxford/New York: Oxford
    University Press, 1989 (Engl. trans. of *L'hindouisme: Anthropologie d'une
    civilisation.* Paris: Flammarion, 1981).
— *Etudes de mythologie hindoue. Vol. II: Bhakti et avatāra.* Paris/Pondichéry:
    Ecole française d'Extrême-Orient, 1994.
— *Le Mahābhārata: Un récit fondateur du brahmanisme et son interprétation.*
    Paris: Editions du Seuil, 2002, 2 Vols.

Bloom, Harold, *Hamlet: Poem Unlimited*. New York: Riverhead Books, 2003.

Blundell, Mary Whitlock, *Helping Friends and Harming Enemies: A Study in Sophocles and Greek Ethics*. Cambridge: Cambridge University Press, 1989.

Bolle, Kees W., *The Bhagavadgītā: A New Translation*. Berkeley, CA/Los Angeles: University of California Press, 1979.

Bordwell, David, *Narration in the Fiction Film*. London: Routledge, 1985.

Bradley, Andrew C., *Shakespearean Tragedy: Lectures on Hamlet, Othello, King Lear, Macbeth*. (1904) London: MacMillan, (1957) 1960.

Bremmer, Jan N., *Greek Religion*. Oxford: Oxford University Press, 1994.

Brennan, Anthony, *Shakespeare's Dramatic Structures*. London/New York: Routledge, (1986) pb 1988.

Brodbeck, Simon Pearse, *Asakta Karman in the Bhagavadgītā*. PhD thesis, School of Oriental and African Studies, London, 2002.

Bryant, Joseph M., *Moral Codes and Social Structure in Ancient Greece: A Sociology of Greek Ethics from Homer to the Epicureans and Stoics*. Albany, NY: State University of New York Press, 1996.

Buitenen, Johannes Adrianus B. van, *The Bhagavadgītā in the Mahābhārata*. Chicago, IL: The University of Chicago Press, 1981.

Bulman, James C., *The Heroic Idiom of Shakespearean Tragedy*. Newark: University of Delaware Press/London, Toronto: Associated University Presses, 1985.

Burian, Peter, 'Myth into *muthos*: the shaping of tragic plot', in: P. E. Easterling (ed.), *The Cambridge Companion to Greek Tragedy*. Cambridge: Cambridge University Press, (1997) 2003[5], 178–208.

Bushnell, Rebecca, 'The Fall of Princes: The Classical and Medieval Roots of English Renaissance Tragedy', in: Rebecca Bushnell (ed.), *A Companion to Tragedy*. Oxford: Blackwell Publishing, 2005, 289–306.

Butler, Judith, *Antigone's Claim: Kinship Between Life and Death*. New York: Columbia University Press, 2000.

Buxton, Richard, 'What Can You Rely on in *Oedipus Rex*? Response to Calame', in: M. S. Silk (ed.), *Tragedy and the Tragic: Greek Theatre and Beyond*. Oxford: Oxford University Press, (1996) pb 1998, 38–48.

Cairns, Douglas L., *Aidōs: The Psychology and Ethics of Honour and Shame in Ancient Greek Literature*. Oxford: Clarendon Press, (1993) 2002.

Calame, Claude, 'Vision, Blindness, and Mask: The Radicalization of the Emotions in Sophocles' *Oedipus Rex*', in: M. S. Silk (ed.), *Tragedy and the Tragic: Greek Theatre and Beyond*. Oxford: Oxford University Press, (1996) pb 1998, 17–37.

Carroll, Noël, *The Philosophy of Horror or Paradoxes of the Heart*. New York: Routledge, 1990.

Cartledge, Paul, '"Deep plays": theatre as process in Greek civic life', in: P. E. Easterling (ed.), *The Cambridge Companion to Greek Tragedy*. Cambridge: Cambridge University Press, (1997) 2003[5], 3–35.

Cessi, Viviana, *Erkennen und Handeln in der Theorie des Tragischen bei Aristoteles*. Frankfurt a/Main: Athenäum, 1987.

Chambers, Edmund K., *The Elizabethan Stage*. Vol. IV. London: Oxford University Press, 1923.

Chattopadhyaya, Debi P., *Ways of Understanding the Human Past: Mythic, Epic, Scientific and Historic*. New Delhi: Centre for Studies in Civilizations, 2001.

Ching, Julia, *Mysticism and Kingship in China: The Heart of Chinese Wisdom.* Cambridge: Cambridge University Press, 1997.

Chirpaz, François, *Le tragique.* Paris: Presses Universitaires de France, 1998.

Cohen, Edward E., 'The High Cost of *Andreia* at Athens', in: Ralph M. Rosen and Ineke Sluiter (eds), *Andreia: Studies in Manliness and Courage in Classical Antiquity.* Leiden/Boston: E. J. Brill, 2003, 145–65.

Colebrook, Claire, *Irony.* London/New York: Routledge, (2004) 2006.

Collins, Dave, and Kremer, John, and Scully, Deidre, 'Psychology in sport', in: *Journal of Psychophysiology* 10/4 (1996), 350–1.

Constructions hagiographiques dans le monde indien—Entre mythe et histoire. Sous la responsabilité de Françoise Mallism. Paris: Librairie Honore Champion, 2001.

Damrosch, David, *What Is World Literature?* Princeton, NJ/Oxford: Princeton University Press, 2003.

— *How to Read World Literature.* Oxford: Wiley-Blackwell, 2009.

Danson, Lawrence, *Shakespeare's Dramatic Genres.* Oxford/New York: Oxford University Press, 2000.

Dasgupta, Surama, *Development of Moral Philosophy in India.* Delhi: Motilal Banarsidass, 1994.

Dhand, Arti, *Woman as Fire, Woman as Sage: Sexual Ideology in the Mahābhārata.* Albany, NY: State University of New York Press, 2008.

Diehl, Huston, 'Religion and Shakespearean Tragedy', in: Claire McEachern (ed.), *The Cambridge Companion to Shakespearean Tragedy.* Cambridge: Cambridge University Press, 2002, 86–102.

Doniger, Wendy, *The Implied Spider: Politics and Theology in Myth.* New York: Columbia University Press, 1998.

— *Splitting the Difference: Gender and Myth in Ancient Greece and India.* Chicago, IL/London: The University of Chicago Press, 1999.

duBois, Page, 'Toppling the Hero: Polyphony in the Tragic City', in: *New Literary History* 35 (2004), 63–81.

Duggan, Anne J., 'Introduction: Concepts, Origins, Transformations', in: Anne J. Duggan (ed.), *Nobles and Nobility in Medieval Europe: Concepts, Origins, Transformations.* Woodbridge: The Boydell Press, (2000) pb 2002, 1–14.

Duindam, Jeroen, *Myths of Power: Norbert Elias and the Early Modern European Court.* Amsterdam: Amsterdam University Press, 1995.

Dux, Günter, *Die Logik der Weltbilder: Sinnstrukturen im Wandel der Geschichte.* Frankfurt a/M: Suhrkamp, 1982.

Eagleton, Terry, *Sweet Violence: The Idea of the Tragic.* Malden, MA/Oxford: Blackwell Publishers, 2003.

— 'Commentary', in: *New Literary History* 35 (2004), 151–9.

Easterling, Patricia E., 'Weeping, Witnessing, and the Tragic Audience: Response to Segal', in: M. S. Silk (ed.), *Tragedy and the Tragic: Greek Theatre and Beyond.* Oxford: Oxford University Press, (1996) pb 1998, 173–81.

— 'A show for Dionysus', in: P. E. Easterling (ed.), *The Cambridge Companion to Greek Tragedy.* Cambridge: Cambridge University Press, (1997) 2003[5], 36–53.

— 'From repertoire to canon', in: Easterling (ed.), *The Cambridge Companion to Greek Tragedy.* Cambridge: Cambridge University Press, (1997) 2003[5], 211–27.

Edwards, Philip, 'Introduction', in: *Hamlet: Prince of Denmark*. Updated edition, ed. Philip Edwards. Cambridge: Cambridge University Press, 2003, 1–32.

Eisenstadt, Shmuel N. (ed.), *The Origins and Diversity of Axial Age Civilizations*. Albany, NY: State University of New York Press, 1986.

— *Multiple Modernities*. Piscataway, NJ: Transaction Publishers, 2002.

Eisenstadt, Shmuel N., *Comparative Civilizations and Multiple Modernities*. 2 vols. Leiden/Boston: Brill, 2003.

Elias, Norbert, *Über den Prozess der Zivilisation. Soziogenetische und psychogenetische Untersuchungen. Vol. I: Wandlungen des Verhaltens in den weltlichen Oberschichten des Abendlandes. Vol. II: Wandlungen der Gesellschaft. Entwurf zu einer Theorie der Zivilisation*. Frankfurt am Main: Suhrkamp, (1939) 1993–94.

Erp Taalman Kip, A. Maria van, 'The Unity of the *Oresteia*', in: M. S. Silk (ed.), *Tragedy and the Tragic: Greek Theatre and Beyond*. Oxford: Oxford University Press, (1996) pb 1998, 119–38.

— *Bokkenzang: Over Griekse tragedies*. Amsterdam: Athenaeum-Polak & Van Gennep, 1997.

Ewans, Michael, 'Patterns of Tragedy in Sophocles and Shakespeare', in: M. S. Silk (ed.), *Tragedy and the Tragic: Greek Theatre and Beyond*. Oxford: Oxford University Press, (1996) pb 1998, 438–57.

Fitzgerald, James L., 'India's Fifth Veda: The *Mahābhārata*'s Presentation of Itself', in: Arvind Sharma (ed.), *Essays on the Mahābhārata*. Leiden/New York: E. J. Brill, 1991, 150–70.

Flood, Gavin, 'Sacred Writings', in: Paul Bowen (ed.), *Themes and Issues in Hinduism*. London/Washington: Cassell, 1998, 132–60.

— 'The Meaning and Context of the Purushārthas', in: Julius J. Lipner (ed.), *The Bhagavad Gītā for our times*. New Delhi: Oxford University Press, 2000, 11–27.

Frackowiak, Richard, Rowe, James, and Friston, Karl, 'Attention to Action: Specific Modulation of Corticocortical Interactions in Humans', in: *Neuroimage* 17/2 (2002), 988–98.

Framarin, Christopher G., 'The Desire You Are Required to Get Rid Of: A Functionalist Analysis of Desire in the *Bhagavadgītā*', in: *Philosophy East and West* 56/4 (October 2006), 604–17.

Friedrich, Rainer, 'Everything to Do with Dionysos?' Ritualism, the Dionysiac, and the Tragic', in: M. S. Silk (ed.), *Tragedy and the Tragic': Greek Theatre and Beyond*. Oxford: Oxford University Press, (1996) pb 1998, 257–83.

Frijda, Nico H., *The Emotions*. Cambridge: Cambridge University Press/Paris: Editions de la Maison des Sciences de l'Homme, 1986.

Frye, Northrop, *Northrop Frye on Shakespeare*. Edited by Robert Sandler. Markham, Ontario: Fitzhenry and Whiteside, 1986.

Gash, Anthony, 'The Dialogic Self in Hamlet', unpublished manuscript.

Geller, Stephen A., 'The God of the Covenant', in: Barbara Nevling Porter (ed.), *One God or Many? Concepts of Divinity in the Ancient World*. Transactions of the Casco Bay Assyriological Institute, 2000, 273–319.

Gerow, Edwin, 'Rasa and Katharsis: A Comparative Study, Aided by Several Films', in: *Journal of the American Oriental Society* 122/2 (April-June, 2002), 264–77.

Gibert, John, *Change of Mind in Greek Tragedy,* Göttingen: Vandenhoeck & Ruprecht, 1995.

Gill, Christopher, *Personality in Greek Epic, Tragic, and Philosophy: The Self in Dialogue.* Oxford: Clarendon Press, 1996.

Girard, René, *La violence et le sacré.* Paris: Grasset, 1972.

— *Des choses cachées depuis la fondation du monde.* Paris: Grasset et Fasquelle, 1978.

— *Le bouc émissaire.* Paris: Grasset, 1982.

Goldhill, Simon, *Language, Sexuality, Narrative: The* Oresteia. Cambridge: Cambridge University Press, (1984) pb 2004.

— 'Mind and madness', in: Simon Goldhill (ed.), *Reading Greek Tragedy.* Cambridge: Cambridge University Press, 1986, 168–98.

— 'The audience of Athenian tragedy', in: P. E. Easterling (ed.), *The Cambridge Companion to Greek Tragedy.* Cambridge: Cambridge University Press, (1997) 2003[5], 54–68.

— 'The language of tragedy: rhetoric and communication', in: P. E. Easterling (ed.), *The Cambridge Companion to Greek Tragedy.* Cambridge: Cambridge University Press, (1997) 2003[5], 127–50.

— *Aeschylus: The* Oresteia. (1992) Second edition. Cambridge: Cambridge University Press, 2004.

Gouhier, H., *Le théatre et l'existence.* Paris: J. Vrin, 1997.

Gould, John, 'Homeric Epic and the Tragic Moment', in: Tom Winnifrith, P. Murray, and K. W. Gransdey (eds), *Aspects of the Epic.* New York: St. Martin's Press, 1983, 32–45.

Grazia, Margreta de, *'Hamlet' without Hamlet.* Cambridge: Cambridge University Press, 2007.

Green, Peter, *A Concise History of Ancient Greece to the Close of the Classical Era.* London: Thames and Hudson, (1973) pb 1981[2].

Greenblatt, Stephen, *Shakespearean Negotiations: The Circulation of Social Energy in Renaissance England.* Oxford: Clarendon, (1988) 2001.

— *Will in the World: How Shakespeare became Shakespeare.* New York/London: W. W. Norton & Company, 2004.

Groot, Ger, 'Ramkoers: Antigone tegenover Kreon', in: Paul Vanden Berghe, Willem Lemmens, and Johan Taels (eds), *Tragisch: Over tragedie en ethiek in de 21e eeuw.* Budel: Damn, 2005, 17–41.

Gupta, Shyamala, *Art, Beauty, and Creativity: Indian and Western Aesthetics.* New Delhi: D. K. Printworld, 1999.

Hall, Edith, 'The sociology of Athenian tragedy', in: P. E. Easterling (ed.), *The Cambridge Companion to Greek Tragedy.* Cambridge: Cambridge University Press, (1997) 2003[5], 93–126.

Halliwell, Stephen, *Aristotle's Poetics.* Chicago, IL: The University of Chicago Press, (1986) 1998.

— 'Plato's Repudiation of the Tragic', in: M. S. Silk (ed.), *Tragedy and the Tragic: Greek Theatre and Beyond.* Oxford: Oxford University Press, (1996) pb 1998, 332–49.

Hamilton, John D. B., 'Antigone: Kinship, Justice, and the Polis', in: Dora C. Pozzi and John M. Wickersham (eds), *Myth and the Polis.* Ithaca, NY/London: Cornell University Press, 1991, 86–98.

Hansen, Mogens Herman, and Naerebout, Frits, *Stad en Staat: De antiek-Griekse poleis en andere stadstaatculturen.* Amsterdam: Amsterdam University Press—Salomé, 2006.

Hattaway, Michael, 'Tragedy and Political Authority', in: Cleare McEachern (ed.), *The Cambridge Companion to Shakespearean Tragedy*, Cambridge: Cambridge University Press, 2002, 103–22.

Haute, Philippe Van, 'Antigone, heldin van de psychoanalyse? Lacans lectuur van Antigone', in: E. Berns, P. Moyaert, and P. van Tongeren (eds), *De God van denkers en dichters: Opstellen voor Samuel IJsseling.* Amsterdam: Boom, 1997, 172–91.

Heering, Herman J., *Tragiek: Van Aeschylus tot Sartre.* 's Gravenhage: L. J. C. Boucher, 1961.

Heesterman, Jan C., *The Inner Conflict of Tradition: Essays in Indian Ritual, Kingship and Society.* Chicago, IL: The University of Chicago Press, 1985.

— 'Self-sacrifice in Vedic Ritual', in: S. Shaked, and D. Shulman, and G. G. Stroumsa (eds), *Gilgul: Essays on Transformation, Revolution and Permanence in the History of Religions. Dedicated to R. J. Zwi Werblowsky.* Leiden: E. J. Brill, 1987, 91–106.

— 'Epic Narrative and Sacrificial Ritual: A Note on the Royal Consecration', in: Eli Franco and Monika Zin (eds), *From Turfan to Ajanta: Festschrift for Dieter Schlingloff on the Occasion of his Eightieth Birthday.* Bhairahawa, Rupandehi, Nepal: Lumbini International Research Institute, 2010, 389–98.

Hegel, Georg Friedrich Wilhelm, *Phänomenologie des Geistes*, (1807) ed. E. Moldenhauer and K. M. Michel. Frankfurt a/M: Suhrkamp, 1986.

Hellemans, Staf, *Het Tijdperk van de Wereldreligies: Religie in agrarische civilisaties en in moderne samenlevingen.* Zoetermeer: Meinema, 2007.

Herman, Arthur L., *A Brief Introduction to Hinduism: Religion, Philosophy, and Ways of Liberation.* Boulder, CO/San Francisco/Oxford: Westview Press, 1991.

Hill, Peter, *Fate, Predestination and Human Action in the Mahabharata: A Study in the History of Ideas.* New Delhi: Mushiram Manoharlal Publishers, 2001.

Hiltebeitel, Alf, 'Brothers, friends, and charioteers: Parallel episodes in the Irish and Indian epics', in: Edgar C. Polomé (ed.), *Homage to Georges Dumézil. Journal of Indo-European Studies.* Monograph 3 (1982), 85–111.

— 'Toward a Coherent Study of Hinduism', in: *Religious Studies Review* 9 (1983), 210.

— *The Ritual of Battle: Krishna in the Mahābhārata.* (New York: State University of New York, 1990) Delhi: Sri Satguru Publications (Indian Books Centre), 1991.

— 'Religious Studies and Indian Epic Texts', in: *Religious Studies Review* 21/1 (January 1995), 26–32.

— *Rethinking the Mahābhārata: A Reader's Guide to the Education of the Dharma King.* New Delhi: Oxford University Press, 2002.

Hiriyanna, M., *The Essentials of Indian Philosophy.* London: Unwin Paperbacks, (1949) 1978.

— *Outlines of Indian Philosophy.* Delhi: Motilal Banarsidass, (1993) 2003³.

Hirst, Jacqueline, 'Upholding the World: Dharma in the Bhagavadgita', in: Julius J. Lipner (ed.), *The Bhagavad Gītā for our times.* New Delhi: Oxford University Press, 2000, 48–66.

Hofstadter, Douglas R., *Gödel, Escher, Bach: An Eternal Golden Braid*. New York: Basic Books, (1979) 1999.

Hopkins, Thomas J., *The Hindu Religious Tradition*. Encino, Calif: Dickenson Publishing Company, 1971.

Hunter, George K., 'Tyrant and Martyr: Religious Heroisms in Elizabethan Tragedy', in: Maynard Mack and George deForest Lord (eds), *Poetic Traditions of the English Renaissance*. New Haven, CT/London: Yale University Press, 1982, 85–102.

Ingalls, Daniel H. H., 'General Introduction, Sanskrit Poetry and Sanskrit Poetics', in: Daniel H. H. Ingalls (ed.), *An Anthology of Sanskrit Court Poetry: Vidyākara's 'Subhāshitaratnakośa'*. Cambridge, MA: Harvard University Press, 1965, 1–56.

— (ed.), *The Dhvanyāloka of Anandavardhana: With the Locana of Abhinavagupta*. Translated by Daniel H. H. Ingalls, Jeffrey M. Masson, and M. V. Patwardhan. Cambridge, MA/London: Harvard University Press, 1990.

Innes, Matthew, '"A Place of Discipline": Carolingian Courts and Aristocratic Youth', in: Catherine Cubitt (ed.), *Court Culture in the Early Middle Ages: The Proceedings of the First Alcuin Conference*. Turnhout, Belgium: Brepols, 2003, 59–76.

Jarcho, Viktor, 'Die Weltanschauung des Dichters und die Verantwortung des Helden in der griechischen Tragödie', in: Heinrich Kuch (Hrsg.), *Die griechische Tragödie in ihrer gesellschaftlichen Funktion*. Berlin: Akademie Verlag, 1983, 41–59.

Jaspers, Karl, *Vom Ursprung und Ziel der Geschichte*. München: Piper, 1949.

Jatavallabhula, Danielle Feller, 'Ranayajña: The Mahābhārata War as a Sacrifice', in: Jan F M. Houben, and Karel R. van Kooij (eds), *Violence Denied: Violence, Non-Violence and the Rationalization of Violence in South Asian Cultural History*. Leiden: E. J. Brill, 1999, 69–103.

Kaeuper, Richard W., *Chivalry and Violence in Medieval Europe*. Oxford: Oxford University Press, (1999) 2002.

Karve, Irawati, *Yugānta: The End of an Epoch*. Poona: Deshmukh Prakashan, 1969.

Katz, Ruth Cecily, *Arjuna in the Mahābhārata: Where Krishna is, There is Victory*. Columbia, SC: University of South Carolina, 1989.

Kaveeshwar, Gajanan W., *The Ethics of the Gītā*. Delhi: Motilal Banarsidass, 1971.

Keay, John, *India: A History*. London/New Delhi: Harper Collins Publishers, (2000) pb 2001.

Keen, Maurice, *Chivalry*. New Haven, CT/London: Yale University Press, 1984.

Kernan, Alvin, *Shakespeare, the King's Playwright: Theater in the Stuart Court, 1603–13*. New Haven, CT/London: Yale University Press, 1995.

Kerrigan, William, *Hamlet's Perfection*. Baltimore, MD/London: The Johns Hopkins University, (1994) 1996.

— '*Macbeth* and the History of Ambition', in: John O'Neill (ed.), *Freud and the Passions*. University Park, PA: Penn State University Press, 1996, 13–24.

Keyishian, Harry, *The Shapes of Revenge: Victimization, Vengeance, and Vindictiveness in Shakespeare*. New York: Humanity Books, (1995) 2003.

Killingley, Dermot, 'Enjoying the World: Desire (kāma) & the Bhagavadgītā', in: Julius J. Lipner (ed.), *The Bhagavad Gītā for our times*. New Delhi: Oxford University Press, 2000, 67–79.

King, Richard, *Indian Philosophy: An Introduction to Hindu and Buddhist Thought.* Edinburgh: Edinburgh University Press, 1999.

Kinsley, David R., *The Sword and the Flute: Kālī and Krishna, Dark Visions of the Terrible and the Sublime in Hindu Mythology.* (Berkeley, CA/Los Angeles: University of California Press, 1975) Delhi: Motilal Banarsidass Publishers, 1995.

Klostermaier, Klaus K., *A Survey of Hinduism.* Albany, NY: State University of New York Press, 1989.

Knott, Kim, *Hinduism: A Very Short Introduction.* Oxford/New York: Oxford University Press, 1998.

Kostof, Spiro, *The City Shaped: Urban Patterns and Meanings Through History.* London: Thames and Hudson, (1991, pb 1999) 2001.

Krieken, Robert van, *Norbert Elias.* London/New York: Routledge, 1998.

Krishnamoorthy, K., *Dhvanyāloka of Anandavardhana.* Critical edition with introduction, translation and notes. Dharwar, 1974.

Kuch, Heinrich, 'Gesellschaftliche Voraussetzungen und Sujet der Griechischen Tragödie', in: Heinrich Kuch (ed.), *Die griechische Tragödie in ihrer gesellschaftlichen Funktion.* Berlin: Akademie Verlag, 1983, 11–39.

Laine, James W., 'Hinduism and the Mahābhārata', in: *Wiener Zeitschrift für die Kunde Südasiens und Archiv für indische Philosophie* 30 (1986), 73–81.

Larson, Gerald James, *Classical Sāmkhya: An Interpretation of its History and Meaning.* (1979) Second, revised edition. Delhi: Motilal Banarsidass, 2005[4].

Lee, John, *Shakespeare's* Hamlet *and the Controversies of Self.* Oxford: Oxford University Press, 2000.

Lele, Jayant, 'The *Bhakti* Movement in India: A Critical Introduction', in: Jayant Lele (ed.), *Tradition and Modernity in Bhakti Movements.* Leiden: E. J. Brill, 1981, 1–15.

Lenoir, Frédéric, *Petit Traité d'histoire des religions.* Paris: Plon, 2008.

Levin, Harry, *The Question of Hamlet.* London/Oxford/New York: Oxford University Press, 1959.

Lipner, Julius, *Hindus: Their Religious Beliefs and Practices.* London/New York: Routledge, (1994) pb 1998.

Lipner, Julius J. (ed.), *The Bhagavad Gītā for our times.* New Delhi: Oxford University Press, 2000 (first published as *The Fruits of our Desiring: An Inquiry into the Ethics of the Bhagavadgita.* Bayeux Arts, 1997).

Liverani, Mario, *Israel's History and the History of Israel.* London/Oakville: Equinox, 2006.

Lloyd-Jones, Hugh, 'Ritual and Tragedy', in: Fritz Graf (Hrsg.), *Ansichten griechischer Rituale. Geburtstags-Symposium für Walter Burkert.* Stuttgart/Leipzig: B. G. Teubner, 1998, 271–95.

Lonsdale, Steven H., *Dance and Ritual Play in Greek Religion.* Baltimore, MD/London: The Johns Hopkins University Press, 1993.

Loraux, Nicole, *La voix endeuillée: Essai sur la tragédie grecque.* Paris: Gallimard, 1999.

Lowe, N. J., 'Tragic and Homeric Ironies: Response to Rosenmeyer', in: M. S. Silk (ed.), *Tragedy and the Tragic: Greek Theatre and Beyond.* Oxford: Oxford University Press, (1996) pb 1998, 520–33.

Machiavelli, Niccolò, *The Prince.* (1513) Translated with an introduction by George Bull. Harmondsworth: Penguin Books, 1982.

Macintosh, Fiona, 'Tragic Last Words: The Big Speech and the Lament in Ancient
    Greek and Modern Irish Tragic Drama', in: M. S. Silk (ed.), *Tragedy and the
    Tragic: Greek Theatre and Beyond*. Oxford: Oxford University Press, (1996) pb
    1998, 414–25.
Mahābhārata. Critical edition, ed. V. S. Sukthankar. Poona: Bori, 1933–59.
Le Mahābhārata, vol.1: Livres I à V, trans. Jean-Michel Péterfalvi, introduction et
    commentaires par Madeleine Biardeau. Paris: Flammarion, 1985.
Maillard, Chantal, 'The Aesthetic Pleasure of Tragedy in Western and Indian
    Thought', in: Mazhar Hussain and Robert Wilkinson (eds), *The Pursuit of
    Comparative Aesthetics: An Interface between East and West*. Aldershot/
    Burlington: Ashgate, 2006, 29–38.
Malinar, Angelika, *Rājavidyā: Das königliche Wissen um Herrschaft und Verzicht.
    Studien zur Bhagavadgītā*. Wiesbaden: Harrassowitz Verlag, 1996.
Manning, Roger B., *Swordsmen: The Martial Ethos in the Three Kingdoms*.
    Oxford: Oxford University Press, 2003.
Margolies, David, *Monsters of the Deep: Social Dissolution in Shakespeare's
    Tragedies*. Manchester/New York: Manchester University Press, 1992.
Martin, John Jeffries, *Myths of Renaissance Individualism*. New Edition.
    Basingstoke: Palgrave Macmillan, 2006.
Martin, Richard P., 'Hesiod, Odysseus, and the instruction of princes', in:
    Transactions of the American Philological Association 114 (1984), 29–48.
— 'Epic as Genre', in: John Miles Foley (ed.), *A Companion to Ancient Epic*.
    Malden, MA/Oxford, UK: Blackwell Publishing, 2005, 9–19.
Martines, Lauro, *Power and Imagination: City-States in Renaissance Italy*.
    (New York: Alfred A. Knopf, 1979) London: Pimlico, 2002.
Matchett, Freda, *Kṛṣṇa: Lord or Avatāra? The Relationship between Krsna and
    Visnu in the context of the avatāra myth as presented by the Harivaṃśa, the
    Visnupurāna and the Bhāgavatapurāna*. Richmond, Surrey: Curzon Press, 2001.
McAlindon, Thomas, *Shakespeare's Tragic Cosmos*. Cambridge: Cambridge
    University Press, (1991) 1996.
McDonnell, Myles, 'Roman Men and Greek Virtue', in: Ralph M. Rosen and Ineke
    Sluiter (eds), *Andreia: Studies in Manliness and Courage in Classical Antiquity*.
    Leiden/Boston: E. J. Brill, 2003, 235–61.
Michaels, Axel, 'Gift and Return Gift, Greeting and Return Greeting in India: On a
    consequential footnote by Marcel Mauss', in: *Numen* 44 (1997), 242–69.
— *Der Hinduismus: Geschichte und Gegenwart*. München: C. H. Beck, 1998
    (transl. into Engl. *Hinduism: Past and Present*. Princeton, NJ/Oxford: Princeton
    University Press, 2004).
Mikalson, Jon D., *Honor Thy Gods: Popular Religion in Greek Tragedy*. Chapel Hill,
    NC/London: The University of North Carolina Press, 1991.
Milner Jr, Murray, *Status and Sacredness: A General Theory of Status Relations
    and an Analysis of Indian Culture*. New York/Oxford: Oxford University Press,
    1994.
Minnema, Lourens, 'Polytheistic and Monotheistic Patterns for Dealing with
    Religious Pluralism', in: *Studies in Interreligious Dialogue* 12/1 (2002), 63–74.
— 'One Dialogue—Four Relationships: The Different Layers of Meaning in the
    Dialogue between Krishna and Arjuna in the *Bhagavadgita*', in: *Studies in
    Interreligious Dialogue* 21/1 (2011), 96–111.

Minor, Robert N. (ed.), *Modern Indian Interpreters of the* Bhagavadgita. Albany, NY: State University of New York Press, 1986.

Mitchell-Boyask, Robin N., 'Dramatic Scapegoating: On the Uses and Misuses of Girard and Shakespearean Criticism', in: M. S. Silk (ed.), *Tragedy and the Tragic: Greek Theatre and Beyond*. Oxford: Oxford University Press, (1996) pb 1998, 426–37.

Mogyoródi, Emese, 'Tragic Freedom and Fate in Sophocles' *Antigone*: Notes on the Role of the "Ancient Evils" in "the Tragic"', in: M. S. Silk (ed.), *Tragedy and the Tragic: Greek Theatre and Beyond*. Oxford: Oxford University Press, (1996) pb 1998, 358–76.

Moyaert, Paul, *Begeren en vereren: Idealisering en sublimering*. Amsterdam: SUN, 2002.

Mul, Jos de, *De Domesticatie van het Noodlot: De wedergeboorte van de tragedie uit de geest van de technologie*. Kampen: Uitgeverij Klement/ Kapellen: Pelckmans, 2006.

Murray, Peter B., 'Hamlet', in: *Shakespeare Criticism Yearbook* 37 (1996), 241–68.

Naerebout, Frits G., and Singor, Henk W., *De Oudheid: Grieken en Romeinen in de context van de wereldgeschiedenis*. Baarn: Ambo, 1995.

Nagy, Gregory, 'The Epic Hero', in: John Miles Foley (ed.), *A Companion to Ancient Epic*. Malden, MA/Oxford, UK: Blackwell Publishing, 2005, 71–89.

Nelson, Janet L., 'Was Charlemagne's Court a Courtly Society?', in: Catherine Cubitt (ed.), *Court Culture in the Early Middle Ages: The Proceedings of the First Alcuin Conference*. Turnhout, Belgium: Brepols, 2003, 39–57.

Nussbaum, Martha C., *The Fragility of Goodness: Luck and Ethics in Greek Tragedy and Philosophy*. Cambridge: Cambridge University Press, 1986.

Nuttall, Anthony D., *Shakespeare the Thinker*. New Haven, CT/London: Yale University Press, 2007.

Olivelle, Patrick, *The Early Upanishads: Annotated Text and Translation*. New York/ Oxford: Oxford University Press, 1998.

Oudemans, Theodorus C. W., and Lardinois, André P. M. H., *Tragic Ambiguity: Anthropology, Philosophy and Sophocles' Antigone*, Leiden/New York: E. J. Brill, 1987.

Padel, Ruth, *Whom Gods Destroy: Elements of Greek and Tragic Madness*. Princeton, NJ: Princeton University Press, 1995.

Palmer, Richard H., *Tragedy and Tragic Theory: An Analytical Guide*. Westport, Connecticut/London: Greenwood Press, 1992.

Parker, Robert, 'Through a Glass Darkly: Sophocles and the Divine', in: Jasper Griffin (ed.), *Sophocles Revisited: Essays Presented to Sir Hugh Lloyd-Jones*. Oxford: Oxford University Press, 1999.

Paster, Gail Kern, 'The tragic subject and its passions', in: Claire McEachern (ed.), *The Cambridge Companion to Shakespearean Tragedy*. Cambridge: Cambridge University Press, 2002, 142–59.

Patel, Ramesh N., *Philosophy of the Gītā*. New York: Peter Lang, 1991.

Pathak, Shubha, 'Why Do Displaced Kings Become Poets in the Sanskrit Epics? Modeling *Dharma* in the Affirmative *Rāmāyana* and the Interrogative *Mahābhārata*', in: *Hindu Studies* 10 (2006), 127–49.

Peck, John, and Coyle, Martin, *How to Study a Shakespeare Play*. (1985) Second edition. Hampshire/New York: Palgrave, 1995.

Peterson, Indira V., 'Arjuna's Combat with the *Kirāta: Rasa and bhakti in Bhāravi's Kirātārjuniya*', in: Arvind Sharma (ed.), *Essays on the Mahābhārata,* Leiden/ New York: E. J. Brill, 1991, 212–50.

Piercey, Robert, 'The Role of Greek Tragedy in the Philosophy of Paul Ricoeur', in: *Philosophy Today* 49/1 (Spring 2005), 3–13.

Platvoet, Jan G., 'De wraak der "primitieven": Godsdienstgeschiedenis van Neanderthaler tot New Age', in: *Nederlands Theologisch Tijdschrift* 47 (1993), 227–43.

Poole, Adrian, *Tragedy: Shakespeare and the Greek Example.* Oxford/New York: Basil Blackwell, 1987.

Prasad, Rajendra, *A Conceptual-Analytic Study of Classical Indian Philosophy of Morals.* (D. P. Chattopadhyaya (gen. ed.), *History of Science, Philosophy and Culture in Indian Civilization,* Vol. 12 Part 1) New Delhi: Concept Publishing Company, 2008.

Pye, Christopher, *The Vanishing: Shakespeare, the Subject, and Early Modern Culture.* Durham/London: Duke University Press, 2000.

Radhakrishnan, Sarvepalli, *The Principal Upanishads.* London: George Allen and Unwin, 1953.

Ramanujan, Attipate K., 'Repetition in the *Mahābhārata*', in: Arvind Sharma (ed.), *Essays on the Mahābhārata.* Leiden/New York: E. J. Brill, 1991, 419–43.

Ram-Prasad, Chakravarti, 'Saving the Self? Classical Hindu Theories of Consciousness and Contemporary Physicalism', in: *Philosophy East and West* 51/3 (July 2001), 378–92.

Raphals, Lisa, 'Fate, Fortune, Chance, and Luck in Chinese and Greek: A Comparative Semantic History', in: *Philosophy East and West* 53/4 (October 2003), 537–74.

Reddy, A. V. Rathna, *The Political Philosophy of the Bhagavad Gītā.* New Delhi: Sterling, 1997.

Redfield, James M., *Nature and Culture in the Iliad: The Tragedy of Hector.* Expanded Edition. Durham/London: Durham University Press, 1994.

Rees, Joan, *Shakespeare and the Story: Aspects of Creation.* London: The Athlone Press, 1978.

Ricoeur, Paul, *Finitude et culpabilité. Livre II: La symbolique du mal.* Paris: Aubier/Éditions Montaigne, 1960, 153–332 (Deuxième Partie: Les 'mythes' du commencement et de la fin).

Riessen, Renée van, *Antigone's bruidsvertrek: De plaats van de* Antigone *in Hegels denken over de vrouw.* Kampen: Kok, 1986.

Robinson, Catherine A., *Interpretations of the* Bhagavad-Gītā *and Images of the Hindu Tradition: The Song of the Lord.* London/New York: Routledge, 2006.

Roche, Mark W., 'The Greatness and Limits of Hegel's Theory of Tragedy', in: Rebecca Bushnell (ed.), *A Companion to Tragedy.* Oxford: Blackwell Publishing, 2005, 51–67.

Roetz, Heiner, *Confucian Ethics of the Axial Age: A Reconstruction under the Aspect of the Breakthrough Toward Postconventional Thinking.* Albany, NY: SUNY, 1993.

Romilly, Jacqueline de, *Hector.* Paris: Editions de Fallois, 1997.

Rosen, Ralph M., and Sluiter, Ineke (eds), *Andreia: Studies in Manliness and Courage in Classical Antiquity.* Leiden/Boston: E. J. Brill, 2003.

Rosenmeyer, Thomas G., 'Ironies in Serious Drama', in: M. S. Silk (ed.), *Tragedy and the Tragic: Greek Theatre and Beyond*. Oxford: Oxford University Press, (1996) pb 1998, 497–519.

Rösler, Wolfgang, *Polis und Tragödie: Funktionsgeschichtliche Betrachtungen zu einer antiken Literaturgattung*. Konstanz: Universitätsverlag Konstanz, 1980.

Rosset, Clément, *La philosophie tragique*. (1960) Paris: Presses Universitaires de France, 1991.

Rutherford, Richard. B., 'Tragic Form and Feeling in the *Iliad*', in: *Journal of Hellenic Studies* 102 (1982), 145–60.

Rykwert, Joseph, *The Seduction of Place: The City in the Twenty-First Century*. London: Weidenfels & Nicholson, 2000.

Sachsenmaier, Dominic, Eisenstadt, Shmuel, and Riedel, Jens (eds), *Reflections on Multiple Modernities: European, Chinese and Other Interpretations*. Leiden/Boston: Brill, 2002.

Sagan, Eli, *At the Dawn of Tyranny: The Origins of Individualism, Political Oppression, and the State*. (New York: Alfred A. Knopf, 1985) London: Faber and Faber, 1986.

Saler, Benson, *Conceptualising Religion: Immanent Anthropologists, Transcendent Natives, and Unbounded Categories*. Leiden: E. J. Brill, 1993.

Sands, Kathleen M., 'Tragedy, Theology, and Feminism' in the Time After Time', in: *New Literary History* 34 (2004), 41–61.

Schechner, Richard, *Between Theater and Anthropology*. Philadelphia, PA: University of Pennsylvania Press, 1985.

Schein, Seth L., *The Mortal Hero: An Introduction to Homer's* Iliad. Berkeley, CA/Los Angeles/London: University of California Press, 1984.

Schiltz, Elizabeth A., 'Two Chariots: The Justification of the Best Life in the *Katha Upanishad* and Plato's *Phaedrus*', in: *Philosophy East and West* 56/3 (July 2006), 451–68.

Schuurman, Cornelis J., *Stem uit de diepte: De mens en zijn bestemming in de symbolische taal der mythe*. Leiden: A. W. Sijthoff, 1970.

Schwartz, Susan L., *Rasa: Performing the Divine in India*. New York: Columbia University Press, 2004.

Seaford, Richard, 'Something to Do with Dionysos—Tragedy and the Dionysiac: Response to Friedrich', in: M. S. Silk (ed.), *Tragedy and the Tragic: Greek Theatre and Beyond*. Oxford: Oxford University Press, (1996) pb 1998, 284–94.

Segal, Charles, *Oedipus Tyrannus: Tragic Heroism and the Limits of Knowledge*. New York: Twayne Publishers, 1993.

— 'The Gods and the Chorus: Zeus in *Oedipus Tyrannus*', in: Charles Segal (ed.), *Sophocles' Tragic World: Divinity, Nature, Society*. Cambridge, MA/London: Harvard University Press, (1995) pb 1998, 180–98.

— 'Catharsis, Audience, and Closure in Greek Tragedy', in: M. S. Silk (ed.), *Tragedy and the Tragic: Greek Theatre and Beyond*. Oxford: Oxford University Press, (1996) pb 1998, 149–72.

Seidensticker, Bernd, '*Peripeteia* and Tragic Dialectic in Euripidean Tragedy', in: M. S. Silk (ed.), *Tragedy and the Tragic: Greek Theatre and Beyond*. Oxford: Oxford University Press, (1996) pb 1998, 377–96.

Sewell-Rutter, Neil James, *Guilt by Descent: Moral Inheritance and Decision Making in Greek Tragedy*. Oxford/New York: Oxford University Press, 2007.

Shakespeare, William, *The Tragedy of Hamlet, Prince of Denmark*, ed. T. J. B. Spencer, with an introduction by Anne Barton. London: Penguin Books, (1980) (1994) 2002.

Shankman, Steven, and Durrant, Stephen, *The Siren and the Sage: Knowledge and Wisdom in Ancient Greece and China*. London/New York: Cassell, 2000.

Sharma, Arvind, *The Hindu Gītā: Ancient and Classical Interpretations of the Bhagavadgītā*. London: Duckworth, 1986.

Sharma, Arvind (ed.), *Essays on the Mahābhārata*. Leiden/New York: E. J. Brill, 1991.

Sharma, Chandradhar, *A Critical Survey of Indian Philosophy*. Delhi: Motilal Banarsidass, 2000.

Sharpe, Eric J., *The Universal* Gītā*: Western Images of the* Bhagavad Gītā. *A Bicentenary Survey*. La Salle, IL: Open Court Publishing Company, 1985.

Shellard, Dominic, *William Shakespeare*. London: The British Library/New York: Oxford University Press, 1998.

Silk, Michael S., 'Tragic Language: The Greek Tragedians and Shakespeare', in: M. S. Silk (ed.), *Tragedy and the Tragic: Greek Theatre and Beyond*. Oxford: Oxford University Press, (1996) pb 1998, 458–96.

Singor, Henk, *Homerische Helden: Oorlogvoering in het vroege Griekenland*. Amsterdam: Amsterdam University Press—Salomé, 2005.

Solomon, Robert C., 'On Fate and Fatalism', in: *Philosophy East and West* 53/4 (October 2003), 435–54.

Sorabji, Richard, *Emotion and Peace of Mind: From Stoic Agitation to Christian Temptation*. Oxford: Oxford University Press, (2000) pb 2002.

Sourvinou-Inwood, Christiane, *Tragedy and Athenian Religion*. Lanham: Lexington Books, 2003.

States, Bert O., *Hamlet and the Concept of Character*. Baltimore, MD/London: The Johns Hopkins University Press, 1992.

Steiner, George, *The Death of Tragedy*. London: Faber and Faber, (1961) pb 1982[5].

— *Antigones*. Oxford: Clarendon Press, 1984.

— 'Tragedy, Pure and Simple', in: M. S. Silk (ed.), *Tragedy and the Tragic: Greek Theatre and Beyond*. Oxford: Oxford University Press, (1996) pb 1998, 534–46.

— '"Tragedy," Reconsidered', in: *New Literary History* 35 (2004), 1–15.

Steinmann, Ralph Marc, *Guru-śishya-sambandha: Das Meister-Schüler-Verhältnis im traditionellen und modernen Hinduismus*. Stuttgart: Steiner Verlag Wiesbaden GMBH, 1986.

Stewart, Frank Henderson, *Honor*. Chicago, IL/London: The University of Chicago Press, 1994.

Struck, Peter T., 'The Ordeal of the Divine Sign: Divination and Manliness in Archaic and Classical Greece', in: Ralph M. Rosen and Ineke Sluiter (eds), *Andreia: Studies in Manliness and Courage in Classical Antiquity*. Leiden/Boston: E. J. Brill, 2003, 167–86.

Sukthankar, Vishnu S., *On the Meaning of the Mahābhārata*. (Bombay: The Asiatic Society of Bombay, 1957) Delhi: Motilal Banarsidass, 1998.

Sutton, Nicholas, *Religious Doctrines in the Mahābhārata*. Delhi: Motilal Banarsidass, 2000.

Suzuki, Mihoko, *Metamorphoses of Helen: Authority, Difference, and the Epic*. Ithaca, NY: Cornell University Press, 1989.

Szondi, Peter, *Versuch ueber das Tragische*. Frankfurt a/Main: Insel-Verlag, 1961.

Taels, Johan, 'Het komische lot van het tragische in de (post)moderne media', in: Paul Vanden Berghe, Willem Lemmens, and Johan Taels (eds), *Tragisch: Over tragedie en ethiek in de 21e eeuw*. Budel: Damon, 2005, 165–84.

— 'Laughing Matters: The Unstoppable Rise of the Comic Perspective', in: Arthur Cools et al. (eds), *The Locus of Tragedy*. Leiden/Boston: E. J. Brill, 2008, 299–318.

Taylor, Charles, *Sources of the Self: The Making of the Modern Identity*. Cambridge, MA: Harvard University Press, 1989.

Temkin, Owsei, *Galenism: Rise and Decline of a Medical Philosophy*. Ithaca, NY/ London: Cornell University Press, 1973.

Thapar, Romila, *A History of India*. Vol. I. (1966) New Delhi: Penguin Books, (1990) 2000[12].

— 'The Historian and the Epic' (1979), in: Romila Thapar (ed.), *Cultural Pasts: Essays in Early Indian History*. New Delhi: Oxford University Press, 2000, 613–29.

— 'The Rāmāyana: Theme and Variation' (1982), in: Romila Thapar (ed.), *Cultural Pasts: Essays in Early Indian History*. New Delhi: Oxford University Press, 2000, 647–79.

— *From Lineage to State: Social Formations in the Mid-First Millenium B. C. in the Ganga Valley*. (Oxford: Oxford University Press, 1984) New Delhi: Oxford India Paperbacks, (1990) 2000[6].

— 'Society and Historical Consciousness: The *Itihāsa-purāna* Tradition' (1986), in: Romila Thapar (ed.), *Cultural Pasts: Essays in Early Indian History*. New Delhi: Oxford University Press, 2000, 123–54.

— *Reinterpreting Ancient India*. Delhi: Oxford University Press, 1993.

— *Early India: From the Origins to AD 1300*. London: Allen Lane, The Penguin Press, 2002.

Trapp, Michael, 'Tragedy and the Fragility of Moral Reasoning: Response to Foley', in: M. S. Silk (ed.), *Tragedy and the Tragic: Greek Theatre and Beyond*. Oxford: Oxford University Press, (1996) pb 1998, 74–84.

Tubb, Gary A., 'Śāntarasa in the *Mahābhārata*', in: Arvind Sharma (ed.), *Essays on the Mahābhārata,* Leiden/New York: E. J. Brill, 1991, 171–203.

Tuchman, Barbara, *The Proud Tower: A Portrait of the World before the War 1890–1914*. New York: Macmillan, 1966.

Turner, Victor, *From Ritual to Theatre: The Human Seriousness of Play*. New York: PAJ Publications, (1982) pb 1992.

Vaidya, Parasurama L., and Pusalker, Achut D., 'The *Mahābhārata*: Its History and Character', in: *The Cultural Heritage of India. Vol. II: Itihāsas, purānas, dharma and other śāstras*. Calcutta: The Ramakrishna Mission Institute of Culture, 1953–62, 51–70.

Vanheeswijck, Guido, 'Vijandige broers, verloren zonen. Halfweg tussen ethische bewustwording en mythische vergelding: de precaire positie van de tragedie volgens René Girard', in: Paul Vanden Berghe, Willem Lemmens, and Johan Taels (eds), *Tragisch: Over tragedie en ethiek in de 21e eeuw*. Budel: Damon, 2005, 43–85.

Veer, Peter van der, *Religious Nationalism: Hindus and Muslims in India*. Berkeley, CA: University of California Press, 1994.

Vernant, Jean-Pierre, 'Le moment historique de la tragédie en Grèce: Quelques conditions sociales et psychologiques', in: Jean-Pierre Vernant and Pierre

Vidal-Naquet (eds), *Mythe et tragédie en Grèce ancienne.* Vol. I. Paris: La Découverte, (1986) 1989, 13–17.

— 'Ébauches de la volonté dans la tragédie grecque', in: Jean-Pierre Vernant and Pierre Vidal-Naquet (eds), *Mythe et tragédie en Grèce ancienne.* Vol. I. Paris: La Découverte, (1986) 1989, 41–74.

Vernant, Jean-Pierre, and Vidal-Naquet, Pierre, *Mythe et tragédie en Grèce ancienne,* Vol. II. Paris: La Découverte, 1986.

Versnel, Hendrik S., *Inconsistencies in Greek and Roman religion. Vol. I: Ter Unus: Isis, Dionysos, Hermes: Three Studies in Henotheism.* Leiden: Brill, 1990.

— 'Thrice One: Three Greek Experiments in Oneness', in: Barbara Nevling Porter (ed.), *One God or Many? Concepts of Divinity in the Ancient World.* Transactions of the Casco Bay Assyriological Institute, 2000, 112–29.

Virtanen, Keijo, 'The Concept of Purification in the Greek and Indian Theories of Drama', in: Mazhar Hussain and Robert Wilkinson (eds), *The Pursuit of Comparative Aesthetics: An Interface between East and West.* Aldershot/Burlington: Ashgate, 2006, 55–84.

Vuyk, Kees, *Homo volens: Beschouwingen over de moderne mens als willende mens naar aanleiding van Nietzsche en Heidegger.* Kampen, 1990.

Waardenburg, Jacques, *Muslims and Others: Relations in Context.* Berlin/New York: Walter de Gruyter, 2003.

Walzer, Michael, 'Liberalism and the Art of Separation', in: *Political Theory* 12/3 (August 1984), 315–30.

Watson, Robert N., 'Tragedies of revenge and ambition', in: Claire McEachern (ed.), *The Cambridge Companion to Shakespearean Tragedy.* Cambridge: Cambridge University Press, 2002, 160–81.

Williams, Bernard, *Shame and Necessity.* Berkeley, CA/Los Angeles/London: University of California Press, 1994.

Williams, Raymond, *Modern Tragedy.* (Stanford, Calif.: Stanford University Press, 1966) Ontario: Broadview Press Encore Editions, 2001.

Winnington-Ingram, Reginald Pepys, *Sophocles: An Interpretation.* Cambridge: Cambridge University Press, (1980) 2002[6].

Woods, Julian F., *Destiny and Human Initiative in the Mahābhārata,* Albany, NY: State University of New York Press, 2001.

Worden, James. W., *Grief Counselling and Grief Therapy: A Handbook for the Mental Health Practitioner.* Third Edition. New York: Brunner/Routledge, 2001.

Author Index

Subject Index

Note: The index of subjects does not include page references to pages in the endnotes section.